TRANSITIONAL JUSTICE AND THE FORMER SOVIET UNION

In the twenty-five years since the Soviet Union was dismantled, the countries of the Former Soviet Union have faced different circumstances and responded differently to the need to acknowledge their communist past and redress the suffering of their people. While some have adopted transitional justice and accountability measures, others have chosen to reject them; these choices have directly affected state building and societal reconciliation efforts. This is the most comprehensive account to date of post-Soviet efforts to address, distort, ignore, or recast the past through the use, manipulation, and obstruction of transitional justice measures and memory politics initiatives. Editors Cynthia M. Horne and Lavinia Stan have gathered contributions from top scholars in the field, allowing the disparate postcommunist studies and transitional justice scholarly communities to come together and reflect on the past and its implications for the future of the region.

Cynthia M. Horne is Professor of Political Science at Western Washington University.

Lavinia Stan is Professor of Political Science at St. Francis Xavier University, Canada.

Transitional Justice and the Former Soviet Union

REVIEWING THE PAST, LOOKING TOWARD THE FUTURE

Edited by

CYNTHIA M. HORNE

Western Washington University

LAVINIA STAN

St Francis Xavier University

CAMBRIDGE
UNIVERSITY PRESS

University Printing House, Cambridge CB2 8BS, United Kingdom

One Liberty Plaza, 20th Floor, New York, NY 10006, USA

477 Williamstown Road, Port Melbourne, VIC 3207, Australia

314-321, 3rd Floor, Plot 3, Splendor Forum, Jasola District Centre, New Delhi - 110025, India

79 Anson Road, #06-04/06, Singapore 079906

Cambridge University Press is part of the University of Cambridge.

It furthers the University's mission by disseminating knowledge in the pursuit of education, learning and research at the highest international levels of excellence.

www.cambridge.org
Information on this title: www.cambridge.org/9781316648056
DOI: 10.1017/9781108182171

© Cambridge University Press 2018

First published 2018
First paperback edition 2019

A catalogue record for this publication is available from the British Library

Library of Congress Cataloging in Publication data
Names: Horne, Cynthia Michalski, editor. | Stan, Lavinia, editor.
Title: Transitional justice and the former Soviet Union : reviewing the past, looking toward the future / Edited by Cynthia M. Horne, Western Washington University, Lavinia Stan, St Francis Xavier University.
Description: New York : Cambridge University Press, 2018. | Includes bibliographical references and index.
Identifiers: LCCN 2017058593 | ISBN 9781107198135 (hardback : alk. paper)
Subjects: LCSH: Transitional justice–Former Soviet republics. | Law reform—Social aspects–Former Soviet republics.
Classification: LCC KLA470 .T73 2018 | DDC 340/.1150947—dc23 LC record available at https://lccn.loc.gov/2017058593

ISBN 978-1-107-19813-5 Hardback
ISBN 978-1-316-64805-6 Paperback

Contents

Figure

Tables

Interviews

Nanci Adler, personal interview with Arsenii Roginskii, Moscow, November 1, 2016

Nanci Adler, personal interview with Arsenii Roginskii, Moscow, October 31, 2016

Nanci Adler, personal interview with Arsenii Roginskii, Moscow, April 9, 2015

Nanci Adler, personal interview with Arsenii Roginskii, Moscow, April 8, 2015

Nanci Adler, personal interview with Semën Samuilovich Vilenskii, Moscow, November 18, 2003

Nanci Adler, personal interview with Semën Samuilovich Vilenskii, Moscow, October 30, 2011

Nelly Bekus, personal interview with Igor Kuznetsov, Minsk, August 28, 2016

Nelly Bekus, personal interview with Zinaida Tarasevich, Minsk, August 26, 2016

Dovilė Budrytė, email communication with Rimantas Jokimaitis, Senior Specialist in the Ministry of Science and Education, February 7, 2017

Violeta Davoliūtė, conversation with Arvydas Anušauskas, November 10, 2016, Vilnius

Violeta Davoliūtė, conversation with Markas Zingeris, September 24, 2016, Vilnius

Violeta Davoliūtė, conversation with Arkadijus Vinokuras, September 12, 2016, Vilnius

Violeta Davoliūtė, conversation with Ronaldas Račinskas, September 9, 2016, Vilnius

Violeta Davoliūtė, personal interview with Arūnas Bubnys, September 8, 2016, Vilnius

Violeta Davoliūtė, personal communication with Birutė Burauskaitė, May 13, 2014, Vilnius

Mark Kramer, personal interview with Yakovlev, at International Democracy Foundation, Moscow, June 11, 2001

Contributors

Nanci Adler is Director of Research and Head of Holocaust and Genocide Studies at the NIOD Institute for War, Holocaust, and Genocide Studies (Royal Netherlands Academy of Arts and Sciences) and Professor of Memory, History, and Transitional Justice at the University of Amsterdam. She has published a number of books, including *Keeping Faith with the Party: Communist Believers Return from the Gulag* (2012) and *The Gulag Survivor: Beyond the Soviet System* (2002). Her many scholarly articles on the Gulag, political rehabilitations, and the consequences of Stalinism have appeared in a variety of peer-reviewed journals, such as *Europe-Asia Studies, Memory Studies*, and the *International Journal of Comparative and Applied Criminal Justice*. Her current research focuses on transitional justice, memory, historical dialog, and the legacies of Communism and mass political repression.

Robert Austin is Associate Professor in the Centre for European, Russian and Eurasian Studies (CERES), at the Munk School of Global Affairs, University of Toronto. He is a specialist on East Central and Southeastern Europe in historic and contemporary perspective. In the past, Austin was a Tirana-based correspondent for Radio Free Europe/Radio Liberty; a Slovak-based correspondent with The Economist Group of Publications; and a news writer with the Canadian Broadcasting Corporation in Toronto. Austin has written articles for *The Globe and Mail, The Toronto Star, Southeast European Times, Orbis, East European Politics and Societies* and *East European Quarterly* along with numerous book chapters and two books published separately in Tirana and Prishtina. He has lectured widely in Europe and North America. His most recent book is *Founding a Balkan State* (2012). At CERES, he coordinates the Undergraduate European Studies Program, the Hellenic Studies Program, and the Hungarian Studies Program.

Onur Bakiner is Assistant Professor of Political Science at Seattle University. His research and teaching interests include transitional justice, human rights, and judicial politics, particularly in Latin America and the Middle East. His book *Truth Commissions: Memory, Politics and Legitimacy* (2016) evaluates the success of truth commissions in promoting political, judicial, and social change. His articles have appeared in a variety of peer-reviewed journals, including *The International Journal of Transitional Justice, Memory Studies, and Nationalities Papers: the Journal of Ethnicity and Nationalism*. His recent piece in *Historical Justice and Memory*, Thompson and Neumann, eds., (2015), entitled "Promoting Historical Justice through Truth Commissions: an Uneasy Relationship," reflects the intersection of his research on transitional justice, social memory, and judicial politics.

Nelly Bekus is Associate Research Fellow in the History Department at the University of Exeter. From 2008 to 2012 she worked as an Assistant Professor at the University of Warsaw. She is the author of *Struggle over Identity. The Official and the Alternative "Belarusianness"* (2010), and has published numerous articles on state- and nation-building under socialism and postsocialism. She is currently doing research, funded by the Leverhulme Trust Research Leadership Award, on the role of the cityscape in the construction of post-socialist identity with a focus on Minsk (Belarus) and Astana (Kazakhstan). She has also been the recipient of fellowships through the Institute of Human Sciences in Vienna (2003), the Remarque Institute, New York University (2007), and, most recently, at the Davis Center for Russian and Eurasian Studies at Harvard University (2012–13). She recently coorganized with Julie Buckler (Harvard University) the seminar "Contested Memory Sites in Post-Socialist Capitals" within the framework of the ACLA Annual Meeting (New York University).

Dovilė Budrytė is a Professor of Political Science at Georgia Gwinnett College. Her areas of interest include memory politics and gender studies. Her publications include articles on various topics related to minority rights and four books: *Taming Nationalism? Political Community Building in the Post–Soviet Baltic States* (2005); *Feminist Conversations: Women, Trauma and Empowerment in Post–Transitional Societies* (coedited with Lisa M. Vaughn and Natalya T. Riegg; 2009); *Memory and Trauma in International Relations: Theories, Cases and Debates* (coeditor with Erica Resende; 2013); and *Engaging Difference: Teaching Humanities and Social Sciences in Multicultural Environments* (coedited with Scott Boykin; 2017). She is currently working on a book titled *Crisis and Change in Post-Cold War International Relations: Ukraine and Beyond* (coedited with Erica Resende and Didem Buhari).

Roman David is a Professor in the Department of Sociology, Lingnan University, Hong Kong. Previously he held positions at Oxford, Wits, Yale, Newcastle, and Harvard. He works in the area of political sociology, specializing on transitional societies and transitional justice. He is the author of *Lustration and Transitional Justice* (2011), which won the triannual Concept Analysis Award by the Committee on Concepts and Methods of IPSA in 2012, and the coauthor (with Ian Holliday) of *Liberalism and Democracy in Myanmar* (in preparation). His work has appeared in indexed journals such as the *American Journal of Sociology, Political Psychology, Journal of Conflict Resolution, Human Rights Quarterly, Law & Social Inquiry*, and the *International Journal of Transitional Justice*. David is well-known for his work on lustration as a method of reckoning in the postcommunist context.

Nenad Dimitrijević is a Professor of Political Science at Central European University, Budapest, Hungary. His core research interests are constitutional theory and transitional justice. He is the author of *Duty To Respond: Mass Crime, Denial, and Collective Responsibility* (2011). Dr. Dimitrijević has written extensively on the former Yugoslavia, with attention to Serbia's transitional justice choices, including multiple entries in the *Encyclopedia of Transitional Justice* (2013) in addition to articles in several edited volumes. He brings a law and constitutionality perspective to transitional justice issues, with publications spanning issues of transitional justice and constitutional theory. His articles have appeared in peer-reviewed journals such as *International Journal of Transitional Justice*, as well as *Philosophy and Social Criticism*.

Violeta Davoliūtė is a Professor at Vilnius University, Institute of International Relations and Political Science and was a Research Associate at Yale University (2015–16). She is the author of *The Making and Breaking of Soviet Lithuania* (2014), coeditor of *Narratives of Exile and Identity in Soviet Deportation Memoirs from the Baltic States* (2016) and coeditor of *Population Displacement in Lithuania in the Twentieth Century* (2016). Dr. Davoliūtė is an Expert Evaluator for the European Commission, Education, Audiovisual and Culture Executive Agency, and the Lithuanian Council of Culture. Her research is focused on the history of cultural elites under Nazi and Soviet rule, questions of trauma and memory, and the social and cultural history of forced modernization, Sovietization, and mass displacement in the Baltic States.

Agata Fijalkowski is a Senior Lecturer-in-Law at University of Lancaster Law School, United Kingdom. Dr. Fijalkowski completed her Ph.D in Law at the University of London. Her main research interest is in transitional criminal justice in postdictatorial and postconflict states. She coedited (with Raluca Grosescu) *Transitional Criminal Justice in Post-Dictatorial and Post-Conflict*

Societies (2015). Dr. Fijalkowski has written about court redress in the Baltic States, retrospective justice and legal culture, and the maladministration of justice in communist Albania and in communist Poland. Her current project, "The Power of Images," considers the way we experience the law when we look at the images of trial proceedings from the period 1945–57 and those that were held in Albania, East Germany, and Poland.

Cynthia M. Horne is a Professor of Political Science at Western Washington University. Her research area of specialty is transitional justice in the post-communist sphere, with attention to the conditions under which lustration and vetting programs have promoted transition goals of democracy, trust in government, trust in public institutions, and inter-personal trust. She has published extensively on the use of lustration, file-access provisions, and public disclosures in the postcommunist transitions in journals such as the *International Journal of Transitional Justice, Comparative Political Studies, Problems of Post-Communism, Law & Social Inquiry,* and *Europe-Asia Studies.* She has contributed to the *Encyclopedia of Transitional Justice* (2012) and *Post-Communist Transitional Justice: Lessons from Twenty-Five Years of Experience* (2015) on similar topics of trust building and transitional justice. Her book *Building Trust and Democracy: Transitional Justice in Post-Communist Countries* (2017) explores the impact of transitional justice on democratization and trust building across Central and Eastern Europe.

Lina Klymenko is a researcher at the Karelian Institute at the University of Eastern Finland. Her research focuses on memory politics, transitional justice, and national identity in post-Soviet countries. Her work has appeared in *Journal of Language and Politics; Journal of Educational Media, Memory, and Society; Canadian Slavonic Papers; Compare: A Journal of International and Comparative Education; Austrian Journal for Political Science; National Identities; Soviet and Post-Soviet Review;* and *Problems of Post-Communism.* At the time of writing she is working on a research project, funded by the Academy of Finland, on coming to terms with the Stalinist past in post-Soviet countries. She held teaching and research fellowships at the University of Tartu (Estonia), the Georg Eckert Institute for International Textbooks Research (Germany), the University of Uppsala (Sweden), and the University of Alberta (Canada).

Mark Kramer is Director of Cold War Studies at Harvard University and a Senior Fellow of Harvard's Davis Center for Russian and Eurasian Studies. He is editor of both the *Journal of Cold War Studies* and the Harvard Cold War Studies Book Series. He has taught international relations and comparative politics at Harvard, Yale, and Brown Universities and was formerly an

Academy Scholar at Harvard and a Rhodes Scholar at Oxford University. He is currently finishing a book on the Polish crisis of 1980–1. Kramer is the author or editor of numerous books and has written more than 200 articles on a variety of topics. His most recent coedited books are *Moscow and German Reunification* (2015); *Imposing, Maintaining, and Tearing Open the Iron Curtain: The Cold War and East-Central Europe, 1945–1989* (2014); *The Kremlin and the Revolutions of 1989* (2014); and *Reassessing History from Two Continents* (2014). Kramer has worked extensively in newly opened archives in all the former Warsaw Pact countries and several Western countries. He has been a consultant for numerous government agencies and international organizations, including as a member of the academic advisory board of the Czech Republic's Institute for the Study of Totalitarian Regimes and formerly as a member of the Scientific Council of the Institute for the Investigation of Communist Crimes in Romania.

Lavinia Stan is Chair of the Department of Political Science and Director of the Centre for Post-Communist Studies at St. Francis Xavier University, Canada. A Comparative Politics specialist, she is the author or editor of eleven books, the most recent of them being the *Encyclopedia of Transitional Justice* and *Post-Communist Transitional Justice at 25* (both coedited with Nadya Nedelsky), and *Transitional Justice in Post-Communist Romania* (Cambridge, 2013, 2013, and 2015, respectively). She has published in a variety of peer-reviewed journals, including *European Journal of Political Research* and *East European Politics and Societies*. Stan is a former member of the Scientific Council of the Institute for the Investigation of Communist Crimes in Romania, editor for *Women's Studies International Forum*, member of the Club of Rome and the scientific boards of twenty scholarly journals in Europe and North America, former member of several Social Sciences and Humanities Research Council of Canada (SSHRCC) adjudicating committees, and current President of the Society for Romanian Studies. Her research has been generously funded by the SSHRCC with multiple research grants. In 2014, she and Lucian Turcescu won a large SSHRCC grant to study religious groups' collaboration/resistance in communist Romania.

Oana-Valentina Suciu is an Assistant Professor in the Political Science Department at the University of Bucharest. She has worked as a civic activist and senior researcher for various nongovernmental organizations and think-tanks, including the Romanian Academic Society and the Institute for Public Policies. She has also collaborated with the World Bank Institute in Washington DC and with the Centre for Research into Post-Communist Economies in London. Between 2007 and 2013 she was the head of the

Domestic Programmes Department of the Romanian Cultural Institute. Her research interests fall within the fields of ethnic minorities' issues, political representation and the transitions in Central and Eastern Europe. She is the author of numerous articles and book chapters on the above-mentioned topics and also a board member of the Society for Romanian Studies. She is also the recipient of several research and academic development grants.

Alexei Trochev is an Associate Professor of Political Science at Nazarbayev University, Kazakhstan. He is the author of *Judging Russia: The Constitutional Court in Russian Politics, 1990–2006* (2008) and many articles and chapters on postcommunist law and politics, including pieces in *Post-Soviet Affairs, East European Law Review, Problems of Post-Communism, Journal of Law and Courts,* and *American Journal of Comparative Law,* to name a few. Two of his most recent book chapters appeared in Cambridge edited volumes, including "How Judges Arrest and Acquit: Soviet Legacies in Post-Communist Criminal Justice," in *The Historical Legacies of Communism in Russia and Eastern Europe,* Beissinger and Kotkin (eds.) (2014) and "Fragmentation? Defection? Legitimacy? Explaining Judicial Roles in Post-Communist 'Colored Revolutions'," in *Consequential Courts: Judicial Roles in Global Perspective,* Kagan et al. (eds.) (2013). Dr. Trochev edits the journal *Statutes and Decisions: The Laws of the USSR and Its Successor States,* which has recently covered issues of judicial politics in Ukraine, police reform in Russia, and criminal justice.

Alexandra Vacroux is a Lecturer in Government and the Executive Director of the Davis Center for Russian and Eurasian Studies at Harvard University. Her research has focused on policy reform in Russia with an emphasis on post-communist health-care systems. She has used the evolution of pharmaceutical regulations as a way of studying how decentralization and recentralization of federal functions have affected outcomes in the health sector, and participated in the preparation of the 2011 *Health Systems in Transition: the Russian Federation* (European Observatory on Health Systems and Policies). She has contributed chapters to the edited volumes: *Building a Trustworthy State in Post-Socialist Transition; Political Evolution and Institutional Change, Local Power and Post-Soviet Politics;* and *Studies of Economies in Transformation.* Vacroux is the Director of Graduate Studies for the M.A. program on Regional Studies, and an active member of the bilateral Working Group on the Future of US–Russia Relations.

Acknowledgments

The idea for this project started with a relatively simple question posed to us while on a roundtable discussing a book project on twenty-five years of transitional justice in Central and Eastern Europe, namely "what about states in the former Soviet Union?" At that moment, we didn't have much to add to the discussion, as little had been written about transitional justice attempts in the former Soviet Union (FSU). The relative dearth of measures in the FSU and outright rejection of accountability measures in many regional states had left this topic underexplored. In many ways, the dog that didn't bark had largely been ignored by both postcommunist and transitional justice scholars. This struck us as problematic. Both the absence and the instrumentalization of measures, not just the implementation of measures, seemed important areas to study, especially as the FSU was approaching its own twenty-fifth anniversary of the dissolution of the USSR. Hence, the idea for this project was hatched from one deceptively simple question.

Tackling this research question proved more challenging than its genesis. We are very pleased that we were able to assemble a group of scholars from diverse research backgrounds and perspectives, willing to collectively dive into this research lacuna. Everyone was empirically challenged to engage with new concepts and cases, or apply narrower research agendas to the broad FSU space. Contributors learned about unfamiliar countries in order to apply their knowledge of transitional justice, or, alternatively, learned about different transitional justice measures in order to evaluate their particular country case(s). We are very grateful for the willingness of many authors to stretch beyond their comfort zones and bring their particular areas of expertise to bear on this collaborative inquiry. We have learned a lot from this opportunity to work with them.

There are many people to thank in the process of bringing a book to frui-
tion. In particular, our editor John Berger at Cambridge University Press was
an enthusiastic supporter of this project from the very beginning. We have
appreciated his support, advice, and patience as we pulled it together, as well
as his enthusiasm for advancing the field of transitional justice in novel ways
theoretically and empirically. We also want to thank Nadya Nedelsky and
Brian Grodsky for enthusiastically supporting this project, and the anonymous
reviewers for kindly allowing it to go ahead.

Personally, Cynthia is most appreciative to have worked with Lavinia on this
project. Lavinia is not only an intellectual power-house, but she is a detail-
oriented, administrative dynamo, capable of providing thoughtful, timely
feedback. Her sense of humor helped pull this project over many a hurdle.
Cynthia feels so fortunate that our chance coffee table conversation morphed
into this project. In turn, Lavinia is no less grateful for Cynthia's willingness
to put up with her hectic administrative duties that often called her attention
for days, even weeks, at a time and slowed down progress for this manuscript.
Indeed, this volume would not have seen its final stages without the unwa-
vering dedication Cynthia demonstrated in contacting contributors, keeping
track of revisions and revisions of revisions, unifying the referencing style,
and bringing all chapters, tables, references, and blurbs together. Lavinia also
wants to thank Lucian and Luc Turcescu for their love and support, and the
Social Sciences and Humanities Research Council of Canada for generously
financing her research on various transitional justice themes.

Despite our best efforts, there is much that remains unexplored in this
volume. Not all FSU cases are covered, not all measures are accounted for,
and the impact of newly implemented measures remains to be seen. We are
hopeful that this volume starts a conversation about the presence and absence
of transitional justice in the FSU for others to build upon.

Introduction

Cynthia M. Horne

A significant amount of scholarly attention has been paid to both the origin and the impact of postcommunist transitional justice measures, and complementary memory politics issues, in Central and Eastern Europe (CEE) since the fall of the Berlin Wall in 1989. This has allowed scholars to compare and evaluate programs across the region in order to better understand the conditions under which transitional justice has (or has not) supported regional postcommunist transitions. In contrast, there has been a relative dearth of scholarship on transitional justice, accountability measures, and/or memory politics in the Former Soviet Union (FSU). To be fair, the absence of robust transitional justice programs in the FSU has left less for scholars to engage with; however, ignoring the use and abuse of measures in the FSU constitutes an oversight in the transitional justice and postcommunist literatures. The FSU republics are important cases both for the measures they adopted and those they rejected. In other words, the origin or rejection of transitional justice in the FSU and the impact of both the presence and absence of transitional justice in the FSU are critical and under-examined research tracks.

This volume aims to fill this lacuna with an examination of the efforts of state and nonstate actors in the FSU to either reckon with or alternately obstruct the recent and more distant communist past, with an eye to how these choices might affect the future. In particular, twenty-five years after the Soviet Union was dismantled and the successor republics moved away from the communist regimes, this volume examines the adoption and rejection of transitional justice measures among the FSU republics, and explores the impact of those transitional justice choices on state-building and societal reconciliation efforts. The volume treats both transitional justice measures and possible transition outcomes or goals broadly, to be maximally inclusive of a range of subtle measures and outcomes given the relative limited use of formal transitional justice in the FSU. To that end, the volume considers traditional transitional justice measures, such as lustration laws, file access provisions, trials, and truth commissions, as well as policies that bleed into memory politics measures, such as memorialization efforts, commemoration initiatives, new national holidays, and history textbook revisions. The volume also engages a range of intentions and outcomes associated with these measures, from traditional state-building initiatives, including the rewriting of national narratives, the fortification of a (re)newed national identity, attempts to promote good governance and trust in public institutions, and anticorruption goals, as well as societal reconciliation measures such as accountability for victims, acknowledgment of past wrongs, and various forms of redress and reparation. In this way, we cast a broad net over measures and outcomes in order to present the most comprehensive account to date of FSU efforts to address, distort, ignore, or recast the past through the use, manipulation, and obstruction of transitional justice measures and memory politics initiatives.

There are three main goals motivating this volume. First, this volume renews the focus on the factors that affect the adoption (or rejection) of efforts to reckon with past human rights abuses in the postcommunist context. Second, the volume examines the limitations of enacting specific transitional justice methods, programs, and practices in the FSU republics, the majority of which have not experienced complete and irreversible democratization. And third the volume explicates the challenge of addressing multiple, competing pasts and the reasons why transitional justice failure, stagnation, and even reversal have been registered in numerous countries in the region.

There are a number of ways this volume distinguishes itself in terms of both transitional justice studies and studies of the FSU. First, this volume is unusual in mixing analyses of cases and "noncases." Most scholarship on postcommunist transitional justice has relied on analyses that included only countries that enacted some type of transitional justice, without addressing noncases.[1] In other words, scholars have inferred impact by comparing across cases of transitional justice, while ignoring countries that eschewed transitional justice. Thoms, Ron, and Paris noted the tendency across the social sciences to focus on the exceptional cases of transitional justice and ignore the failures or worse, the absence of transitional justice.[2] Even large-N studies of transitional justice, such as Olsen, Payne, and Reiter's work on the Transitional Justice Database project, compared across cases of transitional justice omitting similar country cases that failed to implement transitional justice.[3] Admittedly, the noncase is much more challenging to incorporate into such evaluations of transitional justice measures, but it is hard to assess impact if one leaves out similarly situated cases that actively rejected transitional justice.

A comparison of cases and noncases is particularly challenging because one needs similar country cases at similar moments in world historical time and similar justice issues, partially explaining the dearth of such comparative studies. Fortunately, the FSU provides just such a group of similarly situated countries. We have an ability to compare countries with similar communist experiences, which all became sovereign at the same moment in time and had similar transitional justice needs. Moreover, the CEE cases are proximate enough in terms of communist legacies and the timing of independence to make them possible points of comparison to the FSU cases and noncases as well. In other words, we are afforded a fortuitous sample of regionally, temporally, and politically similar countries – some with transitional justice and some without – allowing us the possibility of authentically engaging with the noncase.

To that end, this volume compares cases and noncases within the FSU, and compares cases and noncases across the postcommunist space. For example, noncases like Belarus and Russia are presented alongside cases of limited and/ or failed transitional justice, such as Georgia and Moldova, and compared with cases of multiple and overlapping transitional justice measures, such as Lithuania and Ukraine. In this way, the volume engages across a full range of transitional justice experiences, from the outright rejection of transitional justice, to the manipulation of transitional justice, to iterated attempts at measures. Individual chapters engage targeted comparisons of cases and noncases as well. For example, Mark Kramer compares memory politics measures in Poland to those in Russia, Cynthia Horne compares lustration measures in Ukraine to those in CEE, and Nenad Dimitrijević compares the postconflict and postauthoritarian transitional justice needs of Serbia to those of the FSU, to name a few of the direct comparisons. These chapters gain intellectual leverage over the potential ramifications of choosing or rejecting transitional justice through the intentional comparison of similarly situated cases and noncases in the postcommunist space, attending to the implications for our study of the FSU.

Second, this volume is also unusual in intentionally exploring multiple, competing pasts; a topic largely underdeveloped in postcommunist examinations of transitional justice. Many countries in the FSU have proximate human rights abuses layered on more distant abuses, be they legacies of internal conflict, legacies of war, or legacies associated with different phases of communism. The selection of certain memories to engage with and other memories to set aside reveals the power of both state and nonstate actors to shape and potentially instrumentalize the past. Not engaging with a particular legacy of rights' abuses can be an intentional decision by the state to shape public perceptions about the past and the present, garner electoral support, or prevent popular opposition. For example, Lithuania's engagement with the past, as explored in Dovile Budrytė and Violeta Davoliūtė's chapter, focuses on the layering of communist-era crimes on the atrocities committed under the Nazi oppression, and explores the manner in which the state prioritizes some rights' abuses and memories over others. Budrytė and Davoliūtė focus on the recent turn in Lithuania to engage with Nazi era abuses committed by both foreign occupiers and Lithuanians against their own Jewish countrymen. In this way they engage issues of layered pasts and internal complicity dilemmas, with reverberations through society that the state must juggle as part of transitional justice and accountability programs. Nenad Dimitrijević's chapter presents the Serbian case of layered pasts and selective accountability in order to highlight how the abuses committed during the Yugoslav wars were layered on communist era abuses and on unaddressed abuses committed during World War II. These multiple, unaddressed abuses add layers to the complexity of explanatory frameworks and highlight the serious limitations state and nonstate transitional justice actors face when formulating, promoting, and enacting reckoning programs. Layered rights abuses and state and societal level choices to engage some pasts over others constitute challenges facing most FSU states.

Third, this volume analyzes an array of transitional justice and accountability measures, considering both typical methods and "softer" justice methods. Although there has been less transitional justice in the FSU than CEE, and certainly less than many policymakers and academics have recommended, there are many informal measures that have largely gone unattended. This volume examines both judicial and nonjudicial methods, expanding the definition of transitional justice measures into their intersection with the accountability aspects of memory politics. The first chapter by Lavinia Stan provides an overview of this range of regional accountability and reckoning, from traditional methods such as court trials with resulting verdicts that can be treated as forms of transitional justice, to truth-telling commissions, property restitution and lustration or screening laws, as well as softer methods, such as national days, history textbook rewriting, and public apologies. Stan's chapter presents the most comprehensive overview to date of all attempts to reckon, however limited, with communist era crimes across the entire FSU region. Stan argues that the relative dearth of transitional justice in the region can be explained as a function of several factors: the timing of the worst human rights violations relative to the ousting of the communist regime, the incomplete democratization experienced by many successor republics, the continued political clout of former KGB officers and informers, the balance of forces in postcommunist times, the role of political leadership, and the indifference of international actors. Many of these factors will be explored in greater detail in this volume.

In presenting an overview of transitional justice across the region, Stan lays the foundation for the case studies to follow. For example, Lina Klymenko's chapter engages in such softer forms of transitional justice, examining history textbooks and how the rewriting of aspects of history serves as a form of accountability and a space for memory policies. Alexei Trochev reviews commemoration, rehabilitation, and memorialization in Kazakhstan, echoing similar measures also seen in Russia, Ukraine, and Belarus. Onur Bakiner's chapter engages the explosive popularity of truth commissions as a form of transitional justice around the world, examining the relative dearth of truth commissions, memory institutes, and fact-finding initiatives in the FSU in the context of the global proliferation of this transitional justice measure. Agata Fijalkowski's chapter examines trials and court verdicts as forms of transitional justice and accountability, expanding our understanding of nontraditional forms of transitional justice. Nanci Adler's chapter on Russia's remembering and forgetting highlights national remembrance days, with attention to what they say about current state-building and national narratives in Russia. In sum, the volume presents an array of transitional justice measures, with attention to the role of state and nonstate actors in the process of catalyzing and responding to measures.

BOOK STRUCTURE

The volume is organized into three main sections rather than presenting a country-by-country approach. *Part I, The Long Shadow of the Past* focuses on some of the challenges associated with overcoming communist legacies, and explicates the reasons behind the limited transitional justice enacted in the FSU during the first twenty-five years of postcommunism. Chapters in this section examine how the framing of past communist abuses affects possible courses of action in postcommunist times. Stan, Bekus, Kramer, Trochev, and Adler's chapters explore impediments to reform, delayed transitional justice measures, and the various ways in which the past is being repurposed to advance the political and social objectives in the present.

Part II, Transitional Justice Programs, Practices, and Legislation focuses on the most important methods of transitional justice and accountability attempted in the FSU, including lustration measures, truth commissions, trials and court cases, memory laws, history reeducation, and the (re)construction of historical narratives. Horne, David, Bakiner, Fijalkowski, and Klymenko draw on the transitional justice literature to inform a discussion of how these measures have worked or failed to work in the FSU. Chapters in this section also examine how the selection of certain types of measures over other types of measures has reflected the states' efforts to manage the accountability processes in ways that have not always privileged reckoning over political calculations.

Part III, Layered Pasts and the Politics of Denial draws heavily on scholarship on communist legacies and postcommunist politics in order to examine the rejection of measures to deal with the past. This last set of chapters examines the various state and nonstate actors that have engaged in instrumental manipulation or obfuscation of accountability measures in order to control the way the past is presented or to thwart accountability for both proximate and distant rights abuses. In this way the denial of the past or the selective engagement with the past affect or delimit possibilities for the future. Stan, Austin, Suciu, Davoliūtė and Budrytė, and Dimitrijević's all engage with postconflict and postauthoritarian atrocities layered on each other, both entwining the legacies of state and societal violence and complicating the options for transitional justice.

THEMATIC OVERVIEW

Several broad themes tie the chapters together, presenting findings from this volume that could possibly speak to both FSU transition issues as well as transitions more generally. First, many of the chapters engage *framing, memory, and manipulation issues*, highlighting that transitional justice is not necessarily benign. There is a significant volume of literature on the instrumental manipulation of the past to privilege a certain understanding of the future. Such an intentional framing or manipulation of certain memories or historical experiences could affect the impact of the measures. The state has been particularly active in the FSU reframing the past as a way to control the present. Many contributions in this volume engage with this manipulation of transitional justice, exploring possible perverse consequences of certain transitional justice paths, such as Adler, Kramer, Klymenko, Budrytė and Davoliūtė, Bekus, Trochev, Stan, and Dimitrijević.

For example, Nanci Adler's chapter "Challenges to Transitional Justice in Russia" highlights not only the manner in which the state has suppressed all recognized, institutional transitional justice mechanisms to deal with crimes committed in the past, but also the rehabilitation and valorization of Stalin's achievements, as well as Stalin himself. Instead of reflecting on crimes committed in the past and acknowledging victims, the state has constructed what Adler describes as a "gilded version of the national past," instrumentalized to support current state-building practices, promote patriotism, and justify repressive practices. Although there are some "bottom-up" efforts to remember victims, such as Memorial, such efforts have not resonated as broadly with the general public as a national narrative valorizing Stalin's achievements. Adler's chapter is a cautionary reminder that acts of remembering are political and not necessarily benign.

Mark Kramer's chapter "Public Memory and Communist Legacies in Poland and Russia" similarly engages the rehabilitation of the glory of Stalin in Russia as a means to further the state-building objectives of Vladimir Putin. Kramer's chapter explores how the initial efforts by post-Soviet leaders in Russia to address Stalinist crimes have been intentionally hijacked by Putin, who has instrumentally used a revisionist interpretation of Stalinism to further his own state-building agenda. Alarmingly, Kramer's chapter explicates that, although scholars have meticulously analyzed and made public information about the atrocities associated with Stalinism, the Russian government's reimagining of this valorous past has fueled a wider indifference and lack of interest on the part of the Russian public to engage with the histories of state-led violence. Kramer's chapter is made richer in its comparison with Poland, a country that used formal transitional justice measures, and simultaneously denied parts of its past involving discrimination and violence against Polish Jewry. Kramer's chapter is a reminder of the problems of state instrumentalization of history to advance certain national narratives, both in the presence of transitional justice measures (Poland) and in the absence of such measures (Russia). In a word, public memory framing and (mis)use can happen in a variety of domestic institutional contexts.

Lina Klymenko's chapter "Transitional Justice and the Revision of History Textbooks: the 1932–1933 Famine in Ukraine" traces changes in the narrative surrounding the 1932–3 famine in Ukraine, called the Holomodor, as an example of both historical memory reframing and a soft form of transitional justice. Klymenko identifies the strategies employed in fifth grade textbooks to create a certain national identity for young Ukrainian readers, drawing on the condemnation of the Stalinist totalitarian regime and a sympathy for famine victims. In this way, the rewriting of history textbooks functions as a transitional justice method by presenting a new narrative about the Holomodor that requires both accountability for the past and the acknowledgment of the victims of this state-orchestrated genocide of Ukrainian peasants. Klymenko's chapter is also an example of the use of history textbooks to present Ukraine as a victim of Stalin's collectivization measures, and therefore create an "other" to blame. This reframing of history can be used to cultivate a new national Ukrainian narrative, important for state-building in the post-Soviet period. As such, it is a reminder that the instrumentalization of post-Soviet memory to reframe genocide, repression, and violence is not always to whitewash the past. Memory reframing can also be a way to make up for past misrepresentations of state-led violence and to acknowledge the victims of those abuses. Nonetheless, in divided societies like Ukraine, naming or blaming Russians for the violence threatens to ignite volatile current ethnic divisions in society. In this way, Klymenko's chapter hints at the manner in which transitional justice could undermine societal reconciliation rather than advance it.

A second main theme running through this volume is the challenge of *overlapping transitional justice measures and memory issues*. Multiple, unaddressed regime abuses exist in the post-Soviet space. Proximate aggressions are layered on previous aggressions. The manner in which elites choose to address some crimes of the past but not others can affect the resulting state-building or societal reconciliation processes. If some wrongs are addressed and others are intentionally left unattended, this can result in distorted policies, possibly tainting the transitional justice processes themselves. There is significant variation in the FSU in terms of how states have decided to address these layered historical legacies. This volume presents cases such as Russia (Adler, Kramer), Ukraine (Horne, David), Georgia (Austin), Moldova (Stan), Armenia (Suciu), and the Baltics (Fijalkowski, Budrytė and Davoliūtė), with attention to cases in which Soviet repressions were layered on unresolved World War II atrocities, as well as cases in which atrocities associated with more recent military conflicts are layered on unaddressed Soviet-era offenses.

Roman David considers layered pasts and transitional justice measures in Ukraine in the chapter "Lustration in Ukraine and Democracy Capable of Defending Itself." Ukraine's lustration measures, a regionally specific form of employment vetting widely used in the postcommunist transitions in CEE, were designed to tackle the Soviet communist legacies, the excesses of Viktor Yanukovych's regime, and the human rights abuses committed during the Euromaidan protests. Hence, Ukraine's 2014 lustration measures addressed multiple layered wrongs committed in the proximate and distant past. While the lustration measures focused on the more recent abuses, there was an explicit acknowledgment that the Soviet-era abuses and post-Soviet abuses were related, and that in some ways the unaddressed Soviet past created problems in the post-Soviet present. The larger implication here is the manner in which unresolved previous abuses can taint the foundations on which a new regime is established. Additionally, there is a significant role for civil society in David's chapter. David details the groundswell public support for a lustration of political officials in the wake of the Euromaidan protests. Ukraine therefore presents an example of public activism and calls for accountability that materialized as state-led transitional justice measures, something largely absent in the FSU. The bottom-up push for transitional justice is not without complications and potential rule of law derogations, something explored in detail in David's chapter as well. David directly links lustration and democratization in his exploration of this controversial transitional justice method, as a means by which a democracy is capable of defending itself.

Violeta Davoliūtė and Dovile Budrytė's chapter "Entangled History, History Education and Affective Communities in Lithuania," explores Lithuania's changing perspective on how to address its layered pasts, namely Holocaust-related human rights abuses and abuses committed under Stalinism. In particular, they focus on the use of history textbooks and public reeducation as both transitional justice measures and arenas for memory politics. By exploring how some memories and atrocities are privileged over other memories, they are able to shed light on the politicization of certain historical events and the silencing of others. In environments with such layered abuses, they show how these traumas are in many ways related to each other, and therefore selectively engaging with some human rights abuses and ignoring others creates a problematic approach to transitional justice. By comparing the efforts of two transitional justice institutions involved in history education in post-Soviet Lithuania with the efforts of other civil society agents, they explicate how affective communities developed around acknowledgment and accountability for Lithuania's treatment of its Jewish citizens at the hands of fellow Lithuanians during World War II. Their chapter thus engages aspects of complicity faced by many other FSU states in their transitional justice needs, topics also examined in chapters by Horne and Kramer.

Oana-Valentina Suciu's chapter, "Confronting Multiple Pasts in Post-Soviet Armenia," presents layers of unresolved and unaddressed war atrocities, dating back as far as the 1800s, which affect Armenia's current attitudes toward transitional justice as well as its postcommunist democratization efforts. Suciu describes the Armenian case as a type of Russian matryoshka nesting doll of multiple competing pasts. This visual nicely illustrates how the long shadow of the past is cast over present state-building and societal reconciliation efforts. In particular, Suciu examines the 1915 Genocide perpetrated by the Ottoman Empire, the legacies of Stalinist purges, the on-going conflict in Nagorno-Karabakh with Azerbaijan, and postcommunist abuses, in order to present a complicated story of nested and overlapping rights' abuses. Sucui illustrates how Armenian national history and current politics are driven by a quest for reparations for some but not all past rights' violations. In particular, the 1915 Genocide and the atrocities committed in Nagorno-Karabakh overshadow all other pasts, including the more recent communist past. In fact, addressing the postcommunist past could reveal how Armenians were not just victims but also perpetrators of rights' abuses. Therefore, as with other FSU states in this volume like Ukraine, Kazakhstan, and Georgia, Armenia has instrumentally privileged reckoning with some pasts over others as part of its postcommunist state-building program. Suciu's chapter is especially interesting in addressing both historical abuses and on-going rights' abuses, highlighting that transitional justice is not just about past abuses but could also encompass present and on-going abuses. Her chapter explores how Russia, Turkey, Azerbaijan, the EU, and even the US play a role in treatment of these issues, suggesting an internationalization of transitional justice and memory politics that reverberates in multiple ways with Dimitrijević's chapter on Serbia.

Nenad Dimitrijević's chapter "Learning from Serbian Failure: The Denial of Three Repressive Pasts" explores the dilemmas surrounding the use of transitional justice to address some pasts but not others in the case of postconflict Serbia. He examines three repressive periods in Serbia's history, namely World War II under German occupying powers, the Yugoslav communist period, and the regime of Slobodan Milošević. The case of Serbia is an unusual one of unaddressed or selectively addressed postconflict atrocities layered on postauthoritarian repressions layered on postconflict violence, resonating with other countries in this book such as Georgia, Ukraine, and Moldova. Dimitrijević juxtaposes the limited use of transitional justice in Serbia to address the Yugoslav conflict and the abuses committed under Milošević, against the considerable political legal and cultural efforts directed at addressing the Nazi past and the communist repression. The wrongdoings committed during the Yugoslav conflict are largely ignored and justice efforts are focused on more temporally distant offenses. Those offenses are in turn repurposed as nationalist building measures, in a manner that suggests transitional justice measures are being used to advance Serbia's dominant cultural narrative of denial of wrongdoing. Layered injustices have afforded political elites with a range of offenses to focus on at the expense of others, giving an illusion of transitional justice, albeit one that is disguising denial of wrongs for more proximate state-led violence and abuses. In this way, Dimitrijević draws out the lessons learned from Serbia's misuse of transitional justice and selective engagement with some atrocities over others in order to speak to similar cases of layered, unresolved rights abuses in the FSU cases.

A third main theme running through this volume considers *antireform constituencies*, including state-led opposition to reform and opposition emanating from various civil society groups. Transitional justice is not unproblematic as a set of reforms. There are groups in society and elements of the state structure that benefit economically, socially, and politically from a failure to make the past transparent and from distorting the past by selectively emphasizing certain elements. The efforts by many states in the region to legally block transitional justice reforms or to allow only partial reforms merit close attention. Additionally, the constituencies that mobilize to block transitional justice bear consideration in light of the diverse groups that have thwarted efforts for accountability, such as political elites, special interest groups, and nationalist movements. However, it is not only the absence of reforms that must be considered, but the selection of some types of reforms that distort the past or hijack authentic efforts to engage in accountability. As such both the presence of certain types of choices and the absence of measures altogether could constitute antireform constituencies. Contributions by Stan, Adler, Bekus, and Austin examine the composition and impact of antireform constituencies and their relationship with key political actors representing the government and the opposition in the FSU.

Lavinia Stan examines the understudied case of Moldova in "Transitional Justice Lessons from Moldova," highlighting political elites' efforts to block accountability measures as a way to continue to benefit from a failure to reckon with the past. In particular, she examines how Moldova has chosen to engage with some transitional justice measures, such as rehabilitation, compensation, restitution, and history textbook rewriting, and rejected other measures such as lustration and file access measures. In this way, Moldova's political elites selectively engage with measures that do not threaten them and in some ways could benefit them by increasing their popular support. Additionally, Stan's chapter also considers Moldova's multiple layered pasts, including abuses committed during and after World War II, abuses committed under postwar Soviet occupation, as well as the rights violations committed after Moldovan independence and related to the conflict with Transnistria. She documents that Moldova's reckoning programs of rehabilitation, memorialization, and commemoration selectively prioritized the Stalinist past and ignored the human rights violations perpetrated by later Soviet leaders, in a manner seen in other FSU cases. As such, her chapter resonates with the Russian, Ukrainian, Georgian, and Baltic cases in explicating how unaddressed pasts are entwined, affecting any transitional justice efforts moving forward.

Nelly Bekus presents the under-examined case of Belarus in her chapter "Historical Reckoning in Belarus." She documents a significant number of soft transitional justice measures, including commemorative events and exhibitions, alternative truth-telling and memorialization programs, and even a citizen-organized tribunal, that have largely gone unnoticed by the international community. In comparison to the dominance of state-led narratives in Russia, Bekus explores the efforts of nonstate actors engaging in truth-telling and memorialization efforts to advance an "imagined" Belarusian transition narrative. While efforts to engage in transitional justice were not generally popular across society, various nonstate actors have managed to advance and popularize softer measures. This bottom-up push for a reimagining of history is not necessarily benign, despite the involvement of nonstate actors. On the contrary, Bekus explains how ethnocentric arguments are being instrumentalized by civil society groups to advance a narrative externalizing blame on Russia and the Soviets for excesses committed in the past, and in this way valorizing Belarus and its victimhood. Bekus' chapter presents a cautionary reminder that civil society groups can also advance distorted national narratives to fit parochial political agendas. In other words, while there is evidence in the post-Soviet space of state-led manipulation and distortion of historical memory, civil society groups can also be guilty of such historical manipulation in the way in which previous abuses are selected while others are obscured.

In "Confronting the Soviet and Post-Soviet Past in Georgia," Robert Austin explains that under Mikheil Saakashvili, Georgia embarked on various economic reforms and anticorruption measures without transitional justice, in a curious example of the decoupling of economic reforms and transitional justice. By 2017, Georgia had largely ignoring both the crimes of the Soviet dictatorship and the crimes of the subsequent postcommunist regime of Saakashvili. Austin's detailed narrative ensures that this limited transitional justice is understood as more than simply a state-led initiative to thwart accountability. He shows that while the Georgian political elites engaged in some limited transitional justice, in which the Soviets and Russians were blamed for past atrocities in Georgia, this anti-Soviet narrative was used to construct a sense of both Georgian victimhood at the hands of the Russians and a (re)newed sense of Georgian nationalism. While this might be politically desirable, given Georgia's open conflicts with Russia, the Georgian people's attitudes toward Stalin have reflected a more complicated picture. Support for Stalin's memory is still high in Georgia, with Stalin identified with the Soviet victory over Nazism, and as a favored Georgian son. As such there is bottom-up resistance to framing Stalin as an evil perpetrator of abuses. In short, there are both state and societal forces resistant to transitional justice, for different reasons, but resulting in limited accountability nonetheless.

It is of note that under Saakashvili Georgia was an unusual case of expansive economic reforms, garnering much international praise, distinguishing Georgia from other post-Soviet republics, and yielding significant economic growth. However, the reforms were enacted in a quasi-democratic manner with noticeable rule of law derogations and in the absence of transitional justice. Transitional justice measures are often framed as complements to economic, political, and social reform measures, and in some countries when anticorruption measures are thwarted, transitional justice measures – like lustration – have been used in their place.[4] The success of certain transition goals such as economic development is often linked to transitional justice measures that force bureaucratic change, break up crony networks, promote accountability, and embrace transparency. Austin's chapter on Georgia does not fit with this understanding of transitional justice as necessary complements to other reform measures, prompting questions about the possibility for FSU regional reforms in the absence of complementary transitional justice measures.

Alexei Trochev's chapter "Transitional Justice Attempts in Kazakhstan" reviews the elite-driven transitional justice efforts post-1991, illustrating how they have been largely symbolic or reactive to civil society demands, and often only partially implemented or quickly abandoned. Adopting an approach of officially blaming Soviet rulers for past atrocities without actually naming individuals responsible for past abuses has allowed Kazakh elites to instrumentalize transitional justice measures for political gain. Trochev shows how post-Soviet rulers have used the rehabilitation campaigns to gain political capital by presenting their nation as a victim of Soviet rule rather than as authentic means of seeking the truth or improving accountability for victims and their families. Interestingly, juxtaposing Trochev's chapter against Lina Klymenko's chapter on Ukraine illustrates divergent approaches to the same historical atrocities within the post-Soviet space. For example, the famine in the 1930s has been addressed quite differently in the two republics, with Ukraine officially naming this famine as a case of genocide and Kazakhstan backing away from such an official designation. Trochev examines other state-led atrocities in Soviet Kazakhstan, including riots and purges, to show that the past has been framed or ignored by current leaders in order to advance a Kazakh state-building agenda and as a means of addressing ethnic identity concerns. Like other post-Soviet states covered in this volume, the case of Kazakhstan embodies the manner in which the past continues to cast a long shadow on the future.

A fourth unifying theme in this volume is the placement of the FSU in *a broader comparative context.* To that end, several chapters have made a concerted effort to apply *extra-regional transitional justice lessons to the FSU.* The experiences in CEE with transitional justice are not only regionally proximate but also historically and culturally resonant with the post-Soviet states, constituting a deep and wide base of knowledge to inform our analysis of the FSU. Additionally, several chapters engage *the role of external actors and their influence* on transitional justice in the region. This volume challenges the assumption of FSU exceptionalism seen in some approaches to post-Soviet studies. It is through an intentional comparative approach that we gain leverage over the possible effects of both the presence and absence of FSU transitional justice measures. In other words, comparing across the postcommunist region helps to unpack the possible effects of the noncase.

Onur Bakiner's chapter "Between Politics and History: The Baltic Truth Commissions in Global Perspective" takes the broadest comparative perspective of any of the chapters. He develops a truth commission typology based on memory and truth-telling efforts around the world, and then uses this typology to inform an analysis of Baltic fact-finding bodies. His broad comparative perspective allows him to situate the accomplishments and shortcomings of commissions in Estonia, Latvia, and Lithuania within the context of the global popularity of truth commissions in the 1990s and the 2000s. Although the Baltic commissions did not satisfy most of the definitional criteria used for truth commissions insofar as their forensic investigation, temporal scope, and relationship to victims were concerned, Bakiner argues that the Baltic commissions echo many of the promises and challenges that truth commissions face in their engagement with social memory debates. He shows how the Baltic commissions consciously positioned themselves as arbiters of disagreements over social memory. The Baltic commissions were less concerned with making recommendations for immediate political-institutional reform and more interested in adjudicating debates over history and social memory. This still resembles the work of truth commissions that have produced comprehensive accounts of past wrongs to seek broader state and societal transformations. In sum, Bakiner's broad comparative approach presents us with a range of forms this type of transitional justice could take, as well as some of the strengths and limitations of this type of nonpunitive transitional justice measure. Given the nonpunitive nature of truth commissions, this transitional justice method remains a politically possible options for many states in the FSU.

Cynthia Horne's chapter "Lustration: Temporal, Scope, and Implementation Considerations" takes a narrower comparative approach to assess the post-Maidan lustration program in Ukraine. She draws on the CEE transitional justice scholarship, attending to what we know about the impact of lustration measures on transition goals like the promotion of good governance and democratization, in order to situate Ukraine's legislation in comparative perspective. She highlights that many of the current critiques of Ukraine's laws and intentions resonate with other postcommunist programs. While not minimizing the potential dilemmas associated with measures that could violate due process or retroactivity prohibitions, she also demonstrates that lustration has had a generally positive effect on transition goals in CEE. To the extent that Ukraine's measures can replicate some of the scope and implementation components of CEE that have proven efficacious, there is a real possibility for beneficial reforms to arise from Ukraine's lustration efforts. Moreover, the late timing of lustration in Ukraine raises the question of whether it is too late for Ukraine, and the FSU, to use such transitional justice measures. By utilizing an explicitly comparative perspective, Horne is able to show that there is significantly more latitude in the temporal conditions surrounding the use of this transitional justice measure. Horne's comparative approach helps to adjudicate temporal, scope, and implementation considerations with respect to Ukraine's on-going transitional justice measures.

Other chapters examine external influences on transitional justice in the FSU. Notably, Agata Fijalkowski's chapter "Historical Politics and Court Redress in the Baltic States" explores the way that the European Court of Human Rights (ECtHR) has framed and interpreted communist-era crimes. The chapter is unusual in considering court verdicts and their legal reasoning as forms of transitional justice. More precisely, she explores the way an international actor – the ECtHR – has affected domestic interpretations of history and justice in the Baltics. Fijalkowski argues that legal decisions regarding which communist-era actions are characterized as actionable crimes constitute important practices of transitional justice. Fijalkowski considers cases raised by Estonia, Lithuania, and Latvia and heard by the ECtHR. Through an analysis of three court cases, her chapter illustrates areas in which domestic and international actors contest memory. She argues that the ECtHR is increasingly playing an important role in the validation of key historical narratives in postcommunist Europe, with unexpected consequences for the definition of key crimes and the way these definitions are contested. Saliently for other FSU cases, her chapter hints at the selective manner in which some histories are repressed and others are validated in an effort to create a new national state-building narrative. As such, this chapter presents a third transitional justice method – court trials – that could still be applied to FSU states.

This volume constitutes the first systematic attempt to reflect on what we know about the presence or absence of transitional justice in the FSU on the twenty-fifth anniversary of the end of the Soviet Union. We bring together fourteen scholars with backgrounds in both transitional justice scholarship and a deep historical understanding of the communist system and its unique postcommunist legacies. This is an unusual combination, since the focus of most transitional justice literature has not been on the FSU space and most of the scholarship on the FSU has not engaged with issues of transitional justice. The scholars come from an array of research disciplines, including political science, history, sociology, and law, thereby providing an interdisciplinary perspective on regional transitional justice measures. The temporal and empirical breadth of the volume allows for engagement with both the most important and the most neglected factors shaping transitional justice in the FSU. We hope this volume starts a dialog, raising questions and connecting the postcommunist studies and transitional justice scholarly communities as we move forward together to better understand the past and the future.

Notes

1. Monika Nalepa, *Skeletons in the Closet* (New York: Cambridge University Press, 2010); and Roman David, *Lustration and Transitional Justice* (Philadelphia: University of Pennsylvania Press, 2014). Other foundational pieces in the field of postcommunist transitional justice include: John Moran, "The Communist Tortures of Eastern Europe: Prosecute and Punish or Forgive and Forget?," *Communist and Post-Communist Studies* 27, 1 (1994): 95–109; Helga Welsh, "Dealing with the Communist Past: Central and East European Experiences after 1990," *Europe-Asia Studies* 48, 3 (1996): 413–29; and Nadya Nedelsky, "Divergent Responses to a Common Past: Transitional Justice in the Czech Republic and Slovakia," *Theory and Society* 33 (2004): 65–115.
2. Oskar Thoms, James Ron, and Roland Paris, *The Effects of Transitional Justice Mechanisms: A Summary of Empirical Research Findings and Implications for Analysts and Practitioners* (Ottawa: Centre for International Policy Studies, 2008).
3. Tricia Olsen, Leigh Payne, and Andrew Reiter, *Transitional Justice in Balance: Comparing Processes, Weighing Efficacy* (Washington: United States Institute of Peace Press, 2010).
4. For example, Cynthia M. Horne, "Late Lustration Programs in Romania and Poland: Supporting or Undermining Democratic Transitions?," *Democratization* 16, 2 (2009): 344–76; Lavinia Stan, "The Romanian Anticorruption Bill," *Studies in Post-Communism Occasional Paper*, No. 6 (2004), Centre for Post-Communist Studies, St. Francis Xavier University; and Lavinia Stan, "The Politics of Memory in Poland: Lustration, File Access and Court Proceedings," *Studies in Post-Communism Occasional Paper*, No. 10 (2006), Centre for Post-Communist Studies, St. Francis Xavier University.

PART I

THE LONG SHADOW OF THE PAST

Limited Reckoning in the Former Soviet Union

Some Possible Explanations

Lavinia Stan

Twenty-five years after the collapse of the Former Soviet Union (FSU), it is evident that the fifteen successor republics have engaged in only limited reckoning with the mass human rights abuses perpetrated by the communist regime in 1917–91. The Baltic republics represent the only exception because they made considerable strides by adopting a wide range of transitional justice methods, programs, and practices. By contrast, the other former Soviet republics have done relatively little to reckon with the communist past, therefore demonstrating indifference toward the plight of the former victims and the possibly negative impact on the rule of law from the continued impunity of former communist-era victimizers. In a surprising move, postcommunist Russia and some of its FSU client states have adopted a number of measures designed to counter the very necessity of what the Germans call *Vergangenheitsbewältigung* by negating, justifying or even extolling communist human rights violations.

This chapter reviews the literature available to date to identify the reasons why the FSU has lagged behind the Baltic republics and Central and Eastern Europe in its efforts to come to terms with the legacy of communist crimes. The focus here is on lustration, access to the secret files compiled on ordinary citizens by the KGB, and court trials against communist party officials and secret agents, as well as other nonjudicial transitional justice methods, including history commissions, rehabilitation, property restitution, unofficial truth projects, and public holidays, in order to provide a fuller picture of reckoning in the post-Soviet context.

The chapter is divided into two main sections. The first one pieces together the postcommunist record of transitional justice measures implemented in the successor states to show that those states fall behind Central Europe, and to identify variations within the post-Soviet space. Attention is then given to explaining this weak reckoning effort and the differences among countries.

The incomplete democratization experienced by some successor republics, the continued political clout of former Communist Party leaders, as well as KGB officers and informers, the postcommunist balance of forces between the pro- and antireckoning camps, the role of political leadership, the weakness of civil society groups free of nationalist goals, the indifference of international actors, the timing of the worst human rights violations relative to the ousting of the communist regime, and a local legal culture still rooted in socialist legality explain the relative scarcity of state-led reckoning efforts in the FSU.

Note that this chapter focuses exclusively on programs and methods designed to reckon with the crimes of the communist regime, not with the human rights violations of the Nazi occupation forces or the human rights abuses perpetrated by state agents after 1991 (during the so-called "colored revolutions" or the various wars that have plagued the region). Tables 1.1 and 1.2 visually groups transitional justice measures in both the Baltic states (Table 1.1) and the other FSU states (Table 1.2) to date.

THE TRANSITIONAL JUSTICE RECORD OF THE FSU

Before explaining differences across the postcommunist region and within the FSU, let's first document them. An overview of court trials, file access, and lustration in all postcommunist European countries I conducted in 2008 with some colleagues established the lead of the Baltic states over all of the other successor republics in terms of implementing those three measures, and the FSU's handicap relative to Central and Eastern Europe.[1] Since then no dramatic changes have occurred in the non-Baltic republics that would significantly alter the ranking of these three regions. In addition, the ranking seems to remain largely robust, if additional, nonjudicial transitional justice measures are also considered after surveying the data presented by the Transitional Justice Database Project,[2] legislation published in the region, and the local press.

Ironically, the FSU had an earlier start at transitional justice than its European satellites. Mikhail Gorbachev's policy of *glasnost* (openness), enacted in 1987, challenged some widely held certainties of the communist regime and encouraged the Soviet citizens to denounce the abuses of the regime at a time when Central and Eastern Europeans could only dream of doing so. As a result, Memorial became an important grassroots organization "concerned with history and political symbols, engaged in discovering and revealing the truth, and dedicated to preserving the memory of the victims of successive waves of Soviet repression."[3] Supported by the relatives of the former victims, its regional chapters in the Baltic republics, Russia, Ukraine, and

TABLE 1.1. *Transitional justice measures in the Baltic republics, 1987–2016*

Transitional justice measure	Country program
Access to KGB archives for ordinary citizens	**Estonia** 1994, Law on the collection, conservation and use of materials, inventories of security and intelligence services **Latvia** 1994, Law on the preservation and use of documents of the former state security committee and the determination of individuals' collaboration with the KGB **Lithuania** 1994, Law on the preservation and use of documents of the former state security committee and the determination of individuals' collaboration with the KGB
Lustration, screening, and vetting	**Estonia** 1992, The Constitution of the Republic of Estonia Implementation Act (§ 6-7) 1992, The law on the procedure for taking the oath (amended 1994 and 2001) 1994, Election law on city and town councils, district councils, and pagasts councils 1995, Law on procedure for registration and disclosure of persons who have served in or cooperated with intelligence or counter-intelligence organizations of security organizations or military forces of states which have occupied Estonia 1995, Citizenship law **Latvia** 1994, Election law on city and town councils, district councils, and pagasts councils 1994, Citizenship law 1995, Saeima Election Law **Lithuania** 1991, Decree no. 418 banning KGB employees and informers from government positions 1991, Law no. I-2115 on the verification of mandates of those deputies accused of consciously collaborating with special services of other states 1991, Law no. I-2166 on the security and spy agencies 1994, Law no. 23 on the background checks of individuals holding certain important positions 1999, Law no. VIII-1436 on registering, confession, entry into records and protection of the persons who have admitted to secret collaboration with special services of the former USSR (amended 2010) 1999, Law on the assessment of the USSR State Security Committee (NKVD, NKGB, MGB, KGB) and the current activities of the staff members of this organization

(*continued*)

TABLE 1.1 *(continued)*

Transitional justice measure	Country program
Court trials resulting in a court verdict	**Estonia** 1999, J. Klaassepp, V. Penart, K.-L. Paulov, V. Beskov, M. Neverovski, V. Loginov, and R. Tuvi 2003, A. Kolk, P. Kislyiy 2006, V. Kask, J. Karpov **Latvia** 1993, A. Rubiks 1996, A. Noviks 1999, M. Farbtukh 2000, Y. Savenko 2003, N. Tess 2004, V. Kononov 2005, J. Kirsteins, N. Larionova **Lithuania** 1992, Algis Klimaitis 1995, K. Kurakinas, P. Bartasevicius, and J. Sakalys 1996, M. Burokevičius and J. Jermalavičius 1998, K. Gimzauskas 1999, P. Raslanas; six convicted for involvement in January 1990 events 2000, B. Viater, K. Kregzde, A. Lapinskas, P. Preiksaitis, and I. Tamosiunas 2001, R.J.S., V. Vasiliauskas, and M. Zukaitiene 2002, V. Misiunas 2003, J. Dabulevicius 2004, A. V. 2005, A. Dailide 2006, J. Juskauskas and J. Navickas 2007, Z. D. 2008, J. S. 2009, P. A. Povilaitis 2010, M. Bulatovas and V. Kojalis, T. P. 2011, V. Vasiliauskas and K. Mikhailov 2012, P. Preiksaitis and M. Tabakajev 2013, V. J. Petronis 2014, M. Misiukonis

(continued)

TABLE 1.1 *(continued)*

Transitional justice measure	Country program
Commissions	**Estonia** 1992, State Commission for the Examination of Repressive Policies Carried Out during the Occupations 1998, International Commission for the Investigation of Crimes against Humanity **Latvia** 1992, Commission for the Investigation of Totalitarian Regime Crimes 1998, Commission of the Historians of Latvia **Lithuania** 1998, International Commission for the Evaluation of the Crimes of the Nazi and Soviet Occupation Regimes in Lithuania
Rehabilitation and compensation of former victims	**Estonia** 1988, Law acknowledging the irremediable suffering caused by Stalinist terror 1990, Decree to rehabilitate all individuals convicted for political crimes in the Soviet Russian criminal code 1992, Law on the rehabilitation of persons extra-judicially repressed and wrongfully convicted 1995, Law concerning the determination of repressed status for persons who suffered under the communist and Nazi regimes (amended in 1997, 1998, 1999, 2001, and 2004) 2003, Law on persons repressed by occupying powers **Latvia** 1990, Law concerning the rehabilitation of illegally repressed people 1991, Law concerning amnesty for persons punished for military crimes 1995, Law concerning the determination of repressed status for persons who suffered under the communist and Nazi regimes (amended in 1997, 1998, 1999, 2001, and 2004) **Lithuania** 1990, Law on rehabilitation of persons repressed for resistance to occupation regime (amended 2008) 1997, Law on the legal status of the people of the Republic of Lithuania who fell victims to the occupations of 1939–90 (amended 2007) 1997, Law on state support to the participants of armed resistance 1998, Law on state support to families of the fallen participants of the resistance against the 1940–90 occupations 2000, Law on compensation of damage resulting from the occupation by the USSR

(continued)

TABLE 1.1 *(continued)*

Transitional justice measure	Country program
Property restitution	**Estonia** 1990, Decision of the Supreme Soviet of the Estonian Republic on the restoration of ownership continuity 1991, Principles of Ownership Reform Act 1991, Land Reform Act **Latvia** 1990, Law concerning lands reform in the rural areas of the Republic of Latvia 1992, Law concerning the denationalization of private real estate in the Republic of Latvia and law concerning the return of real estate to lawful owners **Lithuania** 1991, Law on the restoration of the rights of ownership of citizens to the existing real property 1997, Law on the restitution of remaining immovable property rights of the citizens of the Republic of Lithuania
National Days	**Estonia** 1998, June 14 as Day of Mourning 2009, August 23 as Day of Remembrance for Victims of Communism and Nazism **Latvia** 1990, March 8 and June 14 as Remembrance Day to the Victims of Communist Genocide (renamed in 1998) 1998, March 16 as Latvian Soldier's Remembrance Day (removed in 2000) 1998, First Sunday in December as Day for Victims of Genocide against the Latvian People by the Totalitarian Communist Regime 2009, June 17 as Soviet Occupation Day 2009, August 23 as Remembrance Day for the Victims of Stalinism and Nazism **Lithuania** 1991, January 13 as Defenders of Freedom Day 1997, Third Sunday in May as Day of Commemoration of Partisans and Unity of the Army and Society 1997, June 14 as Day of Mourning and Hope 2002, May 14 as Civil Resistance Day 2005, May 8 as World War II Remembrance Day

(continued)

TABLE 1.1 *(continued)*

Transitional justice measure	Country program
Other	**Estonia** 1992, Basic principles for developing the Estonian secret services 1992, KGB Cells Museum in the Grey House, Tartu 1994, Viru KGB Museum in Tallinn early 2000s, Patarei Prison in Tallinn 2003, Tallinn Occupation Museum 2005, Public apology delivered by Prime Minister Andrus Ansip 2008, Law creating the Memory Institute 2008, Maarjamäe memorial and museum in Tallinn **Latvia** 1991, Decision concerning the anticonstitutional activities on the Latvian Communist Party in the Latvian Republic 1991, Decision on the cessation of the activities of the security services of the USSR in the Republic of Latvia 1993, Law on registering public organizations 1993, Museum of the Occupation of Latvia, Riga 1993, People's Front Museum, Riga 2005, Declaration on condemnation of the totalitarian communist occupation regime implemented in Latvia by the Union of Soviet Socialist Republics early 2010s, Tornakalns Deportation Memorial, Riga **Lithuania** 1992, Law I-2477 on responsibility for the genocide of the residents of Lithuania 1992, Genocide Victims' Museum (KGB Museum), Vilnius 1995, Public apology by President Algirdas Brazauskas 1997, Law establishing the Centre of Research of the Genocide and Resistance of the Lithuanian Population 1998, Law on the assessment of the U.S.S.R. Committee of State Security (NKVD, NKGB, MGB, KGB) and present activities of the regular employees of this organization 2000, Vilnius international public tribunal on the evaluation of communist crimes

Source: Lavinia Stan, ed., *Transitional Justice in Eastern Europe and the Former Soviet Union* (London, Routledge, 2009), Chapters 10–11; Peter Hohenhaus, *Dark Tourism*, 2016, available at: www.dark-tourism.com, accessed December 27, 2016; Eva-Clarita Pettai and Vello Pettai, *Transitional and Retrospective Justice in the Baltic States* (Cambridge: Cambridge University Press, 2015); "Estonia," "Latvia," and "Lithuania," *Transitional Justice and Memory in the EU*, 2013, available at: www.proyectos.cchs.csic.es/transitionaljustice/, accessed October 19, 2016.

TABLE 1.2. *Transitional justice measures in other former Soviet states, 1987–2016*

Transitional justice measure	Country program
Access to KGB archives for ordinary citizens	**Russia** 1991, Commission on the transfer of the CPSU and KGB archives to state use 1993, The fundamentals of legislation of the Russian federation on the archival corpus of the Russian federation and on the archives **Ukraine** 1991, Law 962-XII/1991 allowed access to files that contained no information that presented other persons in a negative light 2006, Government creates the Ukrainian Institute of National Remembrance 2009, Presidential Edict no. 37 on declassifying and publishing materials related to the Ukrainian liberation movement, political repressions and Holodomor 2015, Law no. 2540 on access to the archives of repressive bodies of the communist totalitarian regime from 1917 to 1991
Lustration, screening, and vetting	**Georgia** 2011, Liberty charter (includes lustration provisions, unimplemented) **Ukraine** 2014, Law on government cleansing (lustration law) 2014, Law on restoring confidence in the judiciary in Ukraine
Court trials	**Ukraine** 2009, Criminal case is initiated against the Soviet functionaries who carried out the Holodomor. The Kyiv Appellate Court found in 2010 that Stalin and other Soviet functionaries planned and committed genocide, but the case was shelved because defendants were deceased
Commissions	**Azerbaijan** 1990, Parliamentary investigative commission into the Black January events **Moldova** 2010, Presidential commission for the study and evaluation of totalitarian communist regime in the Republic of Moldova **Ukraine** 1997, Commission on the study of the activities of OUN and UPA, created by Council of Ministers. Final report produced in 2004 **Uzbekistan** 1999, Presidential commission for the promotion of the memory of victims

(continued)

TABLE 1.2 *(continued)*

Transitional justice measure	Country program
Rehabilitation and compensation of former victims	**Azerbaijan** 2006, Presidential pension for surviving family members of Black January martyrs **Moldova** 1992, Law no. 1225-XII on rehabilitation of victims of political repressions (amended 1994) **Russia** 1987, Politburo Commission studied repression of the 1930s–50s, and rehabilitated 840,000 individuals 1991, Rehabilitation Commission oversaw the implementation of Law of Rehabilitation 1996, Law enabled the children of "enemies of the people" to claim victim status **Ukraine** 1988, Rehabilitation commissions are created, attached to the regional Communist Party committees 1991, Law no. 962-XII on rehabilitation of victims of political repressions in Ukraine 1993, Law on the status of war veterans recognized UPA members who fought against the German-fascist occupiers of Ukraine in 1941–4 and did not commit crimes against humanity 2014, Law no. 2538-1 on the legal status and honoring of fighters for Ukraine's independence in the twentieth Century
Property restitution	**Azerbaijan** 1991, Law on returning confiscated houses to the owners **Moldova** 2010, Government allocates compensation funds, no commission to distribute them **Russia** 1994, New procedures for returning or paying for illegally confiscated property

(continued)

TABLE 1.2 *(continued)*

Transitional justice measure	Country program
National Days	**Georgia** 2010, February 25 as Occupation Day
	Moldova 2010, June 28 as the Day of Remembrance of Soviet Occupation (canceled)
	Russia 1997, President Boris Yeltsin proposes November 7 as Day of Agreement and Reconciliation. Proposal abolished in 2005 by Putin 2007, October 30 celebrated as Day of Victims of Political Repression
	Ukraine 1993, May 18 becomes the Day of Memory of Victims of the Deportation of Crimean Tatars 1998, Last Saturday of November becomes the Day of Remembrance of the Victims of the Holodomor, later renamed the Day of Remembrance of the Victims of the Holodomor and Political Repressions 2005, October 14 becomes the Day of the Ukrainian Army and the Foundation of UPA
Other	**Azerbaijan** 1994, Parliamentary condemnation of Black January events as a criminal attempt 1998, Presidential decree on "The Martyr of 20 January" for victims of Black January
	Georgia 2006, Museum of Soviet Occupation
	Kazakhstan 2011, KarLag, Museum of Political Repression Victims' Memory of the Dolinka Settlement
	Moldova 2010, President Mihai Ghimpu unveiled commemorative stone to the victims of totalitarianism

(continued)

TABLE 1.2 *(continued)*

Transitional justice measure	Country program
Other	**Russia**

Russia

1990, October, Solovetsky Stone placed near the Lubyanka Prison, Moscow

1991, Decree on the activities of the Communist Party of the Soviet Union and the Communist Party of the Russian Soviet Federated Republic (No. 169)

1991, October 30 as Day of Remembrance of Victims of Political Repression

2001, State Museum of Gulag History, established by historian A.V. Antonov-Ovseenko in Moscow

2002, Memorial to the Victims of Political Repressions in Petrograd – Leningrad, St. Petersburg

2015, New museum dedicated to Gulag victims (1930s–50s) in Moscow

?, Memorial to victims of Stalinist repression in Tomsk, Russia

?, Memorial to Stalin's victims at the Butovsky Firing Range, Moscow

? (apparently closed down in 2015), Museum for the History of Political Repression Perm-36, Urals Region

Ukraine

1988, Party leaders condemn Holodomor

1991, Communist Party is banned, its assets are confiscated (the ban was found unconstitutional in 2003)

1993, President Leonid Kravchuk's edict on measures in connection with the 60th anniversary of the Holodomor recognized Holodomor as genocide

2006, Law 376-V on the Holodomor of 1932–33 in Ukraine, recognizes the Holodomor as a genocide against the Ukrainian people

2007, Museum of Soviet Occupation opened in Kyiv

2008, Holodomor Memorial, Kiev

2012, Lviv Oblast Council banned the use of Soviet, communist and Nazi symbols on official buildings and in mass rallies in the oblast

2012, Museum of the Liberation Struggle of Ukraine opened in Lviv

(continued)

TABLE 1.2 *(continued)*

Transitional justice measure	Country program
Other	2015, Law no. 2538-1 on the legal status and commemoration of the fighters for the independence of Ukraine in the twentieth century
	2015, Law no. 2539 on the perpetuation of victory over Nazism in the World War II, 1939–45
	2015, Law no. 2540 on access to the archives of repressive organs of the communist totalitarian regime 1917–91
	2015, Law no. 2558 on the condemnation of the communist and national socialist (Nazi) regimes, and prohibition of propaganda of their symbols
	Uzbekistan
	2002, Museum of Victims of Political Repression

Sources: Alexei Trochev, "Ukraine," and Nanci Adler, "Russia," both in Lavinia Stan and Nadya Nedelsky, eds., *Encyclopedia of Transitional Justice* (New York: Cambridge University Press, 2013), 490–7 and 404–12, respectively; Giorgi Lomsadze, "Georgia: Tbilisi Creating Black List for Soviet Political Elite, KGB Collaborators," *Eurasianet.org*, June 21, 2011, available at: www .eurasianet.org/node/63718; Oxana Shevel, "Decommunization in Post-Euromaidan Ukraine: Law and Practice," *PONARS Eurasia*, January 2016, available at: www.ponarseurasia.org/memo/ decommunization-post-euromaidan-ukraine-law-and-practice; "Law on the condemnation of the communist and national socialist (Nazi) regimes, and prohibition of propaganda of their symbols," Kyiv, April 9, 2015, available at: www.memory.gov.ua/laws/law-ukraine-condemnation-communist-and-national-socialist-nazi-regimes-and-prohibition-propagan; and Seljan Mammadli, "Transitional Justice in Azerbaijan: Dealing with the Past," no date, available at: www.azadliqciragi .org/pdf/AN/Justice.pdf, all accessed October 19, 2016.

Belarus compiled *Books of Memory* that identified close to one-fourth of the victims of the Great Terror. This initiative ensured that by the time the communist regime collapsed in 1991, the FSU citizens "had become increasingly aware of Stalin's reign of terror and increasingly willing to openly recount their own harrowing personal accounts of life under the hammer and sickle."[4]

Nevertheless, such unofficial reckoning efforts were not accompanied by equally resolute state-led initiatives. The Soviet state officials and agencies did little to unveil the truth about communist crimes, provide justice in courts for the victims, or reform the state structures to prevent a repetition of abuses. For all their reformist talk, Gorbachev and his administration failed to enact meaningful reforms of the police, the KGB and the armed forces; screen, lustrate or prosecute the civil servants, secret agents, and prison guards involved in human rights abuses; provide compensation to and rehabilitate former victims; return property abusively confiscated by the communist authorities; or rewrite history textbooks to acknowledge communist human rights abuses. Thus until 1991 the Soviet transitional justice record was largely limited to unofficial initiatives that engaged state agencies to a limited extent only.

The break-up of the Soviet Union allowed the new successor states to pursue their own transitional justice agendas. For reasons discussed below, these states' transitional justice trajectories have differed markedly. The Baltic republics have aligned themselves with Central and Eastern Europe by doing more transitional justice much earlier during the postcommunist transition period, while the other successor states have done less reckoning and only with considerable delay. Western FSU states (Ukraine, Moldova, but not Belarus) have a slight advantage over their Eastern counterparts (Central Asian countries of Uzbekistan, Tajikistan, Turkmenistan, Kyrgyzstan, and Kazakhstan), whereas Caucasia's more uneven progress falls in between the other two groups. Russia stands in a category by itself, since its government officials have not only refrained from enacting meaningful transitional justice programs, but also tried to completely negate the suffering of the communist-era victims and the crimes of the former victimizers by extolling the virtues of communism.[5]

Let's start by discussing the fate of the secret archives compiled by the KGB on citizens in the FSU, since in Central and Eastern Europe secret documents played such a pivotal role in two other transitional justice methods: court trials against communist officials, and lustration, which restricted members and collaborators of the communist regime from holding a range of postcommunist public offices.[6] As I explained elsewhere, the successor republics' abilities to pursue file access as a method of redress were severely hampered when significant collections from the KGB archive were transferred to Moscow months before the 1991 break of the Soviet Union. Russia alone had direct access to the bulk of the Soviet-era secret archives, but lacked the political will to open them to ordinary citizens and thus to reveal the identity of the thousands of individuals who secretly spied on their workmates, school mates, relatives, and friends.[7] The Russian authorities' unwillingness to open the secret files immediately after 1991 allowed secret agents to destroy key compromising documents, and granted preferential access to selected historians for some research projects, but blocked the ordinary citizens' access to the names of secret agents who collected information on them.[8]

In the other successor states, the number of extant secret documents reportedly depended on the whim of the republican KGB officers charged in 1991 with transferring the files to Moscow: some of these officials transported the bulk of the secret documents to Moscow (Estonia), while others transferred

only part of the collections, leaving some secret files in the republics where
they were produced (Lithuania). After 2006 the collections left behind in the
three Baltic states, although incomplete, were scanned and made available
electronically on a dedicated site.[9] The secret KGB archives left behind in
the Republic of Moldova were few, but the anticommunists who formed the
parliamentary majority in 2010 had the political will to open them. Some
3,000 KGB files on former victims are available at the National Archives, with
plans to transfer 20,000 others from the intelligence services to the National
Archives in the future.[10] It was only after Euromaidan that transitional justice
was seriously considered by the Ukrainian society and political elite. In April
2016 the Ukrainian Institute of National Memory announced plans to make
its KGB collections available electronically, after which most communist-era
archives will be transferred to the Institute, a process to be completed in early
2017.[11] No similar plans were unveiled in other successor republics, and the
size and content of their KGB collections remain poorly understood.

In terms of lustration and court trials, the Baltic republics stand apart from
the other successor states because they have limited the political influence
of former Communist Party officials and KGB employees, and prosecuted a
number of former KGB agents for involvement in rights abuses. By contrast,
none of the other successor states have launched court trials and only Georgia
and Ukraine legislated lustration. Georgia's Liberty Charter of 2011 included
limited lustration provisions that have remained largely unimplemented.[12]
After the Euromaidan, new legislation in Ukraine permitted the screening
of postcommunist officials' past collaboration with the Soviet regime, but
the laws have been only timidly enforced. Moldova, Azerbaijan, and Russia
debated lustration, but their parliaments were ultimately unwilling to screen
the postcommunist elected and nominated public officials for their Soviet-
era ties to the KGB or the Communist Party. Belarus, Armenia, and the five
Central Asian republics have pursued no lustration and no trials, and enter-
tained no public debates on these transitional justice measures.[13]

As in Central and Eastern Europe, there are few commissions in the FSU.
Again, the Baltic states took the lead over the other successor republics. In
a concerted effort to address the legacy of the recent past, in 1998 the Baltic
republics tasked new history commissions to examine the human rights abuses
perpetrated by the Soviet and the Nazi regimes. The focus on crimes of the foreign "occupation" regimes obscured the crimes perpetrated by Baltic nationals, but the commissions successfully put together final reports and unearthed
new information about Soviet and Nazi crimes. Only three other FSU republics created commissions. The Azerbaijani parliamentary inquiry commission
was of little consequence, and its mandate was limited to a single Soviet-era

incident: the 1990 Black January events, when Soviet troops entered Baku to quash the independence movement and killed 130 protesters.[14] In 1999, the Uzbek president created a Commission for the Promotion of the Memory of Victims which ultimately failed to unveil new information about Soviet-era crimes committed in the republic.[15] In 2010, the Republic of Moldova instituted a presidential history commission styled after the 2006 Presidential Commission for the Study of the Communist Dictatorship in Romania. Its final report provided a new in-depth take on Soviet abuses in Moldova. None of these latter three commissions had much public resonance, collected testimonials from victims, or genuinely tried to reconcile the deeply divergent historical narratives put forward by the former communist-era victims, victim-izers, and bystanders.

The Baltic republics have maintained the lead in the rehabilitation of former victims of communist crimes. Starting in the early 1990s, Estonia, Latvia, and Lithuania adopted extensive legislation to address the needs of a large number of communist-era victims, including Gulag prisoners, forced deportees, and victims of other rights abuses inflicted by the state. Only Moldova and Ukraine rehabilitated former Soviet victims soon after 1991, in a move designed to boost their independence claims and move them away from Russia more than to right past wrongs. In Azerbaijan, the president offered limited compensation to a limited number of victims. The packages came late, fifteen years after the country declared its independence, and were made available only to the victims of the Black January events. Ukraine revisited its reparation program after Euromaidan in 2014, when new de-communization laws also touched on the rehabilitation of communist-era victims. Belarus, the Central Asian republics Georgia and Armenia have done nothing in this respect.[16]

The Baltic states have also retained a leading position with respect to the restitution of property abusively confiscated by the communist authorities. Again, in this method they resemble Central and Eastern Europe more than their former Soviet peers. Their restitution programs touched first on land and then on other assets (dwellings), and provided for financial compensation in cases where the confiscated assets were destroyed or could not be returned for various other reasons. Azerbaijan and Russia permitted the return of selected housing units, but those restitution programs satisfied only a tiny fraction of the initial owners. In Central Asia, the states retained ownership of most of the land, and restitution of dwellings or other assets has been almost nonexist-ent. There are signs that even when it was implemented, the restitution program discriminated against ethnic and religious minorities, especially Jewish, German, and Russian claimants in the Baltic republics, but also the minority

Bessarabian Orthodox Metropolitanate in Moldova, and some minority religious groups in other FSU republics.[17]

Outside of the Baltic region, willingness to adopt other methods of transitional justice has been sporadic at best, leading to the implementation of no coherent programs that would help those societies to come to terms with their legacies of Soviet crimes. Tables 1.1 and 1.2 confirm that only the Baltic states have tried to systematically use national days for reckoning purposes. Only three other FSU republics started to celebrate national days dedicated to the memory of communist victims. Belarus, Russia, and the republics in Central Asia and Caucasia have no national celebrations that even remotely evoke the plight of the victims, but instead they still celebrate with great pomp and enthusiasm the Soviet fight against fascism and the patriotism of their armed forces. The Armenian Remembrance Day (24 April) is dedicated exclusively to the Armenian Genocide, whereas the Azerbaijani Martyrs Day (20 January) commemorates only the Black January events. While forgetting the victims, the annual calendar of public festivities in these republics includes Unity Days and Defender of the Fatherland Days that mark the contribution of the police, armed forces, and special forces to the nation's welfare.[18]

The record of other state-led reckoning measures is even spottier outside of the Baltics. The Uzbek Museum of Victims of Political Repression is noteworthy mainly because it remains the only one of its kind in the FSU. In Moldova, Acting President Mihai Ghimpu agreed to symbolically dedicate a stone, instead of an entire museum, to the victims of communist terror, but was removed from office before he could deliver an apology or a condemnation. Only Azerbaijan condemned Soviet crimes, and did so in relation to a very specific event, the Black January of 1990, keeping silent about the many more numerous victims the country lost in the Gulag. Among FSU states only Ukraine condemned the communist regime, and even that condemnation came late in 2015, after Russia threatened the Ukrainian sovereignty by seizing Crimea and fueling armed conflict in Ukraine's eastern provinces. However, the Ukrainian de-communization package of 2014 included provisions to reshape the public space by removing Soviet symbols.[19] In Belarus, Moldova, Caucasia, and Central Asia there have been no apologies, citizens' opinion tribunals or sweeping reforms of the police and secret police forces similar to those delivered, organized, or conducted in Estonia, Latvia, and Lithuania. Outside of the Baltic states memorialization was restricted to eliminating names of streets, parks, and localities related to communist leaders (since there are none named after Stalin and Lenin anymore), but it did not go far enough to ensure a thorough cleansing of the "memoryscape" of Soviet monuments and statues. As such, more than twenty-five years after the breakup of the Soviet Union, many statues of notorious communist leaders continue to adorn public spaces in the region.

Russia, by contrast, stands in a category by itself because of the government's insistence on negating past communist abuses and thus forcing former victims to experience "what they perceived as the injustice of witnessing the official invalidation of their history."[20] The Memorial and the former victims erected monuments and opened a museum dedicated to Soviet repression. Some limited transitional justice was enacted before and after 1991, under the watch of Gorbachev and Yeltsin. Over 840,000 former victims and political prisoners were rehabilitated in 1987–9. In 1991 a new Law on Rehabilitation was adopted, its implementation being overseen by a new Rehabilitation Commission that could rely on secret and state archives to determine individual eligibility to compensation, half-priced medication, free dentures, limited free transportation, and state-subsidized burial. By 2009 "4.5 million victims of political repression were rehabilitated."[21] That same year, however, the Russian government set up a Commission to Counter Attempts to Falsify History to the Detriment of Russian Federation Interests. The Commission was shut down in 2012, but in late 2016 the Russian security experts warned against attempts by foreign scholars to distort Russia's "historical memory" and asked for the Commission to be reinstated with a different name.[22]

EXPLAINING LIMITED RECKONING

The previous section proved the Baltic lead over other successor republics in terms of adopting and implementing programs designed to reckon with communist human rights abuses. Below I discuss some possible explanations which, when taken together, help us understand the relative advantage of the Baltics over the rest of the FSU.

Incomplete Democratization

For all the enthusiasm that accompanied the republics' declarations of independence from the Soviet Union in 1991, it is evident that during the first twenty-five years of the postcommunist transition, the democratic aspirations of citizens in that part of the world have remained largely unfulfilled. True, since 1991 the Baltic republics have made significant strides in implementing democratic reforms that aligned them with Central and Eastern Europe and allowed them to claim membership in the European Union (EU) in 2004. Transitional justice was seen by their national elites and most of their citizenry as a means to distance these countries from Russia and the FSU, and to become accepted into the European democratic club.

By contrast, some of the other republics had tumultuous transitions away from communist rule, marked by high levels of political corruption (Ukraine, Moldova, Russia, and Caucasia), frequent disregard of the rule of law on the part of the postcommunist elites (Russia, Ukraine, and all Central Asian countries), conflict with minority groups (Azerbaijan, Moldova, and Russia), massive popular antigovernmental protests (the Rose Revolution of 2003 in Georgia, the Orange Revolution of 2004 and Euromaidan in 2014 in Ukraine, and the Tulip Revolution of 2005 in Kyrgyzstan), and even armed conflict with Russia or their neighbors (Ukraine, Georgia, Moldova, Armenia, and Azerbaijan).[23] By repeatedly having to turn their attention to problems of political instability, national integrity, and state sovereignty, government actors in these countries had less time and fewer resources at their disposal to direct toward pursuing meaningful reckoning.

Still other republics engaged in no or very little transition, and their postcommunist systems remained more dictatorial than democratic in nature. Today Belarus is the only dictatorship in Europe, having succumbed in 1994 to the autocratic rule of Aleksandr Lukashenko, who continues to serve as president as this chapter goes to print. His regime is steeped in nostalgia for the Soviet times, while his successive governments have retained elements of Soviet rule: state ownership of key industries, recognition of the Russian language on a par with Belorussian, violation of basic human rights, and severe restrictions on the activities of antigovernment opposition groups.[24] Similarly, in the Central Asian republics the collapse of the communist regime allowed former Soviet Communist Party officials to retain power as local strongmen. While Kazakhstan and Kyrgyzstan have recently become more open societies, the other three republics remain known for their governments' serious human rights abuses.[25] Lack of a genuine regime change from communism to democracy annihilated any transitional justice prospects, since postcommunist elites drawn from the former Soviet elites have opposed any reevaluation of a regime with which they actively collaborated.

The Continued Political Influence of Soviet Decision-makers

The post-1991 influence of former Communist Party officials and KGB secret agents represents another explanatory factor, since these individuals used their postcommunist public offices to block, delay or dilute the adoption and implementation of transitional justice legislation out of a refusal to allow the reevaluation and possible condemnation of a regime they had loyally served. Again, the Baltic republics set themselves apart from the other FSU states because in

Estonia, Latvia, and Lithuania, former Soviet decision-makers were unable to retain much political influence after 1991. Independence was seen as intrinsically related to the return of those societies to the time before the World War II and the Soviet occupation, and the marginalization and prosecution of the Russian-speakers who placed ethnic Baltic citizens at a disadvantage. Democratic ideals were assumed to follow ethnic lines, with few ethnic Baltic citizens accepting that Russian-speakers were truly supportive of core democratic ideals. As a result, early on during the postcommunist transition the Baltic societies proved willing to reconstruct the ethnic purity lost in Soviet times when Russian-speakers were encouraged to come to the region to occupy leading public positions.[26]

By contrast, in all other successor states local Soviet decision makers have retained significant political influence which they used to act as gate-keepers against and vocal detractors of reckoning programs. President Vladimir Putin's ties to the former KGB are well documented, as is the impact of the *siloviki* (politicians drawn from the Soviet and post-Soviet security or military services) over the postcommunist Russian state apparatus.[27] In other FSU republics, a string of former Communist Party officials have become presidents, prime ministers, cabinet ministers, members of parliament, regional governors, and mayors, while top public officials drawn from the ranks of the anticommunist opposition forces have been few. The influence of the vast Soviet-era network of secret KGB agents is difficult to document, since their identities remain closely guarded as state secrets across the FSU. It is generally assumed that the KGB officers, a majority of whom were ethnic Russians, took refuge in Moscow when the secret archives were transferred out of the republics. Equally probable is that many secret part-time informers active in the republics belonged to the dominant ethnic group and did not leave for Moscow. Press reports and sporadic revelations from the secret archives seemingly suggest the persistence of their political clout in postcommunist times.

A Weak and Divided Civil Society

The fact that after 1991 civil society has remained weak and divided across the FSU has also made the transitional justice project more difficult to formulate, adopt, and implement. As mentioned earlier, under Gorbachev's rule former victims of the Gulag and/or their surviving relatives were active in recovering the memory of the former political prisoners of Soviet times. Their activism allowed memory projects to come to life at a time when the state was still mainly unreformed and unwilling to fully document, admit, and redress its past history of repression.[28] However, the victims' concerns were ignored by other organized groups and society at large, and as such more than twenty-five years after the break of the Soviet Union there seemingly is no critical mass of nonstate actors supportive of transitional justice programs or able to pressure public officials into considering the merits of reckoning.

With the exception of the Baltic states, and possibly Ukraine after Euromaidan, the FSU societies remain wedded to a "subject" political culture, having been unable to transform themselves into truly "participatory" publics.[29] Opinion polls conducted in postcommunist Russia and other successor republics suggest popular support for strong men and for a strong state. They also suggest that priority is being placed on the collective, not the individual.[30] Election results confirm these general preferences. These sentiments – coupled with beliefs that everybody was placed at a disadvantage by the Soviet dictatorship and therefore there are no victims' groups with additional legitimate claims to suffering, and that the accomplishments of the Soviet regime greatly outnumber its wrongdoings – have meant that transitional justice programs advantageous to former victims have been largely unpopular with both the larger public and other civil society groups. These divisions have grown even wider over time, as fewer and fewer former political prisoners, deportees, and initial owners of property abusively confiscated by the Soviet authorities remain alive.

The general weakness of civil society and the deep divisions within it between the supporters and the detractors of transitional justice explain why in FSU republics, except the Baltic states, political elites have tended to exclude civil society from debates touching on the memory of the Soviet past even when additional electoral capital could have been gained by such inclusion.[31] In many successor republics, the propensity of political elites to use the symbolic capital of Soviet and republican monuments, memorials, and commemorations for nationalist purposes has aligned itself with the nationalist sentiments shared by many segments of the civil society. Instrumentalized nationalism has sometimes rendered transitional justice concerns moot, since they defined the nation by celebrating Soviet-era economic development and political collaboration with Moscow, while at the same time ignoring the destruction of entire communities at the hands of the Soviet repressive apparatus. It was only in the Baltic republics that the Soviet regime was decisively seen as an alien, foreign occupation regime whose influence on the republics was overwhelming negative and thus in need of correction.

The Impact of International Actors

The desire of FSU republics to align themselves with international organizations or foreign governments also influenced the presence/absence and scope of transitional justice. Since declaring their independence, the Baltic states have doggedly pursued an agenda of rapprochement with Europe and were not shy in openly stating their desire to move away from Russia. Europe's attention to transitional justice issues at the 50th anniversary of the end of World War II (celebrated in 1995) led to the formation of presidential history commissions in Estonia, Latvia, and Lithuania in 1998. In response to European concerns for reckoning with the legacy of the Nazi regime, these commissions investigated the Nazi occupation of the Baltic states. But the commissions' mandates were enlarged to examine the crimes of the Soviet occupation, in response to local concerns not fully echoed or understood by Western Europeans. Even before 1998, citizens and state officials in the Baltic states followed closely the debates and implemented some of the transitional justice initiatives adopted in Central and Eastern Europe.

While the European Union was willing to accept the Baltic states into its fold, it was apprehensive toward Russia once Putin replaced Yeltsin. In turn, postcommunist Russia has been nostalgic for its lost empire and the international weight it enjoyed as the main decision-maker in the FSU. Since 2000, Putin has tried to redefine Russia as an important international player, often in opposition to the European Union and occasionally even by asking successor republics to make a clear choice between Moscow and the EU. Russia's influence over the former satellites has also consisted of efforts to block transitional justice initiatives that placed Russians at a disadvantage or negatively portrayed the Soviet regime. It has also transformed these countries into client states by providing them with energy subsidies, access to markets, and military aid at critical moments in time. The Central Asian republics occasionally seemed to reject transitional justice for fear of upsetting Moscow.

Other successor republics have tried to break this bond, and their efforts to distance themselves from Russia and pursue distinct domestic and foreign interests have often been accompanied by transitional justice. In Moldova, for example, late transitional justice programs (the presidential commission, the commemorative stone, the new public holiday) were adopted in 2010 by state officials representing the Alliance for European Integration in a declared move to bring the country closer to the EU. The 2014 Euromaidan and the events leading to it marked a period of intense scrutiny of Ukraine's national commitment to Europe, after more than two decades of acting as a client state of Russia. Euromaidan unleashed a wave of reforms (including transitional justice initiatives) designed to make the country akin to its Western neighbors.

The Timing of Abuses

Another possible explanation lies with the timing of the worst human rights violations relative to the ousting of the communist regime. In Central and Eastern Europe, the most atrocious crimes took place in the first decades of the communist regime, from the 1930s to the 1950s. This meant that in 1989, when those communist dictatorships collapsed, these gross human rights violations were already thirty to fifty years old. In the FSU, the worst crimes were also associated with the rule of Josef Stalin: the great famine of 1932–3, the Great Purge of 1936–8, and the massive deportations of the 1940s, among others.[32] This meant that by 1991, when the independent successor states for the first time had the chance to reckon with the legacy of those wrongdoings, the crimes were forty to sixty years old. Of course, state repression did not stop after Stalin's death in 1953, but the number of deaths decreased substantially when the communist authorities decided to rely primarily on widespread surveillance to keep the society under the Communist Party's thumb.

The longer the time period that separated the commission of crimes from their possible prosecution, the less likely it is to implement meaningful programs that can result in truth, justice, and reconciliation. That is because a longer passage of time makes it more difficult to gather the necessary evidence and to interview witnesses. Fewer victims remain alive to participate in trials and benefit from compensation, property restitution, and related reparation programs. Fewer victimizers are in good health to stand trial and take responsibility for their crimes, and most of them might have already retired from public office without ever being subject to screening or lustration. More properties might become derelict or might be destroyed, thus closing the possibility of their restitution to initial owners. In addition, the Soviet campaigns of selectively rectifying Stalin's crimes might have dampened the public's quest for justice after 1991.

Legal Culture

Grosescu and Fijalkowski argued that a country's legal culture represents another powerful determinant of transitional justice. According to them, the judiciary's understanding of legal formalism, international human rights law, and international criminal law can facilitate, delay or block the implementation of transitional justice.[33] In postcommunist Central and Eastern Europe and the FSU, many of the legal experts called to adjudicate cases of lustration, access to information included in communist archives, property restitution or compensation, and to prosecute former party officials and secret agents involved in human rights violations, had been educated, hired, and promoted by the very communist system against which these transitional justice measures took a stand. In the 1990s before a new generation was able to join their ranks, FSU legal experts were steeped in the Soviet legal culture, which implied an acceptance of the Communist Party's control over the judiciary, a curtailment of the judiciary's independence whenever political issues were at stake, and precedence of state interests over individual rights. True, after Stalin's death the new socialist legality entailed due process and more protection of citizens' individual rights, but still it fell short of the Western legal culture, which placed respect for rule of law at its center. With the exception of the Baltic states, the legal culture in the FSU has undergone fewer and more limited reform since 1991, negatively impacting the transitional justice programs.

CONCLUSION

The more time that passes since the break-up of the Soviet Union, the greater becomes the transitional justice divide between the Baltic republics and the other successor states. In Estonia, Latvia, and Lithuania, democratization and Europeanization reinforced transitional justice, which in turn helped these countries become more democratic by strengthening the rule of law, unveiling the truth about past repression, and providing justice so that state such state-led crimes are avoided in the future. A similar, but vicious, circle is at play in the other successor countries: incomplete transitions to democracy hampered transitional justice, which in turn undermined democratization. Some might argue that for the older Stalinist crimes (and the victims and victimizers associated with them) the window of opportunity for reckoning is rapidly closing.

This chapter summarized the record of transitional justice in the FSU in an effort to then identify the factors that might explain why the Baltic republics are leaders and the other FSU states are laggards in terms of reckoning with Soviet crimes. Lustration, access to secret files, court trials, history commissions, compensation and restitution programs, and public holidays were examined to assess these countries' progress in postcommunist reckoning. The Baltic republics were the only FSU states with coherent, comprehensive, long-term transitional justice programs that were widely regarded as essential for their reconstruction and redefinition as independent states belonging to Europe. Elsewhere in the FSU, transitional justice took place during small windows of opportunity that were opened briefly by the independence movement (Ukraine, Moldova, Azerbaijan), public demonstrations (Euromaidan in Ukraine) or the electoral victory of anticommunist, pro-European politicians (Moldova, Georgia). Even in those cases reckoning programs were not demands put forth by broad segments of the population, but rather initiatives supported by narrow groups. Since the nature of the communist past and the type of exit from communist did not significantly differ within the FSU, country differences were explained by incomplete democratization, the continued presence of former communist decision makers and secret agents in the postcommunist state apparatus, the differential impact of international organizations, the weakness of civil society, and the legal culture.

Notes

1. Lavinia Stan, ed., *Transitional Justice in Eastern Europe and the Former Soviet Union* (London: Routledge, 2009).
2. Transitional Justice Database Project, available at: sites.google.com/site/transitional justicedatabase/, accessed October 15, 2016.
3. Stan, ed., *Transitional Justice in Eastern Europe and the Former Soviet Union*, 222.
4. Ibid.
5. This section overviews judiciary and non-judiciary transitional justice methods adopted in the FSU. Tables 1.1 and 1.2 detail the relevant legislation adopted in the Baltic and non-Baltic successor republics exclusively, and therefore readers must consult other studies to gain information on transitional justice in Central and Eastern Europe. A good starting point is Stan, ed., *Transitional Justice in Eastern Europe and the Former Soviet Union*. A table summarizing the main transitional justice-related laws cannot be included here for lack of space.
6. Monika Nalepa, "Lustration," in Lavinia Stan and Nadya Nedelsky, eds., *Encyclopedia of Transitional Justice* (New York: Cambridge University Press, 2013), 1:46.
7. Stan, ed., *Transitional Justice in Eastern Europe and the Former Soviet Union*, 8. Historians were able to access selected collections for limited time periods.
8. Daria Khubova, "Imprisoned History: The KGB Archives," *The Journal of the International Institute* 1, 1 Winter (1994), available at: http://hdl.handle.net/2027/spo.4750978.0001.103, and Rachel Donadio, "The Iron Archives," *The News York Times*, April 22, 2007, available at: www.nytimes.com/2007/04/22/books/review/Donadio.t.html?_r=0, both accessed October 15, 2016.
9. "KGB in the Baltic States: Documents and Researches," no date, available at: www .kgbdocuments.eu/index.php?2737553734, accessed October 15, 2016.
10. Erin Hutchinson, "Central State and Party Archives in Chisinau, Moldova," *Dissertation Reviews*, February 16, 2015, available at: http://dissertationreviews.org/archives/11591, accessed October 15, 2016.
11. "Ukraine Prepares to Make Soviet KGB Archives Available Online," *Euromaidan Press*, April 11, 2016, available at: http://euromaidanpress.com/2016/04/11/ukraine-prepares-to-make-soviet-kgb-archives-available-online/#arvlbdata, accessed October 15, 2016.
12. Thomas Sherlock, "Georgia," in Lavinia Stan and Nadya Nedelsky, eds., *Encyclopedia of Transitional Justice* (New York: Cambridge University Press, 2013), 2: 186–93.
13. Stan, ed., *Transitional Justice in Eastern Europe and the Former Soviet Union*, 9.
14. Seljan Mammadli, "Transitional Justice in Azerbaijan: Dealing with the Past," no date, available at: www.azadliqciragi.org/pdf/AN/Justice.pdf, accessed October 19, 2016.
15. Brian Grodsky, *The Costs of Justice: How New Leaders Respond to Previous Rights Abuses* (Notre Dame: University of Notre Dame Press, 2011), 171–89.

16. Stan, ed., *Transitional Justice in Eastern Europe and the Former Soviet Union*, Chapter 11.

17. Lavinia Stan and Lucian Turcescu, "Church–State Conflict in Moldova: The Bessarabian Metropolitanate," *Communist and Post-Communist Studies* 36, 4 (2003): 443–65.

18. See *Office Holidays*, 2016, available at: www.officeholidays.com/countries/index.php, accessed October 20, 2016.

19. Part of that drive consisted of demolishing, removing or repurposing statues of communist leaders. One such example that gained the attention of the mass-media was the decision of artist Alexander Milov to turn a statue of Lenin erected in the city of Yuzhne, outside Odessa, into a statue of Darth Vader. "Shedding Its Communist Past, Odessa Converts Lenin Statue into a Monument to Darth Vader," *Meduza Project*, October 22, 2015, available at: https://meduza.io/en/lion/2015/10/22/shedding-its-communist-past-odessa-converts-lenin-statue-into-a-monument-to-darth-vader, accessed October 23, 2016.

20. Nanci Adler, "Russia," in Lavinia Stan and Nadya Nedelsky, eds., *Encyclopedia of Transitional Justice* (New York: Cambridge University Press, 2013), 2: 405.

21. Ibid., 2: 408.

22. Liga Rudzite, "Russia's Fight for the Right History," *Transitions Online*, November 1, 2016, available at: www.tol.org/client/article/26441-russias-fight-for-the-right-history-.html, accessed November 1, 2016.

23. Steven Levitsky and Lucan A. Way, *Competitive Authoritarianism: Hybrid Regimes after the Cold War* (New York: Cambridge University Press, 2010); Taras Kuzio, *Ukraine: Democratization, Corruption and the New Russian Imperialism* (Santa Barbara: Praeger, 2015); Michael Croissant, *The Armenia-Azerbaijan Conflict: Causes and Implications* (Westport: Praeger, 1998); Marcin Kosienkowski and William Schreiber, *Moldova: Arena of International Influences* (Lanham: Lexington Books, 2012); Charlotte Mathilde Louise Hille, *State Building and Conflict Resolution in the Caucasus* (Leiden: Brill, 2010); Archie Brown and Lilia Shevtsova, eds., *Gorbachev, Yeltsin and Putin: Political Leadership in Russia's Transition* (Washington, DC: Carnegie Endowment for International Peace, 2001); and Karen Dawisha, *Putin's Kleptocracy: Who Owns Russia?* (New York: Simon & Shuster, 2014). See also annual corruption rankings of FSU states. For the latest, Transparency International, *Overview of Corruption Perception Index*, no date, available at: www.transparency.org/research/cpi/overview, accessed October 23, 2016.

24. Andrew Wilson, *Belarus: The Last European Dictatorship* (New Haven: Yale University Press, 2011).

25. Olivier Roy, *The New Central Asia: Geopolitics and the Birth of Nations* (London: I.B. Tauris, 2007), 2nd edition.

26. See Table 1 for the election laws and citizenship laws passed in 1994 and 1995.

27. Vladimir Pribylovskiĭ, *The Corporation: Russia and the KGB in the Age of President Putin* (London: Encounter Books, 2008), and Amy Knight, *Spies without Cloaks: The KGB's Successors* (Princeton: Princeton University Press, 1996).

28. Noel Calhoun, *Dilemmas of Justice in Eastern Europe's Democratic Transitions* (New York: Palgrave Macmillan, 2004).

29. I borrow these terms from Gabriel Almond and Sidney Verba, *The Civic Culture: Political Attitudes and Democracy in Five Nations* (Princeton: Princeton University Press, 1963).

30. Among others, Karen Dawisha and Bruce Parrott, eds., *Democratic Changes and Authoritarian Reactions in Russia, Ukraine, Belarus and Moldova* (Cambridge; Cambridge University Press, 1997).

31. Benjamin Forrest and Juliet Johnson, "Unraveling the Threads of History: Soviet-Era Monuments and Post-Soviet National Identity in Moscow," August 2001, 4–5, available at: www.dartmouth.edu/~crn/crn_papers/Forest-Johnson.pdf, accessed October 20, 2016.

32. Robert Conquest, *The Great Terror: A Reassessment* (New York: Oxford University Press, 2008), and Otto Pohl, *Ethnic Cleansing in the USSR, 1937–1949* (Westport: Praeger, 1999).

33. Raluca Grosescu and Agata Fijalkowski, "Retrospective Justice and Legal Culture," in Lavinia Stan and Lucian Turcescu, eds., *Justice, Memory and Redress: New Insights from Romania* (Cambridge: Cambridge Scholars, 2017), 100–23.

2

Challenges to Transitional Justice in Russia

Nanci Adler

During the Soviet terror, particularly in the 1930s, millions of ordinary citizens, well-known political actors, and Party loyalists alike were arbitrarily charged with "counter-revolutionary activities," arrested, and executed, or deported to barely habitable regions in the North and Far East of the Soviet empire. There, they were forced to mine nickel, chop wood, excavate gold, or build railways leading nowhere, but mostly just to waste away through punitively hard labor and hunger under abhorrent physical conditions. Estimates of the fatalities resulting from the Stalinist terror range from a few million to well over 20 million victims, but there is consensus that 17–18 million Russians were sentenced to detention in prisons, colonies, and camps between 1930 and 1956.[1]

Aside from symbolic reparations, the post-Soviet governments have implemented none of the recognized, institutionalized transitional justice mechanisms to reckon with this past. Not one henchman was tried, nor one truth commission instigated, victim compensation was limited, as were official acknowledgments of past injustices and archival access, and the record in the history textbooks remained a political narrative. It was not until 2015 that the state sanctioned a plan for an official monument to the victims of Stalinism, although most victims will not live to see it erected. Indeed, rather than confronting its history of multiple regime abuses, in post-Soviet Russia, there has been a persistent, politically driven, effort to manage national and public memory by repressing, controlling, or even co-opting the memory of repression.

This qualifies post-Soviet Russia as a *non*-case of transitional justice – an exemplar of post- and still-repressive societies that have been unable, unwilling or resistant toward embracing transitional justice measures. A consequence (and symptom) of this status is that twenty-five years after the collapse of the Soviet Union, the achievements of the Stalinist system, and Stalin himself, are again or still being valorized. "Again" reflects the actual chronology of events, because it acknowledges the wave of anti-Stalin revulsion that swept the country after February 25, 1956, when Khrushchev revealed the brutal, capricious excesses of Stalin's purges, and the similar wave set in motion in the late 1980s, when Gorbachev permitted the public to peek into some of the purposively created lacunae in their history. "Still" is also true because it encompasses the current regime's strategy to minimize Stalin's crimes and facilitate the posthumous rehabilitation of Stalin's image in order to promote patriotism and justify current repression. Nevertheless, despite the persistent trend of imposing state control over the Gulag narrative, serious initiatives have been undertaken by the anti-Stalinist organization Memorial as well as other nongovernmental organizations to generate a counter-history. Their efforts to challenge official attempts to ignore or co-opt the history of repression are barely tolerated, leaving them in a legally precarious situation.

This chapter, based on personal interviews, Russian opinion polls, Russian media, exhibitions, archival documents, governmental decrees, and school textbooks, looks at post-Soviet remembrance practices, national memory and the national narrative, the rehabilitation of Stalin, truth and the national narrative, and the recurrent practice of rewriting and reconstructing the past. It also explains why the "bottom-up" efforts have had difficulty finding resonance with the general public, which seems to have construed the gilded version of the national past as more presently relevant than the real, lived history of millions of victims. Finally, it reflects on possibilities for moving beyond this impasse.

REMEMBRANCE PRACTICES: WHICH PAST INFORMS THE PRESENT, AND VICE VERSA

In post-conflict and post-authoritarian societies, remembrance and the claims of surviving victims for redress rely on the willingness of the successor regimes to acknowledge the past repressions and assume some responsibility for compensating the victims. Witness the contrasting ways in which Germany and Russia have approached their repressive histories, displayed on the streets of Berlin and Moscow. Among Germany's many commemorative symbols, Berlin's sidewalks solemnly display over 5,000 *stolpersteine* (stumbling blocks), marking the homes where the victims of Nazism once lived. Inscribed on these blocks are their names, birthdates, deportation points, and dates of death. Over 50,000 such memorial stones have been placed in other European cities.[2] In post-Soviet Russia, markers of the Stalinist terror are rarely observed in the public space, and even when physically visible they are psychologically and politically invisible to the public at large because they refer to an officially redacted or irrelevant past.

Post-Nazi Germany's full, if involuntary, acknowledgment of its repressive history – impelled by the defeat of Nazism – permitted it to progress toward a democratic political system. By contrast, the repression of individual rights continues in an undefeated authoritarian post-Soviet Russia. In 2014, civil society orchestrated the "Last Address" campaign, offering individuals the opportunity to place a name plaque on the buildings from which their relatives were removed, often never to return. These silvery-gray plaques display eight spare lines, for example: "HERE LIVED VLADIMIR ABRAMOVICH NIKOLAEV; PEDIATRICIAN, BORN 1902, ARRESTED 1936, EXECUTED ON 19/12/1938; REHABILITATED IN 1961." To the left of the text, a starkly empty square has been cut in the metal, representing the void that the repression created in the families of millions of Soviet citizens, arrested without warning and executed or incarcerated without a fair trial. It also represents the void recreated by the official avoidance of what actually happened; it bears silent witness to the repression. As of 2015, there were no more than thirty plaques in Moscow, each one the product of a determined struggle with resistant authorities.[3]

WHICH PAST TO REMEMBER?

Among the difficulties of constructing the history of Soviet repression is grasping the intricacy of a process that moved so casually from nonexistent evidence to lethal consequences. Each year since 2007, on the Day of Political Prisoners, Memorial – the most prominent human rights watchdog in Russia – has organized a name-reading commemoration at its monument to the "victims of totalitarianism," a stone from the Solovetsky Islands, the first labor camp under Lenin.[4]

The organizers followed a Western European approach in their conviction that a fundamental component of reconciliation is the official and public recognition of every individual who was victimized. The names they selected were found on "execution lists"[5] of the Narodnyi Komissariat Vnutrennikh Del (NKVD), the precursor to the Komitet Gosudarstvennoy Bezopasnosti (KGB), along with tens of thousands of others – apolitical undesirables who were shot in the back of the neck on the day of sentencing and dumped in a mass grave on the outskirts of Moscow. Memorial hoped that the citizenry and the government would devote the same kind of attention to recalling and recording the names of terror victims as they did to those who fell in the "Great Patriotic War" (World War II). However, this was an unrealistic hope because it ran counter to the state's self-preservative needs. The state was fully

willing to recognize the large number of Russians killed as a consequence of
Nazism, but less willing to acknowledge the large number killed as a consequence of Stalinism.

If transitional justice were on the post-Soviet agenda, such lists of victims
would furnish credible evidence for criminal proceedings against the Soviet
regime. However, trials and/or truth commissions are exceedingly complex
if not impossible undertakings in the aftermath of a seventy-year dictatorship
so devoid of lawfulness. Even such acts as acknowledgment, apology, and
commemoration can be difficult to accommodate, as evidenced by the official
permission to conduct this ceremony only from 10:00 A.M. until 10:00 P.M.,
barely enough time to recite 2000, let alone millions of names. The name-
reading is an annual event, attended mainly by Memorial's constituency, some
foreign ambassadors, and an occasional local news broadcaster. It is regularly
ignored or given low priority by Russian officials.[6]

Until 2015, Moscow had not displayed even a single state-sponsored commemorative plaque for the victims of Stalinism. But in that year, it sponsored
and funded a Gulag Museum. As with other unavoidable acknowledgments of
the repression, the state used this opening to influence the public's perception
of the repression. The Museum's depiction of human rights abuses within
the Gulag is accurate, but avoids mentioning that the system of repression
that existed outside the Gulag was the *modus operandi* of *Soviet* rule. Nor
does its critical appraisal extend to the present regime, whose potential to
strike at any time and place curbs self-expression and induces self-censorship.
The Museum is state-supported and state-controlled. Memorial is not state-
supported, so in theory it should not be subject to state control, but the regime
has used legal means to control Memorial's sources of support, and in so
doing, jeopardized its very survival.

Post-Soviet Russia has found it more expedient to revise its past rather
than acknowledge it, as transitional justice would require. Accordingly, the
fashioning of a good future out of a "bad past" has been facilitated by the
construction of a "usable past" for the national narrative.[7] This has been
accompanied by an emphasis on patriotism that calls for Western franchises
like McDonald's to be replaced by "Edim Doma" (Eat at Home),[8] and by
museum exhibitions that showcase Soviet interpretations of history, such
as "The History of the Return of Crimea," hosted by the Museum of the
Revolution in Moscow.[9] The patriotic fervor has also come to include publications like *Words That Changed the World,* a volume of Putin's collective
wisdom edited by a youth group.[10] Attention to a select past coupled with
historical revisionism has effectively circumvented, or substituted for, transitional justice.

STALIN IN THE PERSONAL SPACE, THE PUBLIC SPACE, AND THE POLLS

A Soviet-era adage proclaimed that: "Lenin is always with us." It alluded to the omnipresence of the leader of the Bolshevik Revolution in public and private spaces. Lenin – though still physically with us as he lays embalmed in a mausoleum on Red Square – has now been relegated to the communist past. The reviled and revered Stalin has not. Twenty-five years after the collapse of the Soviet Union, the history of the crimes of Stalin and Stalinism has been so successfully glossed over that nationwide polls show his popularity edging back toward its pre-de-Stalinization levels, and gaining momentum. It is certain that Stalin is always with us.

In a 2014 poll, half of those surveyed rated Stalin's role in the country's history as positive.[11] In 2015, a poll found that 38 percent of favorable responders agreed that the Soviet people's sacrifices during the Stalinist era were justified by the high goals and results that were achieved in such a short period.[12] The persistence of this trend was demonstrated by another poll conducted around Stalin's birthday in December 2015, when 34 percent of those surveyed considered Stalin's wartime victory of greater importance than any mistakes and transgressions attributed to him. Finally, regarding Stalin himself, 40 percent of those surveyed in 2016 believed that Stalin should not be considered a state criminal, and appraised the Stalin era as being more "good" than "bad."[13] Apparently, the accomplishments of industrialization and the Soviet dictator's wartime victory were more relevant to those polled than the millions of victimizations of that same era that had resulted from those same events. Stalin's burgeoning popularity reflects the longing to restore the country's former prestige and the security of a more strictly, if forcibly, ordered society – a trend led and followed by the present regime.

The official pronouncements on criminalizing pro-Stalin propaganda[14] have been countered by a parallel process of rehabilitating Stalin – streamed to the public on buses, at monuments, in stores, in textbooks, and in the public space. The Communist Party has seized the opportunity to capitalize on this trend by emphasizing the domestic order and international prestige that accompanied Stalin's governance. It declared 2016 to be the year of Stalin, and labeled it the "Stalin Spring,"[15] marking the eightieth anniversary of the 1936 Stalin Constitution that proclaimed the primacy of the Communist Party. Several local parties have subsequently developed initiatives to better educate the populace about Stalin. "Stalin Spring" suggests an affinity to the liberal, democratic expectations of the "Prague Spring" and the later "Arab Spring." In fact, 1936 marked the beginning of the notorious Show Trials, which wiped out the leaders of the Revolution, along with millions of its

followers and ordinary citizens. Such select remembrance led one liberal politician to discredit the subterfuge of propaganda masquerading as education,
"When they talk about the Stalin era, they imagine the holster at the side, but
not the barrel to the back of their neck."[16]

At present, the casual acceptance of repression has been coupled with the
valorization of Stalin, now embedded in a mythologized narrative designed
to raise public morale. This top-down message found bottom-up resonance
among a population increasing concerned about security and stability. The
short-term solution to minimize, where possible, the crimes of the past and
their legacy and focus on Stalin's accomplishments substituted for transitional
justice. Stalin's steady rise in popularity was facilitated by such state-sponsored
measures as restoring an ode to Stalin engraved in a prominent Moscow metro
station and by creating a (now defunct) state commission to guard against
the "falsification of history to the detriment of Russia's interests." This conflu-
ence of exploitation, contrived lies, genuine cynicism, and inadvertent irony
prompted Memorial to presciently recognize the toxicity of Stalinization and
to declare, in 2009, that "de-Stalinization is Russia's acutest problem."[17]

The identification of a human rights issue as Russia's "problem" is true, but
the state asserts a competing truth, and prioritizes a different problem. As a
human rights issue, the politically expedient imposition of a national amnesia
regarding the Gulag, its impact, and meaning marginalizes and revictimizes
the dwindling generation of Gulag survivors, undermines the integrity of the
collective memory, and is an impediment to transitional justice. By contrast,
the issue prioritized by Russia's past and present rulers was not confronting
this criminal history, but rather strengthening the stability and legitimacy
of the regime. They were concerned that de-Stalinization might emerge
uncontrollably from below. Indeed, this apprehension was blatantly mani-
fested in the early years of the Memorial movement (the late 1980s), which
were characterized by official resistance, lest the narrative of past repression
escape the Party's hands.[18] At that time, there was considerable bottom-up resonance for fully confronting the Stalinist past. Today this is much less the case.

The revelations of state-sponsored repression may not have been a major
determinant in facilitating the collapse of the Soviet Union, because it was
only one of many cumulative factors,[19] but the state's assessment of their
importance can be inferred from the effort expended in censoring them. Such
structural clashes of competing priorities identify central issues that impede
transitional justice processes from taking root. Accordingly, rather than following the European example of recognizing the victims and crimes of
Nazism through commemoration, *stolpersteine*, transforming campsites into
memorial museums, and substantive compensation, at present the Russian

authorities have co-opted not only the only museum occupying a former Gulag site, but also its history. In a script that echoes Stalin-era justifications, the camp (Perm) is now being portrayed as a bulwark against fifth column subversives seeking to undermine the Soviet people.[20] This bold effort to manage national and public memory by repressing the memory of repression impedes the emergence of an inclusive, credible, post-repression narrative.

Nuremberg was not a voluntary exercise and it has been much criticized as victors' justice, but it established the principle that the violation of human rights was a prosecutable crime, whether committed by individuals or by the state against its citizens. The legal and moral affirmation of human rights was the local and international justification for bringing down the Apartheid regime in South Africa. It also informed the creation of their Truth and Reconciliation Commission (TRC). Despite its shortcomings, the South African TRC facilitated a dialog between official and personal narratives that forged an inclusive history that reinforced the stability of the new nation. By contrast, decades after Khrushchev's dramatic revelations of Stalin's crimes, the Gorbachev-era glasnost, and the collapse of communism, post-Soviet Russia still has no such history of the Soviet state's repression of its own people.

Why does Russia remain such a "hard case"? While Khrushchev's speech denounced Stalin and Stalin's crimes, it purposively insulated the Communist Party, of which he was a part, from culpability. The reasonable follow-up question regarding why the system of governance permitted Stalin to commit these atrocities was not raised in public. However, a clear answer to that question is provided by an accurate recounting of history. Operationally, Soviet communism was dependent on repression, even as its ideology and propaganda made claims to the contrary. The dominance of the state-sponsored narrative over the victims' accounts reflects the persistence of a *post*-communist repression and totalitarian culture long after its formal demise. The United Russia Party has found it expedient to support its "repression lite" governance by, among other things, permitting the rehabilitation of Stalin. Their policy may be summarized as: those who do not want to be condemned by the past should remember it from a positive perspective.

REMEMBRANCE: OF WHAT AND WHY

A nation's history is always political, but especially so in a repressive state that is attempting to evade its history of repression by crafting an official national history at variance with the personal narratives of its citizens and the physical evidence of its landscape. This is the predicament facing post-Soviet Russia, engaged in a high-maintenance effort to insufficiently officially acknowledge the repression, its victims, and its legacy. Because repression affected so many people, evidence of the Soviet terror is impossible to avoid, but the government apparently hopes it can be minimized by citizens persuaded that those means justified this end. This message found fertile ground, as attested by the polls. Aside from the officially marginalized Memorial and some other nongovernmental organizations that regularly contest past and present human rights violations, there is no push for accountability perhaps because opposing the regime could place individuals and groups in legal and political jeopardy. Transitional justice in Russia would serve the dwindling generation of victims, not to strengthen pride in the nation's past "accomplishments." At best the post-Soviet government is employing an approach-avoidance tactic regarding the crimes of Stalinism.

October 30, 2007 marked the seventeenth anniversary of the year that mass repression and executions began in the Soviet Union. On that day, Vladimir Putin made a symbolic public gesture to commemorate its victims by visiting the Butovo artillery range, an area in the south of Moscow where an estimated 20,765 citizens were executed between August 1937 and October 1938.[21] Many surviving victims considered this a hollow gesture because Putin had done nothing to alleviate their "miserable" existence.[22] Meaningful monetary reparations that might improve their daily life would be only one step in a larger process of recognition. Since the early 2000s, civil society organizations have lobbied the Kremlin to acknowledge the crimes of Stalinism, extend condolences and apologies to the victims and their families, and launch a federal program to remember the repression.[23] Support for these efforts had been provided by Dmitrii Medvedev, the Russian President in 2009, when he asserted that the "memory of national tragedies is just as sacred as the memory of victories."[24] He added that "historical necessity" could provide no justification to those who "destroyed their people."[25]

The petitioners' recommendations included an appeal to the state to admit its culpability, and acknowledge that the whole country was "one big Katyn."[26] They made it clear that their goal was restorative justice and a commemoration of the regime's victims. Suggested ways of accomplishing this included: the establishment of monuments, a national consolidating "unity through consciousness of a common tragic past," a condemnation of the totalitarian regime by the president, the opening of national museums publicizing the history of the terror, social support for victims, and archival access.

Promises to create a state program to eliminate the vestiges of Stalinism were proffered, but genuine official support for such an enormous mandate has been inconsistent and lackluster. For example, Medvedev favored the creation of a database on victims, complete with accurately investigated numbers on the scope of the terror, but stopped short of supporting the request for a "political-legal judgment of the crimes of the communist regime."[27] His objection was that no authority could be empowered to condemn the former totalitarian regime. He also rejected the very idea that the President could admit culpability on behalf of the state by arguing that "legal judgments are passed by judges, not even the president or parliament."[28] Similar ad hoc legalistic impediments typify the arguments that some repressive and post-repressive states have crafted to obstruct transitional justice by ignoring the widely accepted norm that successor states are obliged to acknowledge and condemn a former regime that had been guilty of committing repression.

A major impediment to this recognition is that the history of the state's mass murder and terrorization of its own citizens runs counter to the mythologized Soviet victory over the barbaric Nazi regime, a cornerstone of the state-generated narrative. Indeed, the Director of the State Archive of the Russian Federation – long a champion of promoting access to archives – was demoted in 2016 for publishing an archival document deflating the myth of the heroic wartime defense of Moscow.[29] An acknowledgment of culpability in Stalinist crimes undermines much that was foundational to some citizens today, such as industrialization, the eradication of illiteracy, and other achievements of the Stalinist era.[30]

Notwithstanding all its ambiguity, if not ambivalence, regarding the Stalinist past, in 2015 the Russian government endorsed a bill on the remembrance of victims of political repression.[31] It promoted memorials, books of remembrance, databases, and archival access, along with the recognition of and compensation to victims. It paved the way for a monument to the victims of Stalin's terror to be constructed and placed on the corner of Sakharov Street in central Moscow, and the city of Moscow funded the construction of the previously mentioned Gulag Museum.[32] Concurrently, the state supported a parallel program, labeled "practical patriotism" that it did not precisely define. Since state support for a de-Stalinization program runs counter to the "militant patriotism"[33] it also endorses, civil society is tasked to call attention to the gap between the Russian government's words and deeds.[34]

A quarter of a century after the collapse of the Soviet Union, the work of historians and civil society actors who challenged the official narrative of present or past events became more marginalized and, in some cases, even dangerous. Representatives of human rights organizations have been harassed physically and legally in a manner that has interfered with their activity and damaged their public image. This damage can remain even after the court has found them innocent, because the pernicious charges are widely publicized and the innocent verdict is hardly acknowledged.[35] Addressing a more distant past – namely the human rights violations that took place under Stalin (State Gulag Museum) – is apparently safer than addressing their later Soviet-era trajectories, or the entrenched culture of repression that finds expression in today's human rights violations (Memorial).

Memorial has been accused of political activities and targeted for official harassment with the specious charge that they did not duly declared themselves "foreign agents," in keeping with a 2012 law. They share this politically precarious status with several other nongovernmental organizations, including the Levada Center, a highly respected independent polling agency. In 2013, Memorial headquarters was raided by a state delegation of tax inspectors, who barged into the offices in the early morning accompanied by a television crew. In the fall of 2016, Memorial was officially registered by the state as "foreign agent." It appears that such state-sponsored measures could severely limit the functioning of this grassroots human rights champion, which had emerged with so much hope for individual liberties during Gorbachev's perestroika. Memorial has represented many victims who were forced into signing Stalin-era false confessions (often on ironically similar charges) and subsequently executed. It is not surprising that Memorial steadfastly resisted the state's efforts to compel it to admit to being a "foreign agent" with the intensity of one whose life depended on it.

In my 2015 interview with Arsenii Roginskii, Memorial chairman, he reflected on the grim predicament of the organization. He concluded that the obstructions the state mounted to the work of Memorial were no longer battles, but a prolonged campaign, a "chronic condition."[36] Our interview took place outside of his office, literally outside, owing to some concern regarding surveillance. The stated justification for the regime's persistent efforts to suppress civil liberties was ominously reminiscent of the Soviet justification that it was threatened by capitalist encirclement from without and undermined by internal enemies who were aided and abetted by foreign enemies. One of the charges leveled against Memorial originated from the Ministry of Justice, accusing it of trying to overthrow the Russian government.[37]

Since such accusations, coupled with what the Russian government sees as "anti-Soviet agitation and propaganda," had been employed so frequently to arrest dissidents in the 1970s and the 1980s, what lessons has this government learned from its Stalinist past? The lesson learned seems to be that "repression lite" works, but it should not be seen to resemble Stalinism too closely – at least not the Stalinism associated with the Gulag, purges, and mass graves. Thus, the current regime has finessed this problem by promulgating a select history of the past that recognizes the existence of "some troublesome pages," but does not focus on them.

THE DESTRUCTION OF THE MUSEUM AT LABOR CAMP PERM

In my 2002 *book Gulag Survivor,* I noted that "postwar Europe made the concentration camps an important theme in its efforts to expose the ideology and practices of fascism. Post-Soviet Russia has the potential to do the same. The beginnings are evident."[38] That discussion went on to identify and describe Memorial's efforts to transform the labor camp Perm, which Gorbachev had closed by 1987, into a museum. It was dedicated in 1995, and substantially developed in subsequent years. The museum became a venue for international discussions, and extended its influence by launching an exhibition that traveled the world. Observers and participants in those years had not foreseen that a government that claimed to disown the repression would come to view the museum as a threat that had to be eliminated.

In 2014, as the power and water were shut off by the authorities, and the camp's watchtower bulldozed, it was evident that Perm's physical survival was in peril. The survival of its factual history was also imperiled by a state-run television report featuring interviews with former guards who claimed that only traitors were incarcerated in Perm. The story breezed past the "problematic pages" regarding how citizens came to be labeled as "traitors" or "enemies of the people." Instead, it featured the "self-sacrifice and benevolence" of the camp guards. Irina Flige, chairman of St. Petersburg Memorial, concluded with dismay that "the executioner is masterfully ascending the hero's scaffolding."[39] Perm had become the latest battleground casualty in the contested history of the repression.

NATIONAL MEMORY AND STATE-GENERATED HISTORY

The memory of the Gulag has not yet found an accommodating place in the national memory. Consequently, even attempts at memorialization of the victims have been circumscribed, or sometimes co-opted. While the current Russian administration cannot get the historical genie back into the political bottle, they have attempted to constrain its effects.[40] In the last decade, the government has imposed renewed limitations on archival access, harassed and arrested researchers working in Stalinist archives for "violating victims' rights to privacy,"[41] and skewed the historical narrative in textbooks.

As noted previously, many Soviet leaders were concerned about de-Stalinization, and imposed limitations accordingly. Apparently, an accurate account of the victimizations under seven decades of Soviet rule could not be included in a Soviet history that Russians would be proud of, unless this disclosure was coupled with pride in the government's courage to confront the damage

wrought by Stalin. Rather, the state chose the expedient solution of a purposively incomplete history designed to marginalize the repression as well as the
Gulag. This strategy permits the government to condemn the Soviet terror
and control history at the same time by co-opting some of the tasks of civil
society. Gorbachev had employed this stratagem thirty years earlier when he
imposed limitations on the scope of the emergent Memorial's inquiries so that
the history of Stalinism resided mainly in the hands of the Party.

THE NEXT GENERATION: TEXTBOOKS

The modifications a government imposes on curricula are clear indicators of
what it wants students to learn from the past, and achieve in the future.[42] For
some years, Russia has been promoting a sanitized version of the Stalinist past,
now the approved account of history taught in Russian high schools. Putin
voiced its *raison d'etre* in a nationally broadcast address in 2005, when he
decried the collapse of the Soviet Union as "the greatest geopolitical catastrophe of the twentieth century."[43] He later argued that Russia should not be
made to feel guilty about the Great Purge of 1937, because "in other countries,
even worse things happened."[44] In the passive style of a disowning admission,
Putin acknowledged that there were some "problematic pages" in Russia's history, but he artfully dodged their significance by posing a rhetorical question
regarding what state had not had such events.[45] This ploy is part cause and part
consequence of the fact that Russia made no substantial attempts to come to
terms with the legacy of Soviet communism. On the one hand, it has been
impelled to disapprove of repression by prominent Russians like Aleksandr
Solzhenitsyn, Andrei Sakharov, Khrushchev, and Gorbachev, among others.
On the other hand, its leaders and many of its citizenry have become dependent on repression to maintain stability.[46]

   In 2007, Putin promoted a handbook, titled *The Modern History of Russia,
1945–2006*.[47] Its contents conformed to Soviet-era textbooks, complete with
guidelines dictating several positive ways in which Russian leaders should be
presented.[48] In consequence, educational materials were fashioned to reflect
the political views of the government, though in practice teachers still feel
free to disregard the content of the official textbooks. In 2008, in an effort to
promote patriotism among younger people, a new teachers' manual covering the period 1900–45 was officially approved for use in schools.[49] The use
of *history* to achieve this goal required a considerable manipulation of the
facts and the contrivance of creative interpretations of those facts. For example, the guidelines of a 2012 manual instructed teachers to address the period
of Stalinist repressions by focusing on "what we built in the 1930s."[50] They

were told to explain that "Stalin acted in a concrete historical situation, as a leader he acted entirely rationally – as the guardian of the system."[51] Since the scope of the repression does not readily fit into the concept of "rational governance," the manual suggests working the numbers a bit. For example, it recommends that "a formula could be used wherein only those who received death sentences and those who were executed would be counted."[52] These figures are significantly lower than the established facts because they exclude the additional millions who languished in the Gulag, where they died from disease and forced labor, or were released to die outside of the camp. Other history texts of recent years have advanced similar views.[53] The effectiveness of these history lessons is attested to by the fact that some youth organizations today proudly proclaim, "we leapt forward, we created a country of tanks from a country of plows."[54]

In 2014, the Putin administration commissioned the creation of an authoritative textbook whose narrative would present a "unitary vision," emphasizing the role of Stalin as an "effective manager." The authoritative message was to be: "We are citizens of a Great Country with a Great Past"; Putin recommended that there be no "dual interpretations."[55] A list of thirty-one controversial subjects circulated in the Moscow Russian History Teachers' Association. They ranged in time from the seventeenth century to the present. All these topics would require a deliberately deceptive approach, with a positive spin, to make it into the proposed textbook. Regarding Stalin, attention was directed to the role of his personality, with no reference to his repressions. This subject was circumvented by suggesting that his behavior should be interpreted within the framework of a "one-Party system dictatorship and the autocracy of Stalin."[56] In other words, the one-party system enforced at that time gave this autocrat too much power. Whereas Khrushchev blamed Stalin to save the party, this approach seems to be doing the opposite.

In addition, in 2014 a Soviet-era publisher gained dominance of the textbook market. Notwithstanding the introduction of Solzhenitsyn's *Gulag Archipelago* into the high school curriculum – an initiative supported if not driven by Putin, and completed in 2010 – a subtext of this history lesson is that the political ethos was perhaps not fully ready to change. In fact, that widely publicized gesture was viewed by civil society as "Potemkin-like,"[57] because Solzhenitsyn's text was consigned to literature, and not history, classes. However, while a culture of repression persists, there have been important political changes, which include the fact that the *Gulag Archipelago* and similar works, which were prohibited from being published in the Soviet Union and even illegal to possess, are now readily available. However, such material does not appear to be making a significant step toward the goals of transitional justice. In parallel, the whitewashing of history persists and has found overt expression in 2017 Stalin calendars, prominently displayed in bookstores.

As previously noted, in 2009, a presidential decree empowered the state to manage the historical narrative by establishing a Commission to Counter Attempts to Falsify History to the Detriment of Russian Federation Interests.[58] The commission was composed of state and public officials, along with historians, who were charged with targeting those historical accounts deemed to misrepresent or manipulate facts that cast Russia in a negative light. Civil society organizations expressed their concern that the "struggle against the falsification of history" was becoming an "affair of the state." The danger that alarmed them was that the state could not morally or credibly be the arbiter of the "truth."[59]

The question of who should be the arbiter is beyond complex. It is misleading because it assumes that there is an apolitical arbiter. This assumption is refuted by, for example, the experience of international criminal tribunals that are regularly challenged by the persistence of incompatible and coexisting "truths,"[60] based on the different perceptions of different groups, as well as different interpretations of those perceptions.[61] These differences are generally not resolved by judicial proceedings. In practice, contending parties often enter and leave the court with "their own truths" still intact.[62] The discussion becomes even more complicated when we recognize the coexistence of different truths, some explicit, others implicit.[63] One of Medvedev's last measures as acting President was to dissolve the ill-founded history commission. In 2016, there was talk of resurrecting that commission, or one with a similar mandate.[64] A better contender for the public's trust would be a history commission tasked to identify and analyze areas of agreement, disagreement, and the wide gray area of non-agreement about past events.

RECONSTRUCTING THE PAST

To the extent that Russia succeeds in maintaining a closed society, individual rights will be constrained, and its repressive political system will be shielded from critical public scrutiny and accountability. Unless successfully challenged, the political system will continue to skew its citizens' cognitive and affective appraisals by supplying versions of events that justify its methods of governance, and have gained varying degrees of acceptance. Since Stalin's death, the view of the Stalinist past has been adjusted to fit the state's prevailing needs. Organizations such as Memorial view the attempts to hide the scope and consequences of the repression as counterproductive, because they squander the opportunity to learn from the mistakes of the past.

Semën Vilenskii, whose passing in 2016 marked the end of an era, was incensed by the fact that there had never been a moral condemnation of the Communist Party of the Soviet Union. He spoke with the authority as head of the victims' organization "Vozvrashchenie" (The Return), a Kolyma survivor, a memoir publisher and the only member of the Rehabilitation Commission[65] who had been a Stalin-era prisoner. He has argued that Russia would benefit from a "Nuremberg Trial without blood."[66] Those found guilty of these crimes against humanity could receive the maximum penalty, and then be pardoned. Vilenskii, who died at the age of 88, was one of the last remaining survivors of the Stalinist era. To the end of his life, he called for the state to "recognize and repent."[67] However, Arsenii Roginskii, an ex-prisoner of the (later) dissident era and fellow member of the Rehabilitation Commission, went further. He contended that identifying the victims would be just the first step in dealing with the repression; identifying the oppressors, many still unnamed, would be the next step toward remediating the past and improving the future.[68]

Stalinism and its victims occupy a lacuna in the nation's image of itself, the void in the empty square of the memorial plaque. The vanishing community of Gulag returnees remains determined to remember, record, and publicize the crimes committed in the name of Soviet communism. However, their efforts have been countered by strong official resistance, because Russia has invested heavily in the creation of its purposively incomplete official history. In the Soviet era, there was a fairly consistent recognition that a fuller history of the repression could undermine the legitimacy of the regime. In the post-Soviet era, the gilded version of the past has been promoted as an inspiring rallying point for patriotism and national pride. Thus, twenty-five years after the end of the Soviet Union, Russia crafted an approach to its Stalinist history that burnishes its national image: its citizens were encouraged to flip past the "problematic pages" and focus on the "bright past" of national achievements. Implicit is that the bright future can be achieved without bothering with transitional justice.

CONCLUSION

In real-time history, the chronology of events moves from past to present, and historical scholarship thrives on the assumption that the past produces the present. But in Russia's politicized history, it is the present that produces the past by choosing which parts should be remembered and how they should be construed. In consequence, what could have been a useable "lessons learned" history of Russia has been subverted. It now takes the form of what the needs of the present require the history of Russia to be. While integrating the story of the terror into the mainstream history of Russia is a relatively straightforward undertaking at the level of historical scholarship, it has been frustrated by political obstacles. Overcoming them would require a fundamental shift from a system of governance that devalues human rights toward a democratic ethos that prioritizes them. However, Russians cannot draw on painstakingly evolved democratic traditions and institutions, fine-tuned to balance individual rights with collective responsibilities. For the present, authoritarianism is the default political culture.

The Russian government's efforts to focus attention on the material and military benefits under Stalin and de-emphasize Stalin's crimes suggest that they believe that promulgating this skewed version of history is the best mechanism available for sustaining repressive governance. Thus, organizations pursuing an accurate history of the Stalinist past are at risk of being charged with subversive political activity, and even of attempting to overthrow the Russian government. The blunt coerciveness of the government's response suggests that they are aware of the vulnerability of their claim to legitimacy.

The survival of civil society depends on both the survival of the state and the individuals it governs. The narrative accounts of each should intertwine and inform each other. However, such intertwining is proscribed in a post-Soviet Russia that is attempting to relegate Stalin's repression to the past without recognizing its impact on the present. A major impact of past repression is Russia's dependence on current repression, lest it slip into the kind of unmanageable chaos that followed the dissolution of the Soviet Union.

When looking at the regime's investment in a sanitized Stalin, it appears they have concluded that the Kremlin could not survive a full acknowledgment of the Stalinist repression. This constricted vision has narrowed the field to two major narratives that compete for dominance in the informal marketplace of public opinion: the real story of the victims and survivors, seeking recognition by and compensation from the government, opposed by the official edited and redacted history aiming to persuade the public that the survival of the state required the suppression of individual rights – and still does. The competitive edge given to the official narrative implicitly claims that recognizing the victims and identifying their oppressors should be of less relevance. This message has been challenged by the victims as well as human rights groups, who have asserted that as long as post-Soviet Russia fails to fully acknowledge its history of repression, it will remain mired in its onerous past.

While there is some ambivalent official support for coming to terms with that past, these competing narratives identify deep-seated problems that remain unresolved in post-Soviet Russia. This is relevant because the success of transitional justice in post-Soviet Russia may depend on its ability to forge a dialog between official and personal narratives and create an inclusive history of the Soviet state's repression of its own people, based on credible evidence, and validated by a credible audience. Such a mutually negotiated history would provide a stepping stone rather than a stumbling block on the path to transitional justice – indeed, it might even serve as a mechanism unto itself. This approach might also be relevant beyond Russia. Transitional justice efforts in Ukraine, Belarus, Kazakhstan, and Serbia, for example, are similarly impeded by competing narratives on the communist past and an entrenched culture of repression. The cost of Russia's inability and unwillingness to fully acknowledge its history of repression is one that will be borne by all successor regimes. It can be controlled by constant vigilance, but it is expensive to sustain and has the potential to be destabilizing.

What might facilitate the move beyond the present impasse? The full opening of archives accompanied by gathering and analyzing personal testimonies, and the exhumation and forensic examination of mass graves, would together provide the public with the "shared custody"[69] of a "common past." The "brightness" of the actual past will be dimmed for some, but in this age of transitional justice, a national process of reckoning might achieve sufficient consensus to interrupt the perennial recycling of old repressions into newly justified repressions that have included the repression of the victims' stories. There is support, however limited, for such an approach in Russia. Roginskii, an ardent advocate for nonviolent change, emphasizes the importance of the story we tell to ourselves and to others: "society and the state will need to work together, and historians bear a special responsibility in this process."[70] It may be that an inclusive history that recognizes the victims and their heirs, but also verifies, analyzes, records, acknowledges, and seeks to understand the competing narratives on the past could facilitate a shift from dueling monologs to engaging dialogs, which could break cycles of violence and shorten the long shadow of repression in Russia.

Notes

1. For an apt analysis of various estimates, see Michael Ellman, "Soviet Repression Statistics: Some Comments," *Europe Asia Studies* 54, 7 (2002): 1151–72; J. A. Getty, G. T. Rittersporn, and V. N. Zemskov, "Victims of the Soviet Penal System in the Prewar Years: A First Approach on the Basis of Archival Material," *American Historical*

Review 98, 4 (1993): 1017–49; Steven Rosefielde, "Stalinism in Post-Communist Perspective: New Evidence on Killings, Forced Labour and Economic Growth in the 1930s," *Europe-Asia Studies* 48, 6 (1996): 959–87; Stephen Wheatcroft, "The Scale and Nature of German and Soviet Repression and Mass Killings, 1930–45," *Europe-Asia Studies* 48, 8 (1996): 1319–53.

2. Semen Charnyi, "Odno imia, odna zhizn', odin znak," *30 oktiabria*, 2014, 123, 2.

3. Personal interview, Arsenii Roginskii, Moscow, April 9, 2015.

4. Nanci Adler, *Victims of Soviet Terror: The Story of the Memorial Movement* (Westport: Praeger, 1993).

5. V. Tikhanova, ed., *Rasstrel'nye spiski, volume 1 Donskoe kladbishche, 1934–40* (Moscow: NIPTs Memorial, 1993); *Rasstrel'nye spiski, volume 2, Vagan'kovskoe kladbishche 1926–1936* (Moscow: Memorial, 1995).

6. The Russian government is represented by the Human Rights Ombudsman at this ceremony. Personal observation of ceremonies in 2011 and 2016, confirmed in personal interview with Arsenii Roginskii, Moscow, November 1, 2016.

7. Berber Bevernage, "Writing the Past out of the Present: History and Politics of Time in Transitional Justice," *History Workshop Journal* 69 (2010): 111–31; James Gow, "Dark Histories, Brighter Futures: The Balkans and Black Sea Region: European Union Frontiers, War Crimes and Confronting the Past," *Southeast European and Black Sea Studies* 7, 3 (2007): 345–55.

8. "Mikhalkov Creates Rival to McDonald's," *The Moscow Times*, April 10, 2015.

9. "Krym: Istoriia vozvrashchenie," "Na Puti k pobede," visit to Muzei Revolutsii, Moscow, April 12, 2015.

10. Neil Macfarquhar, "A Book for Discerning Russians: The Words of Putin," *International New York Times*, January 1–2, 2016, available at: www.questia.com/ newspaper/1P2-39136269/a-book-for-discerning-russians-the-words-of-putin, accessed June 24, 2017.

11. "Rol' lichnosti v istorii Rossii," January 20, 2015, available at: www.levada.ru/2015/ 01/20/rol-lichnostej-v-istorii-rossii, accessed June 20, 2017.

12. "Stalin i ego rol' v istorii strany," 2015, available at: www.levada.ru/2015/03/31/ stalin-i-ego-rol-v-istorii-strany/, accessed June 21, 2017.

13. "Rol' Stalina v istorii Rossii," Levada Centre, January 13, 2016, available at: www.levada.ru/2016/01/13/rol-stalina-v-istorii-rossii, accessed January 13, 2016; "Praviteli v otechestvennyi istorii," available at: www.levada.ru/2016/03/01/ praviteli-v-otechestvennoj-istorii/, accessed March 9, 2016.

14. Anna Dolgov, "Russian Senator Introduces Bill Criminalizing Pro-Stalin Propaganda." *Moscow Times*, September 22, 2015, available at: www.themoscowtimes .com/articles/russian-senator-introduces-bill-criminalizing-pro-stalin-propoganda-49720, accessed June 22, 2017.

15. "Lider KPRF ob' iavil o nastuplenii 'stalinskoi vesny,'" *Dozhd TV*, December 21, 2015, available at: http://tvrain.ru/articles/lider_kprf_objavil_o_nastuplenii_ stalinskoj_vesny-400547, accessed June 22, 2017.

16. Alec Luhn, "What Stalin Owes Putin," *International New York Times*, March 12–13, 2016, available at: http://ihtbd.com/ihtuser/print/old%20THT/12-03-2016/ a1203x08xxxxxxxxx.pdf, accessed June 24, 2017.

17. "Russia Marks Day of Victims of Political Repressions," *Itar-TASS*, October 30, 2009.

18. Gorbachev's remarks on Memorial, Zasedanie Politbiuro TsK KPSS, November 24, 1988, RGANI, f. 89, op. 42, d. 23, ll. 1–5.
19. Stephen Cohen, *Soviet Fates and Lost Alternatives* (New York: Columbia University Press, 2009), Chapter 5.
20. Elena Khrustaleva, "Proshchanie s 'Perm'iu-36'," 30 *oktiabria*, 133, 2016, 1–2.
21. L.A. Golovkova, *Butovskii Poligon. 1937–38gg. Kniga pamiati zhertv politicheskikh repressi* (Moscow: Izdatel'stvo 'Al'zo', 2004).
22. "Putin's Visit to Butovo Symbolic – Rights Activist," *Interfax*, October 31, 2007; "President Putin Calls for 'Constructive' Political Rivalries," *AP*, October 30, 2007, available at: www.namibian.com.na/index.php?id=39356&page=archive-read, accessed June 21, 2017.
23. Arsenii Roginskii and Dmitrii Medvedev, "Eta programma ne tol'ko pro istoriiu," February 1, 2011, available at: www.hro.org/node/10218, accessed June 24, 2017.
24. Dmitrii Medvedev, "Repressiiam net opravdaniia," 30 *oktiabria*, 2009, 94.
25. Ibid.
26. "Stenograficheskii otchet o zasedanii Soveta po razvitiu obshchestva i pravam cheloveka," no date, available at: www.kremlin.ru/transcripts/10194, accessed November 6, 2016; Arsenii Roginskii, "Pamiat'o Stalinizme," in *Istoriia stalinizma: itogi i problem izucheniia*, ed. Elena I. Kandrashina (Moscow: ROSSPEN, 2011).
27. "Stenograficheskii otchet o zasedanii Soveta."
28. Ibid.
29. Aleksandr Baklanov, "Gosarkhiv rasskazal o vydumannom 'podviga' 28 panfilovtsev," July 8, 2015, available at: http://snob.ru/selected/entry/94992, accessed November 19, 2016.
30. Irina Flige, "Predmetnaia i material'naia pamiat' o Bol'shom Terror," draft paper, 2007. Document with the author.
31. "Ob utverzhdenii kontseptsii gosudarstvennoi politiki po uvekovecheniiu pamiati zhertv politicheskikh repressii," August 18, 2015, available at: Об утверждении концепции государственной политики по увековечению памяти жертв политических репрессийОб утверждении концепции государственной политики по увековечению памяти жертв политических репрессий Об утверждении концепции государственной политики по увековечению памяти жертв политических репрессий, available at: www.government.ru/docs/19296, accessed November 19, 2016.
32. Vladimir Ryzhkov, "Attitude to Stalin Reveals Russia's Considerable Divide," *Moscow Times*, September 22, 2015, available at: https://themoscowtimes.com /articles/attitude-to-stalin-reveals-russias-considerable-divide-49710, accessed June 22, 2017.
33. Ivan Nechepurenko, "New Policy on Commemorating Victims of Repression at Odds with Actions," *The Moscow Times, John's Russia List* #9, August 20, 2015.
34. Lyudmila Alexandrova, "Russia Condemns Political Repression Officially," *TASS*, August 19, 2015, available at: http://tass.com/opinions/815336, accessed June 21, 2017.
35. On the legal battle of researchers arrested for working in the archives, see Catriona Bass, "Controlling History," *Transitions Online*, December 6, 2011, available at: www.tol.org/client/article/22877-controlling-history.html?print, accessed June 22, 2017.
36. Personal interview, Arsenii Roginskii, Moscow, April 8, 2015.

37. "Miniust obvinil 'Memorial' v podryve konstitutsionnogo stroia RF," November 10, 2015, available at: www.novayagazeta.ru/news/1697854.html, accessed November 6, 2016.
38. Nanci Adler, *The Gulag Survivor: Beyond the Soviet System* (New Brunswick: Transaction Publishers, 2002), 261.
39. Irina Flige, "Prostranstvo Gulaga: opyt i pamiat'," unpublished paper presented at "Theology after the Gulag," Amsterdam, May 2016.
40. Ukaz no. 549, May 15, 2009, available at: www.politru.dokumenty/presidentprosled-it, accessed November 6, 2016.
41. At a May 2012 forum in Moscow, Russian researchers lamented renewed problems with archival access.
42. Elizabeth A. Cole, "Transitional Justice and the Reform of History Education," *The International Journal of Transitional Justice* 1, 1 (2007): 115–37.
43. "Vladimir Putin: 'Raspad SSSR – krupneishaia geopoliticheskaia katasrofa veka'," April 25, 2005, available at: https://regnum.ru/news/polit/444083.html, accessed November 6, 2016.
44. Douglas Birch, "Vietnam Worse than Stalin Purges," *Associated Press*, June 21, 2007, available at: www.washingtonpost.com/wp-dyn/content/article/2007/06/21/AR2007062101885.html, accessed June 22, 2017.
45. Leon Aron, "The Problematic Pages," *The New Republic*, September 24, 2008, available at: https://newrepublic.com/article/62070/the-problematic-pages, accessed June 22, 2017.
46. Adler, *Gulag Survivor*, and Nanci Adler, *Keeping Faith with the Party: Communist Believers Return from the Gulag* (Bloomington: Indiana University Press, 2012).
47. A.V. Filippov, A.I. Utkin, and S.V. Sergeev, eds., *Noveishaia Istoriia Rossii, 1945 – 2006 gg.: Kniga dlia uchitelia* (Moscow: Prosveshchenie, 2007); A.S. Barsenkov, A.I. Vdovin, *Istoriia Rossii. 1917 – 2009* (Moscow: Aspekt Press, 2010).
48. David Brandenberger, "A New Short Course? A.V. Filippov and the Russian State's Search for a 'Usable Past'," *Kritika: Explorations in Russian and Eurasian History*, 10, 4 (2009): 825–33; Elena Zubkova, "The Filippov Syndrome," *Kritika: Explorations in Russian and Eurasian History*, 10, 4 (2009): 861–8.
49. A.A. Danilov, A.V. Filippov, *Istoriia Rossii 1900-1945 gg: Kniga dlia uchitel'ia* (Moscow: Prosveshchenie, 2009).
50. "Stanovlenie mobilizatsionnoi politicheskoi sistemy," no date, available at: www .prosv.ru/ebooks/Danilov_Istoria_1900-1945/12.html, accessed March 14, 2012.
51. "Stanovlenie mobilizatsionnoi," and Danilov and Filippov, *Istoriia Rossii*, 19 and 267.
52. "Uchitel'iam istorii veleno prepodnosit' stalinskii terror kak ratsional'nyi instrument razvitiia strany," no date, available at: www.newsru.com, accessed August 25, 2008.
53. Barsenkov and Vdovin, *Istoriia Rossii. 1917–2009.*
54. "Ensuring Stalin's Victims are not Forgotten," no date, available at: www.bbc.com/news/world-35611709, accessed March 2, 2016.
55. Lyudmila Aleksandrova, "Work on Standard Russian History Manual Proves Really Daunting Task," *Itar-Tass*, September 26, 2013, available at: http://tass.com/opinions/815336, accessed June 21, 2017.

56. Svetlana Bocharova, "Experty perepysivaiut istoriiu Rossii," *Vedomosti*, June 11, 2013, available at: www.vedomosti.ru/politics/articles/2013/06/11/istoriya_po_naryshkinu, accessed June 22, 2017.

57. Arsenii Roginskii, comment at "International Symposium on the Legacy of the Gulag and the Remembrance of Stalinism," Amsterdam, November 8, 2013.

58. Ukaz Prezidenta Rossiiskoi Federatsii ot 15 maia 2009 g. N 549 "O Kommissii pri Presidente Rossiiskoi Federatsii po protivodeistviiu popytkam falsifikatsii istorii i ushcherb interesam Rossii" [On the commission under the President of the Russian Federation to counter attempts at the falsification of history to the detriment of Russia's interests], May 15, 2009, available at: www.politru.dokumenty/ presidentprosledit, accessed November 19, 2016.

59. Paul Goble, "Medvedev Historical Falsification Commission 'Harmful' or 'Useless', Memorial Expert Says." *Window on Eurasia*, May 20, 2009, available at: www.eesti.ca/medvedev-falsification-commission-may-be-harmful-or-useless-memorial-expert-says/article23844, accessed June 22, 2017.

60. Erin Daly, "Truth Skepticism: An Inquiry into the Value of Truth in Times of Transition," *The International Journal of Transitional Justice* 2, 1 (2008): 23–41.

61. Despite the efforts of the International Criminal Tribunal for the Former Yugoslavia to set the record straight, overcome ambiguity, and "police a violent past." Roland Kostic, *Ambivalent Peace: External Peacebuilding, Threatened Identity and Reconciliation in Bosnia and Herzegovina*, Report No. 78 (Uppsala: Department of Peace and Conflict Research, 2007), 33.

62. Andreas Gross, "Draft Resolution and Report on the Use of Experience of 'Truth Commissions'," Report to the Council of Europe, December 4, 2007, 8.

63. Adler, *Keeping Faith*.

64. Personal interview, Arsenii Roginskii, Moscow, October 31, 2016.

65. "Kommissia po reabilitatsii zhertv politicheskikh repressii," no date, available at: http://kremlin.ru/structure/commissions#institution-25, accessed November 19, 2016.

66. Personal interview, Semën Samuilovich Vilenskii, Moscow, November 18, 2003.

67. Personal interview, Semën Samuilovich Vilenskii, Moscow, October 30, 2011.

68. Roginskii, "Pamiat' o stalinizma," 23.

69. Erik Ketelaar, "Truth, Memories and Histories in the Archives of the ICTY," Paper presented at the 60 Years Genocide Convention, The Hague, December 8, 2008, 13.

70. Roginskii, "Pamiat," 27.

3

Public Memory and Communist
Legacies in Poland and Russia

Mark Kramer

In a televised ceremony at the Kremlin in Moscow on November 2, 2007, Russian President Vladimir Putin announced that he had awarded a posthumous Hero of Russia plaque and Gold Star medal to George Koval, an American technician who had been assigned by the US army during World War II to the top-secret Manhattan Project to build a nuclear bomb. Koval, it turned out, also spied for the Soviet military intelligence service under the codename "Delmar" and smuggled highly sensitive information about nuclear weapons' technology to Moscow.[1] At the ceremony honoring Koval, Putin warmly described him as "our comrade" and extolled his "immense contribution to the strengthening of our country's defense capacity."[2] The revelation of Koval's spy work attracted considerable press coverage, but journalists failed to ask why the president of post-Soviet Russia was lauding someone who gave such valuable help to the odious dictatorship of Joseph Stalin. One might assume that by November 2007 Russian leaders would no longer proudly describe a Stalinist agent as "our comrade" and explicitly associate their country with the monstrous policies of the Stalin era. Surely no leader of current-day Germany would even think of bestowing posthumous honors on someone who eagerly colluded with the Nazi regime.

Putin's decision to honor Koval for his service to Stalin is symptomatic of a broader problem in Russia – the failure to come fully to terms with the Soviet past. Starting in the late 1980s under Mikhail Gorbachev and continuing in the 1990s under Boris Yeltsin, leaders in Moscow cast light on the appalling events of the Stalin era, stirring great public interest. In 2008–12, President Dmitrii Medvedev condemned Stalin's crimes, and even Putin has occasionally acknowledged the wanton cruelty of Stalin's regime. These scattered statements have been outweighed by the whitewashing that has been all too common under Putin. The problem is not a lack of information about Stalinist atrocities. Scholars and other experts have overwhelmingly demonstrated that millions were killed under Stalin and have meticulously analyzed the repressive state apparatus. This information is readily available to those in Russia who want to see it. Instead, the problem is a lack of commitment on the part of the Russian government that has fueled a wider indifference and lack of interest on the part of the Russian public.

Although the process of coming to terms with the past has been formidable for many Western countries, it has been even more onerous in former communist countries, especially Russia, which became the "legal successor state" to the Soviet Union in 1991, a status that, for some Russian leaders and elites, tends to blur Russia with the former Soviet Union (FSU). In Russia, as in other countries, public memory has emerged in part from an intra-elite competition that Putin has sought to control. This chapter comparatively assesses the problems that former communist countries have experienced as they reckon with the past. It focuses on two former communist countries: the highly-charged (and often politicized) debates in Poland about historical memory of the communist era and the Russian government's attempts to control public memory of the Soviet era and use it in the service of Putin's political goals.

HISTORICAL RECKONING IN FORMER COMMUNIST COUNTRIES

All of the leading Western democracies have encountered problems in reckoning with abominable events of the recent past, despite the passage of considerable time and change of generations.[3] Even in Germany, the country that is often cited as the model of how societies can try to face up to unspeakable crimes, the process of Vergangenheitsbewältigung (coming to terms with the past) was far from smooth or easy. Historical reckoning has been even more arduous in former communist countries, where the task of reckoning was entirely up to the individual governments and societies. In many cases, especially in the FSU, powerful elites thwarted any real attempt to come to terms with the past.

POLAND AND ITS NAZI PAST

Since 1989, the process of historical reckoning in Poland has been marked by controversy and recriminations about the communist period, and the years that preceded it. The main focus in this chapter is the communist period, but recent debates in Poland about Poles' behavior toward Jews during and immediately after World War II have played such a crucial role in political battles over historical memory that some discussion of them is warranted here.

The main impetus for reassessments of Poles' complicity in the annihilation of Polish Jews has come from the eminent historian Jan Gross. Beginning with *Sąsiedzi* (Neighbors) in 2000, Gross systematically punctured long-held myths about the treatment of Jews by their fellow Poles during and immediately after World War II.[4] In *Sąsiedzi* he recounted how in the town of Jedwabne in July 1941 the local Polish residents turned *en masse* against their Jewish neighbors and brutally killed hundreds of them. This instance of mass violence, Gross argued, was one of numerous pogroms carried out by Poles against Jews in the summer of 1941.

The book struck a raw nerve in Poland and generated fierce debates and recriminations.[5] Some Poles were quick to condemn it, while others took issue with Gross's account of the massacre or his interpretations of why it happened.[6] Still others defended *Sąsiedzi* as a book that "had to be written and was absolutely necessary" to force Poles to "face up to the painful truth of Jedwabne."[7] The discussion in Poland at times took on ugly nationalist and anti-Semitic overtones, and several political commentators, especially those affiliated with the extreme-right Radio Maryja, invoked hoary notions of Judeo-Communism (*Żydokomuna*) and sought to exculpate the attackers.[8]

Despite the viciousness of some of the commentaries, the debate overall had a cathartic effect on Polish society, especially after the parliament officially authorized the Institute of National Remembrance (Instytut Pamięci Narodowej, or IPN) to produce a comprehensive study of the Jedwabne pogrom and the circumstances surrounding it. In 2002, the IPN published a massive compendium of authoritative essays by leading experts and a collection of annotated documents from Polish archives that confirmed Gross's basic findings, but reduced the total death toll and added a wealth of detail.[9] The IPN's successful performance in this high-profile case cemented its reputation as a nonpartisan, professional body that could facilitate historical reckoning in Poland even on the most sensitive topics.

Gross's next two books, *Strach* (Fear) and *Złote żniwa* (Golden Harvest), extended his reassessments of the history of Polish Jews to the late wartime years and early postwar period. In *Strach* he discussed how Polish Christians, especially those who had seized the property of deported or murdered Polish Jews, often reacted with hostility when Polish Jews who had survived the Holocaust returned home as the war ended. The hostility at times gave rise to gruesome anti-Semitic outbursts, including a pogrom in Kielce in July 1946 that left forty-two Jews dead.[10] The cumulative death toll of other attacks against Jews in postwar Poland, including atrocities perpetrated by armed nationalist guerrillas, reached 1,500, according to Gross. As with Gross's first book, the reaction in Poland to *Strach* among professional historians and the wider public was often uneasy. Most scholars accepted the basic facts in Gross's narrative, but many contested his interpretations. Some argued that he had been too sweeping in his characterizations of Polish society and had attributed anti-Semitic motives to people whose actions stemmed from greed or criminality coarsened by the war.[11] A senior figure in the Polish Catholic Church even accused Gross of stoking anti-Semitism by "unfairly maligning the entire Polish nation."[12]

The furor gained even greater intensity with Gross's third book, *Złote żniwa*, which underscored the callousness and antipathy of many Poles toward Jews during the war even as the Holocaust was taking its grisly toll. Gross cataloged instances in which Poles living near Treblinka, Chelmno, and other extermination camps stripped the clothes off Jewish corpses and stole gold fillings from their teeth. He described how Poles waited for their Jewish neighbors to be shot or deported to the gas chambers and then laid claim to their possessions. The small percentage of Poles who tried to save Jews from Nazi death squads were ostracized, physically attacked, or forced into exile by their fellow Poles after the war. In response to the book, many Poles alleged that Gross had dwelt too much on pathologies that were outgrowths of a rampantly destructive war and had therefore "drawn unfair generalizations."[13] Some commentators engaged in ad hominem attacks against Gross, often with anti-Semitic overtones.[14] Gross and his publisher, Znak, responded that the criticisms missed the whole point of the book, which was to show that many Poles behaved with unspeakable cruelty both during and after the war.

Even as Gross's books touched off recriminations and disputes, they stirred greater public curiosity about the history of Polish Jews and spurred many Poles to seek to learn more about the topic. A by-product was the opening in Warsaw in October 2014 of a state-of-the-art Museum of the History of Polish Jews (Muzeum Historii Żydów Polskich), which presents an overview of the destruction of Polish Jewry in the Holocaust and a comprehensive history of Jewish life in Poland.[15] Yet, despite greater public interest in the history of Polish–Jewish relations, the issue has remained politically sensitive in Poland. In 2015, Gross maintained that Poles had killed more Jews during World War II than they had killed Germans.[16] He contended that Poles had killed 17,000 Germans in 1939, 5,000 more over the next four years, and another 5,000 during the August 1944 Warsaw uprising, but the total number of Jews killed by Poles – by ordinary citizens as well as police, paramilitary units, army soldiers, and nationalist guerrillas – was several times higher. Gross's claims were bound to be controversial in a country that had long prided itself on having fought against Germany throughout the war.[17] So vehement was the public reaction that Poland's chief state prosecutor launched a criminal investigation in October 2015 to see whether libel charges should be brought against Gross for having "publicly insulted the Polish nation." If upheld, the charges could lead to a three-year prison sentence.[18]

The criticism of Gross escalated after the right-wing populist Law and Justice (Prawo i sprawiedliwość, or PiS) party of Jarosław Kaczyński won Poland's parliamentary elections and Andrzej Duda, a PiS leader, won the presidency in 2015. Both Duda and the new PiS government endorsed the investigation of Gross. In January 2016, Duda called for the revocation of the Knight's Cross of the Order of Merit awarded to Gross by the Polish government in 1996.[19] That proposal triggered a backlash in Poland among scholars and political commentators, who decried PiS's "stupid and harmful" efforts to use history as a "political weapon." Two open letters to Duda and the government, signed by distinguished Polish historians, warned that such a move would "tarnish Poland's image in the world" and be a "national embarrassment."[20]

Duda had claimed that his move against Gross was part of a wider "offensive" he spearheaded to burnish Poland's image in the face of "malevolent" attempts to "cast aspersions" on the country's historical record and its current global standing. "Historical politics," he asserted in 2016, "should be conducted by the Polish state as an element of the construction of our international position."[21] Yet by trying to expunge all the unpleasant aspects of Poland's treatment of Jews from public memory, Duda undermined what he was trying to achieve and gave the impression that his goal was to sanitize history, not clarify it.

POLAND'S RECKONING WITH THE COMMUNIST PAST

Elite political agendas have also been salient in retrospective debates about Poland's communist past. In Poland, unlike in East Germany and Czechoslovakia, the end of communism came relatively gradually through negotiations between Solidarity and the communist regime at the Round Table talks of February–April 1989. The negotiated nature of the transition induced Solidarity to agree to important compromises in exchange for the formation of a noncommunist government led by Tadeusz Mazowiecki in August 1989. In particular, Solidarity allowed General Wojciech Jaruzelski, the long-time political and military ruler, to remain as president, and General Czesław Kiszczak to remain in charge of the Ministry of Internal Affairs.

Ensconced in those posts over the next several months, Jaruzelski and Kiszczak secretly allowed the removal and destruction of some communist-era files, including state security records. By mid-1990, after Kiszczak and Jaruzelski had been removed from government positions, rumors were circulating that the most incriminating materials had been destroyed and counterfeit docu-ments had been planted.[22] These allegations were exaggerated or false, but destruction of secret police records and other sensitive documents definitely occurred. Conclusive evidence surfaced in February 2016 that when Kiszczak left office in 1990 he took with him numerous highly classified documents and stored them at his home illegally until his death in November 2015.[23] The disclosure that he took these sensitive materials has trammeled even the sincerest of efforts in Poland to reckon with the communist past.

The hardships of the transition fueled a perception that the Round Table had been merely a conspiracy among elites to maintain an inequitable power struc-ture. Many Poles felt that communist elites had used their influence to acquire economic assets that enabled them to live in luxury and to remain dominant in the postcommunist society.[24] Unfortunately, historical memory about the Round Table has often been skewed for political reasons, generating acrimoni-ous debate that sheds little light on the events themselves and gets bogged down in conspiracy theories. Generational change has not helped, in part because the political polarization has converted debates about historical matters into thinly veiled political battles, especially since PiS has been in power.

The most contentious debates about historical memory of Polish com-munism have focused on the role of two important individuals who were on opposite sides in 1980–1: General Jaruzelski and Lech Wałęsa. Was Jaruzelski (who died in 2015) a hero or a traitor? Legal proceedings were under way against Jaruzelski from the early 1990s on for his role in the shootings of work-ers on Poland's Baltic coast in 1970 and the imposition of martial law in 1981. Although the latter charges against him were put on hold in 1996 by a left-wing parliament, they were reinstated in 2005 and remained in place until his death.

Until 1991, Jaruzelski denied that the Soviet Union had intended to invade Poland in 1981, but as soon as the Soviet Union ceased to exist, he repeatedly insisted that he had had no choice but to impose martial law as the "lesser of two evils," that is, as an alternative to a Soviet invasion and military occupation of Poland. He acquired prominent defenders from the ranks of those he once strenuously opposed, notably Adam Michnik, the former dissident intellec-tual. Jaruzelski also had plenty of detractors, some of whom have claimed that Soviet troops would not have dared to invade Poland in 1981 and that Jaruzelski imposed martial law simply to establish a militarized form of communist rule and resist any genuine compromise with Solidarity and the Catholic Church. This debate has been unsatisfactory, in part because these extreme positions have been unconvincing.[25]

Jaruzelski's claims that he acted under enormous Soviet pressure are cer-tainly true. The Soviet Union deployed many divisions of combat-ready troops around Poland's borders, conducted conspicuous Warsaw Pact and bilateral military exercises, informed Polish officials that elaborate plans had been drawn up for a Soviet-led invasion, undertook reconnaissance to carry out those plans, and made vehement exhortations through bilateral and multilateral channels. These various actions, in combination, might well have caused Jaruzelski to fear that Soviet troops would invade Poland unless he imposed martial law. Whether Soviet leaders actually *intended* to invade is a very different matter. But regardless of what Soviet intentions truly were, the key point to bear in mind is that Jaruzelski and other senior Polish officials in 1980 and 1981 were not privy to the internal deliberations of the Soviet Politburo and could never be fully certain about Soviet intentions. Hence, Jaruzelski might have genuinely believed that an invasion would take place if a solution "from within" Poland did not materialize.

Jaruzelski's memoirs accurately depict the excruciating pressure he faced from the Soviet Union, but his account omits a crucial matter: as the decisive moment for the imposition of martial law approached in December 1981, he repeatedly urged Moscow to send Soviet troops into Poland to bail him out. Jaruzelski was appointed head of the Polish United Workers' Party (the Communist party) because Soviet leaders believed he would willingly comply with their demands for a crackdown. Jaruzelski promptly moved ahead with the final preparations for the "lesser of two evils" (martial law), but he also began considering the possibility of relying on the "greater of two evils," Soviet military intervention. His overtures about this option began in October 1981 and continued, with ever greater urgency, until the day martial law was introduced. Apparently, by late 1981 Jaruzelski had come to believe that the martial law operation would be unsuccessful unless it went hand-in-hand with external military intervention.

If Jaruzelski's version of events is problematic, the notion that the Soviet Union was willing to let Poland go its own way is even more dubious. The first step the Soviet Politburo took in August 1980 was to authorize the mobilization of a sizable number of Soviet tank and mechanized infantry divisions "in case military assistance is provided to Poland."[26] From mid-1980 until the fall of 1981, Soviet leaders were fully prepared to send these divisions into Poland to help the communist regime introduce martial law. The only reason troops did not move into Poland is that whenever the Soviet Politburo stepped up its pressure and proposed the deployment to facilitate a vigorous crackdown on the Polish opposition, Polish leaders warned that it would be better if Polish forces imposed martial law on their own. If the Poles had been willing to receive external military support during this period, Soviet troops would have entered Poland to aid them in crushing Solidarity and restoring orthodox communist rule.

In short, the historical evidence reveals a nuanced picture in which Jaruzelski was neither a hero nor a villain. He was operating in a context in which heroes would not have lasted long. Many Polish scholars have published excellent, nuanced analyses of this topic, but public debates have far too often become relentlessly politicized, omitting all nuance.

Much the same is true about recent debates concerning the role of Lech Wałęsa in Polish history. Wałęsa has long been known as the founding leader of the Solidarity (Solidarność) trade union whose image scaling the shipyard fence in Gdańsk in August 1980 is still one of the best-known symbols of the Solidarity era. Wałęsa's term as Poland's first postcommunist president (1990–5) was marred by controversy and political infighting.[27] As early as 1992, rumors circulated that Wałęsa had been an informant for Poland's communist Security Service (SB). Because those allegations initially came from Antoni Macierewicz, a senior official who had been engaged in an acrimonious feud with Wałęsa, most Poles tended to discount them. The accusations tarnished Wałęsa's legacy, but his image was still decidedly positive. However, in the late 1990s, journalists and researchers claimed to have found further evidence that Wałęsa was an SB informant in the 1970s under the codename "Bolek" – charges endorsed by some of his former aides who had split with him in the 1990s. Although a Polish lustration court ruled in 2000 that Wałęsa had been falsely accused, damaging rumors persisted.[28]

The debate about Wałęsa took on a more politically charged tone after Lech Kaczyński was elected president in 2005 and his twin brother, Jarosław, became prime minister in a PiS-headed government. Lech Kaczyński had been a close aide of Wałęsa in the late 1980s and early 1990s, but they eventually had a bitter falling out.[29] As president, Kaczyński lent weight to the rumors that Wałęsa was "Bolek" and encouraged investigations of the matter by journalists and researchers, especially those associated with the IPN. In 2008, two IPN researchers, Sławomir Cenckiewicz and Piotr Gontarczyk, published a 750-page book presenting evidence from the SB archives which allegedly showed that Wałęsa had been an informant in 1970–6 and that later, as president, he sought to cover up his earlier misdeeds.[30] The evidence of Wałęsa's secret work was persuasive, but the documents also suggested that most of the information he provided to the SB was relatively innocuous. More troubling was the evidence that President Wałęsa had relied on his intelligence chief to tamper with the files – an act that was clearly illegal.

The problem with the Cenckiewicz-Gontarczyk book was not the evidence it amassed, but that it made no effort to present a balanced assessment of Wałęsa. It offered no coverage of his invaluable contribution in the 1980–1 crisis or his courageous defiance of the SB in 1982 when officials from the

agency pressured him to turn against Solidarity. Nor did the book acknowledge Wałęsa's crucial role in the Round Table talks or in forcing Jaruzelski to
accept a Solidarity-led government in the summer of 1989. Despite the one-
sided nature of the Cenckiewicz-Gontarczyk book, the controversy tarnished
Wałęsa, who continued to deny even the most persuasive evidence against
him rather than trying to respond to it as fully as possible.

By the time the IPN announced in February 2016 that Kiszczak had illegally
kept a large quantity of classified files at his home, Wałęsa had won another
court ruling against his accusers. Doubts about his integrity had steadily
mounted in the wake of the Cenckiewicz-Gontarczyk book. Hence, the IPN's
disclosure in 2016 of more than 350 pages of SB documents confirming that
Wałęsa was a paid informant in the 1970s caused less of a shock than it might
have in earlier years.[31] Full scanned images of the documents in Wałęsa's personnel and working SB files were made publicly available by the IPN. The
disclosures were seized on by rival political factions, who used Wałęsa as a
symbol in their battles. Jarosław Kaczyński and other PiS officials amplified
their earlier allegations that Wałęsa and Kiszczak colluded in 1989 in fashioning a postcommunist political order that benefited senior former communists.[32] By contrast, Donald Tusk, a critic of PiS who served as prime minister
in 2007–14, dismissed the newly discovered documents as "just a rehash" of old
allegations that "added nothing new."[33] Cenckiewicz denounced Wałęsa and
accused the IPN of mishandling the Kiszczak documents – an accusation that
seemed to be motivated more by politics than by facts.

Had the debate not been so politicized before and after the disclosure of the
Kiszczak files, Wałęsa might have done a better job of explaining his side of the
story, but one of the hazards of the politicization of historical memory is that it
induces participants on all sides to take extreme positions, shifting the discussion away from its proper focus. If Wałęsa had long ago acknowledged a link
with the SB and had explained that he was under great pressure and did his
best to keep his cooperation to a minimum, the controversy most likely would
have subsided relatively quickly with no significant damage to his reputation.
By denying all the evidence against him, he inadvertently fueled the impression that he was covering up something far worse. His failure to come to terms
with his own past laid the groundwork for the partisan attacks against him.

RUSSIA

No sooner had Stalin died in 1953 than Russians began seeking to overcome
his baleful legacy, with the first major de-Stalinization campaign launched
in 1956 by Nikita Khrushchev's secret speech and his further push on

de-Stalinization in 1961. Although Khrushchev's condemnation of Stalin was highly selective (focusing mainly on communist victims of Stalin's terror), it was enormously important in dissipating the godlike aura that had surrounded Stalin even after death. De-Stalinization ground to a halt and was even partly reversed after Khrushchev's ouster in October 1964.

Not until the late 1980s, with the glasnost-era revelations under Gorbachev, did a further drive to face up to the horrors of Stalinism begin in Soviet Russia. Soviet historians, journalists, and public commentators were allowed, for the first time, to discuss sensitive topics in Soviet history, including the Stalinist terror, the "Thaw" and de-Stalinization campaign under Khrushchev, and the stifling conformity of the Brezhnev era. By spring 1988, even foreign policy issues were coming under much harsher scrutiny.[34] Over the next few years the Soviet government acknowledged serious mistakes and misdeeds in its policies toward Czechoslovakia, Poland, and Yugoslavia. These admissions went well beyond what Khrushchev had done.

Nonetheless, the historical reassessments under Gorbachev had their limits, and nearly all of the relevant archival sources remained off-limits. This situation changed fundamentally after the Soviet Union broke apart and Yeltsin became president of an independent Russia. He was willing to facilitate a more accurate and thorough understanding of the Soviet past. Although several of the most important Soviet-era archives remained off-limits to researchers, Yeltsin partly opened numerous archives.[35] In addition, he released selected materials from the archives that were still inaccessible, especially the Presidential Archive, which houses most of the records of the Soviet Communist Party's Politburo as well as many other highly classified collections. In particular, Yeltsin declassified archival collections that Gorbachev had refused to open. Crucial documents pertaining to the Katyń massacres of 1940, the Soviet invasions of Hungary in 1956 and of Czechoslovakia in 1968, the Soviet Union and the crisis in Poland in 1980–1, the shooting down of a South Korean airliner in 1983, to name a few, often during visits by Yeltsin to the relevant countries. The declassification of archival materials thus became an instrument of Yeltsin's foreign policy, as he sought to develop friendly relations with countries like South Korea and Poland that previously had been either dominated by or hostile to the FSU.

Yeltsin also made considerable efforts to come to terms with the internal consequences of Stalinism, making vast quantities of documents available about the Gulag, the Great Famine, the purges and the Great Terror, and the mass deportations of ethnic minorities. However, whereas during the late 1980s Soviet citizens were eagerly following the latest revelations about their country's past, the climate changed after the Soviet Union broke apart in

1991. By the early 1990s, most Russian citizens had little desire to learn about unsavory aspects of communism. Even as Yeltsin released more documents in the early 1990s attesting to Stalin's depraved callousness and criminality, the Russian public barely noticed. The late Aleksandr Yakovlev, who played a central role in promoting reform under Gorbachev and then served as head of an official rehabilitation commission until his death in 2005, said that "reading all these documents about horrible crimes and atrocities and bloodshed and suffering frightens me. It frightens me that people in this country could have behaved that way. But what frightens me more is the fact that the large majority of people in [Russia] are completely indifferent to this information."[36]

Yeltsin missed an opportunity to promote a full-scale historical accounting.[37] He kept several of the most important Soviet-era archives tightly sealed, failed to ensure the systematic removal of statues and monuments glorifying the Soviet regime, and was unwilling to disband (or even scale back) the sprawling state security organs, which were just as symbolic of Stalinist terror as the SS and Gestapo were of Nazi atrocities. The USSR's State Security Committee (KGB) was reorganized in 1991, but its repressive apparatus and personnel were preserved essentially intact in post-Soviet Russia and simply renamed a few times.

Part of the problem in Russia's reckoning with Stalin's legacy is the continued presence of officials who served loyally in the Soviet Communist Party, the Soviet government, and the KGB. These officials have been averse to harsh reassessments of the past and have obstructed the release of sensitive documents that would show the Soviet regime's activities in a sinister light. Putin, for example, has repeatedly said that he profoundly regrets the demise of the Soviet Union, describing it as "the greatest geopolitical catastrophe of the twentieth century," a "catastrophe" that in his view was apparently worse than the rampant bloodshed of the two World Wars and the slaughter of untold millions under Stalin, Hitler, Mao, and the Khmer Rouge.[38] Although Putin has acknowledged that "excesses" occurred under Stalin, he has also frequently hailed the "monumental accomplishments" of the Soviet regime and Stalin. Putin also often speaks with great pride and affection about the Soviet KGB, for which he worked for sixteen years in the 1970s and 1980s. The main postcommunist successors to the KGB, the Federal Security Service (FSB) and Foreign Intelligence Service, extol the KGB's legacy in glossy publications and on their websites.[39]

The strength of the state security organs in post-Soviet Russia was vividly symbolized by the ascendance of Putin, who served as head of the FSB in the late 1990s and then became acting president in 1999 before being elected president the following year. Putin's pernicious impact on historical memory in Russia was evident in a mass survey conducted by the respected Levada Center in 2005.[40] A plurality of respondents chose Stalin as the "greatest leader" in Russia's history. Follow-on surveys over the next decade revealed similar results and widespread public misperceptions of the Stalin era.[41] The distortions became particularly acute after Putin forcibly annexed Crimea in March 2014. Most respondents were either favorable or neutral in their assessments of Stalin, and roughly 25 percent said they would "definitely" vote for Stalin if he were to come back to life and run for president.

The proclivity of Russian leaders to hark back to Soviet and Stalinist symbols and institutions has made it extremely difficult to overcome that terrible legacy. Putin has brought back some of Stalin's trappings and symbols. In May 2000, barely a month after being elected president, Putin authorized the Russian Central Bank to issue 500 special silver coins bearing Stalin's portrait to commemorate the Soviet Union's role in World War II. Days later, at a ceremony marking the fifty-fifth anniversary of the end of the war, Putin unveiled a plaque honoring "Generalissimo Iosif Vissarionovich Stalin" for his "heroic leadership." He also approved the setting up of a bust of Stalin at the Poklonnaya Gora war memorial.[42] In late 2000, he pushed for legislation to bring back the old Soviet national anthem, which had been commissioned by Stalin in 1943 and replaced by Yeltsin in 1991. The anthem was restored in January 2001 (albeit with different words), an event that Putin marked with great solemnity.[43]

When Putin was asked how he could justify the revival of such a blatant symbol of Stalinist repression, he conceded that "many people" associate the anthem with "the horrors of Stalin's prison camps," but he insisted that any such association was unjustified and the anthem should instead be linked with the "many achievements of the Soviet period in which people can take pride."[44] He returned to this theme repeatedly in later years, leaving little doubt that Stalin's transgressions were more than outweighed by his role in having converted the Soviet Union into a "great power" that "commanded the attention of the entire world."[45]

The restoration (or uninterrupted use) of conspicuous Stalinist symbols inevitably mitigates and blurs Stalin's crimes. The continued celebration of Soviet holidays in Russia, particularly the "Day of the Security Organs" on 20 December (the day the notorious Bolshevik secret police, the Cheka, were founded in 1917), conveys callousness toward the millions of victims of the internal security apparatus. Indeed, Putin in 2007 chose to award the posthumous plaque and medal to George Koval on the eve of Military Intelligence Day (5 November), another specialized holiday created by the Stalin-era Soviet government to glorify the intelligence and repressive organs.[46]

Official portrayals of Stalin changed only slightly during Medvedev's presidency (2008–12). Medvedev denounced Stalin and gave hope of a fuller reckoning with Soviet atrocities, but he did not follow up with any concrete, sustained action. In May 2009, Medvedev (with Putin's support) established a presidential commission to "counter attempts at falsifying history against Russia's interests."[47] The commission's Orwellian name had the unintended effect of implying that the Russian government would welcome historical falsifications as long as they were "beneficial to Russia's interests." The commission met repeatedly in 2009, 2010, and 2011, and for a while its formation seemed to portend a stifling clampdown on historical debate, especially regarding the two issues of greatest importance to Putin: the mass famine in Ukraine in 1932–3 and the Soviet Union's role in World War II. However, the commission's work had little concrete impact, confined largely to prolix discussions with little connection to actual history. Even so, its mere existence was a symbolic reminder of Putin's interest in fostering a historical narrative that suited his political agenda. The commission, and the possibility of resurrecting it later, thus had the potential to thwart public discussion of themes and events that could be depicted as "detrimental to Russia's interests." The disbandment of the commission in 2012 meant that it could no longer have a chilling effect on public debate, but the three years of its operation underscored the continued problems in Russia in facing up to the Soviet past.[48]

Even during the far-reaching (albeit temporary) easing of tensions between Russia and Poland after the tragic air crash in Smolensk on April 10, 2010, the Russian government refrained from pursuing a broader historical reckoning. The antifalsification commission continued to meet, and some of the earlier disingenuous assertions about the Katyń massacres (suggesting that they were perpetrated by German, not Soviet, forces) returned to Russia's official discourse.[49] The publication of a remarkable article by Sergei Karaganov in the state-sponsored *Rossiiskaya gazeta* in July 2010, denouncing Stalinism and Stalin's admirers, raised hopes anew that the Russian government would face up to the past, but those hopes proved in vain.[50] Although the theme put forth by Karaganov, a long-time establishment insider, influenced the deliberations of the Valdai Club (whose annual discussions organized by the Russian government are a show of openness and a propaganda vehicle) in September 2010, it had little resonance beyond that. Medvedev proved unwilling to push for a systematic, high-profile reckoning with the Soviet past and the construction of memorials to Stalin's victims. After the Valdai Club's discussions ended the antifalsification commission returned to its standard bromides, a trend that continued until the commission was dismantled shortly before Medvedev stepped down in 2012.[51]

Any remaining effort in Russia to come to terms with the Soviet past ended after Putin returned as president in 2012, and especially after he oversaw the forcible seizure of Crimea from Ukraine in 2014 and then fueled an insurgency in Ukraine's Donbas region. Amid a surge of tensions with the West over Russia's actions in Ukraine, Putin revived sinister rhetoric from the Stalin era, denouncing his liberal Russian critics as "national traitors," a Western "fifth column," and "foreign agents."[52] Pro-Kremlin commentators argued that measures adopted by Stalin in the 1930s to "liquidate traitors" and "uproot the fifth column" in the USSR would be appropriate today to "prevent traitors from undermining morale" and "subverting the Russian state" on behalf of "their sponsors in the West."[53] Putin's supporters who began assailing "traitors" and "fifth columnists" in Russia were often inclined to target Lev Schlossberg, Grigorii Yavlinskii, and other Jews, often in unmistakably anti-Semitic terms.[54]

The revival of Stalin-era rhetoric was accompanied by a further emphasis on Stalin's "great achievements." During the highly publicized ceremonies in 2015 commemorating the seventieth anniversary of the end of World War II, Stalin's portrait was on display and numerous speakers praised him as a "great leader in time of war," implying that Putin was playing the same role.[55] The parallels drawn between Stalin's role in World War II and Putin's role in Ukraine (and later Syria) were featured over and over in state-controlled television broadcasts.

Courageous organizations like Memorial and the International Democracy Foundation have continued to do valuable work in documenting the mass repressions of the Stalin era, but a full reckoning with the Stalinist past must encompass the whole society and polity. The change of generations has not helped. Young Russians are almost as inclined as their elders to look favorably on Stalin, and recent surveys show that most young Russians view the world in roughly the same way that Putin does – they believe that Russia is being unfairly hounded and besieged by "enemies," especially the United States, and that Russia must assert itself as a "great power" to deter "Western" "encroachments" and "prevent the world from falling under the hegemony of the West."[56]

Given these unfavorable trends, the task of facing up to the many horrors of Stalin's rule will require integrity on the part of Russian public officials committed to overcoming Stalin's invidious legacy once and for all. Far from moving in this direction, however, Putin has mostly hindered further attempts to reckon with Stalin's crimes. A museum commemorating the horrors of the Gulag opened in 2015 as a lonely exception in the trend toward obfuscation of the Soviet past. Putin has proven unwilling to "rehash the past" (the dismissive term he regularly uses).

In the absence of a fuller historical reckoning, Stalin's legacy will remain as a blight on Russia's future. The lack of a thorough reckoning with the past has had deleterious effects on the Russian population. Russians who proudly display portraits of Stalin on the streets of Moscow or lay flowers before Stalinist symbols are never chided for condoning a regime and a dictator who engaged in mass murder. On the contrary, Stalin's admirers can now purchase silver coins with his image from the Russian government. This may explain why many Russians regard Stalin as the "greatest leader" in their country's history. In Russia no outcry has emerged over the growing power and size of youth indoctrination organizations that were originally set up by Putin to forestall an orange-style revolution in Russia. These groups not only organize young people in support of Putin but also viciously belittle and threaten human rights and pro-democracy activists. They are akin to the Komsomol, the communist youth organization that indoctrinated millions of Soviet young people and prepared them for lifetime devotion to Stalin's regime.

So long as the symbols and institutions of Stalinist repression are still extant in Russia, the prospects for democracy are dim. Putin's use of these symbols and institutions on behalf of his political agenda has partly undone the imperfect progress achieved under Yeltsin. The longevity of Putin's rule means that efforts to resume historical reckoning will be even more difficult. Many Russians, especially the younger generation, will wonder why they need to reassess issues they assumed had already been settled long ago.

CONCLUSION

Former communist countries that have done the most to encourage a thorough reckoning with the crimes of the communist era have enjoyed greater stability than countries that have avoided any reappraisal of the past or have embarked on the process selectively or halfheartedly. Deep and lasting democratization in Central and Eastern Europe has made the most headway when the iniquities of the communist regimes have been publicly exposed and postcommunist leaders have unequivocally denounced the individuals who were complicit in overseeing systematic cruelty and terror. Even in countries that seemed to have become staunch democratic member-states of the European Union, such as Poland and Hungary, unresolved issues about the past have remained sore points and have contributed to recent setbacks for democratic norms. In these countries, as in Russia, a full reckoning with the past is essential to cement democratic institutions and forestall the rise of lurid conspiracy theories that play into the hands of political leaders intent on thwarting democratization.

Coming to terms with past traumas is bound to be difficult for any society, especially when the trauma was inflicted from within. In the FSU, a full historical reckoning will discomfit people. Millions of ordinary Soviet citizens were complicit in the Stalinist repressions by serving as informers or supporting the regime in other ways. In the post-Stalin era, the KGB continued to recruit millions of informants, whose identities would be disclosed if Soviet records were ever fully opened. Equally important, many powerful individuals who served the Soviet regime have a stake in keeping archives closed and forestalling a thorough historical reckoning.

Much the same is true about the Central and Eastern European countries. Although the Soviet Union imposed and propped up communism there, local elites and millions of ordinary people played crucial roles in the functioning and maintenance of the regimes. The IPN in Poland, the office of the Federal Commissioner (BStU) in Germany who supervises the former East German State Security archives, and the special COMDOS commission in Bulgaria that oversees and makes public the former State Security and military intelligence records have done invaluable work in documenting the communist-era repressions in a professional, nonpartisan manner, but it is hardly surprising that the IPN has come under political pressure during the two governments headed by the PiS (2005–7 and 2015 to the present). It is even less surprising that in Romania and the Czech Republic IPN-like institutes have often been politicized. Over time, one hopes those institutes will emulate the BStU, the IPN, and COMDOS in carrying out highly professional research and publishing huge collections of documents both as books and in digitized form on the Internet. Such activities will greatly facilitate efforts to understand and come to terms with the communist past.

Because less than thirty years has passed since the end of European communism, it is probably too early to expect that a full reckoning with communist crimes and abuses would be possible. In the Baltic countries, which have opened everything in their Soviet-era archives, the problem of coming to terms with the past pertains not to the Soviet era (which is rightly reviled) but to the Nazi period (which is often whitewashed). Until these countries face up to the horrors of *both* periods, their commendable efforts to hold people accountable for Soviet-era repressions will be perceived as selective justice. In the other Central and Eastern European countries and the FSU, historical memory of the communist period is likely to remain controversial for many years to come. Nostalgia for that era, based on a grossly selective "memory" of what communism was truly like, has been common in some quarters and is likely to remain so.

In Russia, Putin has repeatedly expressed nostalgia for the Soviet era, and public opinion polls indicate that his sentiments are widely shared. Until

Russian leaders are committed to facing up to the Soviet horrors, any attempts at historical reckoning by groups like Memorial are bound to reach only a limited segment of the population. Hence, in Russia a true coming-to-terms with Stalinist atrocities and Soviet history may have to wait another twenty years or longer. Elsewhere in the former Soviet bloc, the outlook is brighter, but the process of historical reckoning is bound to be prolonged. Although some degree of "public forgetting" and "selective memory" is inevitable, the more fully that societies come to terms with the past, the less likely it is that past events will one day come back to haunt them.[57]

Notes

1. Koval's identity as "Delmar" was first publicly disclosed by the Russian military newspaper *Krasnaya zvezda* in 2007, months after Koval died in Russia. Vladimir Lota, "Ego zvali 'Del'mar,'" *Krasnaya zvezda*, July 23, 2007, 2. Koval had been identified by name as a Soviet spy much earlier, in Aleksandr Solzhenitsyn, *V kruge pervom [In the First Circle]* (London: Flegon Press, 1968); and Lev Kopelev, *Utoli moya pechali [Ease My Sorrows]* (Ann Arbor: Ardis Press, 1981).

2. William J. Broad, "A Spy's Path: Iowa to A-Bomb to Kremlin Honor," *The New York Times*, November 12, 2007, A1, A10, available at: www.nytimes.com/2007/11/12/us/12koval.html, accessed June 22, 2017.

3. Because of space limitations, examples such as the legacies of slavery in the United States or enduring animosity in the Asian sphere over Japanese regional atrocities in the 1930s and 1940s are not discussed here, but remain highly relevant examples of the challenges many countries face in dealing with the past.

4. Jan Tomasz Gross, *Sąsiedzi: Historia zagłady żydowskiego miasteczka* (Sejny: Fundacja Pogranicze, 2000), translated as Jan Tomasz Gross, *Neighbors: The Destruction of the Jewish Community in Jedwabne, Poland* (Princeton: Princeton University Press, 2001); Jan Tomasz Gross, *Wokół Sąsiadów: Polemiki i wyjaśnienia* (Sejny: Pogranicze, 2003), which contains his responses to the furor about *Neighbors*; Jan Tomasz Gross, *Fear: Anti-Semitism in Poland After Auschwitz* (New York: Random House, 2006), published in Polish as *Strach: Antysemityzm w Polsce tuż po wojnie. Historia moralnej zapaści* (Kraków: Znak, 2008); Jan Tomasz Gross, *Złote żniwa: Rzecz o tym, co się działo na obrzeżach zagłady Żydów* (Kraków: Znak, 2011), published in English as Jan Tomasz Gross with Irena Grudzińska-Gross, *Golden Harvest: Events at the Periphery of the Holocaust* (New York: Oxford University Press, 2012).

5. Antony Polonsky and Joanna B. Michlic, eds., *The Neighbors Respond: The Controversy over the Jedwabne Massacre in Poland* (Princeton: Princeton University Press, 2009); and Andrzej Paczkowski, "Debata wokół 'Sąsiadów': Próba wstępnej typologii," *Rzeczpospolita* (Warsaw), March 24, 2001, A6, available at: http://archiwum.rp.pl/artykul/329564-Debata-wokol.html, accessed June 24, 2017.

6. Natalia Aleksiun, "Polish Historians Respond to Jedwabne," in Robert Cherry and Annamaria Orla-Bukowska, eds., *Rethinking Poles and Jews: Troubled Past, Brighter Future* (Lanham: Rowman & Littlefield, 2007), 164–88.

7. Krystyna Skarżyńska, "Zbiorowa wyobraźnia, zbiorowa wina," *Gazeta wyborcza* (Warsaw), November 24, 2000, 19; Dawid Warszawski, "Odpowiedzialność i jej brak," *Gazeta wyborcza*, December 9–10, 2000, 20–1; Jacek Korczewski, "Mord rytualny," *Wprost* (Poznań), December 10, 2000, 36–7; Dariusz Czaja, "To nie 'oni,' niestety," *Gazeta wyborcza*, December 16–17, 2000, 20–1; Andrzej Żbikowski, "Nie było rozkazu," *Rzeczpospolita* (Warsaw), January 4, 2001, A6–A7; Dawid Warszawski, "Mowa pokutna: Bez także," *Gazeta Wyborcza*, March 9, 2001, 18; and Dawid Warszawski, "Dwie Polski w Jedwabnem," *Wprost* (Poznań), July 21, 2002, 24–6.
8. Jerzy Robert Nowak, *100 kłamstw J. T. Grossa o żydowskich sąsiadach w Jedwabnem* (Warsaw: Wydawnictwo von Borowiecki, 2001); Henryk Pająk, *Jedwabne geszefty* (Lublin: Wydawnictwo Retro, 2001); Lech Z. Niekrasz, *Operacja Jedwabne – mity i fakty* (Wrocław: Nortom, 2001); Antoni Macierewicz, "Rewolucja nihilizmu," *Głos – Tygodnik katolicko-narodowy* (Warsaw), February 3, 2001, 2; Tomasz Strzembosz, "Przemilczana kolaboracja," *Rzeczpospolita*, January 27–8, 2001, A6–A7; Tomasz Strzembosz, "Inny obraz sąsiadów," *Rzeczpospolita*, March 31–April 1, 2001, A6–A7; Marek Jan Chodakiewicz, "Kłopoty z kuracją szokową," *Rzeczpospolita*, January 5, 2001, A6; Piotr Gontarczyk, "Gross kontra fakty," *Życie* (Warsaw), January 31, 2001, 4.
9. Paweł Machcewicz and Krzysztof Persak, eds., *Wokół Jedwabnego*, Vol. I: *Studia*, and Vol. II: *Dokumenty* (Warsaw: Wydawnictwo Instytutu Pamięci Narodowej, 2002). Later research resulted in higher estimates of the numbers of victims and perpetrators, bringing the tallies closer to those originally cited by Gross.
10. Łukasz Kamiński and Jan Żaryn, eds., *Wokół pogromu kieleckiego* (Warsaw: Instytut Pamięci Narodowej, 2006); Leszek Bukowski, Andrzej Jankowski, and Jan Żaryn, eds., *Wokół pogromu kieleckiego* (Warsaw: Instytut Pamięci Narodowej, 2008); Stanisław Meducki and Zenon Wrona, eds., *Antyżydowskie wydarzenia kieleckie 4 lipca 1946 roku*, 2 vols. (Kielce: Kieleckie Towarzystwo Naukowe, 1992).
11. Barbara Törnquist-Plewa, "Coming to Terms with Anti-Semitism: Jan T. Gross's Writings and the Construction of Cultural Trauma in Post-Communist Poland," *European Studies*, 30, 1 (2013): 125–50. Also the interview with Gross in Małgorzata Niemczyńska, "Antysemityzm straszny jak Stalin," *Gazeta Wyborcza*, January 24, 2008, 22.
12. Małgorzata Niemczyńska, "Żydzi nas atakują! Trzeba się bronić," *Gazeta Wyborcza*, February 11, 2008, 7.
13. Comments of participants in roundtable discussion at Deutsches Historisches Institut Warschau, in Warsaw, November 13, 2012.
14. "Internauci chcą zablokować publikację książki Grossa: Grożą bojkotem wydawnictwa," *Rzeczpospolita*, January 10, 2011, 4, available at: www.polskatimes.pl/artykul/355086,internauci-chca-zablokowac-publikacje-ksiazki-grossa-groza-bojkotem-wydawnictwa,4,id,t,nk.html, accessed June 22, 2017.
15. Joanna Podgórska, "Muzeum życia: O tym, jak powstawało Muzeum Historii Żydów Polskich, jak zostało zorganizowane i jakie niesie przesłanie, opowiada Marian Turski," *Polityka* (Warsaw), No. 43, October 22–8, 2014, 108–9; and the guidebook *1000 lat historii Żydów polskich. Miniprzewodnik po ekspozycji* (Warsaw: Muzeum Historii Żydów Polskich POLIN, 2014).
16. "Die Osteuropäer haben kein Schamgefühl," *Die Welt* (Berlin), September 14, 2015, 4.

17. Jerzy Robert Nowak, "Jak prowokator J.T. Gross odsłonił się do końca," Serwis Informacyjny BIBUŁY, October 3, 2015.

18. "Jest śledztwo w sprawie słów Jana T. Grossa – Zarzut: znieważenie narodu polskiego," *Gazeta wyborcza*, October 15, 2015, 6, available at: http://wyborcza .pl/1,75248,19025979,jest-sledztwo-w-sprawie-slow-jana-t-grossa-zarzut-zniewazenie .html, accessed June 22, 2017.

19. Adam Leszczyński, "PiS kole order prof. Jana Tomasza Grossa: I chcą mu odebrać Krzyż Kawalerski," *Gazeta wyborcza*, February 9, 2016, 3; Paweł Wroński, "Zabrać 'zdrajcy' order?," *Gazeta wyborcza*, February 11, 2016, 7.

20. "Apel do prezydenta przeciw postępowaniu ws. odebrania orderu Grossowi," Polish Press Agency, February 12, 2016; and "Prof. Gross zasłużył na ten order: Kancelaria Prezydenta chce reglamentować wolność słowa?," *Gazeta wyborcza*, February 11, 2016.

21. "Prezydent: Państwo polskie powinno realizować 'ofensywną' politykę historyczną," *Rzeczpospolita*, February 16, 2016, 4.

22. Bartłomiej Kaminski, *The Collapse of State Socialism: The Case of Poland* (Princeton: Princeton University Press, 1991); Claudia Kundigraber, *Polens Weg in die Demokratie: der Runde Tisch und der unerwartete Machtwechsel* (Göttingen: Cuvilier, 1997); and Marjorie Castle, *Triggering Communism's Collapse: Perceptions and Power in Poland's Transition* (Boulder: Rowman & Littlefield, 2003).

23. "List Czesława Kiszczaka: Dokumenty publikować po śmierci Lecha Wałęsy," *Rzeczpospolita*, February 22, 2016, 1.

24. Andrzej Stankiewicz, "Nie wierzyli w wybory, większość dziś zmieniła zdanie," *Rzeczpospolita*, June 4, 2014, 13, available at: http://archiwum.rp.pl/artykul/1244268-Nie-wierzyli-w-wybory-wiekszosc-dzis-zmienila-zdanie.html, accessed June 21, 2017.

25. Mark Kramer, "The Soviet Union, the Warsaw Pact, and the Polish Crisis of 1980–1981," in Lee Trepanier, Spasimir Domaradzki, and Jaclyn Stanke, eds., *The Solidarity Movement and Perspectives on the Last Decade of the Cold War* (Kraków: Krakowskie Towarzystwo Eduk, 2010), 27–67.

26. Mark Kramer, "'In Case Military Assistance Is Provided to Poland': Soviet Preparations for Military Contingencies, August 1980," *Cold War International History Project Bulletin* 11, Winter (1998): 102–11.

27. Raymond Taras, *Consolidating Democracy in Poland* (Boulder: Westview Press, 1996); Hubert Tworzecki, *Parties and Politics in Post-1989 Poland* (Boulder: Westview Press, 1996).

28. "Orzeczenie sędziów Sądu Apelacyjnego w Warszawie wraz z uzasadnieniem wyroku w sprawie lustracyjnej Lecha Wałęsy," Sygn. akt V AL. 26100, August 11, 2000, Warsaw.

29. Monika Nalepa, *Skeletons in the Closet: Transitional Justice in Post-Communist Europe* (New York: Cambridge University Press, 2010), 17–19.

30. Sławomir Cenckiewicz and Piotr Gontarczyk, *SB a Lech Wałęsa: Przyczynek do Biografii* (Gdańsk: Instytut Pamięci Narodowej – Komisja Ścigania Zbrodni przeciwko Narodowi Polskiemu, 2008).

31. See the IPN's periodic updates on the materials: IPN, "Informacja dotycząca udostępniania dokumentów z pakietu trzeciego i czwartego z materiałów zabezpieczonych w domu wdowy po Czesławie Kiszczaku," March 7, 2016, available

at:https://ipn.gov.pl/pl/dla-mediow/komunikaty/12235,Informacja-dotyczaca-udostep niania-dokumentow-z-pakietu-trzeciego-i-czwartego-z-.html, accessed June 21, 2017; Agnieszka Sopińska-Jaremczak, "Komunikat o przekazaniu przez prokuratora IPN dokumentów pochodzących z trzeciego i czwartego pakietu materiałów zabezpieczonych w domu wdowy po Czesławie Kiszczaku," March 3, 2016; and Agnieszka Sopińska-Jaremczak, "Komunikat w sprawie ekspertyz dokumentów dotyczących tajnego współpracownika pseudonim 'Bolek'," February 25, 2016.

32. "Macierewicz o archiwum Kiszczaka: To koniec legendy Lecha Wałęsy," *Rzeczpospolita*, February 22, 2016, 7; "Antoni Macierewicz: Lech Wałęsa? Bez wątpliwości 'Bolek'," *Rzeczpospolita*, February 18, 2016, 13; and Paweł Bravo, "'Bolek': Wygodne półprawdy," *Tygodnik Powszechny* (Kraków), No. 8 (February 18, 2016), 17, available at: www.tygodnikpowszechny.pl/bolek-wygodne-polprawdy-32429, accessed June 22, 2017.

33. "Tusk o teczkach z szafy Kiszczaka: Odgrzewana sprawa, przykra dla wizerunku," *Gazeta wyborcza*, February 18, 2016, 3.

34. This trend was initially signaled in May 1988 by the publication of Vyacheslav Dashichev, "Vostok-zapad: poisk novykh otnoshenii – O prioritetakh vneshnei politiki Sovetskogo gosudarstva," *Literaturnaya gazeta* (Moscow), 20 (May 18, 1988), 14. In December, his article was voted one of the best to have appeared in *Literaturnaya gazeta* in 1988.

35. Mark Kramer, "Archival Research in Moscow: Progress and Pitfalls," *Cold War International History Project Bulletin* 3, Fall (1993): 1, 18–39; and Mark Kramer, "Archival Policies and Historical Memory in the Post-Soviet Era," *Demokratizatsiya* 20, 3 (2012): 12–25.

36. Interview with Yakovlev, at International Democracy Foundation, Moscow, June 11, 2001.

37. Nikolai Koposov, "'The Armored Train of Memory': The Politics of History in Post-Soviet Russia," *Perspectives on History* 49, 1 (2011): 23–31; Dina Khapaeva, "Historical Memory in Post-Soviet Gothic Society," *Social Research* 76, 1 (2009): 359–94.

38. "Poslanie Prezidenta Rossii Vladimira Putina Federal'nomu sobraniyu RF: 2005 god," *Rossiiskaya gazeta* (Moscow), April 26, 2005, 1, 2–4.

39. Federal'naya sluzhba bezpopasnosti RF, *Lubyanka 2: Iz istorii otechestvennoi kontrrazvedki* (Moscow: Mosgorarkhiv, 1999).

40. The survey involved a random, nationally representative sample. Sarah E. Mendelson and Theodore P. Gerber, "Failing the Stalin Test: Russians and Their Dictator," *Foreign Affairs* 85, 1 (2006): 2–8.

41. Analiticheskii Tsentr Yuriya Levady (ATsYuL), *Opros: Rol' Stalina v istorii Rossii* (Moscow: ATsYuL, January 2016); Analiticheskii Tsentr Yuriya Levady (ATsYuL), *Opros: Stalin i ego rol' v istorii strany* (Moscow: ATsYuL, March–April 2015); Analiticheskii Tsentr Yuriya Levady (ATsYuL), , *Opros: Rol' lichnostei v istorii Rossii* (Moscow: ATsYuL, January 2015); Analiticheskii Tsentr Yuriya Levady (ATsYuL), *Opros: Otnoshenie k Stalinu v Rossii i stranakh Zakavkaz'ya* (Moscow: ATsYuL, March 2013); Analiticheskii Tsentr Yuriya Levady (ATsYuL), *Opros: Otnoshenie k lichnosti i epokhe Iosifa Stalina* (Moscow: ATsYuL, October 2014); Boris Dubin, *Rossiya nulevykh: Politicheskaya kul'tura, istoricheskaya pamyat', povsednevnaya zhizn'* (Moscow: ROSSPEN, 2011), 111, 141–54, 178–80, 209, 247; and Analiticheskii

Tsentr Yuriya Levady (ATsYuL), *Opros: Rossiyane o Staline* (Moscow: ATsYuL, March 2010).

42. "Iz zhizhni pamyatnikov: Stalin vezli na reabilitatsiyu v kovshe traktora," *Komsomol'skaya Pravda* (Moscow), June 19, 2001, 8.

43. Tat'yana Uklyuchina, "Spory po povodu slov gimna ne prekrashchayutsya," *Vremya novostei* (Moscow), February 1, 2001, 1; "Oshibaetsya li 'Putin s narodom'? Gimn i muki sovesti russkoi intelligentsii," *Nezavisimaya gazeta* (Moscow), December 6, 2000, 1; and Aleksandr Gamov, "Glavnaya pesnya o starom: Pochemu novyi Gimn Rossii tak trudno vkhodit v nashu zhizn'," *Komsomol'skaya Pravda*, January 26, 2001, 4.

44. "Vladimir Putin: Ne zhech' mostov, ne raskalyvat' obshchestvo," *Rossiiskaya gazeta*, December 6, 2000, 1.

45. Maria Lipman, Lev Gudkov, and Lasha Bakradze, *The Stalin Puzzle: Deciphering Post-Soviet Public Opinion* (Washington, DC: Carnegie Endowment for International Peace, 2013); Lev Gudkov, "Zachem Kreml' proslavlyaet Stalina," *Novoe vremya* (Moscow), April 2, 2015, 7; Igor Kharichev, "Putin i Stalin," *Ezhednevnyi zhurnal* (Moscow), May 2, 2013, Item 3.

46. On the carry-over of Soviet holidays into post-Soviet Russia, see Aleksei Makarkin, "Protivorechivye prazdniki v novoi Rossii," *Novoe Literaturnoe Obozrenie* (Moscow) 3 (2015): 13–27. Also Benjamin Forrest and Juliet Johnson, "Unraveling the Threads of History: Soviet-Era Monuments and Post-Soviet National Identity in Moscow," *Annals of the Association of American Geographers* 93, 3 (2002): 524–47.

47. "Ukaz Prezidenta Rossiiskoi Federatsii o Komissii pri Prezidente Rossiiskoi Federatsii po protivodeistviyu popytkam fal'sifikatsii istorii v ushcherb interesam Rossii," Ukaz Prezidenta RF No. 549, May 15, 2009, in *Rossiiskaya gazeta*, May 20, 2009, 2.

48. "Ukaz Prezidenta RF ot 14.02.2012 Nr. 183 'Ob utverzhdeenii sostava Komissii pri Prezidente Rossiiskoi Federatsii po formirovaniyu i podgotovke rezerva upravlencheskikh kadrov, izmenenii i priznanii utrativshimi silu utrativshimi silu nekotorykh aktov Prezidenta Rossiiskoi Federatsii,'" Ukaz Prezidenta RF No. 183, February 14, 2012, in *Sobranie zakonodatelstva Rossiiskoi Federatsii: 2012 g.* (Moscow), Vol. 8, Part III, 988.

49. Among the many vulgar distortions of the history of the Katyń massacres are "Lozh' o Katyni vskryvaetsya," *Segodnya* (Moscow), June 23, 2012, 7; Sergei Kovalev, "Vymysli i fal'sifikatsii v otsenkakh roli SSSR nakanune i s nachalom Vtoroi mirovoi voiny," mil.ru (Russian Ministry of Defense website), June 4, 2009; Arsen Martirosyan, "Kto rasstrelyal plennykh polskikh ofitserov v Katyni," *Pravda* (Moscow), April 14, 2010, 5; "Vystupleniya V. I. Ilyukhina na Plenarnom zasedanii Gosdumy pri obsuzhdenii Zayavleniya 'Pamyati zhertv Katynskoi tragedii,'" *Sovetskaya Rossiya* (Moscow), November 26, 2010, 2; and books by Yurii Mukhin, an ardent Stalinist who has made it his mission to "demonstrate" that German, not Soviet, forces killed the Polish prisoners.

50. Sergei Karaganov, "Russkaya Katyn'," *Rossiiskaya gazeta*, July 22, 2010, 3.

51. "Sostoyalos' sovmestnoe zasedanie Komissii po protivodeistviyu popytkam fal'sifikatsii istorii v ushcherb interesam Rossii i Mezhvedomstvennoi komissii po zashchite gosudarstvennoi tainy," *Rossiiskaya gazeta*, September 8, 2010, 1.

52. "Obrashchenie Prezidenta Rossiiskoi Federatsii, 18 marta 2014 goda, Moskva, Kreml'," *Rossiiskaya gazeta*, March 19, 2014, 1–2.

53. Vladimir Bushin, *Pyataya kolonna* (Moscow: Algoritm, 2014); Evgenii Shestakov, "Mir ostanovitsya vse menee prozapadnym: Nyneshnyaya amerikanskaya politika natselena na smeny rezhima v Rossii," *Rossiiskaya gazeta*, April 24, 2014, 3; Andrei Andreev, "Pyataya kolonna predatelei protiv suvereniteta Rossii," *Novoruss. info*, March 1, 2015. Also Aleksandra Samarina and Ivan Rodin, "'Fultonskaya rech'" Putina: Rossiyu ot zapada snova mozhet otdelit's zhelezhnyi zanaves," *Nezavisimaya gazeta*, March 19, 2014, 3; Valerii Vyzhutovich, "Nuzhna li Rossii gosudarstvennaya ideologiya?" *Rossiiskaya gazeta*, August 15, 2015, 5.

54. Aleksei Gorbachev, "'Natsional-predateli' v kompetentsii uchastkovykh," *Nezavisimaya gazeta*, September 1, 2014, 2.

55. Sergei Medvedev, "Prazdnik bez slez na glazakh: Chto sluchilos' s Dnem Pobedy," *Forbes.ru*, May 8, 2015; "Russia's Victory Day Celebration: Great Patriotic War, Again," *The Economist*, May 2–8, 2015, 54–5; Neil MacFarquhar, "A Parade Hailing Russia's World War II Dead and Marching Further from the West," *The New York Times*, May 8, 2015, A4, available at: www.questia.com/newspaper/1P2-39136269/a-book-for-discerning-russians-the-words-of-putin, accessed June 24, 2017; Ingo Mannteufel, "Opinion: Instrumentalizing History – Moscow and May 9," *Deutsche Welle*, May 9, 2015; "V Moskve mozhet poyavit'sya pamyatnik Stalinu: 'Otkazyvat'sya ot Stalina – znachit otkazyvat'sya ot samikh sebya," *Nakanune.ru*, February 26, 2015, Item 7; Henry Meyer, "Russia Reenacts WWII March after Putin Defends Nazi Pact," Bloomberg News wire, November 7, 2014, Item 5.

56. Analiticheskii Tsentr Yuriya Levady (ATsYuL), *Opros: Bor'ba s 'pyatoi kolonnoi' i oshchushchenie svobody v obshchestve* (Moscow: ATsYuL, December 2015); Analiticheskii Tsentr Yuriya Levady (ATsYuL), "Nastroenie molodykh rossiyan o nastupayushchem godu: Press-vypusk" (Moscow: ATsYuL, December 2011), parts 1–4; Analiticheskii Tsentr Yuriya Levady (ATsYuL), *Obshchestvennoe mnenie – 2011: Ezhegodnik* (Moscow: Levada Tsentr, 2012), 26–28.

57. On the role of "forgetting" in public memory, Vivian Bradford, *Public Forgetting: The Rhetoric and Politics of Beginning Again* (University Park: Pennsylvania State University Press, 2010).

4

Transitional Justice Attempts in Kazakhstan

Alexei Trochev

The Soviet regime left serious wounds in Kazakhstan, yet after declaring its independence in 1991 the republic chose to deal with those legacies through a very narrow transitional justice program that primarily included symbolic commemoration and inconsistent rehabilitation of victims of Stalinist crimes. This chapter is the first to overview efforts to reckon with the Soviet abuses in Kazakhstan; a country that is still engaged in its post-Soviet political, economic, and social transition. Drawing on government documents, media reports, and secondary literature, this chapter explores the ideas, interests, and institutions that have designed and carried out transitional justice for the victims of two large-scale tragedies in Soviet Kazakhstan under Stalin: the famine of 1931–3, and the purges of 1937–53.

President Nursultan Nazarbayev, who declared 31 May as the Remembrance Day of the victims in 1997, the sixty-year anniversary of the Great Purge, repeatedly said that Stalin's repression of millions of people could "not be justified in any way."[1] Yet in 2009, seven out of ten Kazakhstanis negatively viewed Stalin's purges, but only three out of ten viewed Stalin negatively.[2] Blaming Stalinism did not result in any accountability to the public. Instead, Kazakhstani rulers focused on these two recent pasts, both to respond to public demands for dealing with the Soviet past and to champion a nationalist rhetoric in order to underscore the leading role of the Kazakhs in building a multiethnic Kazakhstani nation without impeding the collective discourse about the tragic past. This chapter echoes others in this volume that tie post-Soviet transitional justice to state-led ethnic identity concerns and nation-building.

SOVIET-ERA HUMAN RIGHTS ABUSES IN KAZAKHSTAN

As with other cases presented in this volume, the history of Kazakhstan and the Kazakh people and their relationship with Russia and the Soviet Union is contested and still being rewritten as more information becomes available and current political events engender a reinterpretation of past events. Scholars noted that Kazakhs "participated more fully in the tsarist colonial system and have been better integrated into Soviet policy than other Central Asian nationalities, but the course of Kazakh-Russian relations has been neither peaceful nor without costs to both parties."[3] With this in mind, this section presents some of the history of integration and conflict between Kazakhs and colonial Russia (including the Soviet Union).

The increasingly economically intolerable Russian tsarist colonial policies in Kazakhstan, coupled with the haphazardly administered conscription of Kazakh laborers to the rear of the front lines in Western Russia, culminated in the 1916 Uprising of Kazakhs against Russia on the eve of the February Revolution in 1917. The Kazakhs failed to throw off Russian control and were punished for the uprising. The 1917 Revolution was initially greeted with enthusiasm by Kazakhs, who supported the Provisional Government. When that Government was overthrown, most Kazakhs did not support the Bolsheviks, instead setting up the Alash Orda autonomous Kazakh government. While consisting of many pro-Western officials, the government had no military force of its own to govern the vast steppe region of nomads from December 1917 to mid-1919. It thus sided with the White forces loyal to Tsar Nicholas II against the Bolsheviks. Pockets of resistance to the Bolsheviks remained across Kazakh territory, but by late 1919 most steppe regions acquiesced to the Bolsheviks.[4] In January 1920, the Alash Orda accepted Bolshevik rule, thus ending a Civil War that had divided and exhausted the Kazakhs. October 4, 1920 marked the formation of the Kazakh (initially called Kirgiz) Autonomous Socialist Soviet Republic, thereby officially bringing Kazakhstan into the fold of the Soviet Union. Some members of Alash Orda joined the Soviet republic, while others were purged.[5] The status as an autonomous republic did not protect Kazakhstan against the sweeping waves of political and economic transformations that Moscow imposed with the aim of suppressing the influence of the traditional Kazakh elites and punishing Kazakh resistance. Collectivization, nationalization, and appropriation led to thousands of refugees/victims and considerable unrest, which was met with repeated waves of repression by the Soviet regime.

Some 2.5 million individuals, or over one-third of all ethnic Kazakhs, suffered from the famine of 1931–3.[6] Olcott describes these collectivization and farm appropriation measures as Stalin's efforts to "literally starve into submission" the Kazakh people.[7] During the late 1930s, numerous Kazakh intellectuals and politicians became victims of the Great Purge and Moscow's sustained campaign to suppress Kazakh national identity and culture, traditional clan-based identity, dialects, and networks. Some 1.5 million victims, from many parts of the Soviet Union, were deported to Kazakhstan, which Stalin selected both as the site of some of the largest camps in the Gulag system (such as Karlag and Steplag), and as the "universal laboratory of the friendship of peoples."[8] Survival in those camps was extremely difficult, since the harsh living and working conditions resulted in very high death rates. In addition, over 100,000 residents of Soviet Kazakhstan were imprisoned in the camps, and 27,000 others were executed under Stalin in the 1930s and the 1940s.[9] The republic bordered the Aral Sea, where the Soviet regime tested biological weapons until 1990, and hosted the Semipalatinsk nuclear testing site, at which Soviet authorities conducted in 1949–89 a total of 456 nuclear tests that caused serious damage both to the environment and the health of 200,000 local residents.[10]

After Stalin's death in 1953, those exiled to the Kazakh SSR comprised about 1 million people or 15 percent of the republic's total population. Many of them were banned from returning to their previous places of residence, while others had nowhere to go as their homes had been destroyed or occupied by others, and their families and friendships decimated. Thus, the labor camp officials and many of those released due to mass rehabilitation and the abolition of the labor camp system launched by Nikita Khrushchev in 1956 remained in the Kazakh lands, mostly in cities.[11]

Khrushchev's de-Stalinization did not gain much support in Soviet Kazakhstan.[12] Those charged with anti-Soviet crimes and released from camps were banned from disclosing their conviction for twenty-five years. The names of several denouncers and prosecutors who purged famous Kazakhs were revealed at the time. For example, in 1957, the NKVD investigator, who fabricated a criminal case against the famous Kazakh literary figure Saken Seifullin and tortured him, was deprived of his rank and awards.[13] In 1960–78, the courts rehabilitated 7,112 persons, but Kazakh intellectuals and secret police veterans blocked efforts to raise the issue of personal accountability for repression.[14]

As in other parts of the Soviet Union, the KGB set branches in and recruited secret agents from the republic, placing under surveillance dissidents and other individuals suspected of being critical of the regime, and compiling secret documents on them. This targeted persecution was also directed at loyal Soviet citizens. For example, German deportees (the third largest ethnic group in Soviet Kazakhstan) were rehabilitated in 1964. Those who called for the resurrection of the Volga German Autonomous Republic inside Soviet Russia were blacklisted, banned from contacting the Kremlin, and dismissed from jobs.[15] The Meskhetian Turk activists who lobbied for their return to Soviet Georgia from the Kazakh and Uzbek republics were also blacklisted and imprisoned for anti-Soviet activity.[16] Some of the KGB secret files put together in Kazakhstan were probably transferred to Moscow before the collapse of the Soviet Union.

When Mikhail Gorbachev became Soviet leader in 1985, decades of Sovietization and Russification meant that ethnic Kazakhs amounted only to 40 percent of the 16.5 million citizens living in the Kazakh SSR. Russians represented the second largest group (38 percent).[17] Yet ethnic Kazakhs held more leading positions in the Communist Party, the administration and the Soviets, thanks to the careful cadre policy of the long-time Kazakh leader Dinmukhamed Kunayev, in power since 1964. Gorbachev was set on dismissing and prosecuting Kunayev and his circle for inefficiency, nepotism, and bribe-taking, but high-ranking investigators dispatched from Moscow failed to uncover Kunayev's criminal activities. He resigned in December 1986 and the Kremlin appointed Gennadii Kolbin, an ethnic Russian, in his stead. This act provoked violent student riots in the Kazakh capital of Alma-Ata, the first sign of ethnic strife under Gorbachev. Kolbin saw his appointment to leadership in the republic as a launching pad for further promotion in the Kremlin, and acted hand in hand with Kazakh Premier Nursultan Nazarbayev to purge the rioters and dismiss many of Kunayev's cadres. Moreover, Kolbin took populist actions like promising half-a-million apartments, improving healthcare facilities and meat distribution to the public, and spreading Kazakh-language education and culture.[18]

In response, starting in early 1988, Kazakh intelligentsia used Gorbachev's *glasnost* to criticize Kolbin, framing the December 1986 riots as the failure of the Soviet nationalities policy, and demanding rehabilitation of Kazakh writers and scholars formerly purged by the Bolsheviks, including the Alash Orda leaders.[19] In mid-1989, Gorbachev faced the threat of a Union-level parliamentary commission investigating the 1986 riots (on top of the inquiry commission of the April 1989 clashes in Tbilisi), and well-organized interethnic violent riots and rallies in Kazakh cities. He replaced Kolbin with Nazarbayev, who promptly approved the Kazakh parliamentary investigation of the Alma-Ata riots by a 14-member commission. But local officials endorsed only a few of Gorbachev's de-Stalinization attempts – the ones that victimized famous Kazakh and Soviet figures – despite the burgeoning public debates about the unknown victims of Stalinist terror.

In 1991, the collapse of the communist regime took Kazakhstan by surprise. The republic was the last one to declare independence and break with the Soviet Union, further hinting at its complicated relationship with Russia. Nazarbayev, the First Secretary of the Communist Party, won the presidential elections of December 1991. After becoming president Nazarbayev resigned as Communist Party chairman, and has remained the country's leader as of the

writing of this chapter. Since 1995, the bicameral Parliament has been dominated by political parties sympathetic to the president. To date, Kazakhstan
has been unable to effect full democratization, break with its Soviet past, or
achieve accountability for communist-era human rights violations.

Since 1991 Kazakhstan has made only a handful of largely symbolic attempts
to address the human rights abuses committed by the Soviet regime. Most of
these official attempts blamed the Stalinist regime without considering the
responsibility of individual perpetrators, focusing instead on commemoration
measures, such as renaming public places, building monuments, and rehabilitating victims of the famine of 1931–3 as well as the victims of the deportations and purges of 1937–52. Other reckoning attempts have focused on the
Alash-Orda leaders of 1917–20, and the riots in Alma-Ata of December 1986.
As in other post-Soviet republics (Moldova, Lithuania, and Belarus, examined
in this volume), much less attention has been given to reckoning with the
abuses perpetrated during other time periods, including the vast surveillance
program conducted by the KGB, with the help of local Kazakhs, until the very
last days of Soviet rule.

The Kazakhstani authorities have kept most of the remaining secret police
archives classified, and have taken no measures against the individual perpetrators who conducted the Stalinist purges or collaborated secretly with the
KGB. The first KGB chief of independent Kazakhstan began his career in
the Soviet KGB in 1973, while his successors began in 1963, 1972, and 1979.
There is a disinclination to punish past actions, so even if Soviet-era secret
police officers and informers have been publicly identified, they faced no
trials. In addition, no lustration has been legislated and no court trials have
been launched against communist officials, prison guards, or secret agents. On
the contrary, in 1989, when journalist Ekaterina Kuznetsova published interviews with former Gulag officials still holding prestigious posts, a widow of one
of them successfully sued Kuznetsova for libel in 1991.[20] State and nonstate
actors have supported no broad truth-seeking projects, and the authorities have
rejected the restitution of property abusively confiscated by the Soviet regime.

There have been personnel changes, but not as part of an intentional transitional justice program. Instead, the nationalities policy promoted by post-
Soviet Kazakhstan and the massive emigration of ethnic Russians during the
1990s amounted to a spontaneous lustration, which allowed ethnic Kazakhs
to replace Russians in prestigious positions. This elite replacement has been
seen as a substitute for true legal accountability for the abuses associated with
Russian domination during precommunist and communist times. At the same
time, the Kazakhstani government has permitted rehabilitation, compensation, and memorialization of victims of Stalinism, and has glorified their

memory in museums, monuments, and mass burial sites. Kazakhstan has also encouraged the repatriation of ethnic Kazakhs living abroad, whose ancestors fled the homeland during the 1920s–30s. As a result, in 2016 ethnic Kazakhs accounted for over 66 percent of the total population, whereas Russians represented 20 percent.[21] These informal bureaucratic change processes, together with diverging birth rates, have resulted in significant demographic shifts in postindependence Kazakhstan.

The continuity of the Soviet-era leadership after 1991 explains these narrow transitional justice programs. In contrast, the anti-Soviet presidents of Georgia and Ukraine opened some Communist Party and KGB archives, launched museums dedicated to Soviet-era victims, and attempted to conduct official lustration programs (see the chapters authored by Robert Austin and Cynthia Horne in this volume). Both Kazakhstan and Ukraine greatly suffered from the famine of the 1930s, but they have dealt with this blight on the past differently. Whereas Ukraine declared the famine a genocide and opened (but quickly closed) a criminal case against Stalin and his inner circle (see Lavinia Stan's chapter in this volume), Kazakh leaders used the word "genocide" to characterize that set of human rights abuses only for a short period of time, and did not bring perpetrators to justice. Instead, they largely gave in to pressure from Moscow and the demands from below to refrain from resolute reckoning programs. This explains the choice of rehabilitating only selected victims, and the visibility and sequencing of commemorations.

The adoption of transitional justice has largely depended on the degree of control that the Kazakh government officials could exercise over them.[22] We know from other countries that transitional justice measures are more likely when leaders have already consolidated their power and then introduce accountability mechanisms.[23] Having learned from Gorbachev's failure to rein in societal forces empowered by his reforms, Yeltsin's unproductive rivalry with the Russian Parliament, and transitional justice examples from other countries, Kazakh rulers tried to control transitional justice tightly. They adopted or abandoned reckoning policies in such a way as to gain political capital and improve their reputation at home and/or abroad. Their calculations did not guarantee that these policies' implementation would be smooth or complete, thus, showing dissension within the ruling regime, within society, and between the state and society.

REHABILITATING AND COMMEMORATING THE FAMINE VICTIMS

According to Sarah Cameron, Stalin's "brutal collectivization campaign, compounded on the ground by local cadres, and magnified by longer term changes that made Kazakhs far more dependent on grain and vulnerable to hunger" brought about the famine of 1931–3, during which 1.5 million people perished and another million fled from Soviet Kazakhstan.[24] As a result, ethnic Kazakhs became a minority in the republic (amounting to only 38 percent of the population) and regained the slim majority only in 1990. The Soviet authorities and historians kept the famine (Asharshylyk, in Kazakh) secret and rarely mentioned "certain difficulties with food provision" in the republic. After the end of the World War II, in Balkhash town one street was called Hungry and was built by starving Kazakhs. In 1956, Khrushchev rehabilitated a "true Leninist" and "amazing organizer" Filipp Goloshchekin, who launched and led collectivization in the republic and was executed by Stalin in 1941. That rehabilitation fortified Kazakh rejection of the de-Stalinization campaign mentioned above. A few publications talked about the famine during the late 1980s. Finally, in May 1990 the publication of 50,000 copies of Vladimir Mikhailov's 200-page book in Russian on the famine spurred public interest in this previously forbidden page of history.[25]

In November 1991, acting on requests from historians and civil society activists, the Presidium of the Kazakh Supreme Soviet (equivalent to the parliament) formed an investigative commission to examine the causes of the famine. The commission consisted of legislators, civil society activists, historians, chief editors, and chief law-enforcement officials, who were included to gain access to the secret archives. It examined secret government and party documents, official statistical materials kept on the territory of the Kazakhstan, and witness testimonies. After twelve months of extensive work, in late 1992 the commission was the first to state that based on preliminary historical evidence, on moral grounds, and on its interpretation of the 1948 United Nations Convention on the Prevention and Punishment of the Crime of Genocide, this unprecedented man-made catastrophe amounted to genocide against ethnic Kazakhs and other ethnic groups by the Soviet Kazakh leaders and local officials.[26]

This official recognition of multiethnic genocide victims and the inclusion of the local Kazakh officials as perpetrators departs from Evgeny Finkel's "search for lost genocides." According to him, leaders of states with little or no independence have used the "genocide victim" status of their nations "to brush aside demands to confront injustices and crimes committed by members of the 'suffering nation'."[27] President Nazarbayev chose not to use the word "genocide" and urged citizens to remember yet "depoliticize" the famine in official speeches remembering its victims.[28] While investigating the terror against the rich peasants, the brutal collectivization, the transformation of Kazakh villages, the revolts of the peasants, and their exodus to Russia and

other Soviet republics, the commission also discovered materials documenting the repression of other social groups, which it recognized as a state crime
perpetrated by the Kazakh Republican Communist Party leaders against its
own people.

The commission invoked moral arguments and universally accepted rules
of international law when asking the Supreme Soviet to annul and denounce
the government acts adopted in 1932–3, and recognize the victims of the
famine and collectivization campaigns, as well as the deportees, as victims
of political repression. Such recognition would have automatically triggered
rehabilitation. The commission also asked the Main Archival Department of
the Government of Kazakhstan, the KGB and the MVD to offer researchers
wide access to their archives, and requested the Ministries of Sciences and
Education to fund research in these archives as well as prepare teaching materials for use in high schools and universities.[29] The Supreme Soviet approved
the commission's report, which was published in 1992 in both Kazakh and
Russian in four official newspapers. Historians still debate the accuracy of
the figures on famine victims presented in the report, showing that history
remains contested in Kazakhstan, as in other FSU states.[30] Around the same
time, Mikhailov's book about the famine was translated into Kazakh and published in 5,000 copies without government support. The Kazakh-language
film based on this book was banned from wide circulation in cinemas.[31]

Reacting to the report and pressure from local civil society groups, the
government promised to erect a monument to famine victims in the capital city of Almaty. A black memorial stone was laid in a small park near the
former NKVD headquarters to mark the location of the proposed monument. However, after the capital was relocated to Astana, the government
lost interest in building the monument. In August 2014, the residents of the
apartment blocks surrounding the park proposed to move the black memorial
stone outside of Almaty under the pretext that it blocked their promenades
with children and that monuments devoted to tragedies should not be placed
within the city limits.[32] Two years later, the Almaty mayor launched a contest
to design the monument, and it was finally unveiled on May 31, 2017.[33] This
example highlights the challenges associated with implementing even symbolic accountability measures.

In November 2003, twenty-six states, including Kazakhstan, Russia, and
Ukraine, adopted the UN Joint Statement on the Great Famine of 1932–3
in Ukraine (Holodomor) that commemorated "the memory of millions
of Russians, Kazakhs and representatives of other nationalities who died of
starvation in the Volga River region, Northern Caucasus, Kazakhstan and in
other parts of the former Soviet Union, as a result of civil war and forced

collectivization, leaving deep scars in the consciousness of future generations" and called on the member states "to pay tribute to the memory of those
who perished during that tragic period of history."[34] Hinting at societal divisions regarding how to interpret the past, in April 2009, a public opinion poll
revealed that most Kazakhs positively viewed the collectivization campaign
and the sedentarization of Kazakh nomads in the 1920s–30s.[35] On May 31, 2012,
the eightieth anniversary of the famine, President Nazarbayev unveiled the
monument to famine victims in Astana. He also declared that day, which had
been designated as the Day of the Remembrance of the Victims of Political
Repressions since 1997, to be also known as the Day of Remembrance of the
Victims of the Famine.[36] A similar monument sponsored by the provincial
government was unveiled in the city of Pavlodar. Monuments honoring the
famine victims, but paid for by nongovernment actors, were erected in the
South Kazakhstan Province and near Balkhash city.[37]

In addition to commemorating the famine victims, the Kazakh authorities pledged to bring back the descendants of Kazakh citizens who fled the
republic during Soviet times. Article 7 of the December 1991 Law on State
Independence read that "for all Kazakhs who were forced to leave the territory
of the Republic and live in other states, the right to citizenship of the Republic
of Kazakhstan shall remain alongside with citizenships of other states, unless
it conflicts with the laws of the State that granted the citizenship." Yet dual citizenship was not allowed for other ethnic groups, including Russians. The article further stipulated that Kazakhstan "shall create conditions for the return
to its territory of persons forced to leave the Republic during the period of
mass repression, forced collectivization, as a result of other hostile political
actions, as well as for Kazakhs living in the territories of former Soviet republics and their descendants."[38] According to official figures, close to 1 million
persons repatriated to Kazakhstan since 1991; 5 million ethnic Kazakhs still live
outside of the republic.[39]

After passing the law, the government actively supported repatriation by
offering free transportation, affordable housing, and other incentives. Officials
then proudly reported that the diasporas of other Central Asian nations envied
the Kazakhs who were returning to their historic homeland. Yet, by the mid-
2000s, the returnees faced a number of financial, social, and linguistic barriers.
Moreover, after the 2011 oil worker riots in the Western regions of Kazakhstan,
the authorities began to blame the expatriates for crimes and social tension.[40]
The state-controlled media featured repatriates who were leaving Kazakhstan
because they failed to adapt to local conditions. These reports generated
generalized public animosity toward repatriates.[41]

In sum, the Kazakhstani central and local officials have tried to control the discourse and practice of commemorating and rehabilitating the famine victims, and the repatriation of their descendants. While the work of the investigative parliamentary commission condemned the man-made famine, the government prioritized repatriation, a much more expensive and labor-intensive policy than official condemnation. In 2012, twenty years after the commission published its findings, Kazakh leaders recognized the remembrance national holiday, erected the monument in Astana, and urged individuals not to politicize the famine – clearly trying to control and limit the public discourse about this tragedy. Not declaring the day of remembrance for famine victims as a day separate from the day of remembrance of victims of political repressions helps to hide the famine from the public discourse and from the Kremlin's watchful eye.[42]

COMMEMORATION AND REHABILITATION
OF THE VICTIMS OF STALIN'S PURGES

Kazakhstan's approach to recognizing the victims of Stalin's terror has differed from its efforts to memorialize the victims of the famine in several respects. First, rehabilitation of former victims began during the Soviet period, first under Khrushchev, and then under Gorbachev. These programs enabled the Kazakhstani officials and the local civil society activists to reenact the Soviet-era practices of interacting with and rehabilitating the victims. No similar practices were pursued for the famine victims, who by contrast faced outright denials. Second, the identities of most victims of Stalin's purges were documented on paper in specific locations (prisons, camps, settlements, graves), but those who starved to death in undetermined locations left little or no paper trail. Third, regardless of the attempts to glorify Stalin and portray his purges as necessary for industrialization and for winning World War II, the post-Soviet officials in the FSU agreed that the purges were horrific. This consensus contrasts with the disparity of views on the causes of the famine and its framing as a genocide, which created fissures over if and how victims should be addressed. Fourth, the Kazakhstani authorities were able to borrow from Russia's rehabilitation policies with respect to victims of Stalinism, and implement variants in Kazakhstan. No such policy diffusion was possible with respect to the genocide because the Russian government rejected this interpretation of the famine and urged other post-Soviet states to follow suit.

Although Khrushchev's denouncement of Stalin's cult of personality did not resonate well in Soviet Kazakhstan, Gorbachev's rehabilitations, glasnost, and reexamination of Stalinist history were more popular in Kazakhstan because they provided non-Communist Party members with access to mass media and public fora.[43] In 1988, at the initiative of the head of the Kazakh Union of Writers, the Supreme Court of Kazakh SSR posthumously rehabilitated seventy-one Alash-Orda leaders and members.[44] Initially, the Alash-Orda movement enjoyed support from Lenin, but in 1920 it was banned and in 1931 its leaders were executed. Despite their rehabilitation, the fourteen-volume criminal case against them that was kept in the National Security Committee (KNB) archives was published, without government funding, only in 2011 in Kazakh and then in 2016 in Russian, once the official narrative glorifying Alash-Orda became well entrenched. Even then, the KNB did not release all documents to the researcher, who needed both numerous permissions and supervision by two KNB officers over the course of three years of studying the materials in the Almaty KNB office.[45] This procedure requiring supervision by officers for those working with documents from the KNB archives has not changed.

After the creation of public associations devoted to de-Stalinization in Moscow and riding on the wave of public dissatisfaction with the stalled de-Stalinization in the republic, in early 1989 the Alma-Ata and Karagandy branches of Memorial and Adilet, a Kazakh historical-educational nongovernmental organization, were formed. Local party officials tried to control both organizations by asking them to have monoethnic membership: Adilet for Kazakhs only, Memorial for everyone else.[46] Both organizations rejected this approach, opened membership for all ethnic groups, and agreed to cooperate efforts for opening the KGB archives, commemorating and rehabilitating the victims, and speaking in public about them and Stalin's atrocities. The Almaty-based Adilet secured the cooperation of the Almaty KGB chiefs by enlisting the support of the Soviet KGB leadership. KGB officers revealed the mass burial site of those executed in the Almaty NKVD headquarters, arranged a meeting between the former executioner and "Adilet" activists, and shared the lists of the executed persons with them.[47]

Such meetings were not without controversy. For example, in Karagandy in 1988 the provincial Communist Party committee created a commission to investigate Stalin-era political terror and appointed a former assistant procurator of the Spasskii labor camp, the so-called mass grave of Karlag. He was removed after journalist Kuznetsova complained to Moscow about his past. At a meeting of journalists and NKVD veterans, which was organized in March 1989 after several publications wrote about the labor camps, a veteran screamed that if he had the power he would have executed Kuznetsova for writing about Karlag. The scream was met with general approval by the attending veterans.[48] The widow of a veteran won the libel suit against the journalist in 1991. Reflecting upon these interactions with the former Gulag officials, in 2016 Kuznetsova argued that many officials did not believe in the immorality of their actions and sincerely believed that they had punished true enemies of the people or had simply followed orders from above.[49] In total, procurators rehabilitated 75,000 persons in 1989–93.

Reacting to demands for rehabilitation and commemoration from both the victims of Stalin's terror and their relatives, in 1993 parliament created an interdepartmental commission on declassifying government and Communist Party documents on human rights abuses and another commission on rehabilitating the victims of mass repressions and protecting their rights. These were neither truth nor reconciliation commissions. The first commission, which worked until 2006, helped to reduce bureaucratic barriers among government ministries. For example, in 1994–5 the commission declassified 119 archival documents related to Stalin's Great Purge of 1937–8 and kept them in the Presidential Archive. These documents were published in 1998, with the initials instead of the full names of informers.[50] The second commission worked until 2009. The official justification for closing down both commissions was that the government had fulfilled its duty to rehabilitate the victims of Stalin's terror. There were 350,000 rehabilitated persons registered in Kazakhstan in 2014, up from 327,000 in 2013.[51] The Kazakhstani courts recognized some persons as victims of Stalin's purges as late as 2016.

In 1993, the Law on the Rehabilitation of Victims of Massive Political Repressions, modeled on Russia's Law on Rehabilitation of 1991, was adopted.[52] The Kazakhstani law expanded the scope of the rehabilitation program by including all ethnic groups deported from other parts of the Soviet Union. By 2010, 305,000 of Kazakhstani citizens were rehabilitated as victims of Stalin terror. The procurators and the KNB rehabilitated 80 to 90 percent of all persons for being illegally punished by the Stalinist regime. Rehabilitated persons can claim monetary compensation and nonmonetary benefits, and here bureaucratic resistance to rehabilitation played a role. Some 19,000 Soviet Koreans deported to Kazakhstan from the Russian Far East without any resettlement records had to ask the Supreme Court for recognition as victims of mass repressions.[53] The law made children ineligible for rehabilitation because the social protection officials demanded documents showing the exact dates of imprisonment, exile, and resettlement from the labor camp administration. These documents never mentioned deported, exiled, resettled, or imprisoned children. Kazakh children who had lost to Stalinist terror only one parent or had been taken care of by their relatives after their parents perished were ineligible for rehabilitation because they had no documents from the labor camp administration.[54] As a result, until 1998, the 12,000 children of the purged Kazakhs were ineligible for rehabilitation.

Still, obtaining the status of a rehabilitated person was easier than obtaining the ensuing material benefits. Citing financial hardship, in 1994 and 1999 President Nazarbayev suspended payments and subsidies to the rehabilitated victims of mass repressions. In 2003, the Ministry of Social Protection still claimed that the 1993 law covered only the victims rehabilitated prior to the entry in force of that law. After complaints from the Human Rights Ombudsman and victims to the central government, the Ministry of Social Protection made payments to the victims rehabilitated before and after 1993. Still, the Finance Ministry often failed to disburse funds to the Ministry of Social Protection to pay meager compensation to the victims of Stalinism: 8 USD per month and a one-time payment of 400 USD to each eligible victim.[55]

In total, Kazakhstan paid 10.7 billion tenge to victims in 2003–15, and planned to make payments of a billion tenge in 2016. Some 35,793 persons or 10 percent of all those rehabilitated received a monthly payment of 2,121 tenge (11 USD) as of May 1, 2015, and 35,325 persons as of May 1, 2016, showing an overall declining trend.[56] Local governments have the power to offer additional compensation to Stalin's victims, and usually offer it on 31 May, the Remembrance Day. These amounts, which vary greatly from locality to locality, are always below the amounts paid out to the veterans of World War II and the Soviet invasion in Afghanistan, the victims of the radioactive contamination, and the Chernobyl clean-up workers. For example, in May 2015, the authorities of the Zhambyl district of the North-Kazakhstan Province disbursed 398,000 tenge to forty-three victims, which was less than one-third of the payment made that year to forty-three veterans of the war in Afghanistan. The authorities of the Akzhar district in the same province distributed 71,400 tenge to twelve victims, while 199 victims living in the Glubokoe district of the East Kazakhstan Province received 3,000 tenge each from their local government.[57]

In contrast to those collectively deported, most victims of the Stalinist purges who were charged with crimes had their cases documented by camps, prisons, or troikas (the three-person extrajudicial tribunals). These written documents have remained in the government archives. Memorial and Adilet, in cooperation with the state archives, struggled to declassify these documents and to make public the identity of individual victims. Using the lists of victims provided by the Almaty KGB and the archivists, they created an electronic database of the victims (hosted by the Memorial in Moscow), and published fourteen "Books of Grief" or "Books of Memory" (one for each province of Kazakhstan) with the names of 146,500 Kazakhstanis victimized after 1921.[58] In 2016, the Kazakhstani MVD opened its own online electronic database of victims, searchable by name, based on the KGB archives, in effect, replicating the Memorial database of Stalin's victims.

In April 1992, the KNB signed information exchange agreements with Russia's Ministry of State Security and Ukraine's State Security Service. In the 1990s, the KNB provided the lists of purged persons to all FSU republics and other countries whose citizens perished in the labor camps in the Kazakh SSR. President Nazarbayev personally handed over the lists of victims to Lithuanian and Latvian leaders in 2001 and 2004.[59] During his visit to the United States in 1999, at the meeting with the presidents of major Jewish organizations, Nazarbayev gave the Lubavitcher Library in Brooklyn three binders of files the KGB had compiled on Levi Yitzchak Schneerson. He was the chief rabbi of the Ukrainian city of Dnepropetrovsk for thirty years before he was arrested by the Soviet police in 1939, sentenced to five years of internal exile in the desolate Kazakh village of Chiili, and died in Alma-Ata shortly after his release in 1944. The files, assembled from the secret police archives of Russia, Ukraine, and Kazakhstan, included Schneerson's death certificate, his arrest warrant, and records of his interrogations during his imprisonment and exile. According to Nazarbayev, these files proved "how oddly the totalitarian regime worked and how senseless was the killing of innocent people."[60]

To be sure, state authorities, including the KNB, control which materials are declassified and for which purpose, and many archival documents remain secret.[61] The KNB and the MVD publicly release only names of victims and decisions made against them. They allow relatives to see and to make copies of personal documents that relate only to the victims and do not mention names of other persons, thus, making most files inaccessible. Scholars who want to work in the archives related to Stalin's repressions must obtain clearance from the central government. On May 31, 2016, the National Archive of Kazakhstan organized a week-long exhibition dedicated to famous Kazakhs executed on Stalin's orders, but the exhibited documents were kept under glass and locked so that visitors could not read them because they were still classified "top secret."[62] The archive officials could not explain why the documents remained top secret when visitors could see their title pages. The release of the online database of 41,000 NKVD officers, including 1,000 who served in Soviet Kazakhstan, by the Moscow-based Memorial in November 2016 did not generate broad public discussion in Kazakhstan.[63]

Declassified documents have been published or presented in museums across the country. Kazakhstan's very first Museum for Victims of Political Repressions, founded in Shymkent city in 2001, consists of two halls and is located 80 miles away from the Staryi Ikan village, where residents proudly preserved the only monument to Stalin remaining in Kazakhstan against the wishes of the mayor.[64] The two largest museums dedicated to the victims of Stalinism are located on the sites of former labor camps: the Karlag museum in the Dolinka village, 40 km from Karagandy, and the ALZHIR museum on the site of the demolished Akmolinsk camp for the wives of the "traitors of the motherland" in the Akkol village 30 km from Astana.[65] President Nazarbayev ordered the creation of both museums at the incessant lobbying of local activists, but bureaucratic resistance delayed the start of the museums.[66] The Dolinka mayor, Karagandy activists and historians preserved the abandoned Karlag building from looters in the 1990s after having persuaded the local authorities to expropriate the building.[67] The governor of Karagandy Province approved the Karlag museum in February 2002, but the mayor of Shakhtinsk town, to which Dolinka belongs, allocated only 1 million tenge for the museum.

Initially, the Karlag museum, which opened in 2005, was housed in ten rooms of the better preserved former hospital for labor camp employees. In 2011, at the cost of 238 million tenge it moved to the renovated building of the Karlag headquarters with the torture chambers, underground cells and execution rooms.[68] According to journalist Kuznetsova, the deputy governor insisted on making installations more frightening, which was attractive for tourists yet far from historically accurate – cells, interrogation and execution rooms were located in another (already demolished) building.[69] Local authorities allowed the Memorial and Adilet activists as well as Karagandy branch of the Association of Victims of Political Repressions to set up the Public Council of the Karlag museum, but made sure that activists were not directly involved in the museum administration. In 2016, Karlag museum workers complained about the lack of funds for renovations. They also hoped to organize meetings between the 7,000 victims of repression who received state subsidies in the Karagandy province and museum visitors in order to increase the number of museum visits.[70] According to the Shakhtinsk mayor, over 15,000 visitors came to Karlag museum, 10,000 visitors in the first half of 2014.[71]

In addition, Memorial and Adilet tirelessly lobbied the Kazakh government to convert the former NKVD headquarters in Almaty, the place of actual executions of "enemies of the people," into a museum dedicated to the victims of purges. They succeeded in 2004, when the Almaty mayor Viktor Khrapunov allocated two rooms in that building to the museum. Unlike the ALZHIR museum, constructed under the personal patronage of President Nazarbayev, the Almaty museum of the victims of political repressions was funded from voluntary donations from the victims' relatives, activists, and researchers. In 2006, Mayor Khrapunov sold the building to a commercial bank and moved the museum to the Almaty City Museum. As a result, the exhibition about the victims of Stalin's repressions was placed in storage, making it unavailable to visitors. Relatives of victims have demanded a new location for the museum, to no avail, although such demands have received some support from the public.[72]

In sum, the commemoration and rehabilitation of the victims of Stalin's repression began during Soviet times and has been continued by the post-Soviet Kazakh authorities with varying speed across the country. These are less risky policies for politicians because they replace the risk of being held accountable for past atrocities with glorifying the victims. This is why they began early and they have steadily continued in Kazakhstan. These initiatives – opening archives, setting up museums, erecting monuments, deciding the legal status of the applicant, paying compensation – are under the control of the executive branch, and depend on the discretion of bureaucrats.

CONCLUSION

As the chapter suggests, transitional justice implemented in Kazakhstan has been limited in scope, mostly because of the incomplete break with the communist past effected in 1991. The reproduction of the communist elites, who retained their positions of power and influence after independence, has meant that more radical and resolute reckoning programs such as lustration or court trials were never seriously debated. In addition, transitional justice in the republic has been represented by mostly elite-driven projects, sometimes half-hearted and quickly abandoned, short-term and symbolic, or reactive to civil society demands. The official blaming of the Stalinist regime without naming individuals responsible for past abuses has allowed great flexibility in terms of adopting symbolic transitional justice. The new post-Soviet rulers have used the rehabilitation campaigns to gain political capital by presenting their nations as victims of Soviet rule rather than seeking the truth, improving accountability, and offering meaningful compensation to victims and/or their surviving relatives. Compensation packages offered for physical and moral harm have been largely symbolic. Political expedience and the shadow of Russia determined the scope, sequence, and timing of the transitional justice policies in Kazakhstan.

Two civil society organizations have been at the forefront of the transitional justice effort, without drawing much support from the general population. This is surprising, since Kazakhstan registered high numbers of victims during Soviet times. Perhaps the nation has focused on the more remote Stalinist crimes because it could point the finger to foreign (Russian) perpetrators and thus underscore its victim status. By contrast, the more recent crime of mass surveillance has been largely ignored for fear of dividing the nation, since those crimes involved some Kazakh nationals as secret agents and informers.

Equally important has been the fact that for many in Kazakhstan, late communism was a period of relative stability and order, whereas postcommunism, especially the 1990s, has been a period of decreased living standards. All in all, the political elites, the civil society activists, and the general population have apparently instrumentalized the communist past in various ways at various times after 1991, rendering transitional justice a largely symbolic and rather delayed process.

Notes

1. Zhanat Kundakbayeva and Didar Kassymova, "Remembering and Forgetting: The State Policy of Memorializing Stalin's Repression in Post-Soviet Kazakhstan," *Nationalities Papers* 44, 4 (2006):611–27.
2. Eurasian Monitor, "EM-11: Public Perception of Youth and the New Independent States of the History of Soviet and Post-Soviet Periods," *Analytical Report: Eurasian Monitor*, August (2009), available at: www.eurasiamonitor.org/rus/research/event-162.html, accessed May 6, 2017.
3. Martha Brill Olcott, *The Kazakhs*, 2nd ed. (Stanford: Hoover Institution Press, 1995), xxi.
4. Uyama Tomohiko, "Two Attempts at Building a Qazaq State: The Revolt of 1916 and the Alash Movement," *Dudoignon and Komatsu, Islam in Politics* 3 (2013): 77–98.
5. Dina Amanzholova, "Казахская автономия: от замысла националов к самоопределению по-советски [Kazakh Autonomy: From the Idea of Nationalists to Self-Determination Soviet-Style]," *Acta Slavica Iaponica* 21 (2004): 115–43.
6. Niccolo Pianciola, "The Collectivisation Famine in Kazakhstan, 1931–33," *Harvard Ukrainian Studies* 25, 3–4 (2001): 237–51.
7. Olcott, *The Kazakhs*, xxii.
8. Aleksandr Solzhenitsyn, *The Gulag Archipelago* (Paris: Éditions du Seuil, 1973); Steven Barnes, *Death and Redemption* (Princeton: Princeton University Press, 2011); Sattar Kaziev, "Soviet Nationality Policy and Problems of Trust in Interethnic Relations in Kazakhstan (1917–1991)," PhD Dissertation (Moscow, 2015), 16, 423.
9. Svetlana Eleukhanova, "Istoriia Karlaga: okhrana rezhim i usloviia soderzhaniia." Avtoreferat dissertatsii na soiskanie uchenoi stepeni kandidata istoricheskikh nauk (Karaganda: Karaganda State University, 2009), 3.
10. Gulbarshyn Bozheyeva, Yerlan Kunakbayev and Dastan Yeleukenov, "Former Soviet Biological Weapons Facilities in Kazakhstan: Past, Present, and Future," *Occasional Paper No. 1* (Monterey: Monterey Inst. Cent. Nonproliferation Studies), June (1999); Togzhan Kassenova, "The Lasting Toll of Semipalatinsk's Nuclear Testing," *Bulletin of the Atomic Scientists*, September 28, 2009, available at: http://thebulletin.org/lasting-toll-semipalatinsks-nuclear-testing, accessed March 31, 2017.
11. Natalya Ablazhey, "Kampaniia vnutrennei peredislokatsii spetsposelentsev v nachale 1950-kh gg.: nerealizovannaia direktiva," Proceedings of the International Conference "Znat', chtoby ne zabyt': totalitarnaia vlast' i narod v 20 – nachale 50-kh godov XX veka" May 30–31, 2014. (Ust'-Kamenogorsk: Media-Alians): 37–48.

12. Zbigniew Wojnowski, "De-Stalinization and the Failure of Soviet Identity Build-ing in Kazakhstan," *Journal of Contemporary History* 52 (2017), available at: http://journals.sagepub.com/doi/abs/10.1177/0022009416653457, accessed May 11, 2017.

13. Batyrkhan Zharov and Oleg Taran, "Grazhdanin, patriot, prokuror," *Kazakhstan-skaia Pravda,* June 19, 2015, available at: www.kazpravda.kz/articles/view/grazhdanin-patriot-prokuror/, accessed May 6, 2017.

14. Svetlana Eleukhanova, "Polozhenie repressirovannykh v Kazakhstane," *Reabili-tatsiia i pamiat'* (Moscow: Memorial-Zven'ia, 2016), 193–235; Edward Allworth, *Central Asia, 130 Years of Russian Dominance: A Historical Overview* (Durham: Duke University Press, 1994), 389; and Kaziev, "Soviet Nationality Policy," 419.

15. Kaziev, "Soviet Nationality Policy," 442–8; Zhanna Kydyralina, "Etnichnost' i vlast'" (Sotsialno-etnicheskie konfliktyv Kazakhstane v sovetskii period)," *Obshchestven-nye nauki i sovremennost'*, 5 (2008): 120–8, available at: http://ecsocman.hse.ru/data/2010/09/20/1215005669/Kydaralina.pdf, accessed May 6, 2017.

16. Kydyralina, "Etnichnost' i vlast'," 124.

17. Bhavna Dave, *Minorities and Participation in Public Life: Kazakhstan* (Bishkek: United Nations Office of the High Commissioner for Human Rights, October 2004), available at: www2.ohchr.org/english/issues/minorities/docs/WP5.doc, accessed March 31, 2017.

18. Mikhail Alexandrov, *Uneasy Alliance: Relations between Russia and Kazakhstan in the Post-Soviet Era, 1992–1997* (Boulder: Greenwood, 1999), 18–20.

19. Ibid., 20–2.

20 Svetlana Chekanova, "Sudit zhurnalista," *Media i parvo*, April 11, 2005, available at: http://karaganda-nm.kz/forum/showthread.php?p=702704, accessed May 6, 2017.

21. *Chislennost' naseleniia Respubliki Kazakhstan po otdel'nym etnosam na nachalo 2016 goda* (Astana: Statistics Committee of the Ministry of National Economy of the Republic of Kazakhstan, 2016), available at: www.stat.gov.kz/getImg?id =ESTAT118979, accessed May 6, 2017.

22. Brian Grodsky, *The Costs of Justice: How Leaders Respond to Previous Rights Abuses* (Notre Dame: University of Notre Dame, 2008).

23. Alexei Trochev, "Less Democracy, More Courts: A Puzzle of Judicial Review in Russia," *Law & Society Review* 38, 3 (2004): 513–48.

24. Sarah Cameron, "The Kazakh Famine of 1930–33: Current Research and New Directions," *East/West: Journal of Ukrainian Studies* 3, 2 (2016): 117–32.

25. Valerii Mikhailov, *Khronika velikogo dzhuta* (Alma-Ata: SP "Interbuk," 1990).

26. "Zakliucheniie komissii Prezidiuma Verkhovnogo Soveta Respubliki Kazakhstan po izucheniiu normativnykh pravovykh aktov privedshikh k golodu vo vremia kollektivizatsii," *Kazakhstanskaia Pravda* (December 22, 1992), available at: http://e-history.kz/ru/publications/view/6, accessed May 6, 2017.

27. Evgeny Finkel, "In Search of Lost Genocide: Historical Policy and International Politics in Post-1989 Eastern Europe," *Global Society* 24, 1 (2010): 51–66.

28. Kundakbayeva and Kassymova, "Remembering and Forgetting"; Cameron, "The Kazakh Famine of 1930–33."

29. "Zakliucheniie komissii Prezidiuma."

30. Andrei Grozin, *Golod 1932–1933 godov i politika pamiati v Respublike Kazakhstan* (Moscow: Institut Vostokovedeniia RAN, 2014).

31. Talgat Aitbauly, «Ұлы жұттың жазбалары» [Chronicle of the Great Dzhut] (Alma-Ata: Press, 1992); Film "Great Dzhut" (1992) directed by Kalila Umarov, available at: www.youtube.com/watch?v=Ag6PalmQ7g4, accessed May 6, 2017.

32. "Pamiatnik zhertvam politicheskikh repressii i golodomora predlozhili perenesti za predely Almaty," *TengriNews*, August 7, 2014, available at: https://tengrinews.kz/picture_art/pamyatnik-jertvam-politicheskih-repressiy-golodomora-259271/,accessed May 6, 2017.

33. "Zhertv politicheskikh repressii vspominaiut v Almaty," *Karavan*, May 31, 2016, available at: www.caravan.kz/news/zhertv-politicheskikh-repressijj-vspominayut-v-almaty-376935/; "Programma i usloviia provedeniia otkrytogo konkursa na luchshii proekt pamiatnika zhertvam goloda," *Vechernii Almaty*, July 16, 2016, available at: http://vecher.kz/incity/programma-i-usloviya-provedeniya-ot-krytogo-konkursa-na-luchshij-proekt-pamyatnika-zhertvam-goloda, both accessed May 6, 2017.

34. Morgan Williams, "Ukraine Issues Joint Declaration at the United Nations in Connection with the 70th Anniversary of the Great Famine in Ukraine of 1932–1933," *Art Ukraine*, November 11, 2003, available at: www.artukraine.com/famine-art/ukr_un_decl.htm, accessed May 6, 2017.

35. Eurasian Monitor, "EM-11: Public Perception of Youth."

36. Kundakbayeva and Kassymova, "Remembering and Forgetting," 623.

37. "Pamiatnik zhertvam golodomora vozdvignut v Pavlodare" *KazInform*, May 31, 2012, available at: www.inform.kz/ru/pamyatnik-zhertvam-golodomora-vozdvignut-v-pavlodare_a2468441; "Pamiatnik zhertvam goloda 1930-kh godov ustanovlen v IuKO," *KazInform*, May 31, 2012, available at: www.inform.kz/ru/pamyatnik-zhertvam-goloda-1930-h-godov-ustanovlen-v-yuko_a2467727; Oksana Zhivitskaia, "Smerti predannye zabveniiu," *Balkhashskii rabochii*, October 16, 2014, available at: http://brgazeta.kz/home/2022-2014-10-16-07-34-07.html, all accessed May 6, 2017.

38. Constitutional Law of the Republic of Kazakhstan of December 16, 1991, "On the State Independence of the Republic of Kazakhstan," *Vedomosti Verkhovnogo Soveta Kazakhskoi SSR*, no. 51 (1991), st. 622, available at: http://adilet.zan.kz/eng/docs/Z910004400, accessed May 6, 2017.

39. Zardykhan Zharmukhamed, "Ethnic Kazakh Repatriation and Kazakh Nation-Building: The Awaited Savior of the Prodigal Son?," *Region: Regional Studies of Russia, Eastern Europe, and Central Asia* 5, 1 (2016): 17–34.

40. Oka Natsuko, "A note on ethnic return migration policy in Kazakhstan: changing priorities and a growing dilemma," IDE Discussion Paper No. 394 (March 2013), available at: www.ide.go.jp/English/Publish/Download/Dp/394.html; Sultan Khan-Akkuly, "Sushchestvuet li v Kazakhstane 'oralmanofobiia'?," *Radio Azattyq*, October 12, 2011, available at: http://rus.azattyq.org/a/repatriate_diskrimination_kulibayev_janaozen_phobia_migration/24356665.html, both accessed May 6, 2017.

41. Nuriddin Sultanmuratov, "Repatriatsiia Po-Kazakhski," *Tsentr Azii*, April 2011, 5, available at: www.asiakz.com/repatriaciya-po-kazahski; "Kak pritesniaiut oralmanov v Kazakhstane," *Karavan*, March 13, 2017, available at: www.caravan.kz/news/kak-pritesnyayut-oralmanov-v-kazakhstane-391876/, both accessed May 6, 2017.

42. Bruce Pannier, "Kazakhstan: The Forgotten Famine," *Radio Free Europe/Radio Liberty*, December 28, 2007, available at: www.rferl.org/a/1079304.html, accessed June 21, 2017.

43. Wojnowski, "De-Stalinization and the Failure of Soviet Identity Building in Kazakhstan."
44. The head of the Kazakh Union of Writers, Olzhas Suleimenov, was a son of a purged Alash Orda officer.
45. Tursyn Zhurtbay, *Bol' Moia, Gordost' Moia – Alash!* (Astana: Audarma, 2016), 9.
46. Kathleen Smith, *Remembering Stalin's Victims: Popular Memory and the End of the USSR* (Ithaca: Cornell University Press, 1996), 110, and 114–7.
47. Beibit Koishibayev, "Pravda i mif o zhertvakh repressii," *Turkestan*, 5 (February 2, 2012), available at: www.altyn-orda.kz/pravda-i-mif-o-zhertvax-repressij/, accessed May 6, 2017.
48. Chekanova, "Sudit zhurnalista."
49. Aisulu Toishibekova, "Issledovatel" Karlaga Ekaterina Kuznetsova: "Intelligentsiia v Karagande skladyvalas' iz byvshikh zakliuchennykh lagerei," *Vlast.Kz*, December 19, 2016, available at: https://vlast.kz/life/20875-issledovatel-karlaga-ekaterina-kuznecova-intelligencia-v-karagande-skladyvalas-iz-byvsih-zaklucennyh-lagerej.html, accessed May 6, 2017.
50. *Politicheskie repressii v Kazakhstane v 1937–1938 gg.* (Almaty: Izdatelstvo Kazakhstan, 1998).
51. Pavel Dyatlenko, "Features of Rehabilitation of Victims of Stalin's Political Repressions in Kazakhstan," *Vestnik KRSU* 14, 11 (2014): 29, available at: www.krsu.edu.kg/vestnik/2014/v11/a08.pdf, accessed May 6, 2017.
52. The Law of the Republic of Kazakhstan of 14 April 1993, "On Rehabilitation of Victims of Massive Political Repressions," *Vedomosti Verkhovnogo Soveta Respubliki Kazakhstan*, no. 10 (1993), st. 242, available at: http://adilet.zan.kz/eng/docs/Z930002200, accessed May 6, 2017.
53. Michael Gelb, "An Early Soviet Ethnic Deportation: The Far-Eastern Koreans," *Russian Review* 54, 3 (1995): 389–412.
54. Svetlana Isaeva, "Novye repressii protiv ... repressirovannykh," *Radio Azattyq*, June 4, 2005, available at: http://rus.azattyq.org/a/1180478.html, accessed May 6, 2017.
55. Eleukhanova, "Polozhenie repressirovannykh v Kazakhstane," 193–235.
56. "V Kazakhstane za 12 let zhertvam politicheskikh repressii vyplacheno 9,8 mlrd tenge," *BNews.Kz*, May 31, 2015, available at: http://bnews.kz/ru/news/obshchestvo/v_kazahstane_za_12_let_zhertvam_politicheskih_repressii_viplacheno_98_mlrd_tenge-2015_05_31-1108045; "MZSR: 10,7 mlrd tenge vyplacheno zhertvam politicheskikh repressii v Kazakhstane s 2003 goda," *KazInform*, May 31, 2016, available at: www.inform.kz/ru/mzsr-10-7-mlrd-tenge-vyplacheno-zhertvam-politicheskih-repressiy-v-kazahstane-s-2003-goda_a2909404, both accessed May 6, 2017.
57. "Otchet akima Zhambylskogo raiona Turkova I.I. pered naseleniem raiona," *Ofitsial'nyi internet-resurs akima Zhambylskogo raiona Severo-Kazakhstanskoi oblasti*, July 27, 2016, available at: http://zhb.sko.gov.kz/page.php?page=otchetnyi_doklad_akima_raiona_2015&lang=2; "Informatsiia ob itogakh raboty Akzharskogo otdela zaniatosti i sotsial'nykh programm po sostoianiiu na 1 ianvaria 2016 goda," *Ofitsial'nyi internet-resurs akima Akzharskogo raiona Severo-Kazakhstanskoi oblasti*, April 27, 2017, available at: http://azh.sko.gov.kz/page.php?page=socialnaja_zaschita_naselenija&lang=2; "Ob itogakh sotsial'no-ekonomicheskogo razvitiia raiona za 2015 god i zadachakh na 2016 god," *Ofitsial'nyi Sait Glubokovskii raion*

Vostochno-Kazakhstanskoi oblasti, no date, available at: https://glubokoe.gov.kz/page/socialnaya-zashch, all accessed May 6, 2017.

58. Dyatlenko, "Features of Rehabilitation of Victims of Stalin's Political Repressions in Kazakhstan," 29.

59. "Otkryvaia zavesy tragicheskogo proshlogo," *Press-sluzhba KNB RK*, October 5, 2012, available at: http://knb.kz/ru/history/archive/article.htm?id=10322098@cmsArticle, accessed May 6, 2017.

60. Bill Egbert, "Lubavitchers Given KGB Files on Rabbi," *New York Daily News*, December 20, 1999, available at: www.nydailynews.com/archives/news/lubavitchers-kgb-files-rabbi-article-1.843285, accessed June 22, 2017.

61. Dyatlenko, "Features of Rehabilitation of Victims of Stalin's Political Repressions in Kazakhstan," 31; "Arkhivnye dela, kasaiushchiesia stalinskikh repressii, do sikh por zakryty dlia issledovatelei," *Central Asia Monitor*, June 26, 2015, available at: https://camonitor.kz/16827-arhivnye-dela-kasayuschiesya-stalinskih-repressiy-do-sih-por-zakryty-dlya-issledovateley.html, accessed May 6, 2017.

62. "Kazakhstanskie arkhivy otkryvaiut dostup k sekretnym delam proshlogo," *MK v Kazakhstane*, July 13, 2016, available at: http://mk-kz.kz/articles/2016/07/13/kazakh-stanskie-arkhivy-otkryvayut-dostup-k-sekretnym-delam-proshlogo.html, accessed May 6, 2017.

63. "Kadrovyi sostav organov gosudarstvennoi bezopasnosti SSSR. 1935–1939," Memorial, available at: http://nkvd.memo.ru.

64. Isa Dilara, "Nizverzhennyi Stalin v sele Staryi Ikan," *Radio Azattyq*, May 19, 2015, available at: http://rus.azattyq.org/a/istoria-pamyatnika-stalinu-selo-stariy-ikan/27024370.html, accessed May 6, 2017.

65. Kundakbayeva and Kassymova, "Remembering and Forgetting," 618.

66. Valentina Elizarova, "Komu kusochek istorii?," *Izvetiia-Kazakhstan*, July 15, 2005, available at: www.karlag.kz/art.php?id=71, accessed May 6, 2017.

67. Svetlana Kokhanova, "Arkhipelag Karlag," *Ekspress-K*, August 11, 2009, available at: http://old.express-k.kz/show_article.php?art_id=32202, accessed May 6, 2017.

68. Botagoz Omar, "Muzei Karlaga," *Novoe pokolenie*, May 17, 2011, available at: www.np.kz/events/8262-muzejj_karlaga.html, accessed May 6, 2017.

69. Ekaterina Kuznetsova, "Lecture 3. Karlag i Ego Istoriia," *OpenMind.Kz*, December 22, 2016, available at: http://omind.kz, accessed May 6, 2017.

70. Elena Veber, "Muzei v Dolinke pytaetsia naiti den'gi na rasshirenie," *Radio Azattyq*, May 31, 2016, available at: http://rus.azattyq.org/a/musei-v-dolinke-politicheskie-repressii-31-maja/27770739.html, accessed May 6, 2017.

71. "Shakhtinsk na novom etape razvitiia," *Shakhtinskii vestnik*, July 11, 2014.

72. "V Almaty potomki repressirovannykh nastaivaiut na vosstanovlenii muzeia zhertv politicheskii repressii," *Zakon.Kz*, May 21, 2013, available at: www.zakon.kz/4557618-v-almaty-potomki-repressirovannykh.html, accessed May 6, 2017.

5

Historical Reckoning in Belarus

Nelly Bekus

Belarus is not usually considered a transitional justice case, due to the fact that the country has remained subject to authoritarian rule during most of the postcommunist period. As this chapter goes to print, Belarus is still under the thumb of an authoritarian leader, Alexander Lukashenka, who became president in 1994. But a closer look reveals that Belarus has made efforts to reckon with past rights violations. While they do not amount to a coherent transitional justice agenda, these efforts merit attention for a number of reasons.

First, they show that even authoritarian regimes are eager to ingratiate themselves with former victims in order to prevent civil unrest and gain additional electoral support. Authoritarian leaders show reluctance to ban transitional justice completely from the official agenda, but support only programs that do not undermine their hold on power. Second, these efforts show that even when working in very restrictive circumstances, civil society groups and opposition parties are able to supplement the feeble official reckoning programs with unofficial initiatives (including a citizen's tribunal and a virtual museum). Of course, the authoritarian regime's control over the local mass media and school curricula limits public awareness of many of these efforts, which might remain known to only small segments of the population. Third, such efforts further illustrate that the reevaluation of communist crimes is closely linked to the political elites' contradictory efforts to build a post-Soviet national identity. Twenty-five years after the break-up of the Soviet Union, two contradictory narratives about Soviet history and Belarusian identity developed by the regime of President Lukashenka and the opposition actors are found in Belarus.

While most scholars of postcommunist transitional justice primarily consider the reckoning programs adopted by various former Soviet republics after they declared their independence in 1991, this chapter takes another view. It examines initiatives passed as a result of Mikhail Gorbachev's *glasnost* and *perestroika* in 1987–91, measures introduced in 1990–4, and more recent efforts under Lukashenka. The focus here is on the transitional justice initiatives promoted by the Soviet and post-Soviet governments, as well as those proposed since 1991 by the opposition to Lukashenka, formed from the nationalist Belarusian People's Front (BPF) and civil society organizations such as the Association of Victims of Political Repression, the Saving Kurapaty organization, Memorial, and others.

The BPF, established in June 1989 and registered as a party in 1993, intertwined political liberalization, decommunization, and a new anti-Soviet narrative of Belarusian history and identity. It interpreted Soviet repression as a "national genocide" aimed at exterminating the Belarusian nation. This narrative failed to resonate with large segments of society, and in 1994 Lukashenka won the first post-Soviet presidential election. He capitalized on the Belarusians' social discontent with the collapse of the Soviet Union and promised to reestablish economic ties with former Soviet republics, preserve the social welfare state, and promote egalitarianism and social justice. While he gradually stalled liberalization and democratization, his goals to promote Belarusian collective identity proved popular.[1] Social support for Lukashenka's authoritarianism remains a paradox of his rule.

Belarus is a rare post-Soviet state where Soviet nostalgia has dominated political discourse and morphed into a state ideology. As this chapter shows, the official positive affirmation of the Soviet past as a period of Belarusian nation building makes the memory of Soviet repression ideologically irrelevant. Some opposition actors link Soviet repression with the political discrimination under Lukashenka, thus associating the redress of Soviet abuses with the current political agenda.

The chapter first sketches the Soviet nation-building in Belarus that combined state repression with modernization, and then discusses the Soviet liberalization that created conditions for historical reckoning in the republic. The next part of the chapter introduces the major opposition actors who advanced decommunization in Belarus. After 1994, these actors were disconnected from the official public space, and thus their activities were unofficial. Belarus shows that unofficial transitional justice – citizens' tribunals, lustration proposals, the virtual museum of Soviet repression – can be conducted by memory activists in the absence of state support.

SOVIET NATION-BUILDING IN BELARUS

In 1917 a new Soviet regime was installed in Belarus, accompanied by the brutal repression of "enemies of the revolution." In the 1920s, the Soviet leaders launched a strategic Belarusian nation-building project, initiating affirmative action policies that encouraged ethnic and linguistic particularism among non-Russians, including Belarusians. Radical social changes followed, including the development of national languages, and the transformation of communicative facilities. The press became almost exclusively Belarusian, the use of Russian was discouraged, and the Belarusian language was recognized as the state language. Obligatory language courses were introduced, and the return of Belarusian national elites from exile was encouraged. The number of Belarusian-speaking public officials increased from 26.9 percent in 1925 to 80 percent in 1928, while the number of Belarusian-speaking people in the education system rose from 28.4 percent in 1924–5 to 93.8 percent in 1929–30.[2]

By the late 1920s, nationalization gave way to a new policy, which promoted Russian culture and language as foundations for Soviet unity, centralization, and planning. This push for unity was a way to allay fears that the growing rivalry between national republics could benefit the enemies of the Soviet Union. The Bolsheviks promoted the Belarusian national state, but repressed the people who wanted to turn Belarus away from socialism.

The Great Terror of the 1930s had a catastrophic impact on Belarusian culture. The pre-Soviet leaders were exterminated and most of the intelligentsia educated during Soviet times fell victim to repression. The Belarusian Academy of Sciences lost 90 percent of its members.[3] There is disagreement about the number of victims of repression in Belarus, particularly since the archives of the Belarusian KGB remain sealed. Some studies suggest that the number of victims of inter-war repression reached 132,000. Belarusian history textbooks mention 600,000–700,000 victims, while some historians claim that 1.5 million Belarusians were persecuted.[4] Repression was generally harsher in Belarus than in many other Soviet republics due to proximity to the West.

The Stalinist terror was overshadowed by the extreme brutality of World War II, when Belarus registered the highest number of losses (2.3 to 2.4 million deaths). Moreover, 209 of 270 towns and regional centers were totally destroyed, including the capital city, Minsk.[5] Many Belarusians experienced postwar reconstruction as a "golden age" of development. By 1970 Belarus ranked above other Soviet republics in terms of industrial development and living standards, and by 1991 it had one of the better-managed Soviet economies.[6] The rebuilding of the Belarusian economy and infrastructure with support from the other Soviet republics was perceived as a benefit of intra-Soviet internationalism.

In short, Soviet citizens did not experience oppression the same way during the 1930s, the 1960s, and the 1980s. For them, Khrushchev's condemnation of Stalin's terror launched a new era in Soviet history and symbolically cut late socialism from Stalinist brutality and oppression. Late socialism was stable, prosperous, and nonviolent, marked by progress and well-being that are often overlooked by scholars.[7] In early 1990, such attitudes were common in Belarus. In March 1991, 83 percent of Belarusians voted for the preservation of the Soviet Union.[8] A side effect of Soviet development was the growing Russification of Belarus, which greatly concerned the national intelligentsia. Several informal cultural groups appeared in the mid-1980s to protect the Belarusian language and culture. A new political opposition to Soviet ideology grew out of these nation-minded cultural elites, who used the memory of Stalinist repression to awaken national awareness.

RECKONING WITH THE PAST IN LATE SOVIET COMMUNISM

Historical reckoning started in the late 1980s when *perestroika* and *glasnost* allowed for unprecedented openness and freedom to speak about issues previously omitted in public debates. Under Gorbachev, several measures dealing with the victims of Stalinist repression were adopted (Table 5.1).

The first official document was the 1987 Resolution of the Political Bureau of the Central Committee of the Communist Party of the Soviet Union (September 28, 1987), which initiated the reexamination of Stalinist injustice as a continuation of the historical reckoning started by the 20th Congress of the Communist Party in 1956.[9] The Resolution called for a new commission to gather materials prepared by all post-1953 commissions that investigated Stalinist crimes, other documents housed with the Committee of Party Control, the KGB, the Institute of Marxism-Leninism, the Prosecutor's Office, and the Supreme Court, as well as witness testimonies from citizens. In 1988, the commission instructed the Prosecutor's Office and the State Security Committee of the Soviet Union to reexamine the criminal responsibility of former victims of repression. The commission also initiated the rehabilitation of high officials like Nikolai Bukharin and Alexei Rykov, annulled the forced settlement of Estonian and Latvian citizens, and opened the reexamination of the killings of Polish officers in Katyn as well as the construction of a memorial on the burial site (completed in 2000).[10] In redressing Soviet abuses, the commission actively sought to make policies in a manner that would not contradict *perestroika*.

In July 1988, the Political Bureau ordered the construction of the first memorial to the victims of lawlessness and repression in Moscow. The Solovetsky Stone was inaugurated on October 30, 1990 in Lubyanka Square, Moscow. In January 1989, the Supreme Soviet Presidium initiated the rehabilitation of the victims and the restoration of their pensions, housing, and other rights.

TABLE 5.1. *Selected Soviet legislative acts addressing political repression*

Title of document	Issuing body	Date
Resolution "On the creation of the Commission of the Political Bureau of the Central Committee of the Communist Party of the Soviet Union (CC CPSU) for the additional examination of materials related to the repression of the 1930–40s and the early 1950s"	Political Bureau of CC CPSU	September 28, 1987
Resolution "On the construction of a memorial to the victims of lawlessness and repression in Moscow"	Political Bureau of CC CPSU	July 4, 1988
Decree "On the additional measures of the restoration of justice for victims of the repression of the 1930–40s and the early 1950s"	Presidium of the Supreme Soviet of USSR	January 5, 1989
Resolution "On the preservation of the memory of victims of the repression of 1930–40s and the early 1950s"	Political Bureau of CC CPSU	June 28, 1989
Decree 556 "On the restoration of rights of all victims of political repression during 1920–50s"	President of USSR	August 13, 1990

Source: Reabilitatsiya. Kak eto bylo. Dokumenty Politbyuro TsK KPSS, stenogrammy zasedaniya Komissii Politbyuro TsK KPSS po dopolnitel'nomu izucheniyu materialov, svyazannykh s repressiyami, imevshimi mesto v period 30-40-kh i nachala 50-kh godov, i drugie materialy (Moscow: Materik, 2004).

Resolution of June 28, 1989 of the Political Bureau advised republics to commemorate victims of political repression, build memorials, and establish official cemeteries on former burial sites. Also in 1989, the Decree of 16 January and the Resolution of 28 June allowed for redress and historical justice.

This reconsideration of Stalinist repression aimed at repairing, not deconstructing, the Soviet system. Perestroika was driven by Gorbachev's desire "to reinvigorate the genuine socialist ideas and to revive the radical-democratic system of Soviets."[11] Gorbachev publicly recognized that Khrushchev's campaign was elitist, as thousands of cases remained unconsidered and innocent people were not cleared of unjust charges. Gorbachev' Decree 556 of August 13, 1990 addressed the fate of peasants and other categories of victims overlooked by the 1950s rehabilitation campaign. By doing this, Gorbachev tried once again to reclaim the ideals of the October Revolution: social justice and people's power.

<h2 style="text-align:center">BELARUS: ADVANCING HISTORICAL RECKONING
PRIOR TO INDEPENDENCE</h2>

In October 1988, the informal Martyralog Belarus Committee 58 held its first meeting under the auspices of the state-run Belarusian Cultural Foundation and the leadership of Zianon Pazniak.[12] The 350 participants included prominent Belarusian cultural luminaries, journalists, historians, archeologists, representatives of the Belarusian Academy of Sciences, local councils, the Prosecutor's Office, the Central Committee of the Communist Party of Belarus, public activists, and guests from Armenia and Lithuania.[13] The meeting concluded with the Declaration of the Belarusian Social Historical-Educational Association of Memory of the Victims of Stalinism.[14]

The Declaration set high transitional justice goals for the Association, including opening the secret archives, identifying perpetrators, prosecuting Stalin's supporters, conducting research into Stalinist crimes, financing the construction of monuments and memorials, and returning historical names to villages, towns, and public squares. The Association further supported the return of the Belarusian language to wider public use, and declared 1 November as a national day of memory. The Declaration stated that the Association's activity would rest "on the principles of the XIX Communist Party conference [held in 1952 under Stalin], that affirmed democratic socialism, humanism, and publicity in the society based on the principle of highest historical justice: no one is forgotten, nothing is forgotten."[15] It pledged to initiate an all-union confederation of similar national associations. After 1991, this intra-Soviet focus was replaced by a pro-Europeanism that excluded cooperation within the FSU. Martyralog further advocated truth-telling. It published the bulletin *Martyralog Belarus* in 1989, produced the documentary "Road to Kurapaty" in 1990, organized a conference in 1993, and installed memorial plaques at repression sites.

Other actors further developed Martyralog's activities. The Belarusian Association of Victims of Political Repression, registered in 1992, focused on the judicial, financial, and social support of former victims of repression, and promoted commemorative initiatives such as building memorials and placing plaques. It had regional branches in Babruisk, Hrodna, Brest, Homel, Maladechna, and Pukhavichy. Martyralog's political agenda was taken over by the BPF, which employed historical justice to build an anti-Soviet and anti-Russian national narrative that presented political repression as a "national genocide" aimed at exterminating the Belarusian nation.[16]

The first Belarusian official document on communist repression was Decree 42 of January 18, 1989, which dealt with one burial site. At that time, no political actor possessed comprehensive knowledge of Stalinist repression and its local consequences (Table 5.2). With the archives closed and serious historical studies unavailable, the public and the elites had yet to discover the full scope of Stalinist repression in Belarus.

In 1988, grass-roots memory activists played a major role in advancing this state implemented historical reckoning program, gradually turning it into the full-scale anti-Soviet political program. On 3 June, archaeologist Zianon Pazniak and journalist Yauhenii Shmygalyou in an article on the discovery of a mass grave at Kurapaty, revealed the mass shootings committed by the NKVD (the People's Commissariat for Internal Affairs) in 1937–41, and called for the symbolic punishment of those responsible, since most perpetrators had already passed away.[17] Their article had an unprecedented impact on ordinary Belarusians and Soviet officials. Perestroika compelled communist officials to react to the publication. As such, on 14 June the General Prosecutor opened the first criminal investigation into the crimes of the 1930s.

The following month, a government commission examined the claims in the article and monitored criminal investigations. The commission studied materials with the Prosecutor's Office, archival documents, expert opinions, and the testimonies of fifty-five witnesses. It conducted "selective exhumations" of corpses. Thirty-eight legal experts examined over 3,000 objects found in the graves, and Ministry of Health experts conducted five bone investigations. The Scientific-Research Institute of Legal Expertise, affiliated with the Ministry of Justice, examined cartridges, bullets, coins, fragments of shoes and clothing, and other personal effects found in the graves. The commission identified 510 "assumed burial places" containing the bones of 356 persons. Most skulls had bullet damage at the back or temple. The cartridges and bullets were from Soviet-made Nagan revolvers. Fragments of clothing, shoes, and other objects led the commission to declare that victims belonged to various social groups. Since each grave contained the remains of fifty to sixty people, at least 30,000 victims were buried in the Kurapaty Forest.[18] The mass shootings were attributed to the NKDV.[19] The criminal investigation was eventually closed, since "those responsible for this repression, the NKVD leaders and other individuals, had been [already] sentenced to death or died."[20] As Yazep Brolishs, a former investigator with the Prosecutor's Office, noted "there were no precedents of such investigations, no techniques, no methodologies ... Through trial and error, using proven techniques and methods of criminology, we went out. And we served well all those who dealt with such burial sites after us."[21]

TABLE 5.2. *Selected Belarusian legislative acts addressing political repression*

Title of document	Issuing body	Date
Decree 42 "On memorializing the victims of mass repression of 1937–41 in Kurapaty"	Council of Ministers of Belarusian Soviet Socialist Republic (BSSR)	January 18, 1989
Decree 479–XII "On restoring the rights of citizens who suffered from repression in 1920–50"	Supreme Soviet of BSSR	December 21, 1990
Directive "On restoring rights of citizens who suffered from repression in 1920–50"	Supreme Soviet of BSSR	December 21, 1990
Resolution 349 "On granting benefits to individuals unreasonably brought to criminal liability in the repression of 1920–50s"	Council of Ministers of BSSR	December 29, 1990
Resolution 203 "On the publication of the Book of Memory in the Republic"	Council of Ministers of Republic of Belarus	May 27, 1991
Resolution 847–XII "On rehabilitating victims of political repression in 1930–50s in the Belarusian SSR"	Supreme Soviet of BSSR	June 6, 1991
Resolution 1211–XII "On introducing amendments and additions to some legislative acts of the Republic of Belarus that regulate the restoration of the rights of citizens who suffered from repression in 1920–80"	Supreme Soviet of BSSR	November 1, 1991
Resolution 1349-XII "On introducing amendments and additions to legislative acts of the Republic of Belarus that regulate the restoration of the rights of citizens who suffered from repression in 1920–80"	Supreme Soviet of Republic of Belarus	December 23, 1991
Decree 1791-XII "On completing the rehabilitation of victims of political repression"	Presidium of Supreme Soviet of Republic of Belarus	September 2, 1992
Decree on implementing the legislation on the rehabilitation of victims of political repression of 1920–80 and the restoration of their rights	Presidium of Supreme Soviet of Republic of Belarus	May 24, 1993

(continued)

TABLE 5.2 *(continued)*

Title of document	Issuing body	Date
Resolution 2623-XII "On introducing amendments and additions to some legislative acts of the Republic of Belarus regulating the rehabilitation of victims of repression in 1920–80 and the restoration of their rights"	Supreme Soviet of Republic of Belarus	December 3, 1993
Decree 349 "On regulating some benefits for certain categories of citizens"	President of Belarus	September 1, 1995
Decree 110 "On extending the rehabilitation term for victims of political repression"	President of Belarus	January 28, 1997
Law 30-3 "On introducing amendments and additions to the Directive on the restoration of rights of citizens who suffered from repression in 1920–80"	President of Belarus	April 17, 1997 (amended January 16, 2007)

Source: Aleh Dziarnovich, *Rehabilitation. The Collection of Documents and Normative Acts Pertaining to the Rehabilitation of Victims of Political Repression in 1920–80s* (Minsk: Athenaeum, 2001).

The commission presented its report to the Council of Ministers. The official response to the report (Decree 42 of January 18, 1989) called for the construction of a monument dedicated to political repression (which was never realized), asked the Academy of Science to further research the causes and effects of the mass repression of the 1930s–50s, and urged the publisher of the Belarusian Soviet Encyclopedia to prepare a special edition to commemorate the victims.[22] The Belarusian Decree echoed the Resolution of July 4, 1988 on the construction of a memorial in Moscow, and forecasted the Resolution of June 28, 1989 of the Moscow leaders, which advised republics to commemorate victims of political repression.

NEW LEGISLATION: A BELARUS IN TRANSITION

The discovery, official recognition, and memorialization of Kurapaty in 1988–9 became an important landmark of truth-telling in Belarus. It echoed similar legislative acts adopted in Moscow and informed subsequent Belarusian laws on Stalinist repression. Decree 479–XII regulated the restoration of rights for work, pension, and housing of former victims, and offered compensation for damages to property and other harm. It was supplemented by a Directive (see Table 5.2), which offered benefits such as free housing and free land, either in the locality where former victims currently lived or where they lived before they were repressed. However, only those already registered on special waiting lists qualified for free housing.[23] The free housing provision was retained until 1999.[24] The Directive aimed at implementing Gorbachev's Decree of August 13, 1990, thus showing that the Belarusian governing elites still saw the republic as part of the Soviet Union.

The Supreme Soviet Decree of November 1992 and Article 140 of the Housing Code of 2012 allowed rehabilitated citizens to acquire for free the state-owned dwellings they inhabited.[25] The benefit was granted to the victims of political repression, the children who were in prison or exile together with their parent, the children who were left as minors without parental care due to the political repression of their parents, and the children and unmarried spouses of victims who were executed or who died in prison and were rehabilitated posthumously. Under pressure from the BPF and its supporters, parliament regularly updated the legislation on rehabilitation and restoration of rights, introducing changes that could strengthen the justice-seeking agenda.

Resolution 349 of December 21, 1990 promised free travel on urban passenger transportation systems, a 50 percent reduction in medical prescription expenses (free of charge for disabled individuals), the right to choose the time of annual holidays for former victims who still worked, as well as priority in obtaining free passes for sanatorium-health resort treatment and recreation (issued to employed individuals by trade unions, and to retired individuals by local councils), acquiring air and railway tickets as well as other intercity public transportation, interest-free loans for housing construction, and a free allotment of land for summer house construction.

These benefits showed the government's intention to offer former victims moral and material compensation for suffering under the Soviet regime. The benefits for former victims of repression often equaled those for the veterans of World War II or Socialist Labor, the heroes of the Soviet Union, and the disabled individuals. Benefits symbolically recognized that victims of political repression deserved special treatment from the state. Most of these measures were implemented, although eventually canceled by Lukashenka's Decree 349 of 1995 (see Table 5.2).

Compensation and Rehabilitation Measures Both Pre- and Post independence

Decree 479–XII of December 21, 1990 regulated property restitution. Compensation for time spent in detention was set to half of the minimum salary for each month of imprisonment, up to a maximum of sixty monthly salaries.[26] The amount of compensation, although inadequate, was still larger than the compensation awarded in 1955 by Khrushchev, whose rehabilitation made a one-time payment equal to two months' worth of the victims' last salary. Law 30-3 of 1997 (amended in 2007) set compensation to a maximum of one-hundred minimal salaries at the time of payment. Given the economic crisis, high inflation, and decline in living standards that followed Belarus' independence, compensation packages paid to former victims had little real value. For many former victims, the idea of getting paid for suffering was morally controversial. Some members of the Association of the Former Victims of Political Repression refused compensation, and others who received compensation later regretted it.[27]

Property restitution laws were passed, but implementation proved problematic. According to Decree 479–XII, local authorities administered the in-kind return of confiscated properties or the compensation of losses.[28] Buildings and dwellings could not be returned if they were destroyed during World War II or if they were nationalized or transferred to the municipality under Soviet rule. In-kind restitution was not possible if the confiscated houses were reconstructed, fully rebuilt, or occupied by other individuals. In those cases, the property value was to be paid to the initial owners or their heirs. There is no data on the number of properties involved, and the entire process proved to be very complicated. The law made property return fully dependent on the good will of local councils, which could avoid restitution for unreasonable motives. The independent local press recorded the failed attempts of rehabilitated individuals to receive their property and the inadequate compensation they were offered for lost property.[29]

A significant number of individuals have been rehabilitated in Belarus through various decrees and resolutions. While the number is unknown, over 37,000 citizens were rehabilitated in 1990–2, over 10,000 former victims had their rights restored, and 2,000 rehabilitated individuals received compensation.[30] Under pressure from the BPF, the category of individuals entitled to compensation was widened in 1991–4. The Supreme Soviet Resolution 1349-XII of December 23, 1991 recognized children who were with their parents in prisons, exile, or special settlements as victims of political repression. Resolution 2623-XII of December 3, 1993 added children who remained orphans when both parents were repressed.[31] In October 1994, the category of victims was further expanded to include the children and spouses of individuals who were executed or who died in detention and were rehabilitated posthumously. All these categories of victims were eligible for compensation and they received all other rights assigned to repressed and rehabilitated individuals as well.

Decree 2320–XII of May 23, 1993 recognized as unsatisfactory the speed with which state and law enforcement agencies processed rehabilitation requests. The initial timeframe for considering each request (maximum six months) was not respected because commissions became overloaded with applications. Initially, citizens could apply for rehabilitation only until the end of 1996. This deadline sought to discipline local administrations and prevent delays. It was assumed that three years was sufficient to rehabilitate and compensate all eligible citizens. In addition, to process rehabilitation requests, special commissions were created in the regional and city councils. The deadline to complete rehabilitation terminated the activity of the commissions. On January 28, 1997, President Lukashenka issued Decree 110 to set the deadline for rehabilitation at the end of 2001 and extend its financing. As local councils repeatedly refused to pay compensation after 2001, in 2006 the Constitutional Court confirmed that the councils had no right to refuse indemnification after the deadline had passed. The special administrative structures created to facilitate rehabilitation and compensation were closed down in 2001, but the rehabilitated individuals retained their rights.[32]

Overall, from 1990 to 1994 Parliament adopted twenty-four acts to regulate the rehabilitation, property restitution, and compensation of former victims. These were the only means by which the state compensated former victims for their sufferings. Most of the applications came from victims of repression from the 1930s. The BPF repeatedly stressed the repressive nature of late communism, but the historical record of post-Stalin repression in Belarus did not support this view. According to historian Igor Kuznietsov, in 1961–87 twenty-eight dissidents were convicted in Belarus for anti-Soviet propaganda, and nineteen Belarus-born citizens were convicted in other Soviet republics.[33] The number of rehabilitation requests remains unclear. Some 150 petitioners called for investigations into the use of psychiatry for political and repressive purposes.[34] While the Soviet state continued to practice censorship and to limit freedom in its final decades, repression was rather limited.

NEW MEMORY ACTORS ON THE POLITICAL SCENE

The first elections for the Belarus Supreme Soviet of March 1990 empowered candidates from the Association of Belarusian Language, the Belarusian Ecological Union, the Union of Cooperators, and the Union of Workers, thereby breaking up the monopoly power of the Communist Party. Many of these organizations joined the opposition Democratic Bloc, which also included the BPF, in the Supreme Council.[35] This minority disassociated itself from the Soviet governing elite and party *nomenklatura* to form an alternative to the Communist Party and elected Stanislau Shushkevich as the first vice-chair of Parliament. Shushkevich was a symbolic figure because his father had spent fifteen years in the Gulag. While the Communist Party still commanded a majority of seats, the minority BPF imposed its nationalist agenda as state policy.[36] It replaced the Soviet flag and state symbols in 1991 with a Belarusian flag, introduced Belarusian in schools, the media and public life, and encouraged the rewriting of national history.

Belarus faced political uncertainty from July 1990 to December 1991. The republic declared its sovereignty on July 27, 1990, but the conservative majority of the governing elites hoped that radical changes could be avoided. After the failed coup of August 1991, the conservative parliament leadership resigned. This strengthened the position of the parliamentary opposition and historical reckoning advanced further. Parliament acknowledged the repressive character of the entire Soviet regime, not only Stalin. While previous legislation defined the period of political repression from 1920 to the 1950s, Resolution 1211–XII of November 1, 1991 expanded the timeframe from the 1920s to the 1980s. It rehabilitated individuals convicted on political grounds from 1960 until 1988, or illegally and forcibly placed in psychiatric wards. The Resolution also regulated access to the KGB files of repressed individuals, and stipulated that "rehabilitated individuals and, with their consent or in the event of their death, their relatives have the right to look over the materials of closed criminal or administrative cases and to obtain copies of documents of a nonprocedural nature."[37] In practice, the files are presented to relatives with fragments or full pages blackened or removed. As a rule, information about perpetrators is not made available so as to avoid personal accountability for repression.[38] However, there was a significant shift in accountability associated with this decree.

The Soviet Union collapsed in 1991, but the Soviet government remained intact in Belarus until 1994 when Prime Minister Viacheslav Kebich lost the presidency to Lukashenka. Lukashenka presented himself as an alternative to both the government of Soviet *apparatchiks* and the nationalist, anti-Soviet opposition. His electoral program, "To lead the people off the precipice," leveraged the population's uncertainty about the future following the disintegration of the Soviet Union into political gain.[39]

INDEPENDENT BELARUS: CREATING A NEW NATIONAL IDEA

In Eastern Europe, the memory of communist oppression became the founding myth of the postcommunist states. Emphasis on anticommunist resistance helped postcommunist elites to present Europe as their "true home." After independence, the Belarusian anticommunists reoriented their national framing from the FSU to Europe. In this way, the anti-Soviet opposition built on the memory of political repression to gain geopolitical meaning. Framing Belarus as a part of Europe radically contrasts with the Soviet concept of Belarus as part of a wider East Slavic civilizational space or Lukashenka's Eurasian integration.

To that end, a declared goal of the BPF was the "revival of the European Belarus."[40] In the early 1990s, they supported a union stretching from the Baltic Sea to the Black Sea, comprised of Ukraine, Poland, Belarus, and Lithuania. This idea of Belarus as a "typical country of the region" grouped with the Baltic states and Poland was often reiterated by BPF politicians. According to the BPF program, the anticommunist forces were to implement "national democracy" – a concept blending nationalism and democratization – in the region.[41] Today, the BPF program declares the EU and NATO accession as its main goals. As the influential intellectual and politician Yuri Khadyka stated: "in today's Belarus there is no real choice. In the conditions of a tense inter-civilizational conflict, we have just one way—to the West, to Europe, that is where our legitimate place has been since the fifteenth century."[42]

In part, the nationalist memory narrative used remembrance of Soviet-era victims to other the Soviet experience. The communist political injustices were presented as a reason for society to oppose the Soviet past,[43] but this is not how the Belarusians remembered that past. In 1994–8 they viewed their Soviet experience more positively than other Eastern Europeans: 76–78 percent of Belarusian respondents positively assessed the communist system.[44] The story of Belarus victimhood as a result of Soviet repression also challenged the narrative of the Belarusians' sufferings during World War II, the "hegemonic martyrdom" embraced during Soviet times. The narrative represented a "heroic memory of victimhood" that was a key component of Soviet ideology.[45]

In other postcommunist countries, political elites pursued transitional justice strategically only if it did not interfere with the provision of other expected goods and services.[46] When Lukashenka came to power in 1994, the condemnation of the Soviet past was not seen as helping to restore people's collapsed lives. For many Belarusians the crisis of the early 1990s was not associated with the communist wrongs, but with the collapse of that system and the disintegration of economic ties within the FSU. Despite the flaws of Soviet economic development, Belarusians knew that their economic success was made possible by the larger entity: the Soviet Union. Lukashenka's victory in 1994 was a victory of nostalgic populism. He advanced his own understanding of the Belarusian nation, which stressed the positives associated with Soviet nation-building in Belarus. While not denying the Stalinist terror, the official discourse framed it as a nonpolitical story of "unjustified repressions." Always mentioned in the plural, "repressions" denote senseless acts of violence that specify no agency, elude responsibility, and mean a self-imposed, meaningless social catastrophe.[47]

After 1994, all state initiatives for coming to terms with the repressive and criminal aspects of the Soviet past were effectively marginalized. Lukashenka revived the Soviet selective memory that focused on commemorating the losses of Soviet citizens during World War II, while suppressing public commemoration of the individuals executed under Stalin.[48] The Kurapaty mass grave was registered on the list of Belarusian sites of historical cultural heritage in 1993, but only a small memorial plaque informs visitors of the official status of the wooded area. The 1988 government commission that investigated the Kurapaty mass grave commemorated victims with an entry in the *Belarusian Soviet Encyclopedia*. Indeed, the 1995 edition mentions both Kurapaty and the conclusions of the 1988 investigative commission, which recognized the NKVD as responsible for the crime.

However, four years later, a newer *Belarusian Encyclopedia* posited two competing versions of the mass killings at Kurapaty: one ascribed responsibility to the NKVD, while the other pointed to the Germans.[49] The German role in Kurapaty was first suggested by the independent public commission (IPC) formed in 1992, which included Valentin Korzun and Marya Osipova, a former partisan and Heroine of the Soviet Union. Citing testimony from 50 witnesses, the IPC disagreed with the government commission and blamed the German occupation forces for the executions.[50] The IPC convinced the government to reinvestigate the killings. Early in 1993, the General Prosecutor Vasily Sholodonov stated that the investigation is likely to be protracted.[51] In 1997, the IPC asked Lukashenka again to open a new investigation. This investigation, conducted by the military Prosecutor's Office, led to new excavations in Kurapaty in October 1997 and May 1998. In April 1999, the investigation was closed without any official results. In December 2001, the Prosecutor's Office stated in a letter that investigations "confirmed that in 1937–40 the NKVD transported people from prisons to Kurapaty and killed them."[52] But the letter did not fully refute the "German lead" theory, noting instead that some of the belongings found in Kurapaty were produced in Germany, Poland, Austria, and the Czech Republic:

> Each part of the political fight interprets these pieces of evidence in their own way. For some, they confirm that Germans drove people from Europe to Kurapaty and killed them. For others, they confirm that among the victims were people from Western Belarus, annexed in 1939. It is not possible to confirm or refute these versions with objective pieces of evidence.[53]

Thus, different interpretations of the Kurapaty executions became possible, but the final conclusion remained uncertain.

In 2002, President Lukashenka mentioned Kurapaty in his annual address to the nation, but blurred the issue of accountability:

> there are people buried at Kurapaty. In the 1930s and the 1940s, either Germans carried out the shootings, or someone else did, but [the important thing is that] these were people! And we have to construct [...] a simple memorial to all of the people. This place is for sorrow and thoughts, not for political dancing on the graves.[54]

In 2009, the daily *Belarus Today* attempted to consider the Soviet political repression as a purely historical matter not part of the politics of memory.[55] In itself, such depoliticization of Soviet repression illustrates a lack of political will to remember the crimes of the Soviet state. Such memory clashes ideologically with the positive image of the Soviet past that serves as a foundation for Lukashenka's state ideology.

UNOFFICIAL TRANSITIONAL JUSTICE INITIATIVES

Since 1994, the BPF and various nonstate actors have pursued truth-telling and memorialization programs in order to criminalize the Soviet past. For the anticommunist opposition, the Kurapaty site became a *lieux de memoire* for the Belarusian nation, a people's memorial, and a sanctuary of Belarusian nationhood. Focusing on the victimhood narrative associated with Kurapaty, the BPF repeatedly denied that Polish victims could also be buried there and considered attempts to commemorate Polish victims a provocation.[56] The repeated vandalizing of the Polish memorial signs at Kurapaty by Belarusian nationalist groups illustrates commemorative competitiveness and hostility.[57] Focused on the national character of the mass killings at Kurapaty and other Soviet execution sites, remembrance became instrumentalized as a means of consolidating Belarusian collective identity in opposition to the Soviet past and Russian influence. Patterns of retelling the Soviet past resemble those in the Baltic states and Eastern Europe, where sites of communist violence became important elements of new national history narratives through the recovery of the remains of terror.[58] "Living and dead, we are all one. We are the nation. Although we cannot help the dead, the dead can help us," wrote Pazniak to make the memory of victimhood a foundation for national unity.[59]

In the mid-2000s, new initiatives widened public engagement with the memory of political repression. Looking for models of historical reckoning in

Eastern European and the Baltic states, Belarusian memory activists organized several commemorative projects. In 2007, they founded the Virtual Museum of Soviet Repression in Belarus with the support of the Belarusian Christian Democratic Party. Modeled on the Lithuanian Museum of Genocide Victims, the Belarusian museum collected interviews with victims of the Soviet regime, documents, and photographs. It provides information on the history of repression, the Belarusian legislation on rehabilitation, civic initiatives of historical reckoning, and various memorials dedicated to the victims of repression in Belarus. It also proposes assistance in the search of former victims.[60]

In 2007, a civic group led by Igor Kuznietsov, the leader of the Belarusian branch of Memorial, asked the government to recognize 29 October as the Day of Victims of Stalinist repression, in order to mark the seventieth anniversary of the beginning of the "Great Terror." The initiative was inspired by a day of memory in Russia established on 30 October in 1992. The Belarusian authorities declined the proposition, but unofficial commemorative events have been organized on this date every year since then.

In 2014, the e-book project *Black Book of Stalinism: Belarus, Crime, Terror, Repression* was started to present the losses of the Belarusian people. Nicolas Werth, one of the authors of the *Black Book of Communism* published in France in 1997, was invited to write the introduction to the Belarusian e-book, but the other materials were to be prepared by Belarusian scholars. The first volume covers the 1929–53 period, while the second volume is devoted to the first decade of Bolshevik rule (1917–28) and post-1945 repression. The book is still in preparation, but fragments are available on the site of the civil initiative Return of Memory.[61]

A citizens' tribunal on Stalinist crimes was organized in Minsk in 2015 jointly by the Belarusian Memorial, the Saving Kurapaty association, and the Association of the Victims of Political Repression. The tribunal was the second citizens' tribunal in the FSU after the International Vilnius Public Tribunal of 2000. In interviews with independent media, the organizers emphasized that the symbolic Belarusian tribunal was modeled on the Vilnius precedent, but focused on the crimes committed in that country.[62]

In 2015, the civic initiative Lustration for Belarus was launched to prepare the foundation for enacting lustration in the future.[63] A conference in Vilnius discussed a lustration proposal for Belarus, and included comments from leading Belarusian human rights activists, presentations of other postcommunist lustration programs, and Belarusian translations of key international documents related to lustration and decommunization. While the organizers recognized the symbolic role of this event and the fact that it would remain unknown to the wider public in Belarus, it was important to them to discuss Soviet political repression, prevent amnesia, and equip the Belarusian civil society with means for future transitional justice initiatives. By pursuing unofficial transitional justice, the organizers situated Belarus among other Eastern European states that enacted lustration and argued that Belarus must go through a similar process after the authoritarian regime was ousted. The Belarusian lustration project addresses the crimes of Soviet times and Lukashenka's regime.[64] In this way, the lustration proposal and the politics of history were transformed into a force of opposition to the current regime. A leader from the Experts for Saving Kurapaty civil society groups, Marat Garavy, hoped that the KBG headquarters in Minsk would be transformed into a Belarusian Institute of National Remembrance, similar to the Polish one.[65]

Because of the lack of state support for historical reckoning, Belarusian unofficial programs have secured funding from foreign agencies. The German Bundesstigtung Aufarbeitung supported a project on "Places of Memory of the Victims of Communism in Belarus," and the Konrad Adenauer Foundation helped the Virtual Museum of Soviet Repression. The Experts for Saving Kurapaty organized a project competition on a memorial for the Kurapaty site in 2015. The US Embassy in Minsk funded a traveling exhibition on the history of the site.[66] International agencies provide the Belarusian memory activists with financial support for their projects, and integrate the Belarusian opposition memory politics into the larger European decommunization effort.

Since Belarus remains an authoritarian regime antithetical to decommunization initiatives, it is not surprising that the Virtual Museum, the citizens' tribunal, and lustration are unofficial projects. Unofficial efforts are important, but remain unknown to the wider public; commemorative events are attended by politically engaged memory activists without attracting wider participation. Coverage by the independent media permits these initiatives to maintain a modicum of visibility. They counterbalance the narratives extolling the positive memory of Soviet times maintained by the official discourse and prevent amnesia of Soviet wrongdoings.

CONCLUSION

Transitional justice measures introduced in Belarus in 1989–93 were meant to restore historical justice and victims' rights, but for new nationalist elites, human rights abuses became translated into a national victimhood narrative. This anti-Soviet identity was meant to reassemble society in an independent

Belarus. In the early 1990s, such retrospective construction of Belarusian nationhood in opposition to Soviet identity proved unsuccessful. On the one hand, the perception that the entire Soviet rule was a period of unending national oppression did not match the Belarusians' experience with the successful reconstruction of the republic after the devastation of World War II. On the other hand, the new narrative of victimhood fundamentally challenged the already existing master narrative of national sacrifice – the memory of Belarusian heroic sufferings under the Nazi occupation.

Since 1991, elites have used the memory of Soviet political repression to foster a new Belarusian collective identity. By underlining the repressive nature of Soviet power and its negative effects on the development of Belarus, this Belarusian narrative has othered the Soviet past. Both the new nationalist and former Soviet victimhood narratives generalized individual traumatic experiences to reconstruct collective suffering. As a result, the memory of victimhood in post-Soviet Belarus became polarized between two dominant discourses, Soviet and anti-Soviet. Each of them substitutes the memory of victims with unitary, ideologically instrumentalized myths.

The BPF's discursive reframing of the Soviet experience as colonial oppression was a political failure. Lukashenka's 1994 electoral victory revealed the disparity between the political meaning of collective identity embraced by the nationalist leaders and that held by the larger society. Lukashenka's political strategy reframed Soviet development as an integral part of the Belarusian nation-building narrative. After 1994, justice seeking became a marginal concern. Without denying the Soviet repression, Lukashenka preserved most of the 1990–4 legislation on the rehabilitation of former victims of political repression, but canceled most of the benefits for former victims. The country's new Soviet and political identity made memories of victimhood irrelevant.

Authoritarianism, unlimited subordination of the individual to the state, shrinking political and social autonomy from the regime, and the institutionalization of repression by legal codification of punishment for unwanted political activity characterize Lukashenka's rule. In these conditions, opposition memory activists – political parties and civil society groups – developed transitional justice that symbolically mimicked measures in neighboring Poland and the Baltic states. As Belarus demonstrates, in an authoritarian context the meaning of these activities goes beyond redressing past human rights abuses. By mapping the Belarusian identity as part of Eastern Europe, these activities place Belarus in opposition to the official project of Eurasian integration, and maintain the prospect of future accountability for both past and ongoing repression and human rights abuses.

Notes

1. Vital Silitski, "Signs of Hope rather than a Color of Revolution," in Joerg Forbrig, David Marples and Pavol Demeš, eds. *Prospects for Democracy in Belarus* (Washington: German Marshall Fund, 2006), 23.
2. Terry Martin, *The Affirmative Action Empire Nations and Nationalism in the Soviet Union, 1923–1939* (Ithaca: Cornell University Press, 2001), 160; and Per Anders Rudling, *The Rise and Fall of Belarusian Nationalism. 1906–1931* (Pittsburg: Pittsburg University Press, 2015).
3. Jan Zaprudnik, *Belarus: At a Crossroads in History* (Boulder: Westview Press, 1993), 87, and Nicholas Vakar, *Belorussia. The Making of a Nation. A Case Study* (Cambridge: Harvard University Press, 1956), 146, 150.
4. Tatiana Prot'ko, *Stanovlenie soveskoi totalitarnoi sistemy v Belarusi 1917–1941gg* (Minsk: Tesei, 2002), 606–7; Yaugeni Novik and Genadz Matsul, *Historya Belarusi. February 1917–1997* (Minsk: Universyteckaye, 2000), 158; Mikhail Kostiuk, *Boslevistskaya sistema vlasti w Belarusi* (Moskow: RAN, 2002), 188; and Igor Kuznetsov, "Repressii na Belarusi v 1920–40," in Igor Kuznetsov and Yakov Basin, eds. *Repressivnaya politika sovetskoi vlasti v Belarusi*, Vol. 2 (Minsk: Memorial, 2007), 2–29: 28.
5. Rudling, *The Rise and Fall of Belarusian Nationalism*, 298.
6. David Marples, "History and Politics in Post-Soviet Belarus: The Foundations," in Elena Korosteleva, Colin Lawson and Rosalind Marsh, eds. *Contemporary Belarus: Between Democracy and Dictatorship* (London: Routledge, 2003), 24; and Grigory Ioffe, "Understanding Belarus: Economy and Political Landscape," *Europe-Asia Studies* 56, 1 (2004): 108–9.
7. Neringa Klumbyte and Gulgaz Sharafutdinova, *Soviet Society in the Era of Late Socialism, 1964–1985* (Lanham: Lexington Books, 2013), 5.
8. "Soobschenie Tsentralnoi komissii referendum SSSR. Ob itogakh referendum SSSR sostoyavshegosya 17 marta 1991," *Pravda*, March 27, 1991, available at: www.gorby.ru/userfiles/file/referendum_rezultat.pdf, accessed February 16, 2017.
9. Mikhail Kastiuk, ed., *Narysy historyi Belarusi* (Minsk: Belarus, 1995), 374; and Uladzimir Adamushka, *Palitychnyia represii 20-50 hadou na Belarusi* (Minsk: Belarus, 1994), 142.
10. Protocols of the Commission's meetings are available at Digital Archive of the Foundation of A. Yakovlev, available at: www.alexanderyakovlev.org/fond/issues-doc/66066, accessed February 15, 2014.
11. Stephen Kotkin, *Armageddon Averted: The Soviet Collapse, 1970–2000* (New York: Oxford University Press, 2001), 171–6.
12. The group's name recognized the role of Article 58 in Stalinist repression. "Project of Statute of the Belarusian civic historical-educational association of memory of victims of Stalinism Committee 58," *Public Web-Archive*, no date, available at: http://vytoki.net/?docs=00006123, accessed December 20, 2016.
13. Martyralog. 1989. *Bulleten* (Minsk: Belarusian Association of the Memory of Victims of Stalinism), available at: http//vytoki.net/content/Martyralog.pdf, accessed June 21, 2017.
14. "Declaration," Martyralog Bulleten, Minsk 1989: 6–7, available at: http://vytoki.net/content/Martyralog.pdf, accessed December 14, 2016, 2.

15. Martyralog, *Bulleten*, 10.
16. Zianon Pazniak, "Fizychnaie znishchen'nie belaruskai natsyi," no date, available at: http://pazniak.info/page_fizichnae_znishchenne_belaruskay_natsyi, accessed February 8, 2017, and Zmister Yushkevich, "Nieviadomy genacyd," February 16, 2014, available at: http://mfront.net/nieviadomy-hienacyd.html, accessed January 10, 2017.
17. Zianon Pazniak and Yauhenii Shmygalyou, "Kurapaty – the Road of Death," *Literatura i mastactva*, June 3, 1988, available at: http://kamunikat.org/download .php?item=1865-2.html&pubref=1865, accessed December 11, 2016.
18. David Marples, "Kuropaty: The Investigation of a Stalinist Historical Controversy," *Slavic Review* 53, 2 (1994): 513–23.
19. "Soobshchenie pravitel'stvennoi komissii, sozdannoi resheniem Soveta Ministrov BSSR ot 14 iulya 1988," *Sovetskaia Belorussiya*, January 22, 1989.
20. Georgii Tarnavskii, Valerii Sobolev and Evgenii Gorelik, *Kuropaty: Sledstvie Prodolzhaetsya* (Moscow: Yuridicheskaya kniga, 1990).
21. Igor Kuznetsov, "Zabyt znachit predat," *Belorusskaya delovaya gazeta*, April 14, 2004.
22. "Decree 42 On the memorialization of the victims of mass repressions of 1937–1941 in Kurapaty," January 18, 1989, available at: http://old.bankzakonov.com/obsch/ razdel210/time21/yamf0925.htm, accessed December 13, 2016.
23. For text of Directive, see Aleh Dziarnovich, *Rehabilitation. The Collection of Documents and Normative Acts Pertaining to the Rehabilitation of Victims of Political Repression in 1920–1980s* (Minsk: Athenaeum, 2001), 74–7.
24. In 1992, the Belarusian government privatized public housing. Citizens who lived in state-owned houses could buy their own housing. Some citizens could obtain ownership for free: heroes of Soviet Union, veterans of Socialist Labor and the Great Patriotic War, disabled individuals. "Law of the Republic of Belarus 1593-XII," April 16, 1992, available at: http://pravo.levonevsky.org/bazaby/zakon/ zakb1393.htm, accessed December 12, 2016.
25. Housing Code of the Republic of Belarus, August 28, 2012, available at: www.levonevski.net/pravo/norm2013/num03/d03689/page4.html, accessed December 12, 2016.
26. "Decree 479-XII On restoring the rights of citizens who suffered from repressions in 1920–1950," December 21, 1990, available at: http://pravo.levonevsky.org/bazaby11/republic64/text164.htm, and "Law 183-3 on changes in some legislative acts of the Republic of Belarus," January 4, 2004, available at: http://pravo.levonevsky.org/ bazaby09/sbor43/text43894.htm, both accessed December 12, 2016.
27. Author's personal interview with Zinaida Tarasevich, Minsk, August 26, 2016.
28. The method of calculating the cost of lost properties was specified in Decree of the Supreme Council of the Republic of Belarus of November 3, 1992, December 18, 1992. No 1906-XII, *Vedomosti, Verkhovnogo Soveta Respubliki Belarus*, 1992, No 26: 465, available at: www.pravo.levonevsky.org/bazaby09/sbor88/text88307.htm, accessed June 22, 2017; Dziarnovich, *Rehabilitation. The Collection of Documents and Normative Acts Pertaining to the Rehabilitation of Victims of Political Repression in 1920–80s*.
29. Marat Garavy, "Akhviara Gulagu nia mozha viarnut rodnuyu khatu," *Novy Chas*, August 25, 2014, available at: http://novychas.by/hramadstva/achviara_hulahu_ bezhaty, accessed January 20, 2017.

30. Tatiana Ageeva, "Pravo zhertv politicheskikh repressii na vozmeschenie uscherba osnovano na Konstitutsii i deistvujuschem zakonodatelstve i nie ogranicheno skokami," Belarusian Documents Center, 2016, available at: https://bydc .info/news/444-tatyana-ageeva-pravo-zhertv-politicheskikh-repressij-na-vozmesh chenie-ushcherba-osnovano-na-konstitutsii-i-dejstvuyushchem-zakonodatelstve-i-ne-ogranicheno-srokami, accessed January 20, 2017.

31. "Resolution of the Supreme Council of the Republic of Belarus 2623-XII On the introducing amendments and additions to the legislative acts of the Republic of Belarus regulating issues of rehabilitation of victims of political repressions in 1920-1980 and restoration of their rights," Archive of Belarusian Law, December 3, 1993, available at: http://old.bankzakonov.com/d2008/time83/lav83154.htm, accessed December 15, 2016.

32. Constitutional Court of Belarus, "Decision П-188/ 2006 on the right of citizens – victims of political repression for compensation of harm and payment," May 11, 2006, available at: http://pravo.levonevsky.org/bazaby11/republic25/text542.htm, accessed December 12, 2016.

33. "Obschestvo Memorial: v 1961–1988 v Belarusi bylo osuzhdeno 28 dissidentov," *Naviny.by*, January 24, 2008, available at: http://naviny.by/rubrics/society/2008/01/24/ic_news_116_284382/, accessed January 29, 2017.

34. Uladzimir Mironchyk, "Patryiatyzm – galouny stoup," *Litaratura i Mastactva*, March 5, 1993.

35. Between 30 and 40 Supreme Soviet members supported the Bloc. Aleksander Feduta, Oleg Bogutskii and Viktor Matsinovitch, *Political Parties of Belarus – Essential Part of Civil Society* (Minsk: Friedrich Ebert Stiftung, 2003), 13–14.

36. Lucan Way, "Deer in Headlights: Incompetence and Weak Authoritarianism after the Cold War," *Slavic Review* 71, 3 (2012): 622; and Feduta, Bogutskii and Matsinovitch, *Political Parties of Belarus*, 14.

37. "Resolution 1211–XII On introducing amendments and additions to some legislative acts of the Republic of Belarus regulating the questions of restoration of the rights of citizens who suffered from repressions in the 1920–1980," Archive of Law Library, available at: http://pravo.newsby.org/belarus/postanov28/pst600.htm, accessed January 20, 2017.

38. Author's personal interview with Igor Kuznetsov, Minsk, August 28, 2016.

39. Vital Silitski, "Explaining Post-Communist Authoritarianism in Belarus," in Elena Korosteleva, Colin Lawson and Rosalind Marsh, eds. *Contemporary Belarus. Between Democracy and Dictatorship* (London: Routledge, 2003), 42–3; and David Marples, *Belarus. A Denationalized Nation* (Amsterdam: Harwood, 1999), 86.

40. "Prahrama Patyi BNF," December 2, 2002, available at: http://narodny.org/?p=1116, accessed January 9, 2017.

41. Zianon Pazniak, "My pavinny kiravatcca u Europu," *BPF News*, December 9, 1992; Zianon Pazniak, "Nastaye chas dzieyannyau i rasplaty," *Narodnaya gazeta*, November 8, 1993; and "Prahrama partyi BNF," *BNF Website*, December 2, 2002, available at: http://narodny.org/english/?page_id=2, accessed January 9, 2017.

42. Yuri Khadyka, "Eurapeiskia konteksty belaruskaga mentalitetu," *Filamaty* 4, 7 (2003), available at: http://kamunikat.org/filamaty.html?pubid=5584, accessed January 9, 2017.

43. Zianon Pazniak, *Sapraudnaye abliccha* (Minsk: Palifakt, 1992), 36.

44. Christian Haerper, *Democracy and Enlargement in Post-Communist Europe: The Democratisation of the General Public in 15 Central and Eastern European Countries. 1991–1998* (New York: Routledge, 2002), 9.
45. Simon Lewis, "Overcoming Hegemonic Martyrdom: The Afterlife of Khatyn in Belarusian Memory," *Journal of Soviet and Post-Soviet Politics and Society* 1, 2 (2015): 368.
46. Brian Grodsky, "Transitional Justice and Political Goods," in Lavinia Stan and Nadya Nedelsky, eds. *Post-Communist Transitional Justice: Lessons from 25 Years of Experience* (New York: Cambridge University Press, 2015), 7.
47. Aleksander Etkind, "Post-Soviet Hauntology: Cultural Memory of the Soviet Terror," *Constellations* 16, 1 (2009): 184.
48. Rainer Lindner, "Natsiianal'nyia i prydvornya gistoryki 'lukashenkauskai' Belarusi," *Histarychny almanakh* 4 (2001): 199–215.
49. "Kurapaty," in *Belarus. Encyklapedychny davednik* (Minsk: Belorusskaia Enthiklopedyia, 1995), 411–12; and "Kurapaty," in *Belorusskaia entsiklopediya u 18 tomakh*, tom. 9 (Minsk: Belorusskaia Enthiklopedyia, 1999), 42.
50. Marples, "Kuropaty," 519.
51. Igor Grishan, "Kuropaty: Sledstvie Vozobnovleno," *Sovetskaia Belorussiia*, March 20, 1993, 3.
52. *Kurapaty. Zbornik Materyalau* (Minsk: Arkhiu Nainoushai Historii, 2002), 80–1.
53. Ibid., 81.
54. Annual Address of the President of Republic of Belarus to Parliament, Official Website of the President, April 16, 2002, available at: www.president.gov.by/ru/news_ru/view/fragmenty-iz-vystuplenija-prezidenta-respubliki-belarus-pri-pred-stavlenii-ezhegodnogo-poslanija-parlamentu-5784/, accessed February 2, 2017.
55. "Kuropaty: mir pod sosnami," *Belarus segondnya*, October 29, 2009, available at: www.sb.by/post/93010, accessed January 15, 2017.
56. Zianon Pazniak, "Sutnasc pravakacyi," *Conservative Christian Party BPF*, February 20, 2012, available at: www.narodnaja-partyja.org/oo–Naviny-c_hyphen-minus-Galownac_ja--fr--pg/oo--Naviny-c_hyphenminus-Galownac_ja--bk--an--oi/oo--20121120–06, accessed December 2, 2016.
57. "Zaschitnikam Kuropat nadoelo diskutirovat s Pozniakom," *Belorusskii Partizan*, November 8, 2012, available at: www.belaruspartisan.org/politic/222718/, accessed February 15, 2017.
58. James Mark, "What Remains? Anti-Communism, Forensic Archeology, and the Retelling of the National Past in Lithuania and Romania," *Past and Present* Supplement 5 (2010): 278.
59. Pazniak, *Sapraudnaye abliccha*, 36.
60. Site of Virtual Museum of Soviet Repression in Belarus, available at: http://represii net, accessed January 30, 2017.
61. Fragments of the *Black Book of Stalinism* in Belarusian, available at: http://kurapaty.info/be/black-book, accessed December 13, 2016.
62. Press conference of Igor Kuznetsov, February 12, 2014, *Belorusskii Partisan*, available at: www.belaruspartisan.org/m/politic/257529/, accessed February 14, 2017; and "Lustracyia dla Belarusi. Praekt Kancentcyi lustracyi pry perakhode ad autarytarnaga rezhymu da demakratyi," *Lustacyia dla Belarusi* (Vilnius-Minsk: KontraPress, 2015), 36.

63. Vaclau Areshka, "Ad gramadzianskai inicyiatyvy 'Lustracyia dla Belarusi'," *Lustacyia dla Belarusi* (Vilnius-Minsk: KontraPress, 2015), 6–8.
64. "Lustracyia dla Belarusi," 28–9.
65. Marat Garavy, "Yakim bachycca natsinalny nekropal u Kuraprtakh," *Narodnaya Volya*, March 22, 2016, 4.
66. Anna Kaminski, ed., *Mescy pamaci akhvyarau kamunismu u Belarusi* (Leipzig: Bundesstigtung Aufarbeitung, 2011), and "V posolstve USA w Minske otkrylas vystavka Pravda o Kuropatakh. Fakty, dokumenty, svidetelstva," *Nabiny.by*, March 24, 2016, available at: http://naviny.by/rubrics/society/2016/03/24/ic_news_116_472503, accessed January 14, 2017.

PART II

TRANSITIONAL JUSTICE PROGRAMS, PRACTICES, AND LEGISLATION

6

Lustration in Ukraine and Democracy
Capable of Defending Itself

Roman David

Twenty-two years after regaining independence from the Soviet Union, Ukraine experienced a major political crisis, underwent dramatic political changes, and faced challenges of historic proportions.[1] In February 2013, relentless public protests at the Maidan Independence Square in Kyiv led to the toppling of President Victor Yanukovych. Although democratically elected, pro-Moscow-oriented Yanukovych was widely seen as a corrupt semi-authoritarian leader whose actions put him at odds with the increasingly democratic and pro-European Union (EU) aspirations of Ukrainian citizens. After his escape to Moscow, Ukraine embarked on a course of action taken by other Central and Eastern European countries – to strengthen its ties with the EU. To make the changes irreversible, the Ukrainian public demanded that corrupt public officials and judges associated with Yanukovych's rule be dismissed. To facilitate these dismissals, they called for a lustration law.

The public demands for lustration gained further momentum from the political events that unfolded in the east of the country. Shortly after the Maidan revolution, Russia's proxies organized a bogus referendum in Crimea, which served as a pretext for the annexation of the entire Crimean region of Ukraine. In the following weeks, Russian forces orchestrated and supported separatist movements in the regions of Donetsk and Luhansk, which led to a military confrontation, with the Kyiv government losing control over large parts of the region's territory. Ukrainian democracy thus came under threat internally from the loyalists of Yanukovych and externally from Russia-backed forces clawing at its sovereignty. The creation of a loyal state apparatus staffed with personnel uncompromised by the past was placed high on the political agenda for the new government.

Simultaneous with the increasing demands for lustration, the Council of Europe and other European institutions expressed concern about the structure and function of lustration in Ukraine.[2] They observed that many of the legal provisions that were intended to facilitate lustration may have been in breach of international human rights standards, in particular the European Convention on Human Rights (ECHR). Such concerns were not unwarranted in view of the popular desire for retribution that had simmered in sections of the Ukrainian public in the wake of the bloodshed in Maidan. The European leaders were aware of a similar retributive wave that had swept many western countries in the aftermath of World War II.

While I shared these concerns about retribution during the initial period after the political change,[3] I believe that the case for lustration in Ukraine is justified. This chapter illustrates my argument. I invoke the concept of a democracy capable of defending itself to demonstrate that the ECHR contains provisions for building such democracies, and that the Ukrainian lustration law is an expression of a democracy capable of defending itself. I use a law and society method to elucidate my argument. The law and society method examines laws and legal provisions with the conceptual and methodological apparatuses of social sciences. While legal methods typically focus on "laws in books," the law and society approach studies "laws in society": the former reviews existing legislation, judicial precedents, and comparable legislation in other countries, while the latter is an interdisciplinary arena that examines law in its social, political, and/or historical context. This includes an understanding of the context, motives, and interests in producing laws, their application and interpretation, and it also includes studies of the impact of law on shaping, transforming, or solidifying social relations.

LUSTRATION AND ITS MEANING IN UKRAINE

Lustration has been frequently translated as "vetting," "personnel change," and "purge." Although all these notions concern a reform of the state apparatus in one way or another, it would be unrealistic to expect that lustration would have the same meaning in different countries. The question is how is the social meaning of lustration in Ukraine different from those used in other countries? The question about the meaning is critical: if the meaning of lustration in Ukraine was different, then precedents and lessons from other countries may have limited applicability here. Due to geographic, historical, linguistic, and cultural closeness, Ukrainian legislators and civil society members drew heavily on the experiences of the Czech Republic and Poland.[4] Did lustration have the same social or etymological meaning in Ukraine as in these two countries? Since lustration's social meaning changed over time in both the Czech and Polish cases, one might ask more directly if the Ukrainian understanding of lustration corresponded with the initial Czech and Polish meaning of the term?

Lustration comes from the Latin terms *lustro* and *lustrare*, which in its first meaning suggests "review, survey, examination."[5] Indeed, this is how the term was used in communist Czechoslovakia, where secret police "lustrated" citizens by trying to retrieve any available information on them from its archives. After 1989, Czechs and Slovaks used "lustrace" as a process of retrieving background information about public figures, and conducting background checks to find whether there was evidence of collaboration with the secret police or other agencies of the repressive apparatus in the past.[6] For many Czechs, lustration resembled "lustr," which means "chandelier" and evokes casting light on somebody, putting a public official into a spotlight. In the Czech Republic, lustration has increasingly been associated with its instrumental purpose, which is the dismissal of officials who were found positively lustrated, in other words individuals who are shown to have a record of secret collaboration.

In Poland, "lustracja" used to have the same original meaning as in the Czech Republic: the examination of the background of public figures. For a number of years, almost all the newspapers in Poland published the results of the CBOS opinion poll survey agency, which asked Poles whether it is necessary to conduct lustration and explained "that it is to check the background of public figures."[7] However, the instrumental purpose of lustration in Poland gradually shifted from dismissals to confession, thus defying the wishes of many on the political center-right: owing to political compromise, lustration was used to verify the truthfulness of public self-disclosures concerning the background of politicians, only penalizing in the event that an individual lied about his/her background. Similarly, the Poles implemented "property lustration," which meant the disclosure of the property ownership of politicians. The understanding of lustration as self-disclosure or confession may have been derived from two sources. First, linguistically "lustro" in Polish means a "mirror," which suggests lustration as a self-reflection; and second, Catholicism as the dominant religion places an emphasis on the confession of sins.

The Ukrainian language is close to the other Slavic languages in the region, namely the Czech, Polish, and Slovakian languages. As Russian and Bulgarian, it uses a Cyrillic alphabet. In Ukrainian, the word "lyustratsia" resembles both "mirror" as in Polish and "chandelier" as in Czech. Rather than linguistic influences, the meaning of lustration was understood as a quasi-retributive measure that Ukraine needed to take in order to break free from the past and follow other Central and Eastern European countries toward a prosperous future in the EU.

The quasi-retributive nature of lustration in Ukraine appeared in different forms in different times among different people. For the political and social mainstream, lustration was tantamount to dismissals. This was a critical departure from the Polish reconciliatory model of lustration toward the exclusionary Czech model.[8] However, unlike in the Czech Republic, lustration was not used specifically to mean a process of retrieving background information about public figures to dismiss them; the word "lustration" became directly synonymous with "the dismissal of people associated with the abuses of power." This understanding of lustration in practice comports with the understanding of lustration in the Czech Republic over time.

On the fringes of society, lustration was initially expressed in more radical ways. An imitation of a guillotine with the Ukrainian trident on top and *lyustratsia* written on the bottom, apparently erected by political activists, appeared in the city of Dnipropetrovsk in 2014.[9] The word *lyustratsia* appeared in massive letters on the Maidan Independence Square and was spray painted on the fence of the Supreme Court in Kyiv. In the first case, it represented public demand; in the second case, it represented a threat. Moreover, pictures of tainted politicians were symbolically pelted with tomatoes.[10] In what became known as a "rubbish lustration" or a "trash bucket challenge," about a dozen Ukrainian politicians who had been accused of the abuse of power were thrown into refuse bins in 2014.[11]

One could hardly miss the symbolic meaning evoked here: lustration was meant to lead to the purification of public life of tainted officials. Indeed, the word lustration in its original Latin translation carried another meaning: ritual cleansing and purification by sacrifice. In ancient Rome and contemporary Central and Eastern Europe, lustration acquired similar dual meanings: lustration as an instrumental process; and lustration as a symbolic process. Certainly such instances of public lustration were rather isolated cases and to a certain degree explainable. One can hardly be surprised about the desire for retribution among the Ukrainian public in the wake of the bloody Maidan protests. More than 100 civilians were killed and many others injured during months of standoff between protesters and the government.[12]

LUSTRATION LAWS AND ITS UKRAINIAN VERSION

Lustration laws are special, transitional public employment laws that are typically approved in the aftermath of a regime transition or after civil war.[13] They often, though not always, lead to the dismissal of compromised state personnel from the state apparatus and the prevention of their return for a certain period of time until the new democracy takes root.[14] Lustration laws were applied in the aftermath of communist regimes in some European countries, such as the Czech Republic, Hungary, Poland, Romania, Albania, Lithuania, Latvia, and others.[15] Analogous special public employment laws were applied in many other countries in different historical eras, including the United States, Germany, Iraq, and Libya.[16]

Lustration laws build a bridge between the past and the future. On the one hand, they are forward-looking since they aspire to pursue personnel reform and the establishment of a state apparatus that is loyal to the emerging democratic order and possesses such qualities as efficiency, effectiveness, impartiality, and integrity. On the other hand, the laws are backward-looking since they are typically driven by the fact that holders of administrative positions may be loyal to the previous regime; they may hold records of human rights violations or their departments may have participated in human rights abuses; they may be ineffective in the pursuit of the daily operation of the state; they may be corrupt and their decisions may not have been transparent; and/or they may have held these positions not based on merit but based on their party affiliation, familial ties, and friendship.

Inherited personnel may be not only objectively lacking in competence and integrity, but also subjectively perceived to lack loyalty, impartiality, and trustworthiness. This negatively affects the daily operation of the state, such as the effectiveness of law enforcement, the reliability of tax collection, and the making of nonprejudicial administrative decisions. Performance of the functions of state is inexorably entwined with the credibility of those who perform the functions.

The Ukrainian Parliament adopted two laws that could generally be considered lustration laws: the Law on the Purification of Government (hereinafter the lustration law) and the Law on the Restoration of Trust in the Judiciary.[17] The remainder of this chapter concerns the former. Both laws were approved by the old parliament before the parliamentary elections took place in October 2014, although they were amended afterwards.

The Ukrainian lustration law is a standard exclusive lustration law. It is based on mandatory dismissals of persons who hold positions that are considered incompatible with certain prescribed posts in the past. The removal is temporary, prescribing the period of time out of any public office for five or ten years. Such a temporary provision was also part of the Czech lustration law before it was extended indefinitely. Due to the slow implementation of the law, one may expect it to be extended.

The Ukrainian lustration law contains two sets of substantive provisions. First, it contains backward-looking provisions, which list positions held under the former president Yanukovych, positions during the communist era, including high Communist Party echelons, KGB members and their collaborators, and corrupt officials, for which lustration would be mandated. Second, it contains forward-looking provisions, which list positions in the state apparatus, excluding secret services but including the Army and the judiciary, for which lustration would be required. The judiciary was thus subject to two methods of lustration.

Lustration has been administered by the Lustration Department, which operates under the auspices of the Ministry of Justice. The Department is led by Tetiana Kozachenko, a lawyer and former civil society activist. According to Kozachenko, some 700 officials were dismissed by September 2015, and 940 others by April 2016.[18] The Lustration Commission faced difficulties implementing the lustration law because not all government departments complied with the law. In response, the Commission has taken a proactive stance, criticizing the inaction of state departments.[19] The implementation of the lustration law is monitored and supported by civil society groups, such as the Civic Lustration Committee.[20]

As mentioned earlier, the Council of Europe, via its Venice Commission, expressed concern about the conformity of the Ukrainian lustration law with human rights standards.[21] The Venice Commission appointed a team of experts to assist the Ukrainian lawmakers to draft amendments to the law. The Ukrainian politicians and civil society members found the opinions of the Venice Commission useful while deliberating the legality of the existing lustration law, identifying its deficiencies, and drawing possible avenues for improvement. However, the Commissioners appeared not to fully appreciate the political challenges and historical conditions of Ukraine. I believe that the conformity of the lustration law to European human rights standards cannot be adequately examined without situating it into the theoretical context of a democracy capable of defending itself. Invoking the concept of a democracy capable of defending itself can provide us with the theoretical guidance needed for an assessment of the Ukrainian lustration in light of European standards. The practical advantage of opening this debate now is that the decision about the accord between lustration law and human rights is pending as of the writing of this chapter. An appeal has been lodged with the Constitutional Court of Ukraine, which still has to rule on whether the country's lustration law conforms to the requirements of its own Constitution as well as European human rights standards.[22]

EUROPEAN STANDARDS AND DEMOCRACY CAPABLE OF DEFENDING ITSELF

The implementation of the lustration laws has been typically examined in light of the European standards, which include especially the ECHR and its Protocols, the jurisprudence of the European Court of Human Rights (ECtHR), and Resolution 1096 on Measures to Dismantle the Heritage of Former Communist Totalitarian Systems. Among the national jurisprudence in European countries, the jurisprudence of the Federal Constitutional Court of Germany deserves attention owing to the specific situation of the country that dealt with two totalitarian systems. Beyond Europe, we can look at the jurisprudence of the US Supreme Court that dealt with the legislation of the McCarthy era and with political patronage cases.[23]

None of the sources of European standards in principle prohibits the conduct of lustration in Ukraine or any other country.[24] The ECHR does not specify any right to public employment. Other rights stipulated by the European Convention that are typically applied to lustration laws may be encroached if necessary in a democratic society, for instance, for the protection of national security, to maintain territorial integrity, for public safety, or to uphold the rights of others. The ECtHR has on numerous occasions interpreted the principles of "necessity in democratic society," which may justify the encroachment of certain human rights, and stipulated conditions for such encroachments including the adequacy and proportionality of measure.[25] In cases related to countries with legacies of undemocratic regimes, the ECtHR has applied the concept of *wehrhafte demokratie*, or a "democracy capable of defending itself" when dealing with lustration and other public employment laws.

Any debate about the conformity of the Ukrainian lustration law to European standards needs to center around this key concept of "a democracy capable of defending itself." The concept was coined by Karl Loewenstein in 1937.[26] Based on the analyses of legal and constitutional provisions in prewar Czechoslovakia and other European countries struggling with fascism and Nazism, he observed that the Weimar democracy lacked legal provisions that would grant it a "militant defense" against groups who sought to destroy it. Modern democracies that honor human rights are vulnerable to the undemocratic behavior of individuals, groups, and political parties. Therefore, a democracy should adopt measures to strengthen its capacity to protect itself from potential internal enemies. The concept was enshrined in the Federal German Constitution of 1949.[27] Art. 9(2) prohibited associations that acted against the constitutional order, Art. 21(2) prohibited unconstitutional political parties, Art. 33 stipulated the qualifications required for public office, and Art. 132(1) dismissed judges and civil servants who participated under Nazism. The concept has been both acknowledged and applied by the Federal Constitutional Court.[28]

The concept of a democracy capable of defending itself has also been applied by the ECtHR in lustration cases and similar public employment cases.[29] For instance, in the latest lustration case of *Naidin* v. *Romania*, 2014, concerning a collaborator with the Romanian communist-era secret service Securitate:

> The Court accepted that the difference in treatment applied to Mr. Naidin had pursued the legitimate aims of protecting national security, public safety and the rights and freedoms of others. In order to avoid a repetition of its past, the Romanian State had to be founded on a democracy capable of defending itself.[30]

The court ruled unanimously that there was no violation of Mr. Naidin's right to respect for privacy and family life (Art. 8 of the Convention), which had been assessed in conjunction with the prohibition of discrimination (Art. 14).

THE APPLICABILITY OF "DEMOCRACY CAPABLE OF DEFENDING ITSELF" TO THE UKRAINIAN SITUATION

Generally, the concept of a democracy capable of defending itself is applicable to the Ukrainian situation for several reasons. First, Ukraine qualifies as a democracy, having held free and fair presidential and parliamentary elections in May and October 2014, respectively. According to the Freedom House Report of 2015, "Ukraine's political rights rating rose from 4 to 3 due to improvements in political pluralism, parliamentary elections, and government transparency following the departure of President Viktor Yanukovych."[31] While essentially a democratic state, it does contain an unreformed state apparatus, which is part of the impetus for post-Yanukovych lustration.

Second, it is possible to say that Ukraine is in the process of *state* consolidation. Over the last two decades international organizations have observed the recurrence of abuses of public offices, corruption, and human rights violations. These practices led to public discontent, which manifested vividly in the Orange Revolution of 2004–5 and the Maidan Protests of 2013–14. The recurrence of undemocratic practices in the last two decades can partly be attributed to a failure to deal with the past and an inability to address the problem of personnel continuity in the state apparatus. Although free and fair presidential and parliamentary elections were held in 2014, democracy remained fragile and the state apparatus unreformed. The establishment of reliable state apparatus is necessary for the protection of national security, public safety, and the rights of others.

Third, the concept of *wehrhafte demokratie* has been applied in Germany for decades since World War II. Hence, it is applicable to Ukraine since the country is *currently at war* with powerful enemies inside and outside the country.

As of February 6, 2015, the Office of the United Nations High Commissioner for Human Rights (OHCHR) put the number of fatalities in that war to at least 5,486 persons; at least 12,972 people were wounded and 978,482 were internally displaced.[32] The UN Human Rights Monitoring Mission in Ukraine and the World Health Organization believe that the actual number of fatalities may be significantly higher.[33] By August 2016, according to UN OHCHR, 3.1 million people were in need of humanitarian assistance and 2.5 million people were directly affected by the conflict.[34] Ukraine's official data indeed reported a higher number of fatalities and internally displaced persons (IDPs). On December 5, 2016, Ukraine put the number of officially registered IDPs from Crimea and other occupied territories at 1,656,662; and President Petro Poroshenko estimated the total number of fatalities to be 10,000, among them 7,500 civilians.[35]

Moreover, the current political-security situation in Ukraine is fundamentally different from that of any other country within the Council of Europe system, including Germany, Albania, and Macedonia. None of these countries is currently experiencing open military conflict on its territory, or a breach of its territorial integrity. The ECtHR routinely strives to balance the uniformity of the application of ECHR with country-specific issues, and thus it assesses necessity in a particular democratic society. It is justifiable to believe that the ECtHR will not ignore the political-security situation in Ukraine, including the annexation of part of its territory (Crimea) and the occupation of other parts (Donetsk and Luhank Oblasts).

THE SUBSTANTIVE PROVISIONS OF THE LUSTRATION LAW

The concept of a democracy capable of defending itself allows us to delineate the decisions of the legislator concerning backward-looking substantive provisions of the lustration law. The backward-looking provisions provide for the exclusion from public office of certain categories of personnel. They include the major functionaries of the Communist Party and of its Youth League, collaborators with the secret services, members of the Yanukovych's regime, and corrupt officials.

The Supervising Positions in the Communist Party and the Young Communist League

These organizations were subordinate to Moscow, or in fact were an integral part of the communist apparatus during the Soviet period. The loyalty of their leaders to Ukraine may therefore be questioned in view of the country's current conflict with the Moscow-backed separatists. The current situation in Ukraine thus places certain limitations on the application of Resolution 1096 on Measures to Dismantle the Heritage of Former Communist Totalitarian Systems. The resolution could provide useful political guidance for Ukraine, were it not currently at war. The conflict aggravates the need for urgency in dealing with communist-era personnel whose loyalty is questionable. Loyalty to communism is not seen as a problem of the former Communist Party and communist youth leaders, but loyalty to the external enemy is. By dealing only with the supervisory positions, the law does not apply to the vast majority of functionaries and ordinary Communist Party members. The law applies to supervisory positions in the Communist Party of the Former Soviet Union, Communist Party of Ukraine, and other Union republics of the Former Soviet Union from the level of district committee secretary and above, as well as supervisory positions from the level of secretary of the Central Committee of the All-Union Leninist Young Communist League and above.[36] It thus appears to be a measured response that should be able to satisfy both principles of necessity and proportionality.

Staff Members, Secret Agents of the Secret Services, and Secret Collaborators

As with the Communist Party apparatus, secret services were subordinate to Moscow, and were a part of the same organization, the KGB of the Soviet Union and the Main Intelligence Department of the Soviet Union's Ministry of Defense. The link with Moscow may lead to doubts about the loyalty of personnel and may expose them to blackmail, since Moscow's institutions may have information about them that is not available in Ukraine. Such a possibility may have been strengthened by the defection of the former head of the Security Service of Ukraine (SBU), Oleksandr Yakymenko, (presumably) to Russia in February 2014. He may have been in possession of materials concerning Ukrainian citizens compiled by the SBU and its Soviet-era predecessor. It has also been alleged that Yanukovych, Yakymenko, and former Interior Minister Vitaliy Zakharchenko took an active part in the destabilization of Donbas, and continued to sponsor the separatist militia after their defections to Russia.[37]

Rebuilding intelligence agencies is essentially different from rebuilding other sections of the state apparatus, and therefore it may need to be regulated by separate laws. Lustration law should be limited to preventing the former agents of the KGB and the SBU, and their employees and collaborators, from entering the public service. Substantively, the ECtHR in the cited case of *Naidin* v. *Romania* accepted the exclusion of a collaborator with the Securitate as justifiable grounds for lustration.[38]

The Officials and Officers of Yanukovych's Regime

The lustration law targets officials who were involved in the regime of former President Yanukovych, whose decisions, commissions, and omissions undermined national security, defense, territorial integrity, and human rights. The Yanukovych's regime can be considered illegitimate for a number of reasons. Although the 2010 presidential elections "met most international standards," after his victory Yanukovych quickly reversed many of the changes adopted in the wake of the Orange Revolution, securing Constitutional Court rulings that enabled him to oust Tymoshenko as prime minister and replace her with a loyalist, and to annul the 2004 constitutional compromise that had reduced the power of the presidency. He subsequently launched efforts that systematically reduced Ukrainian citizens' political and civil rights.[39]

By contrast, the parliamentary elections of October 2012 were deeply flawed. Former prime minister Yuliya Tymoshenko, who represented the most outspoken opposition to President Viktor Yanukovych's Party of Regions, remained in jail and was not allowed to compete. The new electoral law, revised at the end of 2011, delivered more seats to the ruling party than it would have won under the previous system. Monitors cited numerous abuses in the elections, which strengthened the position of antidemocratic factions in the parliament. Over the course of the year, the administration continued to exert pressure on the judiciary, media freedom declined, and corruption opportunities increased with the elimination of tendering requirements for state companies.[40]

In addition, the Freedom House analysts concluded that:

[A] crucial factor behind Yanukovych's failure to conclude the EU pact was increasing pressure from Russia, against the backdrop of a fiscal crisis that put Ukraine on the verge of defaulting on its foreign debts. During the latter part of the year, Yanukovych met with Russian president Vladimir Putin several times for secret negotiations, and after he backed away from the EU agreement, Putin on December 17 [2013] pledged to lend Ukraine $15 billion (in $3 billion installments and for just two years) and cut natural gas prices by a third (though the price is reviewed every three months). Moreover, unlike the EU, Putin raised no objections to Yanukovych's authoritarian bent or Tymoshenko's imprisonment, and demanded no economic reforms. Neither leader explained what Ukraine would provide in return for the Kremlin's assistance.[41]

In sum, the regime of Viktor Yanukovych was elected through processes deemed satisfactory by international observers, but it still lacked substantive legitimacy. The regime violated human rights and undermined political processes, judicial independence, and the free press. It used force against its opponents, killing at least seventy-seven people during the Maidan protests.[42]

Corrupt Officials

Targeting corrupt officials is necessary in a country where corruption has been widespread. Corrupt officials need to be removed from positions of influence for three reasons: they engage in criminal activity; subjectively, they threaten the trustworthiness of the state apparatus; and objectively, they serve masters other than the members of the public and their superiors. The 2013 Report of Freedom House considered corruption to be a serious problem in Ukraine:

> Corruption, one of the country's most serious problems, continues to worsen. Business magnates benefit financially from their close association with top politicians. For example, a Forbes study has shown that businessmen affiliated with the Party of Regions win a considerable portion of state tenders. In addition, a new law in 2012 established that state enterprises do not have to use tenders when buying goods, meaning tens of billions of dollars will be disbursed each year without transparency. Separately, Yanukovych has become the de facto owner of a huge estate outside of Kyiv, raising suspicions of illicit wealth, and his two sons have amassed both power and immense personal fortunes. The apparent corruption of the administration, and the precedent set by its politicized pursuit of charges against Tymoshenko and former members of her government, have increased Yanukovych's incentives to remain in power indefinitely. Small and medium-sized businesses continue to suffer at the hands of corrupt bureaucrats, tax collectors, and corporate raiders.[43]

However, dismissals from public office may not be an effective sanction in cases of corruption. The problem is that, according to the lustration law, the same sanction is applied to both corruption and dishonesty in property declarations: dismissal. A corrupt official may be motivated to conceal relevant information in his or her declaration in order to avoid or delay dismissal. Only a successful completion of the verification process may eventually result in his or her dismissal. It would be more effective to charge dishonest officials with perjury and open criminal proceedings against them.

THE "DEMOCRACY CAPABLE OF DEFENDING ITSELF" AND THE LACK OF SUBSTANTIVE LUSTRATION

The current lustration law in Ukraine reflects the time when it was first proposed in spring 2014. At that time, Ukraine faced a particular political and security situation that was soon to change. For this reason, as of late 2016 the law, as it stands, is deficient in terms of failing to provide provisions that would prevent or prohibit the activities of Ukrainian citizens who were involved in political or military subversion of the country. Currently, only those who participated in the annexation of Crimea are affected. In general, the law is deficient in including backward-looking provisions that would prevent anyone who undermines democracy, national security, public safety, and the territorial integrity of the country.

At the same time, the law lacks provisions that would prevent decreasing the operational capacity of the state to a point where the state would be unable to run effectively and defend itself. Widespread dismissals may significantly affect the performance of the state apparatus as a whole, although this is hard to gauge using current impact assessments. Such provisions could provide for threshold levels of personnel after which any dismissal needs to be accompanied by the ability of the particular department to hire a qualified replacement. To avoid the abuse of such provisions, a specific period of time needs to be stipulated for hiring the new staff.

The provisions for exemption from the lustration law also appear insufficient. Currently, the law exempts only those who participated in the antiterrorist operation, which is a euphemism for the military conflict in the East of the country. The record and actions of other persons who have defended the Ukrainian statehood, democracy, and the rule of law need to be taken into account. The loyalty of people is not fixed by their past actions or affiliation. For instance, the events of the past year may have provided an opportunity for Communist Party members to demonstrate their loyalty to the country and commitment to the democratic system in various ways. The case of former Ukrainian President Leonid Kuchma, who had been a member of the Central Committee of the Ukrainian Communist Party in the 1980s and later became a spokesman for Ukrainian interests during the Minsk negotiations with Moscow in 2015,[44] shows that human characters are not fixed. The exclusion of such people may be unwarranted, and in fact it may even diminish the capacity of a democracy to defend itself by depriving the country of qualified personnel. Moreover, unwarranted dismissals may increase the number of those who are hostile to democracy. Dismissals of personnel from the "gray zone" represented by these cases may unnecessarily push them into the "black" zone by making enemies from those who were not enemies in the first place.

RECOMMENDATIONS: THE IMPLEMENTATION OF LUSTRATION LAW

Minimizing the Exclusive Nature of the Lustration Law

Democracy assumes inclusiveness. The Ukrainian lustration law is essentially exclusive in its nature. On the one hand, it is commendable that the law does not affect elected positions, and does not limit the scope of political contestation. On the other hand, there is a risk that the application of the law may exacerbate its exclusive nature. In particular, dismissals implemented together with the publication of the names of positively lustrated positions may have unintended social and political consequences, such as discrimination against the dismissed in the labor market or their joining the administration in the occupied territories.

The public exposure of the dismissed effectively signifies their legal certification as a group unsuitable for democracy. Such perceptions are strengthened by the title of the law on "purification." If the outcome of purification is dismissal then the dismissed are likely to be perceived as "dirty." The dismissed would then face discrimination in the labor market and experience social exclusion in their social spheres.[45] It is essential that the dismissal of personnel under the lustration law is conducted with dignity and respect to the dismissed. Persons dismissed lose their livelihood, they may face discrimination, and they may feel humiliated. Widespread dismissals run the risk that a large number of citizens with the same social status and grievances would work against the fragile democratic system. Giving the dismissed personnel respect and dignity would decrease the risk of them pursuing revenge.

The deleterious effects of de-Baathification in Iraq and the Political Isolation Law in Libya, where special public employment laws lacked the legal safeguards seen with lustration, should nonetheless be taken into account when a large number of personnel is dismissed.[46] Currently, the Ukrainian lustration law is estimated to lead to the dismissal of 2,554 security service personnel.[47] This raises the question of what policies, if any, are currently in place to absorb these personnel. Offering them an employment in the public sector could decrease the risk of them joining the separatist forces and may thus be a better avenue than a social policy that relies on social benefits.

Speedy Reform and Human Rights Standards

The lustration law needs to be implemented without delay. The centrality of the state apparatus and its importance for the establishment of order, security, safety, and human rights warrants urgent implementation of personnel reform. Indeed, in 2016 the Office of the UN High Commissioner for Human Rights acknowledged the need to "*work quickly and effectively* to re-establish the rule of law and the administration of justice in postconflict missions."[48]

The pace of personnel reform may be affected by the required standards of proof. While evidence in most employment and public employment cases needs to meet the standards of "the balance of probabilities," the Venice

Commission in its Interim Opinion on lustration invoked criminal law standards that imply due process guarantees and stringent criterion for evidence "beyond reasonable doubt."[49] Obviously, such standards would manifest the best practices at the ECtHR, but the postulated adherence to such high standards may run the risk of delays and new human rights violations created by an unreformed state apparatus. The procedural standards need to be balanced against the objectives and urgency needed to conduct personnel reform. For instance, the need to conduct speedy dismissals of discredited members of the police force, pursued by the UN mission in Bosnia and Herzegovina, prevented it from applying the right to be heard and led to the relaxation of the standards of proof.[50]

Nonetheless, the emphasis on the speed of personnel reform and its lower standards of evidence in contrast to criminal law do not give new political elites a license to use the process for their own political purposes. Legislators should adopt a measured approach. According to Kritz, lustration laws "can be used to process large numbers of cases quickly, not being burdened by the procedural rigors of the criminal process. They cost far less than trials in both financial and human resources. They are a measured response, allowing those less culpable to avoid trials or prison."[51] Kritz adds that "precisely because they are lower profile than trials, however, generally hidden from public scrutiny, and not subject to the same due process guarantees, noncriminal sanctions are much more apt to be used for purely political reasons, to pursue vendettas or to empty bureaucracies in order to install one's own loyalists."[52] As such, lustration could be consistent with such a measured approach to transitional justice.

Steps by the Legislators

A "democracy capable of defending itself" is essentially an extra-legal concept that permits flexibility in taking into account the current situation in the country, especially challenges to its territorial integrity, national security, and public safety, as well as the potential future risks that stem from them. For this reason, the lustration law needs to be introduced by a preamble that stipulates the law's political objective of establishing a state apparatus that will uphold principles and values such as loyalty, integrity, trustworthiness, impartiality, effectiveness, and efficiency. The lustration law could be accompanied by a parliamentary memorandum that stipulates its legislative intent and explains its individual provisions. Such a memorandum could be approved by Verkhovna Rada (parliament) or its relevant committee.

It is obviously the responsibility of the Ukrainian political leadership to take into account all remaining recommendations of the Venice Commission to the maximum extent possible, to implement them, and to continue dialog with the Commission. The concept of a democracy capable of defending itself does not give any government a blank check to ignore human rights. At the same time, the elected leadership is responsible to the people of Ukraine to quickly establish the state apparatus that will be able to protect the emerging democracy and uphold human rights.

CONCLUSION

The meaning and purpose of the Ukrainian lustration law are different from the meaning and purpose of other lustration laws approved in Central and Eastern Europe. While other lustration laws were dealing with the legacies of totalitarian regimes, the Ukrainian lustration is dealing with a posttotalitarian danger that challenges the very survival of the country. The situation in Ukraine, which recently experienced the loss of some of its territory and an open war on other parts of its territory, is different from the situation in other countries of the Council of Europe. The application of European standards needs to take into account both of these facts. The European jurisdiction provides for the possibility to apply the concept of militant democracy that would serve as a defense against militant tendencies in Ukraine.

The question remains: what lessons for other FSU countries one can be draw from this case? The answer is not straightforward. First, some countries such as Estonia, Latvia, Lithuania, and Georgia already implemented lustration laws. Second, other countries such as Belarus and Russia have – due to popular support for the regimes of Lukashenko and Putin – very little chance of having lustration laws in the near future. Third, the annexation of Crimea and the open conflict in Ukraine make the situation in Ukraine fundamentally different from that in other countries of FSU. Hence, the direct lessons from Ukraine can have a limited impact there. On the other hand, the case of Ukraine teaches us that lustration can have a role to play in the aftermath of all types of regime changes. The authoritarian rule of Yanukovich in Ukraine did not even match the intensity of authoritarianism and repression in Russia and Belarus. Hence, an eventual regime change may prompt legitimate calls for dealing with the protagonists of Putin's and Lukashenko's regimes. Moreover, in the case of Russia, one can consider dismissals of those who participated in the Russia-led conflicts in Ukraine and other countries of the FSU.

Notes

1. I am indebted to the USAID's Fair Justice project for their support of my work in Ukraine. Parts of this chapter appeared in the USAID funded research report: Roman David,

"Ukrainian Lustration and European Standards: Building Democracy Capable of Defending Itself," Kyiv: USAID FAIR, February 24, 2015.

2. European Commission for Democracy through Law (Venice Commission), *Interim Opinion on the Law on Government Cleansing (Lustration Law) of Ukraine, Adopted by the Venice Commission at its 101st Plenary Session*, Venice, December 12–13, 2014; European Commission for Democracy through Law (Venice Commission), *Final Opinion On The Law On Government Cleansing (Lustration Law) Of Ukraine as would result from the amendments submitted to the Verkhovna Rada on 21 April 2015*, Opinion No. 788/2014, CDL-AD(2015)012, Venice, June 19–20, 2015.

3. Roman David, "Beyond Lustration: Personnel Reform in the State Apparatus in Ukraine," Kyiv: USAID FAIR, April 19, 2014.

4. In addition to the Czech Republic and Poland, Georgia was also an inspiration for the Ukrainian lustration program. Both Ukraine and Georgia share a similar historical experience: they were both under the Soviet rule, declared independence at approximately the same time, tried to deal with the remnants of the communist regime in the Rose Revolution of 2003 (Georgia) and the Orange Revolution of 2004–5 (Ukraine), and have been bullied by Russia, which occupies territory of both countries.

5. For etymology of lustration, see Roman David, *Lustration and Transitional Justice: Personnel Systems in the Czech Republic, Hungary and Poland* (Philadelphia: University of Pennsylvania Press, 2011).

6. Roman David, "Lustration Laws in Action: The Motives and Evaluation of Lustration Policy in the Czech Republic and Poland (1989–2001)," *Law and Social Inquiry* 28, 2 (2003): 387–439.

7. The original CBOS survey question was: *Czy, pana(i) zdaniem, powinno się obecnie przeprowadzać w Polsce lustrację, to znaczy sprawdzać, czy osoby pełniące ważne funkcje w państwie nie współpracowały w przeszłości ze służbą bezpieczeństwa, czy też nie powinno? CBOS, Powracające dylematy lustracji i dekomunizacji w polsce*, BS/43/2005, Warsaw, March 2005.

8. David, *Lustration and Transitional Justice*.

9. "Lustration Stele in Ukrainian City – Reminder to Officials," *Life in Ukraine*, September 15, 2014, available at: http://lifeinua.info/lustration-stele-ukrainian-city-remainder-officials-video/, accessed October 7, 2016.

10. David Stern, "Ukraine's Politicians Face Mob Attacks," *BBC News*, October 20, 2014, available at: www.bbc.com/news/world-europe-29536641, accessed October 7, 2016.

11. Roland Oliphant, "Up to a Dozen Ukraine Officials Dumped in Wheelie Bins," *The Telegraph*, October 7, 2014, available at: www.telegraph.co.uk/news/worldnews/europe/ukraine/11145381/Up-to-a-dozen-Ukraine-officials-dumped-in-wheelie-bins.html, accessed October 7, 2016.

12. Borislaw Bilash II, "Euromaidan Protests – The Revolution of Dignity," *Euromaidan Press*, February 20, 2016.

13. Neil Kritz has conceptualized lustration laws as noncriminal sanctions, Teitel as administrative justice, and David as personnel systems. Neil Kritz, ed., *Transitional Justice: How Emerging Democracies Reckon with Former Regimes* (Washington: U.S. Institute of Peace, 1995); Ruti Teitel, *Transitional Justice* (Oxford: Oxford University Press, 2000); and David, *Lustration and Transitional Justice*.

14. Vojtěch Cepl and Mark Gillis, "Making Amends after Communism," *Journal of Democracy* 7, 4 (1996): 118–24; and Roman David, "From Prague to Baghdad: Lustration Systems and their Political Effects." *Government & Opposition* 41, 3 (2006): 347–72.

15. Lavinia Stan, ed., *Transitional Justice in Eastern Europe and the former Soviet Union: Reckoning with the Communist Past* (London: Routledge, 2009); Lavinia Stan and Nadya Nedelsky, eds., *Encyclopedia of Transitional Justice* (New York: Cambridge University Press, 2013); Lavinia Stan and Nadya Nedelsky, eds., *Post-Communist Transitional Justice: Lessons from 25 Years of Experience* (New York: Cambridge University Press, 2015).

16. For overview of various measures, see Alexander Mayer-Rieckh and Pablo de Greiff, eds., *Justice as Prevention: Vetting Public Employees in Transitional Societies* (New York: Social Science Research Council, 2007). There has been no consensus about the nomenclature of these measures. Neil Kritz defines them as noncriminal sanctions, Ruti Teitel as administrative justice, Roman David as personnel systems, and Alexander Mayer-Rieckh and Pablo de Greiff as vetting.

17. Law of Ukraine on the Purification of Government, September 16, 2014 (Закон України Про очищення влади, Відомості Верховної Ради (ВВР), 2014, № 44, ст.2041); and Law of Ukraine on the Restoration of Trust in the Judiciary, April 8, 2014 (Закон України Про відновлення довіри до судової влади в Україні, Відомості Верховної Ради (ВВР), 2014, № 23, ст.870).

18. Ukrinform, "Only 940 Officials in Ukraine Dismissed in Line with Law on Lustration," *Ukrinform*, May 6, 2016.

19. Ukrinform, "Justice Ministry Posts List of Persons in Prosecutor's Office Subject to Lustration Law," *Ukrinform*, April 9, 2016.

20. Civic Lustration Committee, "[A] Year of Lustration in Ukraine: History of Victories and Sabotage," Kyiv: Report of the Non-Government Organization «Civic Lustration Committee», 2015.

21. Venice Commission.

22. The review is not without controversies. Some members of the Rada suggested that seven judges of the Constitutional Court should recuse themselves from hearing the lustration case since they might fall within the scope of the lustration law. Human Rights Information Centre, "Constitutional Court Postpones Consideration of Lustration Law," April 16, 2015, available at: https://humanrights .org.ua/en/material/konstitucijnij_sud_vidklav_rozgljad_zakonupro_ljustraciju, accessed October 17, 2016.

23. *Rutan v. Republican Party of Illinois*, 497 U.S. 62 (1990).

24. Cynthia M. Horne, "International Legal Rulings on Lustration Policies in Central and Eastern Europe: Rule of Law in Historical Context," *Law & Social Inquiry* 34, 3 (2009): 713–44.

25. Roman David, "Transitional Injustice? Criteria for Conformity of Lustration to the Right to Political Expression," *Europe-Asia Studies* 56, 6 (2004): 789–812.

26. Karl Loewenstein, "Militant Democracy and Fundamental Rights I," *The American Political Science Review* 31, 3 (1937): 417–32; Karl Loewenstein, "Militant Democracy and Fundamental Rights II," *The American Political Science Review* 31, 4 (1937): 638–58.

27. Basic Law for the Federal Republic of Germany, Promulgated on May 23, 1949, available at: www.bundestag.de/blob/284870/ceod03414872b427e57fccb703634dcd/basic_law-data.pdf, accessed November 21, 2016.
28. Donald P. Kommers and Russel A. Miller, *The Constitutional Jurisprudence of the Federal Republic of Germany*, 3rd ed. (Durham: Duke University Press, 2012), 51–2.
29. European Court of Human Rights, *Vogt v. Germany*, 1995 *(Application no. 17851/91)*.
30. European Court of Human Rights, *Naidin v. Romania*, 2014 *(Application no. 38162/07)*.
31. Freedom House, *Freedom in the World 2015: Ukraine*, 2015 available at: https://freedomhouse.org/report/freedom-world/2015/ukraine#.VOaY6odiBbw, accessed October 13, 2016.
32. OCHA, *Ukraine Situation Report No. 26 as of 6 February 2015*, February 6, 2015, available at: http://reliefweb.int/sites/reliefweb.int/files/resources/ukraine%20sitrep%2026.pdf, accessed October 13, 2016.
33. Ibid.
34. *Ukraine: Humanitarian Dashboard January*, August 2016, available at: www.humanitarianresponse.info/en/system/files/documents/files/humanitarian_dashboard_august_2016_v6.pdf, accessed October 13, 2016.
35. Ukrinform, "Over 1.6 million IDPs registered in Ukraine," *Unkrinform.net*, available at: www.ukrinform.net/rubric-society_and_culture/2133980-over-16-million-idps-registered-in-ukraine.html, accessed December 7, 2016; CTK, "Válka v Donbasu si podle Porošenka vyžádala 10.000 mrtvých," *Ceske Noviny*, December 6, 2016, available at: www.ceskenoviny.cz/zpravy/valka-v-donbasu-si-podle-porosenka-vyzadala-10-000-mrtvych/1424064, accessed December 7, 2016.
36. Article 3, Part 4, Sections 1 and 2.
37. Interfax-Ukraine, "Security Service Chief Says Former Ukrainian Officials Sponsor Arms Supplies to Separatists," *Kyiv Post*, July 8, 2014.
38. Stern, "Ukraine's Politicians Face Mob Attacks."
39. Freedom House, *Freedom in the World 2013: Ukraine*, available at: https://freedomhouse.org/report/freedom-world/2013/ukraine#.VOaaXodiBbw, accessed October 13, 2016.
40. Ibid.
41. Freedom House, *Freedom in the World 2014: Ukraine*, available at: https://freedomhouse.org/report/freedom-world/2014/ukraine#.VOaUIIdiBbw, accessed October 13, 2016.
42. Laura Smith-Spark and Frederik Pleitgen, "Ukraine Marks Year since Maidan Bloodshed amid Simmering Conflict," *CNN*, February 20, 2015, available at: http://edition.cnn.com/2015/02/20/europe/ukraine-conflict/index.html, accessed October 13, 2016.
43. Freedom House, *Freedom in the World 2013: Ukraine*.
44. Samuel Ramani, "From Disgraced President to Ukraine's Lead Diplomat: The Unlikely Redemption of Leonid Kuchma," *Huffington Post*, September 16, 2016, available at: www.huffingtonpost.com/samuel-ramani/from-disgraced-president-b8130424.html, accessed October 13, 2016.
45. David, *Lustration and Transitional Justice*.
46. David, "From Prague to Baghdad"; Roman David and Houda Mzioudet, "Personnel Change or Personal Change? Rethinking Libya's Political Isolation

Law," Brookings Doha Center, Stanford University "Project on Arab Transitions" Paper Series, No. 4 (March 2014).

47. Number of Public Employees Dismissed according to Law on Purification of Government of Ukraine starting from October 16, 2014 (as of November 24, 2014), USAID FAIR.

48. United Nations, *Rule of Law Tools for Post-Conflict States, Vetting: Operational Framework* (New York and Geneva: United Nations, 2006), italic added.

49. European Commission for Democracy through Law (Venice Commission), 2014. *Interim Opinion on the Law on Government Cleansing (Lustration Law) of Ukraine, Adopted by the Venice Commission at its 101st Plenary Session.* Venice, 12–13 December, para. 103.

50. Alexander Mayer-Rieckh, "Vetting to Prevent Future Abuses: Reforming the Police, Courts, and Prosecutor's Offices in Bosnia and Herzegovina," in Alexander Mayer-Rieckh and Pablo de Greiff eds., Justice as Prevention: Vetting Public Employees in Transitional Societies (New York: Social Science Research Council) 190.

51. Neil J. Kritz, "Dealing with the Legacy of Past Abuses: An Overview of the Options and their Relationship to the Promotion of Peace," in M. Bleeker and J. Sisson, eds., *Dealing with the Past: Critical Issues, Lessons Learned, and Challenges for Future Swiss Policy* (Bern: Swisspeace, 2004), 25.

52. Ibid.

7

Between Politics and History: The Baltic Truth Commissions in Global Perspective

Onur Bakiner

Memory and *truth* initiatives (broadly understood as the investigation and dissemination of facts about human rights violations and the context in which they took place) became an important component of transitional justice practice in many regions of the world in the 1990s and the 2000s, including postcommunist transition countries such as Estonia, Germany, Latvia, Lithuania, Moldova, Romania, Serbia, and Uzbekistan. Postcommunist fact-finding bodies have remained challenging to label, as some observers characterized them as truth commissions, while others found these efforts did not qualify as formal truth commissions due to problems with their mandate limits, autonomy, or other operational aspects.[1] This chapter focuses on Baltic fact-finding bodies, examining the accomplishments and shortcomings of commissions in Estonia, Latvia, and Lithuania by situating them in the context of the global popularity of truth commissions in the 1990s and the 2000s. While the Baltic commissions do not satisfy most of the definitional criteria used for truth commissions insofar as their forensic investigation, temporal scope, and relationship to victims were concerned, their work highlights many of the promises and challenges that truth commissions face in their engagement with social memory debates.[2] They are part of a broader trend in which truth commissions are created years after a regime change to investigate not only recent violence and violations, but also those rights violations that took place in the distant past.

In particular, this chapter shows that the Baltic commissions have little in common with truth commissions that prioritize agent-centered historical narratives and seek institutional reform, reconciliation, or noncriminal sanctions. In contrast, the Baltic commissions consciously position themselves as arbiters of disagreements over social memory. The Baltic commissions are less concerned with making recommendations for immediate political-institutional reform and more interested in adjudicating debates over history and social memory. However, their attentiveness to re-narrating past violence and violations through various levels of analysis resembles the work of truth commissions that have produced comprehensive accounts of past wrongs to seek broader transformation. The Baltic commissions differ from other fact-finding institutes also established in the region, such as institutes of memory and historic preservation, institutions tasked with the preservation of communist state security archives, and the memorials, museums, oral history projects, and memory-related civil society initiatives that seek to educate citizens about the horrors of the past regimes. As such, they constitute analytically separate but complementary forms of truth and memory initiatives in the postcommunist region.

The Baltic commissions' interest in historiography reflects the challenges of rewriting history through memory and truth initiatives: absent forensic investigation and clear recommendations for immediate social and political change, their success or failure is measured by the extent to which they resolve questions around local collaboration, the moral and historical complexity of victimhood, and the affective distance between the past and the present. Country-level differences notwithstanding, the Baltic commissions have had very limited impact in terms of outreach and adjudicating historical controversies.[3] The fact that organizationally they are somewhere between the truth commission and memory institute models accounts for part of this failure. The absence of domestic ownership may be another shortcoming.

It is important to maintain analytical distinctions between different kinds of memory and truth initiatives, but it should be acknowledged that agents of memory and truth often blur the distinctions between truth commissions, memory institutes, and other initiatives in light of their interests, values, and goals.[4] The postcommunist memory and truth initiatives described in this chapter have renegotiated the boundaries between *ad hoc* human rights investigation and ongoing human rights documentation. Nonetheless, maintaining analytical distinctions, even while acknowledging the fluidity of initiatives, is important because initiatives exhibit considerable variation in their sources of support, tasks identified in their mandate, criteria for membership, the degree to which they are immune from political pressure, and their final product.[5] Keeping in mind these definitional differences, this chapter illustrates the ways in which the Baltic commissions renegotiate the variety of tasks and goals associated with truth commissions, memory institutes and other memory and truth initiatives.

To examine the ways in which the Baltic commissions' goals, tasks, and methods reflect or diverge from the historical evolution of truth commissions around the world, this chapter is structured in three main parts. The first section overviews the commissions in the FSU, with a focus on the Baltic countries because other commission-like bodies in the FSU had little or no autonomy from political forces, and thus no capacity to spark public debates over social memory. The second section discusses the goals and tasks of truth commissions in other regions of the world in two respects. First, it assesses their claims of contributing to social and political change in the wake of past atrocities, documenting the empirical evidence that suggests commissions make modest contributions to political and social change in practice. Second, this section examines how truth commissions make sense of past violence. I propose a fourfold categorization of the levels of analysis found in truth commissions' historical narratives of past violence: (1) agent-centered; (2) ideological-cultural; (3) contextual; and (4) structural explanations.[6] Drawing on these distinctions, the third section situates the Baltic commissions within this analytical framework. The conclusion makes suggestions for future memory and truth initiatives in the FSU region.

MEMORY AND TRUTH INITIATIVES IN THE FORMER SOVIET UNION

The Baltic states, Moldova, and Uzbekistan established commissions to investigate past crimes and re-narrate national history. The Baltic commissions have generally been discussed together because they shared common features: they were set up at the same time (1998) by the presidents of those republics, they were comprised of local and/or foreign experts, they had similar mandates to investigate the Nazi and Soviet crimes, and they were created in part because the dominant memory narratives tended to blame past suffering on the German and Russian occupation forces, thus overlooking the crimes committed by Baltic nationals. Unlike the somewhat autonomous commissions in the Baltic region, Uzbekistan set up parliamentary commissions formed of members of parliament – note that Estonia also had a pre-1998 parliamentary commission. The Moldovan presidential commission was similar to its Baltic counterparts, but enjoyed far less independence from the politicians who sponsored it. I will briefly describe these commissions.

The Commission for the Promotion of the Memory of Victims in Uzbekistan was established in 1999 with the goals of shoring up an increasingly repressive regime's international image and strengthening diplomatic ties to the West. This commission did not enjoy autonomy from the government, and little is known of its work.[7] The Estonian parliamentary commission was created in 1992, one year after independence. Both commissions had little capacity for outreach beyond the parliament.

The Moldovan commission was established in 2010 for a short five-month mandate. The process of reckoning with communist-era wrongs was delayed for two decades, in part because the communists were strong in local politics until 2009. The narrow election victory of a center-right party made the commission possible the following year.[8] Although observers saw narrow political instrumentalization in the creation of the commission, disagreements among the commissioners show the extent to which even a narrowly instrumental commission can overcome the limitations of its mandate and work with some degree of operational autonomy. However, the final product reflected political interference, and explains why observers rarely consider the Moldovan body a truth commission: the president edited the content of the commission's final report.[9] In conclusion, the Uzbek, Estonian (parliamentary), and Moldovan commissions enjoyed little or no political autonomy during their operation and in the publication of their final report, which limited their capacity to have political and societal impact.

All three Baltic commissions were decreed by presidents at a time when the international community demanded, on the eve of their accession to the European Union, a more open and honest engagement with past wrongs. All three commissions were expected to address the Nazi occupation during World War II, the Holocaust, and the Soviet period, focusing on atrocities committed by foreign actors and domestic collaborators. State security and party archives became chief sources of information for all commissions.

Also named the Max Jacobson Commission after its chairman, the all-foreigner Estonian International Commission for Investigation of Crimes Against Humanity (active in 1998–2007) represents a second effort to come to terms with the nation's past, after the parliamentary commission mentioned above failed to spark national-level debate around memory.[10] The new presidential commission published three reports, two reporting on the Soviet and Nazi occupations during World War II, and one on the Soviet occupation after 1944. It is the only Baltic commission to identify perpetrators by name.[11] Also, the commission recognized the responsibility of local Estonian actors in past atrocities.[12] The commission's outreach was limited, in part because the factual analysis was found to be dry.[13] In the end, the Estonian Memory Institute was created in 2008 to follow up on the international commission's work.

As its name implies, the Commission of the Historians of Latvia, established in 1998 by the president, brought together local and foreign historians. Instead of publishing a single final report, the commissioners took an alternative approach to knowledge dissemination: they published 27 volumes until 2013, containing not only a report of facts about the past wrongs, but also conference proceedings, monographs, and articles.[14] Both the commission's self-portrayal as a panel of historians and its somewhat vague area of focus meant that it operated less like a truth commission, and more like a memory institute.

The International Commission for the Evaluation of the Crimes of the Nazi and Soviet Occupation Regimes in Lithuania was a mixed panel of seven Lithuanians and five foreigners. Instead of focusing on a large number of historical episodes, the Lithuanian panel selected specific events to examine. Thus, there was little fact-based investigation compared to the Estonian or Latvian commissions.[15] More problematically, the commission was discontinued as a result of political obstruction. The fundamental conflict that led to its collapse was the incompatibility of the narrative of national self-victimization, which many local social and political actors emphasized, with the narrative on the centrality of the Holocaust, which the Jewish community as well as the international actors insisted on.[16]

The Baltic commissions had more autonomy and a longer time span to complete their work than the three other commissions organized in the FSU, but it remains questionable whether they undertook tasks and fulfilled the expectations that a truth commission normally does. The divisiveness of the issues discussed by the Lithuanian panel, which had always prioritized historiographic debates over fact-finding, led to its collapse.[17] The Latvian commission operated as a truth commission for some time, but lacked a clear demarcation of its tasks, and therefore turned into a semi-permanent historical institute over time.[18] Perhaps the Estonian commission resembles a truth commission the most among its Baltic counterparts, insofar as it carried out a fact-finding mission and published final reports at the end of its work.[19] Nonetheless, all three commissions excluded the participation of those who were affected by past wrongs, did not set clear limits on which historical events to investigate, and thus operated more like memory institutes than truth commissions.[20]

Were the Baltic commissions outliers in a time period when the truth commission format dominated memory debates around human rights violations around the world? In order to situate these commissions in the broader evolution of truth commissions it is worth looking into the global context in which truth commissions were shaped. Memory and truth initiatives around the world, and especially truth commissions, have undergone transformations since the mid-1990s. Most truth commissions between the early 1980s and the mid-1990s were established within a year or two of a country's transition from dictatorship and/or armed conflict to democracy and/or peace. The mandates of these transitional truth commissions reflected the immediacy of political, judicial, and rights-related issues, such as the investigation of past violations, redress for victims, provision of justice, the promotion of the rule of law, and political stability.

Transitional commissions have remained popular, as more countries transitioned from authoritarianism and/or conflict in the 1990s and the 2000s, yet alongside transitional commissions, a new type of nontransitional truth commissions emerged in countries that had lived through transitions decades before in the absence of officially mandated truth-finding efforts. Since political stability was less of a concern, and the provision of justice had already been delayed, these nontransitional commissions focused more on investigating past violations and less on reforming existing political and judicial institutions. As I describe later, a small number of nontransitional commissions have produced extensive narratives on the underlying causes of violence and violations, while most others have limited themselves to describing the violations, without explaining why they happened and what that history of violence says about the nation's present.

Most postcommunist memory and truth initiatives resemble the nontransitional typology for two reasons. First, with the exception of the Study Commission for Working Through the History and the Consequences of the SED Dictatorship in Germany (also known as the Enquete Kommission), the Federal Commissioner for the Records of the State Security Service of the former German Democratic Republic, and the abortive Truth and Reconciliation Commission for Serbia and Montenegro, all these initiatives were established five to ten years after the collapse of repressive regimes. The Baltic commissions were established seven years after the regime change; the truth commission in Romania was established in 2006; memory institutes in Poland, Slovakia, Ukraine, Estonia, and Lithuania were opened in the late 2000s. Second, these memory and truth initiatives reflected the goals and priorities of nontransitional commissions: they were focused on documentation of abuses and preservation of historic memory more than reform of political and judicial institutions or redress for victims. None of the FSU commissions adopted a victim-driven approach, which would have included collecting testimonies, publicizing individual suffering, and seeking redress for past wrongs. Yet, the Baltic commissions' goal of investigating violations perpetrated in the distant past, and willingness to open debates on historical memory, also reveals their similarities with some nontransitional truth commissions that combine minimal forensic work with interest in engaging intellectual and policy debates on the nation's past. Their achievements and challenges, therefore, can be instructive for future memory and truth initiatives in the region and beyond.

The postcommunist initiatives blur boundaries between truth commissions (even nontransitional ones) and other memory and truth initiatives in an important way: they examine such a long period of time, so many violations, and so many *types* of violations that their work often resembles that of human rights organizations, not *ad hoc* truth commissions. In addition, the complexity of the political histories that produced these violations push the postcommunist initiatives to constantly make judgments on the political and ideological character of past regimes. While the 1990 truth commission in Chile had (in) famously ignored the political-ideological nature of the 1973 coup and the military regime by exclusively focusing on that regime's human rights violations, postcommunist initiatives could not possibly avoid such judgment. These initiatives' politically charged character was taken for granted from the start.

SOCIAL AND POLITICAL CHANGE THROUGH TRUTH COMMISSIONS

Truth Commissions' Claims

Some claim that a well-designed commission will uncover human rights violations, satisfy victims' demands for truth, promote reconciliation between actors with a history of mutual distrust and hostility, and help to preserve a society's historical memory.[21] Commissions are also expected to prevent the recurrence of violence by "acknowledging what took place during conflict."[22] Drawing upon these claims, empirical analyses of impact have evaluated the extent to which truth commissions foster truth recovery and reconciliation, improve a country's human rights conduct and democracy. Some studies find that truth commissions have a negative impact on human rights and democracy if they are used alone; others find a positive impact or no impact at all.[23] The multiplicity of answers should be considered an opportunity to rethink the theoretical frameworks that explain truth commissions' impact on desirable outcomes, such as the promotion of democracy, respect for human rights, and the nonrecurrence of violence.

Priscilla Hayner notes that truth commissions' contributions are often assessed against the standard of impact; that is, whether or not the desired outcome was observed. The product (the quality and comprehensiveness of the final report) and process (the extent to which a commission encourages broad participation in society by including victims and perpetrators in the search for truth and understanding of past abuses) are important measures of success.[24] Thus, this chapter identifies the potential mechanisms through which truth commissions contribute to desired outcomes through their product and process. The underlying methodological premise is that only a theoretically grounded account that pays attention to causal mechanisms can fully explain truth commissions' contributions to political and social change:

(1)   *Reform*: Truth commissions make recommendations for legal, institutional, and socioeconomic reform in order to prevent future human rights violations.[25] Some of these recommendations have been relatively

institutional in character (judicial reform, for example), but several commissions have also asked for sweeping changes in social structure and/or political culture. Although commissions are responsible for proposing reforms, their implementation is at the discretion of politicians, military leaders, and courts. Therefore, a commission's impact depends critically on political endorsement and implementation.

(2)   *Reconciliation*: Commissions are alleged to reduce the incentives for violence and to facilitate peace processes.[26] They are expected to defuse tensions between former enemies through their outcome and process: they call for an ethics of nonviolence, reconciliation, and sometimes forgiveness in their final reports, and, may contribute to peace by giving voice and setting the stage for the participation of victims and perpetrators alike in the new system.[27]

(3)   *Noncriminal sanctions*: Commissions may remove potentially violent actors from public life by recommending a policy of vetting, sharing information about violations with the judiciary, or by delegitimizing political and military leaders who took part in initiating and aggravating past abuses.[28] Needless to say, vetting/lustration has been implemented in the absence of truth commissions, as well; this chapter only examines suggestions for noncriminal sanctions and delegitimation coming from a truth commission.

(4)   *Awareness raising*: Commissions are expected to raise human rights awareness and promote a human rights culture by educating the public about the causes, patterns, and consequences of past violence and violations.[29] The underlying assumption is that a commission opens or shapes a debate about the nation's past by providing the public with factual information and historical narratives, which will result in society-wide acknowledgment. Toward that end, commission findings and recommendations may be covered by the media, incorporated into educational curricula, and disseminated in art exhibits and memorials.

Assessing Truth Commissions' Claims[30]

Commissions create an impulse for reform: most transitional commissions have generated some degree of impact in terms of political and institutional change. Governments may endorse and publicize the final report, establish follow-up institutions to monitor the postcommission reform process, and institute a reparations program. In some cases, they adopt recommendations within the first year of the final report, but the reformist attitude is more likely owing to pressures by human rights associations and victims' groups.[31] Indeed, no society has effected a comprehensive overhaul of its basic political, social, and economic institutions in light of a truth commission's findings and recommendations; reform has been piecemeal and limited. Nonetheless, commission-inspired reforms have produced concrete, if limited, progress in human rights policy and public-sector reform in various countries.

Evidence on the effects of reconciliation is mixed. In many contexts commissions have not facilitated conflict prevention through reconciliation, at least in the short run. To the contrary, the commission and immediate post-commission processes are usually marked by heightened tensions and disagreements. Individual and institutional actors accused of committing human rights violations often react angrily to a commission's final report even if they do not have grounds to deny the facts.[32] Military leaders, politicians, and judicial authorities often use threats of regime instability, renewed violations, and even a military coup. Victims are rarely satisfied with the commission process, in great part because the mere telling of truth may fail to offer a sense of justice or symbolic and material compensation.[33] Research on broader societal dynamics and long-term trends reveals more optimistic results in some cases. James L. Gibson's research on South Africa contends that even if many people do not endorse reconciliation, those who accept the "truth" of a commission are more likely to feel reconciled, and the effect is strengthened as contact across communities increases.[34] The possibility of long-term reconciliation at the cost of short-term instability is also mentioned in the literature.[35]

Commissions have not succeeded in persuading governments to remove violent actors through noncriminal sanctions: the call for vetting was partially met in El Salvador, whereas political authorities in Chad, Timor-Leste, and Liberia ignored commissions' similar demands.[36] Official sanctioning has not worked as expected, but commissions delegitimized presumed perpetrators in some contexts. Eight transitional commissions have identified individual human rights violators, and in Argentina the press leaked the list of perpetrators. Commissions have also contributed to the delegitimation of individual and institutional actors with their findings and by detailing those actors' roles in committing and condoning past abuses.[37]

Conflict prevention through the removal of violent actors can take place if former perpetrators lose their political clout, popularity, and ability to incite large-scale violence. While success is noted in some countries, it is unclear whether truth commissions can discard some of the notorious offenders in others. Augusto Pinochet and Efraín Ríos Montt continued to hold considerable political power during the transition in spite of public acknowledgment of their role in human rights abuses in Chile and Guatemala, respectively. Military and judicial institutions can refuse to initiate significant personnel or mentality changes in the wake of a truth commission report. Political parties and movements that wholeheartedly endorse the legacy of a past dictator and human rights violator may run relatively successful electoral campaigns, as narrow losses of Keiko Fujimori, dictator Alberto Fujimori's daughter, in the 2011 and 2016 presidential elections in Peru demonstrate. In conclusion, delegitimation through truth commissions has worked in some contexts, and produced more limited results in others.

Truth commissions take their promise of raising awareness around human rights seriously, and find innovative ways to popularize their work both during their activity (through public hearings and televised sessions) and in the postcommission period (publishing the final report as a book or in a newspaper, producing an accessible version of the final report for adults or children, organizing outreach activities, etc.). They also try to incorporate the findings into school curricula, but even in the best of cases (like Guatemala) such incorporation has limited success.[38] It also remains inconclusive whether a truth commission transforms the attitudes of citizens. There is evidence of broad-based support for the findings and conclusions of some truth commissions, or varying degrees of acceptance,[39] but support for a commission's results does not necessarily translate into unambiguous rejection of political violence and rights violations.

Judging from the empirical record on truth commissions' claims to foster a human rights culture and prevent future violence and violations through reform proposals, reconciliation, noncriminal sanctions, and education, it can be concluded that they have made modest contributions. Needless to say the positive effects of truth commissions may have been greater if their findings, narratives, and recommendations found more substantial political support. Yet it is also worth rethinking truth commissions' own understanding of past conflict. All the possible ways in which commissioners can contribute to a society's future refer back to how they understand and explain the past. Their focus on the immediate causes of conflict and insistence on reconciling former enemies has fueled the suspicion that these commissions do not consider the underlying causes and fail to provide remedies against the recurrence of violence and violations.[40] Instead of assuming that truth commissions address the underlying causes, the next section analyzes truth commissions' explanations of the causes and patterns of violent conflict.

WRITING HISTORY THROUGH TRUTH COMMISSIONS

Which factors do truth commissions emphasize to explain the remote and immediate causes of political violence? Few commissions clarify whether they address questions of conflict onset, patterns and repertoires of violence and its severity and duration, or conflict termination. Despite their reluctance to use the language of causality, commissions' historical narratives bear striking similarities to social-scientific research on conflict. Besides claims to promote a nonviolent and democratic transition, they identify the main factors that caused the onset of conflict, magnified its severity or duration, and obstructed peace efforts in particular historical contexts. Truth commissions constantly negotiate levels of analysis, temporal scope, and meta-theoretical approaches in formulating causal explanations. In other words, they consider agency and structure in the short and long term, and immediate and remote causes. They provide responses that combine various epistemologies, methodologies, and causal mechanisms, which guide their proposals for institutional, legal, and political-cultural reform.

Some truth commissions limit themselves to reporting abuses and provide no explanation for the causes of political conflict and violence. Commissions in El Salvador, Haiti, Uruguay, South Korea (2000), Panama, and Morocco did not deal with causal questions.[41] One might think that nontransitional commissions ignore historical explanation, since they are not mandated to serve national reconciliation and reconstruction in the immediate wake of conflict. Nontransitional commissions in Uruguay, South Korea (2000), and Panama were established more than a decade after the transition. In Morocco, there was no regime transition preceding the creation of the commission. These commissions offered no historical explanation of the causes of violence and violations in their final reports. But commissions in South Korea (2005), Ghana, Chile (2003), Paraguay, and Mauritius produced extensive narratives about the origins of civil conflict or violations, although they were not transitional in nature. In short, nontransitional truth commissions do not necessarily ignore historical debates about the underlying causes of violence and violations. Moreover, some commissions approach political violence from multiple perspectives and levels of analysis, whereas others rest content with limited accounts that emphasize a small number of factors, such as personal greed or the geopolitical context.

I identify four levels of explanation used by truth commissions: agent-centered, ideological-cultural, contextual, and structural. Commissions exercise discretion in choosing their narratives. Variation in their causal explanations is a result of the different experiences of political violence, mandate limits, and the commissioners' own agency in narrating those contexts.

Agent-centered explanations trace the responsibility of individuals and institutions for creating and tolerating an atmosphere in which human rights were violated, or for committing the violations. Commissions have highlighted the role of authoritarian and violent dictators, like Chad's Hissène Habré, Peru's Alberto Fujimori, and Paraguay's Alfredo Stroessner. The Sierra Leonean commission points at Liberia's former president Charles Taylor for inciting the civil war. Alongside top leaders, commissions often mention individual politicians, judges, generals and rebel commanders who enabled, or did not stop, violence. Most commissions also identify responsibility at the institutional level. State and nonstate armed groups receive much of the blame everywhere. In El Salvador and Guatemala the judiciary was found complicit in gross rights violations. In Peru, Nigeria, Guatemala, Sierra Leone, Liberia, and Ecuador, commissions pointed the finger at the entire political class for creating a violent atmosphere through "bad governance"[42] and/or actively provoking violence.

Agent-centered explanations are sometimes complemented by more sophisticated causal accounts of violence. One explanation emphasizes the role of ideology and political culture. Various truth commissions take issue with violent ideologies that have structured political institutions and the mindset of rulers. Apartheid in South Africa, the anticommunist National Security doctrines in Argentina and Guatemala, and Stroessner's blend of anticommunism and strongman rule in Paraguay are violent ideologies explored in commission reports.

Other commissions criticize the extent to which ideological polarization led to conflict. For example, the absence of a civic and democratic political culture is seen as the root cause of war. In Argentina, the commission's mention of "terror from both the extreme right and the far left" grounds violence "in psychological and cultural patterns deeply entrenched in national history,"[43] a narrative that divided the left-leaning human rights community and the commissioners. South Korea's 2005 commission combines ideologically motivated violence with a political-cultural explanation of societal apathy: "Influenced by the extreme rightist ideology of Japanese nationalism and the sophisticated manipulation skills of the U.S. military, the Park military junta introduced an extreme right-wing Fascist regime into Korean society during a time when the nation lacked thoughts, values, and awareness of democracy."[44]

Commissions invoke the broader historical and geopolitical context in explaining violence and violations. Commissions in Nigeria, Ghana, Sierra Leone, Liberia, and Mauritius place colonialism at the root of postcolonial political and social problems. The South African, Guatemalan, and Peruvian commissions describe continuities between colonial and postcolonial patterns of marginalization, inequality, and poverty in less directly causal terms. The Cold War received special attention from bodies in Argentina, Chile, Chad, South Africa, Guatemala, Timor-Leste, South Korea, and Liberia, which explained how the Cold War caused, aggravated, and/or justified violent conflict, and clarified the responsibility of foreign actors without whitewashing the domestic ones. Most other commissions, however, tend to shy away from investigating the connection between national and international (or transnational) levels.[45]

Finally, some commissions portray past wrongs in structural terms. As Louise Arbour notes, "truth commissions lend themselves particularly well to the investigation and protection of economic, social, and cultural rights."[46] Indeed, various truth commissions consider socioeconomic and cultural stratification, discrimination, racism, and exclusion from democratic decision-making as underlying causes of political violence. Commissions in Guatemala, South Africa, and Peru devote chapters to detailing the inequality and marginalization that fueled conflicts. The Guatemalan commission states: "structural injustice, the closing of political spaces, racism, the increasing exclusionary and anti-democratic nature of institutions, as well as the reluctance to promote substantive reforms that could have reduced structural conflicts, are the underlying factors which determined the origin and subsequent outbreak of the armed confrontation."[47] Commissions in Nigeria, Ghana, and Liberia describe the underlying social-structural causes of civil conflict in shorter paragraphs. For the Nigerian commission, the nation's problems were "historically deep-rooted and structurally-determined."[48] Its Liberian counterpart writes: "The major root causes of the conflict are attributable to poverty, greed, corruption, limited access to education, economic, social, civil and political inequalities; identity conflict, land tenure and distribution."[49]

In light of this analysis, postcommunist commissions' historical narratives deserve closer attention. The three Baltic commissions, the 1992 German Enquete Kommission, and the 2006 Presidential Commission for the Study of the Communist Dictatorship in Romania provide long descriptions of the political and institutional conditions under which basic rights were violated. The German and Latvian commissions go farthest in contextualizing violence and violations.[50] Agent-centered analyses are dominant, as these commissions condemn the institutions that violated citizens' basic bodily integrity and civil and political rights. In addition, criticism of communist ideology as an underlying cause of violations is a common thread; especially the Romanian commission has been explicit about its condemnation of communism.[51]

Truth commissions' recommendations for the reconstruction of democratic and nonviolent polities reflect their causal narratives. Since almost all commissions use agent-centered, ideological, and political-cultural explanations, their recommendations emphasize the removal of violent individuals, restructuring of institutions, and the promotion of a political culture based on respect for human rights. Some commissions demand the removal of violent actors from public life through trials or vetting. The final reports in El Salvador, Chad, Timor-Leste, and Liberia call for the removal of some or all individuals responsible for past violence. Various commissions have advocated human rights trials, and in Argentina and Peru the information collected by the commissions was shared with the judiciary. Some countries emphasize the importance of human rights education for military personnel (Chile) and the broader public (Uganda). The creation of human rights monitoring institutions is another proposal (Chile and Sri Lanka). Others demand the overhaul of the judiciary (El Salvador and Sri Lanka), and security institutions (Chad, Guatemala, and Nigeria). The repeal of laws that justify violations is on some commissions' agendas (Uganda and Liberia). Contextual differences notwithstanding, truth commissions uniformly advocate some form of legal or institutional reform to avoid a fallback into political violence and human rights violations.

Commissions in Guatemala, Nigeria, and Peru go beyond legal and institutional reform to argue that addressing national tragedy requires a comprehensive transformation of how the nation is structured, and national belonging is understood. For the Nigerian commission, "justice and the protection of human rights in Nigeria must be anchored on fundamentally redesigned and restructured institutional (constitutional-legal, cultural, political and social) and structural (economic and resource-distributive) frameworks."[52] The Peruvian panel calls for a "new social contract" in which all Peruvians, urban and rural, *criollo* and indigenous, are recognized as first-class citizens under conditions of formal and substantive equality.[53]

In conclusion, truth commissions exhibit considerable variation in terms of causal explanations and recommendations. Almost all commissions have identified the institutional actors responsible for past violations, and a few of them have labeled specific individuals, as well. Fewer commissions have taken into account political-cultural, contextual, and structural factors. Those that analyze the geopolitical context (like the Cold War) tend to portray the context as historical backdrop, rather than investigate the responsibility of foreign actors. Finally, some commissions point the finger at the country's deep structural inequalities, but political decision-makers have largely ignored their calls for comprehensive reform.

SITUATING THE BALTIC COMMISSIONS IN CONTEMPORARY TRANSITIONAL JUSTICE PRACTICE

The three Baltic commissions demonstrated little or no interest in three of the four mechanisms through which truth commissions produce impact (political-institutional reform, reconciliation between social and political actors, or noncriminal sanctions). This makes sense if the context in which the commissions came into existence is acknowledged: by 1998, the immediate concerns around political and institutional reform were less pressing, and noncriminal sanctions had already been applied in the absence of truth commissions in many postcommunist societies. Instead, the Estonian and Latvian commissions did take the possibility of raising awareness seriously, and the disagreements that led to the interruption of the Lithuanian commissions' work may have raised awareness unwittingly.

The Baltic commissions' legacy presents questions and challenges that all truth and memory initiatives struggle with in some way. First is the issue of collaboration: in these countries (especially in Lithuania, which had a relative large Jewish population before the Holocaust, compared to Estonia and Latvia) commissions were set up to adjudicate debates on the collaboration of local ethnic majorities with the Nazis during the Holocaust, a discomforting fact overshadowed by dominant narratives of ethnic majority victimhood at the hands of the Nazi and Soviet regimes. The Soviet period lasted much longer, and produced even more difficult questions around domestic participation in the regime. The question of collaboration is particularly acute for societies that suffered foreign occupation and/or totalitarian domination, but acknowledging the participation of bystanders or mainstream political actors in regimes that violate fundamental rights divides social memory in all types of regimes by undermining narratives of victimhood and resistance. For example, Chilean Christian Democrats' initial support for the 1973 military coup and Ellen Sirleaf's funding of Charles Taylor in the late 1980s (which the Liberian commission cited as a reason to ban her from politics in its 2010 final report) were brought up decades later as examples of collaboration. These cases reveal that collaboration, which the Baltic commissions tackled in their own contexts, needs to be addressed by all memory and truth initiatives.

Historical and moral complexity stands out as a related issue. Many (but by no means all) memory and truth initiatives tend to narrate the violent past in terms of victims and perpetrators. While this characterization may be correct for regimes marked by one-sided violence and repression, many countries live through a complex set of events that either engender multiple types of victimization, or blur the victim-perpetrator distinction at the individual and collective levels. Although there is no logical reason not to recognize multiple victimization as such, it is not uncommon for politicians and citizens to prioritize one population's experiences in narrations of the past, thereby presenting the notion of victimhood in zero-sum terms. A key reason for the creation of the Baltic commissions was the fear, voiced by some domestic constituencies and the international community, that the narrative of suffering under the Nazi and Soviet occupations endured by the ethnic majorities in each Baltic state de-emphasized Jewish suffering during the Holocaust. This is not a uniquely Baltic problem, as postrepressive nation-building strategies tend to refer to victimhood in relatively narrow and instrumental terms. Efforts to forge a shared memory of Yugoslavia's dissolution have thus far proven impossible, in great part because dominant memory narratives in each community stress the primacy of the wrongs suffered by that community.

A related issue is how these initiatives conceptualize the affective distance between the past and the present. Politicians, intellectuals, civil society groups, and citizens want to distance themselves from an undesirable, abusive, violent past, but their personal and collective histories are constituted in that past. The Baltic commissions considered the past as radically alien to the present, by characterizing 1940–91 as occupation regimes. While national suffering under occupation is true, it is hardly the whole picture. Repressive regimes not only kill, torture, rape, and imprison, but also build alliances with local actors, establish stable political, economic and social institutions, and perhaps even draw sympathy and legitimacy from the population. While the first Soviet invasion (1940–1) and the following Nazi invasion (1941–4) may not have resulted in the formation of stable institutions, the Soviet period (1944–91) shaped two generations in the Baltic republics. Therefore, acknowledging the continuity between the present and the past remains a lasting challenge for memory and truth initiatives in the FSU.

Finally, the Baltic commissions' methodological choices should be scrutinized further. Most truth commissions around the world have combined a predominantly forensic mode of investigation with a short narrative about the causes and consequences of past violence. The Baltic commissions have adopted an alternative approach since they reflect, first and foremost, the willingness to rethink the nation's history. Fact-driven investigation is secondary to the effort to adjudicate disagreements over the nation's past, and it is largely absent in the Lithuanian commission. It may be tempting to interpret this historiographic interest as a deviation from the conventions of truth commissions, but it is also possible that the Baltic commissions' adjudication of debates over history by combining some of the tasks and goals of conventional truth commissions with the more permanent role played by memory institutes may serve as a new model for future memory and truth initiatives. The Baltic commissions have engaged in debates around the nature and significance of collective suffering in the past, rather than prioritized the identification of individual crimes and their victims (or perpetrators). Seen this way, they are dissimilar to truth commissions established in the immediate transitional period, and to posttransitional truth commissions (in Uruguay or Morocco) that ignore historiography altogether, but quite similar to truth commissions in South Korea and Ghana that have combined human rights investigations with historical narratives.

CONCLUSION

Truth commissions have conventionally served to investigate past human rights violations, narrate the causes and consequences of violence, and propose recommendations for reform, especially in transitional contexts where documenting facts surrounding violations and repressive institutions stand out as pressing concerns. Within this framework, engaging debates around social memory has been considered an auxiliary function for most commissions. However, the interest in adjudicating historical controversies defies the strictures of the transitional paradigm: as the example of the Baltic commissions suggests, and commissions in countries as diverse as South Korea and Brazil, Ghana, and Chile confirm, an increasing number of initiatives take issue with the interpretation of past events even in the absence of transition-era needs and constraints. Yet, the posttransitional paradigm raises the question of what the expectations from a truth commission should be. Are they simply established by politicians to signal the political elite's commitment to an ethic of self-reflection over past wrongs? The Baltic commissions suggest that beyond this narrow political goal, truth commissions are also expected to raise awareness about, and perhaps adjudicate over, difficult questions about a nation's past.

Observers agree that these commissions have made very limited contributions to debates around social memory, in great part because societal outreach was lacking. Some of these limitations arise from the intrinsic difficulties of describing potentially divisive events that took place in the not-so-recent past. However, a commission's organization may play an important role, as well. The blurring of the boundary between a truth commission and memory institute overcomes the temporal and scope limits of a truth commission, but may limit the potential for outreach. The boundary is not merely a scholarly question around definitions: truth commissions undertake investigation of a limited list of human rights violations, operate for a fixed period of time, and carry the hope of government endorsement (and the accompanying policy implementation) of their findings, conclusions and recommendations; however, memory institutes may or may not invoke the language of human rights, are often permanent or semi-permanent, and do not make recommendations for immediate political or institutional reform.

What can be said about the Baltic experiences in light of truth commission efforts around the world? First, they are not outliers, but represent a posttransitional moment in the theory and practice of transitional justice in which memory and truth initiatives are expected to adjudicate long-standing disagreements over social memory rather than attend to the immediate concerns of political stability, rule-of-law reform and societal reconciliation. The unique feature of Baltic commissions has been their fluidity: unlike the temporary and limited truth commissions in other countries, these commissions (especially those in Latvia and Lithuania) have evolved into semi-permanent memory institutes.

The Baltic experiences exemplify the promises of renegotiating the boundaries of truth commissions and memory institutes, but also suffer the shortcomings of this ambiguous format. I argue that memory and truth initiatives that will follow up on the work of these commissions should maintain their ambitious mandate for producing historiography, but do so within the more constrained truth commission model. The work of memory is always accompanied by a variety of moral and political frameworks from which to view the past; investigating *human rights violations* as the basis of historical explanation (a task associated with truth commissions) serves to discuss the historical controversies in a normative framework in which all claims to victimhood, individual and collective, are evaluated rigorously. In addition, having a clear focus on certain historical events and periods, following a constrained temporal mandate helps to structure discussions and disagreements, avoiding the pitfall of treating any and all issue relevant for a commission's work. Finally, an identifiable final report is more likely to draw society's attention and spark debates among historians, politicians, and ordinary citizens than a permanent, ongoing engagement with national history. This is not to deny permanent memory institutes their legitimate place in historiography; rather, it is to argue that such institutes would work better as a follow-up to, rather than in lieu of, *ad hoc* truth commissions that undertake investigations with time and scope limits, and are expected to produce final reports.

Finally, a note on historical controversy: the idea that a truth commission will overcome a society's disagreements about the past is misleading. Since the suspension of the Lithuanian commission's work is attributed to the unending contentiousness of disagreements, the controversial nature of commissions has particular relevance for postcommunist countries in general, and the Baltic region in particular. Despite all the optimism for reaching some sort of reconciliation through truth, discovering and debating of facts of past violence often result in heightened social and political tensions. Therefore, members and sponsors of the Baltic commissions should embrace the difficult, comprehensive and at times divisive historical narratives produced by these past efforts. They should not shy away from narrative pluralism and conflict, for the invigorated public debate as a result of such discordance can be a truth commission's lasting contribution.

Notes

1. Andrew Beattie, "Post-Communist Truth Commissions: Between Transitional Justice and the Politics of History," in Lavinia Stan and Nadya Nedelsky, eds., *Post-Communist Transitional Justice: Lessons from Twenty-five Years of Experience* (New York: Cambridge University Press, 2015), 213; Jennifer Yoder, "Truth without Reconciliation: An Appraisal of the Enquete Commission on the SED Dictatorship in Germany," *German Politics* 8, 3 (1999): 59–80.
2. I define a truth commission as "a temporary body established with an official mandate to investigate past human rights violations, identify the patterns and causes of violence, and publish a final report through a politically autonomous procedure." Onur Bakiner, *Truth Commissions: Memory, Power, and Legitimacy* (Philadelphia: University of Pennsylvania Press, 2016), 31. Their temporary character distinguishes them from memory institutes, and since they are quasi-official by mandate, they are not civil society fact-finding panels. Also Eric Brahm, *Truth and Consequences: The Impact of Truth Commissions in Transitional Societies*. Ph.D. Dissertation, Department of Political Science, University of Colorado at Boulder, 2006; Priscilla Hayner, *Unspeakable Truths: Confronting State Terror and Atrocity* (New York: Routledge, 2011); and Mark Freeman, *Truth Commissions and Procedural Fairness* (New York: Cambridge University Press, 2006).
3. Kirstyn Hevey, *Estonian Transitional Justice: Predicated on a Collective Memory*, Diss. Central European University, 2014; and Eva-Clarita Pettai, "Negotiating History for Reconciliation: A Comparative Evaluation of the Baltic Presidential Commissions," *Europe-Asia Studies* 67, 7 (2015): 1098.
4. Memory and truth initiatives include officially mandated truth commissions. Unofficial fact-finding panels, parliamentary investigation commissions, institutions managing former police archives, memory and historic preservation institutes, scholarly and journalistic oral history projects, memorials and museums are among the mechanisms through which societies reckon with a violent and divisive past. Different kinds of initiatives often perform similar or identical tasks and serve similar social functions, which explains why conceptualizing and naming these initiatives may be a daunting task.
5. Their mandates usually require truth commissions to identify the individual victims of rights violations that took place over a limited period of time. Memory institutes tend to examine a broad pattern of violations for longer time periods. Truth commissions are assumed to enjoy independence from politicians, while parliamentary investigation commissions are run by politicians.
6. As of mid-2016, twenty-seven commissions have submitted final reports to political authorities. Of the twenty-three that produced publicly available final reports, seventeen have written historical narratives.

7. Brian Grodsky, "Justice without Transition: Truth Commissions in the Context of Repressive Rule," *Human Rights Review* 9, 3 (2008): 281–97, and Brian Grodsky, "Beyond Lustration Truth-Seeking Efforts in the Post-Communist Space," *Taiwan Journal of Democracy* 5, 2(2009): 21–43.
8. Andrei Cușco, "Commission for the Study and Evaluation of the Totalitarian Communist Regime in the Republic of Moldova/Comisia pentru studierea si aprecierea regimului comunist totalitar din Republica Moldova," in Lavinia Stan and Nadya Nedelsky, eds., *Encyclopedia of Transitional Justice* (New York: Cambridge University Press), Vol. 3: 52.
9. Ibid.
10. Lavinia Stan, "Truth Commissions in Post-Communism: The Overlooked Solution," *The Open Political Science Journal* 2 (2009): 1–13.
11. Eva-Clarita Pettai and Vello Pettai, *Transitional and Retrospective Justice in the Baltic States* (Cambridge: Cambridge University Press, 2014).
12. Grodsky, "Beyond Lustration," 32.
13. Pettai, "Negotiating History for Reconciliation."
14. Andrejs Plakans, "The Commission of Historians in Latvia: 1999 to the Present," *Journal of Baltic Studies* (2014): 1–18; and Matthew Kott, "Estonia 1940–1945: Reports of the Estonian International Commission for the Investigation of Crimes against Humanity," *Holocaust and Genocide Studies* 21, 2 (2007): 321–3.
15. Pettai, "Negotiating History for Reconciliation," 1081.
16. Ibid., 1098.
17. Ibid.
18. Pettai and Pettai, *Transitional and Retrospective Justice in the Baltic States*, 265.
19. Beattie, "Post-Communist Truth Commissions," 214.
20. Hevey, *Estonian Transitional Justice: Predicated on a Collective Memory*.
21. Martha Minow, *Between Vengeance and Forgiveness: Facing History after Genocide and Mass Violence* (Boston: Beacon Press, 1998); and Desmond Tutu, *No Future without Forgiveness* (New York: Doubleday, 1999).
22. Fionnuala Ní Aoláin and Colm Campbell, "The Paradox of Transition in Conflicted Democracies," *Human Rights Quarterly* 27, 1 (2005): 207.
23. Tricia D. Olsen, Leigh A. Payne and Andrew G. Reiter, *Transitional Justice in Balance: Comparing Processes, Weighing Efficacy* (Washington: US Institute of Peace Press, 2010); Hunjoon Kim and Kathryn Sikkink, "Explaining the Deterrence Effect of Human Rights Prosecutions for Transitional Countries," *International Studies Quarterly* 54, 4 (2010): 939–63; and David Mendeloff, "Truth-Seeking, Truth-Telling, and Postconflict Peacebuilding: Curb the Enthusiasm?," *International Studies Review* 6, 3 (2004): 355–80.
24. Priscilla B. Hayner, "Past Truths, Present Dangers: The Role of Official Truth Seeking in Conflict Resolution and Prevention," in Paul Stern and Daniel Druckman, eds., *International Conflict Resolution after the Cold War* (Washington: National Academies Press, 2000), 369; Geoff Dancy, "Impact Assessment, Not Evaluation: Defining a Limited Role for Positivism in the Study of Transitional Justice," *International Journal of Transitional Justice* 4, 3 (2000): 355–76.
25. Jeremy Sarkin, "The Necessity and Challenges of Establishing a Truth and Reconciliation Commission in Rwanda," *Human Rights Quarterly* 21, 3 (1999): 767–823.

26. Minow, *Between Vengeance and Forgiveness*; Hayner, "Past Truths, Present Dangers"; and Eric Brahm, "Judging Truth: The Contributions of Truth Commissions in Post-Conflict Environments," in Noha Shawki and Michaelene Cox, eds., *Rethinking Sovereignty and Human Rights after the Cold War* (Burlington: Ashgate, 2009).
27. José Zalaquett, "Confronting Human Rights Violations Committed by Former Governments: Applicable Principles and Political Constraints," *Hamline Law Review* 13, 3 (1990): 623–55; Leigh A. Payne, *Unsettling Accounts: Neither Truth nor Reconciliation in Confessions of State Violence* (Durham: Duke University Press, 2008); and Chandra Lekha Sriram and Johanna Herman, "DDR and Transitional Justice: Bridging the Divide?," *Conflict, Security & Development* 9, 4 (2009): 455–74.
28. Lisa Magarrell, "Reparations for Massive or Widespread Human Rights Violations: Sorting out Claims for Reparations and the Struggle for Social Justice," *Windsor Yearbook of Access to Justice* 22 (2003): 85–98.
29. Lisa Laplante and Kimberly Theidon, "Truth with Consequences: Justice and Reparations in post-Truth Commission Peru," *Human Rights Quarterly* 29, 1 (2007): 228–50.
30. The findings in this subsection are based on Bakiner, *Truth Commissions*.
31. Onur Bakiner, "Truth Commission Impact: An Assessment of How Commissions Influence Politics and Society," *International Journal of Transitional Justice* 8, 1 (2014): 6–30.
32. Bronwyn Anne Leebaw, "The Irreconcilable Goals of Transitional Justice," *Human Rights Quarterly* 30, 1 (2008): 95–118.
33. Brandon Hamber and Richard A. Wilson, "Symbolic Closure through Memory, Reparation and Revenge in Post-Conflict Societies," *Journal of Human Rights* 1, 1 (2002): 35–53; Laplante and Theidon, "Truth with Consequences"; and Leebaw, "The Irreconcilable Goals of Transitional Justice."
34. James Gibson, *Overcoming Apartheid: Can Truth Reconcile a Divided Nation?* (New York: Russell Sage Foundation, 2004).
35. William Long and Peter Brecke, *War and Reconciliation: Reason and Emotion in Conflict Resolution* (Cambridge: MIT Press, 2003).
36. Mike Kaye, "The Role of Truth Commissions in the Search for Justice, Reconciliation and Democratisation: The Salvadorean and Honduran Cases," *Journal of Latin American Studies* 29, 3 (1997): 693–716.
37. Mark Freeman and Priscilla Hayner, "Truth-Telling," in David Bloomfield, ed., *Reconciliation after Violent Conflict: A Handbook* (Stockholm: International Institute for Democracy and Electoral Assistance, 2003), 126–7; Madeleine Fullard and Nicky Rousseau, "Truth Telling, Identities, and Power in South Africa and Guatemala," in Paige Arthur, ed., *Identities in Transition: Challenges for Transitional Justice in Divided Societies* (New York: Cambridge University Press, 2011), 88; and Eric Wiebelhaus-Brahm, *Truth Commissions and Transitional Societies: The Impact on Human Rights and Democracy* (New York: Routledge, 2009), 12.
38. Elisabeth Cole, "Transitional Justice and the Reform of History Education," *International Journal of Transitional Justice* 1, 1 (2007): 115–37; Elizabeth Oglesby, "Historical Memory and the Limits of Peace Education: Examining Guatemala's *Memory of Silence* and the Politics of Curriculum Design," in Elizabeth Cole, ed.,

Teaching the Violent Past: History Education and Reconciliation (New York: Rowman and Littlefield, 2007): 175–202.

39. Gibson, *Overcoming Apartheid*.
40. Michael Humphrey, "Reconciliation and the Therapeutic State," *Journal of Intercultural Studies* 26, 3 (2005): 213–14.
41. Chile and South Korea had two truth commissions each: Chile in 1990 and 2003, and South Korea in 2000 and 2005. I denote the specific commission by writing the year in parenthesis throughout the text.
42. Sierra Leone Truth and Reconciliation Commission, *Witness to Truth: Report of the Sierra Leone Truth and Reconciliation Commission*, Volume I. 2004: 10.
43. Greg Grandin, "The Instruction of Great Catastrophe: Truth Commissions, National History, and State Formation in Argentina, Chile, and Guatemala," *American Historical Review* 110:1 (2005): 49.
44. Truth and Reconciliation Commission, Republic of Korea, *Truth and Reconciliation: Activities of the Past Three Years*, 2009: 6.
45. Leebaw, "The Irreconcilable Goals of Transitional Justice," 111.
46. Louise Arbour, "Economic and Social Justice for Societies in Transition," *NYU Journal of International Law and Politics* 40, 1 (2007): 14.
47. Commission for Historical Clarificatoon, *Guatemala: Memory of Silence — Report of the Commission for Historical Clarification [Tz'inil Na'tab'al]*, 1999, Conclusion 12.
48. *Synoptic Overview of HRVIC Report: Conclusions and Recommendations [Nigeria]*, 2009: 1.42.
49. Truth and Reconciliation Commission, Republic of Liberia, *Volume II: Consolidated Final Report*, (TRC of Liberia: Monrovia, 2009), 9.
50. Andrew Beattie, "An Evolutionary Process: Contributions of the Bundestag Inquiries into East Germany to an Understanding of the Role of Truth Commissions," *International Journal of Transitional Justice* 3, 2 (2009): 229–49.
51. Cristian Tileagă, "Communism in Retrospect: The Rhetoric of Historical Representation and Writing the Collective Memory of Recent Past," *Memory Studies* 5, 4 (2012): 462–78.
52. *Conclusions and Recommendations* [Nigeria] 1999: 1:40.
53. *Hatun Willakuy: versión abreviada del Informe final de la Comisión de la Verdad y Reconciliación del Perú*, Lima, 2004, Chapter 8.

8

Lustration: Temporal, Scope, and Implementation Considerations

Cynthia M. Horne

What have we learned from the lustration experiences in Central and Eastern Europe (CEE) that could inform our understanding of the possibilities and limitations of lustration in the Former Soviet Union (FSU)? In reviewing and critiquing the 2014 lustration laws in Ukraine, the European Commission for Democracy Through Law (Venice Commission) grounded their review in both the Council of Europe's original 1996 lustration guidelines, as well as the structure and function of CEE's lustration laws.[1] In this way the postcommunist lustration measures, particularly the vanguard programs in the Czech Republic and Poland, have exerted a legal and normative gravity on what we have come to assume about lustration. However, we have twenty-five years of experience with lustration across a diverse range of postcommunist countries and experiences. Taking a broader view of lustration in practice across CEE provides lessons about the structure, limitations, and temporal conditions associated with more and less effective programs, which in turn might be useful in updating and modifying original understandings of this measure of transitional justice for possible application to the FSU.

This chapter examines lustration in post-Euromaidan Ukraine through the lens of the CEE experiences with lustration measures and public disclosure programs. I use the definition of lustration from the *Encyclopedia of Transitional Justice* as a starting point: "lustration – a form of vetting – describes the broad set of parliamentary laws that restrict members and collaborators of former repressive regimes from holding a range of public offices, state management positions, or other jobs with strong public influence (such as in the media or academia) after the collapse of the authoritarian regime."[2] Public disclosure programs refer to the informal lustration measures seen in countries like Bulgaria, Romania, and Slovakia, by which individuals were vetted in a manner similar to lustration, and the information about previous collaboration was publicly disclosed.[3] Drawing on the twenty-five years

of postcommunist experience with these transitional justice measures, this
chapter argues that some of the presumptions about lustration based on the
original design in 1991 might need to be reconsidered. In particular, there
appears to be more flexibility in the scope and timing of measures than originally assumed. Measures enacted later in the transition can be effective at
catalyzing reform. Contrary to assumptions, more exclusionary and punitive
measures were associated with the most efficacious programs, and wide and
deep measures did not undermine bureaucratic capacity or government effectiveness. However, the CEE experience illustrated possible limitations on the
capacity of lustration to effect any and all transition goals. While lustration has
been shown to support certain kinds of political trust-building, promote good
governance, and support democratization, its effects are often indirect, forcing
us to rethink the parameters and possibilities of lustration as an all-purpose
instrument for reform. Most salient for this chapter, there was little evidence
that lustration acted as a direct anticorruption mechanism in CEE. These
findings apply particularly to the Ukrainian case, but also resonate more
generally across the FSU.

This chapter is structured as follows. First, I summarize the two main lustration laws in Ukraine, namely the Law on Government Cleansing and the Law
on Restoring Confidence in the Judiciary in Ukraine. Second, the similarities
and differences between the Ukrainian program and those of regional counterparts are examined, with particular attention to areas of difference critiqued
by both international and domestic actors. Third, drawing on the lessons
learned from impact assessments of the postcommunist lustration programs,
I engage some of the contested components of the Ukrainian law, attending to
what we know about the scope, implementation, and temporal conditions of
effective programs. The conclusion considers how these findings might apply
to the FSU.

BACKGROUND: LUSTRATION MEASURES IN UKRAINE

After the 1991 break-up of the Soviet Union, Ukraine abolished the KGB
and banned the Communist Party but chose not to pursue lustration.[4]
Following the Orange Revolution in 2004–5, two lustration bills were proposed in 2005 but rejected by both the President and Parliament.[5] The active
rejection of lustration bears note; lustration was an option at various turning
points in Ukraine, but was rejected. A new push for lustration came after the
Euromaidan uprising, following the removal of President Viktor Yanukovych
in 2014. There was significant bottom up support for lustration, with social
groups riding a post-Maidan wave of popular calls for reforms under the "Pure

Government" slogan.[6] Civil society groups and parliamentarians worked in parallel on lustration bills, some competing and others complementary. In the end, two primary lustration measures were passed: the first focused on the judiciary and the second addressed the government and public sector more broadly.

Law on Restoring Confidence in the Judiciary in Ukraine was signed into law by President Petro Poroshenko on April 10, 2014.[7] This lustration measure focused narrowly on the judicial system, requiring all court chairs appointed under Yanukovych to be fired, and all judges to be screened for corruption and/or evidence that they acted against Euromaidan protesters. The lustration would be focused on events between November 21, 2013 and February 21, 2014, targeting breaches of ethics and unfairness under Yanukovych.[8] With respect to broader lustration efforts across the public sector, the Verkhovna Rada (Ukrainian Parliament) registered four different draft lustration laws between February 2014 and April 2014, and two others after that, giving a total of six drafts that were independently submitted for consideration. The drafts came from Oleh Tyahnybok from the Svoboda party, Volodymyr Ariev from Batkivshchyna (formerly Our Ukraine bloc), as well as Valeriy Patzkan and Roman Chernehy from the Ukrainian Democratic Alliance for Reform (UDAR). Concepts were also proposed by various local social committees, including the Kharkiv Human Rights Group represented by Yevhen Zakharov.[9] There was a range of lustration ideas presented in the drafts, from very wide and punitive measures like the Czech Republic's to less punitive and more confessional measures like Poland's. The Lustration Committee, chaired by Yehor Sobolev, was tasked with reviewing and synthesizing these voices and proposals into a coherent draft lustration proposal.[10]

The resulting Law on Government Cleansing (Lustration Law), ratified on September 25, 2014, reflected multiple voices and perspectives on lustration.[11] While David's chapter (Chapter 6) provides more elaborate treatment of the lustration laws in Ukraine, this law's most salient elements for a comparison of Ukraine with other postcommunist lustration measures included: screening across decision-making positions in all state institutions at the central, regional and local levels; an automatic employment ban on officials found guilty of lustratable offenses for five to ten years; the creation of a Social Lustration Council to support work on lustration within the Ministry of Justice; and the recording of a lustration registry within the Lustration Department of the Ministry of Justice to keep track of the process.[12] Screening was decentralized, with the head of each public administration unit accountable for the vetting of his/her institution. In addition to traditional confessions of previous regime involvement, individuals were required to submit financial audits and income information to be considered in the concomitant anticorruption campaign. The original drive was for the removal of Yanukovych-appointed officials and bureaucrats, but there were also elements of decommunization, including the removal of KGB officials, individuals trained in KGB universities, and communist *nomenklatura*. Finally, the law punished anyone who acted against Euromaidan protesters, taking a very proximate approach to crimes of the past. Therefore there were three targets to the "government clean-up": Yanukovych and Party of Regions' officials, communist era *nomenklatura*, and individuals that punished Euromaidan protesters.[13]

These two main lustration laws were parts of a constellation of other lustration/vetting measures and supporting agencies, bills and amendments. For example, a separate lustration amendment for the intelligence services and security sector reforms targeted more specific parts of the public sector. A Council for Judiciary Reform, a Lustration Commission and the Ministry of Justice were all intended to complement and oversee aspects of the broader lustration processes. In this way, lustration in Ukraine constituted a decentralized, layered process with multiple, different executors, oversight agencies, and provisions for screening a range of categories of public servants.[14]

COMPARING UKRAINE TO OTHER POSTCOMMUNIST CASES

There are a number of similarities and differences between lustration in CEE and post-Euromaidan Ukraine. In many ways the measures in Ukraine were less atypical than they have been described by critics, while in other ways they forced more malleability in what we as a transitional justice field have come to expect from lustration measures. Before thinking about how the experiences in CEE might inform the processes in Ukraine, it is important to highlight some of the most salient similarities and differences.

First, Ukrainian politicians and political activists linked lustration measures to multiple transition goals, such as trust-building, corruption fighting, reform of the judiciary, the break-up of oligarchic networks, the decentralization of economic control, and improvements in the efficiency of the public sector.[15] President Poroshenko argued that lustration would both promote judicial reform and fight against more general corruption.[16] The Law on Restoring Confidence in the Judiciary in Ukraine was translated by the Council of Europe as the "Law on Restoration of Trust in the Judiciary," leaving no ambiguity surrounding the goals of the vetting mechanism.[17] The preamble of the Law on Government Cleansing (or the "Clean Power" Law) started out by explicitly linking lustration to democracy. "The law defines legal and organizational principles of clean power (lustration) for protecting and promoting democratic values, the rule of law, and human rights in Ukraine."[18] As such there were many complementary and overlapping goals motivating the lustration laws.

The Ukrainian framing of lustration as a multi-faceted elixir capable of tackling a set of diffuse and somewhat inchoate goals has been critiqued by domestic and international actors for being both unachievable and not in keeping with the letter and spirit of lustration.[19] In particular, the use of lustration as an anticorruption device has been criticized as incompatible with the feasible and appropriate goals of this transitional justice measure.[20] This line of argument is often linked to the Council of Europe's lustration guidelines or the European Court of Human Rights'(ECtHR) rulings on lustration, which describe lustration as a democracy promoter or a mechanism by which "a democracy [is] capable of defending itself."[21] Cleaving narrowly to this understanding unnecessarily delimits the range of reasonable goals associated with lustration.

In fact, the Ukrainian reform goals mirrored those cited by other postcommunist countries in the letter of their lustration laws, in policy debates surrounding the adoption of laws, and by policy makers and activists trying to justify the laws. For example, Stan documented a variety of goals for lustration articulated in Romanian parliamentary debates, including: trust-building, moral cleansing, securing a break with the past, retributive justice for victims, fighting corruption, catalyzing elite replacement, and preventing (re)newed violence.[22] Other scholars have linked lustration and vetting to the goals of restoring trust in public institutions, fighting corruption, and preventing the abuse of power by remnants of the former regime.[23] As such, the mere fact that Ukraine has framed lustration measures as more than a democracy promoter is not in and of itself different from the similar elixir-like framing of lustration in CEE. Later this chapter will engage with realistic expectations for what lustration might or might not be able to accomplish, drawing on the similar experiences in CEE. However, the narratives surrounding lustration in Ukraine and CEE are remarkably consistent.

Second, the *scope of positions* in the Ukrainian legislation has also been criticized as inconsistent with regional practices. The main lustration law included an expansive array of public positions: the Prime Minister and Vice Prime Ministers, the National Bank, and the Chairman of the State Committee for Television and Radio (Article 2§1), the Prosecutor General, and the Heads of the Foreign Intelligence Service, the State Guard, and the Tax Police and related positions (Article 2§2), military officers (Article 2§3), heads of state-owned enterprises related to the military-industrial complex (Article 2§9), and officers of the Interior Ministry (Article 2§6). The lustration of various

departments and categories targeted individuals at the state and regional levels, described as the top three levels of government.[24] Certain judiciary-related
positions were included in the Law on Government Cleansing provisions as
well, including "members of the High Council of Justice, members of the
High Qualification Commission of Judges of Ukraine, professional judges,
[and] Head of the State Judicial Administration of Ukraine" (Article 2§4).[25]

Criticisms have included concerns that this broad scope would denude
bureaucracies, the measures would take too long to implement and not
address the root problem of corruption, and Ukraine had larger post-Maidan
issues to address than lustration. While quite broad, the scope of positions
mirrored other postcommunist lustration experiences. Article 1 of the initial Czechoslovak lustration law of 1991 included all of the aforementioned
positions,[26] Lithuania included semi-public positions, and Poland's 2006 law
expanded the scope of lustrated positions. In many ways, even twenty-three
years later, the scope of lustration in the Czechoslovak vanguard case and
the case of Ukraine showed remarkable overlap, without the predicted dire
bureaucratic effects.

A salient difference in the scope of positions worth highlighting is that the
Ukrainian provisions excluded *elected positions*, while most of the CEE lustration measures included them. Critics suggested that this provision would
shield political candidates from necessary vetting.[27] Ukraine still required political candidates to provide financial statements, but grounded its decision to
allow candidates to run for elected positions in Council of Europe Resolution
1096, which states: "Lustration shall not apply to elective offices, unless the
candidate for election so requests – voters are entitled to elect whomever they
wish (the right to vote may only be withdrawn from a sentenced criminal
upon the decision of a court of law – this is not an administrative lustration,
but a criminal law measure)."[28] Although Ukraine has been heavily criticized
for deviating from other postcommunist countries that lustrated elected positions, these scope conditions remain consistent with the Council of Europe's
argument that compulsory removal from election lists was unnecessary for
lustration.

Third, the lustration processes in Ukraine have different *temporal dimensions* than in CEE. Most postcommunist states focused on addressing wrongs
committed under the communist system up until the overthrow of the totalitarian regimes, generally understood as 1989 in CEE and 1991 in the Baltic states.
In several countries, specific periods were included in the lustration provisions:
March 6, 1945 until December 22, 1989 in Romania; February 25, 1948 until
December 29, 1989 in the Czech and Slovak Republics; and September 12,
1944 until November 10, 1989 in Bulgaria.[29] In this way there was a clear temporal

framing of lustration as a means of addressing crimes committed in the communist past. In contrast, Ukraine's lustration laws included three time periods for accountability. Like the measures in CEE the Ukrainian lustration provisions included decommunization elements, lustrating individuals with connections to the secret police, KGB agents, Komsomol members, and members of Ukrainian Soviet Socialist Republic security bodies. However, unlike CEE measures, Ukraine's also included more proximate wrongdoings, lustrating individuals in public office from the February 25, 2010 to February 22, 2014 to address wrongs committed under President Yanukovych. Additionally, anyone who took action to punish Euromaidan protestors between November 21, 2013 and February 23, 2014 would also be lustrated. This gave the lustration laws both a distant and a proximate temporal element significantly different from the other CEE measures. In some ways the Ukrainian measures were *post-communist* and *post-post-communist measures*, raising questions regarding what part of the "past" and the "present" they meant to capture.

Fourth, the *timing of reforms*, compared to the start of the regime transition in Ukraine, raised questions as well. Discussions abound regarding when is *too late* to initiate measures and how long is *too long* to continue measures. The Council of Europe suggested that "lustration measures should preferably end no later than December 31, 1999, because the new democratic systems should be consolidated by that time in all former communist totalitarian countries."[30] A number of ECtHR rulings, drawing on the Council of Europe's temporal parameters, highlighted that while fledgling democracies needed to defend themselves from domestic forces that might try to thwart their transitions, over time such measures were harder to justify on democracy protection grounds.[31] A decade after a regime transition there was less of a justification for measures that might bend due process safeguards or rule of law criteria in order to safeguard democracy.[32] Finally, the examples of late lustration in Poland and Romania highlighted the potential instrumentalization of lustration measures by political parties against their opponents.[33] While political manipulation of lustration was not exclusive to late lustration measures, the cycles of lustration in Poland and Romania focused attention on the real possibility that the introduction of late lustration measures, like the kind enacted in Ukraine, could be used as a tool of party politics rather than an authentic transitional justice measure.

Fifth, the lustration measures in Ukraine were *layered* in a manner that differentiated them from the CEE experiences. Lustration measures were adopted in CEE after authoritarian transitions, which were largely peaceful except for the contained violence of the Romanian overthrow of Nicolae Ceauşescu.[34] In contrast, Ukraine has both postauthoritarian and postconflict offenses layered on each other. The active conflict in the Donbass region, the conflict in Crimea, and the violent actions taken against Euromaidan protestors all layered an element of conflict-related offenses over the postauthoritarian crimes. As such, the layering of postconflict offenses on postauthoritarian offenses, with areas of possible overlap and reticulation, certainly complicated the framing of the Ukrainian measures in comparison to the clearly postauthoritarian measures in CEE.

Six, in Ukraine lustration laws have been enacted in conjunction with and *layered on other reform measures*, covering similar groups and similar offenses. While it is true that governments in CEE experimented with different types of economic and political reforms simultaneous with lustration, lustration's purview was complementary not redundant with most of these structural reforms. Separate lustration laws captured overlapping elements of the public sector, including a lustration law focused on the judiciary, a lustration law for general public sector positions, a security sector reform for the police and a separate lustration amendment for the Intelligence Services.[35] In Ukraine, the central problem – corruption – is being tackled with overlapping reforms, some of which are partially redundant, complementary, and/or substitutes to lustration. For example, packages of lustration laws, anticorruption laws, anticorruption institutions, and security sector reform measures were all layered on each other in related and somewhat overlapping measures.[36] In this way, there were layers of legislation triangulating core bureaucratic problems in Ukraine, muddying legal responsibilities for reform, and blurring the implementing of the laws. This layering of related reforms differentiates the Ukrainian case from that in CEE.

Seventh, the *decentralized structure* of lustration in Ukraine stands in contrast to the more centralized structure of other postcommunist lustration programs. The Council of Europe's original guidelines suggested "lustration should be administered by a specifically created independent commission."[37] Deviating from this recommendation, Ukraine designed a decentralized system. The senior officials in government agencies were tasked with vetting their own personnel and passing this information on to the Lustration Commission. The Venice Commission criticized this design choice, highlighting that "There is a risk that the practice under the Law, which is to be implemented by a range of public agencies, could either lack uniformity or open space for settling accounts on a personal/political basis or lead to too lenient an approach toward some of the lustrated individuals."[38] There is an expediency to measures that are decentralized, which fits with Ukraine's perceived urgency to have a swift and broad lustration program, but the potential for such measures to be corrupted or manipulated poses a real policy tradeoff.

In the end, Ukraine opted to maintain its decentralized system, with some modifications that brought it in line with the Venice Commission.

In sum, this section highlighted areas of difference between Ukraine's lustration measures and those of other postcommunist cases, with attention to those differences that have been most criticized. Building on these areas of similarity and difference the next section examines how CEE's experience with lustration might inform an understanding of the possibilities and limitations of lustration in Ukraine and other FSU states.

APPLYING LESSONS FROM CEE TO UKRAINE

The postcommunist experience with lustration affords us twenty-five years of evidence about the relative efficacy of different lustration programs and approaches. While all national accountability and transitional justice needs and programs are somewhat unique, and what has worked or not worked in nine other postcommunist countries cannot guarantee similar results in Ukraine, this section draws on some of the findings regarding lustration and related measures in order to contextualize the Ukrainian experience and examine possible impact.

First, one of the primary goals of vetting measures like lustration is to build trust in public institutions specifically and government more generally. We have some confirmatory evidence in the postcommunist transitions of a relationship between lustration measures and higher levels of trust in government.[39] In David's work on personnel systems in the Czech Republic, Hungary, and Poland, he found positive effects from lustration on trust in government.[40] While Horne did not find such a clear and direct positive relationship between lustration and trust in government, she did find indirect relationships between lustration programs and more trustworthy governments.[41] Moreover, Horne illustrated that public institutions directly targeted by lustration measures and/or public disclosures showed higher levels of political trust. To be more precise, trust in public institutions that were *not highly politicized*, showed improvements over time. A variety of oversight institutions like the judiciary, the police, and the press evidenced clear positive relationships between all types of lustration measures and more trust.[42] These findings corresponded with the United Nations' findings in other regions, showing direct, positive relationships between the vetting of the judiciary and the police and more trust in those institutions.[43] Mayer-Rieckh and de Greiff similarly found evidence of a positive relationship between the vetting of oversight institutions through targeted security sector reforms and more trust.[44] These finding suggest that the lustration of public institutions in Ukraine, including but not

limited to the judiciary, the police, and a variety of supporting public institutions like the National Bank, the army and the press, could be enhanced
through lustration measures.

Some critics have highlighted design and/or implementation problems
with the Ukrainian lustration program. Examples abound of individuals using
their clientilistic networks to illegally evade lustration, or traveling to combat
zones to claim exemptions from measures.[45] Lustration in CEE also suffered
from implementation problems. While the decentralization of lustration
authority is unique to Ukraine, allegations of unfair or incomplete implementation mirrored similar struggles in CEE.[46] The political manipulation
of lustration measures by political parties, the problems with incomplete or
missing files, and the manner in which lustration missed many higher ranking
officials whose files were destroyed were some of the implementation flaws
documented in CEE. Despite these known (and many unknowable) implementation problems, across the region there were consistently positive relationships between lustration measures and trust in targeted public institutions.

Moreover, the Ukrainian examples of individuals evading removal must be
considered in light of the thousands of individuals screened and the hundreds removed from positions. For example, as of January 2015, 1,360 civil
servants had lustration checks in the Ministry of Justice, Ministry of Interior,
Fiscal Service and Security Service.[47] By March 2015, 24,000 officials were
lustrated.[48] As of October 2015, the register of lustration held by the Ministry
of Justice listed 772 individuals banned from holding public office for five
to ten years, and 86,730 names on register as having completed lustration
reviews.[49] As of March 2016, the Ministry of Justice reported the prosecution of
387 positions and 401 persons, with an additional 311 self-lustrating.[50] In sum,
while there have been problems with implementation of measures, this would
hardly be unique to Ukraine. Moreover the lustration numbers suggest actual
bureaucratic change is taking place. *In general, the postcommunist experience
suggests that lustration could enhance the trustworthiness of public institutions
and perhaps government, even if the implementation of lustration was flawed.*

Second, since lustration of the judiciary was so important in Ukraine that
a specific judicial lustration law was passed before the general lustration law,
it bears individual attention here. Popova was especially critical of the Law
on Restoring Confidence in the Judiciary in Ukraine, arguing that lustration
sidestepped the real problem of corruption and that judicial independence
would be dangerously compromised through a punitive lustration program.[51]
Judges in Ukraine were also vocal about the legal problems with the lustration measures, arguing that the collective rather than individual guilt criteria in the lustration measures violated the constitution.[52] A progress report in

March 2016 detailed glaring examples of the lax implementation of lustration, and judges evading lustration by drawing either on their judicial networks for reappointment in other regions, or securing appointment to lesser positions.[53] Despite significant implementation problems, the report also documented the successful removal of judges from their positions. As of March 2015, forty-four judges failed lustration and were being dismissed.[54] By the end of 2015, 127 judges were dismissed with a motion to dismiss 400 more, and in 2016 the process of screening 8,000 judges continued.[55] In essence, there was forced bureaucratic change in the judiciary, even if many judges managed to avoid lustration.

It is difficult to adjudicate the claims by judges that the lustration laws violated various aspects of the constitution, since self-interested judges would be materially affected by said laws.[56] Arguments related to individual accountability problems with the law remain true, but mirror similar problems with lustration legislation in other CEE countries that still managed to implement the laws to positive effect. In fact, the judiciary was one of the public institutions showing the largest benefits from lustration measures in the postcommunist space. The relationship between trust in the judiciary and lustration was robust in CEE, irrespective of the timing of the onset of measures or whether the programs were punitive or reconciliatory.[57] Popova acknowledged a similar positive relationship in Georgia.[58] *As such, the evidence from the postcommunist experiences suggests that lustration of the judiciary could build trust in Ukraine.*

Third, the lessons from CEE could inform the scope conditions of beneficial lustration measures. CEE showed us that not all public institutions responded the same to lustration. Horne demonstrated that highly politicized public institutions, like parliament or political parties, did not show the consistently robust trust-building relationships noted with oversight institutions.[59] There was some evidence that early lustration measures, meaning measures enacted very soon after a regime transition, could have positive trust-building effects on politicized institutions, but those effects were less stable, smaller, and more temporally contingent that the previously discussed positive associations between lustration and trust in the judiciary. Horne's findings resonated with other studies documenting problems with the political instrumentalization of lustration by political parties, especially during late lustration programs. For example, Kiss highlighted how the manipulation of lustration measures in Hungary negatively affected both the process and the perceptions of political parties.[60] Stan documented a similar instrumentalization by political parties in Romania trying to gain political advantage over opponents.[61] Szczerbiak explored the problems with late lustration in Poland, in particular its use as a tool of party politics.[62] The instrumental manipulation of lustration as a tool against other political parties has been associated with less trust in politicized public institutions not more.

These findings are directly relevant to the case of Ukraine. The country has come under domestic criticism for excluding elected officials from its lustration net.[63] In practice this means that the President, the Prime Minister and elected members of government would not be subjected to lustration. While civil society actors have been highly critical of this exclusion, it comports with the Council of Europe's recommendations for lustration programs in general, and specific Venice Commission suggestions following its review of the Purification Law.[64] The research findings related to politicized institutions similarly suggested such lustration was not particularly efficacious, and could undermine trust rather than enhance it. *In sum, highly politicized institutions, like parliament and political parties, have not benefited greatly from lustration; therefore the exclusion of these elected offices from lustration in Ukraine does not raise an implementation red flag.*

Fourth, lustration and anticorruption measures have gone hand in hand in Ukraine. The Purification Act is about "clean power" or the removal of corrupt individuals from public affairs.[65] Lustration laws were enacted in conjunction with and supported by other corruption measures, including a package of anticorruption laws passed in October 2014, and the creation of two new institutions, the National Anti-Corruption Bureau and the National Agency for Prevention of Corruption.[66] While these agencies have struggled with staffing and financial support impediments similar to the Lustration Commission, implementation challenges do not obviate the clear and direct framing of lustration as an anticorruption mechanism in Ukraine. The inclusion of a financial assets disclosure component for both lustration laws was unusual in forcing the reporting of income, possibly accrued through the use of public office for personal gain.[67] The use of overlapping lustration and anticorruption laws and committees has resembled a kitchen sink approach to solving the enormous corruption problem. These modifications to traditional lustration caused some, such as the Venice Commission, to argue that lustration should not be contorted into an anticorruption mechanism.

Despite the framing of lustration as a direct corruption corrective, empirical evidence to support this assertion is less certain. Horne found that lustration could have indirect effects on corruption, but no direct, positive relationships between the use of lustration measures, either punitive or reconciliatory, and lower levels of corruption were evident in CEE cases.[68] Corruption levels are lower when government is more effective, public institutions uphold rule of law practices, and a more robust civil society is in place. Since research has shown that lustration was associated with improvements in the quality of government, levels of democracy, trust in targeted public institutions and a more robust civil society in postcommunist states, then one could assert possible indirect effects between lustration and corruption. If this is the case, Ukraine might have been wise to include reinforcing policies, namely anticorruption measures *and* lustration measures. Moreover, the inclusion of an explicit financial statement audit in the Ukrainian provision might enhance the corruption fighting component in a way absent from the CEE lustration measures. Although critics have warned that this financial disclosure aspect was too different from traditional lustration seen in CEE, it might constitute an improvement if the goal is to fight corruption. *In sum, Ukraine's multi-layered approach to lustration and corruption combined with the inclusion of financial audits might actually improve the manner in which lustration addresses underlying corruption problems.*

Fifth, there are many assumptions surrounding the timing and duration of reform measures in the transitional justice literature. These temporal assumptions were part of the Council of Europe's lustration guidelines, recommending a maximum window of ten years for the use of lustration measures, only until democracies were consolidated. According to the Council of Europe's recommendations, the maximum period for disqualification should not exceed five years.[69] While these recommendations reflected logical thinking about lustration and vetting in 1996 when they were codified, we now have two more decades of information about the actual effects of lustration with which to modify initial assumptions about the measures. We know that many CEE countries engaged in late lustration in a manner which appeared to support trust-building and democratization. For example, Poland's late lustration programs started in 1997 near the time the Council of Europe thought reforms should be concluding.[70] Even the vanguard Czech case repeatedly extended the time period for lustration until in 2000 it extended the time period indefinitely.[71] This suggests that the lustration processes in CEE required more than a decade. Moreover, analyses of the timing of lustration measures late and delayed measures were still associated with trust-building and democracy promotion.[72]

In terms of how this applies to Ukraine, the country initially proposed a two-year period to complete lustration. Such efforts to force a two-year period for lustration would be short sighted. While there are different estimates as to how many people would be reviewed in a lustration process, varying from Prime Minister Arseniy Yacenyuk's public announcement of a million people to the approximately 4,000 individuals that the Ukrainian authorities reported to the Venice Commission, in either case a proposed 2015–16 time period for the entire process would be very short compared to other regional programs.[73] The experience in CEE suggests a couple of important temporal qualifications for the Ukrainian experience: lustration measures have taken much longer to implement than two years, and their effects might not be immediately visible. One could not expect immediate and visible reform in Ukraine after one year, despite the contention of critics.[74] The window of opportunity for instituting beneficial measures was longer than originally envisioned. *The CEE experience has taught us that lustration is a longer term process than originally assumed.*

Sixth, in terms of the design of lustration measures, the punitive dimension of lustration measures in Ukraine has drawn criticism. The automatic dismissal of individuals from positions for five to ten years combined with collective, rather than individual, guilt criteria led to a review of the law by the Venice Commission.[75] Part of the dilemma involved whether exclusionary or inclusionary policies were more efficacious in promoting trust-building and democracy. What are the possible merits of an exclusionary lustration program versus an inclusionary program? David's analysis of lustration measures in CEE found that dismissals were most effective at increasing trust in government in CEE, with confessions also working but with one-third of the effect of dismissals.[76] His findings echoed Horne's work that showed that all types of lustration systems – punitive and truth telling, or exclusionary and inclusionary – improved perceptions of trust in public institutions and contributed to democracy, but the largest and most robust effects were associated with compulsory or punitive systems.[77] This goes against the intuition suggesting inclusionary or truth-telling measures might be less divisive and thus more supportive of trust-building and reconciliation. While reconciliatory or non-punitive measures could support transitions, intuitions that they would be as or more effective than punitive programs would not be supported by the CEE empirical evidence thus far. *In sum, the exclusionary and compulsory vetting program in Ukraine comports with the findings from CEE that exclusionary programs might have the largest positive effects on trust and democracy.*

CONCLUSION: THINKING MORE BROADLY ABOUT THE FSU

The comparison of lustration in CEE and Ukraine highlights both the malleability of lustration as well as its limitations. Reflecting on the lustration lessons from CEE, Ukraine's amendments and modifications to the scope and temporal parameters of its lustration measures might remain productive and consistent, depending on the quality of implementation. This begs the question: what are the lessons the CEE experiences and the Ukrainian case present for the FSU? I suggest three main messages for the FSU in terms of the timing of measures, the structure of measures and the goals of measures.

First, the experience with lustration in Ukraine presents some temporal lessons. It could be argued that Ukraine is an example of late lustration, since its measures were passed twenty-three years after the dissolution of the Soviet Union. In terms of lustration as a decommunization mechanism, impact assessments from the postcommunist space suggest that this was outside of the window of opportunity for lustration to support those goals. In a word, twenty-five years after the end of the Soviet Union might be too late for other FSU states to reap the benefits of lustration on such a distant past. However, Ukraine's lustration law primarily targeted the temporally proximate offenses associated with Yanukovych, and only secondarily encompassed more distant communist legacies. While communist *nomenklatura* networks and the corruption of the Yanukovych regime were intertwined, the specific time parameters of the lustration law focused on cleaning the government of bureaucrats, public officials and the judiciary associated with the Party of Regions and appointed by Yanukovych. From this perspective, there is nothing inherently too late about these lustration measures. While lustration might not be effective against communist era officials, it could still be used as a political cleansing tool in a post-post-communist environment. Although the CEE experiences suggested that lustration was most associated with decommunization, nothing suggests that lustration must only be about decommunization.

In practice, there is significant overlap between lustration and vetting. The definition of lustration from the *Encyclopedia of Transitional Justice* frames it as a type of employment vetting.[78] Vetting public officials whose credibility or integrity render them unsuitable for public service remains a temporally open possibility for many FSU countries. In particular, countries with current or future leadership change (Turkmenistan or Kazakhstan), human rights abuses (Uzbekistan), and enduring communist power structures (Belarus) could be amenable to lustration measures. While lustration is most frequently considered at the moment of regime change or the end of conflict, all of these countries could potentially fall into that category in the near future. The use of lustration in Georgia hints at possibilities for its use in other FSU countries. We know that lustration has promoted trust-building, good governance, and democratization in other postcommunist countries, and there is nothing to suggest it could not have positive effects in the FSU if used in a manner that authentically tackled both proximate and more distant regime abuses.

Second, the postcommunist experiences with lustration have shown that both exclusionary and inclusionary measures supported transition goals, but more punitive or exclusionary measures were associated with the greatest benefits. Ukraine has come under fire for its compulsory vetting and employ-ment exclusion. The idealization of nonpunitive lustration measures by inter-national actors is not consistent with what we have come to know about the mechanisms by which lustration prompts change. With respect to the FSU, this means that ideally the processes would be exclusionary. Importantly, if a norm was generalized that lustration could and would include punitive dimensions, it could be a deterrent to future rights' derogations. As Mayer-Rieckh and de Grieff highlighted in their exploration of vetting as a form of transitional justice, measures are both for present accountability and the pre-vention of future abuses.[79] Given on-going rights abuses in some FSU cases, such a deterrent could impact current politics.

Third, the Venice Commission criticized lustration measures in Ukraine for trying to tackle two goals, namely the right of a democracy to protect itself and anticorruption measures.[80] We know from the CEE's experience with lustration that there are limits to what lustration can effect. While there was support for the assertion that lustration promotes political trust-building, good governance, and democratization, there was limited evidence in the postcom-munist cases that lustration directly affected levels of corruption. Lustration appeared to indirectly support the fight against corruption via the manner in which it affected trust in public institutions, but was not the much touted corruption corrective. This suggests that the layering of lustration and anticor-ruption legislation could prove highly effective in the FSU. Should countries find themselves contemplating vetting style reforms to counter endemic cor-ruption, a combination of anticorruption and lustration measures might prove most effective at tackling the complementary but distinct goals of supporting democracy and stamping out corruption. In other words, while lustration or vetting could be a good start to the reform process, lustration would not be sufficient to tackle the myriad transition reforms necessary in many of the FSU states.

Notes

1. European Commission for Democracy Through Law (Venice Commission), *Final Opinion on the Law on Government Cleansing (Lustration Law) of Ukraine*, Opinion No. 788/2014, CDL-AD (2015)012, Venice, June 19, 2015; Council of Europe, *Measures to Dismantle the Heritage of Former Communist Totalitarian Systems*. Resolution 1096 and Doc. 7568, June 3, 1996 Parliamentary Assembly (Strasbourg France, 1996).
2. Monika Nalepa, "Lustration," in Lavinia Stan and Nadya Nedelsky, eds., *Encyclopedia of Transitional Justice* (New York: Cambridge University Press, 2013), 1:46.

3. Cynthia Horne, "Silent Lustration: Public Disclosures as Informal Lustration Mechanisms in Bulgaria and Romania," *Problems of Post-Communism* 62, May (2015): 131–44.

4. Alexei Trochev, "Ukraine," in Lavinia Stan and Nadya Nedelsky, eds., *Encyclopedia of Transitional Justice* (New York: Cambridge University Press, 2013), 2: 490–7.

5. Lavinia Stan, ed., *Transitional Justice in Eastern Europe and the Former Soviet Union: Reckoning with the Communist Past* (New York: Routledge Press, 2009), 239.

6. Agnieszka Piasecka, *Summary of Legislative Work on Lustration Act No. 4359 'On Purification of Government,'* The Open Dialogue Foundation, November 19, 2014.

7. Law of Ukraine No. 1188-VII, "On Restoring Confidence in the Judiciary in Ukraine," Verkhovna Rada (VVR), 2014, No. 23, st. 870, [in Ukrainian], Act of April 8, 2014. http://zakon4.rada.gov.ua/laws/show/1188-18/ accessed October 14, 2016.

8. See Article 3, Section 9, "On Restoring Confidence in the Judiciary in Ukraine."

9. Piasecka, *Summary of Legislative Work.*

10. Tom Balmforth, "Former Journalist Spearheads Ukraine's Lustration Effort," *RFE/RL*, April 12, 2014.

11. While there are various translations of this law including "Purification of Government" and "Clean Government" law, this chapter uses the English translation in the Venice Commission. Law of Ukraine No. 1682-VII, "On the Law on Government Cleansing (Lustration Law)," Verkhovna Rada (VVR), 2014, No. 44, st. 2041, [in Ukrainian], Act of April 8, 2014, available at: http://zakon4.rada.gov.ua/laws/show/1682-18/, accessed September 25, 2016.

12. Articles 2, 3 and 5 in particular, "On Government Cleansing."

13. Article 1, sections 1 and 2, "On Government Cleansing"; Tadeusz Olszański, *The Ukrainian Lustration Act*, Ośrodek Studiów Wschodnich, October 1, 2014.

14. Wojciech Konończuk, Tadeusz Iwański, Tadeusz Olszański and Piotr Żochowski, *The Bumpy Road. Difficult Reform Process in Ukraine*, OSW Commentary, Centre for Eastern Studies, No. 192, November 30, 2015.

15. Ibid.

16. "Poroshenko Decides to Sign Law on Lustration," *Ukraine General Newswire* [Kiev], October 3, 2014.

17. The Council of Europe, *Assessment of the Law on the Restoration of Trust in the Judiciary in Ukraine of 8 April 2014* (Strasbourg: Council of Europe, 2014).

18. Introduction, "On Government Cleansing."

19. Agnieszka Piasecka, *Report: Purification of Government or Vetting Ukrainian Style. The First Year's Experience* (The Open Dialog Foundation, November 5, 2015); Robert Coalson, "Ukraine's Lustration Process Unlikely to be Smooth Sailing," RFE/RL, April 12, 2014."

20. Maria Popova, "Ukraine's Legal problems: Why Kiev's Plans to Purge the Judiciary Will Backfire," *Foreign Affairs*, 15 April (2014).

21. Roman David's chapter engages deeply with this concept. European Court of Human Rights, *Vogt v. Germany*, Final 7/1994/454/535. 26, September (Strasbourg: Council of Europe, 1995).

22. Lavinia Stan, "Witch-hunt or Moral Rebirth? Romanian Parliamentary Debates on Lustration," *East European Politics and Societies* 26, 2 (2012): 287.

23. Jon Elster, ed., *Retribution and Reparation in the Transition to Democracy* (New York: Cambridge University Press, 2006); Brian Grodsky, *The Costs of Justice: How New*

Leaders Respond to Previous Rights Abuses (Notre Dame: University of Notre Dame Press, 2010); and Alexander Mayer-Rieckh and Pablo de Greiff, eds., *Justice as Prevention: Vetting Public Employees in Transitional Societies* (New York: SSRC, 2007).

24. Piasecka, *Summary of Legislative Work*, 13.

25. Piasecka, *Purification of Government or Vetting Ukrainian Style*; "On Restoring Confidence in the Judiciary."

26. "Czech and Slovak Federal Republic: Screening ('Lustration') Law, Act No. 451/1991 (October 4, 1991)," translated in Neil Kritz, ed., *Transitional Justice*. Vol. III (Washington: United States Institute of Peace Press, 1995).

27. Piasecka, *Summary of Legislative Work*.

28. Council of Europe, "Guidelines to ensure that lustration laws and similar administrative measures comply with the requirements of a state based on the rule of law," in *Measures to Dismantle the Heritage*, §g.

29. "Bulgaria: Law on Political and Civil Rehabilitation of Oppressed Persons (June 15, 1991)," translated in Neil Kritz, ed., *Transitional Justice* (Washington: United States Institute of Peace Press, 1995): 672–84; "Czech Republic: Constitutional Court Decision on the Act on the Illegality of the Communist Regime (December 21, 1993)," translated in Neil Kritz, ed., *Transitional Justice* (Washington: United States Institute of Peace Press, 1995): 620–7; and Chamber of Deputies of Romania, *Legea lustratiei* 2012, adopted February 28, 2012, Bucharest, Romania.

30. Council of Europe, "Guidelines," §g.

31. European Court of Human Rights, *Case of Bobek v. Poland*, § 62. 68761/01, July 17, 2007 (Strasbourg: Council of Europe, 2007); European Court of Human Rights, *Case of Matyjek v. Poland*, § 69. 38184/03. April 24, 2007 (Strasbourg: Council of Europe, 2007).

32. Martha Minow, *Between Vengeance and Forgiveness: Facing History after Genocide and Mass Violence* (Boston: Beacon Press, 1998).

33. Aleks Szczerbiak, "Explaining Late Lustration Programs: Lessons from the Polish Case," in Lavinia Stan and Nadya Nedelsky, eds., *Post-Communist Transitional Justice: Lessons from Twenty-Five Years of Experience* (Cambridge: Cambridge University Press, 2015); Cynthia M. Horne, "Late Lustration Programs in Romania and Poland: Supporting or Undermining Democratic Transitions?," *Democratization* 16, 2 (2009): 344–76.

34. Sabrina Ramet, *Social Currents in Eastern Europe: The Sources and Consequences of the Great Transformation* (Durham: Duke University Press, 1995).

35. "National security & defense reform to involve lustration in intelligence agencies," *Ukraine General Newswire* [Kiev], November 17, 2014; Bohdan Butkevych, "Yehor Sobolev: 'Lustration has been blocked'," *The Ukrainian Week* [International Edition], August 15, 2014; and Kononczuk, Iwański, Olszański and Żochowski, *The Bumpy Road*.

36. These reforms are documented in Kononczuk, Iwański, Olszański, and Żochowski, *The Bumpy Road*.

37. Council of Europe, "Guidelines," §a.

38. European Commission for Democracy Through Law (Venice Commission), *Final Opinion*, Section D §80, "Administration of Lustration: Decentralized Nature of the Lustration Procedure."

39. Roman David, *Lustration and Transitional Justice: Personnel Systems in the Czech Republic, Hungary, and Poland* (Philadelphia: University of Pennsylvania Press, 2011).
40. Ibid., 193.
41. Cynthia M. Horne, "Assessing the Impact of Lustration on Trust in Public Institutions and National Government in Central and Eastern Europe," *Comparative Political Studies* 45, 4 (2012): 412–46.
42. Cynthia M. Horne, *Building Trust and Democracy: Transitional Justice in Post-Communist Countries* (Oxford: Oxford University Press, 2017).
43. United Nations, *Rule of Law Tools for Post-Conflict States: Vetting: An Operational Framework*, United Nations HR/PUB/06/5 (New York: Office of the UN High Commission on Human Rights, 2006).
44. Mayer-Rieckh and de Greiff, *Justice as Prevention*.
45. Katya Gorchinskaya, "Avoiding Lustration in Ukraine: Senior Prosecutor Evades Sweep of Yanukovych-Era Officials," *RFE/RL*, July 18, 2015; Katya Gorchinskaya, "Gifts, Prizes, Winnings: A Windfall for Ukraine Judges," *RFE/RL*, June 15, 2015.
46. Problems include incomplete files, missing false, the intentional falsification of information in files, and problems associated with an inherently incomplete process. See Helga Welsh, "Dealing with the Communist Past: Central and East European Experiences after 1990," *Europe-Asia Studies* 48, 3 (1996): 413–29; and Adam Michnik and Václav Havel, "Justice or Revenge," *Journal of Democracy* 4, 1 (1993): 20–7.
47. "Third Wave of Lustration in Ukraine Will Start in March, Will Concern Civil Ministries," *Ukraine General Newswire* [Kiev], January 29, 2015.
48. "Lustration Covers 24,000 Officials, Next Stage in Late March," *Ukraine General Newswire* [Kiev], March 17, 2015.
49. Piasecka, *Purification of Government*, 6.
50. Evgen Solonina, "Yegor Sobolev: 80% of Lustration, 20% Imitation," *Radio Svoboda*, March 10, 2016.
51. "Address of Judges of the Constitutional Court of Ukraine to European and International Organizations and Human Rights Institutions," February 24, 2014, available at www.ccu.gov.ua/en/print/14158, accessed May 10, 2017.
52. "Supreme Court's Appeal to Constitutional Court against Lustration Law Shows Judicial System's Reluctance to Be Cleansed," *Ukraine General Newswire* [Kiev], November 18, 2014.
53. Alexei Trochev, "Patronal Politics, Judicial Networks, and Collective Judicial Autonomy in Post-Soviet Countries," Paper presented at *European Consortium for Political Research*, September 2016, Prague, Czech Republic; Evgen Solonina, "80% of Lustration, 20% Imitation."
54. "Lustration Covers 24,000 Officials."
55. Kononiczuk, Iwański, Olszański and Żochowski, *The Bumpy Road*; Evgen Solonina, "80% of Lustration, 20% Imitation."
56. "Supreme Court's Appeal to Constitutional Court against Lustration Law Shows Judicial System's Reluctance to Be Cleansed."
57. Horne, *Building Trust and Democracy*.
58. Popova, "Ukraine's Legal Problems."
59. Horne, *Building Trust and Democracy*.

60. Csilla Kiss, "The Misuses of Manipulation: The Failure of Transitional Justice in Post-Communist Hungary," *Europe-Asia Studies* 58, 6 (2006): 925–40.
61. Lavinia Stan, *Transitional Justice in Post-Communist Romania: The Politics of Memory* (Cambridge: Cambridge University Press, 2012).
62. Szczerbiak, "Explaining Late Lustration Programs."
63. Piasecka, *Purification of Government*, 13.
64. Ibid., 14; "Venice Commission Confirms that Ukraine's Lustration Law is in Line with International Standards and Resolutions of the Council of Europe," *State News Service* [Kiev], June 19, 2015; and Council of Europe Resolution 1096.
65. "On Government Cleansing."
66. Kononczuk, Iwanski, Olszanski and Zochowski, *The Bumpy Road*, 5.
67. Articles 4 and 5 in particular, Law of Ukraine No. 1682-VII, "On Government Cleansing."
68. Horne, *Building Trust and Democracy*.
69. Council of Europe, "Guidelines," §g and §j.
70. The Lustration Act. 11 April, 1997, The Law on Disclosing Work for or Service in the State's Security Services or Collaboration with them between 1944 and 1990 by Persons Exercising Public Functions.
71. Czech Republic, Act No. 422/2000 and 424/2000 amended Act No. 451/1991 (Lustration Law), available at: www.ustrcr.cz/data/pdf/normy/act451-1991.pdf, accessed October 15, 2016.
72. Cynthia M. Horne, "The Timing of Transitional Justice Measures," in Lavinia Stan and Nadya Nedelsky, eds., *Post-Communist Transitional Justice: Lessons from Twenty-Five Years of Experience* (Cambridge: Cambridge University Press, 2015), 123–47.
73. "Ukraine Lustration Will Cover 1 mln Officials, Law Enforcers," *Ukraine General Newswire* [Kiev], September 17, 2014; European Commission for Democracy Through Law (Venice Commission), *Final Opinion*, 8.
74. Kononczuk, Iwanski, Olszanski and Zochowski, *The Bumpy Road*; Katya Gorchinskaya, "Avoiding Lustration in Ukraine."
75. European Commission for Democracy Through Law (Venice Commission), *Final Opinion*.
76. David, *Lustration and Transitional Justice*, 191.
77. Horne, *Building Trust and Democracy*.
78. Nalepa, "Lustration."
79. Mayer-Rieckh and de Greiff, *Justice as Prevention*.
80. Venice Commission, Section III.A. "Aims of the Law on Government Cleansing," 6.

9

Transitional Justice and the Revision of History Textbooks

The 1932–1933 Famine in Ukraine

Lina Klymenko

In 1989, following the breakdown of communist regimes, countries across Central and Eastern Europe embarked on a process of state rebuilding and a series of related reforms toward capitalism and democracy.[1] The governments of most of those countries adopted various transitional justice measures to condemn the repressions of the communist regimes and deliver justice to the victims of communist crimes as part of their reform measures. Such mechanisms included trials, lustration (screening to ban former communist officials from holding positions in certain postcommunist institutions), reforms of the state security police, the disclosure of information in secret files compiled by the state security services on citizens, the revision of history textbooks, and the commemoration of victims of the repressions in the form of monuments and memorials, to name but a few.[2] In comparison, transitional justice in the Former Soviet Union (FSU) has been narrower and shallower, relying more on nonjudicial methods than the combination of judicial and nonjudicial measures seen in Central and Eastern Europe.[3]

This chapter engages with one such nonjudicial accountability measure that has been used in the FSU, namely the rewriting of history textbooks. In particular, the chapter focuses on textbooks' narration of the 1932–3 famine in Ukraine, known as the Holodomor. As Heorhiy Kasianov points out, the Holodomor was a taboo subject in the Soviet Union, only revealed to the public in the late 1980s. The communist authorities long denied that a famine took place in Soviet Ukraine, Russia, and Kazakhstan in 1932–3.[4] Numerous forms of state oppression and censorship, such as the repression of the Ukrainian intelligentsia from 1940 through the 1970s, as well as the imposed narratives during and after World War II prevented the story of the 1932–3 famine from being brought to public attention. Reports of the mass starvation of peasants reached the foreign public through diplomatic channels, private contacts, as well as through the efforts of journalists and Ukrainian organizations abroad.

Mentioning the famine was considered a counter-revolutionary activity, or an example of anti-Soviet agitation and propaganda. Only those who openly opposed the Soviet regime risked publishing *samizdat* materials on the famine. Stories about the famine (particularly about the starvation of relatives, their survival strategies, and cases of cannibalism) were passed on from generation to generation through families. Soviet academic literature only referred to "some difficulties with food provisions" in 1932–3, and the discussions of Western research and the Ukrainian diaspora regarding the famine were considered ideological sabotage in the Soviet Union.[5]

This chapter investigates how the 1932–3 famine is narrated in contemporary Ukrainian school history textbooks as a transitional justice method. By taking the Ukrainian revision of history textbooks as a case study of transitional justice, the chapter argues that Ukrainian history textbooks function as a mechanism of knowledge creation. In this case, the knowledge relates to the famine, a state crime that had been long denied by the communist repressive regime. The recovery of the famine memory constitutes a nonjudicial transitional justice mechanism. More precisely, the chapter compares how two textbooks framed the Holodomor, condemning the Stalinist totalitarian regime and creating sympathy for the famine victims in order to galvanize a sense of national identity in young readers – the identity that is based on the collective remembrance of this important, but previously muted, historical event. By encouraging students to ask their grandparents about their experiences during the famine, the history textbooks also give voice to the victims of oppression, previously suppressed by the Soviet regime. Moreover, by elaborating on the causes and consequences of this Stalinist crime, the Ukrainian history textbooks prompt students to critically reflect on the relations between state and society in the Stalin era with potential reverberations for current politics.

Following the dissolution of the Soviet Union in 1991, Ukraine has embarked on the creation of a nation-state with its own distinctive national identity. The affirmation of Ukraine's distinctness has often been through an articulation of Ukraine's difference from Russia as the former Soviet central power, and the use of perpetrator and victim designations (Ukraine as victim and Russia/the Soviet Union as perpetrator of state-led atrocities). The creation of national history in Ukraine and the positioning of Russians as the Ukrainian "other" have often produced tensions in the Russian–Ukrainian relations. Yet the Ukrainian textbooks analyzed in this chapter attempt to create a national narrative without jeopardizing the Russian–Ukrainian relations. On the one hand, the textbooks underline the distinctness of Ukrainians vis-à-vis Russians; on the other hand, they refrain from the construction of antagonistic Russian–Ukrainian relations. A peculiarity of the history textbook revision in Ukraine is the designation of particular ethnic groups as victims and perpetrators of the famine. This victim/perpetrator categorization in contemporary Ukrainian school history textbooks is analyzed in this chapter in order to better explicate how the framing of the past has potential current political implications.

The chapter proceeds as follows. First, I examine the nexus between transitional justice policy and history textbook revision, situating this alternative method of transitional justice in the context of accountability measures. Second, I review Ukrainian efforts to come to terms with the Stalinist past, with attention to new narratives and commitments to acknowledge the past in post-Soviet Ukraine. Third, I present a comparative review of two fifth-grade textbooks' treatment of the 1932–3 famine narrative: *Introduction to the History of Ukraine* by Viktor Mysan (2010), and *Introduction to the History of Ukraine* by Vitalii Vlasov and Oksana Danylevska (2010).[6] The paired comparison illustrates the subtle but important reframing of this important event in Ukrainian history, and the manner in which it functions as part of the new national narrative. The conclusion draws attention to the specificity of history textbook revisions in Ukraine as part of the FSU.

REVISION OF HISTORY TEXTBOOKS AS A TRANSITIONAL
JUSTICE MECHANISM

History education can play an important role for societies after a transition, in terms of both understanding and accounting for the past as a type of transitional justice measure.[7] As Elizabeth Cole argues, history education in general and the content of history textbooks in particular are important to help transform young people into citizens. In essence, history education contributes to mechanisms of state-sponsored transitional justice such as "truth telling, official acknowledgment of harm, [...] reconciliation, and public deliberation, understood as [the] creation of a more democratic culture."[8] As Cole points out, history education should be an integral part of a state's policy of transitional justice as it can deepen the state's accountability for the past. Changes in history textbooks can function as a mechanism that shows a state's commitment to the institutionalization of transitional justice. Moreover, it can act as an official gesture of acknowledgment of harm previously committed by the state, and a commitment to the repair of state–society relations.[9]

A critical assessment of the past and accepting responsibility for past wrongs can be important for trust building in inter-state relations following international conflicts or wars. Critical understandings of past injustices can lead states to commit to avoiding the recurrence of such atrocities in the future and to developing more reliable relations between states.[10] Clara Ramírez-Barat and Roger Duthie add that history education within the state should aim to provide society with knowledge about its past, thereby creating opportunities to forge relations between citizens, to develop respect for human rights, and to contribute to civic trust and social cohesion. In other words, history education should function as an important form of acknowledgment and a means of redressing past violence on behalf of the state.[11]

As a transitional justice mechanism, one of the purposes of history textbook revision is to forge a group's new identity. In essence, as Cole argues, during history education reform the memory of mass atrocities inflicted on a particular group often becomes a source of this group's new identity. Frequently, the group that suffered makes a request for its suffering to be acknowledged. This request involves not only the understanding of their own group's suffering – and thus themselves as victims – but also a conception of others, who are often designated as perpetrators.[12] Iwona Irwin-Zarecka highlights that sharing stories of those who suffered serves to bolster the solidarity of the community. Particularly, when the numbers of survivors are dwindling, the need for active memory work and the urge to establish a moral obligation to commemorate the victims of the atrocities can increase. In this context, the definition of victims and oppressors often functions as a boundary between "us" and "them"; and in this identity-building narrative, the oppressor is often assigned the role of the "other."[13]

Huma Haider argues that the purpose of textbook revisions as part of transitional justice policy is to reveal the truth and to preserve the memory of victims, to acknowledge harm done by the state, to promote political and societal reconciliation, and to develop a new collective identity among the youth. According to Haider, this process cannot be undertaken only by history educators, but should also involve academic historians, political actors, and civil society groups. The revision of textbook content should engage with questions regarding which historical events are considered, what facts should be included about actors and events, and how groups considered as historical enemies should be portrayed.[14] As Haider further notes, there is an ongoing debate on how history should be taught at school – whether history teaching should focus on memorizing facts or on the development of young people's critical thinking skills. Most history educators agree that there should be a middle ground, where training for peace and developing civic values occurs alongside the memorizing of historical facts.[15] This argument therefore emphasizes that questions should be raised not only in regard to the information conveyed, but also to the way it is conveyed in the textbooks. The next section will take up some of these issues in the context of the revision of the famine narrative in Ukrainian history textbooks.

COMING TO TERMS WITH THE STALINIST PAST IN UKRAINE

A policy of Holodomor denial dominated textbooks during Soviet times. The school history textbook *History of the Ukrainian SSR* by F. Los and V. Spitskiy (1973) is emblematic of such a textbook adhering to the Soviet policy of famine denial.[16] In this textbook, approved by the Ministry of Education of the Ukrainian Soviet Socialist Republic (Ukrainian SSR), there was no reference to the 1932–3 famine. The year 1932 is depicted as a peak of modernization in the Ukrainian SSR, which from the authors' perspective improved the well-being of workers and peasants. According to the textbook, during the five-year plan, Ukraine was turned into a progressive and modern industrial–agricultural republic. Successful industry secured workers' welfare, resulting in the elimination of unemployment and an increase in workers' salaries. As the textbook explained, in 1932, on the anniversary of the October Revolution, the working day was reduced to seven hours without a decrease in salaries. Changes in rural areas were described positively as well:

> In the decade of the first five-year plan, important changes took place in the countryside. By the end of 1932, collectivization was mostly completed. As a result, the most numerous exploiting class – the affluent peasants (*kulachestvo*) – was eliminated. The decisive role in the agricultural sector was now played by collective farms (*kolkhozy*). The agricultural sector was technically modernized. Collective farms were served by 600 car and tractor stations, which possessed 25,600 tractors, almost 2,000 threshers and numerous cars.[17]

Starting in the late 1980s, the famine became a more open part of public discussion, some of it motivated by domestic and international changes. Kasianov provides an extensive account of how the famine was slowly acknowledged by the Ukrainian communist authorities, and of how the memorialization practices for the famine victims started. In October 1984, a US Commission on the Ukraine Famine was established to conduct a study of the 1932–3 famine, which included the public hearings of famine survivors. The US Commission's findings were delivered to the US Congress in April 1988, publicly revealing the existence and extent of the famine.[18] In 1986, a special commission was created by the Central Committee of the Communist Party of Ukraine (CPU) at the Academy of Sciences of the Ukrainian SSR, tasked with denouncing the results of the then on-going US Congress Commission. Rather than refuting the US assertions, the Ukrainian researchers who gained access to the archives proved the opposite; they provided evidence of the mass starvation of peasants in 1932–3 in Ukraine. As a result, both external and internal information was becoming public about the extent of the famine in Ukraine.[19]

In 1987, the head of the CPU, Volodymyr Shcherbytskyi, acknowledged the famine.[20] The following year, a representative of the party-sponsored Union of Writers of the Ukrainian SSR mentioned the famine in one of his public speeches. Numerous reports about the famine were published in the Ukrainian press at that time. In 1990, the Central Committee of the CPU supported the publication of a book about the famine, and the same year it issued a resolution on the 1932–3 famine in which it urged historians to give an objective account of socialist development in Ukraine. The same year, the Central Committee of the CPU included the topic of collectivization and the 1932–3 famine in its research program on the history of the Ukrainian SSR. In the late 1980s, writers and historians also launched the first project based on the collection of testimonies of famine survivors. Their findings were published in a book that appeared in 1991, before the Ukrainian independence referendum. Kasianov argues that these revelations of the Stalinist crimes in Soviet Ukraine should be interpreted in the context of Ukraine's push for independence from the Soviet Union and its desire to discredit the communist regime.[21]

Since Ukraine gained its independence in 1991, both the state and the civil society have turned the commemoration of the famine into a national tradition. The 1932–3 famine became a national symbol of the collective suffering of Ukrainians in the Soviet Union, in direct opposition to Russia's interpretation of the famine.[22] Over the course of Ukraine's transition, the Ukrainian parliament, the Cabinet of Ministers, and the Ukrainian president have laid out an agenda for the commemoration of the famine victims. Two official documents in particular have influenced the public understanding of the 1932–3 famine in Ukraine. In 2003, following special parliamentary hearings, the Ukrainian parliament issued an address to the Ukrainian people. In the address, the parliament condemned the Stalinist totalitarian regime and recognized the famine as a genocide of Ukrainians.[23] In 2006, on the initiative of the Ukrainian president Viktor Yushchenko, the Ukrainian parliament adopted a law that likewise condemned the Soviet totalitarian regime and classified the famine as a genocide of the Ukrainian people. Moreover, the Holodomor Law of 2006 made the public denial of the 1932–3 famine unlawful.[24] Although the designation of the famine as a genocide of Ukrainians remains debated in both Ukraine and abroad, the fact of the famine is not contested.[25] A public survey from September 2016 indicated that 72 percent of Ukrainians considered the famine to be a genocide of Ukrainians, 14 percent disagreed with the statement, and 14 percent remained undecided.[26]

As part of the official program of commemoration of the famine victims, state authorities instructed Ukrainian educational institutions to raise awareness about Stalinist crimes. For example, in 2003 the Ukrainian parliament rec-ommended the Ukrainian Cabinet of Ministers to supervise the publication of archival documents, academic studies, and a special school textbook on the famine.[27] The Holodomor Law of 2006 explicitly stated that state authorities were expected to ensure that the history of the famine was studied in educa-tional institutions in Ukraine.[28] In the context of Ukrainian transitional justice policy, it became important for the Ukrainian state to acknowledge the fact of the famine, to establish an official record of the famine's causes, to condemn the perpetrators, and to pay tribute to the famine victims. How this was mani-fested in Ukrainian history textbooks will be considered below.

<h3 style="text-align:center">THE NARRATIVE OF THE 1932–1933 FAMINE IN UKRAINIAN
HISTORY TEXTBOOKS</h3>

This analysis of how the 1932–3 famine is depicted in Ukrainian school text-books follows the principles of narrative analysis, meaning I examine the nar-ratives or discourses surrounding a national account of historical events in post-Soviet textbooks.[29] A narrative is a particular type of discourse that pre-sents a story of what happened to a group of people within a particular tempo-ral and spatial setting – referred to in the analysis as "the plot."[30] Narratives that are told by a person or an organization about themselves are grounded in the individual or group's experience. People describe their life stories by select-ing particular events that happened to them at a particular time and place, and link them causally.[31] This section therefore explores the narrative plot of the 1932–3 famine, identifies how the historical event is defined, and shows how the victims and perpetrators of the atrocities are named. Additionally, it focuses on an exploration of didactic devices created by textbook authors as a means to enhance students' understanding of the famine (see Table 9.1 for a summary of the famine as conceptualized in the textbooks).[32]

The focus of this analysis is on the treatment of the 1932–3 famine nar-rative in two textbooks: *Introduction to the History of Ukraine* by Viktor Mysan (2010) and *Introduction to the History of Ukraine* by Vitalii Vlasov and Oksana Danylevska (2010). These textbooks were approved by the Ministry of Education and Science of Ukraine for use in the fifth grade in schools throughout the country, with Ukrainian as the language of instruction. Thus the textbooks are for students who are approximately ten to eleven years old.[33] These textbooks are among four history textbooks recommended by the Ukrainian Ministry of Education for the academic year 2015–16.[34] History edu-cation in Ukraine is embedded in a centralized educational system, closely

TABLE 9.1. *Conceptualizations of the 1932–3 famine in Ukrainian school history textbooks*

Elements of the narrative	Name of textbook author and year of textbook publication	
	Mysan (2010)	Vlasov and Danylevska (2010)
Title of the subchapter	Collective farm life and the Holodomor of 1932–3	Why did the Ukrainian peasants oppose the creation of collective farms?
Naming of the historical event	Great famine called the Holodomor	Deliberately organized famine called the Holodomor
Plot: what happened to particular actors in particular time and space?	The Soviet government's industrialization policy, which required the confiscation of grain from Ukrainian peasants, led to the famine in 1932–3 in Soviet Ukraine	The Bolshevik authorities organized the famine in 1932–3 in Soviet Ukraine to punish Ukrainian peasants that opposed the collectivization policy
Definition of victims and their number	Millions of Ukrainian citizens	Five million Ukrainian people
Definition of perpetrators	Soviet government under the leadership of Stalin	Bolshevik authority
Additional didactic techniques	Photographs, sections with questions, an excerpt from a historical document, and a glossary of terms	Photographs, sections with questions, a map, an excerpt from a historical document, an anecdote, and a short story

supervised by the Ministry of Education, the National Academy of Sciences, and the Academy of Pedagogical Sciences, with the Ministry overseeing the selection of school textbooks on the subjects of the "History of Ukraine" and "World History."[35] The Ministry of Education adopts a national teaching curriculum and also a list of textbooks and teacher guides to be used in schools throughout the country. The selection of textbooks is closely supervised by the Ministry of Education through an annual competition. The textbooks that win the competition are tested in schools, revised if necessary, and then sealed with official approval by the Ministry of Education. Usually, several textbooks are adopted for each grade.[36] As such, this paired case comparison focuses on two of these nationally selected textbooks.

"Introduction to the History of Ukraine" by Mysan (2010)

In Mysan's textbook, the section on the famine is entitled "Collective farm life and the Holodomor of 1932–3" and is part of the chapter called "The Bolsheviks in Ukraine." Along with the section on the 1932–3 famine, the textbook chronologically discusses the war between the Bolshevik Russian government and the Ukrainian People's Republic (UNR) of 1918–20 that ended with the Bolsheviks' takeover of the territory of Ukraine; the creation of the Ukrainian SSR; the formation of the Union of the Soviet Socialists Republics (USSR) in 1922; the collectivization policy adopted in the late 1920s; and state repressions in the 1930s against various strata of the Ukrainian population. The chapter also discusses what it calls "positive changes" in the Soviet Union in the 1930s, and as examples cites the elimination of illiteracy, the introduction of compulsory primary education, and the creation of new higher education institutions.[37]

The section on the famine – which is condensed to half a page – tells a story of the Soviet policy of industrialization and collectivization, which resulted in the famine of 1932–3 through the confiscation of grain from Ukrainian peasants.[38] The narrative begins with a description of the formation of collective farms (*kolhospy*) in Ukrainian villages and the punishment imposed on peasants who refused to join the collective farms. According to the textbook, the peasants who opposed collectivization were punished, deprived of their land, and sent into exile to Siberia. At the same time, the Soviet leadership demanded more and more grain from the peasants, motivating them with an explanation that the profit from the sale of grain was used for the construction of new factories, hydroelectric plants, and houses. The autumn of 1932 was no worse than in previous years, the textbook explains, but the peasants had to pay tax to the state. In this pursuit, special provision brigades were formed which took away all of the foodstuffs from the peasants. It is mentioned in the textbook that people tried to hide grain and potatoes in lofts, under roofs, and also in wells.

The textbook thus defines Ukrainian peasants as famine victims and holds the Soviet government under Stalin responsible for the famine. Yet, there is a certain lack of clarity in this textbook's depiction of the perpetrators. On the one hand, at the beginning of the chapter on the Bolshevik rule in Ukraine, the textbook points to the Russian Bolsheviks' takeover of the territory of Ukraine and terms the Russians "occupiers."[39] On the other hand, in the famine narrative, the textbook author does not assign any ethnic characteristics to the famine perpetrators but is explicit about the ethnicity of the victims. The textbook strongly condemns the Soviet authorities by emphasizing that the famine was the Soviet government's deliberate policy of oppression of Ukrainian peasants. Moreover, the textbook presents the experiences of Ukrainian peasants as the experiences of Ukrainian citizens – thus encouraging students reading the textbook to identify with the famine victims. As the textbook says:

> And a great famine (*velykyi holod*) broke out in Ukraine, followed by death. Whole families, corners, streets, and villages were dying out. Exhausted people were falling everywhere. Horse carts were driven through villages; the dead were picked up and then buried in common graves. Millions of Ukrainian citizens died from hunger in 1932–33 only because the Soviet authorities took grain from them.[40]

The textbook further increases the students' awareness of Stalinist repressions and the collective suffering of Ukrainians through several other techniques. The section on the famine contains a photograph entitled "Collective farm workers (*kolhospnyky*) deliver grain to the state. Early 1930s."[41] The photograph portrays horse-drawn carts loaded with sacks and led by men, and it is used in the textbook as evidence of the historical account of Soviet tax policy. The same section has a column called "Let us think."[42] In this section, the textbook author invites students to think critically about state–citizen relations as it asks the young readers to explain the causes of the famine and possibilities for its avoidance.

Yet it remains confusing how the students are meant to think about the Stalinist era in general. On the one hand, in the last section of the chapter on the Bolshevik rule in Ukraine the textbook author associates the 1930s with positive development in Ukraine and gives examples, such as the elimination of illiteracy, the development of the educational system, and giant construction projects. Yet on the other hand, the textbook remains firm about the state sponsorship of the 1932–3 famine and the repressions of the 1930s. The chapter also contains a glossary of terms consisting of the definition of three words: collective farm, Soviet authorities, and repressions – it defines repressions as a state policy of compulsion and punishment.[43]

At the end of the chapter there is a section called "We work with historical sources" that shows a letter from collective farm workers from the village of Horby to Stalin in 1932. This letter serves not only as an authentic source proving the fact of the famine, but it also appeals to students' emotions. In the letter, the peasants draw Stalin's attention to the food shortages in collective farms. The authors of the letter question the state industrialization and collectivization policies by pointing to their starvation and the starvation of their children. The textbook author's selection of a historical document that mentions the starvation of children could be read as an attempt to evoke sympathy for famine victims, a great number of whom were children. The letter is followed by a set of questions that aim at developing the students' abilities to recognize injustice and repression toward the Ukrainian population. The questions from this section read as follows:

> 1. Can we believe this document? Why? 2. What do you think: did this letter reach Stalin? 3. Are the questions of the collective farm workers fair? Who had to answer those questions?[44]

At the end of the chapter, the students are also given several tasks to perform. Among them is a request to memorize the date of the famine, and to report on the history of the famine in Ukraine in the classroom.[45] This textbook both encourages students to empathize with the famine victims and frames the famine as an act against Ukrainian citizens in an effort to cultivate a sense of Ukrainian collective identity, without explicitly naming another ethnic group as the perpetrator.[46]

"Introduction to the History of Ukraine" by Vlasov and Danylevska (2010)

In the textbook by Vlasov and Danylevska, the 1932–3 famine is described in the section entitled "Why did the Ukrainian peasants oppose the creation of collective farms?," which occupies approximately half a page.[47] The section is part of the chapter entitled "Establishment of Bolshevik rule in Ukraine," which also discusses topics such as the creation of the Ukrainian SSR, the entry of the Ukrainian SSR into the USSR in 1922, and the industrialization of Soviet Ukraine in the 1930s – similar to Mysan's textbook. The latter topic is associated with the heroic labor of millions of people who worked for the construction of giant plants, including the Dniprovska hydroelectric plant, which was the biggest hydroelectric plant in Europe at that time. Moreover, this chapter covers the topics of the repressions committed by the Bolshevik government against Ukrainian teachers, scientists, and artists who disagreed with the Bolshevik party.[48]

The textbook's description of the 1932–3 famine is embedded in the narrative of the Soviet policy of collectivization.[49] The famine is conceptualized as a response of the Bolshevik government to the opposition of the Ukrainian peasants to collectivization. As the textbook explains, in the second half of the 1920s, the Bolshevik government started the forceful creation of collective farms. This meant that land, horses, cattle, and agricultural tools were taken away from peasants. According to the textbook, peasants opposed this policy. The Bolsheviks called those who resisted collectivization *kurkuli* and forcefully exiled them with their whole families to Siberia. In this way, the textbook assigns the Bolsheviks an active role in the organization of the famine, and portrays Ukrainian peasants as famine victims. Similar to Mysan's textbook, this textbook remains silent about the ethnicity of the famine's perpetrators. On the one hand, it highlights the establishment of the Bolshevik rule in Ukraine in 1919.[50] Yet on the other hand, in the famine narrative, the ethnicity of the perpetrators is not disclosed. However, similar to Mysan's textbook, this textbook is explicit about the ethnicity of the victims. The textbook also encourages students to identify with the famine victims and attempts to generalize the experiences of Ukrainian peasant victims to the Ukrainian people as a whole. As the textbook argues:

> The most horrible disaster of those years was the Holodomor. The most difficult were the winter and spring of 1932–33, when people were dying in large numbers from hunger on fruitful Ukrainian lands. The total losses of the Ukrainian people from deliberately organized famine (*navmysnyi holod*) were around five million.[51]

This narrative of the 1932–3 famine is supplemented in the textbook by several didactic techniques that aim to enhance the students' understanding of the famine, and to evoke disapproval of the famine's perpetrators and sympathy for the famine's victims. For example, the textbook contains four photographs that portray the process of collectivization. Similar to the textbook analyzed previously, the photographs seem to serve not only as primary evidence of the famine, but also as an appeal to the students' emotions. In the first photograph, entitled "Activists bring out personal belongings of the *kurkul*. Podillia region in 1929," two men are taking away furniture from a house while children watch. The second photograph, "Cars with the harvest. Kherson region in 1930," shows a line of trucks loaded with sacks. The car in the foreground is decorated with a banner reading "Instead of the *kulak* [Russian for *kurkul*] grain there is socialist grain."[52]

Two other photographs document additional repressions against Ukrainian peasants, and appeal particularly to the students' emotions. The first is entitled "A *kurkul* family being expelled from its own yard. Donetsk region in 1930," and shows a woman with a child dragging a cart full of personal belongings. In the background there is a man in a military uniform observing the event. The second is entitled "De-kulakization of peasants in the village of Udachne in the Donetsk region in 1931." This photo shows a group of peasants and a man in a uniform standing behind sacks. The two women in the photo are standing with their heads bowed, in a manner suggesting they are sad. The textbook poses questions to the students, specifically asking them to engage with their feelings about the photos, and leading them toward a certain normative assessment of the photos:

> What mood are the depicted people in? Do the photographs lead to the conclusion that *kurkuli* were rich people who obtained their affluence unjustly? How can you explain the presence of an armed person during the de-kulakization process? What feelings do these historical events evoke in you?[53]

The textbook also includes several tasks that encourage students to memorize the date of the famine, and prompt their independent thinking about the issue. For example, an anecdote told by the academician Serhii Yefremov, who was repressed in the 1930s, condemns the Soviet government's pejorative definition of an affluent peasant as *kurkul*, and instead suggests that *kurkul* could be understood as a very hardworking peasant.[54] The textbook additionally cites a paragraph from a report by British diplomats in 1932, in which they inform their authorities about the peasants' suffering caused by state repression. The report says that with the exile of *kurkuli*, the villages lost the most energetic and diligent part of their populations.[55] By asking students why the Ukrainian peasants considered de-kulakization as an act of injustice and arbitrariness on the part of the state, the textbook problematizes the state–society relations of the Stalinist era.

The textbook additionally fosters students' understanding of the history of the famine by focusing on the geography and time frame of the famine. For example, in one of the tasks, the students are asked to indicate on a map the regions of Ukraine which suffered the most from the famine, and to calculate the number of years between the creation of the USSR and the famine and between the famine and today. Ultimately, the textbook facilitates the transfer of knowledge about the famine between Ukrainian generations by asking students to think about the importance of the preservation of the memory of the famine. The textbook authors do this by asking the students the following questions:

> What feelings did the material for this lesson provoke? Have you heard about these events before? Is it important to cherish the memory of these events? Why?[56]

Perhaps the most expressive feelings toward the famine victims are evoked through a short story called "The Red Broom."[57] This two-page story at the end of the chapter on Bolshevik rule in Ukraine is about a small boy Vasylko and his father, and it appeals to young readers who can potentially empathize with the child. Bolshevik activists caught the boy and his father trying to hide grain in a hollow tree. Vasylko's father is then sent into exile following his imprisonment as an enemy of the people. The last paragraph of the story is particularly evocative: "It was snowing for the first time. It was December of 1932. The red broom was sweeping across the villages prophesying famine and death."[58] The story is a telling example of the brutality of the Stalinist collectivization policy which led to the starvation of Ukrainian peasants.

The ethnic distinction between the perpetrators and the victims remains fuzzy in this story. The perpetrators are named metaphorically as *zaidy*, a term which denotes strangers or foreign occupiers, but their ethnicity is not explicitly stated. The story also draws attention to the local village activist Fedko who, accompanied by armed men and a dog, confiscated foodstuff from the peasants. The metaphor "red broom" used as the title of this story denotes the Soviet policy of "sweeping away" food from peasants, which resulted in the starvation of millions of Ukrainians. The textbook authors intentionally evoke students' sympathy for famine victims by asking them a set of questions after the short story:

> 1. What did you learn about the life of Ukrainian peasants in the 1930s?
> 2. Why is the famine of the 1930s in Ukraine called by the horrible word "Holodomor"? 3. Do you have witnesses of the famine in your family? Ask your grandparents about it.[59]

The textbook authors emphasize that the short story is based on authentic testimonies of famine survivors. In urging students to ask their grandparents about the events of 1932–3, the textbook facilitates the transmission of the famine memory from an older generation to the younger generation of Ukrainians.

CONCLUSION

This chapter explained how history textbook revisions can be understood as a type of transitional justice policy. It situated the narration of the Ukrainian famine in history textbooks within the context of post-Soviet transitional justice. The chapter provided two examples of how the 1932–3 famine is presented in recent Ukrainian fifth-grade history textbooks, showing the manner in which they attempted to forge an identification of Ukrainian students with the famine victims and urged students to condemn the Stalinist repressions. The photographs in the textbooks serve not only as authentic evidence of the famine, but also as an appeal to students to express their sympathy for the famine victims. The textbooks prompt students to problematize the state–society relations of the 1930s in Soviet Ukraine, and contribute to the development of students' critical thinking regarding state-sponsored injustice inflicted on the Ukrainian population. In this way, the textbooks create a particular narrative of a historical event with potential implications for the current Ukrainian nation-building.

The textbooks make distinctions between victims and perpetrators of the famine, and encourage students to empathize with the victims. By inviting students to identify with the famine victims and generalizing the suffering of the Ukrainian peasants – a social class – to the suffering of the Ukrainian people as a nation, the textbooks aim to intentionally foster a sense of Ukrainian collective identity. In other words, the suffering of Ukrainians in the past becomes a marker of national identification for Ukrainians in the present. This is distinctly visible also in the textbooks' definition of the famine as the Holodomor, which denotes the specificity of the Ukrainian experience in 1932–3 in comparison to the experiences of the famine by other nationalities in the Soviet Union. The depiction of the famine as a narrative of suffering functions as an appeal to the young readers of the textbooks to identify themselves as descendants of the famine's victims.

It has been argued elsewhere that the construction of national identity in Ukrainian history textbooks often involves the positioning of Russians as the Ukrainian ethnic "other."[60] Yet the textbooks analyzed do not fit this stark interpretation. In fact, the ethnic identity of the perpetrators of the famine is somewhat ambiguous in the two textbooks reviewed here. Both textbooks attribute responsibility for the famine to the Soviet government under the leadership of Stalin. However, rather than portraying this victim/perpetrator dichotomy in ethnic terms, a dichotomy between "us" and "them" is drawn between the state and society. The textbooks suggest that national belonging is not necessarily grounded in the "othering" of a particular ethnic group. This is not to say that there are no implied ethnic "othering" elements in the textbooks. The textbooks point to Bolshevik Russia's takeover of the territory of Ukraine in 1919–20. In the short story "Red Broom" in one of the textbooks, the perpetrators are metaphorically called "strangers" or "foreigner occupiers," although this textbook also includes the role of local activists in the confiscation of foodstuff. In this light, the textbook authors' omission of the ethnicity of the perpetrators could be read as an indirect way of conceptualizing Russians as the Ukrainian ethnic "other," while at the same time refraining from the overt construction of an antagonism between Ukrainians and Russians. Ultimately, this fuzziness in the textbooks leaves room for students and teachers to interpret the famine in their own way.

It is beyond the scope of this chapter to explore the impact these history textbooks may have on students. In a 2010 study on the content of history textbooks on the subjects of "The History of Ukraine" and "World History" in the seventh through eleventh grades, Ukrainian teachers and educational policy experts emphasized the point that a history textbook remains the primary systematic source of history teaching, followed by the internet, media, and the like. For 75 percent of students, the textbook functions as the mainstay for their knowledge accumulation, and students use the textbook while preparing for school exams and papers. Yet at the same time, some teachers in Ukraine underlined that in the classroom they seldom use history textbooks, or may not use them at all. If a teacher believes that the textbook interpretation of a historical event contradicts his/her own conception of the event, then he/she might employ additional teaching material to present alternative interpretations.[61] Previous studies have indeed shown how in the classroom, Ukrainian history teachers negotiate between the textbook content and their own conceptions of historical events. By promoting their own vision of Ukrainian nationhood, they often alter textbook narratives and thus the history teaching curriculum.[62]

Notes

1. The author would like to thank the editors of this book for their helpful comments during the revision of this chapter, as well as the Academy of Finland for funding the author's research project on coming to terms with the Stalinist past in post-Soviet countries [decision no. 274356].
2. Lavinia Stan, *Transitional Justice in Post-Communist Romania: The Politics of Memory* (New York: Cambridge University Press, 2013); Monika Nalepa, *Skeletons in the Closet: Transitional Justice in Post-Communist Europe* (New York: Cambridge University Press, 2010); Cynthia Horne, *Building Trust and Democracy: Transitional Justice in Post-Communist Countries* (Oxford: Oxford University Press, 2017).
3. Lavinia Stan, *Transitional Justice in Eastern Europe and the Former Soviet Union* (London: Routledge, 2009), 222; Kathleen E. Smith, *Remembering Stalin's Victims: Popular Memory and the End of the USSR* (Ithaca: Cornell University Press, 1996).
4. Heorhiy Kasianov, *Danse Macabre. Holod 1932–1933 Rokiv u Pol…tsi, Masovii Svidomosti ta Istoriohrafii (1980-ti–Pochatok 2000-kh)* (Kyiv: Nash Chas, 2010), 12–14.
5. Ibid.
6. Viktor Mysan, *Vstup do Istorii Ukrainy* (Kyiv: Heneza, 2010); Vitalii Vlasov and Oksana Danylevska, *Vstup do Istorii Ukrainy: Pidruchnyk dlia 5 Klasu Zahalnoosvitnikh Navchalnykh Zakladiv* (Kyiv: Heneza, 2010). For an analysis of the earlier edition of the textbook by Mysan (1997) see Nancy Popson, "The Ukrainian History Textbook: Introducing Children to the 'Ukrainian Nation'," *Nationalities Papers* 29, 2 (2001): 325–50. For the earlier edition of the textbook by Vlasov and Danylevska (1999) see Jan Janmaat, "History and National Identity Construction: The Great Famine in Irish and Ukrainian History Textbooks," *History of Education* 35, 3 (2006): 345–68.
7. Stan, *Transitional Justice in Post-Communist Romania*; Elizabeth Cole and Karen Murphy, "History Education Reform, Transitional Justice and the Transformation

of Identities," International Center for Transitional Justice, April 20, 2011, available at: www.ictj.org/publication/history-education-reform-transitional-justice-and-transformation-identities, accessed January 30, 2017; Clara Ramírez-Barat and Roger Duthie, "Education and Transitional Justice: Opportunities and Challenges for Peacebuilding," International Center for Transitional Justice, November 16, 2016, available at: www.ictj.org/publication/education-transitional-justice-opportunities-challenges-peacebuilding, accessed January 30, 2017.

8. Elizabeth Cole, "Transitional Justice and the Reform of History Education," *International Journal of Transitional Justice* 1, 1 (2007): 123.

9. Ibid.

10. Ibid., 125.

11. Ramírez-Barat and Duthie, "Education and Transitional Justice," 5–6.

12. Cole, "Transitional Justice and the Reform of History Education," 118–19, and 123; Charles Maier, "Doing History, Doing Justice: The Historian and the Truth Commission," in Robert I. Rotberg and Dennis Thompson, eds. *Truth v. Justice: The Morality of Truth Commissions* (Princeton: Princeton University Press, 2000), 261–78.

13. Iwona Irwin-Zarecka, *Frames of Remembrance: The Dynamics of Collective Memory* (New Brunswick: Transaction Publishers, 1994), 57–60.

14. Huma Haider, "Rewriting History Textbooks," in Lavinia Stan and Nadya Nedelsky, eds. *Encyclopedia of Transitional Justice* (New York: Cambridge University Press, 2012), 94.

15. Ibid., 97.

16. F. Los and V. Spitskiy, *Istoriya Ukrainskoy SSR (Posobiye dlya 9-10 Klassov)* (Kiev: Radyanska Shkola, 1973), 114.

17. Ibid.

18. Kasianov, *Danse Macabre*, 21–2.

19. Ibid., 27–33

20. Ibid.

21. Ibid.

22. Lina Klymenko, "The Holodomor Law and National Trauma Construction in Ukraine," *Canadian Slavonic Papers* 58, 4 (2016): 341–61; Heorhiy Kasianov, "The Great Famine of 1932–33 (Holodomor) and the Politics of History in Contemporary Ukraine," in Stefan Troebst, ed. *Postdiktatorische Geschichtskulturen im Süden und Osten Europas: Bestandsaufnahme und Forschungsperspektiven* (Göttingen: Wallstein, 2010), 619–41; and Wilfried Jilge, "Geschichtspolitik in der Ukraine," *Aus Politik und Zeitgeschichte*, 8–9 (2007): 24–30.

23. Verkhovna Rada Ukrainy, "Pro Zvernennia do Ukrainskoho Narodu Uchasnykiv Spetsialnoho Zasidannia Verkhovnoi Rady Ukrainy 14 Travnia 2003 Roku Shchodo Vshanuvannia Pamiati Zhertv Holodomoru 1932–1933 Rokiv," May 15, 2003, available at: http://zakon4.rada.gov.ua/laws/show/789-15, accessed January 30, 2017.

24. Verkhovna Rada Ukrainy, "Pro Holodomor 1932–1933 Rokiv v Ukraini," November 28, 2006, available at: http://zakon4.rada.gov.ua/laws/show/376-16, accessed January 30, 2017.

25. In fact, international and Ukrainian historians have engaged in a bitter debate on the question of whether the famine can be classified as a genocide of the Ukrainian nation. See David R. Marples, *Heroes and Villains: Creating National History in*

Contemporary Ukraine (Budapest: Central European University Press, 2007); Nicolas Werth, "Case Study: The Great Ukrainian Famine of 1932–33," *Online Encyclopedia of Mass Violence*, April 18, 2008, available at: www.massviolence.org/the-1932-1933-great-famine-in-ukraine, accessed January 30, 2017; Andrea Graziosi, "The Soviet 1931–1932 Famines and the Ukrainian Holodomor: Is a New Interpretation Possible, and What Would Its Consequences Be?," in Halyna Hryn, ed. *Hunger by Design: The Great Ukrainian Famine and Its Soviet Context* (Cambridge: Harvard University, 2008), 1–19; Liudmyla Grynevych, "The Present State of Ukrainian Historiography on the Holodomor and Prospects for Its Development," *Harriman Review* 16, 2 (2008): 10–20.

26. Rating Group Ukraine, "Dynamika Stavlennia do Holodomoru," November 22, 2016, available at: http://ratinggroup.ua/research/ukraine/dinamika_otnosheniya_k_golodomoru.html, accessed January 30, 2017.
27. Verkhovna Rada Ukrainy, "Pro Rekomendatsii Parlamentskykh Slukhan Shchodo Vshanuvannia Pamiati Zhertv Holodomoru 1932–1933 Rokiv," 2003, available at: http://zakon4.rada.gov.ua/laws/show/607-15, accessed January 30, 2017.
28. Verkhovna Rada Ukrainy, "Pro Holodomor 1932–1933 Rokiv v Ukraini."
29. For a narrative analysis see Lina Klymenko, "Narrating the Second World War: History Textbooks and Nation-Building in Belarus, Russia, and Ukraine," *Journal of Educational Media, Memory, and Society* 8, 2 (2016): 36–57.
30. Eleftherios Klerides, "Imagining the Textbook: Textbooks as Discourse and Genre," *Journal of Educational Media, Memory, and Society* 2, 1 (2010): 32.
31. Donald Polkinghorne, "Narrative Configuration in Qualitative Analysis," *International Journal of Qualitative Studies in Education* 8, 1 (1995): 6–8.
32. See also Janmaat, "History and National Identity Construction;" Jan Janmaat, "The 'Ethnic Other' in Ukrainian History Textbooks: The Case of Russia and the Russians," *Compare: A Journal of Comparative Education* 37, 3 (2007): 307–24; Johan Dietsch, *Making Sense of Suffering: Holocaust and Holodomor in Ukrainian Historical Culture* (Lund: Lund University, 2006).
33. The topic of the 1932–3 famine is also covered in the tenth grade in the subject "History of Ukraine."
34. Ministry of Education and Science of Ukraine, "Perelik Navchalnykh Prohram, Pidruchnykiv ta Navchalno-Metodychnykh Posibnykiv, Rekomendovanykh Ministerstvom Osvity i Nauky Ukrainy," no date, available at: http://mon.gov.ua/activity/education/zagalna-serednya/perelik-navchalnix-program.html, accessed January 21, 2017.
35. Karina Korostelina, "Shaping Unpredictable Past: National Identity and History Education in Ukraine," *National Identities* 13, 1 (2011): 3–4.
36. Ibid.
37. Mysan, *Vstup do Istorii Ukrainy*, 142–9.
38. Ibid., 146–7.
39. Ibid., 142–3.
40. Ibid., 146.
41. Ibid., 145.
42. Ibid., 146.
43. Ibid., 147.
44. Ibid., 148.

45. Ibid., 149.
46. It is of note that there are some differences in the treatment of the famine between the 1997 edition of Mysan's textbook and the 2010 edition, suggesting modifications to the national narrative. For example, in the 1997 edition, the section on the famine is called the "Holodomor" and consists of around three pages, including a historical account of the famine, the testimony of a famine survivor, and also a glossary of terms. This is in comparison to the half-page treatment in the 2010 edition under the heading "Collective farm life and the Holodomor of 1932–33." Following the "Holodomor" chapter, the 1997 textbook has a chapter called the "Genocide," which differs from the 2010 edition. In the 1997 edition, the famine was narrated as a story of the Soviet policy of collectivization that through grain confiscation resulted in the starvation of Ukrainian peasants. While this narrative is similar to the 2010 version, in the 1997 version the author conceptualizes the Stalinist repressions of the 1930s (including the famine) as a genocide of Ukrainians, something not asserted in the 2010 version. Viktor Mysan, *Opovidannia z Istorii Ukrainy* (Kyiv: Heneza, 1997), 174–9.
47. Vlasov and Danylevska, *Vstup do Istorii Ukrainy: Pidruchnyk dlia 5 Klasu Zahalnoosvitnikh Navchalnykh Zakladiv*, 167.
48. Ibid., 165–72.
49. Ibid., 167.
50. Ibid., 158.
51. Ibid., 167.
52. Ibid., 168.
53. Ibid., 169.
54. Ibid., 168.
55. Ibid.
56. Ibid., 169.
57. Ibid., 170–1.
58. Ibid., 171.
59. Ibid., 172.
60. Karina Korostelina, "War of Textbooks: History Education in Russia and Ukraine," *Communist and Post-Communist Studies* 43 (2010): 129–37; Janmaat, "The 'Ethnic Other' in Ukrainian History Textbooks."
61. International Renaissance Foundation, *Zmist Pidruchnykiv z Istorii Ukrainy ta Vsesvitnioii Istorii: Stavlennia ta Ochikuvannia Uchniv ta Batkiv v Konteksti Profesiinoi Otsinky Uchyteliv* (Kiev: International Renaissance Foundation, 2010), 6.
62. Peter W. Rodgers, "'Compliance or Contradiction'? Teaching 'History' in the 'New' Ukraine. A View from Ukraine's Eastern Borderlands," *Europe-Asia Studies* 59, 3 (2007): 503–19; Karina Korostelina, "Constructing Nation: National Narratives of History Teachers in Ukraine," *National Identities* 15, 4 (2013): 401–16.

10

Historical Politics and Court Redress in the Baltic States

Agata Fijalkowski

This chapter examines the Baltic states' efforts to frame and interpret communist-era crimes through the lens of three European Court of Human Rights' (ECtHR) decisions.[1] The cases were driven by petitions from citizens from Estonia, Latvia, and Lithuania who, after 1991, failed to get redress in domestic courts on issues related to communist-era actions and offenses. The verdicts in themselves are documents that reflect a certain understanding of the history of the region. In other words, both the decisions and the ways in which communist-era actions are characterized as actionable crimes according to domestic and international law constitute important practices of transitional justice.

This chapter considers three salient narratives about the communist past: first, the narratives put forth by the Baltic states themselves in which they interpret certain Soviet-era actions as crimes perpetrated by the KGB on the occupied Baltic states; second, the narratives put forward by the defendants in domestic and European courts regarding actionable crimes and who holds responsibility for them; and third, the narratives set out by ECtHR judges in both the verdicts and their dissenting opinions regarding these Soviet-era offenses. All of these narratives and interpretations are important transitional justice documents. This chapter focuses on three ECtHR decisions, and the way they reflect the understanding of past crimes shared by the judges, the prosecutors, and the defense counsels. These external actors label certain actions as crimes (including imprescriptible crimes) and by so doing, they change or consolidate the historical narrative in the country from which the case originated.

In particular, this chapter argues that these court cases illustrate areas in which domestic and international actors contest memory. They demonstrate that the ECtHR judges can have a wide variety of opinions on whether acts perpetrated during Soviet times on the territory of the three Baltic states are punishable after 1991. The ECtHR judges come from diverse educational and legal cultural backgrounds, with potential implications for their understanding of twentieth century European history. The ECtHR is playing an increasingly important role in the validation of key historical narratives in postcommunist Europe, with unexpected consequences for the definition of key crimes and the way these definitions are contested. The judiciary's legal interpretation and understanding of international human rights law is crucial in criminal justice cases that entail a conflict between the duty to prosecute heinous crimes and the prohibition of *ex-post facto* punishment.[2] To illustrate the way that these changes in definition and legal remedy come about, the chapter engages both the legal reasoning put forward by domestic courts before the cases reach the ECtHR, and the legal reasoning and verdict of the ECtHR on these cases.

At present, the ECtHR includes forty-seven judges nominated by the states parties to the European Convention of Human Rights. At least twenty-two judges come from former communist countries and the FSU, including one judge from Russia. A case that comes before the Chamber of the ECtHR is heard by a bench composed of the President of the Section to which the case is assigned, the national judge (the judge with the nationality of the state against which the application is lodged) and five other judges. In exceptional cases, a case may be referred or relinquished to the Grand Chamber. In such a situation, the bench is composed of a larger panel of seventeen judges.

In the Baltic republics in particular, and the Former Soviet Union (FSU) more generally, the transition from the repressive communist regimes to more democratic forms of government catalyzed new perspectives on national history. The power struggle between the old and new elites produced different narratives, some shared by the former oppressors, others championed by the former oppressed. The transition also created debates about the significance of key historical events and persons and, more broadly, about right and wrong. In this context, the domestic courts have become critical forums in which different versions of the communist history have prevailed at times through the venue of legal cases.

Occasionally, some of the cases related to communist crimes have then moved to international courts, when individuals believed that due process or legal safeguards were not met in their national jurisdiction. As a result, the ECtHR has become an important "dispenser of transitional justice."[3] The "narratives" about the communist past that the ECtHR has heard, produced, and accepted have in turn determined the shape, form, and success of an important transitional justice measure: court trials as a method of redress. Interestingly, that redress consequently takes place at the national level, reflecting the manner in which the external framing of measures is nationally situated. While it does not replicate the type of foreign transitional justice seen in the International Criminal Tribunal for the Former Yugoslavia (ICTY), it does represent an important international influence on interpretations of history and justice.

Importantly, versions of history could also be appropriated for varied political ends.[4] In this chapter, "historical politics" refers to the political use and abuse of history. An examination of the way in which memories of violent periods are interpreted and used reveals the active appropriation and the use of the past as a basis on which to take prosecutorial action.[5] All cases considered here concerned retrospective justice, and required the courts to define and debate the communist crimes to see if they amounted to imprescriptible crimes (war crimes, crimes against humanity, and genocide). While retrospective justice is important for transitional justice, since it comprises the key points that underpin it (justice and truth), it is legally complex. The court can be challenged when asked to look at provisions permitting the law to work backwards to address egregious rights violations. The Baltic states illustrate the ways in which transitional justice, legal culture, historical politics, and retrospective justice can come together. Ultimately, these cases point to changes in the way international courts interpret communist crimes as imprescriptible crimes. International courts can thus render rulings that impose a different view of history, in contradiction to the domestic courts' interpretations. This chapter highlights the manner in which the ECtHR has shaped legal and political developments and historical narratives in the Baltic states.

THE BALTIC STATES AND THEIR SOVIET PAST

Further to the Molotov-Ribbentrop Agreement concluded between the Soviets and the Germans, the Baltic states were militarily occupied and annexed by the Soviet Union in 1940. The states became part of the Soviet Union *de facto*, although most Western countries refused to recognize this annexation as legal.[6] The Soviet occupying forces initiated, *inter alia*, two main repression campaigns in the Baltic states.

During the first occupation of 1940–1 the Soviets carried out mass deportations in all three countries. In Estonia, it is estimated that 9,267 persons were deported (the number does not include victims of repression or of extrajudicial executions). In Latvia 15,424 persons were deported, and in Lithuania 17,500.[7] Other forms of widespread repression extended to all segments of the Baltic populations, including the political and economic elites, and racial and religious minorities, such as Jews, Roma, and Jehovah's Witnesses. This first repression campaign is often seen as evidence of the Soviet Union's intent to destroy Estonia, Latvia, and Lithuania.[8]

During the first twelve years of the second occupation of 1944–91 further deportations were carried out against local guerrilla movements (the so-called "forest brethren"), the wealthy peasants (the kulaks), and various religious minorities.[9] It is estimated that 20,702 Estonians, 42,231 Latvians, and 78,735 Lithuanians were deported during this second wave.[10] The number of casualties is perhaps even higher, but cannot be estimated in the absence of full access to Russian communist-era archives. Estimates of the total number of Baltic inhabitants repressed, executed or deported to remote regions in the Soviet Union in 1940–53 range from several hundred thousand to over a million,[11] and do not include the people executed or killed, or the thousands who fled westwards upon the return of the Soviet Red Army in 1944.[12] Archival materials suggest that these deportations were planned and executed by the local Soviet security services at the direct order of Moscow, but could not have taken place without high levels of cooperation on the part of the Estonians, Latvians, and Lithuanians.[13] The Baltic states condemned their incorporation into the Soviet Union as forcible military occupation, and asserted that these two deportation campaigns amounted to genocide by the Soviet occupying regime. It was not until the Soviet Union collapsed in 1991 that state responsibility for Soviet-era crimes became a tangible possibility. During the early 1990s, Russia reached out to the Baltic states to establish joint history commissions. These early attempts were rejected by Estonia and petered out in Latvia, because the Baltic republics were not convinced that such commissions could lead to a meaningful outcome. Under Russian Presidents Dmitry Medvedev (2008–12) and Vladimir Putin (1999–2008, 2012–present) historical politics included the following:

> 1) evasive dealings with Stalinism with infrequent critical utterances; 2) tactical "willingness" to acknowledge historical facts and responsibility (not always offering an apology) of the Soviets for such undeniable criminal actions ...; 3) large-scale recreation and popular diffusion of the myth of the "Great Patriotic War," especially the glorification and self-sacrificing and heroic contribution of the Soviets to the victory against fascism and the liberation of Europe; 4) thorough counteraction against the denial or distortion of "the results of the Second World War" that were decided and confirmed at Yalta, Potsdam, Nuremberg and Tokyo.[14]

In contrast to the narrative about the past that would comport with Russia's version of the Baltics as willing Soviet Union republics, most people in the Baltic states experienced Soviet rule as imposed from the outside. After 1991, the Baltic states pushed a dominant historical narrative that treated the Soviet occupation and the entire Soviet regime as an externally inflicted tragedy.[15]

By so doing, they ignored the large role played by ethnic Estonians, Latvians, and Lithuanians in supporting the occupation, consolidating communist rule, and carrying out the surveillance program (see Bekus in this volume). The three court cases discussed in this chapter speak to these aspects of historical politics in postcommunist Russia and the Baltics, highlighting the layered and complex history of the Baltics as part of, and oppressed by, the Soviet Union. Since 1991, the oppressed have been rehabilitated by the Estonian, Latvian, and Lithuanian states, but the Russian state has rejected both the criminal prosecution of Soviet or Russian offenders and its responsibility to compensate Baltic victims. Russia's rejection of responsibility and compensation has prompted commentators to recall the eagerness with which Nikita Khrushchev condemned Stalinist crimes at the twentieth Communist Party Congress in 1956, but not the other crimes perpetrated by the Soviet state after Stalin's death in 1953.[16] The selective manner in which some histories are repressed and other histories are validated highlights the potential instrumental use of the past to forge a new national narrative. These tensions are evident in the three ECtHR cases explored in depth in the following section. Court petitions and cases challenge narratives underscoring the Soviet heroism against fascism, and by doing so, in the eyes of the Russian officials, they distort World War II reality. In this way, the Baltic cases are not just about the Baltics, they reverberate through other FSU states, in particular Russia, as they legitimize or reject certain narratives about the past that are critical for state building.

RETROSPECTIVE JUSTICE THROUGH THE BALTIC COURT CASES

Measures supporting retrospective justice are an important subject of study. Retrospective justice ideally aims at ascertaining the truth and achieving justice, yet not all truth and justice policies may automatically contribute to such a process, and the links between truth and justice are varied and require consideration.[17] Retrospective justice has its roots in the old criminal law principle that the law should not work backwards. This principle was enshrined in Article 7 of the European Convention on Human Rights.[18] The Convention was formulated in 1950, when its drafters responded to previous developments in Nazi Germany and other parts of Europe that allowed authoritarian regimes to pass retroactive laws that made criminal, without warning, acts that had been lawful under the previous democratic regime.[19] These developments also resonated after World War II, when the international community developed the Nuremberg principles, further to the Charter of the International Military Tribunal of August 8, 1945, which permitted individuals to be prosecuted for crimes against humanity that had not been criminal according to the Nazi legislation and practice in force at the time when those acts had been committed.[20] In general, Article 7 prohibits the legislature and the courts from creating or extending the existing law to criminalize acts or omissions that were not illegal at the time of their commission or omission, or to increase a penalty retroactively. It also expects the law to be clearly defined.[21] Article 7 reads:

> No one shall be held guilty of any criminal offence on account of any act or omission which did not constitute a criminal offence under national or international law at the time when it was committed. Nor shall a heavier penalty be imposed than the one that was applicable at the time the criminal offence was committed. This article shall not prejudice the trial and punishment of any person for any act or omission which, at the time when it was committed, was criminal according to the general principles of law recognized by civilized nations.[22]

Criminal law, which is based on individual guilt and is used to confront past injustice, has important retrospective justice components pertaining to legal certainty and clarity that will be explored in this piece through court cases. As will become clear in the next section, both the requirement for individual culpability and the reservation that individuals shall not be punished retrospectively mean that certain forms of retrospective justice might sit uneasily with the legal guarantees enshrined in Article 7.

The Nuremberg Trials drew the attention of the international legal community to principles of natural justice, which were eventually embraced by University of Heidelberg law professor Gustav Radbruch, after he rejected the idea that the horrendous acts of the Holocaust (and other crimes) could go unpunished because they were positive laws. Positive laws are laws laid down by statute by a properly instituted and recognized branch of government. To him, the principle of natural justice could be overcome if the contradiction between the laws in force and the need for justice reached an unbearable degree where the statute constituted incorrect law.[23] Radbruch's solution to this legal conundrum was readily embraced by the international legal community, and allowed for the prosecution of past crimes as a method of transitional justice.

In the Baltic states, retrospective justice has been connected primarily with the crimes committed by the Soviet state and its agents. The use of retrospective justice through court cases demonstrates how certain historical narratives are validated, thereby privileging certain interpretations of the past in a region with layered histories of atrocity. In particular, three rulings handed down by the ECtHR directly engage with regional retrospective justice dilemmas: *Kolk and Kislyiy v. Estonia* (decision of January 17, 2006), *Kononov v. Latvia* (decision of May 17, 2010), and *Vasiliauskas v. Lithuania* (decision of October 20, 2015).[24] These three cases have been selected for this analysis based on key characteristics that lie at the core of legal arguments: the nature of the crime, the identity of the perpetrator(s) and of the victim(s), as well as the tensions between diverging historical narratives and retrospective justice goals that infringe procedural guarantees and human rights.

The crimes of concern for these cases were war crimes, crimes against humanity, and genocide. Of special note is the definition and treatment of the crime of genocide. The 1948 United Nations Convention on the Prevention and Punishment of the Crime of Genocide defined that crime very narrowly.[25] The Convention refers to protected national, ethnical, racial, and religious groups, but in one of the three Baltic cases examined in this chapter, the ECtHR was asked to extend the definition of genocide to include national political groups. The confirmation by the ECtHR of such an extension did not occur. The chapter examines the way crimes were defined and understood by the state prosecutor, defense counsel, and the national courts, and whether the ECtHR upheld the state's narrative in its rulings. Such an investigation is pertinent to transitional justice because it demonstrates that redress through the courts can validate or invalidate the official historical narrative of a country.

Estonia

The Estonian International Commission for the Investigation of Crimes against Humanity (EICICAH) was created in 1998.[26] Its mandate was to establish the crimes against humanity that occurred in Estonia under the Nazi and Soviet occupation regimes (the German occupation of 1941–4 and the Soviet occupation 1940–1 and 1944 onward). Its remit included documentation, not prosecution. In its final report (published in 2008), the Commission used Article 7 of the 1998 Rome Statute of the International Criminal Court, not the Nuremburg definition of 1945, to define crimes against humanity. While the actions may qualify as genocide under both documents, the choice to use the Rome Statute was justified on the grounds that the crimes researched by the EICICAH fell under the Rome Statute's definitions of war crimes, crimes against humanity, and genocide. The decision to use the Rome Statute also avoided the heated debated about the Nuremberg definition requiring a nexus between the crime and war. Thus, the decision was a prudent one, since to tie the definition to the Nuremberg principles might have potentially created problems for prosecutors seeking a charge of genocide. The EICICAH began its work in 1998, at the same time as the Commission of Historians in Latvia, and the International Commission for the Evaluation of the Crimes of Nazi and Soviet Occupation Regimes in Lithuania. All three transitional justice bodies used the Rome Statute to legitimate their aims.[27] By relying on an international treaty, the Baltic states had the confidence to demand the reevaluation of their historical narratives about World War II.[28]

The 1992 Estonian Constitution established that the general principles and norms of international law were part of the country's domestic law. Before the adoption of the new Criminal Code in 2001, amendments were made to the Soviet Criminal Code (which remained in force in postcommunist Estonia) to include crimes against humanity and genocide. Neither crime was known in the Soviet Criminal Code, but after the amendments took force both crimes were included in paragraph 61.[29] By putting the two concepts together, the resulting definition created confusion with respect to the applicable law. The new Criminal Code's definition referred to the definitions of crimes against humanity and genocide in international law, but also went beyond them. For example, according to the new Code the *corpus delicti*, or requisite elements of the crime, included acts against social and political groups, defined as "anti-occupation resistance and other social groups."[30] This extension of the internationally accepted definition to include social and political groups was in direct reference to the repressive acts of deportation committed by the Soviet occupation forces in Estonia. Starting in 1996, the Estonian prosecutors initiated criminal proceedings against a number of persons involved in the mass deportation of civilians. In many investigations related to paragraph 61, most of the defendants had passed away, and in one case the court chose to relieve the defendant from punishment owing to ill health.[31]

The applicants in the case of *Kolk and Kislyiy* v. *Estonia* were of Estonian and Russian nationalities. Both were charged under paragraph 61 for their participation in the mass deportation of civilians from Estonia to remote areas of the Soviet Union during the Soviet occupation in 1949. Kolk was an investigator in the Ministry of National Security of Soviet Estonia, whereas Kislyiy was an inspector in the Ministry of Interior. The Estonian domestic courts upheld their convictions. Before the ECtHR, the defendants argued that it was not established by the Estonian courts that deportation had been a crime against humanity under international and domestic law in 1949 (as the Soviet Criminal Code in force at the time recognized no such crimes). The applicants questioned the reasonableness that they could foresee, at that time, that they were committing an offense.

In its ruling, the ECtHR upheld the Estonian Supreme Court's reasoning. The ECtHR referred to the loss of statehood as a result of the

Molotov-Ribbentrop agreement as an occupation period when Estonia was unable to fulfill its international commitments. The ECtHR observed that the deportation of the civilian population had been expressly recognized as a crime against humanity in the 1945 Charter of the Nuremberg Tribunal.[32] Although the Nuremberg Tribunal was established for trying the major war criminals of the European Axis countries for the offenses they committed before or during World War II, the universal validity of the principles concerning crimes against humanity was subsequently confirmed by Resolution 95 of the General Assembly of the United Nations adopted in 1946. Paragraph 2 of Article 7 does not prevent the trial and punishment of a person for any act or omission which, at the time it was committed, was criminal according to the general principles of law recognized by civilized nations. Furthermore, the Soviet Union had been a party to the 1945 Nuremberg Charter and a United Nations member when the General Assembly adopted Resolution 95. According to the ECtHR, therefore, it could not be argued that those principles had been unknown to the Soviet authorities.[33]

The judgment attracted criticism mainly because of the inconsistencies in the reasoning surrounding the Nuremberg principles. The ECtHR could have more convincingly argued that the applicants' actions were connected to the execution of crimes attributable to the Soviet Union leaders, which fell under the Nuremberg Charter.[34] In other words, the criminal nature of deportations was inferred from international criminal law, not from the fact that the Soviet officials and leaders had to be aware of the criminal nature of deporting civilians. Under the European Convention regime, for conduct to be punishable it should be set out as such under either national or international law. The ECtHR's position in *Kolk and Kislyiy* reflects its position on Article 7, paragraph 2, which stipulated that at the time of its commission the act was criminal according to the general principle of law. In cases where only international rules are at play, or when they conflict with domestic criminal law, the requirements of accessibility and foreseeability disappear. The values upholding human dignity, which is a foundational legal value found at every level of the European constitutional legal order and is also the essence of the European Convention on Human Rights, tip the balance in favor of international law, to the detriment of the accessibility and foreseeability of criminal law.

This case is important for thinking about historical memory and politics because these historical events, and accountability for them, rest at the heart of the legal rationale for retrospective justice. The events took place under Soviet occupation, whose legality has been disputed by Estonia and Russia. As such, *Kolk and Kislyiy* also speaks to larger transitional justice issues in the

FSU, because the case confirms the illegality of the Soviet occupation, which was not limited only to the Baltic states, but extended to other FSU republics. Critically, the ECtHR recognized the illegal actions of the occupying power. In so doing, this application of retrospective justice upheld the victims' dignity over other rights specified in Article 7, as well as over the foreseeability clause. Judge Nicolas Bratza (United Kingdom), the presiding judge in the case, led the unanimous decision. He is known for his opinions on other key cases, including *The Border Guards* cases.[35] In those rulings, Bratza empathized with the defendant and wondered whether the young soldier could have foreseen that his actions at the Berlin Wall would result in a later criminal conviction. Yet Bratza and the ECtHR were more convinced by the German Federal Court of Justice and the Federal Constitutional Court's argument and application of the Radbruch formula. In *Kolk and Kislyiy* the ECtHR referred to the "totalitarian communist regime of the Soviet Union that conducted large-scale and systematic actions against the Estonian population" and saw no reason to depart from the Estonian courts' confirmation that the actions constituted crimes against humanity. *Kolk and Kislyiy* speaks to larger transitional justice issues that court redress can bring a sense of justice and closure to the oppressed (in this instance, the victims of the deportation and the survivors of the occupation and the repressive rule). Despite this important ruling, the ECtHR approach to retrospective justice is not entirely consistent, as will be seen in the next two cases.

Latvia

In 1993, Latvia amended its Criminal Code. As with Estonia, it collapsed crimes against humanity and genocide into a single article, and expanded the number of protected groups by adding "social class" as an actionable group in Article 68 paragraph 1.[36] General principles of international law were incorporated into domestic law. Further to Article 68, paragraph 1, Latvian prosecutors prepared charges against several former Soviet security police officials, in connection with the deportation campaigns from 1940–1 and in 1949.[37]

The case of Alfons Noviks, a high-ranking officer in the secret police, presents a rare example of a former KGB leader being charged and convicted successfully. He was held responsible for committing genocide against the Latvian people, understood as the complete or partial destruction of a group.[38] The *Noviks* case acknowledged that common problems for the three Baltic states in pursuing retrospective justice were the absence of witnesses, the passing away of the perpetrators, and/or the lack of material evidence. For Latvia, getting closer to the truth was difficult also because many answers lay potentially hidden in the still unavailable Russian archives.[39] The Russian leaders proved uncooperative in providing information to facilitate accountability for communist crimes.[40]

The ECtHR decision in the *Kononov* case also highlighted a certain historical narrative for the Baltic states. In May 1944, Kononov and a partisan group (that is, a group of communists fighting against the German troops), attacked a village whose inhabitants were suspected of collaborating with the Nazis. Kononov, viewed as a war hero in Soviet Latvia, was shocked when he was prosecuted for war crimes in the 1990s. The case against him was highly politicized by the time it reached the ECtHR, because it forced a retelling of historical events that was driven less by World War II realities and more by the needs of various Latvian postcommunist institutions to contradict the Soviet narrative and portray Latvia's Soviet annexation as an unlawful occupation. In his statement, Judge Egbert Myjer (the Netherlands) admitted that a judge "should not normally express his private thoughts in relation to a judgment on which he voted. In this exceptional case, however, I think that my comments may at least clarify that there are many ways of thinking behind the legal wording in which this Strasbourg judgment has been drafted."[41] The remark is significant, for it questioned the value of retelling historical narratives about World War II, and reidentifying who was on the "right" or "wrong" side. If Kononov was "right," this would challenge the dominant narrative about World War II and the Soviet fight against fascism as told by Russia.[42] If Kononov was "wrong," this would reaffirm Latvia's alternative narrative of being an occupied country. The ECtHR ultimately found that Kononov's Article 7 rights were violated. The Latvian government then appealed this verdict.

In the appeal before the Grand Chamber, the *Kononov* case hinged on whether the Nuremberg principles constituted a universal standard or if they applied to the victorious Allies only. While the final ruling went on to uphold the view that the Nuremberg principles are universal and applicable to all, it did not follow the precedent set out in *Kolk and Kislyiy* about the illegality of the Soviet occupation. The Court could have extended this precedent to the Latvian occupation regime, but such a move proved too much for the ECtHR. Instead the case established that individuals who found themselves in between two occupying forces were presented with impossible choices that blurred the distinction between moral and legal duties.[43] As a result, the ECtHR's observations concerning the alliances that the villagers could have possibly forged with either the Nazi and/or the Soviet occupiers become hollow.[44] In other words, the identification of who is the victim and who is the perpetrator of crimes against humanity becomes a complex issue. As this case shows, there were very limited choices to make between two competing occupiers. Is survival a war crime when an individual is trying to stay alive either at the frontline or by giving (under duress at times) information about one warring side to another? The moral ambiguities that arise when stark choices for survival are at play are not addressed in this definition of the crime.

The *Kononov* case also illustrates competing historical politics. The Russian Federation exercised their right of third party intervention in the case. The Russian officials voiced the sentiments of the partisans, giving the impression that "with whatever methods one fought against Nazism, it was in any case good."[45] For Russia, Kononov's actions were justified because the Soviet takeover of the Baltic states in 1940 was not an illegal occupation and Russia reinforced the positive contribution that was made by individuals like Kononov in the fight against fascism. The multilayered discourse centered on universal standards and the boundaries of concepts of war crimes and crimes against humanity; the *Kononov* case shows how Russia's legal thinking is distinct from Europe's mainstream liberalism and its European human rights machinery. Russian officials warned, "two or three more judgments concerning revision of the results of World War II – and countries may denounce the [European] Convention [of Human Rights], which will shorten the life-span of the [European] Court."[46] Following a 2015 law that allows constitutional law to take precedence over international law, including the European Convention on Human Rights, Russia is no longer bound to implement the rulings of the ECtHR.[47] That decision reinforced the divide between European and Russian historical narratives about World War II.

The Latvian and Estonian cases are important for transitional justice because they present differing positions on the same past events as retold by two different parties: the Baltic states and Russia. In both cases the legal provisions for imprescriptible crimes were expanded, but in neither case did the ECtHR really comment on this extension. In *Kolk and Kislyiy* the ECtHR examined whether crimes against humanity constituted an international law offense at that time of their commission. In *Kononov*, the ECtHR was keen to show that the Nuremberg principles applied to victors and losers alike, thereby supporting the Nuremberg standard. For historical politics, "legal procedures involving former personnel of the Soviet authorities meant the retelling of past events, from the Soviet forms of narratives to the forms congruous with the regime transition, and constituted an important part of history and memory politics."[48] More generally, "each transition from a repressive regime to more democratic forms of government has led to new perspectives in a country's history. The power struggle between the new and old powers produces different narratives of the oppressor and the oppressed, about the significance of key events and persons and more broadly about right and wrong."[49] For transitional justice the fact that the ECtHR has become the "dispenser of transitional justice" shows that international courts can render rulings that validate or impose a different view of history, in support of, or in contradiction to, the domestic courts' interpretations. An example of the ECtHR not validating the national courts' position is considered in the following section.

Lithuania

Like Estonia and Latvia, the general principles of international law were incorporated into domestic law, further to the 1992 Lithuanian Constitution. In 1992 Lithuania passed the Law on the Liability for Genocide against the People of Lithuania (to complement ratification of the 1948 Convention and the 1968 New York Convention).[50] The 1992 law collapsed the crimes committed by the Soviets and the Germans against the Jews and the Lithuanians into one provision, a decision with broad implications for the law's application and the understanding of those historical events. The law was later widened and the newer version served as the basis of the challenge before the ECtHR in the case discussed in this section. Lithuanian lawyers paid close attention to how successful their Estonian and Latvian counterparts were at the ECtHR, and modified their argument in the *Algirdas Paleckis* case.[51] As such, in contrast to Estonia, Lithuania had a more coherent legal approach to tackling those issues.

In *Vasiliauskas* v. *Lithuania*, the ECtHR found a violation of Article 7. The narrow split vote of 9 to 8 indicated key retrospective justice issues of legal certainty and legal clarity. Vytautas Vasiliauskas was a Lithuanian national retroactively convicted of genocide under Article 99 of the Lithuanian Criminal Code of 2000.[52] The ruling concerned actions committed in 1953 after the annexation of Lithuania by the Soviet Union. At the center of it were the Lithuanian partisans, defined by the domestic courts as a political group that belonged to the underground resistance against the Soviet regime. Vasilauskas argued that his conviction violated Article 7, pointing to the Lithuanian courts' wide interpretation of genocide, which included political and social groups. Most of the court justices found that the conviction under Article 99 of the Lithuanian Criminal Code amounted to a violation of Article 7.

Although genocide was a recognized as a crime under international law in 1953, at the time when the actions were committed, the ECtHR debated whether the applicant's actions qualified as genocide according to the 1948 Convention. The Court held that, in this case, there were no convincing reasons to depart from the groups listed in the 1948 definition. Political groups had been intentionally excluded from the protected categories identified by that definition, a position supported by other international law instruments, such as the Convention on the Non-Applicability of Statutory Limitations to War Crimes and Crimes against Humanity of 1968, the International Criminal Tribunal for the Former Yugoslavia Statute of 1993, and the Rome Statute on the International Criminal Court of 1998.

In turn, the Lithuanian government argued that the Lithuanian partisans were "part" of a national group (the ethnic Lithuanians), and as such were a protected group. While this argument did not fit with international law, it was consistent with the state narratives about the Soviet occupation of Lithuania. The Lithuanian authorities created a historical commission to research and document this view. With Estonia and Latvia expanding their definitions of genocide, Lithuania did so as well. In its 2003 ruling in the *Vasiliauskas v. Lithuania* case, the Lithuanian Supreme Court rejected the position that the definition of genocide should be understood narrowly, indicating that the state's accession to the European Convention on Human Rights did not deprive it of its right to interpret the 1948 Convention so as to permit the evaluation of the crimes committed under the Soviet occupation. But the ECtHR adhered to the narrow interpretation, as set out in international law, and rejected the "part of a part" approach because such an interpretation was not foreseeable to the applicant in 1953, and therefore could not serve as a legal basis for conviction under international law. Thus, the ECtHR concluded that the defendant's Article 7 rights were violated. Moreover, in the cases referring to "in part" normally the distinct part of the protected groups is numerically large in terms of the prominence of the targeted group. In this case, Lithuanian partisans are considered as a distinct part of the wider ethnic Lithuanian group.

The dissenting Judges Mark Villiger (Liechtenstein), Ann Power-Forde (Ireland), Paulo Pinto de Albuquerque (Portugal), and Egidijus Kūris (Lithuania) argued that there had been no violation of Article 7. For these judges, the applicant's conviction was foreseeable in 1953, and the decision to restrict the application of the definition without taking the investigation further was equivalent to adopting an overly formalistic approach. They supported the Lithuanian courts' reasoning that sought a wider approach based on an evaluation of historical facts. In this way, the dissenting judges indicated that Lithuanian partisans were not just a political group, but also a significant part of the national group of ethnic Lithuanians. Therefore, the killing of Lithuanian partisans was consistent with and could be understood as part of the broader objective to destroy ethnic Lithuanians. The judges were convinced of the importance of the partisans in the country's social context, and of the symbolic significance of their destruction to a society that attempted to resist Soviet occupation. For Judge Ineta Ziemele (Latvia), the

Kononov ruling provided an important basis upon which to find for Lithuania in the ECtHR consideration of Article 7 standards. The other dissenting judges, András Sajó (Hungary), Nebojša Vučinić (Montenegro), and Ksenija Turković (Croatia), agreed and found the majority view incorrect and misguided. Indeed, in *Kononov*, the ECtHR approved a standard requiring that offences be defined in law with sufficient accessibility and foreseeability.[53] Yet in *Vasiliauskas*, apart from the dissenting judges, historical politics could not find support in the ECtHR.

The divergent majority and minority positions adopted by the judges reveal the divisions even within the ECtHR in defining genocide. The *Vasiliauskas v. Lithuania* case could result in further challenges under Article 7 of the European Convention of Human Rights. Case commentators worry that individuals convicted of genocide by the International Criminal Court (or the International Tribunal for the Former Yugoslavia) may be tempted to challenge their conviction before the ECtHR, relying on Article 7 of the European Convention in holding the state into account for not protecting them properly from the enlarged, domestic interpretation of genocide.[54] All court judges agreed on the list of protected groups included in the 1948 Convention, but they disagreed on identifying as genocidal the targeting of a part of a part.

In the *Stanislovas Drėlingas* case from April 2016, the Lithuanian Supreme Court ignored the genocide judgment the ECtHR handed down in the *Vasiliauskas* case. *Drėlingas* was convicted for his participation in the capture of Lithuanian partisans, in a plan that was coordinated by the Soviet secret services. *Drėlingas* was neither the leader of the plan, nor involved in the torture of those captured. He was, however, convicted for genocide of a national-ethno-political group. In its verdict, the Lithuanian Supreme Court only superficially referred to the *Vasiliauskas* case, and news media outlets failed to note that the ruling contradicted the ECtHR. In the end, *Drėlingas's* six-year prison sentence was reduced to six months' imprisonment.[55] Victims and survivors of the Soviet occupation in Lithuania might not be satisfied with the ECtHR decision, but they will most likely applaud the Lithuanian Supreme Court ruling. The Supreme Court, however, is rendering rulings that do not conform to ECtHR decisions, and are arguably unconstitutional. Supporters of retrospective justice will question the inconsistencies that have opened up domestically and internationally as a result of these Lithuanian cases.

CONCLUSION

In the Baltic states, transitional justice has included important methods of accountability associated with court trials and verdicts. These methods are not always seen as overt and direct forms of transitional justice, but this chapter demonstrated that these cases led to the (re)construction of historical narratives about the Soviet past. In this way both the domestic court verdicts and their challenges before the ECtHR explored retrospective justice questions related to actions carried out by the Soviet occupying powers in the Baltics. Court rulings validated the Baltic states' narratives with respect to the framing of the offenses as crimes against humanity and/or genocide. The verdicts are documents that reflect a certain understanding of the history of the region, and thus function as a type of transitional justice.

Note that the ECtHR judges and the domestic courts in the Baltic states upheld a wide diversity of opinions on whether acts perpetrated during Soviet times in the Baltic states can be considered as crimes punishable after 1991. The salient areas of contestation were historical narratives, as put forth by the Baltics and by the Russians, and whether the crimes fell under the statutes of limitations. The Baltic retelling of the past was upheld by the ECtHR, but not without some debate about historical contexts, as seen in the *Kononov* case, before the Chamber and Grand Chamber (see Table 10.1). In this case, the dominant (Western) European historical narrative, and the Russian position toward its country's contribution in the fight against fascism, was challenged. In fact, *Kolk and Kislyiy* laid the groundwork for the ECtHR to recognize the illegality of the Soviet occupation of Latvia. It did not do so, but the ECtHR held that the Nuremberg principles apply equally to the Allies and Axis powers.

The differences arise in the way that genocide is defined, as seen in *Vasiliauskas*. There are several issues at stake. One, taken from *Vasiliauskas*, is whether the Lithuanian definition of genocide that includes national political groups will lead to a change on the part of the ECtHR in its approach to genocide. At present this is a minority view. If not, states (such as Lithuania) will go on to ignore the ECtHR rulings. Without clarity on the part of the ECtHR, a state's move to expand a definition of a crime (such as genocide) will mean opening itself up to challenges from those individuals convicted of genocide. This becomes a transitional justice issue for the victims and survivors of a repressive regime, who are hoping for accountability and some sort of validation of their human dignity through the court's (domestic and/or international) endorsement of their suffering. All three cases concerned retrospective justice, and debated the definition of war crimes, crimes against humanity and genocide. While the state narratives converged in their position on crimes committed during the Soviet occupation, the ECtHR revealed a less consistent approach in its validation of domestic legal provisions and state historical narratives. While the ECtHR did not confirm the petition

TABLE 10.1. *Votes in three cases from Baltic states*

Judge	Representing state	Vote for domestic interpretation							
		Kolk and Kislyiy v. Estonia (Chamber decision, January 17, 2006)		*Kononov v. Latvia* (Chamber decision, July 24, 2008)		*Kononov v. Latvia* (Grand Chamber decision, May 17, 2010)		*Vasiliauskas v. Lithuania* (Grand Chamber decision, October 20, 2015)	
		For	Against	For	Against	For	Against	For	Against
Isabelle Berro	Monaco								X
Ledi Bianku	Albania					X			
Corneliu Bîrsan	Romania				X				
David Thór Björgvinsson	Iceland			X					
Javier Borrego Borrego	Spain	X							
Nicholas Bratza	UK	X				X			
Ireneu Cabral Barreto	Portugal					X			
Josep Casadevall	Andorra	X				X			X
Jean-Paul Costa	France						X		
Elisabet Fura-Sandström	Sweden			X					

Name	Country							
Alvina Gyulumyan	Armenia					X		
Khanlar Hajiyev	Azerbaijan	X						
Päivi Hirvelä	Finland				X			
Renate Jaeger	Germany				X			
Sverre Erik Jebens	Norway				X			
Zdravka Kalaydjieva	Bulgaria			X				
Işıl Karakaş	Turkey	X						
Jon Fridrik Kjølbro	Denmark	X						
Egidijus Kūris	Lithuania		X					
Peer Lorenzen	Denmark				X			
Alan Vaughan Lowe	United Kingdom				X			
Rait Maruste	Estonia						X	
Egbert Myjer	Netherlands							X
Matti Pellonpää	Finland						X	
Stanislav Pavlovschi	Moldova						X	

(continued)

TABLE 10.1 (continued)

Judge	Representing state	Kolk and Kislyiy v. Estonia (Chamber decision, January 17, 2006)		Kononov v. Latvia (Chamber decision, July 24, 2008)		Kononov v. Latvia (Grand Chamber decision, May 17, 2010)		Vasiliauskas v. Lithuania (Grand Chamber decision, October 20, 2015)	
		For	Against	For	Against	For	Against	For	Against
Paulo Pinto de Albuquerque	Portugal							X	
Mihai Poalelungi	Moldova						X		
Dragoljub Popović	Serbia					X			X
André Potocki	France								X
Ann Power-Forde	Ireland							X	
Guido Raimondi	Italy								X
Christos Rozakis	Greece					X			
András Sajó	Hungary							X	
Ján Šikuta	Slovakia	X							

Name	Country					
Dean Spielmann	Luxembourg	X		X		
Françoise Tulkens	Belgium			X		
Ksenija Turković	Croatia		X	X		
Mark Villiger	Lichtenstein		X			
Nebojša Vučinić	Montenegro		X	X		
Ineta Ziemele	Latvia		X			X
Boštjan M. Zupančič	Slovenia				X	

(in *Vasiliauskas*), the split vote demonstrated a possible change in the way that international courts will interpret crimes. Moreover, the three cases involved the ECtHR as the European forum in which these state narratives were challenged and debated.

I argue that through these and other cases, the ECtHR is shaping legal and political developments in the FSU. These three cases demonstrate that the ECtHR has become an important "dispenser of transitional justice," and a critical European forum in which various versions of history supersede at different times. However, the diversity of the ECtHR judges and differences in court practices mean that consistency across cases will not always prevail. Importantly, a court composed of forty-seven judges will mean differences in approach to the interpretation of the law and in the understanding of peculiar state histories. All three cases saw important contributions from judges representing either former communist states or the FSU, such as Judges Ziemele and Kūris whose dissent strongly criticized a majority position that they saw as narrow, short-sighted, and unable to embrace a wider definition of genocide. The Dutch ECtHR Judge, Egbert Myjer, cannot be ignored. His contribution reflected and supported the Russian position on the Allies' critical role in fighting fascism during World War II. This view, as shown in this chapter, is being revised, with the help of the ECtHR. In sum, the decisions depended on the judges' understanding of past crimes, and whether the action qualified as crimes according to domestic and international law.

For the FSU and transitional justice, this points to the selective manner in which some histories are repressed and other histories are validated, highlighting the instrumental use of the past to forge a new national narrative through prosecutorial action. Court petitions and cases challenge narratives underscoring the Soviet heroism against fascism, and by doing so, in the view of the Russian officials, they distort World War II reality. In this way, the Baltic cases are not just about the Baltics. These cases reverberate through other FSU states, in particular Russia, as they legitimize or reject certain narratives about the past that are critical for state-building.

Notes

1. No new data were created in this study.
2. Raluca Grosescu and Agata Fijalkowski, "Retrospective Justice and Legal Culture," in Lavinia Stan and Lucian Turcescu, eds., *Justice, Memory and Redress: New Insights from Romania* (Cambridge: Cambridge Scholars, 2017), 101.
3. Antoine Buyse and Michael Hamilton, "Introduction," in Antoine Buyse and Michael Hamilton, eds., *Transitional Jurisprudence and the ECHR: Justice, Politics, and Rights* (Cambridge: Cambridge University Press, 2011), 18.

4. Helga Welsh, "Dealing with the Communist Past: Central and East European Experiences after 1990," *Europe-Asia Studies* 48, 3 (1996): 413–28.
5. Katherine Hite, Cath Collins, and Alfredo Joignant, "The Politics of Memory in Chile," in Cath Collins, Katherine Hite, and Alfredo Joignant, eds., *The Politics of Memory in Chile: From Pinochet to Bachelet* (Boulder: First Forum Press, 2013), 1–29.
6. Eva-Clarita Pettai and Vello Pettai, *Transitional and Retrospective Justice in the Baltic States* (Cambridge: Cambridge University Press, 2015), 45.
7. Ibid., 55.
8. Ibid., 46.
9. According to the Estonian Supreme Court, "hiding oneself was a form of fighting for independence of the Republic of Estonia and against the injustice done to the Estonian people," cited in Lauri Mälksoo, "Soviet Genocide? Communist Mass Deportations in the Baltic States and International Law," *Leiden Journal of International Law* 14 (2001), 776.
10. Pettai and Pettai, *Transitional and Retrospective Justice in the Baltic States*, 55.
11. Ibid., 54.
12. Ibid.
13. Ibid., 56.
14. Nobuya Hashimoto, "Maneuvering Memories of Dictatorships and Conflicts," in Paul Corner and Jie-Hyun Lim, eds., *The Palgrave Handbook of Mass Dictatorship* (London: Palgrave Macmillan, 2016), 179.
15. Ibid., 58.
16. Mälksoo, "Soviet Genocide?" 761.
17. Alexandra Barahona de Brito, Carmen Gonzaléz-Enríquez, and Paloma Aguilar, "Introduction," in Alexandra Barahona de Brito, Carmen Gonzaléz-Enríquez and Paloma Aguilar, eds., *The Politics of Memory: Transitioning Justice in Democratizing Societies* (Oxford: Oxford University Press, 2001), 2.
18. *European Convention on Human Rights*, 2010, available at: www.echr.coe.int/Documents/Convention_ENG.pdf, accessed December 13, 2016.
19. Robin C.A. White and Claire Ovey, *Jacobs, White and Ovey: The European Convention on Human* Rights (Oxford: Oxford University Press, 2014).
20. *Charter of the International Military Tribunal*, August 8, 1945, available at: https://ihl-databases.icrc.org/ihl/INTRO/350?OpenDocument (accessed December 13, 2016).
21. In *Achour v. France*, the ECtHR stated that "the criminal law must not be extensively construed to an accused's detriment" (para 41). *Achour v. France*, Application no. 67335/01, [2007] 45 EHRR 9 (March 29, 2006), *Charter of the International Military Tribunal*.
22. Ibid.
23. Peter Quint, "The Border Guards Trials and the East German Past – Seven Arguments," *American Journal of Comparative Law* 48(2000): 541–72.
24. *Kolk and Kislyiy v. Estonia* (Application no. 23052/04, decision January 17, 2006), available at: http://echr.ketse.com/doc/23052.04-24018.04-en-20060117/view/, accessed January 4, 2017; *Kononov v. Latvia* (Application no. 36376/04, decision May 17, 2010), available at: http://hudoc.echr.coe.int/eng#{"fulltext":["Kononov%20v%20Latvia"],"documentcollectionid2":["GRANDCHAMBER"],"itemid":

["001-98669"]}, accessed January 4, 2017; and *Vasiliauskas v. Lithuania* (Application no. 35343/05, decision October 20, 2015), available at: https://lovdata .no/static/EMDN/emd-2005-035343.pdf, accessed January 4, 2017.

25. *Convention on the Prevention and Punishment of the Crime of Genocide*, January 12, 1951, available at: www.ohchr.org/EN/ProfessionalInterest/Pages/CrimeOfGeno cide.aspx, accessed December 17, 2016.
26. *Introduction*, n.d., available at: www.mnemosyne.ee/hc.ee/index_frameset.htm, accessed December 13, 2016.
27. Hashimoto, "Maneuvering Memories of Dictatorships and Conflicts," 174–5.
28. Ibid., 180.
29. *Estonian Criminal Code*, 2001, available at: www.legislationline.org/documents/ section/criminal-codes, accessed December 13, 2016.
30. Ibid.
31. Mälksoo, "Soviet Genocide?" 776–81.
32. *Charter of the International Military Tribunal.*
33. Estonia acceded to the 1968 Convention on the Non-Applicability of Statutory Limitations to War Crimes and Crimes against Humanity in 1991. The 1968 Convention creates the possibility for the state to overcome any obstacle in the form of statute of limitations for these crimes.
34. Antonio Cassese, "Balancing the Prosecution of Crimes against Humanity and Non-retroactivity of the Law: The *Kolk and Kislyiy v. Estonia* Case before the ECHR," *Journal of International Criminal Justice* 4, 2 (2006): 410–18; and Mälksoo, "Soviet Genocide?" 758.
35. *Streletz, Kessler and Krenz v. Germany* [2001] 33 EHRR 751, available at: www .menschenrechte.ac.at/orig/01_2/Streletz.pdf, accessed January 4, 2017; and *K-HW v. Germany* [2003] 36 EHRR 108, available at: http://hudoc.echr.coe.int/eng#{"ap-pno":["37201/97"], "itemid":["001-59352"]}, accessed January 4, 2017.
36. *Latvian Criminal Code*, 1993, available at: www.legislationline.org/documents/ section/criminal-codes, accessed December 14, 2016.
37. In 1995, the Criminal Division for the Investigation of Crimes Committed on Latvian Territory started to investigate Soviet crimes against humanity. It worked closely together with the Centre for the Documentation of the Consequences of Totalitarianism, which was founded in 1992 as a research institution.
38. Katja Wezel, "Latvia's Soviet Story: Transitional Justice and the Politics of Com-memoration," *Satori*, October 25 (2009), available at: www.satori.lv/raksts/3111, accessed December 17, 2016.
39. Lavinia Stan, "The Former Soviet Union," in Lavinia Stan, ed., *Transitional Justice in Eastern Europe and the Former Soviet Union* (London: Routledge, 2009), 227–30.
40. Such as the Katyń massacre concerning the execution of Polish prisoners-of-war at various killing sites in 1940 by the Soviet secret police. *Janowiec and Others v. Russia*, Applications nos. 55508/07 and 29520/09, decision October 21, 2013, available at: www.menschenrechte.ac.at/orig/13_5/Janowiec.pdf, accessed January 4, 2017.
41. *Kononov v. Latvia* (Application no. 36376/04, [2008] ECHR 695 (July 24, 2008), para 10), available at: http://echr.ketse.com/doc/36376.04-en-20080724/view/, accessed January 4, 2017.
42. Ibid.

43. Timothy Snyder, *Bloodlands: Europe between Hitler and Stalin* (London: The Bodley Head, 2010), 391–4.

44. *Kononov* v. *Latvia*, 2010, para 221; Lauri Mälksoo, "Case Commentary," *American Journal of International Law* 105, 1 (2011): 101–8, at 107.

45. Mälksoo, "Case Commentary," 107.

46. Ibid.

47. BBC, "Russia Puts Its Laws above European Court Rulings," July 14, 2015, available at: www.bbc.co.uk/news/world-europe-33521553, accessed November 7, 2016.

48. Hashimoto, "ManeuveringMemories of Dictatorships and Conflicts," 175.

49. Antoine Buyse, "The Truth, the Past and the Present: Article 10 and Situations of Transition," in Antoine Buyse and Michael Hamilton, eds., *Transitional Jurisprudence and the ECHR: Justice, Politics, and Rights* (Cambridge: Cambridge University Press, 2011), 138.

50. Eva-Clarita Pettai, "Prosecuting Soviet Genocide: Comparing the Politics of Criminal Justice in the Baltic States," *European Politics and Society* 17, 4 (2016): 1–14, 5–8.

51. Justinas Žilinskas, "Introduction of the 'Crime of Denial' in the Lithuanian Criminal Law and the First Instances of Its Application," *Jurisprudencija/Jurisprudence* 19, 1 (2012): 315–29; Domatas Glodenis, "Lithuania's Supreme Court Upholds Verdict for Paleckis'," *Lithuania Tribune*, January 22, 2013, available at: www.liberties.eu/en/news/lithuania-genocide-unlawful-conviction, accessed January 4, 2017.

52. *Lithuanian Criminal Code*, 2003, available at: www.legislationline.org/documents/section/criminal-codes, accessed December 14, 2016.

53. Dissenting opinion Judge Ziemele, *Vasiliauskas* v. *Lithuania*, Application no. 35343/05, decision October 20, 2015, para 21, available at: http://lrv-atstovas-eztt.lt/uploads/VASILIAUSKAS_2015_GC_judgment.pdf, accessed January 4, 2017.

54. Anika Bratzel, "The ECHR's Recent Encounter with Genocide: A Closer Look at the Judgment in *Vytautus Vasiliauskas* v. *Lithuania*," December 1, 2015, available at: http://jean-monnet-saar.eu/?p=1100, accessed December 22, 2016.

55. Domatas Glodenis, "Lithuanian Supreme Court Ignores Strasbourg Genocide Judgment," May 23, 2016, available at: www.liberties.eu/en/news/lithuania-genocide-unlawful-conviction, accessed January 4, 2017.

PART III

LAYERED PASTS AND THE POLITICS OF DENIAL

11

Confronting the Soviet and Post-Soviet Past in Georgia

Robert C. Austin

Georgia presents students and practitioners of transitional justice with some complex questions. As a former Soviet republic and indeed the birthplace of Soviet dictator Joseph Stalin, Georgia appears as a necessary place for transitional justice or at least for a reassessment of its difficult and complex past, following the collapse of the Former Soviet Union (FSU) and subsequent independence in 1991. However, serious and sustained transitional justice did not take place. In fact, a kind of transitional justice, never really embraced by the elite, came only in 2013 and it dealt essentially with the abuses and crimes committed not by the Soviet regime during 1921–91, but by the postcommunist government of Mikheil Saakashvili (2004–13) that was at least quasi-democratic in nature and by some measures a good government. This chapter examines the limited transitional justice program effected to date in Georgia, which inadequately addresses the crimes of both the Soviet dictatorship and the postcommunist regime of Mikheil Saakashvili.

FROM INDEPENDENCE TO A FAILED STATE

Georgia's trajectory after the collapse of the FSU in 1991 was grim. The new independent republic was a deeply criminalized, failed state due to the overwhelming influence of criminal groups and the limited reach of the government. Between 1991 and 2003 state institutions barely existed, except as places that provided a venue for extortion, and thus Georgia lacked the capacity to enact transitional justice. Civil society, often suggested to be a cornerstone of the promotion of transitional justice programs, hardly existed. In addition to a near permanent state of domestic crisis, in 1992 Georgia confronted and ultimately lost two separatist insurgencies in Abkhazia and South Ossetia, two regions which historically were not part of the country and where the ethnic majority Abkhaz and Ossetians pushed for independence. Both wars witnessed extraordinary violence, and resulted in over 200,000 internally displaced persons (IDPs). These wars and their outcomes did not invite the international scrutiny that took place in the Balkans, leaving the Russians largely in charge as somewhat dubious peacekeepers.[1]

Georgia's first postindependence government of Zviad Gamsakhurdia (1991–2) ended in civil conflict due primarily to his own harsh and undemocratic style, his rabid Georgian nationalism, and the collapse of the economy. In 1992, former Soviet foreign minister Eduard Shevardnadze returned to his homeland to legitimize the putsch that had overthrown Gamsakhurdia.[2] In office until 2003, President Shevardnadze in the end failed to stabilize the country. Under him Georgia was simply not governed, and many individuals got rich undeservingly. Citizens faced a government tied to the so-called "thieves-in-law," essentially mafia-style criminal groups. At the same time, state capture prevailed and top-to-bottom corruption, especially from the bloated police services, became a fact of life at every level. Public assets went to criminals, state positions were up for sale with known prices, and Georgians faced an extraordinary crisis of confidence in the government. In 2003, Transparency International noted that Georgia was one of the most corrupt countries in the world.[3] Shevardnadze inherited a bleak situation in 1992, but he did bring some stability. As Thomas de Waal noted, had he resigned in 2000 he would have been remembered as Georgia's "savior," but instead his last three years in power were characterized by "drift and corruption."[4]

FROM WEAK STATE TO STRONG STATE

Georgia entered 2003 on the verge of political and economic collapse. Saakashvili, the youthful and energetic former Minister of Justice (2000–1) and one time Shevardnadze protégé, educated in the United States, led a popular revolution after Shevardnadze attempted to steal the November 2003 parliamentary elections. The Rose Revolution, the very first of the colored revolutions, toppled Shevardnadze and forced new elections at the parliamentary and presidential levels in 2004. The elections brought Saakashvili to power as president, together with a team of young, often Western-educated and committed idealists. Saakashvili's mandate was simple: rebuild the Georgian state almost from scratch and make it a success story. As Lincoln Mitchell noted, "the decision of the Saakashvili government to prioritize state building was rational and probably wise. However, the decision to do this at the expense of democracy not only undermined the democratic promise of the Rose Revolution, but ultimately made the state building process itself significantly more difficult and less successful."[5] In short, democracy had to wait, since state-building was to be pursued at the expense of rule of law and respect for human rights.

The new government was handed an extraordinary mandate for change: Saakashvili won the new presidential elections in January 2004 with 96 percent of the vote. His political party, the United National Movement (UNM), took more than 70 percent of the popular vote and had near total control of the parliament in the March 2004 vote. Moving from street opposition movement to government, the UNM actually faced no opposition in the new parliament. Saakashvili promised Euro-Atlantic integration within two decades. Even more difficult and controversial, he also promised to restore Georgia's territorial integrity by reincorporating the breakaway regions of Abkhazia and South Ossetia.

Saakashvili did not come to power with a mandate for effecting transitional justice, but he undertook a somewhat superficial discussion of the Soviet legacy, focused on discrediting Russia, which had provided support to the separatists in Abkhazia and South Ossetia. What he wanted was rule of law and a strong state, two goals for which he had obtained the mandate to proceed from the Rose Revolution. His first term as president (2004–8) was as breathtaking as it was revolutionary, encompassing a number of reform programs such as reorganizing the government, streamlining bureaucracy, introducing new laws, simplifying the tax code, and cracking down on petty crime and corruption. It earned him extraordinary respect inside and outside of Georgia with many analysts pointing to his policies as something that could be exported as successful state-building strategies, particularly the much-touted police reform program which put an end to corruption, at least within the notoriously sinister traffic police.

The United States, the European Union (EU), and the World Bank lauded the country's rapid and successful transformation and provided extraordinary assistance, with Georgia fast becoming a top destination for international aid and record amounts of foreign direct investment. The United States in particular stood by Saakashvili even after it was clear that Georgian democracy had shortcomings during his second mandate as president (2008–12). He not only paid the pensions but raised them, got the electricity and natural gas flowing to everyone, restored public infrastructure, and cleaned the streets.[6] He loved building projects too, and the face of Tbilisi changed. The public sector faced an extraordinary shake up with tax code changes, massive dismissals, and a focus on accountability. The new government made access to social services easier with new service centers; no longer did one pay a bribe to get a new passport or driver's license. These were lasting and important changes. The most telling statistic is tax collection: revenue from taxes increased almost

700 percent between 2003 and 2008.[7] The World Bank singled out Georgia as the best reforming economy of 2006–10. While there are numerous competing narratives about Saakashvili's eight-year-long rule, there can be no doubt that one of his lasting legacies is that he restored Georgian state institutions and improved state services.

However, it was the focus on crime and justice that later created problems for Saakashvili and the UNM. Unlike the rhetorical wars taking place in other FSU republics and the Balkans, Saakashvili's wars were real and often fought with an astonishing lack of fairness, thus setting the stage for hesitant Georgian transitional justice measures after his ousting in 2012. In tackling crime and corruption, the government adhered to a zero tolerance policy in 2006. "We want zero-tolerance. And it works. It is a fact that it works," Saakashvili said, adding that he was "cleaning our streets of this rubbish."[8] In practice, this declaration meant that the state began to use extra-legal methods to enforce the new policies. The courts worked hand in hand with the government to enforce the new rules, and thus send a strong message to criminals and regime opponents. In short, the courts were politically dependent.

One of the most documented aspects of the Saakashvili government is its success in eliminating petty bribery. All the statistics point to a simple fact: after his reforms took effect, Georgians were paying fewer bribes, cops were doing their jobs, and government officials were no longer expecting gifts. He cut the public service in half, and raised the salaries of those who were fortunate enough to keep their jobs.[9] His most celebrated reform, which has nothing to do with transitional justice, involved firing all the traffic cops, and then rehiring a much smaller number on higher salaries. The Ministry of Internal Affairs dismissed 16,000 of 25,000 employees in the first two years following the Rose Revolution.[10] In love with bold action and symbolism, Saakashvili even changed the "look" of the police services by building glass police stations and a transparent headquarters for the Ministry of Interior. Success was not found in reestablishing Georgia's territorial integrity: Saakashvili was able to reintegrate Ajaria,[11] but not Abkhazia and South Ossetia.

The down side was that Georgia went from a near failed state under Shevardnadze to a highly centralized presidential republic with extraordinary power in the president's hands. Decision-making was limited to Saakashvili and his inner circle. "From the beginning of its time in office the government de-emphasized democracy, even weakened democratic institutions, by shifting power away from the legislature, undermining the independence of the judiciary and restricting media, as part of an attempt to hasten state-building efforts."[12] The constitutional changes of 2004, which concentrated power in the presidency, reflected Saakashvili's vision for the way ahead. The strong executive, Saakashvili argued, was required if reform was to be successful. He promised to return power to the legislature when the job was finished. That Saakashvili was concentrating far too much power in his hands went largely unnoticed as observers lauded the fight against corruption and the economic reform agenda. As Henry Hale notes, the combination of patronalism and presidentialism did serious harm to democratic prospects in Georgia, and many other countries in Eurasia.[13]

Early in his term critics inside and outside of the country were noting flaws in Georgian democracy. People were apparently willing to tolerate this democratic deficit as long as the government made progress in key areas such as poverty and unemployment. This progress, however, did not happen. With hindsight, it now seems obvious that the war on crime and corruption had other targets too. Some argued that the president was using the criminal justice system to retain power and quash dissent.[14] International observers noted that Georgia was going too far in its quest for law and order, and the strong state. The facts are indeed telling. Zero tolerance not only sent the formerly powerful "thieves-in-law" and other mafia figures to jail, but many people found themselves incarcerated for even minor crimes. The courts played an important role, as Georgia witnessed an unprecedented conviction rate of 99.6 percent and a per capita incarceration rate of 531/100000. In 2010, for example, the Tbilisi court had 7,296 criminal trials with only three full acquittals.[15] Average sentences went from one year to five years. At the same time, civil society activists were calling for an end to government pressure on judges to deliver guilty verdicts.[16] Saakashvili simply pushed ahead.

In 2003–12, the prison population grew by 300 percent, according to a report on prisons prepared by Georgia's Open Society Foundation.[17] The country had to build prisons and allocate more cash to the prison system, and this took resources away from the antipoverty or other social programs. Many Georgians wrongly claimed or believed that every family had at least one person in prison. Georgia joined Russia and the United States at the top of the list for people behind bars. Moreover, Saakashvili's critics argued that assets seized by the state were delivered not to the state, but to the UNM instead. However, as Gavin Slade and Alexander Kuptadze note, "the results were dramatic: by 2010, a person in Georgia was half as likely to be a victim of burglary, four times less likely to be robbed and ten times less likely to be assaulted than in law-abiding Germany."[18] In addition to dramatic incarceration rates, a controversial plea-bargaining system also raised controversy. In essence, in exchange for guilty pleas, defendants were allowed to pay fines instead of going to prison. Thomas de Waal and Anna Dolidze noted that thousands of cases were decided in this manner and that it created huge, often illegal, revenue for the government and the UNM.[19] As S. Neil Macfarlane added, from the perspective of those from whom the government was trying to take large sums of money, "the situation may seem little better than the previous era of corruption."[20] None of these programs constitute transitional justice, however, as the aim was zero tolerance in crime and revenue for the government rather than justice for past abuses.

Alongside zero-tolerance that permeated almost every aspect of life, Georgian democracy was weak. Moreover, the government's neo-liberal economic policies failed to tackle pervasive poverty and unemployment, and this oversight drained its popular support. Saakashvili's response to his weakening domestic position was ultimately repression, but it is worth keeping things in perspective: Georgia was not Azerbaijan or Russia, where repression was far more serious. This is the reason why, in addition to accusations that the government was directly linked to high-profile murders, the population grew weary of the president. In November 2007, in an act that would later come back to haunt the UNM, the government violently broke up an opposition protest and took over an opposition television station. Police used rubber bullets, water cannon and other forms of violence, sending 250 people to hospital. Saakashvili then called early presidential elections in January 2008. He barely won those elections.

The UNM won a second majority government in May 2008 amid accusations of fraud, media control, and misuse of state funds to secure victory. His second term in office, which included a disastrous war with Russia that effectively detached, more than likely on a permanent basis, Abkhazia and South Ossetia from Georgia, also witnessed less democracy and more authoritarianism. The decision to go to war was a mistake and confirmed suspicions that Saakashvili was governing with incredible disregard for dissenting voices. Indeed, as Freedom House noted, between 2005 and 2012 Georgia made no gains in terms of its democracy indicators.[21]

GEORGIA, STALIN AND THE SOVIET PAST

Alongside Saakashvili's state-building and law and order program, he did offer a modest and far less meaningful or significant attempt to reckon with Georgia's Soviet past. Reassessing Stalin or Stalinism was not easy in Georgia, as "Stalin is still an important symbol but one with little political content. Georgians have a tendency to avoid discussion of painful topics and find it difficult to reevaluate values. A reassessment has failed to take place regarding one of its most enduring legends—the 'famous son of Georgia,' Stalin."[22]

After Georgia achieved independence, both Gamsakhurdia and Shevardnadze framed the Soviet period as a foreign occupation that started when the Democratic Republic of Georgia was crushed in 1921. The number of human rights abuses raised exponentially under the Soviet occupation, although Georgia was one of the most prosperous Soviet republics. As de Waal notes, the Soviet state "modernized, terrorized and Russified the Caucasus but also gave it new kinds of nationalism."[23] Georgian resistance to Soviet rule, especially after an uprising in western Georgia in 1924, resulted in as many as 4,000 people killed and even more sent into exile. The Caucasus as a whole did escape the "worst of Stalin's excesses until the 1930s."[24] In 1936, however, Lavrenti Beria, another ethnic Georgian whom Stalin appointed first secretary of the Transcaucasian Federation, started his own version of the Great Terror in the region, and wiped out the old Georgian Bolsheviks along with the Georgian intelligentsia. Poets Titsian Tabidze and Paolo Iashvili, writers Michail Javakhishvili and Grigol Robakidze, old Bolshevik leader Mamia Orakhelashvili and almost one-fourth of the Georgian Communist Party leaders condemned for their Trotskyist deviationism, agricultural specialists, peasants and kulaks blamed for poor crops and slow collectivization, hundreds of *raikom* secretaries, enterprise directors, commissars, newspaper editors, and thousands of the lowest level party and state bureaucracy, fell victims to the Great Terror. In 1938, one year after the Transcaucasian Federation was dissolved and Georgia regained its status as a distinct Soviet republic, Beria became head of the NKVD (the precursor of the KGB).[25] The Great Terror was put to an end at around the same time, although the practice of mass arrests, exiles, political executions, and purges continued long afterwards, complementing a wide surveillance program through which the KGB collected information secretly about anticommunist political dissidents.

Before 1991, the official Soviet-sanctioned narrative had claimed that the Democratic Republic of Georgia was just a brief moment before the Bolshevik triumph. With Mikhail Gorbachev's *glasnost* in the late 1980s, Georgian historians started to reject the Soviet interpretation of history, and to underscore instead the violence that accompanied Georgia's Sovietization.[26] In 1991, President Gamsakhurdia said simply that Russia occupied Georgia. Shevardnadze, despite impeccable Soviet credentials, said the same thing years later. President Saakashvili took the anti-Russian occupation narrative to a whole new level. The August 2008 war with Russia, which by any measure was a debacle for Georgia, only reinforced this viewpoint.

While the Georgian political elites have seen the Soviets and Stalin as demons, Georgian people's attitudes toward Stalin have reflected a more complicated picture. Surveys commissioned by the Carnegie Endowment in 2012 in Russia, Armenia, Azerbaijan, and Georgia showed "worryingly high levels of admiration" for Stalin.[27] According to de Waal, the poll suggested "feelings of dependency and confusion" more than genuine support for the return to a dictatorship. Other findings showed that Stalin continues to be identified with World War II, as a victorious leader over Nazism, de-Stalinization has been "half-hearted" or superficial, but young, educated and urban post-Soviet citizens are more critical of his legacy.[28] Lasha Bakradze also argued that Georgians take pride in Stalin as a native son who turned the Soviet Union into a superpower, but separate him from the totalitarian regime that ruled them. "Georgians made a crude trade-off: the Russians 'have us where they want us,' but 'our boy has them'."[29] Their approval of Stalin did not amount to tacit approval for totalitarianism.

Looking back to 1956, Khrushchev's Secret Speech triggered mass demonstrations in Tbilisi, which indicated antipathy toward Soviet rule, heralded the end of Georgian support for communist ideology, and produced an upsurge in Georgian nationalism during Soviet times. Soviet national myths (Moscow as the "Third Rome"; the Great Patriotic War as a triumph over Nazism) were not Georgian national myths.[30] The Carnegie survey's results show that Georgians take pride in their role in World War II and associate the victory with Stalin, rather than with the Soviet Union.[31] While in Russia Stalin is admired as "a symbol of order and autocracy," Georgians see him as a "rebel" who rose to power in a system led by Russians. Moreover, "weak identification" with the Soviets is shown in Georgia's lack of an influential post-FSU Communist Party and minimal nostalgia for the Soviet era. Stalin is therefore "an object of local patriotism and popular devotion."[32]

In comparison to post-Hitler Germany where de-Nazification policies tried to sideline the former supporters of the Third Reich, the Soviet Union never completed the process of de-Stalinization started by Khrushchev. Much of the communist leadership that supported Stalin remained in place after his death in 1953, and few questioned the underlying totalitarian ideology and repressive system until Gorbachev launched his *perestroika*, but that policy did not amount to a full-scale reassessment of the past. With Georgian independence in 1991, "there was no interest in any serious analysis of recent history as the country wrestled instead with complex social and political problems."[33] This remains as true in 2017, as it did in 1991.

Saakashvili ramped up the victimhood narrative that placed Russia more firmly as an aggressor and an occupier. His signature project was the somewhat underwhelming Museum of Soviet Occupation, which opened in Tbilisi in 2006 on 26 May, the day Georgia declared independence from the Russian Empire in 1918. Given the length of the Soviet "occupation" of Georgia, the museum is a disappointment, occupying a very small space on the top floor of the national museum. As visitors travel through the museum, they come to see the Soviet era as external to and in contradiction to Georgian national history.

Like other museums in Central and Eastern Europe that commemorate the occupation (Riga, Tallinn, and Budapest), the museum in Tbilisi negates Georgian agency during the seventy years under Soviet rule. This museum's interpretation of Georgian history is best understood in the context of the Rose Revolution. The exhibits also provide a black and white interpretation of the past with the emphasis on violence and Georgian victimhood from 1918 to 1989. The first exhibit the visitor encounters is a bullet-ridden railway car where Georgians taking part in the aforementioned anti-Bolshevik uprising of August 1924 were shot. Its critics also noted that the museum seems more concerned with demonizing Russia than engendering a sophisticated reassessment and discussion of Georgia's place in the FSU. Alongside the museum, the government encouraged academics to study Georgia's relationship with Russia to confirm the occupation narrative. The Ministry of Education proposed a new textbook on Russian occupation and a "Russian Occupation Week" was initiated. The first Georgian republic is presented in the textbook as a "multi-ethnic, democratic and united Georgia."[34]

In June 2010, Saakashvili also removed the statue of Stalin in his hometown of Gori. Like many of his initiatives, it was a top-down move with little public discussion, and the removal took place at night. Saakashvili argued that it was simply impossible to commemorate the victims of Stalinism when the statue still stood in Gori. As one observer noted, "The removal of the most famous surviving monument to Joseph Stalin has been broadly welcomed in Georgia, although many were upset at the secrecy with which the statue was whisked away in the Soviet dictator's home town of Gori. Some went as far as accusing Saakashvili of using 'Stalinist tactics to efface traces of the past'."[35] Other symbols of the Soviet past were removed and street names were changed. Tellingly, the Gori municipal leadership rebuked Saakashvili after he lost power in 2012, and the statue reappeared inside the local museum grounds. The monument's reappearance was probably less a manifestation of pro-Stalin feelings than the need for the curious to visit Gori. The new government clearly did not care what Gori did with the statue.[36]

In May 2011, in what was the only formal lustration process, the Freedom Charter was introduced. The law sought to strengthen national security, prohibit Soviet and Fascist ideologies and remove all symbols, and create a commission to vet and investigate officials who are accused of involvement with foreign special forces. This meant that any Soviet-era functionary could be banned from any kind of public office. Lustration had been considered before, first by Gamsakhurdia who was not in power long enough to do anything, and later as a cornerstone of the 2003 Rose Revolution. With Shevardnadze and his FSU cronies in power, lustration was impossible to implement. But why did lustration take so long, given that the conditions enabling it were met in 2004 when lustration had been at the top of Saakashvili's agenda. For Saakashvili, lustration had already been effected when Georgia skipped a generation once Shevardnadze was ousted. More sinister minds pointed to Saakashvili's past collaboration with the KGB, while others noted that one of the most important figures in the UNM, Nino Burjanadze, was Shevardnadze's goddaughter and a vocal opponent of lustration. When the law did appear, it was not the UNM that proposed it, but an anticommunist opposition party.

Finally, in 2011, Saakashvili announced plans to move the Georgian parliament to Kutaisi, a city some 250 km west of Tbilisi. At the same time, the former parliament, as the seat of the Georgian Soviet Socialist Republic, was demolished. Prior to the move, Saakashvili had ordered the destruction of the Soviet-era Glory Memorial in Kutaisi in December 2009. The memorial, a 35-m concrete arch, honored the dead and missing from World War II. The destruction of the arch was done by explosives and killed a woman and her daughter when they were struck by flying bits of concrete. Saakashvili's critics accused him of disgracing the legacy of the 300,000 Georgians killed in the war. Others noted that Saakashvili moved the parliament in Kutaisi only as a pretext to destroy the monument.[37] In any case, Georgia got a brand new parliament and Saakashvili's pledge to regional development was upheld.

THE STALIN MUSEUM

Opened in the 1930s and moved to its present location in the 1950s, the Museum was left almost to decay after Stalin's death. After *perestroika* was introduced in the late 1980s the museum "was closed in order to permit it to present a more balanced image of Stalin. Following the collapse of the Soviet Union [in 1991] it was reopened but the exhibits omitted reference to Stalin's repressions."[38] Nanci Adler noted that "while the museum is no longer visited by Soviet-era busloads, this burnished depiction of the dead dictator, along with the proliferation of his busts and statues in Georgian homes and restaurants, points to a need to valorise a selective past."[39]

The contents of the Museum have remained largely untouched since the 1950s. Visitors learn about Stalin's life beginning with his early childhood years in poverty. The exhibition follows him to seminary in Tbilisi, and then on to his career as a revolutionary in Moscow. The biggest draw is Stalin's musty and creepy railcar used for trips and meeting with world leaders. Visitors quickly note the lack of written information in English, and the silence surrounding Stalin's role in the Great Terror, the Gulag, and the development of the Soviet Union's harsh economic plans. Guides provide a detached view of the period seemingly leaving the visitor to decide just what happened. Saakashvili hoped to turn the place into a Museum of Stalinism that would have offered a critical assessment of Stalin and his crimes. He expected to raise the funds for the project, aiming for something that told the story of Stalin's crimes similar to a Holocaust museum, but that never happened. In an attempt to deal with mounting pressure to conform to the Saakashvili government's anti-Soviet narrative, a separate room was built in 2010 to discuss Stalinist repression. Despite the addition, the visitor still ends the tour in a gift shop with mugs, shirts, lighters, and replicas of Stalin's pipe.

Resistance to changing the Museum's current narrative and correcting its many silences has come from locals, many of whom felt that Saakashvili's pro-Georgian and pro-Western approach sidelined their personal memories of the communist period. Irina, a curator at the Museum, explained that they wanted the Museum to reflect the fact that some people were happier during the communist period.[40] In this respect, the Museum's glorification of Stalin might be better interpreted as one community's attempt to reclaim some of the more positive elements of Georgia's communist past. Lacking money for heat, the museum maintains a generally forlorn atmosphere. The Museum lives off modest funds from the Ministry of Culture and ticket sales to the curious. Chinese tourists come in the biggest numbers, according to local staff. Staying open is likely a matter of economic necessity for the town of Gori, which also boasts its own miniature Reichstag.

According to the Carnegie poll, 45 percent of Georgians have a positive view of Stalin.[41] Breaking the respondents down by age and social group reveals little differences: urban and educated Georgians have a slightly less positive view of him, and younger people are largely indifferent (more than 25 percent).[42] Bakradze concluded that the modernization brought about by the Rose Revolution was superficial, and did not change Georgian consciousness: "Georgia is still in the grip of Soviet-style thinking, and even Georgian nationalism still has a quite Soviet character."[43] The Carnegie poll results paradoxically showed little support for authoritarianism, and high levels of support for democracy (68 percent).[44] But this does not mean that Georgians are clamoring for transitional justice. Georgia still requires a reexamination of the past, but such reexamination is unlikely to happen when poverty and unemployment remain the state's key challenges.

AFTER SAAKASHVILI

Georgia headed to parliamentary elections in October 2012. By then, Saakashvili and his team had already rewritten the constitution from a super-presidency to a parliamentary republic, based on Saakashvili's promise to put power back in the legislative branch. Many speculated that Saakashvili would copy Vladimir Putin and move from President to Prime Minister – we will never know, as he did not get the chance. The electoral climate was fraught and all early indications suggested that victory for the UNM would be easy. The main challenge came from a coalition of eight political parties named the Georgian Dream. They were brought together by Georgia's richest man and one time Saakashvili ally, Bidzina Ivanishvili, who had bankrolled some of the President's more lavish building projects. Like many ordinary Georgians, Ivanishvili decided to break with the president shortly after the failed war with Russia in 2008.

Ivanishvili and the parties he brought together faced an uphill battle, but they were unified by a collective hatred of the president and the extraordinary cash of their patron. In the run up to the elections, the UNM played extremely dirty. An early tactic, in the hope that Saakashvili could prevent Ivanishvili from entering Georgian politics, was to strip him of his Georgian citizenship in 2011. The Georgian court maintained that Ivanishvili had violated Georgian law in March 2010 when he took French citizenship. That move made him a citizen of three countries (Georgia, Russia, and France), which was illegal under Georgian law.[45] Under international pressure, the government eventually backed down. Next, hastily passed electoral finance laws sought to limit the impact of Ivanishvili's wealth, and lots of unexpected auditors visited parties allied with the billionaire. A report from Transparency International Georgia noted "intimidation of opposition activists," "physical reprisals against opposition supporters," "detention and arrest on political grounds," "use of legal resources for political and electoral purposes," "disproportional sanctions imposed on opposition parties," "obstructing party activities," "pressure on businesses," "the use of the country's public resources for political and electoral purposes," and "voter bribing."[46] In broad terms, the preelection environment was demonstrably oriented in favor of the ruling UNM and pointedly against opposition challengers, including Georgian Dream.[47]

While it looked like an easy UNM victory, the mood changed when the Georgian television broadcast horrific videos showing the rape and torture of prisoners in the Number 8 Gldani prison outside Tbilisi. The video of prison torture so decisively shaped the election outcome because of the legacy of eight years of often ill-conceived law and order policies. With so many people in prison, Georgians reacted, and the prison videos served as a catalyst not only for a change in government but also toward a new standard in human rights. Prior to the release of the video, which the UNM claimed was made by the Kremlin, Georgia's prison system was showing signs of strain. An Open Society report pointed to overcrowding and a culture of silence and ill treatment.[48] Saakashvili's zero-tolerance policy was blamed for prison overcrowding. All these, taken together, ensured a victory of Georgian Dream.

Despite Saakashvili's enormous accomplishments, his critics argued that his government was not as liberal as everyone thought. The Gldani video was just one of many pieces of evidence suggesting that the whole era needed a serious reappraisal. As de Waal noted, Saakashvili was far more authoritarian than most people realized, and his all-powerful Interior Ministry "turned Georgia into a police state."[49] When the vast numbers of wrongly imprisoned individuals were considered, Georgia seemed set for a reckoning with the Saakashvili era. As Lincoln Mitchell noted, "simply moving forward as if October 2012 was just a normal election, and not instead a judgment of a criminal past, would be a miscarriage of justice, as it would let people involved with high-level corruption, illegal surveillance, abuse, and even torture, go free."[50]

Immediately after assuming the office, the new Georgian Dream government arrested senior officials from the Saakashvili government on the assumption that they had "a popular mandate to investigate and punish allegedly very serious abuses committed by its predecessors."[51] The new government promised to deliver justice, and as such it needed to respond to three categories of crimes allegedly committed under Saakashvili's rule, all of which are perceived to have political elements. The first category encompasses physical crimes, including extrajudicial killings, torture, inhuman and degrading treatment, beatings, illegal arrests, and imprisonment. The second includes crimes against privacy and personhood, such as illegal surveillance, wiretapping, harassment, and threats. And the third involves economic issues, such as the arbitrary deprivation of property and business.[52]

Foreign observers like de Waal and Dolidze and Human Rights Watch unsuccessfully called for the creation of a Truth and Reconciliation Commission for Georgia. The Georgian Dream government lacked the political will to look at the recent past and the task proved too daunting given the other, arguably more serious challenges the government faced. But that did not stop them from pursuing some high level former officials. Fearing for their futures and a potential witch-hunt, several officials fled Georgia as soon as the election results were clear.

The decision to bring charges against Saakashvili was not an easy one. Outside interests, particularly in the United States, counseled against the move and there was no unanimity in the Georgian Dream coalition. There were good reasons for charging him (nobody should be above the law) and good reasons not to (it could set Georgia on a permanent path of political vengeance similar to the one taken by Albania).[53] Before the government made up its mind, Saakashvili fled Georgia shortly after his presidential term expired in November 2013. In July 2014, he was formally charged with abuse of power, primarily related to the violent suppression of an opposition rally in 2007, the illegal seizure of an opposition television station, and other illegal actions. The charges related to the opposition protest were telling, as they accused Saakashvili of giving "criminal orders" to the police services, who employed tear gas, pursued fleeing protestors, and beat them with truncheons and wooden poles. Not all of the charges were political; many were economic and related to alleged embezzlement and the misuse of state funds. Although out of the country at the time, Saakashvili was held in "pre-trial detention in absentia." The new regime was clearly prepared to hold the Saakashvili regime accountable for human rights and other abuses, but observers inside and out of Georgia denounced the process as political. For the Georgia Dream coalition, the priority was the recent past, not the distant Soviet past.

In August 2014, new charges were added when Saakashvili was accused of organizing an assault on one of his opponents, Georgian lawmaker Valeri Gelashvili. In a subsequent clarification of the charges, the Prosecutor General noted that "Saakashvili exceeded his official powers by using violence and affronting human dignity of a victim, which caused substantial damage to the rights of individuals and legal entities, legitimate public and state interests."[54] Saakashvili and his allies called the charges a political witch hunt designed to destroy the opposition UNM. In June 2015, Saakashvili gave up his Georgian citizenship to avoid prison. He subsequently took the offer of Ukrainian citizenship from President Petro Poroshenko, and became the governor of the Odessa oblast until November 2016 in hopes that he could do for Odessa what he did for Georgia in terms of eliminating corruption and restoring confidence in state institutions.

Since then several prominent former officials, including former Defense Minister Bacho Akhalaia and former Interior Minister and Prime Minister Vano Merabishvili, have been brought to trial. Akhalaia was acquitted of subjecting special-forces personnel to torture or inhumane treatment, but still faced charges of beating prisoners in 2006 when he was in charge of the penitentiary system and the subsequent alleged torture of detainees in 2011.[55] Merabishvili received four and a half years in prison for exceeding his authority by condoning unnecessary violence during the dispersal by force of opposition demonstrators in Tbilisi in May 2011. As analysts noted, "he is also well-known for presiding over a range of alleged abuses, including an expansive surveillance apparatus, the frequent arrest of opposition members."[56] Merabishvili faces additional charges for the murder in 2006 by the Interior Ministry personnel of banker Sandro Girgvliani.[57]

Together with former Defense Minister David Kezerashvili, former Justice Minister Zurab Adeishvili, and former Tbilisi Mayor Gigi Ugulava, Merabishvili is charged jointly with Saakashvili in connection with the November 2007 crackdown on the opposition. Arrest warrants were issued in 2013 for Adeishvili. Ugulava was arrested in July 2014 at Tbilisi airport (he claimed he was not fleeing, but expected to return the next day) on suspicion of money-laundering and using budget funds to finance the UNM parliamentary election campaign in 2012. Ugulava's trial proved controversial as it often ignored provisions for pretrial detention. He received a four and a half years sentence in September 2015. These actions against former Saakashvili regime members did not go unnoticed outside the country. Criticism came from the United States, the EU, and NATO, urging the Georgia Dream government to avoid politically motivated prosecutions.[58] The government did not pull back, the more so since the prosecutor's office consulted with a number of foreign experts in criminal law.[59]

Not only were charges laid against top officials. As noted, many ordinary Georgian citizens expected both justice, and maybe restitution. Thousands of people came forward, but documentation was thin and proving crimes was difficult as many of the events had occurred in 2006. The governing coalition established the Commission on the Miscarriage of Justice, but lacked the resources to deal with the 20,000 cases it faced. With the Prime Minister promising cash payments to victims, the possibility of false claims was never far from anyone's mind.

In the end, very little was done to deal with Georgia's legacy of human rights abuses for Saakashvili or the Soviet crimes in a systematic way. A general amnesty released roughly 14,000 inmates from prison after the 2012 elections. Saakashvili, hanging on as president after the 2012 parliamentary election, called the former prisoners "Russian spies and coup plotters."[60] The new head of the Parliamentary Human Rights Committee called the prisoners Saakashvili's "personal convicts."[61] The move did undo some of the worst effects of the zero tolerance policy, and took pressure off the overcrowded prisons. However, even the amnesty procedure lacked seriousness as there was no rigorous screening procedure and it made no allowances for rehabilitation programs.

By contrast, the Georgia Dream coalition made serious headway in reforming Saakashvili's monstrous Interior Ministry and the judiciary with the aim of depoliticizing them both. The governing coalition promised to restore the independence of the Prosecutor's Office and to depoliticize law enforcement. The courts also changed in one simple way: they could examine on a case-by-case basis, instead of merely rubber stamping the decisions of the Prosecutor's Office. As such, judges began to exercise more independence from the executive. This meant that fewer people went to jail, bail was also improved with the judge taking into account the financial capacity of the defendant, jury selection was made more transparent, the previously dubious plea bargaining system disappeared, and judges were no longer merely passive observers but actively engaged particularly in ensuring that defendants knew their rights.[62] However, no screening or lustration process affected the judiciary, so judges and prosecutors who once collaborated with Saakashvili retained their jobs if they played by the new rules.

CONCLUSION

Georgia's story is both complicated and emblematic of transitional justice efforts in the FSU and elsewhere, especially the Balkans where the process often struggled and stalled. Inheriting a Soviet legacy and a very mixed attitude toward Stalin, postcommunist Georgia's domestic crisis meant that the past stayed largely untouched, beyond asserting the natural right of Georgian independence in the wake of the country's Soviet occupation in 1921. There was no serious effort at examining Georgia's Soviet experience. The very fact that the dissident Gamsakhurdia, who was eager to have serious transitional justice, was replaced by Shevardnadze, a former Politburo member and Foreign Minister of the FSU, says it all. Shevardnadze left the past in the past.

When Saakashvili took power in the Rose Revolution of 2003 he shook everything up, leaving behind a mixed legacy. He achieved some successes in state-building, charted Georgia's course away from the Russian sphere toward the EU and NATO, and his reforms created the very conditions that allowed for the peaceful transfer of power in 2012. These are undeniable accomplishments. His nation-building exercise also showed some gains by an attempt to frame Georgian identity as distinctively European.

His landmark projects, outside his war on corruption and police reform, included monuments going up and coming down, museums built, a reenergized and even edgy Tbilisi, and modest reassessments of the communist past insofar as it reinforced his anti-Russian narrative. It never really went much further than that even after the failed August 2008 war, Saakashvili had less success with his efforts to transform Gori and the Stalin Museum into a critical assessment of Stalin and Stalinism, and even less success with altering some of the fundamental beliefs held by most Georgians toward Stalin. Like many of his projects, transitional justice was half-baked and half-completed when he lost power. Saakashvili, as indicated by the destruction of the World War II memorial or the removal of Stalin's statue under the cover of darkness, only reinforced assumptions that he was not a true democrat – he was prone to monolog, not dialog. He was closer to Ataturk, his real role model, than Václav Havel.

In hoping to remake Georgia and assert its Europeanness, Saakashvili went too far. By choosing a revolution from above after a revolution from below in 2003, he laid the groundwork for his own subsequent undoing. His heavy-handed methods, zero-tolerance policy, and climate of fear meant that when he lost power Georgians needed transitional justice for the very recent past, as well as the Soviet past. A small and poor state like Georgia could hardly manage both projects. The zero-tolerance policy, which filled Georgia's prisons, led to an unprecedented crisis as there were far too many people in jail under dubious circumstances. As the Gldani videos made clear, the prisons were violent and nasty places. Georgia's current justice concerns loomed large and in some ways may be even larger than its transitional justice concerns.

The Georgian Dream government did its best to adequately deal with the abuses of the recent Saakashvili regime, but never in a systematic way despite the fact that this was something the people genuinely wanted. They provided amnesty for thousands of prisoners, freed up the courts from political influence, and arrested roughly 200 officials. However, there was no political will for real and comprehensive compensation and rehabilitation of victims, along the lines of a truth and reconciliation commission. The economy and health-care proved more important. Stalin and Stalinism were even further from the government's agenda. Georgia needed transitional justice for two periods: the deep or Soviet past and the recent past. The Georgian Dream government decided that while the recent past deserved attention, the deep past did not. It seemed fair to conclude that while they were willing to provide a new narrative for the Saakashvili years, they were not prepared to do the same for the Soviet period.

Notes

1. Thomas de Waal, *The Caucasus: An Introduction* (Oxford: Oxford University Press, 2010), 164.
2. Ibid., 142.
3. Alexander Kapatadze, "Georgia's Break with the Past," *Journal of Democracy* 26, 1 (2016): 110.
4. De Waal, *The Caucasus*, 189.

5. Lincoln A. Mitchell, "Compromising Democracy: State-building in Saakashvili's Georgia," *Central Asian Survey* 28 (2009): 172.
6. S. Neil MacFarlane, "Post-Revolutionary Georgia On the Edge?" Briefing paper for Chatham House, March 2011, 8, available at: www.chathamhouse.org/sites/files/ chathamhouse/public/Research/Russia%20and%20Eurasia/bp0311_macfarlane .pdf, accessed November 2, 2016.
7. Mitchell, "Compromising Democracy," 175.
8. Gavin Slade, "Georgia's Prisons: Roots of Scandal," *Open Democracy*, September 24, 2012, available at: www.opendemocracy.net/gavin-slade/georgias-prisons-roots-of-scandal, accessed October 23, 2016.
9. Kapatadze, "Georgia's Break with the Past," 113.
10. Matthew Light, "Police Reforms in the Republic of Georgia: The Convergence of Domestic and Foreign Policy in an Anti-Corruption Drive," *Policing and Society* 24, 3 (2014): 324.
11. Ajaria, in the southwest of the country, emerged as a kind of one-man fiefdom under Shevardnadze. Saakashvili managed to remove the local leader and restore Tbilisi's control. See de Waal, *The Caucasus*, 196.
12. Mitchell, "Compromising Democracy," 178.
13. Henry E. Hale, "25 Years After the USSR: What's Gone Wrong?," *Journal of Democracy* 27, 2 (2016): 26.
14. Kapatadze, "Georgia's Break with the Past," 115.
15. Charles H. Fairbanks Jr. and Alexi Gugashvili, "A New Chance for Georgian Democracy," *Journal of Democracy* 24, 1 (2013): 118.
16. MacFarlane, "Post-Revolutionary Georgia On the Edge?" 9.
17. *Crime and Excessive Punishment: The Prevalence and causes of Human Rights Abuse in Georgia's Prisons* (Tbilisi: Open Society Georgia Foundation, 2014), iv.
18. Gavin Slade and Alexander Kupatadze. "The Failed 'Mental Revolution': Georgia, Crime and Criminal Justice," *openDemocracy*, October 1, 2014, available at: www .opendemocracy.net/gavin-slade-alexander-kupatadze/failed-mental-revolution-georgia-crime-and-criminal-justice, accessed October 23, 2016.
19. Anna Dolidze and Thomas de Waal, "A Truth Commission for Georgia," *Carnegie Europe*, December 5, 2012, available at: http://carnegieeurope.eu/2012/12/05/truth-commission-for-georgia-pub-50249, accessed October 1, 2016.
20. MacFarlane, "Post-Revolutionary Georgia On the Edge?" 13.
21. Michael Cecire, "Georgia's 2012 Elections and Lessons for Democracy Promotion," *Orbis* 57, 2 (2013): 236.
22. Lasha Bakradze, "Georgia and Stalin: Still Living with the Great Son of the Nation," Rpt. in *The Stalin Puzzle: Deciphering Post-Soviet Public Opinion* (Washington: Carnegie Endowment for International Peace, 2013), 53.
23. De Waal, *The Caucasus*, 71.
24. Ibid., 81.
25. George Tarkhan-Mouravi, "70 years of Soviet Georgia," January 19, 1997, available at: http://rolfgross.dreamhosters.com/Texts/KandA-Web/Giahistory.htm, accessed November 29, 2016.
26. Malkhas Toria, "The Soviet Occupation of Georgia in 1921 and the Russian-Georgian War of August 2008: Historical Analogy as a Memory Project," in

Stephen Jones, ed., *The Making of Modern Georgia, 1918–2012* (London: Routledge, 2014), 316–35.
27. Bakradze, "Georgia and Stalin," 59.
28. Ibid.
29. Ibid., 47.
30. Ibid., 48.
31. Ibid., 49.
32. Ibid.
33. Ibid., 50.
34. Toria, "The Soviet Occupation of Georgia," 324.
35. Natia Kuprashvili, "Georgians Finally Topple Stalin," *The Messenger* (Tbilisi), No. 28, July 7, 2010, 7.
36. Ibid.
37. Nina Gachava, "Georgian President Blasted Over Monument's Demolition," *Radio Free Europe/Radio Liberty*, December 21, 2009, available at: www.rferl.org/a/Georgian_President_Blasted_Over_Monuments_Demolition/1910056.html, accessed November 11, 2016.
38. Nanci Adler, "The Future of the Soviet Past Remains Unpredictable: The Resurrection of Stalinist Symbols Amidst the Exhumation of Mass Graves," *Europe-Asia Studies* 57, 8 (2005): 1096.
39. Ibid.
40. Katrine Bendtsen Gotfredsen, "Void Pasts and Marginal Presents: On Nostalgia and Obsolete Futures in the Republic of Georgia," *Slavic Review* 73, 2 (2014): 255.
41. Bakradze, "Georgia and Stalin," 51.
42. Ibid., 52.
43. Ibid.
44. Ibid., 53.
45. "Ivanishvili Loses Court Case over Georgian Citizenship," *Civil.ge*, December 27, 2011, available at: www.civil.ge/eng/article.php?id=24309, accessed November 23, 2016.
46. Cecire, "Georgia's 2012 Election and Lessons for Democracy Promotion," 238.
47. Ibid.
48. *Crime and Excessive Punishment: The Prevalence and causes of Human Rights Abuse in Georgia's Prisons.*
49. Thomas de Waal, "So Long, Saakashvili," *Foreign Affairs*, 29 October (2013), available at: www.foreignaffairs.com/articles/russia-fsu/2013-10-29/so-long-saakashvili, accessed November 7, 2016.
50. Lincoln A. Mitchell, "Duelling Narratives: Storytelling and Spin in Georgia," *World Affairs* 176, 3 (2013): 2.
51. Dolidze and de Waal, "A Truth Commission for Georgia," available at: http://carnegieeurope.eu/2012/12/05/truth-commission-for-georgia-pub-50249, accessed November 28, 2016.
52. Ibid.
53. Robert C. Austin, "Transitional Justice as Electoral Politics," in Lavinia Stan and Nadya Nedelsky, eds., *Post-Communist Transitional Justice: Lessons from 25 Years of Experience* (New York: Cambridge University Press, 2015), 30–50.

54. "Georgia Modifies Charges against Ex-officials Including Saakashvili," *Democracy and Freedom Watch*, March 14, 2015, available at: http://dfwatch.net/georgia-modifies-charges-against-five-ex-officials-including-saakashvili-34314, accessed November 28, 2016.

55. "Interior Ministry Remains Georgian Government's Achilles Heel," *RFE/RL*, June 2013, available at: www.rferl.org/a/georgia-interior-ministry-achilles-heel/25005620.html, accessed December 3, 2016.

56. Sam Patten and Michael Cicere, "Victors' Justice in Georgia?" *The National Interest*, December 7, 2012, available at: http://nationalinterest.org/commentary/victors-justice-georgia-7817, accessed November 3, 2016.

57. Ibid.

58. "NATO Warns Georgia against Political Persecution of Ex-officials," *Reuters*, June 27, 2013, available at: http://uk.reuters.com/article/uk-georgia-nato-idUKBRE95Q0WQ20130627, accessed December 3, 2016.

59. These included "British barrister Sir Geoffrey Nice, who led The Hague tribunal prosecution of former Yugoslav president Slobodan Milošević; former Israeli state prosecutor Moshe Lador, who indicted ex-president of Israel Moshe Katzav and former PM Ehud Olmert, and Paul Coffey, former director of the UN Mission in Kosovo (UNMIK) department of justice and formerly chief of the organized crime and racketeering section of the U.S. Department of Justice." "Prosecutors Invite Foreign Experts to Help in Handling 'Politically Sensitive Cases'," *Civil.ge*, July 24, 2014, available at: www.civil.ge/eng/article.php?id=27516, accessed November 7, 2016.

60. "Georgia Begins Freeing Political Prisoners Under Amnesty," *Deutsche Welle*, January 13, 2013, available at: www.dw.com/en/georgia-begins-freeing-political-prisoners-under-amnesty/a-16518706, accessed November 28, 2016.

61. Ibid.

62. Tinatin Avaliani, *Results of Pre-Year Trial Monitoring Project: Initial Problems, Changes in Trends, and Existing Challenges* (Tbilisi: Georgian Young Lawyers' Association, 2014).

12

Transitional Justice Lessons from Moldova

Lavinia Stan

Among the successor republics of the Former Soviet Union (FSU), Moldova unjustly remains an understudied case, largely ignored by transitional justice scholars. There is to date no single case or comparative study speaking at length about this small independent republic of only 3.5 million people. The lack of attention stems from the dearth of scholars with intimate knowledge of Moldovan realities, the country's unimportance relative to its neighbors (Ukraine and Romania), the prolonged frozen conflict between Moldova and the secessionist region of Transnistria, and postcommunist Moldova's wavering record of reckoning with the recent past. Nevertheless, I argue that the study of the Republic of Moldova could shed light on important topics relevant for transitional justice scholarship and practice.

To make this argument, this chapter discusses the main ways in which the Moldovan case can further our knowledge of transitional justice and of the need to address multiple sets of human rights violations perpetrated by different state structures at various times. The focus here is on the questions arising, insights gained, and lessons learned from the study of this neglected country. As such, this analysis offers neither a comprehensive overview of the pasts that post-Soviet Moldova sought to redress after gaining independence in 1991, nor an in-depth analysis of the transitional justice methods and programs that it pursued until 2016. While I appreciate the need for such descriptive progress reports, especially since none has been published to date, here I use the historical pasts and the postcommunist record as background for a more theoretical examination of what the Moldovan case can contribute to transitional justice scholarship.

MOLDOVA'S LAYERED PASTS

Moldova's controverted history resembles in many respects the history of other former Soviet republics, whose territories repeatedly shifted hands among different state structures and whose borders changed regardless and often in spite of the wishes and interests of the population residing within them. Empires and kingdoms ruled from afar – by leaders who often never set foot on Moldovan territory, and had little understanding of local needs or the desire to consider Moldovan interests in the pursuit of their policy agendas – asserted control over Moldovan towns and villages, only to be pushed back by other plundering occupation forces. The mixed make-up of the local population meant that foreign occupiers were not always seen with suspicion and were even sometimes welcomed as liberators.

In 1812, the river Prut became a state border separating communities that belonged to the Principality of Moldova, by then a vassal of the Ottoman Empire. That same year, the Ottomans recognized the de facto situation on the ground and ceded Moldova to the Russians, whose military forces had already occupied the territory. State-imposed assimilation through Russification of the local Romanian-speaking population started in 1828, and was accompanied by a sharp erosion of local autonomy and a dramatic decrease of Romanian speakers from 86 percent in 1816 to 52 percent in 1905.[1] Those policies, diligently enacted by the Russian authorities for nine decades, remain a sour point for Romanian speakers even today.

Prut ceased to serve as a state border in 1918, when the Moldovan Parliament voted for independence from Bolshevik-controlled Russia and unification with the neighboring kingdom of Romania. While cheered by the Romanian speakers, the unification (which was less a marriage between equals than a take-over by the Romanian state of the politically weaker and economically backward province) became a point of contention for the Russian-speakers, who by then accounted for almost half of Moldova's population. Romania's discrimination of ethnic, linguistic, and religious groups in Moldova – which included the Romanianization of local groups and the allotment of some of the best local bureaucratic and academic jobs to Romanians brought from other regions – left the impression that the tightly centralized government in Bucharest considered none of them, not even Moldova's Romanian-speakers, an equal partner.

Another layer of grievances was added during and after World War II. In 1940, Romania ceded Moldova to the Soviet Union. By then, Stalin's Great Terror had already ended, but Soviet authorities engaged in other crimes on Moldovan territory. Some 136 individuals branded as traitors of the Soviet Union for collaborating with the Romanian authorities were killed in 1940–1. Moreover, Romanian-speakers were barred from Moldovan Communist Party leadership positions, and thousands of Moldovan citizens were deported to Central Asia in 1941.[2] With the support of Nazi Germany, Romania reoccupied Moldova in 1941, but lost it again in 1944, this time for good. The brief Romanian control of Moldova was memorable in the number of rights violations committed by the fascist state of Marshall Ion Antonescu. The Romanian authorities deported 300,000 Jews, including 147,000 from Moldova, to Transnistrian camps, where 90,000 of them met their death in squalid conditions.[3] The Romanianization legislation passed by the Antonescu regime was enforced on Moldovan territory, affecting other non-Romanian groups. Local Ukrainians were particularly affected by these policies, which also closed down some of their schools and allowed for the nationalization of land.

Under the Soviet occupations of 1940–1 and 1944–91, Moldova registered new rights violations. In 1940, for the first time Moldova was brought together with Transnistria, formerly a Ukrainian land with few Romanian-speakers, into the Moldovan Soviet Socialist Republic. The amalgamation ensured that the Romanian- and Russian-speakers accounted for equal percentages of the Soviet republic's population, thus eroding Romanian-speakers' claims to a special status. Subsequent economic policies made Transnistria home to Soviet Moldova's industrial complex, while agriculture remained predominant in other parts of the republic where Romanian-speakers formed the majority. Russification reversed the legacy of Romanianization, closed down schools in Romanian, and ensured that leadership positions went to Russian-speakers. Soviet crimes affected Moldovans in a number of ways: 40,500 Moldovans were killed after being drafted into the Soviet army in 1944; 60,000 local residents were deported to Siberia and Central Asia; over 8,300 executions and numerous political arrests resulted in at least 216,000 deaths; 350,000 cases of dystrophy resulted from the 1946–7 famine; anticommunist resistance groups were executed or deported in 1944–53; and pro-independence activists were imprisoned during the 1970s and the 1980s.[4] Additionally, the KGB placed many Moldovan citizens under tight surveillance, recruiting others as secret informers.

A new set of rights violations were perpetrated after Moldova gained independence from the Soviet Union in 1991. The new state included Transnistria, whose historical ties to Moldova were weak, and where Russian-speakers accounted for a majority of the 0.5 million residents. The Romanian-speakers' vocal support for unification with Romania, and the absence of strong guarantees for the protection of minority rights, prompted Transnistria to break away from Moldova and to ask Moscow for support. Moldovan efforts to bring Transnistria back into its fold led to military conflict in 1992, which subsequently became an unsolved frozen conflict. Transnistria remains unrecognized by the United Nations, and therefore is absent from official maps. River Nistru, which separates Transnistria from the rest of Moldova, is de facto a state border, preventing Moldovan authorities from exercising effective control over the breakaway region. Thus, after 1991 the record of human rights abuses has expanded to include an undetermined number of casualties on both sides resulted from the 1992 military war, and the abuses perpetrated after the war by the Transnistrian authorities, which have imposed a dictatorial one-party state embellished with communist symbols and supported militarily by the former Soviet fourteenth Army (currently part of the Russian army). Over the years, Transnistrian agents have been accused of conducting illegal kidnappings, arrests, beatings, and torture of religious minorities and Moldovans critical of the breakaway regime or the Russian military presence in the territory.[5]

In sum, postcommunist Moldova has had to reckon with multiple recent pasts, one more brutal than the other. Many of the victims and victimizers of earlier abuses (Romanianization and Stalinist crimes) have long been dead, the memory of their suffering or impunity being forgotten or seen as secondary in importance to the pressing political, social, and economic problems that plague the republic today. Many of the victims and victimizers of more recent abuses (of late communism or the war with Transnistria) are among the estimated 615,000 who work abroad.[6]

AN OVERVIEW OF POST-1991 REDRESS EFFORTS

Transitional justice efforts in Moldova have included a combination of failed and limited programs enacted by state and/or civil society actors that have delivered little truth, justice, or redress. This section summarizes some of the main efforts aimed at dealing with the multiple pasts, whose legacies have impacted the independent republic. This summary speaks about rehabilitation and compensation, lustration, access to the KGB archives, rewriting of history textbooks, the presidential history commission, the use of communist symbols, and the presence of statues of communist leaders in public spaces. It does not touch on court trials, since no former prison guard or Communist Party leaders were indicted for human rights abuses in post-Soviet Moldova. This section ends with a short description of the very limited reckoning efforts made to date in Transnistria.

Rehabilitation, Compensation, and Restitution

Rehabilitation and compensation for lost property were among the first transitional justice policies pursued in Moldova, even before independence. On April 10, 1989, the Council of Ministers of Soviet Moldova annulled its decision of 1949 on the deportation of *kulaks* (wealthy farmers) and former landowners wronged by the Stalinist regime. After the collapse of the Soviet regime this modest rehabilitation program was expanded by Law 1225 on the Rehabilitation of Political Victims of December 8, 1992, which benefited all those deported, arrested or executed by the Soviet regime until 1991. Survivors received a monthly pension of 200 Moldovan Lei, which was equivalent to only 16 US dollars but represented a significant burden for the republic's impoverished budget.[7]

In June 2006, legal amendments entitled all political victims of the Soviet regime to receive compensation for dwellings abusively nationalized before 1991. Former victims criticized the shortage of funds, the payment of some compensation packages in installments over a five-year period, and the resistance of the local authorities to disburse compensation.[8] The program got an unexpected injection of additional funds in April 2009, when the ruling Party of Communists for the first time reached out to the former victims in part to prevent an electoral loss. Some 13 million Lei (equivalent to 1 million US dollars) were earmarked for Stalinist victims, but victims of post-1953 rights violations received nothing. Overall, the rehabilitation and compensation programs have failed to satisfy former victims.

Postcommunist Moldova did not allow for the wide restitution in kind of dwellings, community centers or industrial buildings, thus placing many citizens and religious groups at a disadvantage. Among the few exceptions was the Choral synagogue in Chisinau, nationalized in 1940 and returned after 1991. Gorbachev's policies did not affect the ownership of land, which remained with the collectives from the early 1950s until 1991. After independence, agricultural land was transferred from the state to individuals, some but not all former owners and their descendants. Families residing in rural areas gained ownership of small plots of up to 0.75 hectares. This meant that some land went to families who had no ownership rights before collectivization, but lived in rural areas at the time the land allocation took place. The distorted policy left former owners with nothing, if they had moved to urban areas or emigrated. By 1999, 344,500 hectares had been transferred to private hands in this program.[9] The Land Code of 1991 and the Law on Peasant Farms of 1992 further slighted former owners, who were denied restitution of the land belonging to the cooperatives in favor of the workers, peasants, and administrative staff working for the cooperatives.[10] Thus, these land privatization programs were not based on the principle of restitution.

Lustration and Access to Secret Files

Since 1991 several lustration proposals have been publicly discussed, but none has been approved by parliament, although the political and managerial elite inherited by independent Moldova was mostly non-Romanian and drawn from among the former Soviet elite. As the Moldovan Intelligence Service head admitted in the 1990s, "if the lustration law will be adopted, the Moldovan parliament might remain without MPs."[11] Moldova needed lustration to renew its postcommunist elites, but the war in Transnistria and the region's de facto secession put a lid on such demands during the 1990s.

Moldova was the first of the FSU republics to debate a lustration proposal, introduced in parliament in 2000 by deputies representing the Popular Christian Democratic Party. The proposal banned former secret agents from the presidency, parliament, cabinet, the judiciary, and mass-media, and offered Moldovan citizens access to their NKVD and KGB files. In presenting the bill, Christian Democrat deputy Stefan Secareanu lamented the fact that former spies were "in control of [important] economic sectors" and were "blackmailing" politicians with a tainted past.[12] Secareanu's remark was confirmed on May 31, 2001, when the Party of Communists parliamentary majority rejected the bill that would have put a stop to the political careers of many of its members. After the vote, Christian Democrat leader Iurie Rosca argued that self-identification of former KGB agents was better than no identification at all, but this sort of unofficial confession-based lustration was not embraced by other Moldovan politicians.[13]

In 2005, lustration became the focus of a public debate in which 200 local political and intellectual luminaries evaluated its pros and cons. The majority of the respondents criticized lustration and defended Soviet-era secret collaboration as a patriotic act. Another feeble attempt to bring lustration back on the public agenda was made in 2015, when the independent Political Criminality Forum announced its intention to submit a draft law that targeted officials involved in both Soviet-era repression and Transnistrian separatism.[14] That promise was never fulfilled. It is generally accepted in Moldova that lack of lustration allowed the old communist elites to retain their political and economic clout, and to create a veritable mafia diverting public assets for their own private gain.[15]

Part of the difficulty in enacting lustration is the fact that Moldova inherited few KGB archives, as the majority of the secret collections were moved in 1991 either to Transnistria or to Moscow. This deprived Moldova of the most important method of identifying former secret informers and their victims.[16] The few KGB collections left in the republic were kept under lock and key until the mid-2000s, thus Moldovans accused of past collaboration with the KGB cannot refute those claims, while journalists and state agencies have no evidence to unmask former secret agents.[17] Some 3,000 KGB files were moved to the National Archives in 2009, and 20,000 others were processed for transfer in 2015.[18]

In 2010, the presidential Commission for the Study of the Communist Dictatorship in Moldova (discussed below) gained limited access to the 70,000–80,000 former KGB files housed with the Moldovan Information and Security Service, and the 100,000–170,000 files at the Ministry of Interior.[19] According to Moldovan law, communist-era documents remain closed for twenty-five years, but it is unclear whether that is measured from the moment they are produced or archived.[20] The Ministry of Interior and the Information and Security Service have used this legal provision to progressively tighten access to the archives, and keep extant post-Stalinist documents inaccessible.[21] Even more important is the fact that access was never extended outside a narrow group of historians to ordinary citizens once placed under surveillance by the Soviet authorities. In this sense, Moldova still lacks a true policy on access to the secret files.

Rewriting History Textbooks

During Soviet times, schools in Moldova offered "History of the Moldavian SSR" as a compulsory subject in grades 7 to 10. The course taught students about the "common Soviet past" Moldova shared with other republics, more than the history of the Moldovan people or Moldovan lands (which were intrinsically linked with Romania). Since 1991, writing history for preuniversity students has pitted the so-called "unionists" against the "Moldovenists."[22] The former group wants history textbooks to talk about the common past shared by Moldova and Romania and to bear the title "History of Romanians." Such textbooks were introduced in schools for grades 5 to 9 in 1995. The latter want to impose an "integrated" "History of Moldova" that focuses on the accomplishments of the communist period, ignores Moldova's links to Romania, and claims that Moldovan and Romanian identities are distinct. Both groups have sought acceptance with the Ministry of Education, whose approval is needed for textbooks to reach schools. In 2011, the Ministry added fuel to the debate by soliciting proposals for textbooks that would bear the title "History."[23]

After forming the government in 2001, the Party of Communists tried to replace "History of the Romanians" with textbooks that denied historical ties with Romania and fostered a distinct Moldovan identity similar to the one promoted by the Soviets. It also reintroduced Russian as a compulsory subject in primary schools throughout Moldova. These efforts ignored the wishes of significant segments of the population and the main professional associations of historians, and therefore were met with prolonged and massive street protests in the capital Chisinau. Nevertheless, the Party of Communists was bent on promoting a version of history that legitimized its claim to power, and undermined its political enemies.

In 2002, the communist-dominated government replaced "History of Romanians" with "History of Moldovans," which in turn was abandoned in favor of "Integrated History." In 2006, the Ministry of Education introduced "Integrated History," without consulting historians, teachers, parents, or the general public. The textbooks have been heavily criticized for their factual errors and erroneous interpretation. The ninth and twelfth grade textbooks, in particular, include numerous photos of and citations from communist leaders, prompting critics to suggest that the rewriting of history textbooks has been used by the ruling Party of Communists (and the Minister of Education) for electoral purposes. The "unionist" school teachers have apparently continued to use the revised history textbooks in defiance of the Ministry's order.[24] The textbook war is unlikely to conclude anytime soon.

The History Commission

The Commission for the Study of the Communist Dictatorship in Moldova was styled after its Romanian counterpart, deliberately ignoring the Baltic precedent. The Moldovan commission shares some characteristics with the Presidential Commission for the Study of the Communist Dictatorship in Romania.[25] The Moldovan commission was a presidential body with no subpoena powers because legislators of the Party of Communists and other political formations disputed its creation. It had to investigate two broad historical periods (1940–1 and 1944–91) that spanned both Stalinist and later Soviet crimes. It had little time at its disposal, being asked to report back to an active president who was to be replaced within a year. More importantly, the Moldovan commission looked at Soviet crimes in isolation from the crimes of fascist Romania, Transnistria, or postcommunist Moldova. As such, it was a history body focusing mostly on archival material, not a truth commission collecting testimonials from victims or helping victims to reconcile with victimizers.

In addition, the Moldovan commission included no international members, and no representatives of the "victimizing" groups (the Russian-speakers, the former KGB agents, or the former Communist Party leaders). Its outreach activities were rather limited; tellingly, its first major conference was organized in Bucharest, not Chisinau. The commission branded the Soviet regime as an unlawful occupation regime, thus appropriating the terms employed by its Baltic counterparts and ignoring the position of Moldova's Russian-speakers, who believe the term is unjust. In contrast to the Romanian commission, the Moldovan body was shunned by the Moldovan Parliament, which refused to acknowledge or discuss the commission's work. It also failed to produce a final report, drafting instead a sixteen-page executive summary that was heavily corrected and amended by President Mihai Ghimpu. The Moldovan commission inspired no similar effort in other countries, and facilitated no further transitional justice progress in Moldova (leading to no condemnation of communist crimes, as was the case in Romania). It is thus not surprising that truth commission experts regard the Moldovan body as a failed commission (see Bakiner in this volume).

Memorialization Efforts

As other former Soviet states, Moldova had a multitude of communist symbols in its public spaces: names of streets, parks, and schools, as well as statues and monuments. Some communist symbols remained present well after the collapse of the Soviet Union. As late as 2012, communist symbols still elicited vigorous debates between those who wanted them removed from public sight and those who wanted them to stay. A report released that year talked about the fate of statues of Lenin, which in villages like Riscani were removed by anticommunist mayors only to be reinstalled later by mayors representing the Party of Communists. The report argued that the statues no longer represented communist symbols that inspired political action or ideological preferences, but rather had been reduced to the level of touristic attractions similar to any other museum pieces.[26] Such a view does not seem to be embraced by Moldovan politicians, who still believe that public symbols, such as street names, statues, and monuments, influence the way in which citizens conceive of their political regimes. The debates led to the adoption on July 12, 2012 of Law 192, which the Venice Commission criticized for banning the propaganda of "totalitarian regimes" without clearly identifying which regime it referred to.[27] The law was aimed at the Party of Communists, which unapologetically retained communist symbols (the hammer and sickle) in its electoral campaigns, and tried to rehabilitate Joseph Stalin and Vladimir Lenin as positive figures in the history of Moldova.

As in other countries, in Moldova memorialization also extended to efforts to revamp old museums and exhibitions and open new ones. In November 2012, for example, the National Museum of Archeology and History in Chisinau included a permanent exhibition that presented the Romanian kingdom as a benevolent ruler responsible for great prosperity, and Russia as an evil occupation regime. The smaller temporary exhibitions on "Gulag" and "Soviet Moldova between Myths and Gulag" were found wanting in terms of their content, which consisted mostly of Lenin statues more than artifacts attesting to rights violations.[28] The Jewish Heritage of Moldova Museum, also in

Chisinau, offers information about the Holocaust, pogroms, and Jewish life on Moldovan territory.

Transitional Justice in Transnistria

The Transnistrian authorities see Moldova and Romania as the main aggressors, Russia as its protector, and Soviet times as the golden age of unparalleled prosperity and ethnic harmony. As such, Transnistria has made little efforts to reckon with the crimes of a regime it never condemned. Instead, funding was allocated to the Museum of Genocide allegedly committed against the Transnistrian people by the Moldovan government in the 1992 war. The museum is located in Bender town. The History Museum in Tiraspol has a Lenin statue at its main entrance. In 2012, it included two exhibitions on the "Defenders of Transnistria" and "Tiraspol is 220 year old," both united by photos of President Igor Smirnov (1990–2011) and the soldiers who died in the 1992 war.[29] Russian is the working language in all these museums.

In Transnistria, schools use Russian history textbooks that are written in Russian and claim that the region was never part of Romania historically, a point that boosts the region's claim to independence.[30] The two Transnistrian textbooks – *World History* and *History of the Fatherland* – make no mention of Soviet human rights abuses, Transnistria's common history with Moldova, or the persecution of the Romanians, the breakaway region's largest ethnic group. A hammer and a sickle are incorporated into the Transnistrian flag and its coats of arms, and its public spaces are littered with communist symbols.

Since 2015, foreign nongovernmental organizations like The Causeway Institute for Peace-Building and Conflict Resolution have tried to facilitate a process of reconciliation between Moldova and Transnistria by using the success of the Northern Ireland example. Discussions have not led to significant results, either because not enough time has passed since they were started, or because Moldova and Transnistria have remained reluctant partners.[31]

TRANSITIONAL JUSTICE LESSONS FROM MOLDOVA

There are several important lessons that can be gleaned by looking closely at the case of Moldova. Let me detail what I consider the three most important, noting that the list detailed in this section is far from comprehensive. These lessons relate to the difficulty of pursuing a transitional justice agenda in situations where multiple states must share responsibility for redress, identity politics is too tightly linked to reckoning initiatives and programs, and/or transitional justice is instrumentalized by political actors, especially unreformed communists opposed to any acknowledgment of past rights violations.

Multistate Responsibility for Redress

As the previous section explained, varied crimes were perpetrated at different times on the territory of Moldova by the authorities of four, often inimical, states – Moldovan, Transnistrian, Romanian, and Soviet/Russian. However, the governments of Romania, Russia, and Transnistria have been largely unwilling to atone for their past crimes, preferring instead either to reject or to deflect attention from their responsibility for rights violations.

In Romania, the final reports of the Commission for the Study of the Communist Dictatorship in Romania (active in 2016) and of the International Commission on the Holocaust in Romania (active in 2003–4) mentioned some crimes committed in Moldova against Romanian-speakers by the Soviet regime and against Jews by the Romanian fascist authorities. Beyond that, the Romanian state has been unwilling to revisit in full the crimes of the fascist regime and the legacy of Romanianization, partly because it has tended to see Romania as a victim more than a victimizer in relation to Moldova. For a multitude of reasons, Bucharest has embraced the view that granting Romanian (and by extension European Union) citizenship to Moldovans is sufficient compensation for any past wrongs they and their families might have suffered at the hands of the Romanian state. That many former victims (especially Jews, Ukrainians, and Moldovan citizens who emigrated elsewhere) are overlooked by this scheme remains a point that none in Romania talk about.

The Russian and Transnistrian authorities have denied Soviet crimes and preferred to shift attention from the suffering of Romanian-speakers to postcommunist Moldova's discrimination against Russian-speakers. For them, discrimination refers to all policies meant to erase the disadvantage to which Romanian-speakers had been placed during Soviet times (such as the introduction of Romanian language instruction in Moldovan schools and recognition of Romanian as the official language). Both claim to be successors of the Soviet Union, and both selectively acknowledge only the few Soviet achievements in Moldovan territories, insist that Soviet troops "liberated" not "occupied" Moldova, and ignore or even deny the large number of rights abuses perpetrated during Soviet times. Russia and Transnistria have further rejected responsibility for the casualties and property destruction of the 1992 war, although their military involvement in the war is well documented. In addition, both Russia and Transnistria have adopted legislation that aims at countering any critical assessment of the Soviet past. For example, on June 27, 2016

Transnistrian authorities adopted a law that banned criticism of the Russian Army in the breakaway territory, and encouraged an emphasis on its "positive" role.[32] Both Russia and Transnistria continue to refuse access to the secret KGB files compiled on Moldovan citizens that are housed in their territories.

In sum, unwillingness on the part of Transnistria, Romania, and Russia to revisit past crimes for which they are responsible has meant that the Moldovan state and nonstate actors could rely on little, if any, outside support for efforts to right such a complex layered past. However, satisfying all victims and punishing all victimizers requires the involvement of all these states in the transitional justice process. The Moldovan Jews deported to the Transnistrian camps by the Romanian fascist authorities would want to hear from the Romanian state, as the successor of the fascist state. The victims of Stalinist deportations and their descendants, for example, would require an apology (even compensation) not only from the Moldovan government, but also from the Russian state, as the successor of the Soviet Union. Equally, identifying the state agents who organized and facilitated those deportations, and understanding their share of responsibility, would also require cooperation from the other states involved. However, that cooperation has not been forthcoming. Moreover, Russia has defended some perpetrators, including members of the fourteenth Soviet Army stationed in Transnistria.

The impossibility of reckoning with all pasts at the same time has prompted some in Moldova to challenge individual transitional justice programs and initiatives. For example, some historians criticized the presidential commission as a futile and incomplete exercise, because its mandate did not include an analysis of the crimes perpetrated by the Romanian fascist state on the Moldovan territory. These critics accuse all transitional justice efforts of being instrumentalized for political or electoral purposes (on this point, see more below). Nevertheless, a fair evaluation of these programs should take into account the limitations imposed by other states' refusals to admit responsibility. Thus, Moldova and other FSU republics raise a question of general relevance for transitional justice scholarship. When multiple states must share the burden of responsibility for a significant number of past rights' abuses, all national transitional justice programs will remain partial and limited in the absence of cooperation from the other states.

Identity Politics and Transitional Justice

Moldova further illustrates the perils of tying transitional justice too closely to identity politics. Indeed, in those territories the past is so complicated and multilayered that no ethnic, religious, or linguistic group was only a victim suffering at the hands of others or only a victimizer benefiting at the expense of others. The categories of victims and victimizers therefore overlap, each group having a past suffering for which it wants redress and another past as a perpetrator that it wants to downplay, or even hide.

Moldova's Romanian-speakers aligned themselves with the Romanian state authorities to perpetrate crimes against ethnic and religious minorities in the 1940s. Since 1991, their efforts to reverse Soviet Russification policies have made other Moldovan citizens feel like second-class citizens in their republic. At the same time, Moldova's Romanian-speakers were placed at a disadvantage by the Romanians from Romania, and suffered greatly under a Soviet regime that promoted Russian-speakers to positions of power and influence. Romanian-speakers registered additional casualties during the Transnistrian war, and those living in the secessionist region continue to face discrimination and persecution to this day. Similarly, Russian-speakers benefited from the Soviet Russification policies, which allowed them to access the best employment and education in the republic. After 1992, the Russian-speakers in Transnistria have imposed an authoritarian regime that is intolerant of minority groups, especially Romanian-speakers. At the same time that Russian-speakers take pride in the fact that they liberated Moldova from fascist Romania and helped the backward republic develop economically during Soviet times, they lament the casualties they registered in the Transnistrian war.

The transitional justice policies pursued by Romanian-speakers in Moldova, and politicians representing their interests, have often been premised on the need to redress that group's suffering. Accountability for involvement in past crimes was never factored in, as though the group engaged in no past violations. For example, rehabilitation, compensation, and the history commission were pursued largely because they could offer evidence of Romanian-speakers' suffering at the hands of the Soviets and Russian-speakers. Almost all calls for opening the secret archives have been directed to Russia and Transnistria, not to Romania, where documents about Romanianization and the Holocaust could be found. Romanian-speakers were not the only ones to prioritize their suffering over their involvement in past crimes. Russian-speakers have done the same, pursuing transitional justice policies only to the extent that they could unveil their suffering at the hand of the Romanian majority. While Romanian-speakers kept silent about Romanian responsibility for fascist crimes, Russian-speakers downplayed the crimes of the Soviet regime and Russia's involvement in the Transnistrian war.

This perpetual competition of reckoning projects proposed by Romanian- and Russian-speakers, and the parties that represent their interests (the most recent of which are the Alliance for European Integration and the Party of

Communists, respectively), has completely ignored the interests of other minority groups and of diaspora members, and has bred distrust among all these groups. In Moldova, for example, rewriting history textbooks has reinforced exclusivist narratives that underscore the group's suffering and the guilt of the others. The lesson here is not that alternative programs able to reshape narratives, debunk myths, encourage cooperation, and neutralize harmful elites should be promoted, but that such alternative programs would find very little support in a divided society where major groups see politics (and reckoning) as a zero-sum game. This is especially the case since no other country has ever implemented programs reaching all these goals at once. In spite of proposals coming from some transitional justice practitioners,[33] in the absence of foreign intervention, divided societies must first forge a common identity to even consider implementing alternative reckoning programs that could bridge the identity gap.

The Political Instrumentalization of Transitional Justice

Moldova exemplifies a danger well known to transitional justice scholars and practitioners: the use of reckoning programs by political actors for their narrow electoral interests. Indeed, since 1991 transitional justice has been pursued (or rejected) by various state actors not so much because they believed in the need to right past wrongs, but in the hope of undermining their political opponents and protecting their own electoral advantage. Examples can be offered of political parties situated on both sides of the political spectrum.

Take the left-wing Party of Communists, which dominated the Moldovan government until 2008. The Communist Party was outlawed in 1991 by the new political actors who advocated for independence and unification with Romania. The country's subsequent descent into war with Transnistria undermined the front's legitimacy, and bolstered support for the former Communist Party, which was resurrected as the Party of Communists in 1994. Its decisive win in the parliamentary elections of 2001 made Moldova the only post-Soviet state where unreformed communists returned to power. The party gained the largest number of votes in subsequent elections, making it a political force to be reckoned with, although its agenda asked for the re-creation of the Soviet Union. This point converged with the wishes of as many as 48.6 percent of Moldovans, who in 2009 regretted the disappearance of the former communist empire.[34] The same opinion survey showed that a clear majority of Moldovans believed that living standards, housing conditions, health care, education, order, and employment opportunities were better under the Soviet Union.

Nevertheless, the Party of Communists refused to investigate Soviet crimes less out of a desire to follow the popular mood than to protect its own interests. More radical transitional justice methods like lustration, court trials and access to the secret files by ordinary citizens would have affected their rank and file more than their political opponents. As the direct heir to the Soviet-era Communist Party, the Party of Communists had the largest number of members and leaders tainted by collaboration with the Soviet regime. Similarly, property and land restitution would have eroded their economic clout and benefited former owners and Romanian-speaking segments of the population, which more often than not voted for the anticommunist forces. Even the refusal to remove Soviet symbols from public spaces and an insistence in rehabilitating notorious Soviet killers like Stalin and Lenin stemmed from a desire to normalize Soviet crimes and block criticism of a regime the party had once dominated.

In 2010, a more coherent transitional justice program was embraced by a center-right pro-European (as well as anti-Russian and anticommunist) coalition government and facilitated by the resignation of President Vladimir Voronin, the Party of Communists leader. Senate Speaker Mihai Ghimpu, a supporter of the common Moldovan-Romanian identity, became Acting President. On January 14, 2010 Ghimpu created the Commission for the Study of the Communist Dictatorship in Moldova to analyze the responsibility of the Soviet regime in perpetrating crimes in Moldova. In June, he decreed 28 June as the Soviet Occupation Day, and unveiled a commemorative stone in Chisinau, Moldova's capital. Unfortunately, the Constitutional Court promptly revoked the festive day, the commission had mixed results, and a Monument to the Victims of Soviet Occupation is yet to replace the stone. These hastily adopted transitional justice agenda had few, if any, long-term effects and were unable to boost public support for reckoning, but all aimed at undermining the legitimacy of the Party of Communists, the government coalition's political enemy.

These two examples provide ample evidence that instrumentalization has deeply undermined even the very narrow transitional justice program this post-Soviet republic has implemented. Of course, a certain degree of instrumentalization is present in almost any country that enacts reckoning measures. But in the case of Moldova the unmediated and gross involvement of political actors has seriously undermined even the most honest transitional justice programs and institutions. Indeed, Moldova is one of the very few documented cases of failed commissions that ultimately are unable to produce a substantial final report, and possibly the only country where the politician who created the commission took it upon himself to write history to his liking by amending and correcting the brief executive summary the commission managed to produce. This direct involvement undermined the commission's activities even in the eyes of its supporters, and confirmed the worst fears of the unrepentant communists and their followers that the commission (and reckoning in general) was part of a political vendetta directed against them.

CONCLUSION

More than a quarter of a century after the collapse of the communist regime, no ethnic and linguistic group in Moldova seems willing to acknowledge itself as both victim and victimizer; instead, all groups claim redress for their suffering exclusively, ignoring the plight of all others. Due to the frozen military conflict with the break-away region of Transnistria, frequent squabbles among self-interested parties, social and political unrest generated by government corruption and mismanagement, escalating economic problems, deep divisions between Romanian- and Russian-speakers, and the lack of a common vision/ identity of Moldova as an independent state (from both Romania and Russia) have resulted in a country unable to pursue transitional justice coherently since it gained independence from the Soviet Union in 1991. As if this was not enough, political parties on both sides of the ideological spectrum have used, misused, and abused reckoning initiatives for their own narrow interests. Transitional justice, as a result, has been generally patchy, partial, and largely ineffective in righting the wrongs of Moldovia's many pasts.

Nevertheless, Moldova is far from representing a noncase, a country where no reckoning has been pursued, as the transitional justice literature seems to suggest. As this chapter demonstrates, Moldova resembles in many ways other FSU republics that started reassessing their past during the late 1980s, while the communist regime allowed a degree of openness and activism. True, those reckoning programs of rehabilitation, memorialization, and commemoration selectively prioritized the Stalinist past and ignored the human rights violations perpetrated by later Soviet leaders. To those programs, mostly but not all led by the civil society, a variety of timid state-led efforts were added after 1991. Unfortunately for Moldova, a new set of human rights abuses occurred in postcommunist times once Transnistria claimed its independence.

The Moldovan transitional justice record, while limited in scope, teaches us three important lessons with applicability to other settings in the FSU and beyond: the responsibility for past rights violations of multiple states that resist or refuse to engage in reckoning; the intricate relationship between national identity and transitional justice; and the resilience of political actors' attempts at instrumentalizing reckoning. Multiple states were involved in perpetrating violations on the territories of Estonia, Lithuania, and Latvia (which were subjected to Soviet and Nazi occupations), Ukraine (which endured abuses as a Soviet state and more recently after Russia occupied part of its territory), as well as Georgia, Armenia, and Azerbaijan (which faced wars with break-away regions after decades of Soviet abuses). Some of these issues are addressed in other chapters on Georgia's, Serbia's, Lithuania's, and Ukraine's layered transitional justice needs. Similarly, a host of other FSU republics are facing an identity crisis that divides their loyalty between Russia and Europe, with Ukraine and Belarus of particular note. Last, instrumentalization of transitional justice programs by self-interested politicians is another recurrent theme relevant in a number of the other countries discussed in this volume. In this way, Moldova speaks to many of the central themes associated with incomplete reckoning in the FSU.

Notes

1. Ion Nistor, *Istoria Basarabiei* (Bucharest: Humanitas, 1991).
2. Igor Casu, "Moldova under the Soviet Communist Regime: History and Memory," in Vladimir Tismaneanu and Bogdan Iacob, eds., *Remembrance, History and Justice: Coming to Terms with Traumatic Pasts in Democratic Societies* (Budapest: Central European University Press, 2015), 355.
3. Comisia Prezidentiala pentru Analiza Dictaturii Comuniste din Romania, *Raport Final*, Bucharest (2006), 748–9, available at: www.wilsoncenter.org/sites/default/files/RAPORT%20FINAL_%20CADCR.pdf, accessed February 5, 2017; and Stefan Cristian Ionescu, "'Californian' Colonists versus Local Profiteers? The Competition for Jewish Property during the Economic Colonization of Bukovina, 1941–1943," *Yad Vashem Studies* 44, 2 (2016): 121–46.
4. Comisia Prezidentiala pentru Analiza Dictaturii Comuniste din Romania, *Raport Final*, 747–52; Michael Ellman, "The 1947 Soviet Famine and the Entitlement Approach to Famines," *Cambridge Journal of Economics* 39, 24 (2000): 603–30; "Political Repressions in the Moldavian Soviet Socialist Republic after 1956: Towards a Typology Based on KGB files Igor Casu," *Dystopia* I, 1–2 (2014): 89–127.
5. US Department of State, *Moldova*, March 6, 2007, available at: www.state.gov/j/drl/rls/hrrpt/2006/78828.htm, accessed February 5, 2017.
6. Data from 2012. See Migration Policy Center, *Moldova*, June 2013, available at: www.migrationpolicycentre.eu/docs/migration_profiles/Moldova.pdf, accessed February 13, 2017.
7. "Lege nr. 1225 privind reabilitarea victimelor represiunilor politice," December 8, 1992, available at: http://lex.justice.md/index.php?action=view&view=doc&id=313312, accessed March 4, 2017.
8. Casu, "Moldova under the Soviet Communist Regime," 366.
9. Matthew Gordon, "Agricultural Land Reform in Moldova," no date, p. 9, available at: www.staff.ncl.ac.uk/matthew.gorton/moldlandpapers.pdf, accessed February 12, 2017.

10. Ibid.
11. Institute of World Policy, *How to Get Rid of Post-Sovietness?* (Kyiv: Institute of World Policy, 2012), 102.
12. "Moldovan Parliament Rejects Lustration Bill," *RFE/RL Newsline*, June 1, 2001.
13. For further details, see Lavinia Stan, ed., *Transitional Justice in Eastern Europe and the Former Soviet Union* (London: Routledge, 2009), 222–46.
14. "Experts: Moldova Must Adopt Lustration Law," *Teleradio Moldova*, January 9, 2015, available at: www.trm.md/en/politic/experti-moldova-trebuie-sa-adopte-legea-lustratiei/, accessed February 5, 2017.
15. Declaration of Iurie Rosca, cited in "Georgia, Moldova and Bulgaria: Dismantling Communist Structures Is Hardly Extremism. Interview with Irina Sarishvili-Chanturia, Iurie Rosca and Philip Dimitrov," *Demokratizatsiya*, November 23, 2001, 318, available at: www2.gwu.edu/~ieresgwu/assets/docs/demokratizatsiya%20 archive/GWASHU_DEMO_12_2/P225677W77561736/P225677W77561736.pdf, accessed February 5, 2017.
16. "Georgia, Moldova and Bulgaria," 314.
17. See the *Petrenco v. Moldova* case at the European Court of Human Rights. James A. Sweeney, *The European Court of Human Rights in the Post-Cold War Era: Universality in Transition* (London: Routledge, 2013), 169.
18. Erin Hutchinson, "Central State and Party Archives in Chisinau, Moldova," February 16, 2015, available at: http://dissertationreviews.org/archives/11591, accessed February 12, 2017.
19. "Societatea trebuie să-şi cunoască trecutul, chiar dacă uneori doare şi e prea dur," *Timpul*, April 29, 2010, available at www.timpul.md/articol/societatea-trebuie-sa-si-cunoasca-trecutul-chiar-daca-uneori-doare-si-e-prea-dur-9992.html; and "Hundreds of thousands of cases to be examined by commission for combating Communism," *Moldova Azi*, January 18, 2010, available at: www.azi.md/en/print-story/8511, both accessed February 26, 2017.
20. "Hundreds of Thousands of Cases to Be Examined by Commission for Combating Communism".
21. Ecaterina Deleu, "Condamnarea comunismului nu înseamnă scoaterea PCRM în afara legii," *Flux*, January 15, 2010, available at: http://archiva.flux.md/articole/8586, accessed February 26, 2017.
22. Wim van Meurs, *History Textbooks in Moldova* (Strasbourg: Council of Europe, 2003), available at: www.cap.uni-muenchen.de/download/2003/2003_History_Text books.pdf; and Sergiu Musteata, *About Us and Our Neighbors: History Textbooks in the Republic of Moldova, Romania and Ukraine* (2017), available at: http://repository .gei.de/handle/11428/213, both accessed March 4, 2017.
23. Cornel Ciurea, "Historical Politics in the Republic of Moldova – An Unfulfilled Obsession," *Moldova's Foreign Policy Statewatch* 34, August (2011): 3.
24. Igor Casu, "Nation-Building in the Era of Integration: The Case of Moldova," in Konrad Jarausch and Thomas Linderberger, eds. *Conflicting Memories. Europeanizing Contemporary History* (New York: Berghan Books, 2007), 237–53.
25. For the Romanian commission, see Lavinia Stan, *Transitional Justice in Post-Communist Romania: The Politics of Memory* (New York: Cambridge University Press, 2013).
26. Institute of World Policy, *How to Get Rid of Post-Sovietness?* 99.

27. Venice Commission, "Moldova – Ban of Communist Symbols," 2013, www.venice.coe.int/Newsletter/NEWSLETTER_2013_02/3_MDA_EN.html, accessed February 5, 2017.
28. Adi Schnytzer and Alina Zubkovych, "Comparative Symbolic Violence: The Chisinau and Tiraspol National Historical Museums," no date, 3, available at: www.jewishgen.org/Bessarabia/files/ComparativeViolenceInMoldova_article.pdf, accessed February 12, 2017.
29. Ibid.
30. Schnytzer and Zubkovych, "Comparative Symbolic Violence: The Chisinau and Tiraspol National Historical Museums," 9.
31. Causeway Institute for Peace-Building and Conflict Resolution, "Moldova," no date, available at: www.cipcr.org/moldova/, accessed March 4, 2017.
32. Sorin Alexandru, "La Tiraspol pana la 7 ani de inchisoare daca negi rolul 'pozitiv' al armatei ruse," *Capital*, June 29, 2016, available at: www.capital.ro/la-tiraspol-faci-pana-la-7-ani-de-inchisoare-daca-negi-rolul-pozitiv-al-armatei-ruse.html, accessed February 5, 2017.
33. Paige Arthur, *Identities in Transition* (New York: International Center for Transitional Justice, 2009), available at: https://idl-bnc.idrc.ca/dspace/bitstream/10625/50118/1/IDL-50118.pdf, accessed February 26, 2017.
34. Institute of World Policy, *How to Get Rid of Post-Sovietness?* 93.

13

Confronting Multiple Pasts in Post-Soviet Armenia

Oana-Valentina Suciu

Motto

A listener asks Radio Yerevan: Is it possible to foretell the future?

Radio Yerevan replies: Yes, no problem. We know exactly what the future will be.

Our problem is with the past: that keeps changing.[1]

Armenia represents a challenging case study of post-Soviet transitional justice because the country did not adopt lustration or provide access to secret files, did not officially condemn the Soviet regime, did not set up a history commission, and did not offer reparations. Only rarely did it address the recent communist past with the help of judicial and nonjudicial, state and nonstate reckoning measures. Lustration featured on the public agenda as late as 2011, but will most probably be abandoned in the near future, since the bills dealing with the accountability of the former KGB agents were rejected by the government in September 2011, and again in December 2016 by Parliament.

War atrocities, dating back as far as the 1800s, created multiple competing pasts that are as closely intertwined as Russian matryoshka nesting dolls. The 1915 Genocide perpetrated by the Ottoman Empire has been layered onto unsolved communist rights trespasses, as well as postcommunist abuses, such as the on-going conflict in Nagorno-Karabakh located in the southern Caucasus. Ironically, Armenia has been interested in addressing a set of abuses that took place close to a century ago, while generally neglecting the more recent legacies of the Stalinist purges and the secret collaboration of ethnic Armenians with the KGB. This chapter focuses on Armenia's multiple competing pasts, and the ways in which the reckoning process was shaped by its imperfect, but stable, postcommunist democracy. The focus here is mainly on lustration and memorialization as transitional justice programs.

ARMENIA'S COMPETING PASTS

Soviet Armenia inherited the lands known as Eastern or Russian Armenia before World War I. They were a remnant of Great Armenia, whose western territories fell under Ottoman rule in the seventh century and under Persian rule in the sixteenth century.[2] Geography, religion, and language have shaped Armenian history.[3] The Christian Armenian population of the predominantly Muslim Ottoman Empire perished or was driven into exile in 1915–23, thus augmenting an older diaspora. Currently, the 6-million-strong Armenian diaspora is twice as large as the population of the Armenian republic. Some 1.5 million Armenians died in the 1915 massacres perpetrated by the Ottoman Empire (see below). After 1915, only the eastern population – in and around the capital Yerevan – remained in its original location, thanks to Soviet support.

Surrounded by nondemocratic and illiberal states, Armenia has remained a prisoner of geography with a history defined by conflict.[4] Explicit nation- and state-building was possible only briefly after World War I (1918–21) when Armenia was an independent state.[5] Threatened by Turkey (the successor of the Ottoman Empire) and bordering Iran on the eastern side, the newly founded Republic of Armenia sought "salvation" in rapprochement with the Soviet Union. This protection proved to be a poisoned apple, since Stalin took gerrymandering to the extremes and decided in 1921, during a plenary session of the Bureau of Caucasian Affairs (Kavburo), to establish the mountainous region of Nagorno-Karabakh as an autonomous oblast of Soviet Azerbaijan – not Soviet Armenia. The Soviet authorities denied the Armenian character of the region, although Armenians made up the majority of its population.[6] Stalin's decision was rejected by many ethnic Armenians. During the 1930s, Soviet security head Lavrentiy Beria shot the Armenian Party Secretary Aghasi Khanjian for openly endorsing Nagorno-Karabakh's unification with Armenia. Such an extreme measure was taken because "Stalinism meant that there could be no discussion or expression of grievances with relation to the national boundaries."[7]

The communist history of Armenia can be broken down into several stages. First, the migration of stateless Armenians (bearers of special League of Nations passports) during the late 1920s and of Armenian citizens of Soviet Armenia in the late 1940s and the 1960s shaped a distinctive Armenian diaspora element. Second, a brief opening brought about during the 1950s by the rule of Soviet leader Nikita Khrushchev allowed Armenian Soviet leaders to petition the First Secretary of the Communist Party about the poor living conditions in the republic and the (lack of) rule of law in Nagorno-Karabakh. Third, the Soviet policy of building a "nationless" state and society encouraged the all-inclusive identity of the "new Soviet man" in Armenia, with lingering postcommunist effects.[8]

Until the 1960s Armenia promoted a "quiet nationalism" that placed the ethnic group at the core of the nation.[9] Moscow allowed – even encouraged – a degree of cultural nationalism in the republic, although nationalism was officially prohibited in the Soviet Union. This prohibition was temporarily lifted in 1965, when Armenians organized massive public demonstrations on 24 April to commemorate the fiftieth anniversary of the Genocide, something they had previously done only in private. Shortly afterwards, the First Secretary of the Armenian Communist Party, Yakov Zaroubian, supported by the government of Soviet Armenia, obtained the approval of the central authorities in Moscow to build a monument for the Genocide victims.[10] If this symbolic nationalism was encouraged to irk Turkey, a NATO member, territorial nationalism remained off-limits. In fact, the Armenian foreign affairs minister Jan Kirakosian regularly raised the subject of the Armenian Genocide with the Supreme Soviet to no avail.[11]

Between 1987 and 1991, Mikhail Gorbachev's policies of perestroika and glasnost allowed the republics to voice demands for border shifts within the Soviet Union. Gorbachev still believed that Soviet internationalism was more important than the rights of any national group. Nevertheless, in Armenia the Karabakh Movement gathered close to 1 million protesters (that is, roughly one-third of the republic's population) in the Opera Square of Yerevan in February 1988, an unprecedented degree of popular mobilization at the republican level. That same month witnessed the systematic killing of Armenians by Azeri in the town of Sumgait, a Caspian Sea city in Azerbaijan inhabited by a sizable Armenian community. According to de Waal, the killings in Sumgait were the worst case of interethnic violence in the seventy years of the Soviet Union, fuelled by the developments related to Nagorno-Karabakh. Hundreds of Armenians were forced to leave Sumgait, an industrial town that was the pride of industrial development in the Soviet Union. Mass violent Azeri rallies targeting the Armenian community unleashed a bloody conflict, soon to turn into a genuine pogrom, with Armenian properties ransacked, burned down and their inhabitants attacked, raped, and murdered.[12] Sumgait brought increased pressure on the Soviet Armenian authorities to support unification with Nagorno-Karabakh.

Multiple voices have proffered different narratives about problems and solutions for Armenia. Some Soviet and postcommunist politicians have claimed that the Soviet authorities saved and preserved the national Armenian identity and developed the country economically. In contrast, the nationalist opponents of the communist regime have blamed the Communist Party for not defending the Armenian national interest. For both groups, the main enemies are not the Russians, whose protection is indispensable for Armenia's national security, but "the Turks" (a group including both the Azeri and the Turks).[13] In 1988–90, Soviet rule was placed under scrutiny by a third group formed of noncommunist intellectuals, such as Levon Ter-Petrossian, who became the first postcommunist president of independent Armenia in 1992. A fourth group represented by the "revolutionaries," that is militants for the Nagorno-Karabakh cause (demanding the region's incorporation into Armenia), saw themselves as replacements for the communist bureaucrats removed in 1988–91. The "revolutionaries," part of a liberal intelligentsia who itself was the product of Soviet heavy industrialization, lost their jobs during the 1990s when a market economy replaced the Soviet command economy. This is why in Armenia the regime change of 1991 is ironically labeled as the "revolution of mathematicians," who had to build the independent state from scratch.[14]

During the early stages of independence (1992–4) the "revolutionaries" dominated Armenian politics, and technocrats were appointed to public offices requiring specific expertise (especially positions in the economic sphere, where a shock therapy approach was applied to effect marketization). Between 1995 and 2000, the influence of these politicians decreased to the point of being totally excluded from senior offices and in fact being replaced by members of the military and the law enforcement agencies. The 2000–10 decade saw the strengthening of the institution of the president, the rise of a new oligarchic economic elite that acquired leverage over political structures, and the general professionalization of the public administration and bureaucracy. A need for consensual crisis management and institution building has characterized the country after 2011, as the politically independent technical experts have become politically more powerful than the corrupt businesspeople. The political turmoil of independent Armenia briefly outlined here suggests that little room was left for dealing directly and openly with the Soviet past. Any calls for accountability and historical reckoning have focused on condemnation of, reparations for and/or international recognition of atrocities related to Turkey and Azerbaijan.

The latest parliamentary elections of April 2017, in which the nationalist, conservative Republican Party won a plurality of the vote, supports an interpretation of an Armenia unwilling to address its Soviet past. The Republicans, widely seen as a "party of oligarchs" and a "typical post-Soviet party of power," have been accused of corruption and of rigging past elections.[15] They are supported by the leftist Armenian Revolutionary Federation (Dashnaktutsiun), which was founded in Tbilisi in 1890, but was repeatedly banned before and after 1991 for its radicalism against the Turkish authorities.[16] The new government must help the country transform from a presidential to a parliamentary democracy by 2018, step up the fight against corruption, and bring Nagorno-Karabakh within Armenian borders.[17] Transitional justice was not a declared priority during the electoral campaign, which focused mainly on social, economic, and corruption issues, and most surely will not be pursued by the new rulers.

ARMENIA'S LUSTRATION AND FILE ACCESS ATTEMPTS

Lustration was discussed only by the small pro-EU opposition party, Heritage (Jarangutyun), founded in 2002 by Raffi Hovhanissyan, an American-born, wealthy Armenian. In September 2011, Heritage submitted to Parliament a lustration bill that would have allowed the identification and dismissal of those civil servants who, before 1991, worked for the domestic or foreign branches of the Soviet KGB, or worked as investigators or collaborators with the secret services of other states. After critics pointed out that this lustration bill could start a veritable witch-hunt and called it a "treachery" and a "shame,"[18] the government rejected the lustration bill, despite support from some segments of the population. The bill was harshly criticized by Gorik Hakobyan, head of the Armenian National Security Service, on grounds that "no special service operates without a network of agents and even the precedent of disclosing agents who cooperated in the past will strike a significant blow to the entire security system."[19]

Human rights activists Mikail Danielyan and Vardan Harutunyan explained that lustration could help post-Soviet Armenia to identify individuals who secretly spied on their family, friends, and neighbors for the benefit of the secret police, and that it was not too late to adopt this long overdue transitional justice program.[20] Nevertheless, their plea fell on deaf ears, and the topic did not make it on the official agenda, regardless of its importance. Journalist Hakob Badelyan similarly observed that "since Armenia's independence, no government has ever supported the adoption of the law on lustration."[21] This is partly because lustration has been understood as nothing more than "political cleansing," in other words, a process that could be easily manipulated by political actors to undermine the credibility and legitimacy of their opponents.[22]

Academics argue that Soviet political and institutional legacies have persisted in Armenia because of the continuity of communist political and business leaders, who got a new lease on their political lives after the collapse of the communist regime.[23] According to historian Gerard Libaridian, after Armenia's independence there were "no witch hunts, no zeal to avenge the abuses of the past or punish former leaders for the state of affairs at the time the ANM [the pro-independence Armenian National Movement] took over the government from the Communists."[24] On the contrary, Libaridian points out that there was a high degree of continuity of personnel from the Soviet system in the ANM ranks. This elite continuity meant that internal conflicts were avoided, and also that the new government embraced no critical approach of the communist regime. As such, there was

> no evaluation of the impact of Soviet rule on the economy, political culture, morals, and intellectual health of the society. The 'intellectual' class failed to examine the values by which intellectuals, writers, and artists were promoted and the impact of the values they represented on the spiritual and cultural well-being of society. By and large industry managers did not address the financial bankruptcy, management failure, infrastructural decay, and obsolete machinery that would make economic recovery difficult. Physicians failed to expose the antiquated and disastrous health system and medical practices (...) Educators failed to challenge an educational system that was antiquated and [driven by] colonial mentality, Stalinist pedagogy, and rotten to the core.[25]

In this context, it is understandable that the bill on lustration was rejected again after being included on the legislative agenda in November 2016. After the bill was repeatedly postponed by extensive and divisive floor debates, as many as 70 of the 104 legislators voted against it.[26] The reasons given were the same – it was felt that it would destroy Armenia's intelligence network and thus expose the country to the risk of being destabilized by domestic and foreign agents.[27] Like other post-Soviet states, Armenian voters are not yet ready to reckon with the Soviet past through a radical program like lustration.

Some information on former KGB full-time agents and part-time collaborators is publicly available at Cambridge University – not in Armenia. Cambridge holds thirty-three boxes of manuscript notes, notebooks, and typescripts collected by the Soviet defector Vasiliy Mitrokhin, a former archivist for the Chief KGB Directorate. These archival documents were donated by Mitrokhin's son to the university and are available for consultation, both in print at the Churchill Archive Centre and in electronic format on the Janus website.[28] Based on these documents, rights activist Felix Corley argued that:

> An initially surprising number of individuals who figure in Mitrokhin's voluminous notes as KGB operatives, agents, trusted contacts or in other capacities are ethnic Armenians. Perhaps more of those mentioned are Armenian than of any other Soviet nationality. However, it is important to note that Armenians were not solely a Soviet nationality. Although the titular nation of a Soviet republic (...), more than half the Armenian population were

not from Soviet Armenia and were not Soviet citizens. (...) the KGB could exploit the wide geographic spread of the Armenian population, the links many [of them] had through residence or relatives to Soviet Armenia, diaspora Armenians' residence in Soviet Armenia where recruitment was easier, and the widespread acceptance among Armenians (except among hardline members of the Dashnak party) that Soviet Armenia represented at least some kind of national homeland towards which loyalty was not necessarily wrong.[29]

Some of the Armenian agents and informants were recruited while they were studying in the Soviet Union and were blackmailed by the KGB prior to returning back to their home countries as a condition to obtain permission to leave the USSR. Corley lists 135 individuals and their codenames, as they appear in the secret files, followed by the type of activity they conducted, the target they were assigned to pursue, and the reason why they agreed to spy, if known.

Considering how powerful and oppressive the Soviet regime was, these files provide scant information on how "free" the choice to cooperate with the KGB was. In addition, it is difficult to assess the level of harm produced by these secret agents and informants without full access to the entire KGB archive. The post-Soviet Armenian authorities have continued to ignore the importance of granting file access to ordinary citizens, enacting lustration and vetting programs, and piecing together the truth about the communist repression system. This is mostly because the republic's entire political system relies on political parties, as well as military and economic agents who belong to various self-interested cartels eager to keep their former involvement with the communist repression system out of the public eye.

Additional documents related to the Soviet past can be accessed through the National Archives of Armenia in Yerevan, which contain numerous archival funds and hundreds of thousands of files, microfilms, and tapes dating from 1855 to 2003. These funds include documents on parties such as the Armenian Revolutionary Federation (Dashnaktiun) and the Communist Party of Armenia, as well as top state institutions once controlled by the latter.[30]

Current efforts to deal with the past in Armenia are also affected by the ongoing conflict in Nagorno-Karabakh and attempts to get recognition of the Armenian Genocide by Turkey. The propensity of the Armenian authorities to downplay the communist past and praise the Soviet regime as a benevolent protector is rational, since the Armenian branch of the KGB not only defended national security in the mid-1980s and the early 1990s, but also played a role in Nagorno-Karabakh by participating in hostage negotiations and the disarming the local militias. However, the Soviet regime also quietly fuelled the ethno-religious conflict in an effort to weaken both Armenia and Azerbaijan and keep them as client states, thereby further complicating Armenia's framing of and willingness to address its past.[31]

THE NAGORNO-KARABAKH ISSUE

Among the conflicts that engulfed the Caucasus after 1988, the one in Nagorno-Karabakh proved to be the longest and the bloodiest, claiming thousands of lives on both sides (Armenian and Azeri) and threatening the peace of post-Soviet Eurasia.[32] The new permissiveness allowed by glasnost and perestroika after 1987 triggered vocal reactions in Yerevan and the Karabakh region. In Stepanakert, the capital of this autonomous region, people took to the streets on February 13, 1988, releasing grievances accumulated during seventy years of Soviet rule and calling for the region to be recognized formally as part of Armenia.[33] These events impacted domestic politics in both Soviet Armenia and Soviet Azerbaijan by positioning the Armenian-based Karabakh Movement at the very heart of these countries' political, economic, social, and cultural developments.

The first protests that occurred in Armenia in early 1988 were not anti-Soviet in character, since demonstrators in Yerevan carried portraits of Gorbachev. People took to the streets in unprecedented numbers to protest against the violent clashes in Sumgait, a city in Azerbaijan proper but with a considerable-sized Armenian population, which claimed the lives of many civilian Armenians in what is described as a pogrom.[34] Initially, their slogans did not overstep the limits imposed by glasnost and perestroika and did not call for border realignment or regime change.[35] Radicalism grew only after the Soviet leaders in Moscow completely ignored these moderate demands and labeled the protesters "hooligans" and "extremists."[36] The discontent gathered more steam by the end of that year when Armenia was hit by a serious earthquake, which killed between 25,000 and 50,000 people and left half a million Armenians homeless. This natural catastrophe and the destruction it caused prompted Gorbachev to allow, for the first time since the end of World War II, the affected areas in Armenia to receive international humanitarian aid. As some analysts noted, this gesture signified a turning point in the history of the Cold War.[37]

By 1990, Armenian nationalist militias were continuously attacking border points with Azerbaijan, forcing Gorbachev, who otherwise had chosen after 1988 not to pay too much attention to this region, to threaten to declare martial law if the attacks did not stop. In 1991, a national referendum overwhelmingly called for Armenia's secession from the Soviet Union. By that point, politics already had the stamp of nationalism, which looked like the only solution for the smallest Soviet republic surrounded by violent neighbors and largely ignored by central authorities. Nation-building efforts and inclusive, civic nationalism were virtually absent during the early 1990s. That was because the nation was already defined along ethnic lines, united by past traumas, and surviving in spite of the foreign others, such as Turkey or Azerbaijan. The nature and degree of Moscow's involvement in the armed conflict of Sumgait (1988) or in the peaceful Nagorno-Karabakh movement in Yerevan (1988–91) remains unknown. The quick rejection of the lustration bill two decades later means the involvement of the Soviet central authorities in these events will remain speculative for now. Meanwhile, questions still linger regarding how and why a loyal communist government, such as the Armenian one in the late 1980s to early 1990s, pursued a course of action that eventually led to the independence of the republic and the implosion of the Soviet Union.

After independence, Armenian politics became more radicalized. The conflict over Nagorno-Karabakh disrupted trade and transport routes, led to energy cuts, a blockade and closed borders imposed by Azerbaijan and Turkey (which increasingly mentored the newly born Azeri state). This was followed by Armenia's exclusion from regional development projects, with negative effects felt even today. The conflict fostered authoritarianism within Armenia and a highly dangerous political and military overdependence on Moscow, which became Armenia's main security partner.[38] Politicians who took a moderate stand were labeled traitors, thus leading political actors into a vicious cycle of radicalization, outbidding their political enemies in an effort to constantly prove their patriotic credentials.[39] The trend, which is mirrored by the local media and the universities, has expanded the disconnection between politicians and voters, who fear the possibility of being "sold to the enemy."[40] Nevertheless, most Armenian political parties express a wish to balance the "strategic partnership" with Russia with good relations with the United States, the EU, and Iran. This policy of "complementarity"[41] seeks to achieve security by bringing together foreign partners with radically different agendas, values, and interests, obviously complicating policy making even more.

Since the Nagorno-Karabakh conflict erupted, Armenia and Azerbaijan have engaged in a war of words, with conflicting claims for historical legitimacy, numerous military threats, and a plethora of conspiracy theories, one more unbelievable than the next. They both have misrepresented the reality on the ground, used fear and hatred, and promoted stories of atrocities and displacement.[42] For each side, only a complete victory could put an end to the conflict and compensate for the losses incurred.[43] Today, under the unsuccessful supervision of third parties like the Organization of Security and

Cooperation in Europe, this "no war, no peace" situation finds no solution given the permanent arms race and weekly increases in victims on both sides.[44] As negotiations are unable to break the deadlock, the Nagorno-Karabakh conflict retains the potential to turn the Caucasus into a battleground involving Russia, Turkey, and Iran, as it once was in the seventeenth and eighteenth centuries. Despite the common economic interests of these three powers in the region, the conflict remains a matter of concern especially as these states are becoming increasingly authoritarian, an aspect that might impede the "complementarity" approach used by Armenian actors.

As far as Armenia and Azerbaijan are concerned, "there are virtually no economic, cultural, or other contacts between the two communities today, and the best term to describe the bilateral relations is a familiar zero-sum-game."[45] In Armenia, the conflict with Azerbaijan summons vivid memories of Armenians' past suffering at the hands of the Ottomans. Sumgait reminded the Armenians of the massacres of World War I, prompting them to equate the Azeris with the Ottoman armies and the Sumgait massacre to the Genocide. All these memories reinforced the Armenians' belief that they could not cohabitate with "barbarian Turks."[46]

Unsurprisingly, these tragic historical legacies and the quest for national survival have taken precedence over other reckoning programs, even twenty-five years after independence. The ongoing conflict has made related transitional justice programs very difficult to be put into practice. It has also reinforced the view that reckoning with the communist past, in a more critical, resolute, and comprehensive way, would damage post-Soviet Armenia's relations with its Russian protector. As such, most reckoning efforts have focused on the most distant past: the Genocide.

TRANSITIONAL JUSTICE AND THE ARMENIAN GENOCIDE

Many pages have been written on the Armenian Genocide by scholars, diplomats, priests, doctors, soldiers, Armenians, and foreigners alike, with varying degrees of involvement in the events. Started by the Ottoman authorities on April 24, 1915 in the city of Istanbul (the former Constantinople), the Genocide represented the first ethnic cleansing of the twentieth century. As many as 1.5 million Armenians were killed in state-led massacres between 1915 and 1923. All testimonies and analyses point to the collective memory and trauma the Genocide inflicted on the Armenians living inside and outside Armenian borders. A century-old conflict thus shapes the images that Armenians and Turks hold of each other, Armenia's domestic politics, and its foreign policy. Every year, around 24 April, Armenians all over the world come together under the slogan "Remember. Recognize. Reconcile" in an attempt to increase international awareness of the Genocide and convince important international actors such as the United States and Israel to take a clearer stand against the denial of the Genocide by Turkish authorities. The Genocide is the main focus of Armenia's transitional justice efforts.

Scholars identify several inter-related dimensions of the Armenian–Turkish relationship that led to an asymmetry of power benefiting Turkey, but not Armenia: (1) psychological and cognitive factors (the image of the other, negative stereotypes, the historical trauma and collective memory, the lack of healing and closure, the historical memory of the Genocide and Turkey's denial); (2) structural barriers (the lack of communication with, knowledge about, and diplomatic and economic relations with the other); (3) need for justice (to correct historical and ongoing injustice); and (4) Realpolitik (the regional power dynamics, including relations with Russia, Azerbaijan, and Georgia, Turkey's support for Azerbaijan in the Nagorno-Karabakh conflict, and Turkey's sealed border with Armenia).[47] Turkey recognized Armenia as an independent state in 1992, but maintains closed borders to Armenians.[48] As almost no communication is possible, the average Armenian perceives Turkey as the hostile state depicted in history textbooks. Turkey is not a neighbor, but the old, repressive Ottoman Empire.

Starting in the late 1990s, the Armenian authorities called for the recognition of the 1915 events as a Genocide in order to pressure Ankara. Every time Turkey made peace in Nagorno-Karabakh a precondition for normalizing relations with Armenia, Armenia toughened its stand on the recognition of the Genocide by appealing for support from its diaspora and various Western governments. The aim is to pressure Ankara into making concessions as part of the reconciliation process.[49] Public attitudes toward Turkey and Azerbaijan are slightly more critical of these countries than Armenia's official position. Armenians consider both countries hostile enemies, and show deep distrust of both Turks and Azeris. Most Armenians do not support reconciliation, and are disappointed with their leaders' insufficiently tough stance toward Turkey. Turkey is seen as a "strong evil force," and Armenians as "gullible victims." Polls suggest that the Armenians should claim compensation for the Genocide, including land gains.[50] These sentiments have remained largely unchanged after 2000 despite the alleged Armenian–Turkish rapprochement, which is often described somewhat ironically in Armenia and by the international media as "football diplomacy."[51]

In 2001, President Robert Kocharyan sought to improve relations with Turkey by creating the Turkish-Armenian Reconciliation Commission (TARC), under the auspices of the US State Department. Unfortunately,

TARC's activity lacked the transparency and representation of a legitimate transitional justice mechanism because the Armenian Revolutionary Federation (Dashnaktsutiun), the strongest political voice supporting the recognition of the Armenian Genocide, was excluded. TARC commissioned an independent legal analysis conducted by the International Center for Transitional Justice (ICTJ) to determine whether the UN Genocide Convention could retroactively apply to the Armenian case. The ICTJ concluded that "the events, viewed collectively ... include all of the elements of the crime of genocide as defined in the Convention,"[52] but added that the Convention does not permit retroactive compensation for damages, and obligations could be imposed only on the states party to it. Thus, "no legal, financial or territorial claim arising out of the events could successfully be made against any individual or state under the Convention."[53] As such, TARC failed to bring about Armenian–Turkish reconciliation, although it was a first step toward it.[54] Moreover, TARC's technical analysis was unable to change collective memories.

The Turkish representatives at the OSCE have proposed the creation of a joint truth commission, but such a body would be useless unless the Ottoman Archives, which contain many documents directly related to the organization of the massacres, were made available.[55] Given Turkey's recent turn toward authoritarianism, which led to thousands of journalists, academics, activists, and novelists being fined and/or imprisoned for publicly speaking out for human rights, the likelihood of obtaining this information is not high. The Turkish Penal Code defines truth as "an insult to Turkishness," while the April 2017 referendum granted unlimited powers to the president. Reconciliation seems highly unlikely in the near future not only from the Turkish side, but also because of the bellicose, hardened position of the Armenian government toward Turkey and Azerbaijan, and its quest to obtain the approval of voters.

COLLECTIVE MEMORY AND THE PUBLIC SPACE(S)

Collective memory is manifested in the public space through urban architecture, memorials, and public buildings. References to the Soviet past are ubiquitous but hidden, from the architecture of buildings (recognizable throughout the former Soviet bloc), to the urban structure of the city (with wide, straight avenues), and through various public monuments evoking post-Soviet Armenian identity politics. The 1990s were characterized by the tendency to remove traces of the Soviet past and rename public squares, streets, and buildings to reflect what was depicted as a glorious precommunist history. The trend was common to all postcommunist countries. Removing Lenin's statue from downtown Yerevan on April 13th, 1991 was a symbolic gesture, and legend has it that the statue circled the square three times, like a typical funeral procession.[56] At the same time, there was a bizarre continuity with the Soviet past, illustrated by the monumental statue of Mother Armenia (Mayr Hayastan) in Victory Park, which marks the victory in "the patriotic antifascist war," and the Tsitsernakaberd memorial for the victims of the Armenian Genocide.

For the citizens of Armenia, the Soviet regime is associated with modernization and political and societal institutions that served the national interest, the formation of a national identity, and the promotion of a high-brow "Soviet Armenian culture." Thus, the "Soviet Armenian" – the bearer of the modernized Armenian identity – is a hybrid construction that indivisibly blends "the Soviet" and "the Armenian" identities.[57] Mother Armenia reflects this trend in Soviet monument art. Unveiled in 1967, five years after Stalin's statue had been removed from the top of the Victory Monument, "the image of the mother was not new to Soviet aesthetics. She became The Mother, calling her sons to combat and instilling wartime values in her children. This symbolic role gained strength through the course of the war, appearing time and again as a representation of the collective and a symbol of the Soviet nation."[58]

At the time of its unveiling on November 29th, 1967, the Tsitsernakaberd monument was "the most direct physical manifestation of an ethno-national issue in Soviet Armenia."[59] It was preceded in April 1965 by the largest demonstration in the Soviet Union, during which hundreds of thousands of people asked the Soviet Armenian and central governments to allow the official commemoration of the Genocide. According to the Armenian Genocide Museum-Institute, a transitional justice institution established in Yerevan in 1995, the official competition called for a design that embodied "the creative Armenian nation's life that has been full of struggle, its inexhaustible vitality to survive, the progress it has made as well as representing its present and the bright future while eternalizing the memory of millions of victims of the Genocide of 1915."[60]

As such, it would be impossible to imagine any "pure Armenian quality," free from Soviet admixtures or a Soviet nation, free of ethnic or national attributes. For the Armenians who were socialized under the Soviet regime, the national tradition was available only in this hybrid form, depicted by public monuments that represent Armenian officers who belonged to the Soviet army or were Marxist revolutionaries. This is why many perceive the Soviet Armenian identity as the true national identity, a position supported by the high ethnic and religious homogeneity of the population. The history of Soviet Armenia is yet to be reconsidered by the cultural and academic luminaries, some of whom have asked the authorities to facilitate a genuine public debate on the Soviet past and its symbolic legacies (such as public monuments and street names).[61]

The population of Soviet Armenia included many formerly stateless refugees. Another wave of repatriation occurred in 1945–8 when, encouraged by the Stalinist policies, "about 100,000 Armenians from Bulgaria, Greece, Egypt, Iraq, Iran, Lebanon, Syria, the USA, Romania, France and other countries were repatriated to Armenia. These included doctors, teachers, scientists, artists, and musicians, with financial support again provided by the Armenian diaspora." These were guided by the idea that "let it be Soviet, it is still Armenia!"[62] Fooled by the Soviet propaganda, and in search of a land that would provide a territorial basis for their national identity, many of these refugees were soon confronted with the totalitarian system of repression, deportation and imprisonment, were labeled "bourgeois," "agents of the USA and of capitalism," and, in the happiest situations, were faced with the scarcities and continuous KGB surveillance of daily life.

Memoirs and letters were created during those decades, depicting real-life stories that probably formed the basis of Radio Yerevan's infamous jokes. These personal writings were a mechanism for coping with the naïve patriotism and nostalgic romanticism that cost many their lives. Many of the letters sent from the "Soviet paradise" echoed these lines:

> An Armenian repatriated from Italy to the USSR agrees with his brother who remains in Italy to write in ordinary ink if life in the USSR is good, in green ink if things are bad. Sometime later a letter arrives written in ordinary ink: "Everything is first-rate, I got an apartment, work, the shops are full of stuff. There are shortcomings, but minor ones: for instance, it's difficult to get hold of green ink."[63]

Even today memories of Soviet Armenia conjure a sense of pride in citizen as it is perceived as a protector of Armenian identity during times of discontent and as the only viable alternative to the obliteration of a country and a nation, surviving against tremendous odds.[64]

CONCLUSION

Like many of the FSU states covered in this volume, Armenia's post-Soviet transition has been marked by numerous political, economic, social, and cultural challenges: state-building being at the top of the public agenda. The Armenian collective memory and state building program (both in Armenia and in the diaspora) cannot be understood without placing the trauma of genocide at its very center. Its national history and current politics are driven by the quest for reparations for this and other past injustices, including the long simmering conflict with Azerbaijan. Seventy years of communism and the collective memory of the Genocide created a strange love-hate relationship with Moscow, still perceived by ordinary Armenians and the political elites alike as the savior of a nation that otherwise would have perished.

As this chapter illustrated, the formation of a national identity has been an on-going feature of domestic politics both during the Soviet period and after the break-up of the Soviet Union. In fact, the brief political liberalization in the 1960s allowed the Soviet Armenian authorities to play the nationalist card, an unconventional behavior accepted by Moscow because Armenia never directly challenged the Communist Party and the authority of the center. Moscow even tolerated Armenia's restructuring of the public space to stress an Armenian identity more than a Soviet identity. This liberalization is visible in monuments such as Mother Armenia (which replaced Stalin's statue) and the Tsitetsernakaberd memorial (also a pilgrimage destination for all Armenians). Both monuments embody a primordial identity forged around ethnicity, language, religion, traditions, and a shared traumatic history. The manner in which this historical narrative was and continues to be used to leverage symbolic reparations also points toward a certain degree of instrumentalization of this identity, consistent with some of the other FSU national experiences examined in this volume. Armenia, like neighboring Georgia, is the bearer of a pre-1918 nationhood, although not of a clear statehood. The quest to align nationhood and statehood is an enduring feature of the Armenian national narrative.[65]

The post-1991 transitional justice attempts to address past traumas through a joint international commission bore little fruit, especially in light of the ongoing conflict with Azerbaijan over the Nagorno-Karabakh enclave. This conflict has led to closed borders with Turkey and Azerbaijan, and contributed to slow economic reforms, increased levels of corruption and unemployment, a self-censored media, and the migration of over 1 million Armenians to other countries, especially Russia. For Armenians, justice means winning the war with Azerbaijan and obtaining reparations, as well as solidifying an alliance with international actors like Russia, who is still perceived as the main ally. These are hard goals to achieve since Armenian elites behave less like political parties and more like cartels and economic oligopolies. While this type of ideological continuity undermines reform efforts, it is unfortunately consistent with that seen in other FSU states like Russia, Belarus, and Moldova.

More radical approaches to postcommunist-related transitional justice would have affected the rank and file of Armenian current elites, something political parties did not support. Although survey results indicate Armenians are highly distrustful of political institutions and the judiciary, there still was limited societal support for lustration measures. In fact, the Heritage party, which championed lustration, was forced out of Parliament in 2017, suggesting that voters had other concerns. Survey results indicated that Armenians consider Azerbaijan and Turkey as their main enemies, confirming the dominance of an "us versus them" narrative and partially explaining why the communist past is unlikely to be addressed as long as older and deeper wounds are left unhealed.

For the time being, Armenia has failed to obtain the unconditional recognition of the Armenian Genocide by Turkey, the end of the conflict with Azerbaijan, the international recognition of Nagorno-Karabakh as independent, or the public unveiling of former KGB collaborators. Failure to address these issues contributes to stalled democratic developments and could lead to an escalation of conflict, like that seen in the way conflicts in Ossetia and Abkhazia affect Georgia's internal political life and the manner in which the conflict in Transnistria affects Moldova's development. By adopting a transitional justice agenda, even an informal one, Armenia might promote democratization and minimize the chances that conflicts could escalate.

Armenia's multilayered past occupies a huge role in the Armenian collective sense of self as a people; it is also the source of Armenian unity in recent decades. Armenia stands out from the other former Soviet republics both due to its legacy of collective trauma and its ability to start reassessing its pre-Soviet pasts starting in the mid-1960s. In particular, the price for this privilege of limited reassessment and budding nationalism was that Armenia ignored other human rights violations, such as the Stalinist deportations.[66] Therefore, the biggest challenge for Armenians going forward is to reconcile and address the competing pasts, to be able to engage memories of Stalinist repression and deportations, legacies of the Genocide, as well as the casualties and forced migration resulting from the Nagorno-Karabakh conflict. Since transitional justice measures are relevant to both conflict-resolution processes and the larger democratization process, utilizing them more directly could prove a productive means of educating both the public and the political body about these layered traumas and promoting broader state-building goals. However, for the time being, Armenia remains a prisoner of its history and geography.

Notes

1. Tony Judt, *Postwar: A History of Europe since 1945* (London: The Penguin Press, 2005), 830.
2. Christopher Walker, *Armenia: The Survival of a Nation* (London: Palgrave Macmillan, 1990), 2nd edition, 1.

3. Armenia adopted Christianity as its state religion in 301 AD. James Fearon and David Laitin, *Armenia*, July 5, 2006, available at: https://web.stanford.edu/group/ethnic/Random%20Narratives/ArmeniaRN1.4.pdf, accessed May 2, 2017.
4. Richard Giragosian, "Armenia's Search for Independence," *Current History. A Journal of Contemporary World Affairs* 113, 765 (2014): 284–9; Maria Raquel Freire and Licínia Simão, *The Armenian Road to Democracy – Dimensions of a Tortuous Process*, CEPS Working Document No. 267, May 2007, 1; Alla Mirzoyan, *Armenia, the Regional Powers and the West* (London: Palgrave MacMillan, 2010), 7; and Phil Gamaghelyan, "Rethinking the Nagorno-Karabakh Conflict: Identity, Politics, Scholarship," *International Negotiation* 15, 1 (2010): 33–56.
5. Shushanik Makaryan, *Impacts of Nationhood and the World Society on Nation-State building: Has the Nation Disappeared?* (Florence: European University Institute, 2009), 10.
6. Walker, *Armenia*, 395.
7. Ibid., 396.
8. Rogers Brubaker, "Nationhood and the National Question in the Soviet Union and Post-Soviet Eurasia: An Institutional Account," *Theory and Society* 23, 1 (1994): 47–78.
9. Razmik Panossian, "Post-Soviet Armenia. Nationalism and its Discontent(s)," in Lowell W. Barrington, ed., *After Independence. Making and Protecting the Nation in Postcolonial and Post-communist States* (Ann Arbor: Michigan University Press, 2006), 225–48.
10. "History of Tsisernakaberd Memorial Complex," no date, available at: www.genocide-museum.am/eng/Description_and_history.php, accessed April 30, 2017.
11. Walker, *Armenia*, 398.
12. Thomas de Waal, *The Caucasus. An introduction* (New York: Oxford University Press, 2010), 111 and 98–138.
13. Panossian, "Post-Soviet Armenia," 2.
14. Alexander Iskandaryan, "Armenia, between Autocracy and Poliarchy," *Russian Politics and Law* 50, 4 (2012): 28; and Alexander Iskandaryan, Hrant Mikaelian and Sergey Minasyan, *War, Business and Politics: Informal Networks and Formal Institutions in Armenia* (Yerevan: Caucasus Institute, 2016), 29.
15. "Armenia's Murky Politics," *The Economist*, April 11, 2007, available at: www.economist.com/node/8993685, accessed May 29, 2017.
16. Gaïdz Minassian, *Le rêve brisé des Arméniens – 1915* (Paris: Flammarion, 2015).
17. Katy E. Pearce, "Political Institutional Trust in the Post-Attempted Coup Republic of Armenia," Paper presented at the annual meeting of the NCA 96th Annual Convention, San Francisco, November 13, 2010, available at: www2.gwu.edu/~ieres gwu/assets/docs/demokratizatsiya%20archive/GWASHU_DEMO_19_1/J37082196087WVG8/J37082196087WVG8.pdf; and Freedom House, *Nations in Transit 2016*, 2016, available at: https://freedomhouse.org/report/nations-transit/2016/armenia, both accessed May 29, 2017.
18. "Former Deputy Minister of National Security of Armenia Is against the Draft Law on Lustration," *MediaMax*, December 1, 2011, available at: www.mediamax.am/en/news/politics/3286/, accessed May 18, 2017.
19. Ibid.
20. "Opinions on Armenia's Lustration Law: Were They Informers or Are They Serving the People?," *Epress.am*, December 6, 2011, available at: http://epress.am/

en/2011/12/06/opinions-on-armenias-lustration-law-were-they-informers-or-are-they-serving-the-people.html, accessed May 18, 2017.

21. Hakob Badalyan, "Armenia's Lustration," *Lragir.am*, November 15, 2011, available at: www.lragir.am/index/eng/0/comments/view/24195, accessed May 18, 2017.

22. Aram Abrahamyan, "Lustration Pros and Cons," *Aravot.am*, December 3, 2016, available at: http://en.aravot.am/2016/12/03/184901/, accessed May 18, 2017.

23. Armin Ishkanian, *Democracy Building in Post-Soviet Armenia* (London: Routledge, 2008), 120–1; and Ken Jowitt, "The Leninist Legacy," in Vladimir Tismaneanu, ed., *The Revolutions of 1989: Rewriting Histories* (London: Routledge, 1999), 213–30.

24. Gerard J. Libaridian, *Modern Armenia: People, Nation, State* (New Brunswick: Transaction Publishers, 2004), 211.

25. Ibid.

26. "The National Assembly Began the Works of the Last Regular Four-days Sitting of the Convocation," December 5, 2016, available at: www.parliament.am/news .php?cat_id=2&NewsID=8932&year=2016&month=12&day=05&lang=eng, accessed May 19, 2017.

27. In 2017, the legislator who introduced the bill – Zaruhi Postanyan – left Heritage, after which Heritage lost its parliamentary representation.

28. The Mitrokhin archives are available at: https://janus.lib.cam.ac.uk/db/node .xsp?id=EAD%2FGBR%2F0014%2FMITN, accessed May 29, 2017. The documents are comprehensively analyzed in Christopher Andrews, *The Sword and the Shield* (London: Basic Books, 2001).

29. Felix Corley, *Armenians in the Mitrokhin's notes*, August 2015, 4, available at: www .academia.edu/15177390/Armenians_in_Mitrokhins_KGB_notes, accessed May 29, 2017.

30. More details on the website of the Armenian National Archives, available at: www .armarchives.am/en/content/113/, accessed May 27, 2017.

31. Martin Ebon, *KGB: Birth and Rebirth* (London: Praeger, 1994), 147–9.

32. Svante Cornell, *Small Nations and Great Powers. A Study of Ethnopolitical Conflict in the Caucasus* (Caucasus World: Courzon Press, 2001), 125.

33. Marina Kurkchiyan, "The Karabakh Conflict. From Soviet Past to Post-Soviet Uncertainty," in Edmund Herzig and Marina Kurkchiyan, eds., *The Armenians. Past and Present in the Making of National Identity* (London: Routledge, 2005), 147.

34. According to Thomas de Waal,

> the Sumgait killings were a watershed for the Soviet Union. It goes without saying that they were a catastrophe for the Armenians. Between 26 and 29 Sumgait Armenians lost their lives and hundreds more were injured. Almost all the 14,000 Armenians of Sumgait left the city. Outside Sumgait, the violence shocked the community of around 350,000 Armenians throughout Azerbaijan, thousands of whom left the republic. Sumgait was also a catastrophe for Azerbaijan, which, as it struggled to react to the unexpected events in Karabakh, had produced the most savage intercommunal violence in the Soviet Union in living memory. The brutality was a painful contrast to the more peaceful demonstrations in Armenia, and ordinary Azerbaijanis were horrified and confused.

Thomas de Waal, *Black Garden. Armenian and Azerbaijan through Peace and War* (New York: New York University Press, 2003), 40.

35. Panossian, "Post-Soviet Armenia," 231; Walker, *Armenia*, 398–9; and Ishkanian, "Armenia, between Autocracy and Poliarchy," 116.

36. Panossian, "Post-Soviet Armenia."

37. Robert O. Krikorian, "Armenia's Political Transition in Historical Perspective," *Global Dialogue* 7, 3–4 (2005): 97.

38. Giragosian, "Armenia's Search for Independence," 284; and Sulamith Begemann and Ivo Meli, "Armenia's Stalled Transformation Process," in *Swiss Study Foundation Summer School – History, Threats and Opportunities. The Case of Georgia and Armenia*, August 27–September 6, 2014, 17–28, available at: www .studienstiftung.ch/wp-content/uploads/2016/08/Studies-of-the-South-Caucasus-Region-2014_Booklet.pdf.

39. Lucan Way, "State Power and Autocratic Stability. Armenia and Georgia Compared," in Christopher Stefes, ed., *The Politics of Transition in Central Asia and the Caucasus: Enduring Legacies and Emerging Challenges* (London: Routledge, 2009), 103–23.

40. Gamaghelyan, "Rethinking the Nagorno-Karabakh Conflict," 39.

41. Giragosian, "Armenia's Search for Independence," 284–5.

42. Ibid., 150. Also Sergey Minasyan, *Nagorno-Karabakh After Two Decades of Conflict: Is Prolongation of the Status Quo Inevitable?* (Yerevan: Caucasus Institute, 2010).

43. Larisa Deriglazova and Sergey Minasyan, "Nagorno-Karabagh: The Paradoxes of Strength and Weakness in an Asymmetric Conflict," *Caucasus Institute Research Papers*, No. 3, June (2011).

44. The casualty figures vary, depending on the information source – Armenian, Azeri, or independent news agency. However, according to BBC and the Al Jazeera estimates, more than 30,000 people died on both sides until the 1994 ceasefire. In April 2016, both sides reported "dozens of victims," (Al Jazeera gives 110 dead, including civilian casualties) but an exact figure is difficult to ascertain. The Armenian media reports often about casualties, both military and civilian, but it is difficult for these figures to be verified. Similar information can be found in "Nagorno–Karabagh profile," April 6, 2016, available at: www.bbc.com/news/world-europe-18270325, and "Nagorno-Karabakh. Azerbaijan hits Armenia defence unit," May 17, 2017, available at: www.aljazeera.com/news/2017/05/nagorno-karab akh-azerbaijan-hits-armenian-air-defence-170516104753249.html, both accessed June 22, 2017.

45. Sergey Minasyan, Hrant Mikaelyan, and Nina Iskandaryan, "The Silent Guns of August. Why the Karabakh War Has Not Begun Anew," *Policy Brief Caucasus Institute*, No. 1, September (2014): 127.

46. Cornell, *Small Nations and Great Powers*, 70, and Krikorian, "Armenia's Political Transition," 97.

47. Esra Çuhadar and Burcu Gültekin Punsmann, *Reflecting on the Two Decades of Bridging the Divide: Taking Stock of Turkish-Armenian Civil Society Activities* (Ankara: Tepav, 2012), 23, available at: www.tepav.org.tr/upload/files/1326455092-5 .Reflecting_on_the_Two_Decades_of_Bridging_the_Divide___Taking_Stock_ of_Turkish_Armenian_Civil_Society_Activities.pdf, accessed May 4, 2017; Alexander Iskandaryan and Sergey Minasyan, *Pragmatic Policies vs. Historical Constraints: Analyzing Armenia-Turkey Relations* (Yerevan: Caucasus Institute,

January 2010), 15–16; and Uğur Ümit Üngör, "The Armenian Genocide: A Multi-Dimensional Process of Destruction," *Global Dialogue* 15, 1 (2013): 97–106.

48. Çuhadar and Punsmann, *Reflecting on the Two Decades*, 35.
49. Iskandaryan, Mikaelian and Minasyan, *War, Business and Politics*, 31–2.
50. Narek Galstyan and Aram Terzyan, "The Portrayal of 'The Other' in Foreign Policy Discourse and Public Consciousness in Armenia (2008–present)," *Caucasus Analytical Digest* 77, 14 (2015): 1–6.
51. A brief analysis of when the Turkish and the Armenian presidents met to discuss politics during a World Cup football qualification game in 2009 can be found in "Turkish-Armenian Relations. Football Diplomacy," *The Economist*, September 3, 2009, available at: www.economist.com/node/14380297, and Ivan Watson, "Armenian Leader in Turkey for 'Soccer Diplomacy'," CNN, October 14, 2009, available at: http://edition.cnn.com/2009/WORLD/europe/10/14/turkey.armenia.soccer.diplomacy/, both accessed June 22, 2017.
52. D. Nigar Göksel, "Turkey and Armenia Post-Protocols: Back to Square One?" *TESEV Foreign Policy Bulletin*, 2012, 17, available at: www.css.ethz.ch/content/specialinterest/gess/cis/center-for-securities-studies/en/services/digital-library/publications/publication.html/154171, accessed April 30, 2017.
53. "International Center for Transitional Justice (ICTJ) Report prepared for TARC," 10 February (2003), 4, available at: www.armenian-genocide.org/Affirmation.244/current_category.5/affirmation_detail.html, accessed April 30, 2017.
54. Simon Payaslian, *The History of Armenia. From Origins to the Present* (London: Palgrave MacMillan, 2007), 199–227.
55. *A Century of Denial: The Armenian Genocide and the Quest for Justice*, April 23, 2015, available at: www.gpo.gov/fdsys/pkg/CHRG-114jhrg95113/html/CHRG-114jhrg95113.htm, accessed May 29, 2017.
56. Elen Aghekyan, "Lenin in Yerevan," *The Abovyan Group*, August 31, 2014, available at: https://abovyangroup.org/2014/08/31/lenin-in-yerevan, accessed May 6, 2017.
57. Hrach Bayadyan, "Hierarchy," *Atlas of Transformation*, 2011, available at: http://monumenttotransformation.org/atlas-of-transformation/html/h/hierarchy/hierarchy-hrach-bayadyan.html; and Hrach Bayadyan, *Short Essays on Post-Soviet Yerevan. The Changing Meaning of Urban Space in Yerevan*, December 3, 2007, available at: http://acsl.am/wp-content/uploads/2008/11/guidelines_Short%20Essays%20on%20Post-Soviet%20Yerevan.pdf, both accessed May 14, 2017.
58. Elen Aghekyan, "The Mother of All Statues," *The Abovyan Group*, December 10, 2013, available at: https://abovyangroup.org/2013/12/10/mother-of-all-statues, accessed May 29, 2017; and Bayadyan, "Hierarchy."
59. Elen Aghekyan, "Memory and Memorial: April 24 Atop Tsitsernakaberd," *The Abovyan Group*, April 24, 2014, available at: https://abovyangroup.org/2014/04/24/memory-and-memorial-april-24-atop-tsitsernakaberd/, accessed May 29, 2017.
60. The Armenian Genocide Museum-Institute, "Tsitsernakaberd Memorial Complex," no date, available at: www.genocide-museum.am/eng/Description_and_history.php, accessed May 29, 2017.
61. Kristin Kavoukian, "Soviet Mentality? The Role of Political Culture in Relations between the Armenian State and Russia's Armenian Diaspora," *Nationalities Papers* 41, 5 (2013): 722.

62. Nona Shahnazarian, "Letters from the Soviet 'Paradise': The Image of Russia among the Western Armenian Diaspora," *Journal of Eurasian Studies* 4, 1 (2013): 8–17.
63. Ibid.
64. Walker, *Armenia*, 14.
65. Judt, *Postwar*, 652–3.
66. Among the former Soviet republics, the term "genocide" is also used by Western-oriented Ukrainians. See Klymenko's chapter for a discussion of the politics surrounding the use of this term in the case of Ukraine's 1930 famine.

14

Learning from Serbian Failure

The Denial of Three Repressive Pasts

Nenad Dimitrijević

This chapter discusses transitional justice processes, achievements, and set-backs in Serbia in an effort to establish whether the Serbian case provides useful lessons for dealing with the past in the Former Soviet Union (FSU). The focus is on how Serbia addressed or ignored the legacies of its layered repressive pasts. Serbia experienced three periods of repression: the collaboration of the Serbian government with the German occupying forces during World War II (1941–4), the Yugoslav communist regime of 1944–90, and the regime of Slobodan Milošević (1990–2000). The first was a puppet regime complicit with Nazi crimes, the second was an authoritarian regime, while the third was a façade democracy heavily involved in inter- and intra-state war. All these regimes committed crimes and violated human rights, thus a complete account of transitional justice in Serbia must address methods for dealing with three related but still distinct sets of wrongdoings and their legacies.

Serbia applied limited transitional justice after Milošević's ousting from power in 2000. The measures focused mostly on the crimes committed during the wars of the 1990s. Lack of political support and a widespread culture of denial have impeded effective engagement with the mass atrocities in the 1990s. In recent years considerable political, legal, and cultural efforts have been directed at addressing the Nazi past and the communist repression, but these efforts have been heavily instrumentalized, serving mainly to justify the politically and culturally dominant interpretation of Serbian nationalism. This misuse of transitional justice reached its peak with the rehabilitation of fascist collaborators from World War II. These overlapping transitional jus-tice processes have considerably enlarged the body of documentary knowl-edge about the past, but this newly acquired knowledge did not contribute to societal and political acknowledgment of the truth about victims' suffering, wrongdoers' misdeeds and responsibility, or the character of the three recent pasts. The transitional justice record thus far has been decidedly mixed, and dominated by denial. Denial works both as the dominant popular attitude to wrongdoings, and as the main strategy of political and cultural elites. It appears in different forms, ranging from claims that the Serbs did not commit crimes (literal denial) to claims that crimes committed by the Serbs were justifiable (interpretive denial).

The chapter consists of four sections. The first section identifies the features of the Nazi, communist and nationalist repressive pasts, outlines the Serbian transitional dynamics, and presents the popular attitudes toward confronting the three repressive pasts after the regime change of 2000. The second section explores the legal mechanisms and political and cultural ambiguities of Serbia's treatment of the Nazi and communist crimes. While these two repressive pasts are clearly distinct, they were addressed simultaneously with the same transitional justice mechanisms, therefore they will be considered in tandem. Section two therefore aims to explain the political and ideological preferences behind the choice to concomitantly deal with the two pasts, and the consequences for the democratic transition. The third section presents methods for addressing the crimes of the 1990s. The fourth section asks whether the Serbian case offers lessons relevant to the FSU.

In terms of lessons learned from transitional justice experiences, some might argue that the Serbian case is irrelevant for the FSU. Particularities of the Serbian case, such as its three repressive pasts, or the manner in which it has suffered from political manipulation of these pasts, or the involvement of the international community in its transitional justice measures might make Serbia a nongeneralizable case. Others might argue that the significant differences between Serbia and the FSU do not invalidate the comparison. First, the FSU and Serbia became newly independent states after the fall of communism, a fact that tied nation-building to the confrontation with past wrongdoings. Second, Serbia's decision to deal with the Nazi and communist repressions simultaneously could present some lessons to FSU countries with multiple repressive pasts, such as the Baltic republics. Third, the wars of the 1990s could make Serbia comparable to FSU republics that experienced armed conflict after 1991: Moldova, Georgia, Armenia, Azerbaijan, Russia, and Ukraine. Fourth, Serbia's dominant culture of denial is comparable to Russia's official attitude toward the communist past. Finally, in contrast to most FSU countries, Serbia has tried numerous mechanisms of transitional justice, and its experience could provide valuable insights for countries trying to decide whether and how to address the past.

THE REPRESSIVE PASTS AND THE AMBIGUITY OF TRANSITION

This section outlines the characteristics of the three repressive regimes that are the subject of transitional justice in Serbia: the Nazi regime (1941–4), the Yugoslav communist federation (1944–90) of which Serbia was a unit, and the regime of Slobodan Milošević (1990–2000). Accordingly, Serbia under-went three regime changes: in 1944 from pro-Nazi to the communist regime of Yugoslavia, in 1990 from communism to the Milošević regime, and in 2000 from the Milošević regime to (illiberal) democracy.

During World War II Serbia was ruled by a collaborationist totalitarian regime established after the Nazi occupation in 1941. The government installed by the German forces was supported by the Chetnik military units and the Serbian Volunteer Corps, a paramilitary Nazi organization. The regime com-mitted mass crimes against the Jews, Roma, and those Serbs identified as com-munist supporters.[1] The Chetnik movement was composed originally of units of the Yugoslav Royal Army who refused to recognize Yugoslavia's capitulation in April 1941, and instead pledged to fight against the Nazi occupying forces. In October 1941, their extreme nationalist ideology prompted the Chetniks to collaborate with the Axis powers against the communists.[2] During the war the Chetniks committed many crimes against the Serbian population in Serbia, the Muslims in Bosnia, and the Croats in Bosnia and Croatia.[3]

The second repressive regime was Yugoslavia under communism. This regime committed many human rights violations, with the mechanisms, types, and targets of repression corresponding roughly with the regime's changing political and ideological needs. Three waves of repression can be identified. The first wave (1944–5), which accompanied the country's liberation from the Nazis and the establishment of the communist regime, effected wide purges of war criminals, fascist collaborators, and "class enemies" through judicial and extrajudicial measures.[4] Reprisals also targeted ethnic groups accused of collaboration with the Nazi regime, primarily Germans and Hungarians.[5] Dealing with Nazi war crimes was broadly comparable to similar actions undertaken in other postwar European countries. On the other hand, purges of those identified as "class enemies" became acts of unjustifiable repres-sion of innocent people. The second wave of repression (1948–53) followed Yugoslavia's split with the Soviet Union and targeted mainly the communists who remained loyal to Stalin.[6] The third wave occurred during late com-munism, when repressive episodes were regular, but less severe. The regime suppressed occasional mass protests guided by social or nationalist causes with police brutality, mass arrests, and significant curtailment of liberties.

In addition, the regime remained wary of the intellectual opposition, and those identified as dissidents worked under constant ideological and police surveillance.[7]

The end of communism was not the beginning of democracy. In 1990 Yugoslavia transitioned from authoritarian rule to a long and devastating series of inter-ethnic conflicts that led to its violent dissolution. The Milošević regime was a façade democracy. The loyalty of the citizens was achieved through ideological manipulation and threat of force. The constitutional system was reduced to an arbitrary, authoritarian tool. Human rights were routinely violated, and the repression selectively targeted the non-Serbs and the ethnic Serbs who opposed the official nationalist ideology and participated in antiwar activities.

The three wars in Croatia (1991–5), Bosnia-Herzegovina (1992–5), and Kosovo (1998–9) produced an enormous number of casualties, significant material destruction, and serious human rights abuses, including rape, torture, imprisonment, and the forced expulsion of entire ethnic groups.[8] Most of the atrocities were committed by the Serbian government, the different paramilitary units under its control, and the puppet regimes it established in the occupied parts of Croatia and Bosnia. Importantly, the regime and its criminal practices enjoyed the support of significant segments of the Serbian population, which endorsed the official nationalism presented as "protection of the Serbian national interests."[9]

The regime change of 2000, the result of the popular mobilization that culminated in the electoral victory of the anti-Milošević Democratic Opposition of Serbia, created the promise of a break with the continuity of repression. Unfortunately that promise has largely failed to materialize. To date, Serbia's democratic transition has been unsuccessful due in large part to its failure to address the past more than problems with institutional design or incomplete and biased implementation.

In particular, two opposing strategies toward the past emerged soon after the regime change. Led by the then newly elected President Vojislav Koštunica, several parties from the victorious coalition effectively joined forces with Milošević's Socialist Party and with radical nationalist parties and organizations to deny past wrongs and insist on institutional continuity with the nationalism of yesterday. This camp opposed the removal of notorious officials of the Milošević regime, obstructed reform projects in parliament, and protected war criminals indicted before the International Criminal Tribunal for the Former Yugoslavia (ICTY). The second strategy was embraced by Prime Minister Zoran Đinđić and his cabinet (2001–3). Pragmatically favoring the design and implementation of economic and political changes, the reformists accepted the need to confront past crimes, but only after the new democracy was stabilized. This government started cooperating with the ICTY, arrested Milošević in March 2001, and sent him to The Hague. Still, the reformists failed to realize the full moral and political weight of the past. This became tragically obvious in March 2003, when Ðinđić was assassinated by officers of a special police unit of the repressive apparatus inherited from the Milošević's regime. Despite its involvement in war crimes, the apparatus continued its existence after Milošević was gone.

TRANSITIONAL JUSTICE I: DEALING WITH NAZI AND COMMUNIST CRIMES

When Milošević became the unchallenged leader of Serbia, zenophobic nationalism became the dominant ideology.[10] The nationalist cultural elite supported this change, by presenting the communist repression as part of a conspiracy that other Yugoslav nations used to minimize Serbia and the Serbian people in the federation.[11] Since Milošević and his regime never officially renounced socialist ideology, there was no attempt to deal systematically with communist repression, or to reassess Nazi collaboration. Instead of addressing past crimes, a new layer of injustice was added during the wars of the 1990s.

The question of the relationship to past crimes was politically opened only after the regime change of 2000. As described above, 2001–3 occasioned a fierce ideological battle over the past. Ðinđić's assassination in 2003 was followed by the electoral victory of the nationalist bloc of the anti-Milošević Democratic Opposition of Serbia, who pursued continuity with the nationalism of the past. They dealt with long delayed transitional justice questions, based on a nationalist revision of the recent Serbian history. This revision included questions of what counted as a crime, who were the wrongdoers and the victims, and what counted as relevant harm. This strategy first called for denial of Serbian responsibility for the war crimes of the 1990s, as part of the defense of Milošević's nationalist legacy. Second, both the Nazi and communist regimes were reevaluated, by rehabilitating the political and military leaders, institutions, and organizations of the Serbian collaborationist regime of World War II, and by acknowledging communist wrongdoings. This was the ideological framework of the first Serbian transitional justice program, whose dynamics are presented below.

The methods of dealing with the two repressive pasts included rehabilitation of both victims of communist human rights abuses and Nazi collaborators, property restitution, the rewriting of history textbooks, and other forms of memorialization, but not the opening of the communist secret police archives. Limited access to secret files was granted by a government decree in 2001, but declared unconstitutional in 2003. This move legally blocked efforts to raise questions about the repressive and criminal activities of the secret police, the army, and different paramilitary units active during the Yugoslav wars of the 1990s. In a word, the old repressive apparatus stayed in place, largely unreformed.

The simultaneous rehabilitation of Nazi collaborators and victims of communism represented an important misuse of transitional justice in Serbia. In 2004, Law 137 on Rights of Veterans, Disabled Veterans and Their Families recognized the Serbian Chetniks as antifascist freedom fighters and granted them the same social entitlements that partisan veterans had enjoyed since 1945. In 2012, the Constitutional Court struck down the provisions that provided equal benefits to the Chetniks and the partisans, without denying the Chetniks' status of "freedom fighters."

In 2006, Law 33 on Rehabilitation sought "the rehabilitation of persons who were – without judicial or administrative procedure, or in judicial or administrative procedure – deprived, for political or ideological reasons, of life, liberty, or some other rights in the period between April 6, 1941 [the day of the German attack on Yugoslavia] and the day this Law enters into force" (Article 1).[12] Since the law extended to the period of Nazi rule, it allowed for the rehabilitation of both the victims of communist repression and of the Nazi collaborators of World War II. Celebrated by revisionist historians as the "only mechanism of transitional justice in Serbia that has been implemented to some extent,"[13] the law rehabilitated a string of prominent collaborators, most notably the Chetniks leader Draža Mihailović. Mihailović was sentenced to death and executed in 1946 for crimes of treason, collaboration, terrorism, and mass murder of civilians and captured partisans. Immediately after the enactment of the law, several parties, organizations, and individuals asked for his rehabilitation. Mihailović was rehabilitated in May 2015 by the Belgrade District Court, which annulled the 1946 sentence.

This judicial decision was the culmination of a long process of rehabilitation of Mihailović and the Chetniks. While the court heard the formal rehabilitation case, the Serbian government established in April and September 2009, respectively, the State Commission for the Establishment of the Circumstances of the Execution of General Draža Mihailović, and the Commission for Discovery and Memorialization of Secret Mass Graves of Persons Executed after Liberation in 1944. The formation of the first commission was met with enthusiasm by the nationalist media, right-wing political parties, organizations, and intellectuals. Despite their violent past, the Chetniks and their leader have retained among Serbian nationalists the mythical status of anticommunist liberation fighters and national heroes. Such public support for the Commission's work, followed by celebrations of Mihailović's judicial rehabilitation, was the most visible sign that transitional justice turned into a defense of fascist collaboration.

The second commission sought to locate graves of those executed after 1944, establish the exact number of victims, and identify each victim.[14] The Commission had to reveal and acknowledge the truth about communist crimes by memorializing the sites of crime, publishing the names of the victims, and encouraging their rehabilitation. The importance of these tasks cannot be overestimated. As of November 2016, the Commission identified 60,000 individuals killed and disappeared after the end of World War II.[15] However, independent investigations pointed to many inconsistencies and factual errors in the Commission's record, showing that the number of victims was substantially lower.[16] This Commission enriched the scant knowledge about communist repression, but its creation also demonstrated the continuing cultural and political confusion affecting Serbia, including the lack of readiness to search for truth about communist crimes in an objective way, free of ideological preferences.

In 2011, Law 92 on Rehabilitation partly revised the 2006 law by denying the right to rehabilitation to "the members of the collaborationist formations who committed war crimes" (Article 2).[17] Importantly, war criminals were identified as those convicted after 1944 by the socialist courts. The law also stipulated that those members of the collaborationist political apparatus and military units who had not participated in war crimes were entitled to rehabilitation as unlawfully harmed persons. In this way, the 2011 law sent a conflicting message: by accepting the legitimacy of the socialist judiciary and its verdicts, it narrowed the possibility to rehabilitate fascist collaborators, but it also effectively decriminalized membership in the fascist apparatus.

Like many other postcommunist countries, Serbia has also used memorialization to revisit the official memory of its troubled communist past. In 2001, public holidays celebrating the liberation struggle and the formation of the socialist state were replaced by religious holidays and holidays commemorating precommunist events. Many communist monuments were destroyed or removed, while thousands of streets, squares, and public institutions received new names.[18] Some of those "places of memory" are today named after prominent fascist collaborators.[19] While the use of other transitional justice methods balanced an incomplete condemnation of the communist regime and rehabilitation of Nazi collaborators, memorialization was the only measure that focused exclusively on the communist symbols, removing them in favor of a new reading of national history.

Finally, the restitution of confiscated property remains slow, mostly because the state is not ready to address this problem. The restitution of property lost under the Nazi occupation is limited to "the victims of the Holocaust without living rightful heirs," whose property is transferred to Jewish councils (according to the 2016 Law 13 on the Restitution of Property of the Victims of the Holocaust Without Rightful Heirs). The restitution of property confiscated by the communist regime was addressed by the 2011 Law 72 on the Return of Confiscated Property; however, the state kept postponing its full implementation. Claimants expressed dissatisfaction with the adequacy of the restitution mechanisms and the financial compensation through treasury bonds scheduled to start in December 2018.[20] Lack of legal certainty and transparency, and the state's apparent hesitation to systematically return property, has made some suspicious that the government is protecting those powerful actors who continue to use the property that would be subject to restitution demands.[21]

This overview of methods for dealing with the first two Serbian repressive pasts shows a heavily instrumentalized abuse of transitional justice. Rather than acknowledging injustices committed under both regimes, the regime essentially opened the question of communist crimes as a way to pave the way for a revisionist legitimation of the Serbian fascist regime. This revisionism minimized the crimes of Nazi collaborationists by pointing to the crimes of the communist partisans and of the Yugoslav communist regime. At work was an "overlaying of one devastating experience by another ... [where] very few have tried to overcome this false binary opposition, with one revisionism attacking another."[22] This approach effectively abandoned the search for the truth about these two periods. A peculiar proposal for overcoming this binary opposition was found in calls for "national reconciliation." This was where ideological revisionism reached its peak, with its demand for rendering both the fascist and communist past politically and culturally irrelevant, in the name of a new reading of national solidarity for all Serbs. In October 2008, the centrist Democratic Party and the Socialist Party (the party established by Milošević in 1990, as the heir to the Communist Party) signed the Declaration of Reconciliation that proclaimed an "end of confrontations."[23] Given the close ties of the secret police and the army with the Socialist Party under Milošević, the Declaration exonerated both the party's higher echlons and the heads of the repressive apparatus of legal and political responsibility.

In addition to being morally corrupt, this policy effectively undermined both the internal stability of the regime and its international credibility. Internally, it created a public divide between the regime supporters and a broad alliance of self-identified antifascists. Externally, it was met with disbelief and protest in Croatia and Bosnia-Herzegovina, where the Chetniks committed numerous atrocities. A potentially important lesson, revisited in more detail in section four, suggests that failing to distinguish between two repressive pasts in order to solidify a preferred reading of national history does normative harm without achieving the desired policy goals.

TRANSITIONAL JUSTICE II: DEALING WITH THE CRIMES OF THE 1990S

Milošević's rule was decisively marked by the Yugoslav wars, in which mass crimes were committed under the guise of protecting the Serbian minority in the other republics of the federation. Since the regime change of 2000, the denial of responsibility for the crimes of the 1990s has remained the dominant cultural and political attitude. At the same time, an outspoken group of liberal civic organizations (Humanitarian Law Center, Women in Black, and Helsinki Committee for Human Rights in Serbia) is committed to opposing denial, silence, and forced forgetting. In addition, Serbia has been under pressure from the international community to cooperate with the ICTY, and to follow up this cooperation by establishing domestic judicial and investigative bodies. The interplay of these conflicting domestic approaches and external pressures has produced a checkered transitional justice landscape. This section summarizes the accountability mechanisms used to date.

Serbia has applied a range of judicial and nonjudicial, domestic and international transitional justice mechanisms, with the ICTY as the most important among them. This *ad hoc* international court was established in May 1993 by the UN Security Council Resolution 827 to deal with the crimes committed during the Yugoslav wars.[24] Serbia was widely criticized for its refusal to fully cooperate with the ICTY. The gravest problems included the regime's reluctance to capture defendants, or provide ICTY investigators access to both sites of atrocities and official documentation related to the crimes, and failure to secure the availability and protection of witnesses. Under the sustained pressure of the international community, successive Serbian governments provided minimum cooperation.[25] Popular perceptions of the ICTY have remained mostly negative.[26] Most state institutions and parliamentary parties have continued to manipulate nationalist sentiments, working with nationalist cultural elites to reinforce the claim that the ICTY's very existence and activity provided evidence of an anti-Serbian bias. As such, while the ICTY contributed enormously to the authority of international law in general and the fight against impunity in the region in particular, and although the Tribunal invested a lot of effort in its outreach program,[27] its contribution to Serbia's return to democracy has remained limited.[28] This is due to the lack of readiness of the political elites as well as the population to confront the truth about atrocities, and their selective compliance with the transitional justice demands of external actors.

The "completion strategy" laid down by the UN Security Council Resolutions 1503 (2003) and 1534 (2004) required the ICTY to complete all proceedings by November 2017.[29] Rather than anticipating the end of trials after the ICTY's closure, the strategy insists on strengthening the capacity of domestic courts to deal with war crimes. In response, governments in Bosnia-Herzegovina, Serbia, and Croatia established specialized bodies for war crimes investigations and proceedings.[30] Created by domestic authorities under the decisive influence of the UN, these bodies did not fit the classic transitional justice distinction between domestic, international, and mixed judiciary organs. In July 2003 the Serbian Parliament passed the Law 67 on the Organization and Jurisdiction of Government Authorities in Prosecuting War Crimes Perpetrators ("War Crimes Law"), setting up three special institutions for handling war crimes: the Office of the War Crimes Prosecutor, the War Crimes Chamber of the District Court in Belgrade, and the War Crimes Investigation Service of the Serbian police. The work of these institutions has been hampered by political obstacles mounted by successive governments and radical nationalist opposition parties. The lack of investigative support from the unreformed police, frequent intimidation of witnesses by former perpetrators and members of the public, and a general lack of resources have all impeded the functioning of these institutions as well.[31] Against all odds, the Prosecutor and the Chamber have demonstrated a degree of independence from the Serbian government and the dominant public opinion, and the capacity to apply legal expertise to the cases presented before them. By October 2016, forty-five trials were completed, with seventy-three defendants sentenced to 857 years in prison; thirty-seven persons were acquitted; several cases are ongoing.[32] Critical evaluations of the work of these bodies point to the small number of indictments and the failure to prosecute high-ranking perpetrators.[33] The impact of the relative success of domestic judiciary in prosecuting crimes is similar to that of ICTY: while their work revealed the truth about some of the most atrocious crimes committed by the Serbian citizens and state units, this knowledge has changed neither the dominant policy of denial, nor the public's prevailing attitude of denial.

Serbia witnessed an aborted attempt to establish the truth about past atrocities through a truth commission. The Truth and Reconciliation Commission of Yugoslavia ("Yugoslavia" in the title refers to the federation of Serbia and Montenegro) was established in 2001 by presidential decree to carry out research on the social, interethnic, and political causes of the wars of the 1990s.[34] The Commission was established amid a fierce ideological struggle among reformists and conservatives in the coalition that ousted Milošević. It was widely seen as an attempt by the conservatives led by President Koštunica to prove their readiness to cooperate with the international community, which insisted on Serbia confronting its recent wrongs.[35] The Commission had a poorly designed mandate and poorly articulated competencies. It defined its task as the search for causal explanations in a wide historical perspective, based on the assumption that dealing with the recent mass atrocities required an exploration of the region's modern political and cultural history reaching back to the nineteenth century.[36] Its implicit goal was to diminish Serbian responsibility for the atrocities of the 1990s.[37] The Commission called for an "unbiased multidisciplinary approach to history," and repeatedly made references to the suffering endured by the Serbian people. This approach rested on a relativistic view that each of the nations engaged in the 1990s wars had a legitimate right to defend its own truth about atrocities. While not denying the crimes committed by the Serbs, the Commission invoked the "complexity of history" to diminish the responsibility of the Serbs and point to the responsibility of other ethnic groups and political regimes in the atrocities.[38] Lack of government and social support paralyzed the activities of the Commission, which faded away before its three-year mandate expired without fulfilling any of its tasks and goals.

In 2003, the Serbian Parliament passed Law 58 on Accountability for Human Rights Violations (lustration law). The parliamentary debate and voting once again reconfirmed the deep rupture within the Serbian political elite. While its presenters insisted that the law was necessary for accounting with the authoritarian past, and especially for revealing the activities of the secret police, the opponents denounced it as a mechanism aimed at retaliation, the removal of political opponents, and/or the imposition of collective responsibility.[39] The law established an extensive list of candidates and officeholders who would be subjected to lustration. The process was to be carried out by a special commission, whose members would be elected by Parliament. The law opted for an accusation-based procedure, meaning the commission would search archival records for evidence of possible violations of human rights of each candidate or officeholder.[40] The law was never applied, since the legislators representing the nationalist parties prevented the election of the commission. The law expired in 2013 without implementation.

The mass atrocities committed by the Serbian regime called for reparations for victims. Consistent with the dominant attitude of denial, Serbia ignored the needs of the victims of atrocities committed by the Milošević regime in Bosnia-Herzegovina, Croatia, and Kosovo. According to Article 35 of Serbia's 2006 Constitution, any person "shall have the right to compensation of material or nonmaterial damage inflicted on him by the unlawful or irregular activity of a state body, [or] entities exercising public powers."[41] Further legal guidelines remain unclear. The 1996 Law 52 on the Rights of Civilian Invalids of War applies only to the citizens of Serbia. Their access to reparation remains heavily constrained, violating both the international conventions Serbia has ratified and European standards.[42] The only option for the larger category of those who could claim reparations – foreign nationals harmed by the Serbian state during the wars of the 1990s – is the lawsuit against the Serbian state. Between 2006 and 2010, the Belgrade nongovernmental organization Humanitarian Law Center submitted 52 charges against the state on behalf of 188 citizens of Bosnia-Herzegovina, Montenegro, and Kosovo, requesting financial compensation for harms they suffered.[43] The vast majority of these cases were dismissed by different judicial instances in Serbia.[44]

In conclusion, the Serbian record of dealing with war crimes of the 1990s reveals political, social, and cultural dynamics decisively shaped by the denial of those crimes. The prevalent attitude toward the recent past in Serbia was based on the assumption that Serbs did not actually commit unjustifiable crimes: even if their actions caused harm and suffering, they should be reinterpreted "in the historical context." Proper contextualization would allegedly demonstrate that such acts were necessary, thus politically and morally legitimate. Another important feature of this dynamic was the regime's peculiar attitude to the externally imposed normative requirements and mechanisms of transitional justice. The ICTY is an international institution requiring local action, but domestic war crimes judicial bodies and the truth commission were created as local institutional responses to external demands. Paradoxically, the heavy involvement of the international community created a leeway for domestic actors. The broad normative aims of the international intervention (with criminal justice understood as a mechanism for achieving truth, peace, stability, and reconciliation) allowed domestic actors to play a complex bargaining game.[45] First, externally imposed obligations were accepted, in order to gain benefits like EU candidacy and financial support. Second, the successive governments reinterpreted these obligations, and adapted them to their narrow political interests of preserving legitimacy with the domestic constituents by employing nationalism.[46]

SERBIA AND THE FORMER SOVIET UNION: SOME LESSONS

Can Serbia's incomplete transitional justice record offer valuable lessons for the FSU? As stated in the introduction, Serbia can be seen as a unique case of transitional justice that defies comparison. It is a country confronted with three waves of massive crimes committed under the auspices of three different ideological justifications and political preferences. In addition, its transitional justice was shaped by supranational institutions that exclusively pressured Serbia to address the wrongdoings of its most recent past, something not common in the former communist sphere. Nevertheless, comparability among different transitional justice cases does require exact comportment in the nature and number of pasts, their legacies, and the responses to them. The fact that both Serbia and the FSU had difficult pasts that remained problematic during postcommunism justifies the search for possible lessons. The following comments identify similarities and differences among events, attitudes, or mechanisms of transitional justice that appeared in Serbia and at least one FSU country. The goal is to enhance understanding of each analyzed case.

Transitional justice rarely follows the purely principled choice of acknowledging victimhood, punishing perpetrators, and revealing the truth about the past without considering the (legitimate or illegitimate) political constraints of the present. Transitional justice is an inherently political process, in which almost every important issue – from the question of what will count as crime to the question of who will be held responsible – calls on the new elites to make political choices.[47] Serbia's transitional justice experience demonstrates the controversial politicization of the past by means of enforced silence, interpretive denial, and instrumental dealing with only those aspects of the past that are deemed politically prudent for a self-interested postcommunist political elite.

Both Serbia and the FSU republics emerged as new states from the fall of communism. There was a double discontinuity to reckon with: the first break concerned abandoning the communist rule in favor of (formal) democracy; the second break rejected the hitherto dominant communist ideology for a new form of state identity, based on ethnicity. These two choices affected attitudes toward the repressive past and the choice of transitional justice measures. To rephrase, identity politics proved extremely important in shaping transitional justice. Ideally, the interplay between new national identity and the history of repression would integrate the repressive past(s) into a narrative that would become acceptable for different groups and political actors, while remaining sensitive to the demands for truth and accountability for wrongdoings. However, this balance was achieved in none of the new states. One shared feature of the postcommunist nation-building is the insistence on valorizing the positive aspects of their national histories, accompanied by the tendency to minimize wrongdoings committed in the name of the nation.

One lesson to be drawn from Serbia's modest transitional justice record relates to the importance of carefully attending to the temporal dimension of injustices. In communist Yugoslavia, the Communist Party dealt with the Nazi past, but ignored its own crimes. In the 1990s, the Serbian regime denied its involvement in the Yugoslav wars. After 2000, the simultaneous effort to deal with three repressive pasts amounted to delayed and inadequate justice. In terms of temporal conditions, regimes often addressed pasts that did not directly affect the current political environment. The conflation of methods and instrumental manipulation of pasts created conflict-ridden approaches, demonstrating repeatedly the lack of readiness on the part of the political elites to confront the nationalist agenda driving their approach toward the past. In other words, transitional justice was used to further certain nationalist state-building goals rather than as an authentic attempt to deal with wrong-doings in the past.

The Serbian case shows that a viable approach to the complexity of postauthoritarian and postconflict justice must address several related questions: the presence or absence of transitional justice, the appropriate methods and their timing, as well as the reasons and interests that affect the regime's choice of methods. Each country must first identify its repressive past, especially when there are multiple repressive pasts to reckon with, each with its distinct types of crimes, victims, wrongdoers, repressive apparatuses, and ideological justifications. The Serbian case demonstrates that addressing different repressive pasts with one set of transitional justice methods disregards those distinctions and results in legal, political, and normative confusion. The long communist rule cannot be disregarded as irrelevant, and the World War II crimes may need to be assessed separately from the communist and postcommunist abuses. These points are summarized below.

First, the way in which the communist past is viewed and acknowledged affects a country's decision to adopt or to reject transitional justice. The Baltic countries, which condemned communism as a repressive regime and framed it as a Soviet occupation, employed different transitional justice methods to acknowledge victimhood, punish perpetrators, and reveal the truth about the communist past. In other post-Soviet countries, the continuity of the old communist elites and their transformation into nationalist leaders meant that the communist past was hardly addressed and transitional justice never took off. By contrast, Serbia's assessment of communism remains incomplete and controversial. The uneasy coalition between the anticommunist political parties and the communist successor party not only blocked lustration, but also thwarted reform of the repressive apparatus, and access to secret files. Rather than dealing comprehensively with the communist repression, these parties came together as defenders of the extreme nationalism of the Milošević regime. In Russia the Putin regime forcefully imposed and in some ways reinforced a positive memory of communism, but Serbia's attitude to communism remained ambiguous. Nevertheless, in both countries communist wrongdoings are insufficiently and inadequately addressed. The absence of systematic efforts to identify and acknowledge victimhood promoted the *de facto* rehabilitation of Stalin and Milošević as important national heroes. Both countries "measured" the use of rehabilitation, property restitution, and victims' compensation against possible political risks and gains.[48] For victims, such misuse of transitional justice was a cynical abuse of political power, as illustrated by the repeated changes in the estimates of the number of victims in both countries.[49] Those killed, imprisoned, sent to labor camps, forcefully displaced, or deprived of property remained robbed of human dignity and were transformed into pawns of a narrow-minded "politics of the present."

The second point concerns the need for a noninstrumental reckoning with the Nazi regime, and a careful reflection on the limits to comparing the Nazi and communist crimes. Post-Milošević Serbia committed a grave revisionist mistake by rehabilitating Nazi collaborators and equating them with communist partisan fighters in the name of national reconciliation. Serbian revisionism is broadly comparable to the concept of "double genocide" used in the Baltic countries and most clearly expressed in the Prague Declaration of 2008, which proposed a common reading of Europe's twentieth century history that would "recognize Communism and Nazism as a common legacy and bring about an honest and thorough debate on all the totalitarian crimes of the past century."[50] Simply put, the argument is that some European countries suffered equally from Stalin's and Nazi crimes. While both repressive regimes are undeniably criminal, remembering them under one label remains controversial. This approach tends to dismiss the unique aspects of each repressive regime. Their careful comparison is more appropriate for establishing a shared European memory of repression. In addition, as in Serbia, this approach opens room for minimizing and relativizing one past by reference to another past for the sake of sanitizing collective identity. The strong feelings about historical injustice and past suffering of the Baltic populations and elites deserve respect. But one troubling consequence of the dominant attitudes to the layered Nazi and communist crimes in these countries is the use of memorialization to minimize and even exonerate the involvement of the ethnic Baltic citizens in the Holocaust and anti-Jewish pogroms. Serbia shows that, after a difficult past, a country's return to democracy remains dependent on its readiness to openly confront its dark historical episodes, regardless of how unpleasant they are for national groups.

Third, Serbia's case shows the limits of applying transitional justice in a conflict situation and in a postconflict context shaped by disputes over the legacies of repression. A lesson for postconflict countries is that a "frozen conflict" (such as Georgia and Abkhazia, Moldova and Transnistria, Armenia and Azerbaijan over Nagorno-Karabakh, and Ukraine) might not allow for the effective use of transitional justice. This is most likely when the sides in the conflict keep insisting on their ostensibly irreconcilable positions, denying any room for dialog. The competing narratives point to disputes about the facts, their interpretation, and their political use.[51] A counter-example is the experience of RECOM, a joint initiative of 1,800 civic groups from the former Yugoslavia, which campaigned for the establishment of a regional truth commission. While achieving this goal will ultimately depend on the support of the regional governments, RECOM has already shown that yesterday's enemies can deliberate and potentially reach a common understanding of acknowledgment of victimhood and responsibility for crimes.[52] Rather than embracing the dominant closed narratives of "our victimhood" and "others' guilt," the sides in "frozen conflicts" could start working together by "delineating the areas of agreement, disagreement, and negotiability."[53] Only afterwards could they agree on political solutions to the conflict. While this is a difficult political choice, "frozen conflicts" do not express "primordial hatred": their persistence is a matter of political preferences.

CONCLUSION

Serbia's attitude to its repressive pasts is based on a nationalistic, revisionist project centered on extolling the country's history. However, such a one-sided reading undermines any transitional justice possibilities that fail to reify that narrow, positive narrative. Serbia used some transitional justice mechanisms, but was neither concerned with authentically revealing past crimes nor was it focused on acknowledging victims' suffering or punishing perpetrators.[54] Its ultimate aim was to establish a new dominant memory of an unblemished Serbian past free of human rights abuses in order to create the basis of a new ethnic identity.

Since Serbia is one among many postcommunist countries confronted with multiple past repressions layered on each other, its modest transitional justice record offers important lessons for the FSU republics with similar multiple unaddressed pasts. First, the choice to ignore past crimes wrongly assumes that the presence or absence of the legacies of wrongdoings can be politically controlled. In reality, the legacies remain regardless of whether they are (or they are not) acknowledged by the new governments. Second, selectively dealing with some past episodes while sidelining others is wrong, because it makes an unacceptable distinction between relevant and irrelevant victimhoods and sufferings. In this way, it tries to achieve political stability by imposing silence, denial, partial truth, or outright institutionalized lies. Rather than providing for a common understanding of the past, the oppressive imposition of an official narrative of the past is deeply divisive and requires political rulers to invest increasing resources and use higher levels of repression to preserve this narrative (as the cases of Memorial in Russia detailed in Adler's chapter on Russia illustrates).

In Serbia the failure to address the past and the instrumental misuse of transitional justice established a high degree of continuity between the past repressive regimes and the present democratic governments. Such continuity undermined democracy and justice. The rule of law was sidelined in favor of the arbitrary use of political power. Criminal justice, lustration, rehabilitation, and truth-revealing mechanisms were either rejected, or used as means of defending "our cause" against our "enemies." The human dignity of victims was further harmed by using their past suffering as a political bargaining chip. The population remained a prisoner of its own intentional ignorance of historical reality and its own moral indifference to the suffering of fellow human beings.

Notes

1. For a detailed analysis of collaboration of these institutions, organizations, and movements, see Olivera Milosavljević, *Potisnuta istina. Kolaboracija u Srbiji 1941–1944* (Belgrade: Helsinški odbor za ljudska prava u Srbiji, 2006); Milan Radanović, *Kazna i zločin. Snage kolaboracije u Srbiji* (Belgrade: Rosa Luxemburg Stiftung, 2015).
2. Milivoj Bešlin, "Četnički pokret Draže Mihailovića – najfrekventniji objekat istorijskog revizionizma u Srbiji," in Momir Samardžić, M. Bešlin, and S. Milošević, eds., *Politička upotreba prošlosti. O istorijskom revizionizmu na postjugoslovenskom prostoru* (Novi Sad: AKO, 2013), 94; Jozo Tomasevich, *Chetniks* (Stanford: Stanford University Press, 1975), 166.
3. Radanović, *Kazna i zločin*, 44.
4. Srđan Cvetković, *Između srpa i čekića. Likvidacija narodnih neprijatelja 1944–1953* (Belgrade: Institut za savremenu istoriju, 2006), 140; Srđan Milošević, *Istorija pred sudom. Interpretacija prošlosti i pravni aspekti u rehabilitaciji kneza Pavla Karađorđevića* (Belgrade: Fabrika knjiga, 2013), 15.
5. Michael Portmann, "Communist Retaliation and Persecution on Yugoslav Territory during and after World War II," *Tokovi istorije* 1–2 (2004): 61.
6. Ivo Banac, *With Stalin Against Tito. Cominformist Splits in Yugoslav Communism* (Ithaca: Cornell University Press, 1988), 145.
7. Nebojša Popov, "Traumotology of the Party-State," in Nebojša Popov, ed., *The Road to War in Serbia. Trauma and Catharsis* (Budapest: Central European University Press, 2000), 89.

8. Nataša Kandić, ed., *Victims' Right to Reparation in Serbia and the European Court of Human Rights Standards. 2014–2015 Report* (Belgrade: Humanitarian Law Center, 2015), 5.

9. For example, Organization for Security and Cooperation in Europe Mission to Serbia and Belgrade Cetre for Human Rights, *Attitudes toward War Crimes, the ICTY and the National Judiciary*, October 2011, available at: www.bgcentar.org.rs/bgcentar/eng-lat/citizens-perceptions-of-human-rights-law-and-practice/stavovi-prema-ratnim-zlocinima-haskom-tribunalu-domacem-pravosudu-za-ratne-zlocine/, accessed December 12, 2016.

10. Nenad Dimitrijević, "Words and Death: Serbian Nationalist Intellectuals," in Andras Bozoki, ed., *Intellectuals and Politics in Central Europe* (Budapest: Central European University Press, 1999), 124.

11. The most important act of this nationalist revision is the 1989 Memorandum of the Serbian Academy of Sciences and Arts. See Kosta Mihajlović and Vasilije Krestić, eds., *Memorandum of the Serbian Academy of Sciences and Arts. Answers to Criticisms* (Belgrade: Serbian Academy of Sciences and Arts, 1995). For a critical analysis of this document, Latinka Perović, "The Flight from Modernization," in Nebojša Popov, ed., *The Road to War in Serbia. Trauma and Catharsis* (Budapest: Central European University Press, 2000), 109; and Olivera Milosavljević, "The Abuse of the Authority of Science," in Nebojša Popov, ed., *The Road to War in Serbia. Trauma and Catharsis* (Budapest: Central European University Press, 2000), 274.

12. Zakon o rehabilitaciji, *Službeni glasnik Republike Srbije*, 33/2006, available at: http://www.stojkovic.co.rs/pdf/rehabil.pdf, accessed December 12, 2016.

13. Quoted in Milan Radanović, "Zakonodavna politika Vlade Republike Srbije (2004–2011) u službi revizije prošlosti. Zakon o rehabilitaciji i njegova primena kao paradigma istorijskog revizionizma u Srbiji," in Milivoje Bešlin and Petar Atanacković, eds., *Antifašizam pred izazovima savremenosti* (Novi Sad: AKO, 2012), 91.

14. "Rules of the Procedure of the Commission," 2010, available at: www.komisija1944.mpravde.gov.rs, accessed December 12, 2016.

15. For the list of identified victims and locations of mass graves, see "Spisak žrtava i lokacije grobnica," available at: www.komisija1944.mpravde.gov.rs, accessed December 12, 2016.

16. Milan Radanović, "Kontroverze oko kvantifikovanja i strukturisanja stradalih u Srbiji nakon oslobođenja 1944–1945," in Momir Samardžić et al, eds., *Politička upotreba prošlosti. O istorijskom revizionizmu na postjugoslovenskom prostoru* (Novi Sad: AKO, 2013), 184.

17. Zakon o rehabilitaciji, *Službeni list Republike Srbije*, 92/2011, available at: www.paragraf.rs/propisi/zakon_o_rehabilitaciji.html, accessed December 12, 2016.

18. Nebojša Dragosavac, "'Prepakivanje istorije' masovnim preimenovanjem beogradskih ulica," in Momir Samardžić et al, eds., *Politic̆ka upotreba prošlosti. O istorijskom revizionizmu na postjugoslovenskom prostoru* (Novi Sad: AKO, 2013), 333.

19. Srđan Radović, "Istorijski revizionizam i imenovanje javnih prostora u savremenim balkanskim društvima," in Momir Samardžić et al, eds., *Politička upotreba prošlosti. O istorijskom revizionizmu na postjugoslovenskom prostoru* (Novi Sad: AKO, 2013), 328.

20. Vladimir Todorović, Siniša Rajić and Danijela Kožul, "Denacionalizacija u Republici Srbiji," *Projuris* (2016), available at: http://projuris.org/fokus1.html, accessed December 12, 2016.
21. Mile Antić, "Država nije dobar domaćin," *BizLife*, July 26, 2016, available at: www.bizlife.rs/biznis/poslovne-vesti/mile-antic-predsednik-mreze-za-restituciju-za-bizlife-drzava-nije-dobar-domacin/, accessed December 12, 2016.
22. Vladimir Petrović, "(Ne)legitimni revizionizam: pravo i (pseudo)istoriografske revizije na zapadu i istoku," in Vera Katz, ed., *Revizija prošlosti na prostorima bivše Jugoslavije* (Sarajevo: Institut za istoriju, 2007), 32.
23. "Deklaracija o pomirenju DS i SPS," *Politika Daily*, October 21, 2008, available at: www.politika.rs/scc/clanak/59971/, accessed December 12, 2016.
24. "Resolution 827 (1993) Adopted by the Security Council at its 3217th meeting on 25 May 1993," available at: www.icty.org/x/file/Legal%20Library/Statute/statute_827_1993_en pdf, accessed December 12, 2016.
25. ICTY Annual Reports, 1994–2017, available at: www.icty.org/en/documents/annual-reports, accessed December 12, 2016.
26. For empirical data on the dynamics of the popular attitudes to the crimes and their legacies, see *Organization for Security and Cooperation in Europe Mission to Serbia, Attitudes*, available at: http://www.osce.org/serbia/90422, accessed October 15, 2017; and Diane Orentlicher, *Shrinking the Space for Denial: The Impact of the ICTY in Serbia* (Belgrade: Center for Transitional Processes, 2008), 37.
27. The ICTY defines its outreach program as "work with the communities in the region to reflect on the Tribunal's achievements and carry that legacy forward [...] and an extensive and methodical information campaign targeted at the region." International Criminal Tribunal for the Former Yugoslavia, *Outreach Programme*, 2017, available at: www.icty.org/en/outreach/outreach-programme, accessed December 12, 2016.
28. Patrice McMahon and David Forsyth, "The ICTY Impact on Serbia: Judicial Romanticism Meets Network Politics," *Human Rights Quarterly* 30, 2 (2008): 412.
29. International Criminal Tribunal for the Former Yugoslavia, Completion Strategy Report, Letter of November 17, 2016, available at: www.icty.org/sites/icty.org/files/documents/161117_icty_progress_report_en.pdf, accessed December 12, 2016.
30. International Criminal Tribunal for the Former Yugoslavia, *Development of the Local Judiciaries*, n.d., available at: www.icty.org/en/outreach/capacity-building/development-local-judiciaries, accessed December 12, 2016.
31. Sandra Orlović, ed., *Report on War Crimes Trials in Serbia during 2014 and 2015* (Belgrade: Humanitarian Law Center, 2015), 21.
32. Statistical Report of War Crime Prosecutor of Serbia, October 2016, available at: www.tuzilastvorz.org.rs/sr/predmeti/statistika, accessed December 12, 2016.
33. Orlović, ed., *Report on War Crimes Trials in Serbia*, 8–10.
34. *Odluka o osnivanju Komisije za istinu i pomirenje*, Official Gazette of the Federal Republic of Yugoslavia, 15/2001.
35. Dejan Ilić, "The Yugoslav Truth and Reconciliation Commission," *Eurozine*, April 2004, available at: www.eurozine.com/articles/2004-04-23-ilic-en.html, accessed December 12, 2016.
36. *Odluka o osnivanju Komisije.*
37. Mark Freeman, "Serbia and Montenegro: Selected Developments in Transitional Justice," International Center for Transitional Justice, *Case Study Series*, October

2004, p. 5, available at: www.ictj.org/sites/default/files/ICTJ-FormerYugoslavia-Serbia-Developments-2004-English.pdf, accessed December 12, 2016.

38. Vojin Dimitrijević, "Facts Versus Truth: The Dilemmas of a Reluctant Member of a Truth and Reconciliation Commission," in Okwui Enwezor, Carlos Basualdo, Ute Meta Bauer, eds., *Experiments with Truth: Transitional Justice and the Processes of Truth and Reconciliation. Documenta 11_Platform2* (Ostfildern-Ruit: Hatje Cantz, 2002), 205–13.

39. Milan Cakić, "Lustracija u Evropi i Srbiji: Motivacija za donošenje Zakona o lustraciji i njegove društvene funkcije," *Sociologija* 52, 3 (2010): 300.

40. For the distinction between accusation-based and confession-based lustration procedures, see Monika Nalepa, "To Punish the Guilty and Protect the Innocent: Comparing Truth Revelation Procedures," *The Journal of Theoretical Politics* 20, 2 (2008): 224–5.

41. Constitution of the Republic of Serbia, *Official Gazette of Republic of Serbia*, No. 83/2006, available at: www.constituteproject.org/constitution/Serbia_2006 .pdf?lang=en, accessed December 12, 2016.

42. Kandić, ed., *Victims' Right to Reparation in Serbia*, 18.

43. Ibid., 38.

44. For a detailed analysis of these cases, legal proceedings, and judicial decisions, see Kandić, ed., *Victims' Right to Reparation in Serbia*, 37–96.

45. Jelena Subotić, "Truth, Justice, and Reconciliation on the Ground: Normative Divergence in the Western Balkans," *Journal of International Relations and Development* 18, 3 (2015): 362.

46. Ibid.

47. Jon Elster, "Emotions and Transitional Justice," *Soundings: An Interdisciplinary Journal* 86, 1–2 (2003): 19–21.

48. For the use of rehabilitation, restitution, and compensation in Russia, see Kora Andrieu, "An Unfinished Business: Transitional Justice and Democratization in Post-Soviet Russia," *International Journal of Transitional Justice* 5, 2 (2011): 203.

49. For Russia, Nanci Adler, "Reconciliation with – or Rehabilitation of – the Soviet Past?," *Memory Studies* 5, 3 (2012): 328–9. For Serbia, Radanović, "Kontroverze," 184.

50. "Prague Declaration on European Conscience and Communism," June 3, 2008, available at: www.webcitation.org/640tCtAyz, accessed December 12, 2016.

51. Nanci Adler, "'The Bright Past', or Whose (Hi)story? Challenges in Russia and Serbia Today," *Filozofija i društvo* 23, 4 (2012): 122.

52. Coalition for RECOM, What Is RECOM?, 2015, available at: www.recom.link/, accessed December 12, 2016.

53. Adler, "The Bright Past," 133.

54. Jelena Subotić, "The Mythologizing of Communist Violence," in Lavinia Stan and Nadya Nedelsky, eds., *Post-Communist Transitional Justice: Lessons from Twenty-Five Years of Experience* (New York: Cambridge University Press, 2015), 200.

15

Entangled History, History Education, and Affective Communities in Lithuania

Violeta Davoliūtė and Dovilė Budrytė

In September 2016, the commemoration of the seventy-fifth anniversary of the massacre of Jews in Molėtai, a small town in Lithuania, attracted some 4,000 people, including Holocaust survivors, and prominent Lithuanian politicians and luminaries. Never before had an event commemorating the Holocaust enjoyed this level of participation, or received as much media coverage in Lithuania. By contrast, in early 2011 the appearance of anti-Semitic press articles, a radical nationalist rally in the capital, and attempts by the state prosecutor to question former Holocaust survivors about war crimes committed by Soviet partisans set a very different tone on matters of historical reckoning related to World War II.[1]

Since Lithuania regained its independence in 1991, national efforts to address the abuses of past occupational regimes have centered largely on the Soviet period, with comparatively little attention given to the short, but brutal German occupation, and the murder of over 90 percent of Lithuania's Jewish population during the Holocaust.[2] Transitional justice measures in post-Soviet Lithuania had to focus first on the crimes of the outgoing and long-lasting Soviet regime (the lustration of former members of repressive state agencies, restorative justice for victims, and criminal prosecution of former perpetrators), but the German occupation of Lithuania in 1941–4 makes it difficult to disentangle the legacy of Soviet and Nazi rule.

In particular, the rapid alternation of totalitarian regimes – Soviet and Nazi – aggravated social and ethnic divisions, generating polarized patterns of collaboration and resistance among the local population that pitted one community against the other, vastly compounding the social devastation of war.[3] After the first year of Soviet occupation (1940–1), many Lithuanians came to see the arrival of German troops in June 1941 as an opportunity to restore Lithuanian sovereignty, although the Nazi genocide drove Jews to perceive the Soviets as the "lesser of two evils."[4] Nazi war propaganda reinforced the perceived identification of the Jews with the communist regime, while Soviet propaganda falsely labeled all Lithuanian nationalists as fascists and Nazi collaborators. The result was what Saulius Sužiedėlis called the "geopolitics of hatred," a legacy that complicates state-building and historical reconciliation in Lithuania to this day.[5]

Transitional and retrospective justice efforts in post-Soviet Lithuania have struggled to shape historical consciousness and public awareness of this layered past. In keeping with international trends, the "right to history" has become integral to the transitional justice discourse: "historical knowledge, responsibly rendered, has now come to be seen as a critical step toward justice, and the suppression of such knowledge (or its absence) is now understood as the continuation and/or renewal of earlier injustices."[6] Yet, as noted by Elizabeth A. Cole, the connections between transitional justice and history education must be investigated in their own right.[7] This chapter explains changes in historical consciousness in Lithuania by asking *how* historical trauma is framed, *when* a past event is brought to the forefront of public memory, by *whom*, and *why*. In essence, this chapter looks at history framing and education as forms of transitional justice.

Historical commissions have often played an important role in these processes. Broadly defined as "investigative bodies charged with providing new understanding(s) of past events on the basis of fresh archival research,"[8] such commissions may acquire enough power to develop their own narratives, become a forum for testimonies, legitimize or delegitimize certain narratives, and facilitate reconciliation.[9] State-supported memory institutions (museums, universities, and research centers) and nonstate actors interested in promoting their own historical narratives play similar roles. This chapter focuses on "pivotal traumatic events" that play major political roles in making and breaking communities.[10] World War II, the Holocaust, the anti-Soviet resistance, and Soviet repression, especially Stalin's mass deportations, can be seen as "pivotal traumatic events" with a long-lasting impact on political and cultural identities in Lithuania. The impact of various "agents of memory" on changes in historical consciousness related to pivotal traumatic events is not often documented. Therefore, in addition to analyzing the strategies of various "agents of memory," this chapter draws on interviews with prominent actors who engaged in history education and the construction of historical narratives, to bring out their subjective understanding of their mission and environment.[11]

The chapter is structured as follows. First, it outlines the emergence of a "memory regime" in Lithuania during the late 1980s, focused primarily on the Stalin-era mass deportations, the formation of an "affective community"[12] around the trauma, and a corresponding "externalization" of the Soviet regime.

Second, it reviews the engagement of these memories in Lithuanian history textbooks. The third section looks closely into the roles of two state-sponsored agents of memory: the Genocide and Resistance Research Center of Lithuania and the International Commission for the Evaluation of Crimes of the Nazi and Soviet Occupation Regimes in Lithuania. The fourth section turns to the role of nonstate actors, describes the more recent recognition of Lithuanian collaboration with both the Soviet and Nazi regimes, and concludes by noting the emergence of an affective community based less on a sense of victimhood and more on a sense of responsibility to atone for and learn from the past.

TRAUMA, AFFECTIVE COMMUNITIES AND THE MEMORY REGIME OF POST-SOVIET LITHUANIA

The lifting of censorship during Gorbachev's *glasnost* in the late 1980s unleashed an enormous wave of popular interest in the circumstances surrounding Lithuania's incorporation into the Soviet Union, the postwar, anti-Soviet resistance, and its suppression through the collectivization of agriculture and mass deportations. Seizing upon the openness provided by *glasnost*, the first public demonstration in Vilnius of August 23, 1987 commemorated the forty-eighth anniversary of the signing of the Molotov-Ribbentrop Pact in 1939, which presaged the annexation of the Baltic States by the Soviet Union in 1940. The Vilnius rally coincided with demonstrations in the two other Baltic capitals – Tallinn and Riga – and was repeated on a yearly basis with ever increasing crowds until the collapse of the Soviet Union.[13]

That same year, Lithuanians began to buy the latest issue of *Komjaunimo tiesa*, a leading reformist newspaper that printed historical materials, and reached a daily circulation of a half million issues in 1988. History books and memoirs published at the time had circulations of 50,000–75,000 with the more popular reaching 100,000. For example, 90,000 copies of the memoirs of the prominent inter-war Lithuanian diplomat Juozas Urbšys, *Lithuania during the Fateful Years 1939–1940*, were published in 1989.[14] The memoirs of deportees played a critical role in unveiling the crimes of the Stalinist regime and articulating the suffering of the Lithuanian people. For example, the memoirs of journalist Valentinas Gustainis, *Be kaltės: Sibiro tremtyje ir lageriuose* (Innocent: In Deportation and Lagers in Siberia), sold out almost immediately upon publication in 1989 with a print-run of 100,000 copies.[15]

Mass rallies, the publication of deportee memoirs, and commemorative events were supplemented by efforts to collect personal written evidence of oppression. In July 1988, Sąjūdis created the Commission for Investigation of Stalinist Crimes to establish the truth about Stalinist crimes. The commission distributed questionnaires on Soviet deportations in Lithuania, collected data about camps, mass killings, and the numbers of victims, as well as provided the information to the Sąjūdis press and the public.[16] For most Lithuanians, the full scale of Soviet crimes was unknown and their public disclosure created shock and public indignation, which Sąjūdis successfully used for political mobilization.

The "return of memory" also took on a performative dimension of mourning and commemoration. Lithuanian families engaged in widespread efforts to commemorate the loss of relatives who had been killed or deported during Soviet times. The first open commemorations began in 1987, and numerous Lithuanians made pilgrimages to deportation sites in Siberia and Kazakhstan, erecting crosses and monuments at former prisons and forced labor camps. Many took a further step and brought the remains of former prisoners and deportees back to Lithuania for reburial, often accompanied by large street processions.

The initial process of coming to terms with the past in the late 1980s was dominated by various nonstate actors that coalesced under the wing of Sąjūdis, such as the Freedom League of Lithuania and the Union of Political Prisoners and Deportees of Lithuania. These nonstate groups publicized Soviet crimes through mass rallies, cultural events and independent press outlets such as *Sąjūdžio žinios* and *Atgimimas*. They contributed to the creation of a powerful narrative about the "fighting and suffering" Lithuanian nation, with a focus on the mass deportations and repressions conducted under Stalin and on the anti-Soviet resistance. Adopting the vocabulary used by the politically active Lithuanian diaspora members in the West, these nonstate actors started to use the term "genocide" to condemn Stalinist deportations and repressions. This term later became part of a name used by a state-supported memory institution, the Genocide and Resistance Research Center of Lithuania, and its subsidiary, the Museum of Genocide Victims. As recalled by Birutė Burauskaitė, the head of the Genocide and Resistance Research Center of Lithuania, the inclusion of the word "genocide" in its title had nothing to do with the Holocaust, but reflected a strong emotional impulse to signal the suffering of the Lithuanian nation at the hands of the Soviet occupying power.[17] The intention was to strengthen the common front against Soviet rule, not to raise issues that could prove divisive, such as the complicity of Lithuanians with the Soviets.

The emerging memory regime focused on commemoration of deportations and the war of resistance that tended to portray the anti-Soviet partisans in an idealized and one-sided manner.[18] Arūnas Bubnys, one of the first historians to analyze the Holocaust, points out: "At that time the discourse was very self-centered. We were not interested in what we, Lithuanians, may have done wrong. The focus was on what we did right."[19] Since then some journalists and scholars have challenged the idealized portrayal of heroic sacrifice, but treatments of this subject that would undermine the image of unsullied heroism continue to generate acrimony.[20]

The focus on the atrocities under Soviet rule de-prioritized the trauma of the Holocaust. As Holocaust survivor and Sąjūdis activist Irena Veisaitė recalls, "we had meeting after meeting where people were sharing their experience of suffering, but there was no room here for my experience."[21] The entangled history of the Nazi and Soviet occupations renders it hard to address one set of atrocities and not the other. For example, by spring 1991 the Law on the Reconstitution of Legal Rights of the People Repressed for the Resistance to Occupation Regimes (May 2, 1990) rehabilitated over 50,000 people,[22] some of whom had participated in the Holocaust.[23] Thus, layered pasts render it difficult to selectively address atrocities in this region.

That said, the memory of the Holocaust also saw a revival during this period. Throughout the Soviet period, the specific character of the Holocaust as the genocide of the Jews was denied. Memorials and monuments that were raised at Jewish mass killing sites generically noted the sacrifice made by "Soviet citizens." This included the Paneriai site near Vilnius, where 70,000 Jews were killed next to 20,000 Poles and 8,000 Russians. The Vilna Gaon Lithuanian State Jewish Museum was established in 1989. Parliament made the first official admission of Lithuanian involvement in the Holocaust in 1990 in the "Declaration on the Jewish Genocide in Lithuania." In 1994, 23 September was declared the National Memorial Day for the Genocide of Lithuanian Jews, and it has been commemorated every year since. Aside from these official gestures, grass-roots commemoration efforts were led by Lithuania's small Jewish community and visitors from Israel, America, and Western Europe, who visited the towns and villages in Lithuania where their ancestors had lived. Still, these travelers were often shocked to see that cemeteries and memorial sites were neglected, overgrown with grass and weeds, sometimes without even a sign showing the way to the site of a mass killing.[24]

In sum, the World War II, the anti-Soviet resistance and its repression through mass deportations came to be seen as "pivotal traumatic events" with a long-lasting impact on political identities. Emma Hutchison defines "affective communities" as communities "wielded together, at least temporarily, by shared emotional understandings of tragedy."[25] In her words, "what a community makes of traumatic occurrences – that is, the social and political significance of trauma – is thus linked to, and contingent upon, the emotional resonance of the events at issue."[26]

HISTORY EDUCATION AND TEXTBOOKS

In Lithuania, the teaching of history is closely intertwined with efforts to boost national identity. Drawing on a heightened awareness of the postwar resistance movement, the development of civic consciousness and national identity has been a core objective in successive national security strategies since at least 1996. The preamble to the 1996 strategy states: "the Lithuanian nation has never consented to occupation, has opposed enslavement and sought liberation by all possible means."[27] The assertion of consistent national resistance to foreign rule is essential to Lithuania's position that its incorporation into the Soviet Union was illegitimate.

The postwar resistance and mass deportations under the Soviets have served as focal points for the raising of civic consciousness in successive national and civic education programs. For example, the program for 2006 includes activities for youth centered on the "battles, victories and losses" of the resistance movement, and related civic education programs centered on current security and defense issues.[28] According to Rimantas Jokimaitis, a specialist in the Lithuanian Ministry of Science and Education, history of anti-Soviet resistance and Soviet occupation is accorded "exceptional attention from the state," and therefore schools are provided with textbooks that comment on these subjects and additional materials (partisan diaries, films, and maps).[29] Over time, these themes were complemented with greater commemoration of the Holocaust. For example, the program for 2016–20 not only includes the same activities promoting awareness of the anti-Soviet resistance, but also emphasizes broad civic engagement, including Holocaust commemoration and awareness of Lithuania's Jewish heritage, media literacy, and participation in local, national, and EU-level politics.[30]

Not surprisingly, textbooks used in Lithuanian schools track closely with the main themes of the post-Soviet memory regime. Christine Beresniova's study of six commonly used textbooks published in 1998–2009 highlighted several key themes: resistance and the fight for independence; victimization of the nation; and the culpability of (mostly) the Nazis in carrying out the Holocaust on Lithuanian soil.[31] She revealed a highly simplified, glorified, and romantic portrayal of Lithuanian resistance movements, particularly the Lithuanian Activist Front (LAF). The texts ignored the collaboration of the LAF leadership with the Nazis, and created the false impression that all Lithuanians resisted foreign occupation. The suffering of the Lithuanian nation, defined in historical, linguistic, and ethnic terms, was given the most detailed and emotional coverage, while the Holocaust was described in a distant and abstract manner.

Most but not all textbooks discussed the participation of Lithuanians in the Holocaust; however the issues of personal responsibility, empathy, tolerance, and human rights were only partially addressed.[32]

According to research conducted by Algis Bitautas, 101 history textbooks were published in Lithuania in 1990–2014. Some of them attempted to depict the complicated nature of the postwar period. Others chose to avoid the discussion of this controversial historical period (the postwar) altogether. For example, the whole anti-Soviet partisan war was covered in one single paragraph in *Lietuvos istorijos problemos 11 klasei*.[33]

Bitautas detected the emergence of an "ethnocentric perspective" in the history textbooks used in Lithuania after 2003. The postwar experiences of ethnic Lithuanians were highlighted, but the participation of minorities in postwar partisan fights against the Soviets was obscured.[34] A "civic consciousness program" for high school students adopted by the Ministry of Education in 2011 was nation-centric, fitting the paradigm of "fighting and suffering." This program, developed by Vidmantas Vitkauskas, a director of a high school in the town of Garliava, used teaching about the partisan war and other forms of resistance to strengthen civic consciousness. Vitkauskas characterized Lithuanian history as "a chronicle of ruthless struggle for freedom and independence" and mentioned "national genocide" (the Stalinist deportations and repressions) as part of this "chronicle."[35] He described his program as "an enrichment" of the study of modern history in high schools, featuring the heroism of certain personalities and highlighting national traditions, but leaving out the complexities of the anti-Soviet partisan war.

Holocaust studies are better integrated into the national curriculum, but in practice teaching remains uneven.[36] According to Christine Beresniova, Holocaust education remains a "source of contention" for many teachers and school administrators, who feel that they do not receive adequate professional rewards for "spending more than the required time" on the topic.[37] Beresniova identified the "potential for conflict" with fellow teachers as an obstacle to successful teaching of the Holocaust in Lithuania.[38] That is because developments in history education, such as the creation of textbooks and teaching history from multiple perspectives in the classrooms, lag behind academic research and public debates.[39] In sum, attempts have been made in Lithuania to integrate complicated traumatic events, including the Holocaust, World War II, and the postwar period into history education, but individual teachers still interpret the national directives associated with these attempts.

MAKING SENSE OF THE CHANGING NARRATIVES:
ACTORS AND MEMORY AGENTS

These observations about multiple memory narratives in Lithuania's memory landscape raise questions about the ways in which they are constructed and by whom. The concept of mnemonic actors, or "agents of memory," helps to understand the selective appropriation of facts and the creation of coherent and appealing narratives.[40] Drawing on this framework, we analyze relevant state and nonstate actors that have influenced the formation of historical consciousness in Lithuania, including the Genocide and Resistance Research Center of Lithuania, the International Commission, and nonstate actors.

The Genocide and Resistance Research Center of Lithuania

The history education programs created by the Center have targeted mostly high school students. Since the 1990s, in cooperation with the Ministries of Defense and Education, the Center has organized a popular student contest titled "Lietuvos kovų už laisvę ir netekčių istorija" (History of Lithuania's struggles for freedom, armed forces, and losses) during which students are invited to use writing and other creative talents to depict historical themes related to "national traumas" (that is, the Stalinist deportations and repression campaigns) and the anti-Soviet war of resistance. The Center has also organized summer camps for contest participants. In 2015, 1,000 students participated in the contest, with winning works exhibited on public property next to the Museum of Genocide Victims and published as collections of essays.[41]

The members of the Union of Political Prisoners and Deportees of Lithuania have been an integral part of these programs. When reporting on the fifteenth annual student contest in 2015, *Genocidas ir rezistencija*, a publication of the Center, quoted Algirdas Blažys, a former political prisoner and a Union member. Blažys thanked the "enthusiastic teachers" who inspired students to participate in this contest, and expressed a hope that the contest will strengthen the "desire for freedom" that is part of "a guarantee of the fatherland's freedom" (tėvynės laisvės garantas). Other history education programs pursued by the Center, such as the collection of testimonies related to the postwar period, have involved former deportees and political prisoners, including those who are still politically active.

The Center has cooperated with several nongovernmental organizations on memory issues, and has worked with community groups such as Lemtis (Fate) on organizing joint educational events. Since the times of Sąjūdis (the late 1980s), groups interested in preserving memories of deportations under Stalin organized "expeditions" to the deportation sites, took care of the abandoned graveyards in Siberia, and brought the remains of deportees to Lithuania. Misija Sibiras (Mission Siberia) is one of the best-known projects. Its young members have already made eleven trips to Siberia. Lemtis created joint programs with high school students who also travel to Siberia.

The Center has actively collaborated with the Union of Political Prisoners and Deportees of Lithuania to build monuments for anti-Soviet resistance fighters, collect witness memoirs, and organize public commemorations. Sometimes such relations led to tension, as the Union has embraced a dogmatic, almost religious, sense of history related to deportations and anti-Soviet resistance, while the Center has attempted to publish critically oriented research on similar topics.[42]

The Center also leads activities related to Tuskulėnų rimties parkas (Tuskulėnai Peace Park), where two major political traumas – the Soviet repressions and the Holocaust – intersect. During World War II, the owners of the manor located in this park saved Jews, and this was also the site of Soviet traumas. Since 1998, the park has become associated with the victims of the KGB-NKVD repressions of 1944–7. This memorial complex includes a chapel where victims murdered by the KGB-NKVD are buried.[43] The Center leads educational activities at the park, such as explaining the structure of the death penalty used by the Soviet regime in the 1940s, recounting the life stories of former victims, and retelling examples of how Jews were saved during the Holocaust.[44] These activities target middle school and high school students.

Overall, the Center's history education programs focus on the traumas of the Soviet period, especially deportations and repressions conducted under Stalin. Only recently did the Center start to focus on the more recent Soviet past, developing an interactive game for high school students called "The Soviet Incubator" that recreates everyday life in the former Soviet Union, and confronts the players with choices, such as whether to join the Communist youth, whether to read forbidden literature (for which they could be imprisoned), or how to get desired but scarce goods (that is, deal with "deficit").[45]

The Center has recently turned attention to the Holocaust, creating one room devoted to the Roma Holocaust and another room to World War II, and integrating Holocaust-related materials into teacher education programs focused on the anti-Soviet war of resistance and related themes, such as the partisan publications and everyday life during the struggle. However, many aspects of the anti-Soviet resistance are omitted, particularly the fate of the guerilla members who survived the battle, the Soviet trials of the anti-Soviet guerrillas, or the fate of the guerillas who survived deportation and returned to Lithuania. These omissions perpetuate a simplified and decontextualized picture of

resistance as a timeless, heroic struggle, "forgetting" about the moral dilemmas it entailed, the perspective of noncombatants and the intra-communal
tensions that were part and parcel of the war of resistance and its aftermath.

This simplified picture of resistance is evident in the educational materials made available to school teachers.[46] The publications produced for youth
by the Center, such as Rūta Gabrielė Vėliūtė's *Partizanai* (The Partisans),
embrace the "fighting and suffering" paradigm that reinforces a one-sided view
of the anti-Soviet resistance.[47] This book, which can be used as a supplemen-
tary material in secondary education, draws heavily on Nijolė Gaškaitė's, an
anti-Soviet resistance fighter and a self-taught historian, presenting a roman-
ticized depiction of anti-Soviet partisan resistance, and setting the actors on
the "right" side of history (the Lithuanian partisans) apart from their enemies
(the Soviet occupying forces).[48] As early as 2003, such history education programs were criticized by Liudas Truska, a well-known historian and one of
the first scholars to bring forth the unpopular issue of Lithuanian collaboration with the Nazis during the Holocaust.[49] For him, such programs did not
promote critical thinking skills, but instead strengthened an idealized view of
the anti-Soviet partisan war.[50] Specifically, he was concerned with the yearly
contest organized by the Center, which presented the partisans and their help-
ers in a one-dimensional light.[51] In response, Dalia Kuodytė, who served as
the Center Director in 1997–2008, argued that these history contests fostered
"the joy of discovery" (of new historical facts and stories that were unknown
to students), and even inspired some critical thinking as the students started
asking questions about the meaning of January 13, 1991 (associated with the
defense of Lithuania against the Soviet Union) and the fate of the Jews during
World War II.[52]

According to Holocaust historian Arūnas Bubnys, the current Center
director Birutė Burauskaitė has been "much more open to the Holocaust"
when compared to the former director.[53] Under Burauskaitė's leadership,
the Museum of Genocide Victims incorporated two sections devoted to the
Holocaust and World War II. Furthermore, the Center sponsored the translation and publication of Kazimierz Sakowicz's *Ponary Diary* (1941–3), which
documented the involvement of many Lithuanians in the killing of the Jews
in Paneriai, a town close to Vilnius.[54] *Genocidas ir rezistencija*, an academic
journal published by the Center, has devoted more attention to the Holocaust,
and the Lithuanian participation in it (as perpetrators, not only saviors of
the victims). Burauskaitė has not shied away from publicly discussing controversial topics, such as the involvement of the former Lithuanian anti-Soviet
partisans in the Holocaust. Thus, the Center has become much more secure
in addressing multiple historical traumas, rather than maintaining a selective

focus on the Soviet past, thus contributing to the historical truth finding associated with transitional justice.

The International Historical Commission

The International Commission for the Evaluation of the Crimes of the Nazi and Soviet Occupation Regimes in Lithuania was formed by President Valdas Adamkus on September 7, 1998.[55] Whereas the Center emerged in the context of the movement against Soviet rule, the Commission emerged in the context of Lithuania's political, social, and cultural integration with Europe. The Lithuanian body was formed at the same time with analogous presidential commissions in Latvia and Estonia, part of a joint Baltic strategy of pursuing memory politics. Toward the end of the 1990s, recurrent controversies and intense criticism by Western state actors and organizations over issues of historical accountability with respect to the Holocaust were perceived as obstacles to further integration into the European Union and the international community.[56] As such, the establishment of the presidential commissions was "a conscious effort by the states to mediate in this conflict and to facilitate a reconciliation of interpretive and mnemonic divisions within and beyond their borders."[57]

While the aims of the International Historical Commission are similar to those of the Center (establishing the truth about the crimes of totalitarian regimes, commemorating the victims, and educating the population), the structure of the Commission ensures that the Holocaust in Lithuania receives as much attention as the Soviet crimes. The first members of the Commission were divided equally between Lithuanian and international scholars, including Jewish historians from Israel, the United Kingdom and the United States. The participation of Yitzhak Arad, then director of Yad Vashem, the Holocaust Martyrs' and Heroes' Remembrance Authority in Israel, who survived the Holocaust by escaping from the Vilnius ghetto to join a Soviet partisan unit, lent credibility to the Commission's intention to uncover the truth about the participation of Lithuanians in the Holocaust. The goals of the Commission are described as follows:

> To fill in gaps in the modern history of Lithuania, by academic research and investigation conducted by specialists and experts, and disseminate the documented information both in Lithuania and abroad. To bring to Lithuania historical and sociological research, which has been generated in the west during the past fifty years, in essence, to reverse the isolation and separation from historical information, which characterized the Soviet period. To publicize and disseminate the information generated, and inform citizens

and students of all ages concerning the Holocaust and crimes committed by the Soviet regimes, and their consequences for Lithuanian society and the international community.[58]

The Commission is divided into two sub-commissions – one for the Soviet occupations and one for the Nazi occupation – intended "to clearly distinguish between the crimes committed by the two occupational regimes and to avoid superficial analogies during their analysis and evaluation."[59] The sub-commission on the Nazi occupation published three volumes and several studies, and the sub-commission on the Soviet occupation published six volumes.[60]

At the April 2005 meeting of the Commission, its members agreed to continue research on the Holocaust and the Stalinist phase of the second Soviet occupation (1945–53). However, the Commission's work was quickly enveloped in controversy, caused by an investigation launched by Lithuania's Prosecutor's Office into crimes against humanity allegedly committed by a Soviet partisan unit in January 1944. Arad was summoned as a witness. Given Lithuania's perceived reluctance to prosecute collaborators with the Nazi regime, the Prosecutor's activism in questioning a Holocaust survivor caused an international furor. The Prosecutor's Office "took pains to emphasize that no criminal charges were being considered against Arad," but "the mere fact that a Holocaust survivor was being questioned in connection with a war crimes investigation caused an international outcry."[61] The Lithuanian President criticized the Prosecutor, but did not interfere in the judicial process. The investigation was dropped in 2008 for lack of evidence, but the scandal resulted in a long hiatus in the truth-finding work of the Commission, even as established educational programs (described below) continued unabated.

The Commission was formally reinstated in August 2012 by a presidential decree that appointed new researchers to the two sub-commissions. The first included two representatives of the Israel-based Yad Vashem organization (Dina Porat and Arkadiy Zeltser), Andrew Baker of the American Jewish Committee, Saulius Sužiedėlis of Millersville University, and Kęstutis Grinius of Vilnius University. The second sub-commission on Soviet crimes includes Alexander Daniel of the Russia-based Memorial organization, Nicolas Lane of the American Jewish Committee, Timothy Snyder from Yale University, Françoise Thomas from Sorbonne University, Hungarian historian Janos M. Rainer, and Arvydas Anušauskas, chairman of the Seimas Committee on National Security and Defense.

The Commission is yet to resume a significant level of historical investigation. According to Arūnas Bubnys, the Commission lacks funding to embark on an ambitious research and publication program. Instead, the Vilnius State

Gaon Jewish Museum has gained recognition for publications and discussions on the Holocaust.[62] Ronaldas Račinskas, the Commission's executive director, admits that the state-funded organization "works like a nongovernment organization," with project funding coming almost exclusively from the European Union and other grants.[63] In 2007–9, the Commission published several reports on Soviet crimes.[64]

The educational programs of the Commission are administratively separate from its historical investigations. They have received consistent funding from external sources, and have continued without interruption. In 2002, the Commission was tasked with implementing broad-based educations programs designed to inform young people about the crimes of the totalitarian regimes, as part of Lithuania's membership in the Task Force for International Cooperation on Holocaust Education, Remembrance, and Research, recently renamed the International Holocaust Remembrance Alliance. In 2003, the Commission established a special program on tolerance education called Teaching about the Crimes of Totalitarian Regimes, Prevention of Crimes against Humanity and Tolerance Education. The program, implemented in schools across the country, includes: (a) developing a tolerance education network; (b) training teachers of secondary schools; (c) preparing comprehensive national curriculum; and (d) initiating and coordinating secondary school project activities. Thus far, the Tolerance Education Network has established forty-six Tolerance Education Centers (TECs) at secondary schools, nongovernmental organizations, and museums in eight administrative units of Lithuania.

The Commission is currently developing a Comprehensive National Curriculum that will consist of an educational program, pedagogical and methodological publications, a list of recommended historical and fictional literature, and visual materials (posters, maps, and documentary and feature films). The Commission also provides support to schools, nongovernmental organizations, museums, and other groups seeking to initiate their own tolerance education projects with information and consultations on the preparation, fundraising, and implementation of projects. To date, the Commission has assisted nearly 1,500 teachers at secondary schools involved in tolerance-oriented education activities.

Specifically, trainers from the Commission assist in the organization of seminars for teachers and school administrators. The TECs provide educational modules for use in various school subjects, organize seminars on human rights and historical themes, and commemorate the victims of totalitarian regimes, including field trips for students to maintain and visit local monuments and graves. Teacher training activities aim at creating experienced and trained professionals. From 2002 to 2009, some forty-six conferences and seminars (totaling 402 hours) were held, including twenty-one conferences and seminars (317 hours) devoted to Holocaust education. Lithuanian teachers participated in another eighteen conferences in the United States and Israel. The focus on the Holocaust education was probably influenced by international donors; however, the Genocide Research and Resistance Center has provided intensive training on Soviet crimes and the war of anti-Soviet resistance to teachers. In total, in 2002–9, 2,064 people participated in seminars offered by the Center, of whom fifty-two were qualified as teacher-trainers. Translations of foreign-language works, including classical texts like *The Diary of Anne Frank*, were made available to preuniversity students through TEC outreach as well.[65]

According to a survey conducted in 2004, students who participated in the TECs have "a better knowledge of history, higher level of personal historical responsibility, a more developed culture of remembrance and an understanding of crimes against humanity, and more positive attitudes toward minorities and ethnic groups."[66] The *Vilmorus* public survey of September 2001 interviewed 1000 respondents about research into the Nazi and Soviet crimes committed in Lithuania.[67] Asked whether it is worth researching these crimes, 41 percent responded positively, and 47 percent negatively. Over 64 percent believed that an international (not national) agency could be best trusted to research World War II. The results reflected two major tendencies: the growing public willingness to learn about past abuses, and the fact that the occupations are still remembered as highly painful and traumatic. Public willingness to learn about past abuses has increased recently, partially as a result of activities pursued by nonstate actors.

Nonstate Actors

Since 1991, the (re)integration of Lithuanian society into Europe has led to a reconfiguration and empowerment of nonstate actors across the political spectrum. On the right, the Lithuania for Lithuanians movement has sought to capture public attention during the annual 11 March Lithuanian independence celebrations by organizing marches in Vilnius. These marches grew in prominence after the economic crisis of 2008, but lost their appeal after Russia's aggression against Ukraine in 2014, and amid suspicions that Russia supported right-wing movements in Europe. Rūta Vanagaitė and Efraim Zuroff represent another transnational configuration. A popular Lithuanian author paired with a renowned international Holocaust justice/remembrance activist to write *Mūsiškiai* (Our People), a book that activated popular media attention in 2016 by discussing Lithuania's participation in the Holocaust.[68] Although the book added few facts to existing studies, it broke public indifference.

At a book presentation, Zuroff admitted his surprise at how extensively Lithuanian historians had covered the Holocaust, but said that "almost everything about the Holocaust in Lithuania has been written but almost none of it has been read."[69] Now in its third printing, *Our People* has brought this painful memory into the mainstream. It used the KGB records of people tried for collaboration with the Nazis. From 1943 to 1953 over 320,000 Soviet citizens were arrested in the Soviet Union for collaboration with the Germans, and their trials took place until the 1980s. The records of these trials have only recently become available for historical research, contributing to the study of the Holocaust by bringing to light many acts of Lithuanian collaboration with the Nazis in the perpetration of the Holocaust.[70]

The book reached people who had never read diaries or testimonies about the Holocaust, or had "distanced themselves from the facts through various logical and psychological techniques."[71] As an individual of local fame, Vanagaitė's perspective on any matter carried authority, and her book cleverly brought the issue home through its title. *Mūsiškiai* is the Lithuanian first person plural possessive pronoun, "ours," which in this case signifies "our people" or "our own kind." In writing a popular book about Lithuanian Holocaust perpetrators, calling them "our own kind," Vanagaitė revealed the experience of the Holocaust in the tribal, national memory of ethnic Lithuanians. Moreover, by noting that one of her own relatives participated in the murder of Jews, Vanagaitė challenged the Stalinist moral code that held children responsible for the acts of their parents, and had encouraging children to cover up shameful events of the past for which their parents should take responsibility.

Zingeris was critical of the book's factual inaccuracies and the simplistic portrayal of complex events. Contrasting her book to the professional approach of the scholars of the International Historical Commission, which focused on "institutions and not personalities," Zingeris admitted to having been troubled initially by the book's appearance. But he strongly approved of the book as a tool of raising awareness: "Why not? It's good. The masses need shock therapy, with all of its mistakes and inadequacies. She has renewed discussion of the Holocaust among the masses. Scholarly work does not reach the grass roots because even Holocaust educators cannot afford to buy or spend the time to read these scholarly works."[72] Other commentators betrayed a deep discomfort with any suggestion that Lithuanians today should "own up" to these acts. "Those freaks are not our people," exclaimed journalist and public activist Vidmantas Valiušaitis.[73] Vilnius University historian Nerijus

Šepetys reprimanded the authors for oversimplifying the historical context, and insisted that "your people are not our people."[74]

As Arkadijus Vinokuras pointed out, it is the media and local celebrities who can carry the message in society most effectively.[75] This insight explains the influence of Rūta Vanagaitė and Marius Ivaškevičius in popular memory making. Vanagaitė's coauthored book *Mūsiškiai* is written as a dramatic story with clear villains and innocent victims. The fact that she discusses the perpetrators as real people, as one of "us," the Lithuanians, makes her story especially powerful. Vinokuras described the power of Vanagaitė's story this way:

> In Lithuania it is still common to distinguish people between "us" and "them." And so a Lithuanian woman steps forth who is writing, not in a dry academic style, as historians would – nobody reads their works, except for a narrow circle of people, but a publicist, knowing how to write so that simple people read, knowing how to talk, with Zuroff, "the enemy of Lithuania," delivers this message: "our own people also killed." She said something that was taboo to say out loud.[76]

Marius Ivaškevičius, a famous playwright known for his play "Išvarymas" (Getting out) about the lives of the Lithuanian migrants in the United Kingdom, made another important contribution to the recent "memory turn" in Lithuania. In 2016, he published several essays on the absence of Holocaust commemoration in his hometown of Molėtai. In one of them, titled "I am not Jewish" (Aš—ne žydas), he wrote:

> This summer, as I was visiting the Paneriai memorial, my daughter asked me a childish question: How many more people were killed here, compared with Molėtai? The arithmetic is simple: Here one hundred thousand, there two thousand. This means fifty times more. Then why am I more moved by Molėtai? I did not know what to tell her. Maybe because I was able to somehow conceptualize two thousand people, but one hundred thousand— not yet. Because one hundred thousand equals ten full "Siemens" halls. (Siemens is a huge hall in Vilnius.) This is more than the whole Marakana stadium in Brazil, the stadium which I have never visited. It takes time to understand this; I can't suddenly get out from this shell of naivety and indifference where I was hiding for forty years.[77]

Ivaškevičius's approach has had enormous influence on public views of the Holocaust. He connected with the tragedy of the Holocaust in his hometown and through his personal charisma attracted thousands of people to the commemoration ceremonies in this town. Because Ivaškevičius was a "relatively young" Lithuanian, he was able to appeal to the younger generation.

His public demonstration of emotion (reprimanding the mayor of Mólėtai, who represented an "old" Soviet nomeklatura disinterested in the Holocaust commemoration) added appeal to his memory politics and mobilized the youth. Shortly after the publication of his essays, various debates, talkshows and round tables multiplied Ivaškevičius' effect, inviting local luminaries to reflect on the Holocaust commemoration. Thus, Ivaškevičius became a powerful memory entrepreneur, responsible for a shift in historical consciousness in Lithuania.

CONCLUSION

Our case studies and interviews suggest that while the state's sustained engagement in the memorialization and teaching of history is essential to generate public awareness of contemporary history, nonstate actors also play important roles in creating "affective communities" around traumatic, pivotal events of the past. In the late 1980s Lithuanian nonstate actors generated an "affective community" around the experience of Stalinist deportations, and contributed to the more recent change in historical consciousness related to the Holocaust.

As in other contexts associated with transitional and retrospective justice, affective communities were formed in Lithuania around "legitimate emotions" or "public emotional responses" to past oppression and violence. Such public emotions can mobilize people to fight against injustices, but the rights of the accused must not be violated in a way that resembles "legally sanctioned revenge."[78]

The public emotions discussed in this chapter raised questions as to what constitutes legitimate institutional recognition and acknowledgment of such emotions – the crimes that triggered these strong emotions were committed a long time ago and most perpetrators are already dead. In the late 1980s, public emotional responses to the Soviet crimes led to the creation of a commission to investigate Soviet crimes, which later became the Genocide and Resistance Research Center. In 2016, Mólėtai and Vanagaitė's *Our People* coincided with public pressure on the government to name the Lithuanian participants in the Holocaust. Thus, in Lithuania nonstate actors have interacted with state actors and institutions in finding the historical truth and raising historical consciousness.

Our study shows that two state-supported transitional justice institutions were quite effective in raising public awareness of past events and establishing a coherent narrative, but had limited ability to trigger public emotions and form an affective community around the memory of trauma, when compared with nonstate actors. In particular, our investigation of the impact of Vanagaitė's book *Our People* and the mass participation in commemorative activities in Molėtai suggest that nonstate actors were able to stir powerful collective emotions related to the Holocaust that underlie a major change in historical consciousness in Lithuania.

Admittedly, nonstate actors often do not have enough power and resources to institutionalize their version of truth (in museums and textbooks), but the change in historical consciousness may alter public perceptions, as well as teaching and learning in the classroom. History textbooks might not quote Vanagaitė and Ivaškevičius, but their impact on the thinking of individual teachers and families may make the teaching of the Holocaust more meaningful in the future.

It remains an open question as to whether nonstate opinion leaders like Vanagaitė could have achieved the breakthrough of emotions in the absence of the less visible but systemic work to inform and educate a few generations of postindependence Lithuanians about the Holocaust. The research sponsored by the International Commission and the Center revealed historical facts that found their way into history textbooks, classrooms, and scholarly publications. The educational programs sponsored by the Commission might have empowered these nonstate actors, but their impact is difficult to measure.

This chapter further challenges certain positions on the intersection between affective communities built on public emotions and the consolidation of democracy. Mihaela Mihai claims that political mobilization based on public emotions may hinder the entrenchment of democratic norms by triggering cycles of revenge and competitive victimhood.[79] By contrast, our work suggests that the creation of affective communities can facilitate historical truth-finding and the entrenchment of democratic norms. Recent changes of historical consciousness related to the Holocaust in Lithuania strengthen democracy by promoting critical thinking about the past.

Notes

1. Violeta Davoliūtė, "In Vilnius, Shared Pain, Divided Memory," *Transitions Online* (June 30, 2011).
2. Two hundred thousand people out of a prewar population of about 3 million.
3. Jan Gross, "Social Consequences of War: Preliminaries to the Study of Imposition of Communist Regimes in East Central Europe," *East European Politics and Societies* 3, 2 (1989): 198–204.
4. Dov Levin, *The Lesser of Two Evils: Eastern European Jewry Under Soviet Rule, 1939–1941* (Philadelphia: Jewish Publication Society, 1995).
5. Saulius Sužiedėlis, "Collaboration during the Second World War: Past Realities, Present Perceptions," in Joachim Tauber, ed., *"Kollaboration" in Nordosteuropa: Erscheinungsformen und Deutungen im 20. Jahrhundert* (Wiesbaden: Harrassowitz, 2006): 164–73.

6. Alexander Karn, *Amending the Past: Europe's Holocaust Commissions and the Right to History* (Madison: University of Wisconsin Press, 2016), 22.
7. Elizabeth A. Cole, "Transitional Justice and the Reform of History Education," *The International Journal of Transitional Justice* 1 (2007): 115–37.
8. Karn, *Amending the Past*, 4.
9. Onur Bakiner, *Truth Commissions: Memory, Power, and Legitimacy* (Philadelphia: University of Pennsylvania Press, 2016), 5.
10. Emma Hutchison, *Affective Communities in World Politics: Collective Emotions after Trauma* (Cambridge: Cambridge University Press, 2016), 4.
11. Interviews for this chapter were conducted with historian, politician and former employee of the Genocide and Resistance Research Center Arvydas Anušauskas; historian Arūnas Bubnys, currently a GRRC researcher and author of the first extensive historical monograph on the Holocaust in Lithuania; Birutė Burauskaitė, the head of the Genocide and Resistance Research Center; Markas Zingeris, the Head of the Vilna Gaon Museum and a Member of Parliament; Arūnas Streikus, historian, former Genocide and Resistance Research Center researcher and coauthor of a history book for grades 10 and 12; Ronaldas Račinskas, the current head of the International Commission for the Investigation of Nazi and Soviet Crimes; and Arkadijus Vinokuras, journalist, writer, politician, and former advisor to the Prime Minister of Lithuania.
12. Hutchison, *Affective Communities in World Politics*, 4.
13. Alfred E. Senn, *Lithuania Awakening* (Berkeley: University of California Press, 1990).
14. Juozas Urbšys, *Lietuva lemtingaisiais 1939–1940 metais, 1939–1940* (Vilnius: Mintis, 1988).
15. Valentinas Gustainis, *Be kaltės: 15 metų Sibiro tremtyje ir lageriuose* (Vilnius: Mintis, 1989). For a compilation of children deportee testimonies, see Aldona Žemaitytė, *Amžino įšalo žemėje* (Vilnius: Vyturys, 1989).
16. Genocide and Resistance Research Centre of Lithuania, "History of the Centre," available at: http://genocid.lt/centras/lt/823/c/, accessed January 31, 2017.
17. Birutė Burauskaitė, personal communication with Violeta Davoliūtė, May 13, 2014, Vilnius.
18. Interview with Arūnas Bubnys, conducted by Violeta Davoliūtė, September 8, 2016, Vilnius.
19. Ibid.
20. Witness the controversy generated by Rimvydas Valatka, "Ką pagerbė Lietuva – partizanų vadą Generolą Vėtrą ar žydų žudiką?" (Whom did Lithuania Honor: the Leader of Partisans General Vėtra or a Jew killer?), *Delfi*, July 26, 2015, available at: www.delfi.lt/news/ringas/lit/r-valatka-ka-pagerbe-lietuva-partizanu-vada-generola-vetra-ar-zydu-zudika.d?id=68576988, accessed January 31, 2017.
21. Vladas Sirutavičius, Darius Staliūnas, and Jurgita Šiaučiūnaitė–Verbickienė, *Lietuvos žydai: istorinė studija* (Vilnius: Baltos lankos, 2012), 512.
22. Rimgaudas Geleževičius, *Holokausto teisingumas ir restitucija Lietuvoje atkūrus nepriklausomybę, 1990–2003* (Vilnius: Lietuvos teisės universitetas, 2003), 10.
23. Ibid., 14. Eva-Clarita Pettai and Velo Pettai found that in 1991 the Lithuanian government rejected 500 requests for rehabilitation as proof that it was not pursuing "indiscriminate rehabilitation" by rehabilitating those who participated in

genocide and the killing of unarmed civilians. Eva-Clarita Pettai and Velo Pettai, *Transitional and Retrospective Justice in the Baltic States* (Cambridge: Cambridge University Press, 2015), 178.

24. Simon Schama, *Landscape and Memory* (New York: A.A. Knopf, 1995); Stephen Greenblat, "Racial Memory and Literary History," *Proceedings of the Modern Language Association* 116, 1 (2001): 48–63.

25. Hutchison, *Affective Communities in World Politics*, 72.

26. Ibid.

27. *Lietuvos respublikos nacionalinio saugumo pagrindų įstatymas 1996 m.* gruodžio 19 d. Nr. VIII-49 Vilnius.

28. *Dėl ilgalaikės pilietinio ir tautinio ugdymo programos patvirtinimo 2006 m. rugsėjo 19 d.* Nr. X-818, Vilnius.

29. Rimantas Jokimaitis, "Istorija ir istorinė atmintis," a presentation at conference "Lietuvos mokykla ir istorinė atmintis," Lithuanian parliament, November 12, 2015. The text of the presentation was provided by Rimantas Jokimaitis to Dovilė Budrytė via email on February 7, 2017.

30. *Dėl pilietinio ir tautinio ugdymo 2016–2020 metų tarpinstitucinio veiksmų plano patvirtinimo 2016 m. kovo 25 d.* Nr. V-237, Vilnius.

31. Christine Beresniova, "An Unimagined Community? Examining Narratives of the Holocaust in Lithuanian Textbooks," in James H. Williams, ed., *(Re)Constructing Memory: School Textbooks and the Imagination of the Nation* (Boston: Sense Publishers, 2014), 269–92 at 279.

32. Ibid., 288.

33. Algis Bitautas, "Kontroversiškos temos naujausių laikų vadovėliuose: lietuviškų istorijos vadovėlių analizė (1990–2014 m.)," *Istorija* 95 (2014): 3, 58–93.

34. Ibid.

35. Vidmantas Vitkauskas, Pasipriešinimo Istorijos programa: Lietuvos ir užsienio lietuvių pasipriešinimo istorijos mokymo programa X-XII klasei. Approved by the Lithuanian Ministry of Education 2011 (Nr. V-1016).

36. Rimantas Jokimaitis, Senior Specialist in the Ministry of Science and Education, said that according to the Curriculum adopted by the Ministry of Science and Education, the Holocaust is taught in middle school and high school (5, 6, 10, and 12 grades). Questions about the Holocaust are integrated into the final exam for students graduating from high schools. The teaching of the Holocaust is "integrated into the larger context of the history of World War II," and the Holocaust is taught "in the European and Lithuanian contexts." Email communication with Dovilė Budrytė, February 7, 2017.

37. Christine Beresniova, "'Unless They Have To': Power, Politics and Institutional Hierarchy in Lithuanian Holocaust Education," in Zehavit Gross and E. Doyle Stevick, eds., *As the Witnesses Fall Silent: 21st Century Holocaust Education in Curriculum, Policy and Practice* (Cham: Springer, 2015), 391–406.

38. Ibid., 391.

39. Ibid.

40. Michael Bernhard and Jan Kubik, "A Theory of the Politics of Memory," in Michael Bernhard and Jan Kubik eds., *Twenty Years after Communism: The Politics of Memory and Commemoration* (New York: Oxford University Press, 2014), 8–9.

41. Dalė Rudienė, "Atminkime, kas svarbu, arba jubiliejinis XV konkursas 'Lietuvos kovų už laisvę ir netekčių istorija,'" *Genocidas ir Rezistencija*, 1 (2015): 140–2.

Rimantas Jokimaitis, ed. *Skaudžių likimų aidas: nacionalinio mokinių konkurso "Lietuvos kovų už laisvę ir netekčių istorija" rašinių rinktinė* (Vilnius: Lietuvos gyventojų genocido ir rezistencijos tyrimo centras, 2013).

42. Conversation with Arvydas Anušauskas, recorded by Violeta Davoliūtė on November 10, 2016, Vilnius.
43. The Memorial Complex of the Tuskulėnai Peace Park, available at: http://genocid .lt/tuskulenai/en/, accessed February 6, 2017.
44. Edukacija, available at: http://genocid.lt/tuskulenai/lt/419/c/, accessed February 6, 2017.
45. Algirdas Rudis, "Kronika-Edukacinis zaidimas 'Sovietinis inkubatorius'," 2014, available at: http://genocid.lt/centras/lt/2303/a/, accessed January 31, 2017.
46. Žydrūnė Šidagytė, "Partizaninis karas Lietuvoje: Kaip apie tai kalbame šiandien," *Genocidas ir Rezistencija*, 37, 1 (2015): 131–133.
47. Rūta Gabrielė Vėliūtė, *Partizanai [N16]* (Vilnius: Lietuvos gyventojų genocido ir rezistencijos tyrimo centras, 2009).
48. Nijolė Gaškaitė, *Pasipriešinimo istorija 1944–1953 metai* (Vilnius: Aidai, 1997, 2006).
49. Liudas Truska, "1944–53 metai. Ką davė Lietuvai partizaninis karas?" *Akiračiai*, 345, 1 January (2003): 4–8.
50. Ibid.
51. Ibid., 4.
52. Dalia Kuodytė, "Recenzija: Šešėlių žaismas," *Genocidas ir Rezistencija*, 14, 2 (2003): 154–62.
53. Conversation with Arūnas Bubnys, September 8, 2016.
54. Kazimierz Sakowicz and Yitzhak Arad, *Ponary Diary, 1941–1943: A Bystander's Account of a Mass Murder* (New Haven: Yale University Press, 2005).
55. Lietuvos Respublikos Prezidento 1998 m. rugsėjo 7 d. dekretas Nr.159 "Dėl Tarptautinės komisijos nacių ir sovietinio okupacinių režimų nusikaltimams Lietuvoje įvertinti" (Žin., Nr. 80-2248), available at: www.e-tar.lt/portal/lt/legalAct/ TAR.4045F0BAAF21, accessed January 31, 2017.
56. Maria Mälksoo, "The Memory Politics of Becoming European: The East European Subalterns and the Collective Memory of Europe," *European Journal of International Relations* 15, 4 (2009): 653–80.
57. Eva-Clarita Pettai, "Negotiating History for Reconciliation: A Comparative Evaluation of the Baltic Presidential Commissions," *Europe-Asia* Studies 67, 7 (2015): 1080.
58. *The International Commission for the Evaluation of the Crimes of the Nazi and Soviet Occupation Regimes in Lithuania: Fact Sheet* (Vilnius: The Commission, 2000).
59. Ibid.
60. For a full list of the Commission's publications, see Saulius Sužiedėlis, "The International Commission for the Evaluation of the Crimes of the Nazi and Soviet Occupation Regimes in Lithuania: Successes, Challenges, Perspectives," *Journal of Baltic Studies* (2014): 1–16.
61. Pettai and Pettai, *Transitional and Retrospective Justice In the Baltic States*, 259.
62. Conversation with Arūnas Bubnys, September 8, 2016.
63. Conversation with Ronaldas Račinskas, recorded by Violeta Davoliūtė on September 9, 2016, Vilnius.

64. Pettai and Pettai, *Transitional and Retrospective Justice in the Baltic States*, 260.
65. Karn, *Amending the Past*, 138.
66. Tomas Balkelis and Violeta Davoliūtė, "National Report on Lithuania," in *How the Memory of Crimes Committed by Totalitarian and/or Other Repressive Regimes in Europe Is Dealt With*, ed. Carlos Closa Montero, European Commission, Directorate General for Justice, Freedom and security, Direction D: Fundamental rights and citizenship (2009), 45.
67. Ibid.
68. Rūta Vanagaitė, *Mūsiškiai* (Vilnius: Alma littera, 2016).
69. Ibid.
70. Tanja Penter, "Collaboration on Trial: New Source Material on Soviet Postwar Trials against Collaborators," *Slavic Review* 64, 4 (2005): 782–90.
71. Conversation with Markas Zingeris, recorded by Violeta Davoliūtė on September 24, 2016, Vilnius.
72. Ibid.
73. Vidmantas Valiušaitis, "Atkirto Rūtai Vanagaitei: 'Išsigimėliai nėra mūsiškiai,'" January 28, 2016, available at: http://kultura.lrytas.lt/istorija/atkirto-rutai-vanagaitei-issigimeliai-nera-musiskiai.htm, accessed January 31, 2017.
74. Nerijus Šepetys, "Jūsiškiai – mums ne mūsiškiai," Naujasis Židinys – Aidai, April 25, 2016, available at: www.delfi.lt/news/ringas/lit/n-sepetys-jusiskiai-mums-ne-musiskiai.d?id=71032318, accessed January 31, 2017.
75. Conversation with Arkadijus Vinokuras, recorded by Violeta Davoliūtė on September 12, 2016, Vilnius.
76. Ibid.
77. M. Ivaškevičius, "Aš- ne žydas," *delfi*, August 24, 2016, available at: www.delfi.lt/news/ringas/lit/m-ivaskevicius-as-ne-zydas.d?id=72107298, accessed January 31, 2017.
78. Mihaela Mihai, *Negative Emotions and Transitional Justice* (New York: Columbia University Press, 2016), 3–4.
79. Ibid., 3.

Conclusion: The Uses, Lessons, and Questions of Transitional Justice

Alexandra Vacroux

[The Soviet people] need more light than ever before, so that the Party and the people know everything, so that we do not have dark corners, where mold would again start to grow, so that they know what we are now decisively struggling against – and are far from overcoming. That's why we need more light!

We need openness, criticism, self-criticism; these are the most important features of the socialist way of life, and if someone believes that we need this only to criticize the shortcomings of the past, then he is deeply mistaken. The most important thing is that openness, criticism, self-criticism, and democracy is necessary if we are to move forward to solve huge problems. We cannot solve these problems without the active participation of the people. That's why we need all this.

> Mikhail Gorbachev, General Secretary of the Communist
> Party of the Soviet Union, 1987.[1]

Within a year of ascending to power in 1985, Mikhail Gorbachev began arguing that the Soviet Union would not emerge from stagnation without frank introspection. Citizens were asked to shine light into dark corners, to identify problems and discuss possible remedies, and to contribute to a collective understanding of why the Soviet Union could not go on as it had. "This reconsideration of Stalinist repression aimed at repairing, not deconstructing, the Soviet system," notes Bekus.[2] But the wave of dissatisfaction unleashed by Gorbachev's exhortation exposed implacable resentment among many of the Soviet republics and eventually released the Warsaw Pact countries from their Soviet moorings.

Gorbachev's policy of *glasnost*, or openness, resulted in lively consideration of many topics once taboo. Although Khrushchev launched a de-Stalinization campaign in 1956, it had fizzled with his removal in 1964. Open review of political crimes committed in the 1930s and the 1940s only began in the second half of the 1980s, when the Politburo passed a number of resolutions that identified, rehabilitated, and memorialized victims.[3] Given that Moscow initiated these transitional justice measures even before the collapse of the Soviet Union, the failure of the Russian Federation and many post-Soviet states to make any progress on this front is somewhat of a puzzle. The absence of widespread transitional justice efforts in the post-Soviet space has meant that little attention has been directed at understanding why this dog didn't bark – why didn't Gorbachev's suggestion that citizens shine a light into dark Soviet corners gather momentum? Postcommunist scholarship has focused instead on more determined attempts by Central and Eastern European countries to come to grips with their complicated and layered histories of violence and oppression. Meanwhile, twenty-five years after the collapse of the Soviet Union, the lack of genuine, state-led transitional justice measures in most of the post-Soviet states remains largely unexplored.

The authors in this volume address this lacuna by tackling the puzzle of missing or ineffectual lustration in the Former Soviet Union (FSU). The chapters look into the myriad experiences of these countries and ask why some governments attempted transitional justice and others did not. What kind of measures were adopted and why? And what impact did these choices have on the political and social landscape?

WHAT IS TRANSITIONAL JUSTICE SUPPOSED TO ACHIEVE?

Transitional justice measures can take a number of different forms, many of which are discussed in this volume. They may be state-driven, as in the case of lustration of officials (Ukraine); court trials (Baltics); rehabilitation, restitution, and compensation programs for victims (Belarus, Kazakhstan); and access to secret police archives. They may also be nonjudicial, involving historical commissions (Moldova), changes in history textbooks (Ukraine, Lithuania), or removal of communist symbols from public space. Finally, they may be driven by the public, which we observe in informal truth projects (Lithuania, Belarus) or memorials (Russia). In the post-Soviet space, transitional justice is meant to involve a reckoning with the history of the Soviet Union – or more precisely, with human rights abuses committed by the Soviet government at various levels, at various times. In some countries, improprieties committed before communism (as in the case of the occupied Baltics or Moldova) or after communism (as in Georgia and Ukraine) may also be the subject of transitional justice. The underlying assumptions of the transition paradigm are that critical, public awareness of a problematic past is cathartic for victims, discourages impunity among perpetrators, and may be helpful in creating a "mutually negotiated history" from competing narratives about a nation's past, some of which have been imposed from above.[4] In addition, it may facilitate certain types of reform – a proposition that Ukraine is currently putting to the test.[5]

Reckoning with abominable events in a nation's history is never easy; even democracies like the United States and Japan have failed to fully acknowledge having condoned forms of slavery in the past. Doing so is especially difficult when a country has experienced periods of atrocities one after the other, as Russia and Ukraine did through collectivization, followed by Stalinist purges, and the horrors of World War II. Serial human rights abuses have also been a feature of contemporary history in the Baltic countries, Serbia, and Moldova. The victims in one period may be the perpetrators in the next.[6] Each group wants both redress for its suffering and to downplay the role it may have played in other crimes.[7] Ideally, transitional justice can forge a common identity, although it seems unlikely under the best of circumstances. Indeed, one should perhaps ask why any FSU country would pursue transitional justice, rather than why they have not.

WHAT ACTUALLY HAPPENED?

As we survey the rather bleak transitional justice landscape in the FSU, it is useful to look at the overall picture. The lackluster implementation of transitional justice in the FSU stands in contrast to multifaceted programs in Central and Eastern Europe.[8] Once the Berlin Wall fell and the Warsaw Pact dissolved, former Eastern Bloc countries used the memory of communist oppression as foundational myths.[9] Having shaken off Soviet management of foreign and domestic affairs, the Eastern and Central European countries positioned themselves in opposition to Russia.

In contrast, the treatment of the communist past was not uniform across the Soviet space in the years immediately following the collapse of the Soviet Union. At one end of the spectrum, politicians in the western FSU championed broad anti-Soviet narratives that resembled those of their European neighbors. The Baltic states "pushed a dominant historical narrative that treated the Soviet occupation and the entire Soviet regime as an externally inflicted tragedy."[10] The Belarusian parliament passed a series of resolutions that condemned the entire Soviet regime – not just Stalin – as they defined the 1920s to the 1980s as a period of political repression.[11] And in Ukraine, shortly before the 1991 referendum on independence, revelations from Holodomor famine survivors were published "in the context of Ukraine's push for independence from the Soviet Union and its desire to discredit the communist regime."[12]

Other post-Soviet states were more measured in their criticism, choosing to focus on particularly painful periods rather than reject the Soviet era as

348 *Alexandra Vacroux*

a whole. This approach generated political capital for communist-era elites looking to reframe their careers as nation-builders. Denouncing human rights abuses perpetrated by Soviet communists in Kazakhstan in the 1930s, for example, allowed Kazakh rulers to "champion a nationalist rhetoric in order to underscore the leading role of the Kazakhs in building a multiethnic Kazakhstani nation without impeding the collective discourse about the tragic past."[13]

At the other end of the spectrum we find Russia and Belarus understating the horrors of Stalinism, and emphasizing Stalin's contribution to victory in World War II and industrialization. As the successor state to the Soviet Union, Russia's official attitude toward its history is complicated. Khrushchev, Gorbachev, and Yeltsin opened the door (and some archives) for review of past transgressions and political crimes, but President Putin has been reluctant to administer more than light criticism of abuses. For example, Putin has explained that while "many people" associate the music from the Soviet (and now Russian) national anthem with "the horrors of Stalin's prison camps," the proper association is with the "many achievements of the Soviet period in which people can take pride."[14] Kramer believes that countries in which officials who loyally served the Soviet state, the Communist Party, and the KGB feature prominently in post-Soviet governments are less likely to encourage a harsh reassessment of the past.[15] Russia and the Central Asian countries are all dominated by presidents that successfully converted Soviet *nomenklatura* backgrounds into valuable political currency in the post-Soviet period.

The performance of the fifteen FSU countries is clearly mixed. The Baltic states, pulled into the European Union orbit soon after independence, implemented the most diverse set of transitional justice measures, though results have arguably fallen short of expectations.[16] The three Caucasian countries and five Central Asian states have done much less, though Georgia has recently become more interested in such measures and Kazakhstan stands out as having tried more than its neighbors. Ukraine and Moldova have had bursts of transitional justice measures, while Russia and Belarus have not. Can we generalize about how the FSU countries have approached the sensitive questions of transitional justice, and why they have made the choices they did?

HOW CAN WE EXPLAIN TRANSITIONAL JUSTICE (OR LACK THEREOF) IN THE FSU?

As Horne points out in the introduction, the FSU lends itself to comparative study because it comprises countries that share a communist past and became sovereign at the same time. All experienced collectivization and purges, and most suffered intensely during World War II under the Nazi occupation or from Stalin's deportation of populations he suspected of disloyalty. All heard Gorbachev's appeal to look honestly at the past and present, and were subject to Soviet resolutions and decrees that set political rehabilitation in motion.[17] Why did some countries start reckoning with the communist past, while others did not?

This volume reviews the very different experiences of sixteen FSU countries and Serbia, each of which have had their own approach to the complicated issue of transitional justice. In looking over the country cases and their transitional justice choices, political leaders, civil society, and international actors all have a role to play in whether or not transitional justice takes place.

Timing

The Soviet Union was composed of fifteen member republics, eleven of which were incorporated into the federation in the 1920s. The three Baltic countries and Moldova were occupied by the Soviet Union in 1940 as a direct or indirect consequence of the Molotov-Ribbentrop Pact. At the moment of dissolution of the Soviet Union in 1991, these four late-comers had been part of the Soviet Union for about fifty years, while the remaining republics had been part for some seventy years. This difference of twenty years affected whether or not the countries had been subject to some of Stalin's most brutal episodes, like collectivization in the 1930s and the Great Terror of 1936–7. It also played a role in whether or not the countries were ready to contemplate extensive transitional justice in the 1990s.

In Russia, Adler argues that the more time passes and the intensity of the crimes fades, the harder it becomes to implement transitional justice.[18] The victims and victimizers of Stalinist crimes of the 1930s and the 1940s are long dead and "the memory of their suffering or impunity [has been forgotten or is seen] as secondary in importance to the pressing political, social and economic problems" of the day.[19] Most of the FSU transitional justice measures have been more focused on documenting abuses than reforming institutions or providing extensive redress for victims.[20] Stan notes:

> The longer the time period that separated the commission of crimes from their possible prosecution, the less likely [are] meaningful programs that can result in truth, justice and reconciliation. That is because a longer passage of time makes it more difficult to gather the necessary evidence and to interview witnesses. Fewer victims remain alive to participate in trials and benefit from compensation, property restitution, and related reparations programs. Fewer victimizers are in good health to stand trial and take responsibility for

their crimes, and most of them might have already retired from public office without ever being subject to screening or lustration.[21]

Anyone twenty years old in 1935 would now be over hundred, and life expectancy rates in Eurasia make centenarians exceedingly rare. As such, more than twenty-five years after the collapse of the FSU, one must consider both the feasibility and utility of transitional justice measures.

In 1996, the Council of Europe optimistically recommended that "lustration measures should preferably end no later than 31 December 1999, because the new democratic systems should be consolidated by that time in all former communist totalitarian countries."[22] Figure 16.1 presents a timeline capturing key FSU transitional justice measures, and it reveals that several states (Russia, Belarus, Lithuania, Estonia, and Kazakhstan) engaged in important transitional justice measures in the early 1990s. In these same countries, nonstate entities simultaneously pursued a similar agenda. The Lithuanian Genocide and Resistance Center was established in 1990, and both the Belarussian Association of Victims of Political Repression and the Russian Memorial Society were founded in 1992. The rest of the 1990s saw little new developments on this front, presumably in part because devastating economic collapse shifted attention from reviewing the past to surviving the present.

In some countries, interest in transitional justice picked up at the turn of the century, as it did in Eastern Europe, at about the time when the Council of Europe had thought that postcommunist reforms could be concluding.[23] Although late implementation of transitional justice runs the risk of higher politicization, the FSU experience suggests that early implementation is not possible if transitional justice is so depoliticized that it fails to get on the agenda of a country dealing with more urgent problems.[24] In most cases the renewed interest in reviewing Soviet era human rights abuses coincided with a change of political leadership. The importance of leadership, civil society, and international actors is considered in the next three subsections.

Leadership

In the early 1990s, transitional justice was appealing to FSU leaders who wanted to set themselves apart from their Soviet predecessors. Yeltsin wanted to demonstrate that he rejected the Communist Party, and that he could carry Russia far further than Gorbachev. Belarus tried to frame itself as a "typical country of the region" – like the Baltics and Poland.[25] The Baltic countries were the first to claim independence from the Soviet Union, and their first democratically elected leaders did not waste time in articulating a view of

● STATE ACTIONS   ○ NON-STATE ACTIONS

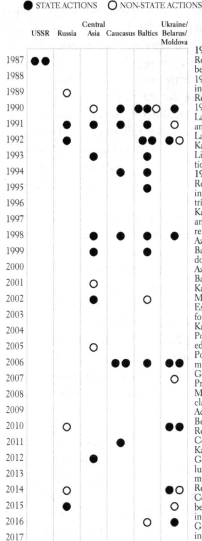

1987 USSR: Gorbachev launches glasnost; Rehabilitation of former victims and political prisoners begins 1989 Russia: "Memorial" society founded 1990 Azerbaijan: Parliamentary Commission investigates Black January (BJ) events; Baltics: Rehabilitation laws passed (restitution laws pass 1990-1992); Belarus: Restitution law, compensation; Latvia: First remembrance days; Lithuania: Genocide and Resistance Research Center 1991 Azerbaijan: Law on returning confiscated houses to owners; Kazakhstan: Commission to investigate famine; Lithuania: Lustration laws; Russia: Law on rehabilitation; Ukraine: testimonies of famine victims published 1992 Belarus: Association of Victims of Political Repression; KGB archives opened; Estonia/Latvia: investigatory commissions formed; Lithuania: Court trials begin; Russia: Yeltsin opens archives 1993 Kazakhstan: Parliamentary commission to declassify and document human rights abuses, and law on rehabilitation; Latvia: Court trials begin 1994 Azerbaijan: Parliamentary condemnation of BJ; Baltics: Laws on preservation and use of KGB documents; 1995 Estonia: Lustration law 1998 Azerbaijan: Presidential decree on martyrs of BJ; Baltics: Presidential History Commissions established; Kazakhstan: Publication of list of informers by initials; Moldova: Truth Commission established 1999 Estonia: Court trials begin; Uzbekistan: Commission for Promotion of the Memory of Victims 2001 Kazakhstan: First Kazakh museum for Victims of Political Repression 2002 Lithuania: Tolerance education initiated; Uzbekistan: Museum of Victims of Political Repression 2005 Kazakhstan: Karlag museum opens 2006 Baltics: Secret files put online; Georgia: Museum of Soviet Occupation; Azerbaijan: Presidential pension for surviving BJ martyrs; Moldova: Property restitution law; Ukraine: Law classifies Holodomor as genocide 2007 Belarus: Activists found virtual museum of Soviet repression 2010 Moldova: 5-month Truth Commission created, KGB files opened; Russia: Karaganov article on decommunization 2011 Georgia: "Liberty Charter" includes (unimplemented) lustration laws 2012 Kazakhstan: Nazarbayev unveils monument to famine victims; declares Day of Remembrance 2014 Belarus: Black Book of Communism published; Russia: Posledny Address begins; Ukraine: Lustration laws 2015 Belarus: Civic initiative "Lustration for Belarus"; Russia: State-funded Gulag museum 2016 Lithuania: "Our People" breaks indifference to Holocaust; Ukraine: Institute of National Memory to make KGB files available

Chart by Hugh K. Truslow

FIGURE 16.1. *FSU transitional justice initiatives: a schematic view*

history that emphasized the crimes committed under the Soviet "occupation," while understating human rights abuses committed by Lithuanians during the Holocaust. The Baltic countries, part of the European Union since 2004, have pursued a transitional justice approach that looks much more like that of the Central and Eastern Europe than the rest of the FSU.

State-sponsored transitional justice in Belarus and Russia stopped when the first post-Soviet presidents were replaced by Lukashenka (1994) and Putin (2000). In both countries, Soviet nostalgia now dominates the political discourse and has "morphed into state ideology."[26] Adler notes that the political system in Russia has become heavily invested in an official, incomplete narrative that prioritizes survival of the state over individual rights.[27] Celebrating Stalin's achievements, most notably the Soviet victory in World War II, reinforces the message that state goals may call for personal sacrifice.[28] Accordingly, textbooks sanitize the past, arguing that Stalin acted "entirely rationally as guardian of the system," though the one-party system "maybe ... gave him too much power."[29] Similarly, while Russian textbooks have noted that Russia's history does contain some "troublesome pages,"[30] by 2015 Stalin had been rehabilitated enough to have his portrait prominently displayed during official ceremonies commemorating the seventieth anniversary of the end of World War II. Stalin's transgressions are outweighed by his having made the Soviet Union a great power.[31] In this environment, state-sponsored justice for victims of Soviet human rights abuses is out of the question.

Most of the other FSU leaders also largely failed to implement transitional justice for victims of the Soviet period, apart from a few desultory efforts by Azerbaijan and Uzbekistan. Kazakhstan's Nazarbayev, in power before and since 1991, has recognized the victims of the 1931–3 famine and 1937–8 purges. Moldova's dynamic political scene has seen justice partially and erratically served. Georgia and Ukraine have more recently taken steps to rectify abuses of post-Soviet presidents Saakashvili and Yanukovych. When political leaders want to distinguish themselves from their predecessors, they often call for an investigation into past crimes – as long as they are sure that they themselves will not be implicated. Postcommunist elites drawn from the Soviet *nomenklatura* and institutions like the KGB are unlikely to call for a reevaluation of a regime with which they collaborated.[32] In Kazakhstan, for example, the incomplete break with communism and the "reproduction of communist elites" means that transitional justice will be parsed and distributed when it serves the leaders by allowing them to "champion a nationalist rhetoric that underscores the leading role of Kazaks in building a multiethnic Kazakh nation."[33] Overall, the Nazarbayev regime finds it as useful as Putin or Lukashenka to define itself by celebrating Soviet-era accomplishments and by leveraging symbolic capital inherent in Soviet accomplishments like World War II.[34]

What about the FSU countries that are run by leaders who have put more distance between themselves and the Soviet past? In the Caucasus, the political elite has been concerned with issues besides transitional justice for victims of communism. The Armenians have focused on the Armenian genocide of one hundred years ago, and have prioritized this crime above all others.[35] In Georgia, transitional justice has come late, and is focused mainly on rectifying abuses of the 2008–13 Saakashvili presidency. The Georgian case for Soviet-era transitional justice is complicated by the fact that Stalin was himself Georgian, and retains a certain cachet as a native son. A 2013 Carnegie poll found that 45 percent of Georgian respondents had a positive view of Stalin, as did 38 percent of Armenians.[36] Meanwhile, Azerbaijan has been run by the same family since before the collapse of the Soviet Union. Ilham Aliyev has been president since his father, Heydar Aliyev, first secretary of the Communist Party of Azerbaijan and then president, died in 2003. The leadership of these countries, as in Central Asia, does not appear to believe it can gain significant political capital by questioning the now-distant Soviet past.

Transitional justice tends to happen when political leadership is convinced that investigating and punishing crimes of the past might serve their interests. In the FSU, most countries do not have consolidated political systems where competing political parties nurture constituencies with grievances that will be served by lustration, court trials, or other transitional justice measures. Moldova is an exception in this respect. Political parties serving Romanian-leaning and Russia-favoring voters have been ready to use transitional justice to advance the interests of their voters over those of others.[37] In Central and Eastern Europe and the Baltics, there were instances in which consolidated political leadership was interested in building a new national narrative based on rejecting the socialist past, Russian influence, and accountability. Where political leadership has been consolidated in the FSU, it has seen advantages to looking at Soviet rule with rose-colored glasses. Where the political system has been volatile and unconsolidated, as for example in Moldova, Ukraine, Georgia, and Serbia (which is not a former Soviet republic but is considered in a chapter of this volume), transitional justice has been deployed as a policy weapon with mixed results. The incomplete democratic transition experienced by these countries has produced leaders who are not interested in spending resources and shouldering the political costs of a meaningful reckoning with the past.[38]

Civil Society

It would not, however, be accurate to characterize post-Soviet societies as completely uninterested in transitional justice for victims of Soviet repression. Even in Russia, a transitional justice "non-case," a 2011 survey found that 71 percent of respondents supported declassification of documents on political repression and 44 percent agreed that school materials "free of the myths of the Stalinist epoch" should be produced. (Half of respondents supported the lustration of officials who deny crimes of the Stalinist regime.[39]) A survey conducted two years later found attitudes largely unchanged, but noted that 36 percent of older respondents expressed respect for Stalin, while 39 percent of younger Russians were indifferent to him.[40] Sergei Karaganov, a political insider unaffiliated with Putin's government, has bravely and persistently called for the "de-Stalinization and de-Communization of the Russian public mind and our country in general."[41] His reasoning echoes the sentiments articulated by proponents of transitional justice:

> I am convinced that modernization of the country will be impossible either at the technical or on the political level without changing the consciousness of society, without nurturing the people's sense of responsibility for themselves and for the country, the feeling of pride in it, albeit bitter at times.
>
> These days all the people live according to the principle "each for himself," society is fragmented, the elites are mostly contemptuous of the masses, and the masses of people are contemptuous of the elites. After a hundred years of Russian history neither the people nor the elites have anything to be respected for. The only thing that one can be truly proud of was the Great Patriotic War, but its uniting potential has been dwindling with years. Society will be unable to respect itself and its country as long as it continues to hide from itself the terrible sin 70 years of totalitarianism, when the people made the revolution and brought to power and supported an anti-human, barbaric regime. They allowed its existence and were involved in self-genocide: the systemic periodic elimination of their very best, strongest and free-minded representatives; the destruction of traditional morals; the demolition of churches and cultural monuments; and the ruin of culture itself...
>
> ... Concealing this history from ourselves would be tantamount to complicity in the crime. If we do not recognize the whole truth, we'll remain heirs not to the best part of our people and not to the best traits of our people, but to the worst traits and the worst part of it: the executioners, police informers, collectivization activists, organizers of "holodomor," and the destroyers of churches.[42]

Karaganov's proposals have not been taken up by the authorities, but non-governmental organizations across Russia have taken it upon themselves to remember the victims of repression. The most prominent, Memorial, was founded in the mid-1980s to challenge the narrative of the Communist Party. Under increasing pressure from the Putin regime, Memorial has been dubbed a "foreign agent" involved in political activities. Nonetheless, its 120 provincial organizations across Russia, Belarus, Ukraine, and Kazakhstan represent a vocal, if underrepresented, element of post-Soviet society.[43] Adler also mentions "Last Address," a project that installs plaques at the final homes of victims of Soviet political repression after 1917.[44] In 2017, the project was taken up by Ukrainian and Czech activists as well.[45] Bekus notes that informal initiatives like the 2014 Belarus edition of the Black Book of Stalinism exist, but awareness of them is limited by aggressive controls on the media.[46] Nevertheless, "memory entrepreneurs" may have an important impact, as writers and memoirists have had in Lithuania.[47]

Several of the authors in this volume suggest that the legacy of Soviet legal culture, and its privileging of state institutions over individual rights, weighs heavily on the population's ability to articulate transitional justice goals. Several authors note ambivalence among groups in the FSU surrounding questions of culpability for past crimes, namely whether an individual executing state orders had the independent moral authority to decide right from wrong, and whether he/she should be retroactively prosecuted for following those orders. Trochev notes that people who worked in the Gulag system do not accept the immorality of their actions.[48] As a consequence, FSU countries have consistently shielded those responsible for human rights abuses from accountability measures. The Karlag museum in Kazakhstan, for example, glorifies victims rather than focusing on who is accountable.[49] Truth commissions in the Baltics (as in South Korea and Ghana), emphasize collective suffering rather than identifying individual crimes and victims.[50] And in Serbia, the Truth and Reconciliation Commission invoked the "complexity of history" as a way of absolving perpetrators of human rights abuses; the actions were necessary at the time, and therefore politically and morally legitimate.[51] Bakinur notes that given the long period of time that has elapsed since the Stalinist crimes took place, transitional justice in these countries will never really be about the victims, and it may be useful to accept these lesser forms of justice if they are what is available.[52]

International Actors

Following the dissolution of the Soviet Union, Central and Eastern European countries were eager to put distance between themselves and Russia, and to be accepted as European. They were therefore willing to sign up for measures promoted by the Council of Europe, whose Commissioner for Human Rights stated firmly in 2014, "While there is no unique package of measures for dealing with past or on-going serious human rights violations, history shows that durable solutions cannot be achieved unless they are based on the pillars of justice, reparations, truth and guarantees of non-recurrence ... impunity for serious human rights violations is a no-go for European states today."[53] Several chapters in this volume describe instances in which the European institutions of justice have not always played an unequivocally productive role in promoting transitional justice. The European Court of Human Rights has been helpful, if uneven, in adjudicating appeals of national court decisions in Estonia, Lithuania, and Latvia.[54] In Serbia, Dimitrijević explains that demands of the United Nation's International Criminal Tribunal for the former Yugoslavia have paradoxically given the elites more flexibility in meeting international demands.[55] International actors use transitional justice to influence domestic policy, and the domestic political elite use transitional justice to manipulate their international position. Kramer cites Andrzej Duda, Polish President since 2015 to this effect: "Historical politics should be conducted by the Polish state as an element of the construction of our international position."[56]

The most important international actor as far as FSU countries are concerned is Russia. Trochev argues that the "shadow of Russia" limits opportunities for transitional justice. Stan agrees that Russian officials oppose efforts that diminish the positive legacy of the Soviet Union because they fear that this will reduce Russian influence today.[57] The complex case of Moldova, in which full-fledged justice would require contrition from four state actors (Romania, Russia, Moldova, and Transnistria), highlights Russia's resistance to negative assessments of the Soviet Union within what it considers its sphere of influence – the FSU. Both Russia and Transnistria have passed legislation that criminalizes critical assessments of the Soviet past.[58] In short, it is not only domestic political actors that are willing to instrumentalize calls for transitional justice – Russia's unwillingness to support reassessment of the Soviet role in developing FSU countries has undoubtedly reduced interest in doing so among FSU elites keen to maintain good relations with the Russian Federation.

CONCLUSION

The authors in this volume make it clear that the transitional justice measures implemented in FSU countries (and Serbia) leave much to be desired. The decision to introduce such measures is a political calculation made by national elites when expedient – that is, when doing so is likely to augment their ability to retain power. The chapters on Kazakhstan, Ukraine, Moldova, and Serbia provide concrete examples of how transitional justice has been instrumentalized by parties across the political spectrum. As Stan writes in the case of Moldova, "since 1991 transitional justice has been pursued (or rejected) by various state actors not so much because they believed in the need to right past wrongs, but in the hope of undermining their political opponents and protecting their own electoral advantage."[59] Bekus notes in reference to Belarus that "even authoritarian regimes are eager to ingratiate themselves with former victims in order to prevent civil unrest and gain additional electoral support."[60] Both domestic and international factors can affect the elite's calculations, and many are addressed in this volume.

The country cases presented in this volume challenge three of the basic assumptions of transitional justice. First, it has been assumed that the choice to implement transitional justice has a positive impact on state-building and reconciliation. The Council of Europe defines lustration, for example, as "a democracy promoter mechanism by which a democracy is capable of defending itself."[61] In Serbia, however, the ultimate aim of transitional justice was "to establish a new dominant memory of an unblemished Serbian past free of human rights abuses in order to create the basis of a new ethnic identity."[62] Elites who choose to introduce transitional justice measures may assume that they can tamp down the bad memories and get some benefit out of the process. But authoritarian-minded leaders in the FSU are likely to be sympathetic to Bakinur's conclusion that truth commissions "are more likely to increase narrative pluralism and societal tension than lead to reconciliation."[63] Given the Baltic experience, and the fact that some of the Central European countries that implemented transitional justice (for example, Hungary and Poland) have experienced backsliding in the democratic process, the assumption that transitional justice is an essential precondition of building a sustainable, democratic political order requires more rigorous testing.

Second, lustration has been characterized as the "engine of reform for the administrative state."[64] Clearing out perpetrators of abuses from the ranks of officialdom is held to be an important element in bureaucratic modernization. For this to be true, however, lustration must take place while the perpetrators still retain power, either formally or informally. Ukraine's 2014 laws, accordingly, target those who benefitted from the Yanukovich government of 2010–14, and aim at simultaneous lustration and anticorruption. Reckoning with the Soviet, and particularly the Stalinist past, however, cannot hope to produce the same effect. Bakinur notes that in the Baltics, truth commissions were "more about investigating the contentious narrative about the past rather than promoting reforms or reconciliation."[65] The very contentiousness of the narrative may itself delay transitional justice and undercut the possibility of building momentum for reforms. In Moldova, the ten years that politicians spent debating lustration, starting in 2000, allowed the communist elite to retain and convert its economic and political clout.[66]

Finally, transitional justice is "supposed to reflect an ethic of self-reflection."[67] The Serbian truth commissions, however, demonstrate that the instrumentalization of transitional justice can actually aggravate the miscarriage of justice.

The 2004 Serbian law on the Rights of Veterans, Disabled Veterans and Their Families simultaneously rehabilitated both Nazi collaborators and victims of communism.[68] As Dimitrijević notes, the "failure to distinguish between two repressive pasts in order to solidify a preferred reading of national history ... does normative harm without achieving policy goals."[69]

Transitional justice has been seen as an important element of democratization. Given that only six of the fifteen post-Soviet countries are seen as democratic by Freedom House in 2017, a volume that considered transitional justice in the FSU must necessarily deal with a variety of cases. Of the six democratic FSU countries (Estonia, Latvia, Lithuania, Georgia, Moldova, and Ukraine), only the first three have implemented systematic transitional justice to reckon with the Soviet past. These are also the three that have the most consolidated democratic systems. This would seem to support the usefulness of transitional justice in democratization. However, Georgia, Moldova, Ukraine, and Serbia suggest that effective transitional justice may not be necessary for democratization. These countries have all initiated some kind of transitional justice measures, but they have either come after democratization (Ukraine, Georgia), or have been extensively manipulated by political actors during the long postcommunist transition (Moldova, Serbia). None of these cases have produced model transitional justice programs or outcomes, and we are hard-pressed to affirm that ineffective transitional justice is better than none at all.

One possible conclusion of this volume is that nonstate transitional justice measures can, if in a limited way, address the communist past when states are unwilling to adopt decisive measures on their own. Russian nongovernmental organizations have quietly pursued recognition for victims of communist political repression across the country, even as the Putin regime downplays the "excesses" of Stalinist governance. The publication of Holodomor testimonies in Ukraine pushed de-communization forward faster than the authorities might have chosen to do so on their own. Memory entrepreneurs in Lithuania used books and memoires to raise civic consciousness of collaboration in the Holocaust in a way that augmented the effectiveness of the state-run research center and historical commission. Of course, Bekus and Adler provide a note of caution to this assessment, as nonstate actors are also susceptible to instrumental manipulation of transitional justice to create a certain beneficial narrative about the past as well.

The political elite of an authoritarian government may not choose to reckon with a past that serves its purposes, as the decision to adopt transitional justice measures like lustration, court trials, or truth commissions is a political calculation that rarely favors exposing past crimes. Dimitrijević notes that both Serbia and Putin's Russia "'measured' the use of rehabilitation, property restitution and victims compensation against possible political risks and gains" and decided not to open a can of worms that might undercut the legitimacy of the governing group or ideology. Adler notes that "historical scholarship thrives on the assumption that the past produces the present. But in Russia's politicized history, it is the present that produces the past by choosing which parts should be remembered."[70]

This highlights a paradox of transitional justice: if you wait too long after the crimes have been committed, the urgency to compensate victims and punish perpetrators is lost. But if you act while those implicated are still active, the political elite will find it less appealing to do a thorough reckoning. Transitional justice requires that the nation's leaders believe that their country will be stronger if they build a new, postcommunist identity that acknowledges a sometimes ugly history. The political elites in the FSU and Serbia have not, for the most part, been ready to face this challenge.

Notes

1. Gorbachev's closing remarks at the Central Committee CPSU Plenum of January 28, 1987, available at: http://soveticus5.narod.ru/88/zakl1987.htm, accessed July 4, 2017. Translated by author.
2. Bekus, Chapter 5.
3. Bekus, Table 5.1. A 1988 Politburo meeting set transitional justice goals for the USSR.
4. Stan, Chapter 1; Bakinur, Chapter 7; and Adler, Chapter 2.
5. Horne, Chapter 8, on combining lustration with anticorruption.
6. Bakiner, Chapter 7.
7. Stan, Chapter 12.
8. Lavinia Stan, ed. *Transitional Justice in Eastern Europe and the Former Soviet Union* (London: Routledge, 2009).
9. Bekus makes this point while noting that the Belarusian anticommunists joined in this sentiment in the early 1990s as a way of framing Belarus as part of Europe.
10. Fijalkowski, Chapter 10, fn 15.
11. Bekus, Chapter 5.
12. Kasianov cited in Klymenko, Chapter 9, fn 21.
13. Trochev, Chapter 4.
14. Kramer, Chapter 3, fn 44.
15. Kramer, Chapter 3.
16. Bakiner's chapter suggests that the Baltic truth commissions made a limited contribution to debates on social memory. Generally created immediately upon the fall of a dictatorship, truth commissions are intended to prompt reform, promote reconciliation, promote noncriminal sanctions such as lustration, and increase awareness of the past. Those created in the last decades of the twentieth century, however, fell short of these objectives.
17. Bekus, Table 5.1.

18. Adler, Chapter 2.
19. Although Lavinia Stan is talking about the case of Moldova, which I've grouped with the Baltics, her comment applies to crimes of the 1930s–40s.
20. Bakiner is discussing the truth commissions set up in several postcommunist countries, noting that they were "focused on documentation of abuses and preservation of historic memory more than reform of political and judicial institutions or redress for victims."
21. Stan, Chapter 1.
22. Horne, Chapter 8, fn 1 and 30 for Guidelines.
23. Horne notes that with two decades of late lustration measures behind us, it seems that "many CE countries engaged in late lustration in a manner which appeared to support trust building and democratization." Indeed, Poland's began in 1997, when the Council of Europe thought they should be concluding.
24. Horne, Chapter 8.
25. Bekus, Chapter 5.
26. Ibid.
27. Adler, Chapter 2.
28. Ibid.
29. Ibid.
30. Ibid.
31. Kramer, Chapter 3.
32. Elites who have monetized their communist connections are also not likely to support transitional justice measures. As Lavinia Stan notes in Moldova, it is "generally accepted ... that lack of lustration allowed the old communist elites to retain their political and economic clout, and to turn into a veritable mafia diverting public assets for their own private gain." Chapter 12.
33. Trochev, Chapter 4.
34. Bekus notes that because World War II was so devastating, Belarus experienced post-Stalinism as a sort of golden age and was reluctant to break up the Soviet Union. Chapter 5.
35. Suciu, Chapter 13.
36. The Carnegie report found that 42 percent of Russian respondents named Stalin as the most influential historical figure. Lev Gudkov, a Russian sociologist, wrote in the report that "Vladimir Putin's Russia of 2012 needs symbols of authority and national strength, however controversial they may be, to validate the newly authoritarian political order. Stalin, a despotic leader responsible for mass bloodshed but still identified with wartime victory and national unity, fits this need for symbols that reinforce the current political ideology." Thomas De Waal, Maria Lipman, Lev Gudkov, and Lasha Bakradze, "The Stalin Puzzle: Deciphering Post-Soviet Public Opinion," *Carnegie Europe*, March 1, 2013, available at: http://carnegieeurope.eu/2013/03/01/stalin-puzzle-deciphering-post-soviet-public-opinion-pub-51075, accessed July 20, 2017. See also Austin, Chapter 11.
37. Stan, Chapter 12.
38. Stan, Chapter 1.
39 Russian Public Opinion Research Center (VCIOM), *DeStalinization in Progress*, Press Release No. 1369, May 17, 2011, available at: https://wciom.com/index.php?id=61&uid=14, accessed July 9, 2017.

40 Or, in the words of VCIOM, felt no emotions. VCIOM, *DeStalinization in Progress*. This resonates with Kramer's assertion that young Russians look favorably upon Stalin (Chapter 3). For a discussion of the reframing of the Soviet experience, see Thomas Sherlock, "Russian Politics and the Soviet Past: Reassessing Stalin and Stalinism under Vladimir Putin," *Communist and Post-Communist Studies* 49, 1 (2016): 45–59.

41 "Speech by Sergei Karaganov at a meeting of the Council on Civil Society and Human Rights discussion of the Project on the Perpetuation of the Memory of Victims of the Totalitarian Regime and on National Reconciliation," *Johnson's Russia List*, February 8, 2011, available at: www.russialist.org/archives/russia-karaganov-project-perpetuate-memory-totalitarian-victims-national-reconciliation-feb-320.php, accessed July 9, 2017.

42 Ibid.

43 Anne White, "The Memorial Society in the Russian Provinces," *Europe-Asia Studies*, 47, 8 (1995): 1343–66.

44 Last Address relies on the 1992 Federal Law "On Rehabilitation of Victims of Political Repression," which notes that "In the years of Soviet power, millions of people were victims of the totalitarian state, suffered repression for political and religious convictions, or for social, national or other characteristics ... The goal of this Law is to rehabilitate all victims of political repression implemented on the territory of the Russian Federation after 25 October (7 November) 1917." See Sergei Parkhomenko, "'Last Address' – An Anti-totalitarian Project Which Gives Voice to Man's Right to Life," *Fund for Last Address*, June 29, 2017, available at: www.poslednyadres.ru/articles/gordon_posledn_adresa_praga.htm, accessed July 9, 2017.

45 Ibid.

46 Bekus, Chapter 5.

47 Davoliūtė and Budrytė, Chapter 15.

48 Trochev, Chapter 4.

49 Although the Kazakh courts rehabilitated 7,000 people between 1960 and 1978, Kazakh intellectuals and secret police veterans refute the idea of personal responsibility for crimes committed under Soviet rule. Alexei Trochev characterizes Kazakh transitional justice as "symbolic attempts" to address human rights abuses without blaming specific individuals, see Chapter 4.

50 Bakiner, Chapter 7.

51 Dimitrijević, Chapter 14.

52 Bakiner, Chapter 7.

53 Nils Muižnieks, "Transitional Justice in the Context of European Convention Obligations: The Right to Life and Dealing with the Past." Speech presented to Council of Europe, Commissioner for Human Rights. University of Ulster: Belfast. November 6, 2014, available at: https://rm.coe.int/ref/CommDH/Speech(2014)10, accessed July 9, 2017.

54 Fijalkowski, Chapter 10.

55 Dimitrijević, Chapter 14.

56 Duda, 2016 cited in Kramer, Chapter 3, fn 19.

57 Stan, Chapter 1.

58. Russia's May 5, 2014 law bans "wittingly spreading false information about the activity of the USSR during the years of World War Two."

59. Stan, Chapter 12.
60. Bekus, Chapter 5.
61. Horne, Chapter 8. This concept is the cornerstone of Chapter 6 by Roman David.
62. Dimitrijević, Chapter 14.
63. Bakiner, Chapter 7.
64. David, Chapter 6.
65. Bakiner, Chapter 7.
66. Stan, Chapter 12.
67. Bakiner, Chapter 7.
68. Dimitrijević, Chapter 14.
69. Ibid.
70. Adler, Chapter 2.

Bibliography

Ablazhey, Natalya. 2014. "Kampaniia vnutrennei peredislokatsii spetsposelentsev v nachale 1950-kh gg.: nerealizovannaia direktiva." *Proceedings of the International Conference "Znat', chtoby ne zabyt': totalitarnaia vlast' i narod v 20 – nachale 50-kh godov XX veka."* May 30–31, 2014. Ust'-Kamenogorsk: Media-Alians, 37–48.

Abrahamyan, Aram. no date. "Lustration Pros and Cons." *Aravot.am*, available at: http://en.aravot.am/2016/12/03/184901/, accessed May 18, 2017.

Adamushka, Uladzimir. 1994. *Palitychnyia represii 20-50 hadou na Belarusi.* Minsk: Belarus.

"Address of Judges of the Constitutional Court of Ukraine to European and International Organizations and Human Rights Institutions." February 24, 2014, available at: www.ccu.gov.ua/en/print/14158, accessed May 10, 2017.

Adler, Nanci. 1993. *Victims of Soviet Terror: The Story of the Memorial Movement.* Westport: Praeger.

2002. *The Gulag Survivor: Beyond the Soviet System.* New Brunswick: Transaction Publishers.

2005. "The Future of the Soviet Past Remains Unpredictable: The Resurrection of Stalinist Symbols Amidst the Exhumation of Mass Graves." *Europe-Asia Studies* 57, 8: 1093–119.

2012. *Keeping Faith with the Party: Communist Believers Return from the Gulag.* Bloomington: Indiana University Press.

2012. "Reconciliation with - or Rehabilitation of - the Soviet Past?" *Memory Studies* 5, 3: 327–38.

2012. "'The Bright Past', or Whose (Hi)story? Challenges in Russia and Serbia Today." *Filozofija i društvo* 23, 4: 119–38.

2013. "Russia," in Lavinia Stan and Nadya Nedelsky, eds. *Encyclopedia of Transitional Justice.* New York: Cambridge University Press, Vol. 2: 404–12.

Ageeva, Tatiana. 2016. "Pravo zhertv politicheskikh repressii na vozmeschenie uscherba osnovano na Konstitutsii i deistvujuschem zakonodatelstve i nie ogranicheno skokami." Belarusian Documents Center, available at: https://bydc.info/news/444-tatyana-ageeva-pravo-zhertv-politicheskikh-repressij-na-vozmeschenie-ushcherba-osnovano-na-konstitutsii-i-dejstvuyushchem-zakonodatelstve-I-ne-ogranicheno-srokami, accessed January 20, 2017.

Aghekyan, Elen. 2013. "The Mother of All Statues." *The Abovyan Group*, December 10, available at: https://abovyangroup.org/2013/12/10/mother-of-all-statues, accessed May 29, 2017.

  2014. "Lenin in Yerevan." *The Abovyan Group*, August 31, available at: https://abovy angroup.org/2014/08/31/lenin-in-yerevan, accessed May 6, 2017.

  2014. "Memory and Memorial: April 24 Atop Tsitsernakaberd." *The Abovyan Group*, April 24, available at: https://abovyangroup.org/2014/04/24/memory-and-memorial-april-24-atop-tsitsernakaberd/, accessed May 29, 2017.

Aitbauly, Talgat. 1992. «Ұлы жұттың жазбалары» "[Chronicle of the Great Dzhut.]". Alma-Ata: Дәуір.

Aleksiun, Natalia. 2007. "Polish Historians Respond to Jedwabne," in Robert Cherry and Annamaria Orla-Bukowska, eds. *Rethinking Poles and Jews: Troubled Past, Brighter Future*. Lanham: Rowman & Littlefield, 164–88.

Alexandrov, Mikhail. 1999. *Uneasy Alliance: Relations between Russia and Kazakhstan in the Post-Soviet Era, 1992-1997*. Boulder: Greenwood.

Alexandrova, Lyudmila. 2013. "Work on Standard Russian History Manual Proves Really Daunting Task." *Itar-Tass*, September 26, available at: http://tass.com/opin ions/763057, accessed June 22, 2017.

  2015. "Russia Condemns Political Repression Officially." *TASS*, August 19, available at: http://tass.com/opinions/815336, accessed June 21, 2017.

Alexandru, Sorin. 2016. "La Tiraspol pana la 7 ani de inchisoare daca negi rolul "pozitiv" al armatei ruse." *Capital*, June 29, available at: www.capital.ro/la-tiraspol-faci-pana-la-7-ani-de-inchisoare-daca-negi-rolul-pozitiv-al-armatei-ruse.html, accessed February 5, 2017.

Allworth, Edward. 1994. *Central Asia, 130 Years of Russian Dominance: A Historical Overview*. Durham: Duke University Press.

Almond, Gabriel and Sidney Verba. 1963. *The Civic Culture: Political Attitudes and Democracy in Five Nations*. Princeton: Princeton University Press.

Amanzholova, Dina. 2004. *"Казахская автономия: от замысла националов к самоопределению по-советски* [Kazakh Autonomy: From the Idea of Nationalists to Self-Determination Soviet-Style]" *Acta Slavica Iaponica* 21: 115–43.

Analiticheskii Tsentr Yuriya Levady (ATsYuL). 2010. *Opros: Rossiyane o Staline*. Moscow: ATsYuL, March.

  2011. *Nastroenie molodykh rossiyan o nastupayushchem godu: Press-vypusk*. Moscow: ATsYuL, December.

  2012. *Obshchestvennoe mnenie – 2011: Ezhegodnik*. Moscow: Levada Tsentr.

  2013. *Opros: Otnoshenie k Stalinu v Rossii i stranakh Zakavkaz'ya*. Moscow: ATsYuL, March.

  2014. *Opros: Otnoshenie k lichnosti i epokhe Iosifa Stalina*. Moscow: ATsYuL, October.

  2015. *Opros: Bor'ba s 'pyatoi kolonnoi' i oshchushchenie svobody v obshchestve*. Moscow: ATsYuL, December.

  2015. *Opros: Rol' lichnostei v istorii Rossii*. Moscow: ATsYuL, January.

  2016. *Opros: Rol' Stalina v istorii Rossii*. Moscow: ATsYuL, January.

Andreev, Andrei. 2015. "Pyataya kolonna predatelei protiv suvereniteta Rossii." *Novoruss.info*, March 1.

Andrews, Christopher. 2001. *The Sword and the Shield*. London: Basic Books.

Andrieu, Kora. 2011. "An Unfinished Business: Transitional Justice and Democratization in Post-Soviet Russia." *International Journal of Transitional Justice* 5, 2: 198–220.

Annual Address of the President of Republic of Belarus to Parliament. 2002. Official Website of the President, April 16, available at: www.president.gov.by/ru/news_ru/view/fragmenty-iz-vystuplenija-prezidenta-respubliki-belarus-pri-predstavlenii-ezhe godnogo-poslanija-parlamentu-5784/, accessed February 2, 2017.

Antić, Mile. 2016. "Država nije dobar domaćin." *BizLife*, July 26, available at: www.bizlife.rs/biznis/poslovne-vesti/mile-antic-predsednik-mreze-za-restituciju-za-bizlife-drzava-nije-dobar-domacin/, accessed December 12, 2016.

"Antoni Macierewicz: Lech Wałęsa? Bez wątpliwości 'Bolek'." 2016. *Rzeczpospolita*, February 18, p. 13, available at: www.rp.pl/Historia/160219249-Antoni-Macierewicz-Lech-Walesa-Bez-watpliwosci-Bolek.html, accessed June 22, 2017.

Aoláin, Fionnuala Ní and Colm Campbell. 2005. "The Paradox of Transition in Conflicted Democracies." *Human Rights Quarterly* 27, 1: 172–213.

"Apel do prezydenta przeciw postępowaniu ws. odebrania orderu Grossowi." 2016. *Polish Press Agency*, February 12.

Arbour, Louise. 2007. "Economic and Social Justice for Societies in Transition." NYU *Journal of International Law and Politics* 40, 1: 1–27.

Areshka, Vaclau. 2015. "Ad gramadzianskai inicyiatyvy 'Lustracyia dla Belarusi'," in Vaclau Areshka, ed. *Lustacyia dla Belarusi*. Vilnius-Minsk: KontraPress, 6–8.

2015. "Lustracyia dla Belarusi. Praekt Kancentcyi lustracyi pry perakhode ad autarytarnaga rezhymu da demakratyi," in Vaclau Areshka, ed. *Lustacyia dla Belarusi*. Vilnius-Minsk: KontraPress, 36–63.

"Arkhivnye dela, kasaiushchiesia stalinskikh repressii, do sikh por zakryty dlia issledovatelei." 2015. *Central Asia Monitor*, June 26, available at: https://camonitor.kz/16827-arhivnye-dela-kasayuschiesya-stalinskih-repressiy-do-sih-por-zakryty-dlya-issledovate ley.html, accessed May 6, 2017.

Aron, Leon. 2008. "The Problematic Pages." *The New Republic*, September 24, available at: https://newrepublic.com/article/62070/the-problematic-pages, accessed June 22, 2017.

Arthur, Paige. 2009. *Identities in Transition*. New York: International Center for Transitional Justice, available at: https://idl-bnc.idrc.ca/dspace/bitstream/10625/50118/1/IDL-50118.pdf, accessed February 26, 2017.

Austin, Robert C. 2015. "Transitional Justice as Electoral Politics," in Lavinia Stan and Nadya Nedelsky, eds. *Post-Communist Transitional Justice: Lessons from 25 Years of Experience*. New York: Cambridge University Press, 30–50.

Avaliani, Tinatin. 2014. *Results of Pre-Year Trial Monitoring Project: Initial Problems, Changes in Trends, and Existing Challenges*. Tbilisi: Georgian Young Lawyers' Association.

Azatyan, Vardan, no date, *Über die Ruinen der sowjetischen Vergangenheit. Einige Gedanken über Religion, Nationalismus und künstlerische Avantgarden in Armenien*, available at: www.springerin.at/dyn/heft_text.php?textid=2136&lang=en.

Badalyan, Hakob. 2011. "Armenia's Lustration." *Lragir.am*, November 15, available at: www.lragir.am/index/eng/0/comments/view/24195, accessed May 18, 2017.

Bakiner, Onur. 2014. "Truth Commission Impact: An Assessment of How Commissions Influence Politics and Society." *International Journal of Transitional Justice* 8, 1: 6–30.

2016. *Truth Commissions: Memory, Power, and Legitimacy*. Philadelphia: University of Pennsylvania Press.

Baklanov, Aleksandr. 2015. "Gosarkhiv rasskazal o vydumannom 'podviga' 28 panfilovtsev," July 8, available at: http://snob.ru/selected/entry/94992, accessed November 19, 2016.

Bakradze, Lasha. 2013. "Georgia and Stalin: Still Living with the Great Son of the Nation," in *The Stalin Puzzle: Deciphering Post-Soviet Public Opinion*. Washington: Carnegie Endowment for International Peace.

Balkelis, Tomas and Violeta Davoliūtė. 2009. "National Report on Lithuania," in Carlos Closa Montero, ed. *How the Memory of Crimes Committed by Totalitarian and/or Other Repressive Regimes in Europe Is Dealt With*. Brussels: European Commission, Directorate General for Justice, Freedom and security, Direction D: Fundamental rights and citizenship.

Balmforth, Tom. 2014. "Former Journalist Spearheads Ukraine's Lustration Effort." *RFE/RL*, April 12, available at: www.rferl.org/a/former-journalist-spearheads-ukraines-lustration-effort/25330909.html, accessed June 22, 2017.

Banac, Ivo. 1988. *With Stalin Against Tito. Cominformist Splits in Yugoslav Communism*. Ithaca: Cornell University Press.

Barahona de Brito, Alexandra, Carmen Gonzaléz-Enríquez, and Paloma Aguilar. 2001. "Introduction," in Alexandra Barahona de Brito, Carmen Gonzaléz-Enríquez, and Paloma Aguilar, eds. *The Politics of Memory: Transitioning Justice in Democratizing Societies*. Oxford: Oxford University Press, 1–39.

Barnes, Steven. 2011. *Death and Redemption*. Princeton: Princeton University Press.

Barsenkov, A. S. and A. I. Vdovin. 2010. *Istoriia Rossii. 1917–2009*. Moscow: Aspekt Press.

Basic Law for the Federal Republic of Germany. May 23, 1949, available at: www .bundestag.de/blob/284870/ceod03414872b427e57fccb703634dcd/basic_law-data .pdf, accessed November 21, 2016.

Bass, Catriona. 2011. "Controlling History." *Transitions Online*, December 6, available at: www.tol.org/client/article/22877-controlling-history.html?print, accessed June 22, 2017.

Bayadyan, Hrach. 2007. *Short Essays on Post-Soviet Yerevan. The Changing Meaning of Urban Space in Yerevan*, December 3, available at: http://acsl.am/wp-content/uploads/2008/11/guidelines_Short%20Essays%20on%20Post-Soviet%20Yerevan.pdf, accessed May 14, 2017.

Beattie, Andrew. 2009. "An EvolutionaryProcess: Contributions of the Bundestag Inquiries into East Germany to an Understanding of the Role of Truth Commissions." *International Journal of Transitional Justice* 3, 2: 229–49.

2015. "Post-Communist Truth Commissions: Between Transitional Justice and the Politics of History," in Lavinia Stan and Nadya Nedelsky, eds. *Post-Communist Transitional Justice: Lessons from Twenty five Years of Experience*. New York: Cambridge University Press, 213–32.

Begemann, Sulamith and Ivo Meli, 2014. "Armenia's Stalled Transformation Process," in *Swiss Study Foundation Summer School – History, Threats and Opportunities. The Case of Georgia and Armenia*, August 27–September 6, Zurich, pp. 17–28, available at: www.studienstiftung.ch/wp-content/uploads/2016/08/Studies-of-the-South-Caucasus-Region-2014_Booklet.pdf, accessed October 17, 2017.

Bendtsen Gotfredsen, Katrine. 2014. "Void Pasts and Marginal Presents: On Nostalgia and Obsolete Futures in the Republic of Georgia." *Slavic Review* 73, 2: 246–64.

Beresniova, Christine. 2014. "An Unimagined Community? Examining Narratives of the Holocaust in Lithuanian Textbooks," in James H. Williams, ed. *(Re) Constructing Memory: School Textbooks and the Imagination of the Nation*. Boston: Sense Publishers, 269–92.

2015. "'Unless They Have To': Power, Politics and Institutional Hierarchy in Lithuanian Holocaust Education," in Zehavit Gross and E. Doyle Stevick, eds. *As the Witnesses Fall Silent: 21st Century Holocaust Education in Curriculum, Policy and Practice*. Cham: Springer, 391–406.

Bernhard, Michael and Jan Kubik. 2014. "A Theory of the Politics of Memory," in Jan Kubik and Michael H. Bernhard, eds. *Twenty Years after Communism: The Politics of Memory and Commemoration*. New York: Oxford University Press, 7–33.

eds. 2014. *Twenty Years After Communism: The Politics of Memory and Commemoration*. Oxford: Oxford University Press.

Bešlin, Milivoj. 2013. "Četnički pokret Draže Mihailovića – najfrekventniji objekat istorijskog revizionizma u Srbiji," in Momir Samardžić, Milivoj Bešlin, and S. Milošević, eds. *Politička upotreba prošlosti. O istorijskom revizionizmu na postjugoslovenskom prostoru*. Novi Sad: AKO, 83–142.

Bevernage, Berber. 2010. "Writing the Past out of the Present: History and Politics of Time in Transitional Justice." *History Workshop Journal* 69: 111–31.

Bilash II, Borislaw. 2016. "Euromaidan Protests – The Revolution of Dignity." *Euromaidan Press*, February 20, available at: http://euromaidanpress.com/2016/02/20/the-story-of-ukraine-starting-from-euromaidan/2/, accessed June 22, 2017.

Birch, Douglas. 2007. "Vietnam Worse than Stalin Purges." *Associated Press*, June 21, available at: www.washingtonpost.com/wp-dyn/content/article/2007/06/21/AR2007062101885.html, accessed June 22, 2017.

Bitautas, Algis. 2014. "Kontroversiškos temos naujausių laikų vadovėliuose: lietuviškų istorijos vadovėlių analizė (1990–2014 m.). *Istorija* 95, 3: 58–93.

Black Book of Stalinism. no date. Available at: http://kurapaty.info/be/black-book, accessed December 13, 2016.

Bocharova, Svetlana. 2013. "Experty perepysivaiut istoriiu Rossii." *Vedomosti*, June 11, available at: www.vedomosti.ru/politics/articles/2013/06/11/istoriya_po_naryshkinu, accessed June 22, 2017.

Bozheyeva, Gulbarshyn, Yerlan Kunakbayev, and Dastan Yeleukenov. 1999. "Former Soviet Biological Weapons Facilities in Kazakhstan: Past, Present, and Future." *Occasional Paper* No. 1. Monterey: Monterey Inst. Cent. Nonproliferation Studies.

Bradford, Vivian. 2010. *Public Forgetting: The Rhetoric and Politics of Beginning Again*. University Park: Pennsylvania State University Press.

Brahm, Eric. 2006. *Truth and Consequences: The Impact of Truth Commissions in Transitional Societies*. Ph.D. Dissertation, Department of Political Science, University of Colorado at Boulder.

2009. "Judging Truth: The Contributions of Truth Commissions in Post-Conflict Environments," in Noha Shawki and Michaelene Cox, eds. *Rethinking Sovereignty and Human Rights after the Cold War*. Burlington: Ashgate, 119–30.

Brandenberger, David. 2009. "A New Short Course? A.V. Filippov and the Russian State's Search for a 'Usable Past'." *Kritika: Explorations in Russian and Eurasian History* 10, 4: 825–33.

Bratzel, Anika. 2015. "The ECHR's Recent Encounter with Genocide: A Closer Look at the Judgment in *Vytautus Vasiliauskas* v. *Lithuania*," December 1, available at: http://jean-monnet-saar.eu/?p=1100, accessed December 22, 2016.

Bravo, Paweł. 2016. "'Bolek': Wygodne półprawdy." *Tygodnik Powszechny (Kraków)*, No. 8, February 18, p. 17, available at: www.tygodnikpowszechny.pl/bolek-wygodne-polprawdy-32429, accessed June 22, 2017.

Brill Olcott, Martha. 1995. *The Kazakhs*, 2nd edn. Stanford: Hoover Institution Press.

Broad, William J. 2007. "A Spy's Path: Lowa to A-Bomb to Kremlin Honor." *The New York Times*, November 12, pp. A1, A10, available at: www.nytimes.com/2007/11/12/us/12koval.html, accessed June 22, 2017.

Brown, Archie and Lilia Shevtsova. eds. 2001. *Gorbachev, Yeltsin and Putin: Political Leadership in Russia's Transition*. Washington: Carnegie Endowment for International Peace.

Brubaker, Rogers. 1994. "Nationhood and the National Question in the Soviet Union and Post-Soviet Eurasia: An Institutional Account." *Theory and Society* 23, 1: 47–78.

Bukowski, Leszek, Andrzej Jankowski, and Jan Żaryn. eds. 2008. *Wokół pogromu kieleckiego*. Warsaw: Instytut Pamięci Narodowej.

"Bulgaria: Law on Political and Civil Rehabilitation of Oppressed Persons (June 15, 1991)." 1995. in Neil Kritz, ed. *Transitional Justice*. Washington: United States Institute of Peace Press, 672–684.

Bushin, Vladimir. 2014. *Pyataya kolonna*. Moscow: Algoritm.

Butkevych, Bohdan. 2014. "Yehor Sobolev: 'Lustration has been blocked'." *The Ukrainian Week*, August 15, available at: http://ukrainianweek.com/Politics/116898, accessed June 22, 2017.

Buyse, Antoine. 2011. "The Truth, the Past and the Present: Article 10 and Situations of Transition," in Antoine Buyse and Michael Hamilton, eds. *Transitional Jurisprudence and the ECHR: Justice, Politics, and Rights*. Cambridge: Cambridge University Press, 131–50.

Buyse, Antoine and Michael Hamilton. 2011. "Introduction," in Antoine Buyse and Michael Hamilton, eds. *Transitional Jurisprudence and the ECHR: Justice, Politics, and Rights*. Cambridge: Cambridge University Press, 1–10.

Cakić, Milan. 2010. "Lustracija u Evropi i Srbiji: Motivacija za donošenje Zakona o lustraciji i njegove društvene funkcije." *Sociologija* 52, 3: 285–306.

Calhoun, Noel. 2004. *Dilemmas of Justice in Eastern Europe's Democratic Transitions*. New York: Palgrave Macmillan.

Cameron, Sarah. 2016. "The Kazakh Famine of 1930-33: Current Research and New Directions." *East/West: Journal of Ukrainian Studies* 3, 2: 117–32.

Cassese, Antonio. 2006. "Balancing the Prosecution of Crimes against Humanity and Non-retroactivity of the Law: The Kolk and Kislyiy v. Estonia Case before the ECHR." *Journal of International Criminal Justice* 4, 2: 410–18.

Castle, Marjorie. 2003. *Triggering Communism's Collapse: Perceptions and Power in Poland's Transition*. Boulder: Rowman & Littlefield.

Casu, Igor. 2007. "Nation-Building in the Era of Integration: The Case of Moldova." in Konrad Jarausch and Thomas Linderberger, eds. *Conflicting Memories. Europeanizing Contemporary History*. New York: Berghan Books, 237–53.

2014. "Political Repressions in the Moldavian Soviet Socialist Republic after 1956: Towards a Typology Based on KGB files." *Dystopia I*, 1–2: 89–127.

2015. "Moldova under the Soviet Communist Regime: History and Memory," in Vladimir Tismaneanu and Bogdan Iacob, eds. *Remembrance, History and Justice: Coming to Terms with Traumatic Pasts in Democratic Societies.* Budapest: Central European University Press, 347–72.

Causeway Institute for Peace-Building and Conflict Resolution. no date. "Moldova." Available at: www.cipcr.org/moldova/, accessed March 4, 2017.

Cecire, Michael. 2013. "Georgia's 2012 Elections and Lessons for Democracy Promotion." *Orbis* 57, 2: 232–50.

Cenckiewicz, Sławomir and Piotr Gontarczyk. 2008. *SB a Lech Wałęsa: Przyczynek do Biografii.* Gdańsk: Instytut Pamięci Narodowej – Komisja Ścigania Zbrodni przeciwko Narodowi Polskiemu.

Cepl, Vojtěch and Mark Gillis. 1996. "Making Amends after Communism." *Journal of Democracy* 7, 4: 118–24.

Chamber of Deputies of Romania. 2012. *Legea lustratiei*, February 28, available at: www.cdep.ro/pls/proiecte/upl_pck.proiect?idp=6394, accessed June 22, 2017.

Charnyi, Semen. 2014. "Odno imia, odna zhizn', odin znak." *30 oktiabria*, 123.

Charter of the International Military Tribunal, August 8, 1945, available at: https://ihl-databases.icrc.org/ihl/INTRO/350?OpenDocument, accessed December 13, 2016.

Chekanova, Svetlana. 2005. "Sudit zhurnalista." *Media i parvo*, April 11, available at: http://karaganda-nm.kz/forum/showthread.php?p=702704, accessed May 6, 2017.

Chislennost' naseleniia Respubliki Kazakhstan po otdel'nym etnosam na nachalo 2016 goda. 2016. Astana: Statistics Committee of the Ministry of National Economy of the Republic of Kazakhstan, 2016, available at: www.stat.gov.kz/getImg?id=ESTAT118979, accessed May 6, 2017.

Chodakiewicz, Marek. January. 2001. "Kłopoty z kuracją szokową." *Rzeczpospolita*, January 5, p. A6, available at: http://archiwum.rp.pl/artykul/317680-Klopoty-z-kuracja-szokowa.html, accessed June 22, 2017.

Ciurea, Cornel. 2011. "Historical Politics in the Republic of Moldova – An Unfulfilled Obsession." *Moldova's Foreign Policy Statewatch* 34: 3.

Civic Lustration Committee. 2015. "[A] Year of Lustration in Ukraine: History of Victories and Sabotage." Kyiv: Civic Lustration Committee.

Coalition for RECOM. 2015. "What Is RECOM?" Available at: www.recom.link/, accessed December 12, 2016.

Cohen, Stephen. 2009. *Soviet Fates and Lost Alternatives.* New York: Columbia University Press.

Cole, Elizabeth A. 2007. "Transitional Justice and the Reform of History Education." *International Journal of Transitional Justice* 1, 1: 115–37.

Cole, Elizabeth and Karen Murphy. 2011. "History Education Reform, Transitional Justice and the Transformation of Identities." *International Center for Transitional Justice*, April 20, available at: www.ictj.org/publication/history-education-reform-transitional-justice-and-transformation-identities, accessed January 30, 2017.

Comisia Prezidentiala pentru Analiza Dictaturii Comuniste din Romania. 2006. *Raport Final*, Bucharest, available at: www.wilsoncenter.org/sites/default/files/RAPORT%20FINAL_%20CADCR.pdf, accessed February 5, 2017.

Commission for Historical Clarificatoon. 1999. *Guatemala: Memory of Silence* – *Report of the Commission for Historical Clarification* [Tz'inil Na'tab'al], available at: www.aaas.org/sites/default/files/migrate/uploads/mos_en.pdf, accessed June 21, 2017.

Conquest, Robert. 2008. *The Great Terror: A Reassessment*. New York: Oxford University Press.

"Constitution of the Republic of Serbia". 2006. *Official Gazette of Republic of Serbia*, No. 83/2006, available at: www.constituteproject.org/constitution/Serbia_2006 .pdf?lang=en, accessed December 12, 2016.

Constitutional Court of Belarus. 2006. "Decision П-188/2006 on the right of citizens – victims of political repression for compensation of harm and payment," May 11, available at: http://pravo.levonevsky.org/bazaby11/republic25/text542.htm, accessed December 12, 2016.

Constitutional Law of the Republic of Kazakhstan of December 16, 1991. 1991. "On the State Independence of the Republic of Kazakhstan," *Vedomosti Verkhovnogo Soveta Kazakhskoi SSR*, no. 51 (1991), st. 622, available at: http://adilet.zan.kz/eng/docs/Z910004400, accessed May 6, 2017.

Convention on the Prevention and Punishment of the Crime of Genocide. 1951. January 12, available at: www.ohchr.org/EN/ProfessionalInterest/Pages/CrimeOfGenocide .aspx, accessed December 17, 2016.

Corley, Felix. 2015. *Armenians in the Mitrokhin's notes*, August, available at: www .academia.edu/15177390/Armenians_in_Mitrokhins_KGB_notes, accessed May 29, 2017.

Cornell, Svante. 2001. *Small Nations and Great Powers. A Study of Ethnopolitical Conflict in the Caucasus*. Caucasus World: Courzon Press.

Council of Europe. 1996. *Measures to Dismantle the Heritage of Former Communist Totalitarian Systems*, June 3, available at: http://assembly.coe.int/nw/xml/xref/x2h-xref-viewhtml.asp?fileid=7506&lang=en, accessed on June 21, 2017.

2014. *Assessment of the Law on the Restoration of Trust in the Judiciary in Ukraine of April 8, 2014*. Strasbourg: Council of Europe.

Crime and Excessive Punishment: The Prevalence and causes of Human Rights Abuse in Georgia's Prisons. 2014. Tbilisi: Open Society Georgia Foundation.

Croissant, Michael. 1998. *The Armenia-Azerbaijan Conflict: Causes and Implications*. Westport: Praeger.

CTK. 2016. "Válka v Donbasu si podle Porošenka vyžádala 10.000 mrtvých." *Ceske Noviny*, December 6, available at: www.ceskenoviny.cz/zpravy/valka-v-donbasu-si-podle-porosenka-vyzadala-10-000-mrtvych/1424064, accessed December 7, 2016.

Çuhadar, Esra and Burcu Gültekin Punsmann. 2012. *Reflecting on the Two Decades of Bridging the Divide: Taking Stock of Turkish-Armenian Civil Society Activities*. Ankara: Tepav.

Cuşco, Andrei. 2015. "Commission for the Study and Evaluation of the Totalitarian Communist Regime in the Republic of Moldova/Comisia pentru studierea si aprecierea regimului comunist totalitar din Republica Moldova," in Lavinia Stan and Nadya Nedelsky, eds. *Encyclopedia of Transitional Justice*. New York: Cambridge University Press, Vol. 3, 48–53.

Cvetković, Srđan. 2006. *Između srpa i čekića. Likvidacija narodnih neprijatelja 1944–1953*. Belgrade: Institut za savremenu istoriju.

Czaja, Dariusz. 2000. "To nie 'oni,' niestety." *Gazeta wyborcza*, December 16–17, pp. 20–21, available at: http://wyborcza.pl/1,75402,182315.html?disableRedirects=true, accessed June 22, 2017.

Czech Republic, Act No. 422/2000 and 424/2000 amended Act No. 451/1991 (Lustration Law), available at: www.ustrcr.cz/data/pdf/normy/act451-1991.pdf, accessed October 15, 2016.

"Czech Republic: Constitutional Court Decision on the Act on the Illegality of the Communist Regime (December 21, 1993)." 1995. in Neil Kritz, ed. *Transitional Justice*. Washington: United States Institute of Peace Press, 620–27.

"Czech and Slovak Federal Republic: Screening ("Lustration") Law, Act No. 451/1991 (October 4, 1991)." 1995. in Neil Kritz ed. *Transitional Justice*. Vol. III. Washington: United States Institute of Peace Press, 312–21.

Czy, pana(i) zdaniem, powinno się obecnie przeprowadzać w Polsce lustrację, to znaczy sprawdzać, czy osoby pełniące ważne funkcje w państwie nie współpracowały w przeszłości ze służbą bezpieczeństwa, czy też nie powinno? CBOS, Powracające dylematy lustracji i dekomunizacji w polsce [Do you think lustration should be carried out in Poland now, that is, to check whether persons with important functions in the state did not cooperate in the past with the security servicet? CBOS, Returning dilemmas of lustration and decommissioning in Poland.]. 2005. BS/43/2005, Warsaw, March.

Daly, Erin. 2008. "Truth Skepticism: An Inquiry into the Value of Truth in Times of Transition." *International Journal of Transitional Justice* 2, 1: 23–41.

Dancy, Geoff. 2000. "Impact Assessment, Not Evaluation: Defining a Limited Role for Positivism in the Study of Transitional Justice." *International Journal of Transitional Justice* 4, 3: 355–76.

Danilov, A. A. and A. V. Filippov. 2009. *Istoriia Rossii 1900–1945 gg.: Kniga dlia uchitel'ia*. Moscow: Prosveshchenie.

Dashichev, Vyacheslav. 1988. "Vostok-zapad: poisk novykh otnoshenii – O prioritetakh vneshnei politiki Sovetskogo gosudarstva." *Literaturnaya gazeta (Moscow)*, 20, May 18, p. 14.

Dave, Bhavna. 2004. *Minorities and Participation in Public Life: Kazakhstan*. Bishkek: United Nations Office of the High Commissioner for Human Rights, October, available at: www2.ohchr.org/english/issues/minorities/docs/WP5.doc, accessed March 31, 2017.

David, Roman. 2003. "Lustration Laws in Action: The Motives and Evaluation of Lustration Policy in the Czech Republic and Poland (1989–2001)." *Law and Social Inquiry* 28, 2: 387–439.

2004. "Transitional Injustice? Criteria for Conformity of Lustration to the Right to Political Expression." *Europe-Asia Studies* 56, 6: 789–812.

2006. "From Prague to Baghdad: Lustration Systems and their Political Effects." *Government & Opposition* 41, 3: 347–72.

2011. *Lustration and Transitional Justice: Personnel Systems in the Czech Republic, Hungary, and Poland*. Philadelphia: University of Pennsylvania Press.

2014. "Beyond Lustration: Personnel Reform in the State Apparatus in Ukraine." Kyiv: USAID FAIR, April 19.

2015. "Ukrainian Lustration and European Standards: Building Democracy Capable of Defending Itself." Kyiv: USAID FAIR, February 24.

David, Roman and Houda Mzioudet. 2014. "Personnel Change or Personal Change? Rethinking Libya's Political Isolation Law." Brookings Doha Center, Stanford University "Project on Arab Transitions" Paper Series, No. 4, March.

Davoliūtė, Violeta. 2011. "In Vilnius, Shared Pain, Divided Memory." *Transitions Online*, June 30, available at: www.tol.org/client/article/22515-in-vilnius-shared-pain-divided-memories.html, accessed June 22, 2017.

Dawisha, Karen. 2014. *Putin's Kleptocracy: Who Owns Russia?* New York: Simon & Shuster.

Dawisha, Karen and Bruce Parrott. eds. 1997. *Democratic Changes and Authoritarian Reactions in Russia, Ukraine, Belarus and Moldova.* Cambridge: Cambridge University Press.

"Declaration." 1989. *Martyralog Bulleten*, Minsk, pp. 6–7, available at: http://vytoki .net/content/Martyralog.pdf, accessed December 14, 2016.

"Decree no. 42 on the memorialization of the victims of mass repressions of 1937–1941 in Kurapaty." 1989. January 18, available at: http://old.bankzakonov.com/obsch/ razdel210/time21/yamf0925.htm, accessed December 13, 2016.

"Decree no. 479–XII on restoring the rights of citizens who suffered from repressions in 1920–1950." 1990. December 21, available at: http://pravo.levonevsky.org/bazaby11/ republic64/text164.htm, accessed December 12, 2016.

"Decree no. 487 of the Belarusian Council of Ministers of 1 July 1994." 1994. available at: www.pravo.levonevsky.org/bazaby11/republic60/text155.htm, accessed June 22, 2017.

"Decree no. 759 of the Belarusian Council of Ministers of 18 December 1992." 1992. available at: http://pravo.levonevsky.org/bazaby11/republic62/text704.htm, accessed June 22, 2017.

"Decree no. 1906-XII of the Supreme Council of the Republic of Belarus of 3 November 1992." 1992. *Vedomosti Verkhovnogo Soveta Respubliki Belarus*, available at: www .pravo.levonevsky.org/bazaby09/sbor88/text88307.htm, accessed June 22, 2017.

"Deklaracija o pomirenju DS i SPS." 2008. *Politika Daily*, October 21, available at: www.politika.rs/scc/clanak/59971/, accessed December 12, 2016.

Deleu, Ecaterina. 2010. "Condamnarea comunismului nu înseamnă scoaterea PCRM în afara legii." *Flux*, January 15, available at: http://archiva.flux.md/articole/8586, accessed February 26, 2017.

Dėl ilgalaikės pilietinio ir tautinio ugdymo programos patvirtinimo 2006 m. rugsėjo 19 d. 2006. Nr. X-818, Vilnius.

Dėl pilietinio ir tautinio ugdymo 2016–2020 metų tarpinstitucinio veiksmų plano patvirtinimo 2016 m. kovo 25 d. 2016. Nr. V-237, Vilnius.

Deriglazova, Larisa and Sergey Minasyan. 2011, "Nagorno-Karabagh: The Paradoxes of Strength and Weakness in an Asymmetric Conflict." *Caucasus Institute Research Papers*, No. 3, June.

de Waal, Thomas. 2003. *Black Garden. Armenian and Azerbaijan through Peace and War.* New York: New York University Press.

2010. *The Caucasus. An introduction.* New York: Oxford University Press.

"So Long, Saakashvili," *Foreign Affairs*, October 29, available at: www.foreignaffairs .com/articles/russia-fsu/2013-10-29/so-long-saakashvili, accessed November 7, 2016.

de Waal, Thomas, Maria Lipman, Lev Gudkov, and Lasha Bakradze. 2013. "The Stalin Puzzle: Deciphering Post-Soviet Public Opinion." *Carnegie Europe*, March 1, 2013, available at: http://carnegieeurope.eu/2013/03/01/stalin-puzzle-deciphering-post-soviet-public-opinion-pub-51075, accessed July 20, 2017.

"Die Osteuropäer haben kein Schamgefühl." 2015. *Die Welt (Berlin)*, September 14, p. 4.

Dietsch, Johan. 2006. *Making Sense of Suffering: Holocaust and Holodomor in Ukrainian Historical Culture*. Lund: Lund University.

Dilara, Isa. 2015. "Nizverzhennyi Stalin v sele Staryi Ikan." *Radio Azattyq*, May 19, available at: http://rus.azattyq.org/a/istoria-pamyatnika-stalinu-selo-stariy-ikan/27024370.html, accessed May 6, 2017.

Dimitrijević, Nenad. 1999. "Words and Death: Serbian Nationalist Intellectuals." in Andras Bozoki, ed. *Intellectuals and Politics in Central Europe*. Budapest: Central European University Press, 123–35.

Dimitrijević, Vojin. 2002. "Facts Versus Truth: The Dilemmas of a Reluctant Member of a Truth and Reconciliation Commission," in Okwui Enwezor, Carlos Basualdo, Ute Meta Bauer, eds. *Experiments with Truth: Transitional Justice and the Processes of Truth and Reconciliation*. Ostfildern-Ruit: Hatje Cantz, 205–13.

Dissenting opinion Judge Ziemele, Vasiliauskas v. Lithuania. 2015. Application no. 35343/05, decision October 20, 2015, para 21, *European Court of Human Rights*. Strasbourg: ECtHR, available at: http://lrv-atstovas-eztt.lt/uploads/VASILIAUSKAS_2015_GC_judgment.pdf, accessed January 4, 2017.

Dolgov, Anna. 2015. "Russian Senator Introduces Bill Criminalizing Pro-Stalin Propaganda." *Moscow Times*, September 22, available at: https://themoscowtimes.com/articles/russian-senator-introduces-bill-criminalizing-pro-stalin-propoganda-49720, accessed June 22, 2017.

Dolidze, Anna and Thomas de Waal. 2012. "A Truth Commission for Georgia." *Carnegie Europe*, December 5, available at: http://carnegieeurope.eu/2012/12/05/truth-commission-for-georgia-pub-50249, accessed October 1, 2016.

Donadio, Rachel. 2007. "The Iron Archives." *The News York Times*, April 22, available at: www.nytimes.com/2007/04/22/books/review/Donadio.t.html?_r=0, accessed October 15, 2016.

Dragosavac, Nebojša. 2013. "'Prepakivanje istorije' masovnim preimenovanjem beogradskih ulica," in Momir Samardžić, Milivoj Bešlin, and Srđan Milošević, eds. *Politička upotreba prošlosti: o istorijskom revizionizmu na postjugoslovenskom prostoru*. Novi Sad: Tramaxion, 333–51, available at: www.rosalux.rs/sites/default/files/publications/Politicka_upotreba_proslosti.pdf, accessed June 21, 2017.

Dubin, Boris. 2011. *Rossiya nulevykh: Politicheskaya kul'tura, istoricheskaya pamyat', povsednevnaya zhizn'*. Moscow: ROSSPEN.

Dyatlenko, Pavel. 2014. "Features of Rehabilitation of Victims of Stalin's Political Repressions in Kazakhstan." *Vestnik KRSU* 14, 11: 29, available at: www.krsu.edu.kg/vestnik/2014/v11/a08.pdf, accessed May 6, 2017.

Dziarnovich, Aleh. 2001. *Rehabilitation. The Collection of Documents and Normative Acts Pertaining to the Rehabilitation of Victims of Political Repression in 1920–1980s*. Minsk: Athenaeum.

Ebon, Martin. 1994. *KGB: Birth and Rebirth*. London: Praeger.

Egbert, Bill. 1999. "Lubavitchers Given KGB Files on Rabbi." *New York Daily News*, December 20, available at: www.nydailynews.com/archives/news/lubavitchers-kgb-files-rabbi-article-1.843285, accessed June 22, 2017.

Eleukhanova, Svetlana. 2009. "Istoriia Karlaga: okhrana rezhim i usloviia soderzha-niia." *Avtoreferat dissertatsii na soiskanie uchenoi stepeni kandidata istoricheskikh nauk.* Karaganda: Karaganda State University.

2016. "Polozhenie repressirovannykh v Kazakhstane," in *Reabilitatsiia i pamiat'.* Moscow: Memorial-Zven'ia, 193–235.

Elizarova, Valentina. 2005. "Komu kusochek istorii?" *Izvetiia-Kazakhstan,* July 15, available at: www.karlag.kz/art.php?id=71, accessed May 6, 2017.

Ellman, Michael. 2000. "The 1947 Soviet Famine and the Entitlement Approach to Famines." *Cambridge Journal of Economics* 39, 24: 603–30.

2002. "Soviet Repression Statistics: Some Comments." *Europe-Asia Studies* 54, 7: 1151–72.

Elster, Jon. ed. 2003. "Emotions and Transitional Justice." *Soundings: An Interdisciplinary Journal* 86, 1–2: 17–40.

ed. 2006. *Retribution and Reparation in the Transition to Democracy.* New York: Cambridge University Press.

"Ensuring Stalin's Victims are not Forgotten." no date, available at: www.bbc.com/news/world-35611709, accessed March 2, 2016.

"Estonia," *Transitional Justice and Memory in the EU.* 2013, available at: www.proyectos.cchs.csic.es/transitionaljustice/, accessed October 19, 2016.

Estonian Criminal Code. 2001. available at: www.legislationline.org/documents/section/criminal-codes, accessed December 13, 2016.

Etkind, Aleksander. 2009. "Post-Soviet Hauntology: Cultural Memory of the Soviet Terror." *Constellations* 16, 1: 182–200.

Eurasian, Monitor. 2009. "EM-11: Public Perception of Youth and the New Independent States of the History of Soviet and Post-Soviet Periods." *Analytical Report: Eurasian Monitor,* August, available at: www.eurasiamonitor.org/rus/research/event-162.html, accessed May 6, 2017.

European Commission for Democracy through Law (Venice Commission). 2014. *Interim Opinion on the Law on Government Cleansing (Lustration Law) of Ukraine, Adopted by the Venice Commission at its 101st Plenary Session.* Venice, December 12–13.

European Commission for Democracy through Law (Venice Commission). 2015. *Final Opinion on the Law on Government Cleansing (Lustration Law) of Ukraine as would result from the amendments submitted to the Verkhovna Rada on April 21, 2015.* Opinion No. 788/2014, CDL-AD(2015)012, Venice, June 19–20.

European Convention on Human Rights. 2010. available at: www.echr.coe.int/Documents/Convention_ENG.pdf, accessed December 13, 2016.

"Experts: Moldova must adopt Lustration Law." 2015. *Teleradio Moldova,* January 9, available at: www.trm.md/en/politic/experti-moldova-trebuie-sa-adopte-legea-lustratiei/, accessed February 5, 2017.

Fairbanks Jr., Charles H. and Alexi Gugashvili. 2013. "A New Chance for Georgian Democracy." *Journal of Democracy* 24, 1: 116–27.

Fearon, James and David Laitin. 2006. *Armenia,* July 5, available at: https://web.stanford.edu/group/ethnic/Random%20Narratives/ArmeniaRN1.4.pdf, accessed May 2, 2017.

Federal'naya sluzhba bezpopasnosti RF. 1999. *Lubyanka 2: Iz istorii otechestvennoi kontrrazvedki.* Moscow: Mosgorarkhiv.

Feduta, Aleksander, Oleg Bogutskii, and Viktor Matsinovitch. 2003. *Political Parties of Belarus – Essential Part of Civil Society.* Minsk: Friedrich Ebert Stiftung.

Filippov, A. V., A. I. Utkin, and S. V. Sergeev. eds. 2007. *Noveishaia Istoriia Rossii, 1945–2006 gg.: Kniga dlia uchitelia.* Moscow: Prosveshchenie.

Finkel, Evgeny. 2010. "In Search of Lost Genocide: Historical Policy and International Politics in Post-1989 Eastern Europe." *Global Society* 24, 1: 51–66.

Flige, Irina. 2016. "Prostranstvo Gulaga: opyt i pamiat'." Unpublished paper presented at "Theology after the Gulag." Amsterdam, May.

————. 2007. "Predmetnaia i material'naia pamiat' o Bol'shom Terror." Unpublished paper.

Forest, Benjamin and Juliet Johnson. 2001. "Unraveling the Threads of History: Soviet-Era Monuments and Post-Soviet National Identity in Moscow." August, available at: www.dartmouth.edu/~crn/crn_papers/Forest-Johnson.pdf, accessed October 20, 2016.

————. 2002. "Unraveling the Threads of History: Soviet-Era Monuments and Post-Soviet National Identity in Moscow." *Annals of the Association of American Geographers* 93, 3: 524–47.

"Former Deputy Minister of National Security of Armenia Is against the Draft Law on Lustration." 2011. *MediaMax*, December 1, available at: www.mediamax.am/en/news/politics/3286/, accessed May 18, 2017.

Freedom House. 2013. *Freedom in the World 2013: Ukraine*, available at: https://freedomhouse.org/report/freedom-world/2013/ukraine#.VOaaXodiBbw, accessed October 13, 2016.

————. 2014. *Freedom in the World 2014: Ukraine*, available at: https://freedomhouse.org/report/freedom-world/2014/ukraine#.VOaUIIdiBbw, accessed October 13, 2016.

————. 2015. *Freedom in the World 2015: Ukraine*, available at: https://freedomhouse.org/report/freedom-world/2015/ukraine#.VOaY6odiBbw, accessed October 13, 2016.

Freeman, Mark. 2004. "Serbia and Montenegro: Selected Developments in Transitional Justice." International Center for Transitional Justice, *Case Study Series*, October, available at: www.ictj.org/sites/default/files/ICTJ-FormerYugoslavia-Serbia-Developments-2004-English.pdf, accessed December 12, 2016.

————. 2006. *Truth Commissions and Procedural Fairness.* New York: Cambridge University Press.

Freeman, Mark and Priscilla Hayner. 2003. "Truth-Telling," in David Bloomfield, ed. *Reconciliation after Violent Conflict: A Handbook.* Stockholm: International Institute for Democracy and Electoral Assistance, 126–7.

Fullard, Madeleine and Nicky Rousseau. 2011. "Truth Telling, Identities, and Power in South Africa and Guatemala," in Paige Arthur, ed. *Identities in Transition: Challenges for Transitional Justice in Divided Societies.* New York: Cambridge University Press, 54–86.

Gachava, Nina. 2009. "Georgian President Blasted Over Monument's Demolition." *Radio Free Europe/Radio Liberty*, December 21, available at: www.rferl.org/a/Georgian_President_Blasted_Over_Monuments_Demolition/1910056.html, accessed November 11, 2016.

Gamaghelyan, Phil. 2010. "Rethinking the Nagorno-Karabakh Conflict: Identity, Politics, Scholarship." *International Negotiation* 15, 1: 33–56.

Gamov, Aleksandr. 2001. "Glavnaya pesnya o starom: Pochemu novyi Gimn Rossii tak trudno vkhodit v nashu zhizn'." *Komsomol'skaya Pravda*, January 26, p. 4.

Garavy, Marat. 2014. "Akhviara Gulagu nia mozha viarnut rodnuyu khatu." *Novy Chas*, August 25, available at: http://novychas.by/hramadstva/achviara_hulahu_bezhaty, accessed January 20, 2017.

——— 2016. "Yakim bachycca natsinalny nekropal u Kuraprtakh." *Narodnaya Volya*, March 22, p. 4.

Gaškaitė, Nijolė. 1997 and 2006. *Pasipriešinimo istorija 1944–1953 metai*. Vilnius: Aidai.

Gelb, Michael. 1995. "An Early Soviet Ethnic Deportation: The Far-Eastern Koreans." *Russian Review* 54, 3: 389–412.

Geleževičius, Rimgaudas. 2003. *Holokausto teisingumas ir restitucija Lietuvoje atkūrus nepriklausomybę, 1990–2003*. Vilnius: Lietuvos teisės universitetas.

Genocide and Resistance Research Centre of Lithuania. no date. "History of the Centre." available at: http://genocid.lt/centras/lt/823/c/, accessed January 31, 2017.

"Georgia Begins Freeing Political Prisoners Under Amnesty." 2013. *Deutsche Welle*, January 13, available at: www.dw.com/en/georgia-begins-freeing-political-prisoners-under-amnesty/a-16518706, accessed November 28, 2016.

"Georgia Modifies Charges against Ex-Officials including Saakashvili." 2015. *Democracy and Freedom Watch*, March 14, available at: http://dfwatch.net/georgia-modifies-charges-against-five-ex-officials-including-saakashvili-34314, accessed November 28, 2016.

"Georgia, Moldova and Bulgaria: Dismantling Communist Structures Is Hardly Extremism. Interview with Irina Sarishvili-Chanturia, Iurie Rosca and Philip Dimitrov." 2001. *Demokratizatsiya*, November 23, p. 318, available at: www2.gwu.edu/~ieresgwu/assets/docs/demokratizatsiya%20archive/GWASHU_DEMO_12_2/P225677W77561736/P225677W77561736.pdf, accessed February 5, 2017.

Getty, J. Arch, Gábor T. Rittersporn, and Viktor N. Zemskov. 1993. "Victims of the Soviet Penal System in the Pre-war Years: A First Approach on the Basis of Archival Material." *American Historical Review* 98, 4: 1017–49.

Gibson, James. 2004. *Overcoming Apartheid: Can Truth Reconcile a Divided Nation?* New York: Russell Sage Foundation.

——— 2013. "Lithuania's Supreme Court Upholds Verdict for Paleckis." *Lithuania Tribune*, January 22, available at: www.liberties.eu/en/news/lithuania-genocide-unlawful-conviction, accessed January 4, 2017.

Giragosian, Richard. 2014. "Armenia's Search for Independence." *Current History. A Journal of Contemporary World Affairs* 113, 765: 284–9.

Goble, Paul. 2009. "Medvedev Historical Falsification Commission 'Harmful' or 'Useless', Memorial Expert Says." *Window on Eurasia*, May 20, available at: www.eesti.ca/medvedev-falsification-commission-may-be-harmful-or-useless-memorial-expert-says/article23844, accessed June 22, 2017.

Göksel, D. Nigar. "Turkey and Armenia Post-Protocols: Back to Square One?" *TESEV Foreign Policy Bulletin*, 2012, p. 17, available at: www.css.ethz.ch/content/specialin terest/gess/cis/center-for-securities-studies/en/services/digital-library/publications/publication.html/154171, accessed April 30, 2017.

Golovkova, L. A. 2004. *Butovskii Poligon. 1937-38gg. Kniga pamiati zhertv politich-eskikh repressi*. Moscow: Izdatel'stvo 'Al'zo'.

Gontarczyk, Piotr. 2001. "Gross kontra fakty." *Zycie* (Warsaw), January 31, p. 4, available at: www.geocities.ws/jedwabne/gross_kontra_fakty.htm, accessed June 22, 2017.

Gorbachev, Aleksei. 2014. "'Natsional-predateli' v kompetentsii uchastkovykh." *Nezavisimaya gazeta*, September 1, p. 2.

Gorbachev, Mikhail. 1987. "Gorbachev's closing remarks at the Central Committee CPSU Plenum of 28 January 1987", available at: http://soveticus5.narod.ru/88/zakl1987.htm, accessed July 4, 2017.

Gorchinskaya, Katya. 2015. "Avoiding Lustration in Ukraine: Senior Prosecutor Evades Sweep of Yanukovych-Era Officials." *RFE/RL*, July 18, available at: www.rferl.org/a/ukraine-lustration-prosecutor-valendyuk/27135678.html, accessed June 22, 2017.

2015. "Gifts, Prizes, Winnings: A Windfall for Ukraine Judges." *RFE/RL*, June 15, available at: www.rferl.org/a/ukraine-judges-declare-windfalls-gifts-prizes/27073624.html, accessed June 22, 2017.

Gordon, Matthew. no date. "Agricultural Land Reform in Moldova," available at: www.staff.ncl.ac.uk/matthew.gorton/moldlandpaper5.pdf, accessed February 12, 2017.

Gow, James. 2007. "Dark Histories, Brighter Futures: The Balkans and Black Sea Region: European Union Frontiers, War Crimes and Confronting the Past." *Southeast European and Black Sea Studies* 7, 3: 345–55.

Grandin, Greg. 2005. "The Instruction of Great Catastrophe: Truth Commissions, National History, and State Formation in Argentina, Chile, and Guatemala." *American Historical Review* 110: 1: 46–67.

Graziosi, Andrea. 2008. "The Soviet 1931–1932 Famines and the Ukrainian Holodomor: Is a New Interpretation Possible, and What Would Its Consequences Be?," in Halyna Hryn, ed. *Hunger by Design: The Great Ukrainian Famine and Its Soviet Context.* Cambridge: Harvard University, 1–19.

Greenblat, Stephen. 2001. "Racial Memory and Literary History." *Proceedings of the Modern Language Association* 116, 1: 48–63.

Grishan, Igor. 1993. "Kuropaty: sledstvie vozobnovleno." *Sovetskaia Belorussiia*, March 20, p. 3.

Grodsky, Brian. 2008. "Justice without Transition: Truth Commissions in the Context of Repressive Rule." *Human Rights Review* 9, 3: 281–97.

2009. "Beyond Lustration Truth-Seeking Efforts in the Post-Communist Space." *Taiwan Journal of Democracy* 5, 2: 21–43.

2010. *The Costs of Justice: How New Leaders Respond to Previous Rights Abuses.* Notre Dame: University of Notre Dame Press.

2015. "Transitional Justice and Political Goods." in Lavinia Stan and Nadya Nedelsky, eds. *Post-Communist Transitional Justice: Lessons from Twenty-Five Years of Experience.* New York: Cambridge University Press, 7–29.

Grosescu, Raluca and Agata Fijalkowski. 2017. "Retrospective Justice and Legal Culture," in Lavinia Stan and Lucian Turcescu, eds. *Justice, Memory and Redress: New Insights from Romania.* Cambridge: Cambridge Scholars, 100–23.

Gross, Jan Tomasz. 1989. "Social Consequences of War: Preliminaries to the Study of Imposition of Communist Regimes in East Central Europe." *East European Politics and Societies* 3, 2: 198–214.

2000. *Sąsiedzi: Historia zagłady żydowskiego miasteczka.* Sejny: Fundacja Pogranicze.

2001. *Neighbors: The Destruction of the Jewish Community in Jedwabne, Poland.* Princeton: Princeton University Press.

2003. *Wokół Sąsiadów: Polemiki i wyjaśnienia.* Sejny: Pogranicze.

2006. *Fear: Anti-Semitism in Poland After Auschwitz.* New York: Random House.

Gross, Andreas. 2007. "Draft Resolution and Report on the Use of Experience of 'Truth Commissions'." *Report to the Council of Europe*, December 4.

Gross, Jan Tomasz. 2008. *Strach: Antysemityzm w Polsce tuż po wojnie. Historia moralnej zapaści.* Kraków: Znak.

2011. *Złote żniwa: Rzecz o tym, co się działo na obrzeżach zagłady Żydów.* Kraków: Znak.

Gross, Jan Tomasz with Irena Grudzińska-Gross. 2012. *Golden Harvest: Events at the Periphery of the Holocaust.* New York: Oxford University Press.

Grozin, Andrei. 2014. *Golod 1932–1933 godov i politika pamiati v Respublike Kazakhstan.* Moscow: Institut Vostokovedeniia RAN.

Grynevych, Liudmyla. 2008. "The Present State of Ukrainian Historiography on the Holodomor and Prospects for Its Development." *Harriman Review* 16, 2: 10–20.

Gudkov, Lev. 2015. "Zachem Kreml' proslavlyaet Stalina." *Novoe vremya (Moscow)*, April 2, p. 7.

Gustainis, Valentinas. 1989. *Be kaltės: 15 metų Sibiro tremtyje ir lageriuose.* Vilnius: Mintis.

Haerper, Christian. 2002. *Democracy and Enlargement in Post-Communist Europe: The Democratisation of the General Public in 15 Central and Eastern European Countries. 1991–1998.* New York: Routledge.

Haider, Huma. 2012. "Rewriting History Textbooks," in Lavinia Stan and Nadya Nedelsky, eds. *Encyclopedia of Transitional Justice.* New York: Cambridge University Press, Vol. 1: 93–98.

Hale, Henry E. 2016. "25 Years After the USSR: What's Gone Wrong?" *Journal of Democracy* 27, 2: 24–35.

Hamber, Brandon and Richard A. Wilson. 2002. "Symbolic Closure through Memory, Reparation and Revenge in Post-Conflict Societies." *Journal of Human Rights* 1, 1: 35–53.

Hashimoto, Nobuya. 2016. "Maneuvering Memories of Dictatorships and Conflicts," in Paul Corner and Jie-Hyun Lim, eds. *The Palgrave Handbook of Mass Dictatorship.* London: Palgrave Macmillan, 171–84.

Hatun Willakuy: versión abreviada del Informe final de la Comisión de la Verdad y Reconciliación del Perú, 2004. Lima.

Hayner, Priscilla. 2000. "Past Truths, Present Dangers: The Role of Official Truth Seeking in Conflict Resolution and Prevention," in Paul Stern and Daniel Druckman, eds. *International Conflict Resolution after the Cold War.* Washington: National Academies Press, 338–82.

2011. *Unspeakable Truths: Confronting State Terror and Atrocity.* New York: Routledge.

Hevey, Kirstyn. 2014. *Estonian Transitional Justice: Predicated on a Collective Memory.* Diss. Budapest Hungary: Central European University.

Hille, Charlotte Mathilde Louise. 2010. *State Building and Conflict Resolution in the Caucasus.* Leiden: Brill.

Hite, Katherine, Cath Collins, and Alfredo Joignant. 2013. "The Politics of Memory in Chile," in Cath Collins, Katherine Hite, and Alfredo Joignant, eds. *The Politics of Memory in Chile: From Pinochet to Bachelet.* Boulder: First Forum Press, 1–29.

Hohenhaus, Peter. 2016. *Dark Tourism*, available at: www.dark-tourism.com, accessed December 27, 2016.

Horne, Cynthia M. 2009. "International Legal Rulings on Lustration Policies in Central and Eastern Europe: Rule of Law in Historical Context." *Law & Social Inquiry* 34, 3: 713–44.

2009. "Late Lustration Programs in Romania and Poland: Supporting or Undermining Democratic Transitions?" *Democratization* 16, 2: 344–76.

2012. "Assessing the Impact of Lustration on Trust in Public Institutions and National Government in Central and Eastern Europe." *Comparative Political Studies* 45, 4: 412–46.

2015. "Silent Lustration: Public Disclosures as Informal Lustration Mechanisms in Bulgaria and Romania." *Problems of Post-Communism* 62, 3: 131–44.

2015. "The Timing of Transitional Justice Measures," in Lavinia Stan and Nadya Nedelsky, eds. *Post-Communist Transitional Justice: Lessons from Twenty-Five Years of Experience.* Cambridge: Cambridge University Press, 123–47.

2017. *Building Trust and Democracy: Transitional Justice in Post-Communist Countries.* Oxford: Oxford University Press.

Housing Code of the Republic of Belarus. August 28, 2012. Available at: www.levon evski.net/pravo/norm2013/num103/do3689/page4.html, accessed December 12, 2016.

Human Rights Information Centre. 2015. "Constitutional Court Postpones Consideration of Lustration Law," April 16, available at: https://humanrights.org.ua/en/material/konstitucijnij_sud_vidklav_rozgljad_zakonupro_ljustraciju, accessed October 17, 2016.

Human Rights Violations Investigation Commission. 2002. *Synoptic Overview of HRVIC Report: Conclusions and Recommendations,* May, available at: www.nigeri anmuse.com/nigeriawatch/oputa/OputaSummaryRecommendations.pdf, accessed June 21, 2017.

Humphrey, Michael. 2005. "Reconciliation and the Therapeutic State." *Journal of Intercultural Studies* 26, 3: 203–20.

"Hundreds of Thousands of Cases to Be Examined by Commission for Combating Communism." 2010. *Moldova Azi,* January 18, available at: www.azi.md/en/print-story/8511, accessed February 26, 2017.

Hutchinson, Erin. 2015. "Central State and Party Archives in Chisinau, Moldova." *Dissertation Reviews,* February 16, available at: http://dissertationreviews.org/archives/11591, accessed October 15, 2016.

Hutchison, Emma. 2016. *Affective Communities in World Politics: Collective Emotions after Trauma.* Cambridge: Cambridge University Press.

Ilić, Dejan. 2004. "The Yugoslav Truth and Reconciliation Commission." *Eurozine,* April, available at: www.eurozine.com/articles/2004-04-23-ilic-en.html, accessed December 12, 2016.

"Informatsiia ob itogakh raboty Akzharskogo otdela zaniatosti i sotsial'nykh programm po sostoianiiu na 1 ianvaria 2016 goda." 2017. *Ofitsial'nyi internet-resurs akima Akzharskogo raiona Severo-Kazakhstanskoi oblasti,* April 27, available at: http://azh.sko.gov.kz/page .php?page=socialnaja_zaschita_naselenija&lang=2, accessed May 6, 2017.

Institute of National Remembrance (IPN). 2016. "Informacja dotyczaca udostępniania dokumentów z pakietu trzeciego i czwartego z materiałów zabezpieczonych w domu wdowy po Czesławie Kiszczaku." March 7, available at: https://ipn.gov.pl/pl/dla-mediow/komunikaty/12235,Informacja-dotyczaca-udostepniania-dokumentow-z-pakietu-trzeciego-i-czwartego-z-.html, accessed June 21, 2017.

Institute of World Policy. 2012. *How to Get Rid of Post-Sovietness?* Kyiv: Institute of World Policy.

Interfax-Ukraine. 2014. "Security Service Chief Says Former Ukrainian Officials Sponsor Arms Supplies to Separatists." *Kyiv Post,* July 8, available at: www.kyivpost.com/

article/content/war-against-ukraine/security-service-chief-says-former-ukrainian-officials-sponsor-arms-supplies-to-separatists-355071.html, accessed June 22, 2017.

"Interior Ministry Remains Georgian Government's Achilles Heel." 2013. *RFE/RL*, June, available at: www.rferl.org/a/georgia-interior-ministry-achilles-heel/25005620 .html, accessed December 3, 2016.

International Center for Transitional Justice. 2003. "International Center for Transitional Justice (ICTJ) Report prepared for TARC," February 10, available at: www.armenian-genocide.org/Affirmation.244/current_category.5/affirmation_detail.html, accessed April 30, 2017.

International Commission for the Evaluation of the Crimes of the Nazi and Soviet Occupation Regimes in Lithuania. 2000. *Fact Sheet*. Vilnius: International Commission for the Evaluation of the Crimes of the Nazi and Soviet Occupation Regimes in Lithuania.

International Criminal Tribunal for the Former Yugoslavia. 2016. *Completion Strategy Report, Letter of November 17, 2016*, November 17, available at: www.icty.org/sites/ icty.org/files/documents/161117_icty_progress_report_en.pdf, accessed December 12, 2016.

International Criminal Tribunal for the Former Yugoslavia. *Annual Reports*, available at: www.icty.org/en/documents/annual-reports, accessed December 12, 2016.

International Criminal Tribunal for the Former Yugoslavia. no date. *Outreach Programme*, available at: www.icty.org/en/outreach/outreach-programme, accessed December 12, 2016.

International Criminal Tribunal for the Former Yugoslavia. no date. *Development of the Local Judiciaries*, available at: www.icty.org/en/outreach/capacity-building/ development-local-judiciaries, accessed December 12, 2016.

International Renaissance Foundation. 2010. *Zmist Pidruchnykiv z Istorii Ukrainy ta Vsesvitnioii Istorii: Stavlennia ta Ochikuvannia Uchniv ta Batkiv v Konteksti Profesiinoi Otsinky Uchyteliv*. Kiev: International Renaissance Foundation.

"Internauci chcą zablokować publikację książki Grossa: Grożą bojkotem wydawnictwa." 2011. *Rzeczpospolita*, January 10, p. 4, available at: www.polskatimes .pl/artykul/355086,internauci-chca-zablokowac-publikacje-ksiazki-grossa-groza-bojkotem-wydawnictwa,4,id,t,nk.html, accessed June 22, 2017.

Ioffe, Grigory. 2004. *"Understanding Belarus: Economy and Political Landscape." Europe-Asia Studies* 56, 1: 85–118.

Ionescu, Stefan Cristian. 2016. "'Californian' Colonists versus Local Profiteers? The Competition for Jewish Property During the Economic Colonization of Bukovina, 1941–1943." *Yad Vashem Studies* 44, 2: 121–46.

Irwin-Zarecka, Iwona. 1994. *Frames of Remembrance: The Dynamics of Collective Memory*. New Brunswick: Transaction Publishers.

Isaeva, Svetlana. 2005. "Novye repressii protiv … repressirovannykh." *Radio Azattyq*, June 4, available at: http://rus.azattyq.org/a/1180478.html, accessed May 6, 2017.

Ishkanian, Armin. 2008. *Democracy Building in Post-Soviet Armenia*. London: Routledge.

Iskandaryan, Alexander. 2012. "Armenia, between Autocracy and Poliarchy," *Russian Politics and Law* 50, 4: 23–36.

Iskandaryan, Alexander, Hrant Mikaelian, and Sergey Minasyan. 2016. *War, Business and Politics: Informal Networks and Formal Institutions in Armenia*. Yerevan: Caucasus Institute.

Iskandaryan, Alexander and Sergey Minasyan. 2010. *Pragmatic Policies vs. Historical Constraints: Analyzing Armenia-Turkey Relations*. Yerevan: Caucasus Institute.

"Ivanishvili Loses Court Case over Georgian Citizenship." 2011. *Civil.ge*, December 27, available at: www.civil.ge/eng/article.php?id=24309, accessed November 23, 2016.

Ivaškevičius, M. 2016. "Aš- ne žydas." *Delfi.lt*, August 24, available at: www.delfi.lt/news/ringas/lit/m-ivaskevicius-as-ne-zydas.d?id=72107298, accessed January 31, 2017.

"Iz zhizhni pamyatnikov: Stalin vezli na reabilitatsiyu v kovshe traktora." 2001. *Komsomol'skaya Pravda* (Moscow), June 19, p. 8.

Janmaat, Jan. 2006. "History and National Identity Construction: The Great Famine in Irish and Ukrainian History Textbooks." *History of Education* 35, 3: 345–68.

2007. "The 'Ethnic Other' in Ukrainian History Textbooks: The Case of Russia and the Russians." *Compare: A Journal of Comparative Education* 37, 3: 307–24.

"Jest śledztwo w sprawie słów Jana T. Grossa – Zarzut: znieważenie narodu polskiego." 2015. *Gazeta wyborcza*, October 15, p. 6, available at: http://wyborcza.pl/1,75248,19025979,jest-sledztwo-w-sprawie-slow-jana-t-grossa-zarzut-zniewazenie.html, accessed June 22, 2017.

Jilge, Wilfried. 2007. "Geschichtspolitik in der Ukraine." *Aus Politik und Zeitgeschichte* 8–9: 24–30.

Jokimaitis, Rimantas. ed. 2013. *Skaudžių likimų aidas: nacionalinio mokinių konkurso "Lietuvos kovų už laisvę ir netekčių istorija" rašinių rinktinė*. Vilnius: Lietuvos gyventojų genocido ir rezistencijos tyrimo centras.

2015. "Istorija ir istorinė atmintis." Presentation at conference "Lietuvos mokykla ir istorinė atmintis," Lithuanian parliament, November 12.

Jowitt, Ken. 1999. "The Leninist Legacy," in Vladimir Tismaneanu, ed. *The Revolutions of 1989: Rewriting Histories*. London: Routledge, 213–30.

Judt, Tony. 2005. *Postwar: A History of Europe Since 1945*. London: The Penguin Press.

"Justice Ministry Posts List of Persons in Prosecutor's Office Subject to Lustration Law." 2016. *Ukrinform*, April 9, available at: www.ukrinform.net/rubric-crime/1997291-justice-ministry-posts-list-of-persons-in-prosecutors-office-subject-to-lustration-law.html, accessed June 22, 2017.

"Kadrovi sostav organov gosudarstvennoi bezopasnosti SSSR. 1935–1939." Memorial, no date. http://nkvd.memo.ru, accessed May 6, 2017.

"Kak pritesniaiut oralmanov v Kazakhstane." no date. *Karavan*, March 13, available at: www.caravan.kz/news/kak-pritesnyayut-oralmanov-v-kazakhstane-391876/, accessed May 6, 2017.

Kaminski, Bartlomiej. 1991. *The Collapse of State Socialism: The Case of Poland*. Princeton: Princeton University Press.

Kaminski, Anna. ed. 2011. *Mescy pamaci akhvyarau kamunismu u Belarusi*. Leipzig: Bundesstigtung Aufarbeitung.

Kamiński, Łukasz and Jan Żaryn. eds. 2006. *Wokół pogromu kieleckiego*. Warsaw: Instytut Pamięci Narodowej.

Kandić, Nataša. ed. 2015. *Victims' Right to Reparation in Serbia and the European Court of Human Rights Standards. 2014–2015 Report.* Belgrade: Humanitarian Law Center.

Karaganov, Sergei. 2010. "Russkaya Katyn." *Rossiiskaya gazeta,* July 22, p. 3.

2011. "Speech by Sergei Karaganov at a meeting of the Council on Civil Society and Human Rights Discussion of the Project on the Perpetuation of the Memory of Victims of the Totalitarian Regime and on National Reconciliation." *Johnson's Russia List,* February 8, available at: www.russialist.org/archives/russia-karaganov-project-perpetuate-memory-totalitarian-victims-national-reconciliation-feb-320.php, accessed July 9, 2017.

Karn, Alexander. 2016. *Amending the Past: Europe's Holocaust Commissions and the Right to History.* Madison: University of Wisconsin Press.

Kasianov, Heorhiy. 2010. *Danse Macabre. Holod 1932–1933 Rokiv u Politytsi, Masovii Svidomosti ta Istoriohrafii (1980-ti–Pochatok 2000-kh).* Kyiv: Nash Chas.

2010. "The Great Famine of 1932-33 (Holodomor) and the Politics of History in Contemporary Ukraine," in Stefan Troebst, ed. *Postdiktatorische Geschichtskulturen im Süden und Osten Europas: Bestandsaufnahme und Forschungsperspektiven.* Göttingen: Wallstein, 619–41.

Kassenova, Togzhan. 2009. "The Lasting Toll of Semipalatinsk's Nuclear Testing." *Bulletin of the Atomic Scientists,* September 28, available at: http://thebulletin.org/lasting-toll-semipalatinsks-nuclear-testing, accessed March 31, 2017.

Kastiuk, Mikhail. ed. 1995. *Narysy historyi Belarusi.* Minsk: Belarus.

Kavoukian, Kristin. 2013. "Soviet mentality? The Role of Political Culture in Relations between the Armenian State and Russia's Armenian Diaspora." *Nationalities Papers* 41, 5: 709–29.

Kaye, Mike. 1997. "The Role of Truth Commissions in the Search for Justice, Reconciliation and Democratisation: The Salvadorean and Honduran Cases." *Journal of Latin American Studies* 29, 3: 693–716.

"Kazakhstanskie arkhivy otkryvaiut dostup k sekretnym delam proshlogo." 2016. *MK v Kazakhstane,* July 13, available at: http://mk-kz.kz/articles/2016/07/13/kazakhstan skie-arkhivy-otkryvayut-dostup-k-sekretnym-delam-proshlogo.html, accessed May 6, 2017.

Kaziev, Sattar. 2015. "Soviet Nationality Policy and Problems of Trust in Interethnic Relations in Kazkahstan (1917–1991)." PhD Dissertation, Moscow.

Ketelaar, Erik. 2008. "Truth, Memories and Histories in the Archives of the ICTY." Paper presented at the 60 Years Genocide Convention, The Hague, December 8.

"KGB in the Baltic States: Documents and Researches." no date, available at: www .kgbdocuments.eu/index.php?2737553734, accessed October 15, 2016.

Khadyka, Yuri. 2003. "Eurapeiskia konteksty belaruskaga mentalitetu." *Filamaty* 4, p. 7, available at: http://kamunikat.org/filamaty.html?pubid=5584, accessed January 9, 2017.

Khan-Akkuly, Sultan. 2011. "Sushchestvuet li v Kazakhstane 'oralmanofobiia'?" *Radio Azattyq,* October 12, available at: http://rus.azattyq.org/a/repatriate_diskrimination_kulibayev_janaozen_phobia_migration/24356665.html, accessed May 6, 2017.

Khapaeva, Dina. 2009. "Historical Memory in Post-Soviet Gothic Society." *Social Research* 76, 1: 359–94.

Kharichev, Igor. 2013. "Putin i Stalin." *Ezhednevnyi zhurnal* (Moscow), May 2.

Khrustaleva, Elena. 2016. "Proshchanie s 'Perm'iu-36'." *30 oktiabria* 133: 1–2.

Khubova, Daria. 1994. "Imprisoned History: The KGB Archives." *The Journal of the International Institute* 1, 1 Winter, available at: http://hdl.handle.net/2027/spo.4750978.0001.103, accessed October 15, 2016.

Kim, Hunjoon and Kathryn Sikkink. 2010. "Explaining the Deterrence Effect of Human Rights Prosecutions for Transitional Countries." *International Studies Quarterly* 54, 4: 939–63.

Kiss, Csilla. 2006. "The Misuses of Manipulation: The Failure of Transitional Justice in Post-Communist Hungary." *Europe-Asia Studies* 58, 6: 925–40.

Klerides, Eleftherios. 2010. "Imagining the Textbook: Textbooks as Discourse and Genre." *Journal of Educational Media, Memory, and Society* 2, 1: 31–54.

Klumbyte, Neringa and Gulgaz Sharafutdinova. 2013. *Soviet Society in the Era of Late Socialism, 1964–1985*. Lanham: Lexington Books.

Klymenko, Lina. 2016. "Narrating the Second World War: History Textbooks and Nation-Building in Belarus, Russia, and Ukraine." *Journal of Educational Media, Memory, and Society* 8, 2: 36–57.

2016. "The Holodomor Law and National Trauma Construction in Ukraine." *Canadian Slavonic Papers* 58, 4: 341–61.

Knight, Amy. 1996. *Spies without Cloaks: The KGB's Successors*. Princeton: Princeton University Press.

Koishibayev, Beibit. 2012. "Pravda i mif o zhertvakh repressii." *Turkestan*, February 2, available at: www.altyn-orda.kz/pravda-i-mif-o-zhertvax-repressij/, accessed May 6, 2017.

Kokhanova, Svetlana. 2009. "Arkhipelag Karlag." *Ekspress-K*, August 11, available at: http://old.express-k.kz/show_article.php?art_id=32202, accessed May 6, 2017.

Kommers, Donald P. and Russel A. Miller. 2012. *The Constitutional Jurisprudence of the Federal Republic of Germany*, 3rd ed. Durham: Duke University Press.

"Kommissia po reabilitatsii zhertv politicheskikh repressii." no date, available at: http://kremlin.ru/structure/commissions#institution-25, accessed November 19, 2016.

Kononczuk, Wojciech, Tadeusz Iwański, Tadeusz Olszański, and Piotr Żochowski. 2015. *The Bumpy Road. Difficult Reform Process in Ukraine*, OSWCommentary, Centre for Eastern Studies, No. 192, November 30.

Kopelev, Lev. 1981. *Utoli moya pechali [Ease My Sorrows]*. Ann Arbor: Ardis Press.

Koposov, Nikolai. 2011. "'The Armored Train of Memory': The Politics of History in Post-Soviet Russia." *Perspectives on History* 49, 1: 23–31.

Korczewski, Jacek. 2000. "Mord rytualny." *Wprost* (Poznań), December 10, pp. 36–37.

Korostelina, Karina. 2010. "War of Textbooks: History Education in Russia and Ukraine." *Communist and Post-Communist Studies* 43: 129–37.

2011. "Shaping Unpredictable Past: National Identity and History Education in Ukraine." *National Identities* 13, 1: 3–4.

2013. "Constructing Nation: National Narratives of History Teachers in Ukraine." *National Identities* 15, 4: 401–16.

Kosienkowski, Marcin and William Schreiber. 2012. *Moldova: Arena of International Influences*. Lanham: Lexington Books.

Kostic, Roland. 2007. *Ambivalent Peace: External Peacebuilding, Threatened Identity and Reconciliation in Bosnia and Herzegovina, Report No. 78*, Uppsala: Department of Peace and Conflict Research.

Kostiuk, Mikhail. 2002. *Boslevistskaya sistema vlasti w Belarusi*. Moskow: RAN.
Kotkin, Stephen. 2001. *Armageddon Averted: The Soviet Collapse, 1970–2000*. New York: Oxford University Press.
Kott, Matthew. 2007. "Estonia 1940–1945: Reports of the Estonian International Commission for the Investigation of Crimes Against Humanity." *Holocaust and Genocide Studies* 21, 2: 321–23.
Kovalev, Sergei. 2009. "Vymysli i fal'sifikatsii v otsenkakh roli SSSR nakanune i s nachalom Vtoroi mirovoi voiny." mil.ru (Russian Ministry of Defense website), June 4.
Kramer, Mark. 1993. "Archival Research in Moscow: Progress and Pitfalls." *Cold War International History Project Bulletin* 3: 18–39.
  1998. "'In Case Military Assistance Is Provided to Poland': Soviet Preparations for Military Contingencies, August 1980." *Cold War International History Project Bulletin* 11, Winter: 102–111.
  2010. "The Soviet Union, the Warsaw Pact, and the Polish Crisis of 1980-1981." in Lee Trepanier, Spasimir Domaradzki, and Jaclyn Stanke, eds. *The Solidarity Movement and Perspectives on the Last Decade of the Cold War*. Kraków: Krakowskie Towarzystwo Eduk, 27–67.
  2012. "Archival Policies and Historical Memory in the Post-Soviet Era." *Demokratizatsiya* 20, 3: 12–25.
Krikorian, Robert O. 2005. "Armenia's Political Transition in Historical Perspective," *Global Dialogue* 7, 3–4.
Kritz, Neil J. ed. 1995. *Transitional Justice: How Emerging Democracies Reckon with Former Regimes*. Washington: U.S. Institute of Peace.
  2004. "Dealing with the Legacy of Past Abuse: An Overview of the Options and Their Relationship to the Promotion of Peace," in M. Bleeker and J. Sisson, eds. *Dealing with the Past: Critical Issues, Lessons Learned, and Challenges for Future Swiss Policy*. Bern: Swisspeace, 15–32.
Kundakbayeva, Zhanat and Didar Kassymova. 2006. "Remembering and Forgetting: The State Policy of Memorializing Stalin's Repression in Post-Soviet Kazakhstan." *Nationalities Papers* 44, 4: 611–27.
Kundigraber, Claudia. 1997. *Polens Weg in die Demokratie: der Runde Tisch und der unerwartete Machtwechsel*. Göttingen: Cuvilier.
Kuodytė, Dalia. 2003. "Recenzija: Šešėlių žaismas." *Genocidas ir Rezistencija*, 14, 2: 154–62.
Kupatadze, Alexander. 2016. "Georgia's Break with the Past." *Journal of Democracy* 27, 110–23.
Kuprashvili, Natia. 2010. "Georgians Finally Topple Stalin." *The Messenger* (Tbilisi), No. 28, July 7, p. 7.
Belorusskaia Enthiklopedyia "Kurapaty." 1995. *Belarus. Encyklapedychny davednik*. Minsk: Belorusskaia Enthiklopedyia, 411–12.
Belorusskaia Enthiklopedyia "Kurapaty." 1999. *Belorusskaia entsiklopediya u 18 tomakh, tom. 9*. Minsk: Belorusskaia Enthiklopedyia, 42.
Arkhiu Nainoushai Historii. *Kurapaty. Zbornik Materyalau*. 2002. Minsk: Arkhiu Nainoushai Historii.
Kurkchiyan, Marina. 2005. "The Karabakh Conflict. From Soviet Past to Post-Soviet Uncertainty," in Edmund Herzig and Marina Kurkchiyan, eds. *The Armenians. Past and Present in the Making of National Identity*. London: Routledge.

"Kuropaty: mir pod sosnami." 2009. *Belarus segondnya*, October 29, available at: www .sb.by/post/93010, accessed January 15, 2017.

Kuzio, Taras. 2015. *Ukraine: Democratization, Corruption and the New Russian Imperialism*. Santa Barbara: Praeger.

Kuznetsov, Igor. 2004. "Zabyt znachit predat," *Belorusskaya delovaya gazeta*, April 14. 2007. "Repressii na Belarusi v 1920–40." in Igor Kuznetsov and Yakov Basin, eds. *Repressivnaya politika sovetskoi vlasti v Belarusi*. Minsk: Memorial, Vol. 2: 2–29.

Kuznetsova, Ekaterina. 2016. "Lecture 3. Karlag i Ego Istoriia." *OpenMind.Kz*, December 22, available at: http://omind.kz, accessed May 6, 2017.

Kydyralina, Zhanna. 2008. "Etnichnost' i vlast' (Sotsialno-etnicheskie konfliktyv Kazakhstane v sovetskii period)." *Obshchestvennye nauki i sovremennost'* 5: 120–8, available at: http://ecsocman.hse.ru/data/2010/09/20/1215005669/Kydaralina.pdf, accessed May 6, 2017.

Laplante, Lisa and Kimberly Theidon. 2007. "Truth with Consequences: Justice and Reparations in post-Truth Commission Peru." *Human Rights Quarterly* 29, 1: 228–50.

Latvia. 2013. *Transitional Justice and Memory in the EU*, available at: www.proyectos .cchs.csic.es/transitionaljustice/, accessed October 19, 2016.

Latvian Criminal Code. 1993, available at: www.legislationline.org/documents/ section/criminal-codes, accessed December 14, 2016.

"Law 10 on Rehabilitation of Victims of Massive Political Repressions." 1993. *Vedomosti Verkhovnogo Soveta Respubliki Kazakhstan*, no. 10, April 14, st. 242, available at: http://adilet.zan.kz/eng/docs/Z930002200, accessed May 6, 2017.

"Law 183-3 on changes in some legislative acts of the Republic of Belarus." 2004. January 4, available at: http://pravo.levonevsky.org/bazaby09/sbor43/text43894.htm, accessed December 12, 2016.

"Law of the Republic of Belarus 1593-XII." 1992. April 16, available at: http://pravo .levonevsky.org/bazaby/zakon/zakb1393.htm, accessed December 12, 2016.

Law of Ukraine on the Purification of Government. 2014. September 16. Закон України Про очищення влади, Відомості Верховної Ради (ВВР), 2014, № 44, ст.2041.

Law of Ukraine on the Restoration of Trust in the Judiciary. 2014. April 8. Закон України Про відновлення довіри до судової влади в Україні, Відомості Верховної Ради (ВВР), 2014, № 23, ст.870.

"Law on the condemnation of the communist and national socialist (Nazi) regimes, and prohibition of propaganda of their symbols." 2015. Kyiv, April 9, available at: www.memory.gov.ua/laws/law-ukraine-condemnation-communist-and-national-socialist-nazi-regimes-and-prohibition-propagan, accessed October 19, 2016.

Leebaw, Bronwyn Anne. 2008. "The Irreconcilable Goals of Transitional Justice." *Human Rights Quarterly* 30, 1: 95–118.

"Lege nr. 1225 privind reabilitarea victimelor represiunilor politice." 1992. December 8, available at: http://lex.justice.md/index.php?action=view&view=doc&id=313312, accessed March 4, 2017.

Leszczyński, Adam. 2016. "PiS kole order prof. Jana Tomasza Grossa: I chcą mu ode-brać Krzyż Kawalerski." *Gazeta wyborcza*, February 9, p. 3.

Levin, Dov. 1995. *The Lesser of Two Evils: Eastern European Jewry Under Soviet Rule, 1939–1941*. Philadelphia: Jewish Publication Society.

Levitsky, Steven and Lucan A. Way. 2010. *Competitive Authoritarianism: Hybrid Regimes after the Cold War*. New York: Cambridge University Press.

Lewis, Simon. 2015. "Overcoming Hegemonic Martyrdom: The Afterlife of Khatyn in Belarusian Memory." *Journal of Soviet and Post-Soviet Politics and Society* 1, 2: 367–401.

Libaridian, Gerard J. 2004. *Modern Armenia: People, Nation, State.* New Brunswick: Transaction Publishers.

"Lider KPRF ob' iavil o nastuplenii 'stalinskoi vesny." 2015. *Dozhd' TV,* December 21, available at: https://tvrain.ru/articles/lider_kprf_objavil_o_nastuplenii_stalinskoj_vesny-400547, accessed June 22, 2017.

Lietuvos respublikos nacionalinio saugumo pagrindų įstatymas 1996 m. 1996. gruodžio 19 d. Nr. VIII-49 Vilnius.

Lietuvos, Respublikos Prezidento. 1998. "Dėl Tarptautinės komisijos nacių ir sovietinio okupacinių režimų nusikaltimams Lietuvoje įvertinti" (Žin., Nr. 80-2248), 1998 m., rugsėjo 7 d. dekretas Nr.159, available at: www.e-tar.lt/portal/lt/legalAct/TAR.4045F0BAAF21, accessed January 31, 2017.

Light, Matthew. 2014. "Police Reforms in the Republic of Georgia: The Convergence of Domestic and Foreign Policy in an Anti-Corruption Drive." *Policing and Society* 24, 3: 318–45.

Lindner, Rainer. 2001. "Natsiianal'nyia i prydvornya gistoryki 'lukashenkauskai' Belarusi." *Histarychny almanakh* 4: 199–215.

Lipman, Maria, Lev Gudkov, and Lasha Bakradze. 2013. *The Stalin Puzzle: Deciphering Post-Soviet Public Opinion.* Washington: Carnegie Endowment for International Peace.

"List Czesława Kiszczaka: Dokumenty publikować po śmierci Lecha Wałęsy." 2016. *Rzeczpospolita,* February 22, p. 1.

"Lithuania." 2013. *Transitional Justice and Memory in the EU,* available at: www.proyectos.cchs.csic.es/transitionaljustice/, accessed October 19, 2016.

Lithuanian Criminal Code, 2003. Available at: www.legislationline.org/documents/section/criminal-codes, accessed December 14, 2016.

Loewenstein, Karl. 1937. "Militant Democracy and Fundamental Rights I." *The American Political Science Review* 31, 3: 417–32.

  1937. "Militant Democracy and Fundamental Rights II." *The American Political Science Review* 31, 4: 638–58.

Lomsadze, Giorgi. 2011. "Georgia: Tbilisi Creating Black List for Soviet Political Elite, KGB Collaborators." *Eurasianet.org,* June 21, available at: www.eurasianet.org/node/63718, accessed October 19, 2016.

Long, William and Peter Brecke. 2003. *War and Reconciliation: Reason and Emotion in Conflict Resolution.* Cambridge: MIT Press.

Los, F. and V. Spitskiy. 1973. *Istoriya Ukrainskoy SSR (Posobiye dlya 9–10 Klassov).* Kiev: Radyanska Shkola.

Lota, Vladimir. 2007. "Ego zvali 'Del'mar'." *Krasnaya zvezda,* July 23.

"Lozh' o Katyni vskryvaetsya." 2012. *Segodnya* (Moscow), June 23, p. 7.

Luhn, Alec. 2016. "What Stalin Owes Putin." *International New York Times,* March 12–13, available at: http://ihtbd.com/ihtuser/print/old%20THT/12-03-2016/a1203x08xxxxxxxxx.pdf, accessed June 24, 2017.

"Lustration Covers 24,000 Officials, Next Stage in Late March." 2015. *Ukraine General Newswire* (Kiev), March 17.

"Lustration Stele in Ukrainian City – Reminder to Officials." 2014. *Life in Ukraine*, September 15, available at: http://lifeinua.info/lustration-stele-ukrainian-city-remainder-officials-video/, accessed October 7, 2016.

MacFarlane, S. Neil. 2011. "Post-Revolutionary Georgia On the Edge?" Briefing paper for Chatham House, March, available at: www.chathamhouse.org/sites/files/chathamhouse/public/Research/Russia%20and%20Eurasia/bpo311_macfarlane.pdf, accessed November 2, 2016.

Macfarquhar, Neil. 2015. "A Parade Hailing Russia's World War II Dead and Marching Further from the West." *The New York Times*, May 8, p. A4.

2016. "A Book for Discerning Russians: The Words of Putin." *International New York Times*, January 1–2.

Machcewicz, Paweł and Krzysztof Persak. eds. 2002. *Wokół Jedwabnego, Vol. I: Studia, and Vol. II: Dokumenty*. Warsaw: Wydawnictwo Instytutu Pamięci Narodowej.

Macierewicz, Antoni. 2001. "Rewolucja nihilizmu." *Głos – Tygodnik katolicko-narodowy* (Warsaw), February 3, p. 2.

"Macierewicz o archiwum Kiszczaka: To koniec legendy Lecha Wałęsy." 2016. *Rzeczpospolita*, February 22, p. 7.

Magarrell, Lisa. 2003. "Reparations for Massive or Widespread Human Rights Violations: Sorting out Claims for Reparations and the Struggle for Social Justice." *Windsor Yearbook of Access to Justice* 22: 85–98.

Maier, Charles. 2000. "Doing History, Doing Justice: The Historian and the Truth Commission," in Robert I. Rotberg and Dennis Thompson, eds. *Truth v. Justice: The Morality of Truth Commissions*. Princeton: Princeton University Press, 261–78.

Makarkin, Aleksei. 2015. "Protivorechivye prazdniki v novoi Rossii." *Novoe Literaturnoe Obozrenie* (Moscow) 3: 13–27.

Makaryan, Shushanik. 2009. *Impacts of Nationhood and the World Society on Nation-State building: Has the Nation Disappeared?* Florence: European University Institute.

Mälksoo, Lauri. 2001. "Soviet Genocide? Communist Mass Deportations in the Baltic States and International Law." *Leiden Journal of International Law* 14, 4: 757–87.

2009. "The Memory Politics of Becoming European: The East European Subalterns and the Collective Memory of Europe." *European Journal of International Relations* 15, 4: 653–80.

2011. "Case Commentary." *American Journal of International Law* 105, 1: 1–8.

Mammadli, Seljan. no date. "Transitional Justice in Azerbaijan: Dealing with the Past," available at: www.azadliqciragi.org/pdf/AN/Justice.pdf, accessed on October 19, 2016.

Mannteufel, Ingo. 2015. "Opinion: Instrumentalizing History – Moscow and May 9." *Deutsche Welle*, May 9.

Mark, James. 2010. "What Remains? Anti-Communism, Forensic Archeology, and the Retelling of the National Past in Lithuania and Romania." *Past and Present* Supplement 5: 276–300.

Marples, David R. 1994. "Kuropaty: The Investigation of a Stalinist Historical Controversy." *Slavic Review* 53, 2: 513–23.

1999. *Belarus. A Denationalized Nation*. Amsterdam: Harwood.

2003. "History and Politics in Post-Soviet Belarus: The Foundations, in Elena Korosteleva, Colin Lawson, and Rosalind Marsh, eds. *Contemporary Belarus: Between Democracy and Dictatorship*. London: Routledge, 21–35.

2007. *Heroes and Villains: Creating National History in Contemporary Ukraine.* Budapest: Central European University Press.

Martin, Terry. 2001. *The Affirmative Action Empire Nations and Nationalism in the Soviet Union, 1923–1939*. Ithaca: Cornell University Press.

Martirosyan, Arsen. 2015. "Kto rasstrelyal plennykh polskikh ofitserov v Katyni." *Pravda* (Moscow), April 14, p. 5.

Martyralog. 1989. *Bulleten.* Minsk: Belarusian Association of the Memory of Victims of Stalinism, available at: http://vytoki.net/content/Martyralog.pdf, accessed June 21, 2017.

Mayer-Rieckh, Alexander 2007. "Vetting to Prevent Future Abuses: Reforming the Police, Courts, and Prosecutor's Offices in Bosnia and Herzegovina," in Alexander Mayer-Rieckh and Pablo de Greiff, eds. *Justice as Prevention: Vetting Public Employees in Transitional Societies*. New York: Social Science Research Council, 180–221.

Mayer-Rieckh, Alexander and Pablo de Greiff. eds. 2007. *Justice as Prevention: Vetting Public Employees in Transitional Societies*. New York: Social Science Research Council.

McMahon, Patrice and David Forsyth. 2008. "The ICTY Impact on Serbia: Judicial Romanticism Meets Network Politics." *Human Rights Quarterly* 30, 2: 412–35.

Meducki, Stanisław and Zenon Wrona. eds. 1992. *Antyżydowskie wydarzenia kieleckie 4 lipca 1946 roku*, 2 vols. Kielce: Kieleckie Towarzystwo Naukowe.

Medvedev, Dmitrii. 2009. "Repressiiam net opravdaniia." *30 oktiabria*, 94.

Medvedev, Sergei. 2015. "Prazdnik bez slez na glazakh: Chto sluchilos' s Dnem Pobedy." *Forbes.ru*, May 8.

Mendeloff, David. 2004. "Truth-Seeking, Truth-Telling, and Postconflict Peacebuilding: Curb the Enthusiasm?" *International Studies Review* 6, 3: 355–80.

Mendelson, Sarah E. and Theodore P. Gerber. 2006. "Failing the Stalin Test: Russians and Their Dictator." *Foreign Affairs* 85, 1: 2–8.

Meurs, Wim van. 2003. *History Textbooks in Moldova*. Strasbourg: Council of Europe, available at: www.cap.uni-muenchen.de/download/2003/2003_History_Textbooks .pdf, accessed March 4, 2017.

Meyer, Henry. 2014. "Russia Reenacts WWII March after Putin Defends Nazi Pact." *Bloomberg News wire*, November 7, Item 5.

Michnik, Adam and Václav Havel. 1993. "Justice or Revenge." *Journal of Democracy* 4, 1: 20–7.

Migration Policy Center. 2013. *Moldova*, June, available at: www.migrationpolicycentre .eu/docs/migration_profiles/Moldova.pdf, accessed on February 13, 2017.

Mihai, Mihaela. 2016. *Negative Emotions and Transitional Justice*. New York: Columbia University Press.

Mihajlović, Kosta and Vasilije Krestić, eds. 1995. *Memorandum of the Serbian Academy of Sciences and Arts. Answers to Criticisms*. Belgrade: Serbian Academy of Sciences and Arts.

Mikhailov, Valerii. 1990. *Khronika velikogo dzhuta*. Alma-Ata: SP "Interbuk".

"Mikhalkov Creates Rival to McDonald's." 2015. *The Moscow Times*, April 10.

Milosavljević, Olivera. 2000. "The Abuse of the Authority of Science," in Nebojša Popov, ed. *The Road to War in Serbia. Trauma and Catharsis.* Budapest: Central European University Press, 274–302.
    2006. *Potisnuta istina. Kolaboracija u Srbiji 1941–1944.* Belgrade: Helsinški odbor za ljudska prava u Srbiji.
Milošević, Srđan. 2013. *Istorija pred sudom. Interpretacija prošlosti i pravni aspekti u rehabilitaciji kneza Pavla Karađorđevića.* Belgrade: Fabrika knjiga.
Minassian, Gaïdz. 2015. *Le rêve brisé des Armeniens – 1915.* Paris: Flammarion.
Minasyan, Sergey. 2010. *Nagorno-Karabakh After Two Decades of Conflict: Is Prolongation of the Status Quo Inevitable?* Yerevan: Caucasus Institute.
Minasyan, Sergey, Hrant Mikaelyan, and Nina Iskandaryan. 2014. "The Silent Guns of August. Why the Karabakh War Has Not Begun Anew." *Policy Brief Caucasus Institute*, No. 1, September.
Ministry of Education and Science of Ukraine. 2017. "Perelik Navchalnykh Prohram, Pidruchnykiv ta Navchalno-Metodychnykh Posibnykiv, Rekomendovanykh Ministerstvom Osvity i Nauky Ukrainy," available at: http://mon.gov.ua/activity/ education/zagalna-serednya/perelik-navchalnix-program.html, accessed January 21, 2017.
"Miniust obvinil 'Memorial' v podryve konstitutsionnogo stroia RF." 2015. November 10, available at: www.novayagazeta.ru/news/1697854.html, accessed November 6, 2016.
Minow, Martha. 1998. *Between Vengeance and Forgiveness: Facing History after Genocide and Mass Violence.* Boston: Beacon Press.
Mironchyk, Uladzimir. 1993. "Patryiatyzm – galouny stoup." *Litaratura i Mastactva*, March 5.
Mirzoyan, Alla. 2010. *Armenia, the Regional Powers and the West.* London: Palgrave Macmillan.
Mitchell, Lincoln A. 2009. "Compromising Democracy: State-building in Saakashvili's Georgia." *Central Asian Survey* 28, 2: 171–83.
    2013. "Duelling Narratives: Storytelling and Spin in Georgia." *World Affairs*, available at: www.worldaffairsjournal.org/article/dueling-narratives-storytelling-and-spin-georgia, accessed June 21, 2017.
"Moldovan Parliament Rejects Lustration Bill." 2001. *RFE/RL Newsline*, June 1.
Moran, John. 1994. "The Communist Tortures of Eastern Europe: Prosecute and Punish or Forgive and Forget?" *Communist and Post-Communist Studies* 27, 1: 95–109.
Muižnieks, Nils. 2014. "Transitional Justice in the Context of European Convention Obligations: The Right to Life and Dealing with the Past." Speech presented to Council of Europe, Commissioner for Human Rights, University of Ulster, Belfast, November 6, available at: https://rm.coe.int/ref/CommDH/Speech (2014) 10, accessed July 9, 2017.
Musteata, Sergiu. 2017. *About Us and Our Neighbors: History Textbooks in the Republic of Moldova, Romania and Ukraine*, available at: http://repository.gei.de/ handle/11428/213, accessed March 4, 2017.
Muzeum Historii Żydów Polskich, *1000 lat historii Żydów polskich. Miniprzewodnik po ekspozycji.* 2014. Warsaw: Muzeum Historii Żydów Polskich POLIN.
Mysan, Viktor. 1997. *Opovidannia z Istorii Ukrainy.* Kyiv: Heneza.
    2010. *Vstup do Istorii Ukrainy.* Kyiv: Heneza.

"MZSR: 10,7 mlrd tenge vyplacheno zhertvam politicheskikh repressii v Kazakhstane s 2003 goda." 2016. *KazInform*, May 31, available at: www.inform.kz/ru/mzsr-10-7-mlrd-tenge-vyplacheno-zhertvam-politicheskih-repressiy-v-kazahstane-s-2003-goda_a2909404, accessed May 6, 2017.

"Nagorno–Karabagh profile." 2016. April 6, www.bbc.com/news/world-europe-18270325, accessed June 22, 2017.

"Nagorno-Karabakh. Azerbaijan hits Armenia defence unit." 2017. May 17, www.aljazeera.com/news/2017/05/nagorno-karabakh-azerbaijan-hits-armenian-air-defence-170516104753249.html, accessed June 22, 2017.

Nalepa, Monika. 2008. "To Punish the Guilty and Protect the Innocent: Comparing Truth Revelation Procedures." *The Journal of Theoretical Politics* 20, 2: 224–5.

2010. *Skeletons in the Closet: Transitional Justice in Post-Communist Europe*. New York: Cambridge University Press.

2013. "Lustration," in Lavinia Stan and Nadya Nedelsky, eds. *Encyclopedia of Transitional Justice*. New York: Cambridge University Press, Vol. 1: 46–51.

"National Security & Defense Reform to Involve Lustration in Intelligence Agencies." 2014. *Ukraine General Newswire* (Kiev), November 17.

"NATO Warns Georgia against Political Persecution of Ex-Officials." 2013. *Reuters*, June 27, available at: http://uk.reuters.com/article/uk-georgia-nato-idUKBRE95Q0WQ20130627, accessed December 3, 2016.

Natsuko, Oka. 2013. "A Note on Ethnic Return Migration Policy in Kazakhstan: Changing Priorities and a Growing Dilemma." *IDE Discussion Paper* No. 394 (March), available at: www.ide.go.jp/English/Publish/Download/Dp/394.html, accessed May 6, 2017.

Nechepurenko, Ivan. 2015. "New Policy on Commemorating Victims of Repression at Odds with Actions." *The Moscow Times, John's Russia List #9*, August 20.

Nedelsky, Nadya. 2004. "Divergent Responses to a Common Past: Transitional Justice in the Czech Republic and Slovakia." *Theory and Society* 33: 65–115.

Niekrasz, Lech Z. 2001. *Operacja Jedwabne – mity i fakty*. Wrocław: Nortom.

Niemczyńska, Małgorzata. 2008. "Antysemityzm straszny jak Stalin." *Gazeta Wyborcza*, January 24, p. 22.

2008. "Żydzi nas atakują! Trzeba się bronić." *Gazeta Wyborcza*, February 11, p. 7.

Nistor, Ion. 1991. *Istoria Basarabiei*. Bucharest: Humanitas.

Novik, Yaugeni and Genadz Matsul. 2000. *Historya Belarusi. February 1917–1997*. Minsk: Universyteckaye.

Nowak, Jerzy Robert. 2001. *100 kłamstw J. T. Grossa o żydowskich sąsiadach w Jedwabnem*. Warsaw: Wydawnictwo von Borowiecki.

2015. "Jak prowokator J.T. Gross odsłonił się do końca." Serwis Informacyjny BIBUŁY, October 3.

"Ob itogakh sotsial'no-ekonomicheskogo razvitiia raiona za 2015 god i zadachakh na 2016 god." no date. Ofitsial'nyi Sait Glubokovskii raion Vostochno-Kazakhstanskoi oblasti, available at: https://glubokoe.gov.kz/page/socialnaya-zashch, accessed May 6, 2017.

"Ob utverzhdenii kontseptsii gosudarstvennoi politiki po uvekovecheniiu pamiati zhertv politicheskikh repressii." 2015. August 18, available at: www.government.ru/docs/19296, accessed November 19, 2016.

"Obrashchenie Prezidenta Rossiiskoi Federatsii, 18 marta 2014 goda, Moskva, Kreml'." 2014. *Rossiiskaya gazeta*, March 19, pp. 1–2.

"Obschestvo Memorial: v 1961–1988 v Belarusi bylo osuzhdeno 28 dissidentov." 2008. *Naviny.by*, January 24, available at: http://naviny.by/rubrics/society/2008/01/24/ic_news_116_284382/, accessed January 29, 2017.

OCHA. 2015. *Ukraine Situation Report No. 26 as of February 6, 2015*, February 6, available at: http://reliefweb.int/sites/reliefweb.int/files/resources/ukraine%20sitrep%2026 .pdf, accessed October 13, 2016.

"Odluka o osnivanju Komisije za istinu i pomirenje." 2001. *Official Gazette of the Federal Republic of Yugoslavia*, 15/2001.

Oglesby, Elizabeth. 2007. "Historical Memory and the Limits of Peace Education: Examining Guatemala's Memory of Silence and the Politics of Curriculum Design," in Elizabeth Cole, ed. *Teaching the Violent Past: History Education and Reconciliation*. New York: Rowman and Littlefield, 175–202.

Oliphant, Roland. 2014. "Up to a Dozen Ukraine Officials Dumped in Wheelie Bins." *The Telegraph*, October 7, available at: www.telegraph.co.uk/news/worldnews/europe/ukraine/11145381/Up-to-a-dozen-Ukraine-officials-dumped-in-wheelie-bins .html, accessed October 7, 2016.

Olsen, Tricia, Leigh Payne, and Andrew Reiter. 2010. *Transitional Justice in Balance: Comparing Processes, Weighing Efficacy*. Washington: United States Institute of Peace Press.

Olszański, Tadeusz. 2014. *The Ukrainian Lustration Act*. Ośrodek Studiów Wschodnich, October 1.

Omar, Botagoz. 2011. "Muzei Karlaga." *Novoe pokolenie*, May 17, available at: www .np.kz/events/8262-muzejj_karlaga.html, accessed May 6, 2017.

"Only 940 Officials in Ukraine Dismissed in Line with Law on Lustration." 2016. *Ukrinform*, May 6, available at: www.ukrinform.net/rubric-politics/2012422-only-940-officials-in-ukraine-dismissed-in-line-with-law-on-lustration.html, accessed June 21, 2017.

"Opinions on Armenia's Lustration Law: Were They Informers or Are They Serving the People?" 2011. *Epress.am*, December 6, available at: http://epress.am/en/2011/12/06/opinions-on-armenias-lustration-law-were-they-informers-or-are-they-serving-the-people.html, accessed May 18, 2017.

Opros: Stalin i ego rol' v istorii strany. Moscow: ATsYuL, March–April 2015.

Orentlicher, Diane. 2008. *Shrinking the Space for Denial: The Impact of the ICTY in Serbia*. Belgrade: Center for Transitional Processes.

Organization for Security and Cooperation in Europe Mission to Serbia and Belgrade Cetre for Human Rights. 2011. *Attitudes toward war crimes, the ICTY and the national judiciary*, October, available at: www.bgcentar.org.rs/bgcentar/eng-lat/citizens-perceptions-of-human-rights-law-and-practice/stavovi-prema-ratnim zlooin ima-haskom-tribunalu-domacem-pravosudu-za-ratne-zlocine/, accessed December 12, 2016.

Orlović, Sandra. ed. 2015. *Report on War Crimes Trials in Serbia During 2014 and 2015*. Belgrade. Humanitarian Law Center.

"Orzeczenie sędziów Sądu Apelacyjnego w Warszawie wraz z uzasadnieniem wyroku w sprawie lustracyjnej Lecha Wałęsy." 2000. *Sygn.akt* V AL. 26100, August 11, Warsaw.

"Oshibaetsya li 'Putin s narodom'? Gimn i muki sovesti russkoi intelligentsia." 2000. *Nezavisimaya gazeta* (Moscow), December 6, p. 1.

"Otchet akima Zhambylskogo raiona Turkova I.I. pered naseleniem raiona." 2016. *Ofitsial'nyi internet-resurs akima Zhambylskogo raiona Severo-Kazakhstanskoi oblasti*, July 27, available at: http://zhb.sko.gov.kz/page.php?page=otchetnyi_doklad_akima_raiona_2015&lang=2, accessed May 6, 2017.

"Otkryvaia zavesy tragicheskogo proshlogo." 2012. *Press-sluzhba KNB RK*, October 5, available at: http://knb.kz/ru/history/archive/article.htm?id=10322098@cmsArticle, accessed May 6, 2017.

"Over 1.6 million IDPs registered in Ukraine." no date. *Unkrinform.net*, available at: www.ukrinform.net/rubric-society_and_culture/2133980-over-16-million-idps-registered-in-ukraine.html, accessed December 7, 2016.

Paczkowski, Andrzej. 2001. "Debata wokół 'Sąsiadów: Próba wstępnej typologii." *Rzeczpospolita* (Warsaw), March 24, p. A6, available at: http://archiwum.rp.pl/artykul/329564-Debata-wokol.html, accessed June 24, 2017.

Pajak, Henryk. 2001. *Jedwabne geszefty*. Lublin: Wydawnictwo Retro.

"Pamiatnik zhertvam goloda 1930-kh godov ustanovlen v IuKO." 2012. *KazInform*, May 31, available at: www.inform.kz/ru/pamyatnik-zhertvam-goloda-1930-h-godov-ustanovlen-v-yuko_a2467727, accessed May 6, 2017.

"Pamiatnik zhertvam golodomora vozdvignut v Pavlodare." 2012. *KazInform*, May 31, available at: www.inform.kz/ru/pamyatnik-zhertvam-golodomora-vozdvignut-v-pavlodare_a2468441, accessed May 6, 2017.

"Pamiatnik zhertvam politicheskikh repressii i golodomora predlozhili perenesti za predely Almaty." 2014. *TengriNews*, August 7, available at: https://tengrinews.kz/picture_art/pamyatnik-jertvam-politicheskih-repressiy-golodomora-259271/, accessed May 6, 2017.

Panossian, Razmik. 2006. "Post-Soviet Armenia. Nationalism and its Discontent(s)," in Lowell W. Barrington, ed. *After Independence. Making and Protecting the Nation in Postcolonial and Post-communist States*. Ann Arbor: Michigan University Press, 225–48.

Parkhomenko, Sergei. 2017. "'Last Address' – An Antitotalitarian Project which Gives Voice to Man's Right to Life," *Fund for Last Address*, June 29, available at: www.poslednyadres.ru/articles/gordon_posledn_adresa_praga.htm, accessed July 9, 2017.

Patten, Sam and Michael Cicere. 2012. "Victors' Justice in Georgia?" *The National Interest*, December 7, available at: http://nationalinterest.org/commentary/victors-justice-georgia-7817, accessed November 3, 2016.

Payaslian, Simon. 2007. *The History of Armenia. From Origins to the Present*. London: Palgrave Macmillan.

Payne, Leigh A. 2008. *Unsettling Accounts: Neither Truth nor Reconciliation in Confessions of State Violence*. Durham: Duke University Press.

Pazniak, Zianon. 1992. "My pavinny kiravatcca u Europu." *BPF News*, December 9.

1992. *Sapraudnaye abliccha*. Minsk: Palifakt.

1993. "Nastaye chas dzieyannyau i rasplaty." *Narodnaya gazeta*, November 8.

2012. "Sutnasc pravakacyi." *Conservative Christian Party BPF*, February 20, available at: www.narodnaja-partyja.org/oo–Naviny-c_hyphenminus-Galownac_ja–fr–pg/oo–Naviny-c_hyphenminus-Galownac_ja–bk–an–oi/oo–20121120–06, accessed December 2, 2016.

no date. "Fizychnaie znishchen'nie belaruskai natsyi." available at: http://pazniak
.info/page_fizichnae_znishchenne_belaruskay_natsyi, accessed February 8, 2017.

Pazniak, Zianon and Yauhenii Shmygalyou. 1988. "Kurapaty – the Road of Death."
Literatura i mastactva, June 3, available at: http://kamunikat.org/download
.php?item=1865-2.html&pubref=1865, accessed December 11, 2016.

Pearce, Katy E. 2010. "Political Institutional Trust in the Post-Attempted Coup
Republic of Armenia." Paper presented at the annual meeting of the NCA 96th
Annual Convention, San Francisco, November 13, 2010, available at: www2.gwu
.edu/~ieresgwu/assets/docs/demokratizatsiya%20archive/GWASHU_DEMO_19_1/
J37082196087WVG8/J37082196087WVG8.pdf

Penter, Tanja. 2005. "Collaboration on Trial: New Source Material on Soviet Postwar
Trials against Collaborators." *Slavic Review* 64, 4: 782–90.

Perović, Latinka. 2000. "The Flight from Modernization," in Nebojša Popov, ed.
The Road to War in Serbia. Trauma and Catharsis. Budapest: Central European
University Press, 109–22.

Petrović, Vladimir. 2007. "(Ne)legitimni revizionizam: pravo i (pseudo)istoriografske
revizije na zapadu i istoku," in Vera Katz, ed. *Revizija prošlosti na prostorima bivše
Jugoslavije*. Sarajevo: Institut za istoriju, 21–42.

Pettai, Eva-Clarita. 2015. "Negotiating History for Reconciliation: A Comparative
Evaluation of the Baltic Presidential Commissions." *Europe-Asia Studies* 67, 7:
1079–101.

2016. "Prosecuting Soviet Genocide: Comparing the Politics of Criminal Justice in
the Baltic States." *European Politics and Society* 18, 1: 52–65.

Pettai, Eva-Clarita and Vello Pettai. 2014. *Transitional and Retrospective Justice in the
Baltic States*. Cambridge: Cambridge University Press.

Pianciola, Niccolo. 2001. "The Collectivisation Famine in Kazakhstan, 1931–33."
Harvard Ukrainian Studies 25, 3–4: 237–51.

Piasecka, Agnieszka. 2014. *Summary of Legislative Work on Lustration Act No. 4359 On
Purification of Government*. Warsaw: The Open Dialogue Foundation, November 19.

2015. *Report: Purification of Government or Vetting Ukrainian Style. The First Year's
Experience*. Warsaw: The Open Dialog Foundation, November 5.

Plakans, Andrejs. 2014. "The Commission of Historians in Latvia: 1999 to the Present."
Journal of Baltic Studies. Published online 8 August: 1–18.

Podgórska, Joanna. 2014. "Muzeum życia: O tym, jak powstawało Muzeum Historii
Żydów Polskich, jak zostało zorganizowane i jakie niesie przesłanie, opowiada
Marian Turski." *Polityka (Warsaw)*, No. 43, October 22–28, pp. 108–109.

Pohl, Otto. 1999. *Ethnic Cleansing in the USSR, 1937–1949*. Westport: Praeger.

Politicheskie repressii v Kazakhstane v 1937–1938 gg. 1998. Almaty: Izdatelstvo
Kazakhstan.

Polkinghorne, Donald. 1995. "Narrative Configuration in Qualitative Analysis."
International Journal of Qualitative Studies in Education 8, 1: 5–23.

Polonsky, Antony and Joanna B. Michlic. eds. 2009. *The Neighbors Respond: The
Controversy over the Jedwabne Massacre in Poland*. Princeton: Princeton University
Press.

Popov, Nebojša. 2000. "Traumotology of the Party-State," in Nebojša Popov, ed.
The Road to War in Serbia. Trauma and Catharsis. Budapest: Central European
University Press, 81–108.

Popova, Maria. 2014. "Ukraine's Legal problems: Why Kiev's Plans to Purge the Judiciary Will Backfire." *Foreign Affairs*, April 15.

Popson, Nancy. 2001. "The Ukrainian History Textbook: Introducing Children to the 'Ukrainian Nation'." *Nationalities Papers* 29, 2: 325–50.

"Poroshenko Decides to Sign Law on Lustration." 2014. *Ukraine General Newswire* (Kiev), October 3, available at: www.kyivpost.com/article/content/may-25-presidential-election/poroshenko-decides-to-sign-law-on-lustration-366846.html, accessed June 21, 2017.

Portmann, Michael. 2004. "Communist Retaliation and Persecution on Yugoslav Territory during and after World War II." *Tokovi istorije* 1–2: 45–74.

"Poslanie Prezidenta Rossii Vladimira Putina Federal'nomu sobraniyu RF: 2005 god." 2005. *Rossiiskaya gazeta* (Moscow), April 26, pp. 1, 2–4.

"Prague Declaration on European Conscience and Communism." 2008. June 3, available at: www.webcitation.org/64otCtAyz, accessed December 12, 2016.

"Prahrama Patyi BNF." 2002. December 2, available at: http://narodny.org/?p=1116, accessed January 9, 2017.

"Praviteli v otechestvennyi istorii." no date, available at: www.levada.ru/2016/03/01/praviteli-v-otechestvennoj-istorii/, accessed March 9, 2016.

"President Putin Calls for 'Constructive' Political Rivalries." 2007. *AP*, October 30, available at: www.namibian.com.na/index.php?id=39356&page=archive-read, accessed June 21, 2017.

Press conference of Igor Kuznetsov. 2014. *Belorusskii Partisan*. February 12, available at: www.belaruspartisan.org/m/politic/257529/, accessed February 14, 2017.

"Prezydent: Państwo polskie powinno realizować 'ofensywną' politykę historyczną." 2016. *Rzeczpospolita*, February 16, p. 4.

Pribylovskiĭ, Vladimir. 2008. *The Corporation: Russia and the KGB in the Age of President Putin*. London: Encounter Books.

"Prof. Gross zasłużył na ten order: Kancelaria Prezydenta chce reglamentować wolność słowa?" 2016. *Gazeta wyborcza*, February 11.

"Programma i usloviia provedeniia otkrytogo konkursa na luchshii proekt pamiatnika zhertvam goloda." 2016. *Vechernii Almaty*, July 16, available at: http://vecher.kz/incity/programma-i-usloviya-provedeniya-otkrytogo-konkursa-na-luchshij-proekt-pamyat nika-zhertvam-goloda, accessed May 6, 2017.

"Project of Statute of the Belarusian civic historical-educational association of memory of victims of Stalinism Committee 58." no date. *Public Web-Archive*, available at: http://vytoki.net/?docs=00006123, accessed December 20, 2016.

"Prosecutors Invite Foreign Experts to Help in Handling 'Politically Sensitive Cases'." 2014. *Civil.ge*, July 24, available at: www.civil.ge/eng/article.php?id=27516, accessed November 7, 2016.

Prot'ko, Tatiana. 2002. *Stanovlenie soveskoi totalitarnoi sistemy v Belarusi 1917–1941gg.* Minsk: Tesei.

"Putin's Visit to Butovo Symbolic – Rights Activist." 2007. *Interfax*, October 31.

Quint, Peter. 2000. "The Border Guards Trials and the East German Past – Seven Arguments." *American Journal of Comparative Law* 48, 4: 541–72.

Radanović, Milan. 2012. "Zakonodavna politika Vlade Republike Srbije (2004–2011) u službi revizije prošlosti. Zakon o rehabilitaciji i njegova primena kao paradigma istorijskog revizionizma u Srbiji," in Milivoje Bešlin and Petar Atanacković, eds. *Antifašizam pred izazovima savremenosti*. Novi Sad: AKO, 81–114.

2013. "Kontroverze oko kvantifikovanja i strukturisanja stradalih u Srbiji nakon oslobođenja 1944–1945," in Momir Samardžić, Milivoj Bešlin, Srđan Milošević, eds. *Politička upotreba prošlosti: o istorijskom revizionizmu na postjugoslovenskom prostoru*. Novi Sad: Tramaxion, 157–220, available at: www.rosalux.rs/sites/default/files/publications/Politicka_upotreba_proslosti.pdf, accessed June 21, 2017.

2015. *Kazna i zločin. Snage kolaboracije u Srbiji*. Belgrade: Rosa Luxemburg Stiftung.

Radović, Srđan. 2013. "Istorijski revizionizam i imenovanje javnih prostora u savremenim balkanskim društvima," in Momir Samardžić, Milivoj Bešlin, and Srđan Milošević, eds. *Politička upotreba prošlosti: o istorijskom revizionizmu na postjugoslovenskom prostoru*. Novi Sad: Tramaxion, 313–32, available at: www.rosalux.rs/sites/default/files/publications/Politicka_upotreba_proslosti.pdf, accessed June 21, 2017.

Ramani, Samuel. 2016. "From Disgraced President to Ukraine's Lead Diplomat: The Unlikely Redemption of Leonid Kuchma." *Huffington Post*, September 16, available at: www.huffingtonpost.com/samuel-ramani/from-disgraced-president-_b_8130424.html, accessed October 13, 2016.

Ramet, Sabrina. 1995. *Social Currents in Eastern Europe: The Sources and Consequences of the Great Transformation*. Durham: Duke University Press.

Ramírez-Barat, Clara and Roger Duthie. 2016. "Education and Transitional Justice: Opportunities and Challenges for Peacebuilding." *International Center for Transitional Justice*, November 16, available at: www.ictj.org/publication/education-transitional-justice-opportunities-challenges-peacebuilding, accessed January 30, 2017.

Raquel Freire, Maria and Licínia Simão, 2007. *The Armenian Road to Democracy – Dimensions of a Tortuous Process*, CEPS Working Document No. 267 (May).

Rasstrel'nye spiski. 1995. *Vagan'kovskoe kladbishche 1926–1936*. Moscow: Memorial, Vol. 2.

Rating Group Ukraine. 2016. "Dynamika Stavlennia do Holodomoru," November 22, available at: http://ratinggroup.ua/research/ukraine/dinamika_otnosheniya_k_golodomoru.html, accessed January 30, 2017.

Reabilitatsiya. Kak eto bylo. Dokumenty Politbyuro TsK KPSS, stenogrammy zasedaniya Komissii Politbyuro TsK KPSS po dopolnitel'nomu izucheniyu materialov, svyazannykh s repressiyami, imevshimi mesto v period 30-40-kh i nachala 50-kh godov, i drugie materialy. 2004. Moscow: Materik.

"Resolution 827 (1993) Adopted by the Security Council at its 3217th meeting on 25 May 1993," 1993. Available at: www.icty.org/x/file/Legal%20Library/Statute/statute_827_1993_en.pdf, accessed December 12, 2016.

"Resolution 1211–XII on introducing amendments and additions to some legislative acts of the Republic of Belarus regulating the questions of restoration of the rights of citizens who suffered from repressions in the 1920-1980." 1991. *Archive of Law Library*, available at: http://pravo.newsby.org/belarus/postanov28/pst600.htm, accessed January 20, 2017.

"Resolution of the Supreme Council of the Republic of Belarus 2623-XII On the introducing amendments and additions to the legislative acts of the Republic of Belarus regulating issues of rehabilitation of victims of political repressions in 1920-1980 and restoration of their rights." 1993. *Archive of Belarusian Law*, December 3, available at: http://old.bankzakonov.com/d2008/time83/lav83154.htm, accessed December 15, 2016.

Rodgers, Peter W. 2007. "'Compliance or Contradiction'? Teaching 'History' in the 'New' Ukraine. A View from Ukraine's Eastern Borderlands." *Europe-Asia Studies* 59, 3: 503–19.

Roginskii, Arsenii. 2011. "Pamiat'o Stalinizme," in Elena I. Kandrashina, ed. *Istoriia stalinizma: itogi i problem izucheniia*. Moscow: ROSSPEN, 21–7.

2013. Comment at "International Symposium on the Legacy of the Gulag and the Remembrance of Stalinism." Amsterdam, November 8.

Roginskii, Arsenii and Dmitrii Medvedev. 2011. "Eta programma ne tol'ko pro istoriiu," February 1, available at: www.hro.org/node/10218, accessed June 24, 2017.

"Rol' lichnosti v istorii Rossii." 2015. January 20, available at: www.levada.ru/2015/01/20/rol-lichnostej-v-istorii-rossii, accessed June 20, 2017.

"Rol' Stalina v istorii Rossii." 2016. *Levada Centre*, January 13, available at: www.levada.ru/2016/01/13/rol-stalina-v-istorii-rossii, accessed January 13, 2016.

Rosefielde, Steven. 1996. "Stalinism in Post-Communist Perspective: New Evidence on Killings, Forced Labour and Economic Growth in the 1930s." *Europe-Asia Studies* 48, 6: 959–87.

Roy, Olivier. 2007. *The New Central Asia: Geopolitics and the Birth of Nations*, 2nd edn. London: I.B. Tauris.

Rudienė, Dalė. 2015. "Atminkime, kas svarbu, arba jubiliejinis XV konkursas "Lietuvos kovų už laisvę ir netekčių istorija." *Genocidas ir Rezistencija*, 1: 140–2.

Rudis, Algirdas. 2014. "Kronika-Edukacinis zaidimas 'Sovietinis inkubatorius'." Available at: http://genocid.lt/centras/lt/2303/a/, accessed January 31, 2017.

Rudling, Per Anders. 2015. *The Rise and Fall of Belarusian Nationalism. 1906–1931*. Pittsburg: Pittsburg University Press.

Rudzite, Liga. 2016. "Russia's Fight for the Right History." *Transitions Online*, November 1, available at: www.tol.org/client/article/26441-russias-fight-for-the-right-history-.html, accessed November 1, 2016.

"Rules of the Procedure of the Commission," 2010. Available at: www.komisija1944.mpravde.gov.rs, accessed December 12, 2016.

"Russia Marks Day of Victims of Political Repressions." 2009. *Itar-TASS*, October 30.

"Russia Puts Its Laws above European Court Rulings." 2015. *BBC*, July 14, available at: www.bbc.co.uk/news/world-europe-33521553, accessed November 7, 2016.

"Russia's Victory Day Celebration: Great Patriotic War, Again." 2015. *The Economist*, May 2–8, pp. 54–5.

Russian Public Opinion Research Center (VCIOM), *DeStalinization in Progress*, Press Release No. 1369, May 17, 2011, available at: https://wciom.com/index.php?id=61&uid=14, accessed July 9, 2017.

Ryzhkov, Vladimir. 2015. "Attitude to Stalin Reveals Russia's Considerable Divide." *Moscow Times*, September 22, available at: https://themoscowtimes.com/articles/attitude-to-stalin-reveals-russias-considerable-divide-49710, accessed June 22, 2017.

Sakowicz, Kazimierz and Yitzhak Arad. 2005. *Ponary Diary, 1941–1943: A Bystander's Account of a Mass Murder*. New Haven: Yale University Press.

Samarina, Aleksandra and Ivan Rodin. 2014. "'Fultonskaya rech' Putina: Rossiyu ot zapada snova mozhet otdelit's zhelezhnyi zanaves." *Nezavisimaya gazeta*, March 19, p. 3.

Sarkin, Jeremy. 1999. "The Necessity and Challenges of Establishing a Truth and Reconciliation Commission in Rwanda." *Human Rights Quarterly* 21, 3: 767–823.

Schama, Simon. 1995. *Landscape and Memory*. New York: A.A. Knopf.

Schnytzer, Adi and Alina Zubkovych. no date. "Comparative Symbolic Violence: The Chisinau and Tiraspol National Historical Museums." available at: www.jew ishgen.org/Bessarabia/files/ComparativeViolenceInMoldova_article.pdf, accessed February 12, 2017.

Senn, Alfred E. 1990. *Lithuania Awakening*. Berkeley: University of California Press.

Šepetys, Nerijus. 2016. "Jūsiškiai – mums ne mūsiškiai." *Naujasis Židinys – Aidai*, April 25, available at: www.delfi.lt/news/ringas/lit/n-sepetys-jusiskiai-mums-ne-musiskiai .d?id=71032318, accessed January 31, 2017.

Shahnazarian, Nona. 2013. "Letters from the Soviet 'Paradise': The Image of Russia among the Western Armenian Diaspora." *Journal of Eurasian Studies* 4, 1: 8–17.

"Shakhtinsk na novom etape razvitiia." 2014. *Shakhtinskii vestnik*, July 11.

"Shedding Its Communist Past, Odessa Converts Lenin Statue into a Monument to Darth Vader." 2015. *Meduza Project*, October 22, available at: https://meduza.io/ en/lion/2015/10/22/shedding-its-communist-past-odessa-converts-lenin-statue-into-a-monument-to-darth-vader, accessed October 23, 2016.

Sherlock, Thomas. 2013. "Georgia," in Lavinia Stan and Nadya Nedelsky, eds. *Encyclopedia of Transitional Justice*. New York: Cambridge University Press, Vol. 2: 186–93.

2016. "Russian Politics and the Soviet Past: Reassessing Stalin and Stalinism under Vladimir Putin," *Communist and Post-Communist Studies* 49, 1: 45–59.

Shestakov, Evgenii. 2014. "Mir ostanovitsya vse menee prozapadnym: Nyneshnyaya amerikanskaya politika natselena na smeny rezhima v Rossii." *Rossiiskaya gazeta*, April 24, p. 3.

Shevel, Oxana. 2016. "Decommunization in Post-Euromaidan Ukraine: Law and Practice." *PONARS Eurasia*, January, available at: www.ponarseurasia.org/memo/ decommunization-post-euromaidan-ukraine-law-and-practice, accessed October 19, 2016.

Šidagytė, Žydrūnė. 2015. "Partizaninis karas Lietuvoje: Kaip apie tai kalbame šiandien." *Genocidas ir Rezistencija*, 37, 1: 131–3.

Sierra Leone Truth and Reconciliation Commission. 2004. *Witness to Truth: Report of the Sierra Leone Truth and Reconciliation Commission*. Available at: www.sierraleo netrc.org/index.php/view-the-final-report, accessed June 21, 2017.

Silitski, Vital. 2003. "Explaining Post-Communist Authoritarianism in Belarus," in Elena Korosteleva, Colin Lawson, and Rosalind Marsh, eds. *Contemporary Belarus. Between Democracy and Dictatorship*. London: Routledge, 36–52.

2006. "Signs of Hope rather than a Color of Revolution," in Joerg Forbrig, David Marples and Pavol Demeš, eds. *Prospects for Democracy in Belarus*. Washington: German Marshall Fund, 20–8.

Sirutavičius, Vladas, Darius Staliūnas, and Jurgita Šiaučiūnaitė-Verbickienė. 2012. *Lietuvos žydai: istorinė studija*. Vilnius: Baltos lankos.

Skarżyńska, Krystyna. 2000. "Zbiorowa wyobraźnia, zbiorowa wina." *Gazeta wyborcza* (Warsaw), November 24, p. 19.

Slade, Gavin. 2012. "Georgia's Prisons: Roots of Scandal." *Open Democracy*, September 24, available at: www.opendemocracy.net/gavin-slade/georgias-prisons-roots-of-scandal, accessed October 23, 2016.

Slade, Gavin and Alexander Kupatadze. 2014. "The Failed 'Mental Revolution': Georgia, Crime and Criminal Justice." *Open Democracy*, October 1, available at: www.opendemocracy.net/gavin-slade-alexander-kupatadze/failed-mental-revolu tion-georgia-crime-and-criminal-justice, accessed October 23, 2016.

Smith, Kathleen. 1996. *Remembering Stalin's Victims: Popular Memory and the End of the USSR*. Ithaca: Cornell University Press.

Smith-Spark, Laura and Frederik Pleitgen. 2015. "Ukraine Marks Year since Maidan Bloodshed amid Simmering Conflict." *CNN*, February 20, available at: http://edi tion.cnn.com/2015/02/20/europe/ukraine-conflict/index.html, accessed October 13, 2016.

Snyder, Timothy. 2010. *Bloodlands: Europe between Hitler and Stalin*. London: The Bodley Head.

"Societatea trebuie să-și cunoască trecutul, chiar dacă uneori doare și e prea dur." 2010. *Timpul*, April 29, available at: www.timpul.md/articol/societatea-trebuie-sa-si-cunoasca-trecutul-chiar-daca-uneori-doare-si-e-prea-dur-9992.html, accessed February 26, 2017.

Solonina, Evgen. 2016. "Yegor Sobolev: 80% of Lustration, 20% Imitation." *Radio Svoboda*, March 10.

Solzhenitsyn, Aleksandr. 1968. *V kruge pervom*. London: Flegon Press.

1973. *The Gulag Archipelago*. Paris: Éditions du Seuil.

"Soobshchenie pravitel'stvennoi komissii, sozdannoi resheniem Soveta Ministrov BSSR ot 14 iulya 1988." 1989. *Sovetskaia Belorussiya*, January 22.

"Soobshchenie Tsentralnoi komissii referendum SSSR. Ob itogakh referendum SSSR sostoyavshegosya 17 marta 1991." 1991. *Pravda*, March 27, available at: www.gorby.ru/userfiles/file/referendum_rezultat.pdf, accessed February 16, 2017.

Sopińska-Jaremczak, Agnieszka. 2016. "*Komunikat o przekazaniu przez prokuratora IPN dokumentów pochodzących z trzeciego i czwartego pakietu materiałów zabez-pieczonych w domu wdowy po Czesławie Kiszczaku.*" March 3. Warsaw: IPN.

2016. "*Komunikat w sprawie ekspertyz dokumentów dotyczących tajnego współpra-cownika pseudonim 'Bolek'.*" February 25. Warsaw: IPN.

"Sostoyalos' sovmestnoe zasedanie Komissii po protivodeistviyu popytkam fal'sifikat-sii istorii v ushcherb interesam Rossii i Mezhvedomstvennoi komissii po zashchite gosudarstvennoi tainy." 2010. *Rossiiskaya gazeta*, September 8, p. 1.

"Spisak žrtava i lokacije grobnica," 2010. Available at: www.komisija1944.mpravde.gov .rs, accessed December 12, 2016.

Sriram, Chandra Lekha and Johanna Herman. 2009. "DDR and Transitional Justice: Bridging the Divide?" *Conflict, Security & Development* 9, 4: 455–74.

"Stalin i ego rol' v istorii strany." 2015. *Levada.ru*, available at: www.levada.ru/2015/03/31/stalin-i-ego-rol-v-istorii-strany/, accessed June 21, 2017.

Stan, Lavinia. 2004. "The Romanian Anticorruption Bill." *Studies in Post-Communism Occasional Paper*, No. 6, Centre for Post-Communist Studies, St. Francis Xavier University.

2006. "The Politics of Memory in Poland: Lustration, File Access and Court Proceedings." *Studies in Post-Communism Occasional Paper*, No. 10. Centre for Post-Communist Studies, St. Francis Xavier University.

2009. "The Former Soviet Union." in Lavinia Stan, ed. *Transitional Justice in Eastern Europe and the Former Soviet Union*. London: Routledge, 227–30.

ed. 2009. *Transitional Justice in Eastern Europe and the Former Soviet Union*. London: Routledge.

2012. *Transitional Justice in Post-Communist Romania: The Politics of Memory*. New York: Cambridge University Press.

2012. "Witch-hunt or Moral Rebirth? Romanian Parliamentary Debates on Lustration." *East European Politics and Societies* 26, 2: 274–95.

Stan, Lavinia and Nadya Nedelsky. eds. 2013. *Encyclopedia of Transitional Justice*. New York: Cambridge University Press, 3 volumes.

eds. 2015. *Post-Communist Transitional Justice: Lessons from Twenty-Five Years of Experience*. New York: Cambridge University Press.

Stan, Lavinia and Lucian Turcescu. 2003. "Church–State Conflict in Moldova: The Bessarabian Metropolitanate." *Communist and Post-Communist Studies* 36, 4: 443–65.

Stankiewicz, Andrzej. 2014. "Nie wierzyli w wybory, większość dziś zmieniła zdanie." *Rzeczpospolita*, June 4, p. 13, available at: http://archiwum.rp.pl/artykul/1244268-Nie-wierzyli-w-wybory-wiekszosc-dzis-zmienila-zdanie.html, accessed June 21, 2017.

"Stanovlenie mobilizatsionnoi politicheskoi sistemy." no date, available at: www.prosv.ru/ebooks/Danilov_Istoria_1900-1945/12.html, accessed March 14, 2012.

Statistical Report of War Crime Prosecutor of Serbia, October 2016, available at: www.tuzilastvorz.org.rs/sr/predmeti/statistika, accessed December 12, 2016.

"Stenograficheskii otchet o zasedanii Soveta po razvitiu obshchestva i pravam cheloveka." no date, available at: www.kremlin.ru/transcripts/10194, accessed November 6, 2016.

Stern, David. 2014. "Ukraine's Politicians Face Mob Attacks." *BBC News*, October 20, available at: www.bbc.com/news/world-europe-29536641, accessed October 7, 2016.

Strzembosz, Tomasz. 2001. "Inny obraz sąsiadów." *Rzeczpospolita*, March 31–April 1, 2001, pp. A6–A7.

2001. "Przemilczana kolaboracja." *Rzeczpospolita*, January 27–28, pp. A6–A7.

Subotić, Jelena. 2015. "The Mythologizing of Communist Violence," in Lavinia Stan and Nadya Nedelsky, eds. *Post-Communist Transitional Justice: Lessons from Twenty-Five Years of Experience*. New York: Cambridge University Press, 188–210.

2015. "Truth, Justice, and Reconciliation on the Ground: Normative Divergence in the Western Balkans." *Journal of International Relations and Development* 18, 3: 361–82.

Sultanmuratov, Nuriddin. 2011. "Repatriatsiia Po-Kazakhski." *Tsentr Azii*, April, available at: www.asiakz.com/repatriaciya-po-kazahski, accessed May 6, 2017.

"Supreme Court's Appeal to Constitutional Court against Lustration Law Shows Judicial System's Reluctance to Be Cleansed." 2014. *Ukraine General Newswire* (Kiev), November 18.

Sužiedėlis, Saulius. 2006. "Collaboration during the Second World War: Past Realities, Present Perceptions," in Joachim Tauber, ed. *"Kollaboration" in*

Nordosteuropa: Erscheinungsformen und Deutungen im 20. Jahrhundert. Wiesbaden: Harrassowitz, 164–73.

2014. "The International Commission for the Evaluation of the Crimes of the Nazi and Soviet Occupation Regimes in Lithuania: Successes, Challenges, Perspectives." *Journal of Baltic Studies.* Published online, 8 August: 1–16.

Sweeney, James A. 2013. *The European Court of Human Rights in the Post-Cold War Era: Universality in Transition.* London: Routledge.

Szczerbiak, Aleks. 2015. "Explaining Late Lustration Programs: Lessons from the Polish Case," in Lavinia Stan and Nadya Nedelsky, eds. *Post-Communist Transitional Justice: Lessons from Twenty-Five Years of Experience.* Cambridge: Cambridge University Press, 51–70.

Taras, Raymond. 1996. *Consolidating Democracy in Poland.* Boulder: Westview Press.

Tarkhan-Mouravi, George. 1997. "70 years of Soviet Georgia," January 19, available at: http://rolfgross.dreamhosters.com/Texts/KandA-Web/Giahistory.htm, accessed November 29, 2016.

Tarnavskii, Georgii, Valerii Sobolev, and Evgenii Gorelik. 1990. *Kuropaty: Sledstvie Prodolzhaetsya.* Moscow: Yuridicheskaya kniga.

Teitel, Ruti. 2000. *Transitional Justice.* Oxford: Oxford University Press.

"Third Wave of Lustration in Ukraine Will Start in March, Will Concern Civil Ministries." 2015. *Ukraine General Newswire* (Kiev), January 29.

Thoms, Oskar, James Ron, and Roland Paris. 2008. *The Effects of Transitional Justice Mechanisms: A Summary of Empirical Research Findings and Implications for Analysts and Practitioners.* Ottawa: Centre for International Policy Studies.

Tikhanova, V. ed. 1993. *Rasstrel'nye spiski, volume 1, Donskoe kladbishche, 1934–40.* Moscow: NIPTs Memorial.

Tileagă, Cristian. 2012. "Communism in Retrospect: The Rhetoric of Historical Representation and Writing the Collective Memory of Recent Past." *Memory Studies* 5, 4: 462–78.

Todorović, Vladimir, Siniša Rajić, and Danijela Kožul. 2016. "Denacionalizacija u Republici Srbiji." *Projuris,* available at: http://projuris.org/fokus1.html, accessed December 12, 2016.

Toishibekova, Aisulu. 2016. "Issledovatel' Karlaga Ekaterina Kuznetsova: "Intelligentsiia v Karagande skladyvalas' iz byvshikh zakliuchennykh lagerei." *Vlast.Kz,* December 19, available at: https://vlast.kz/life/20875-issledovatel-karlaga-ekaterina-kuznecova-intelligencia-v-karagande-skladyvalas-iz-byvsih-zaklucennyh-lagerej .html, accessed May 6, 2017.

Tomasevich, Jozo. 1975. *Chetniks.* Stanford: Stanford University Press.

Tomohiko, Uyama. 2013. "Two Attempts at Building a Qazaq State: The Revolt of 1916 and the Alash Movement," *Dudoignon and Komatsu, Islam in Politics* 3: 77–98.

Toria, Malkhas. 2014. "The Soviet Occupation of Georgia in 1921 and the Russian-Georgian War of August 2008: Historical Analogy as a Memory Project," in Stephen Jones, ed. *The Making of Modern Georgia, 1918–2012.* London: Routledge, 316–35.

Törnquist-Plewa, Barbara. 2013. "Coming to Terms with Anti-Semitism: Jan T. Gross's Writings and the Construction of Cultural Trauma in Post-Communist Poland." *European Studies,* 30, 1: 125–50.

Transitional Justice Database Project. Available at: https://sites.google.com/site/transitionaljusticedatabase/, accessed October 15, 2016.

Transparency International. *Overview of Corruption Perception Index*, available at: www.transparency.org/research/cpi/overview, accessed October 23, 2016.

Trochev, Alexei. 2004. "Less Democracy, More Courts: A Puzzle of Judicial Review in Russia." *Law & Society Review* 38, 3: 513–48.

2013. "Ukraine," in Lavinia Stan and Nadya Nedelsky, eds. *Encyclopedia of Transitional Justice*. New York: Cambridge University Press, Vol. 2: 490–7.

2016. "Patronal Politics, Judicial Networks, and Collective Judicial Autonomy in Post-Soviet Countries." Paper presented at *European Consortium for Political Research*, September. Prague: Czech Republic.

Truska, Liudas. 2003. "1944-53 metai. Ką davė Lietuvai partizaninis karas?" *Akiračiai*, 345, 1: 4–8.

Truth and Reconciliation Commission, Republic of Korea. 2009. *Truth and Reconciliation: Activities of the Past Three Years*, available at: www.usip.org/sites/default/files/ROL/South_Korea_2005_reportEnglish.pdf, accessed June 21, 2017.

Truth and Reconciliation Commission, Republic of Liberia. 2009. *Final Report: Volume II: Consolidated Final Report*. TRC of Liberia: Monrovia.

"Tusk o teczkach z szafy Kiszczaka: Odgrzewana sprawa, przykra dla wizerunku." 2016. *Gazeta wyborcza*, February 18, p. 3.

Tutu, Desmond. 1999. *No Future without Forgiveness*. New York: Doubleday.

Tworzecki, Hubert. 1996. *Parties and Politics in Post-1989 Poland*. Boulder: Westview Press.

"Uchitel'iam istorii veleno prepodnosit' stalinskii terror kak ratsional'nyi instrument razvitiia strany." no date, available at: www.newsru.com, accessed August 25, 2008.

"Ukaz Prezidenta RF ot 14.02.2012 Nr. 183 'Ob utverzhdeenii sostava Komissii pri Prezidente Rossiiskoi Federatsii po formirovaniyu i podgotovke rezerva upravlencheskikh kadrov, izmenenii i priznanii utrativshimi silu utrativshimi silu nekotorykh aktov Prezidenta Rossiiskoi Federatsii.'" 2012. *Ukaz Prezidenta RF*, No. 183, February 14, in *Sobranie zakonodatelstva Rossiiskoi Federatsii: 2012 g.* (Moscow).

Ukaz Prezidenta Rossiiskoi Federatsii ot 15 maia 2009 g. N 549 'O Kommissii pri Presidente Rossiiskoi Federatsii po protivodeistviiu popytkam falsifikatsii istorii i ushcherb interesam Rossii." [On the commission under the President of the Russian Federation to counter attempts at the falsification of history to the detriment of Russia's interests]. 2009. May 15, available at: www.politru.dokumenty/president prosledit, accessed November 19, 2016.

Uklyuchina, Tat'yana. 2001. "Spory po povodu slov gimna ne prekrashchayutsya." *Vremya novostei (Moscow)*, February 1, p. 1.

Ukraine: Humanitarian Dashboard January. August 2016. Available at: www.human itarianresponse.info/en/system/files/documents/files/humanitarian_dashboard_august_2016_v6. pdf, accessed October 13, 2016.

"Ukraine Lustration Will Cover 1 mln Officials, Law Enforcers." 2014. *Ukraine General Newswire* [Kiev], September 17.

"Ukraine Prepares to Make Soviet KGB Archives Available Online." 2016. *Euromaidan Press*, April 11, available at: http://euromaidanpress.com/2016/04/11/ukraine-pre pares-to-make-soviet-kgb-archives-available-online/#arvlbdata, accessed October 15. 2016.

Ümit Üngör, Uğur. 2013. "The Armenian Genocide: A Multi-Dimensional Process of Destruction." *Global Dialogue* 15, 1: 97–106.

United Nations. 2006. *Rule of Law Tools for Post-Conflict States: Vetting: An Operational Framework.* United Nations HR/PUB/06/5. New York: Office of the UN High Commission on Human Rights.

United States Department of State. 2007. *Moldova,* March 6, available at: www.state .gov/j/drl/rls/hrrpt/2006/78828.htm, accessed February 5, 2017.

Urbšys, Juozas. 1988. *Lietuva lemtingaisiais 1939–1940 metais, 1939–1940.* Vilnius: Mintis.

"V Almaty potomki repressirovannykh nastaivaiut na vosstanovlenii muzeia zhertv politicheskii repressii." 2013. *Zakon.Kz,* May 21, available at: www.zakon.kz/4557618-v-almaty-potomki-repressirovannykh.html, accessed May 6, 2017.

"V Kazakhstane za 12 let zhertvam politicheskikh repressii vyplacheno 9, 8 mlrd tenge." 2015. *BNews.Kz,* May 31, available at: http://bnews.kz/ru/news/obshchestvo/v_kazah stane_za_12_let_zhertvam_politicheskih_repressii_viplacheno_98_mlrd_tenge-2015_05_31-1108045, accessed May 6, 2017.

"V Moskve mozhet poyavit'sya pamyatnik Stalinu: 'Otkazyvat'sya ot Stalina – znachit otkazyvat'sya ot samikh sebya." 2015. *Nakanune.ru,* February 26, Item 7.

"V posolstve USA w Minske otkrylas vystavka Pravda o Kuropatakh. Fakty, dokumenty, svidetelstva." 2016. *Nabiny.by,* March 24, available at: http://naviny.by/rubrics/society/ 2016/03/24/ic_news_116_472503, accessed January 14, 2017.

Vakar, Nicholas. 1956. *Belorussia. The Making of a Nation. A Case Study.* Cambridge: Harvard University Press.

Valatka, Rimvydas. 2015. "Ką pagerbė Lietuva – partizanų vadą Generolą Vėtrą ar žydų žudiką?" [Whom Did Lithuania Honor: The Leader of Partisans General Vėtra or a Jew Killer?]. *Delfi,* July 26, available at: www.delfi.lt/news/ringas/lit/r-valatka-ka-pagerbe-lietuva-partizanu-vada-generola-vetra-ar-zydu-zudika.d?id=68576988, accessed January 31, 2017.

Valiušaitis, Vidmantas. 2016. "Atkirto Rūtai Vanagaitei: 'Išsigimėliai nėra mūsiškiai," January 28, available at: http://kultura.lrytas.lt/istorija/atkirto-rutai-vanagaitei-issigi meliai-nera-musiskiai.htm, accessed January 31, 2017.

Vanagaitė, Rūta. 2016. *Mūsiškiai.* Vilnius: Alma littera.

Veber, Elena. 2016. "Muzei v Dolinke pytaetsia naiti den'gi na rasshirenie." *Radio Azattyq,* May 31, available at: http://rus.azattyq.org/a/musei-v-dolinke-politicheskie-repressii-31-maja/27770739.html, accessed May 6, 2017.

Vėliūtė, Rūta Gabrielė. 2009. *Partizanai [N16].* Vilnius: Lietuvos gyventojų genocido ir rezistencijos tyrimo centras.

"Venice Commission Confirms that Ukraine's Lustration Law is in Line with International Standards and Resolutions of the Council of Europe." 2015. *State News Service* (Kiev), June 19.

Verkhovna, Rada Ukrainy. 2003. "Pro Rekomendatsii Parlamentskykh Slukhan Shchodo Vshanuvannia Pamiati Zhertv Holodomoru 1932–1933 Rokiv." available at: http://zakon4.rada.gov.ua/laws/show/607-15, accessed January 30, 2017.

_____ 2003. "Pro Zvernennia do Ukrainskoho Narodu Uchasnykiv Spetsialnoho Zasidannia Verkhovnoi Rady Ukrainy 14 Travnia 2003 Roku Shchodo Vshanuvannia Pamiati Zhertv Holodomoru 1932–1933 Rokiv." May 15, available at: http://zakon4.rada.gov .ua/laws/show/789-15, accessed January 30, 2017.

_____ 2006. "Pro Holodomor 1932–1933 Rokiv v Ukraini." November 28, available at: http:// zakon4.rada.gov.ua/laws/show/376-16, accessed January 30, 2017.

Vitkauskas, Vidmantas. no date. *Pasipriešinimo Istorijos programa: Lietuvos ir užsienio lietuvių pasipriešinimo istorijos mokymo programa X-XII klasei.* Available at: www.upc.smm.lt/naujienos/pasipriesinimas/Pasipriesinimo_istorijos_programa.do, accessed June 21, 2017.

"Vladimir Putin: Ne zhech' mostov, ne raskalyvat' obshchestvo." 2000. *Rossiiskaya gazeta*, December 6, p. 1.

"Vladimir Putin: 'Raspad SSSR – krupneishaia geopoliticheskaia katasrofa veka'." 2005. April 25, available at: https://regnum.ru/news/polit/444083.html, accessed November 6, 2016.

Vlasov, Vitalii and Oksana Danylevska. 2010. *Vstup do Istorii Ukrainy: Pidruchnyk dlia 5 Klasu Zahalnoosvitnikh Navchalnykh Zakladiv.* Kyiv: Heneza.

"Vystupleniya V. I. Ilyukhina na Plenarnom zasedanii Gosdumy pri obsuzhdenii Zayavleniya 'Pamyati zhertv Katynskoi tragedii'." 2010. *Sovetskaya Rossiya* (Moscow). November 26, p. 2.

Vyzhutovich, Valerii. 2015. "Nuzhna li Rossii gosudarstvennaya ideologiya?" *Rossiiskaya gazeta*, August 15, p. 5.

Walker, Christopher. 1990. *Armenia: The Survival of a Nation*, 2nd edn. London: Palgrave Macmillan.

Warszawski, Dawid. 2000. "Odpowiedzialność i jej brak." *Gazeta wyborcza*, December 9–10, pp. 20–1.

2001. "Mowa pokutna: Bez także." *Gazeta Wyborcza*, March 9, p. 18.

2002. "Dwie Polski w Jedwabnem." *Wprost* (Poznań), July 21, pp. 24–6.

Way, Lucan. 2009. "State Power and Autocratic Stability. Armenia and Georgia Compared," in Christopher Stefes, ed. *The Politics of Transition in Central Asia and the Caucasus: Enduring Legacies and Emerging Challenges.* London: Routledge, 103–23.

2012. "Deer in Headlights: Incompetence and Weak Authoritarianism after the Cold War." *Slavic Review* 71, 3: 619–46.

Welsh, Helga. 1996. "Dealing with the Communist Past: Central and East European Experiences after 1990." *Europe-Asia Studies* 48, 3: 413–29.

Werth, Nicolas. 2008. "Case Study: The Great Ukrainian Famine of 1932–33." *Online Encyclopedia of Mass Violence*, April 18, available at: www.massviolence.org/the-1932-1933-great-famine-in-ukraine, accessed January 30, 2017.

Wezel, Katja. 2009. "Latvia's Soviet Story: Transitional Justice and the Politics of Commemoration." *Satori*, October 25, available at: www.satori.lv/raksts/3111, accessed December 17, 2016.

Wheatcroft, Stephen. 1996. "The Scale and Nature of German and Soviet Repression and Mass Killings, 1930-45." *Europe-Asia Studies* 48, 8: 1319–53.

White, Anne. 1995. "The Memorial Society in the Russian Provinces." *Europe-Asia Studies*, 47, 8: 1343–66.

White, Robin C. A. and Claire Ovey. 2014. *Jacobs, White and Ovey: The European Convention on Human Rights.* Oxford: Oxford University Press.

Wiebelhaus-Brahm, Eric. 2009. *Truth Commissions and Transitional Societies: The Impact on Human Rights and Democracy.* New York: Routledge.

Williams, Morgan. 2003. "Ukraine Issues Joint Declaration at the United Nations in Connection with the 70th Anniversary of the Great Famine in Ukraine of 1932-1933."

Art Ukraine, November 11, available at: www.artukraine.com/famineart/ukr_un_
decl.htm, accessed May 6, 2017.

Wilson, Andrew. 2011. *Belarus: The Last European Dictatorship*. New Haven: Yale
University Press.

Wojnowski, Zbigniew. 2017. "De-Stalinization and the Failure of Soviet Identity
Building in Kazakhstan." *Journal of Contemporary History*, available at: http://jour
nals.sagepub.com/doi/abs/10.1177/0022009416653457, accessed May 11, 2017.

Wroński, Paweł. 2016. "Zabrać "zdrajcy" order?" *Gazeta wyborcza*, February 11, p. 7.

Yoder, Jennifer. 1999. "Truth without Reconciliation: An Appraisal of the Enquete
Commission on the SED Dictatorship in Germany." *German Politics* 8, 3: 59–80.

Yushkevich, Zmister. 2014. "Nieviadomy genacyd," February 16, available at: http://
mfront.net/nieviadomy-hienacyd.html, accessed January 10, 2017.

"Zakliucheniie komissii Prezidiuma Verkhovnogo Soveta Respubliki Kazakhstan po
izucheniiu normativnykh pravovykh aktov privedshikh k golodu vo vremia kollektivizatsii." 1992. *Kazakhstanskaia Pravda*, December 22, available at: http://e-history.kz/
ru/publications/view/6, accessed May 6, 2017.

"Zakon 33 o rehabilitaciji." 2006. *Službeni glasnik Republike Srbije*, available at: www
.stojkovic.co.rs/pdf/rehabil.pdf, accessed December 12, 2016.

"Zakon o rehabilitaciji." 2011. *Službeni list Republike Srbije*, 92/2011, available at: www
.paragraf.rs/propisi/zakon_o_rehabilitaciji.html, accessed December 12, 2016.

Zalaquett, José. 1990. "Confronting Human Rights Violations Committed by Former
Governments: Applicable Principles and Political Constraints." *Hamline Law
Review* 13, 3: 623–55.

Zaprudnik, Jan. 1993. *Belarus: At a Crossroads in History*. Boulder: Westview Press.

"Zaschitnikam Kuropat nadoelo diskutirovat s Pozniakom." 2017. *Belorusskii Partizan*,
November 8, available at: www.belaruspartisan.org/politic/222718/, accessed
February 15, 2017.

Żbikowski, Andrzej. 2001. "Nie było rozkazu." *Rzeczpospolita* (Warsaw), January 4,
pp. A6–A7.

Žemaitytė, Aldona. 1989. *Amžino išalo žemėje*. Vilnius: Vyturys.

Zharmukhamed, Zardykhan. 2016. "Ethnic Kazakh Repatriation and Kazakh Nation-
Building: The Awaited Savior of the Prodigal Son?" *Region: Regional Studies of
Russia, Eastern Europe, and Central Asia* 5, 1: 17–34.

Zharov, Batyrkhan and Oleg Taran. 2015. "Grazhdanin, patriot, prokuror."
Kazakhstanskaia Pravda, June 19, available at: www.kazpravda.kz/articles/view/
grazhdanin-patriot-prokuror/, accessed May 6, 2017.

"Zhertv politicheskikh repressii vspominaiut v Almaty." 2016. *Karavan*, May 31,
available at: www.caravan.kz/news/zhertv-politicheskikh-repressijj-vspominayut-v-
almaty-376935/, accessed May 6, 2017.

Zhivitskaia, Oksana. 2014. "Smerti predannye zabveniiu." *Balkhashskii rabochii*,
October 16, available at: http://brgazeta.kz/home/2022-2014-10-16-07-34-07.html,
accessed May 6, 2017.

Zhurtbay, Tursyn. 2016. *Bol' Moia, Gordost' Moia – Alash!* Astana: Audarma.

Žilinskas, Justinas. 2012. "Introduction of the 'Crime of Denial' in the Lithuanian
Criminal Law and the First Instances of Its Application." *Jurisprudencija/
Jurisprudence* 19, 1: 315–29.

Zubkova, Elena. 2009. "The Filippov Syndrome." *Kritika: Explorations in Russian and Eurasian History*, 10, 4: 861–8.

Official websites

Virtual Museum of Soviet Repression in Belarus, available at: http://represii.net, accessed January 30, 2017.

Court cases

Achour v. *France*, Application no. 67335/01, [2007] 45 EHRR 9 (March 29, 2006), Charter of the International Military Tribunal, August 8, 1945, available at: https://ihl-databases.icrc.org/ihl/INTRO/350?OpenDocument, accessed December 13, 2016.
European Court of Human Rights. 1995. *Vogt v. Germany (Application no. 17851/91)*. Strasbourg: Council of Europe.
European Court of Human Rights. 2007. *Case of Bobek v. Poland, § 62. 68761/01, July 17*, Strasbourg: Council of Europe.
European Court of Human Rights. 2007. *Case of Matyjek v. Poland, § 69. 38184/03, April 24*, Strasbourg: Council of Europe.
European Court of Human Rights. 2014. *Naidin v. Romania (Application no. 38162/07)*. Strasbourg: Council of Europe.
Janowiec and Others v. *Russia*, Applications nos. 55508/07 and 29520/09, decision October 21, 2013, available at: www.menschenrechte.ac.at/orig/13_5/Janowiec.pdf, accessed January 4, 2017.
K-HW v. *Germany* [2003] 36 EHRR 108), available at: http://hudoc.echr.coe.int/eng#{"appno":["37201/97"],"itemid":["001-59352"]}, accessed January 4, 2017.
Kolk and Kislyiy v. *Estonia* (Application no. 23052/04, decision January 17, 2006), available at: http://echr.ketse.com/doc/23052.04-24018.04-en-20060117/view/, accessed January 4, 2017.
Kononov v. *Latvia* (Application no. 36376/04, decision May 17, 2010), available at: http://hudoc.echr.coe.int/eng#{"fulltext":["Kononov%20v%20Latvia"], "document-collectionid2":["GRANDCHAMBER"],"itemid":["001-98669"]}, accessed January 4, 2017.
Rutan v. *Republican Party of Illinois*, 497 U.S. 62 (1990).
Streletz, Kessler and Krenz v. *Germany* [2001] 33 EHRR 751, available at: www.menschenrechte.ac.at/orig/01_2/Streletz.pdf, accessed January 4, 2017.
Vasiliauskas v. *Lithuania* (Application no. 35343/05, decision October 20, 2015), available at: https://lovdata.no/static/EMDN/emd-2005-035343.pdf, accessed January 4, 2017.

Movie

"Great Dzhut," movie directed by Kalila Umarov, available at: www.youtube.com/watch?v=Ag6PalmQ7g4, accessed May 6, 2017.

Index

nationalist, 126, 307, 311
political, 10, 11, 32, 38, 104, 109, 122, 149, 171,
218, 249, 267, 296, 304, 311, 313, 315, 316,
352, 356, 358, 359
post-communist, 36, 121, 268, 315
replacement, 92, 181
reproduction, 352
Soviet, 36, 120, 268
Estonian International Commission for
Investigation of Crimes Against
Humanity, 158
Euromaidan, 8, 32, 33, 36, 38, 39, 42, 178
protester, 180, 183, 184
European Convention on Human Rights, 136,
217, 220, 224, 227, 229, 230
European Court of Human Rights, 15, 141,
142, 143, 144, 149, 181, 216, 217, 223, 224,
225, 226, 227, 228, 229, 230, 231, 236, 356
European Union, 35, 39, 80, 135, 158, 245, 273,
333, 335, 348, 351
exile, 69, 99, 101, 111, 118, 119, 205, 210, 249, 283
internal, 101

famine, 7, 13, 197, 208, 211, 265
denial, 201
memory, 210
perpetrator, 205, 208
survivor, 201, 202, 210
victim, 92, 95, 96, 97, 198, 202, 203, 205,
206, 207, 208, 209, 210, 211
victims, 7
fascism, 34, 55, 141, 219, 220, 226, 227, 231, 236
Federal Commissioner for the Records of
the State Security Service of the former
German Democratic Republic, 160
Federal Security Service, 76
file, 31, 70, 73, 74, 101, 121, 186, 269, 288
access, 2, 11, 19, 20, 31, 288, 316
secret, 31, 32, 42, 74, 90, 121, 197, 268, 269,
274, 277, 282, 288, 308, 316
Foreign Intelligence Service, 76
forgiveness, 162

Gamsakhurdia, Zviad, 244, 248, 249, 251, 258
genocide, 7, 13, 93, 94, 97, 202, 218, 219, 222,
223, 225, 228, 229, 230, 231, 236, 293, 295,
317, 323, 326, 327

national, 110, 115, 329
victims, 94, 284
Genocide and Resistance Research Center of
Lithuania, 325, 326, 330, 339
Georgian Dream, 254, 255, 256, 259
Germany, 46, 47, 66, 67, 69, 81, 123, 139, 142,
143, 155, 220, 247, 250, 264
Ghimpu, Mihai, 34, 271, 277
glasnost, 20, 51, 91, 97, 109, 112, 249, 284, 289,
325, 345
Gontarczyk, Piotr, 73, 74
Gorbachev, Mikhail, 20, 30, 35, 37, 46, 51, 54,
55, 56, 66, 75, 76, 91, 93, 97, 109, 112, 113,
114, 118, 249, 250, 267, 284, 289, 325, 345,
346, 348, 349, 350
Gori, 251, 253, 258
grave, 97, 115, 124, 309, 335
common, 206
mass, 47, 54, 61, 98, 115, 123
Great Famine, 40, 75, 78, 88, 89, 92, 93, 94,
95, 96, 97, 197, 198, 199, 200, 201, 202,
203, 205, 206, 207, 208, 209, 210, 211, 347,
352
Great Purge, 40, 56, 88, 89, 99
Great Terror, 30, 75, 111, 125, 249, 253, 264,
349
Gross, Jan, 68, 69, 70
guard, 55
prison, 30, 92, 266
Gulag, 34, 37, 48, 50, 54, 55, 56, 57, 75, 79, 121,
253, 271
narrative, 46
official, 92, 98
prisoner, 33
returnee, 59
site, 51
survivor, 50
system, 90, 355
Gulag Museum, 48, 53, 54

historiography, 156, 171, 172
History Museum, 272
holiday, 77, 118, 309
national, 2, 4, 5, 97
public, 19, 39, 42, 309
religious, 309
Soviet, 77

CPSIA information can be obtained
at www.ICGtesting.com
Printed in the USA
LVHW080933140822
725908LV00013B/685

9 781316 648056